LEE COUNTY LIBRARY
SANFORD, N. C.

W9-AEF-040

THE LEE COUNTY LIBRARY
SANFORD, NORTH CAROLINA

— PRESENTED BY —
Drs. Elizabeth and
John Dotterer

THE COLLECTED WORKS OF
ABRAHAM LINCOLN

THE COLLECTED WORKS OF
ABRAHAM LINCOLN

THE ABRAHAM LINCOLN ASSOCIATION
SPRINGFIELD, ILLINOIS

IV

ROY P. BASLER, *EDITOR*

MARION DOLORES PRATT AND LLOYD A. DUNLAP

ASSISTANT EDITORS

RUTGERS UNIVERSITY PRESS
NEW BRUNSWICK, NEW JERSEY

LEE COUNTY LIBRARY
SANFORD, N. C.

COPYRIGHT 1953 BY
THE ABRAHAM LINCOLN ASSOCIATION

THE HISTORY BOOK CLUB EDITION

———

COMPOSED IN INTERTYPE WAVERLEY
BY H. WOLFF BOOK MANUFACTURING COMPANY, NEW YORK CITY,
PRINTED BY MURRAY PRINTING COMPANY, FORGE VILLAGE, MASSACHUSETTS,
AND BOUND BY THE HADDON CRAFTSMEN, SCRANTON, PENNSYLVANIA

———

TITLE PAGE WOOD ENGRAVING BY STANLEY RICE
DESIGN BY P. J. CONKWRIGHT

SOURCES
AND LOCATION SYMBOLS

DESCRIPTION OF SOURCES

THE following symbols provide a description of sources as cited at the beginning of the first footnote to each item. In addition to the customary symbols for describing manuscripts, the editors have employed symbols or single words to identify other sources which have been cited repeatedly in the first footnote.

AD	Autograph Document
ADS	Autograph Document Signed
ADf	Autograph Draft
ADfS	Autograph Draft Signed
AE	Autograph Endorsement
AES	Autograph Endorsement Signed
AL	Autograph Letter
ALS	Autograph Letter Signed
ALS copy	Autograph Letter Signed, copied by Lincoln and preserved in his papers
Copy	Copy not by Lincoln
D	Document
DS	Document Signed
Df	Draft
DfS	Draft Signed
ES	Endorsement Signed
F	Facsimile—following any of the preceding symbols
LS	Letter Signed
P	Photostat—following any of the preceding symbols

Angle   *New Letters and Papers of Lincoln.* Compiled by Paul M. Angle. Boston and New York: Houghton Mifflin Company, 1930.

Herndon   *Herndon's Lincoln: The True Story of a Great Life.* By William H. Herndon and Jesse W. Weik. 3 volumes. Chicago, New York, and San Francisco: Belford, Clarke & Company, [1889].

Hertz   *Abraham Lincoln: A New Portrait.* By Emanuel Hertz. 2 volumes. New York: Horace Liveright, Inc., 1931.

Lapsley   *The Writings of Abraham Lincoln.* Edited by Arthur Brooks Lapsley. 8 volumes. New York: P. F. Collier and Son, 1905.

NH   *Complete Works of Abraham Lincoln.* Edited by John G. Nicolay and John Hay. 12 volumes. New York: Francis D. Tandy Company, 1905.

OR   *The War of the Rebellion: A Compilation of the Official Records of the Union and Confederate Armies.* 4 series; 70 "volumes"; 128 books. Washington: Government Printing Office, 1880-1901. Roman numerals are used for Series, Volume, and Part (if any); pages are in arabic.

Tarbell   *The Life of Abraham Lincoln. . . .* By Ida M. Tarbell. 2 volumes. New York: The Doubleday & McClure Company, 1900.

Tracy   *Uncollected Letters of Abraham Lincoln.* Edited by Gilbert A. Tracy. Boston and New York: Houghton Mifflin Company, 1917.

Wilson   *Uncollected Works of Abraham Lincoln.* Edited by Rufus Rockwell Wilson. 2 volumes. Elmira, New York: Primavera Press, 1947-1948.

LOCATION SYMBOLS

CCamStJ   St. John's Seminary Library, Camarillo, Calif.
CLCM   Los Angeles County Museum Library, Los Angeles, Calif.
CSmH   Henry E. Huntington Library, San Marino, Calif.
CoHi   State Historical Society of Colorado, Denver, Colo.
CoU   University of Colorado Library, Boulder, Colo.
Ct   Connecticut State Library, Hartford, Conn.
CtHi   Connecticut Historical Society, Hartford, Conn.
CtLHi   Litchfield Historical Society, Litchfield, Conn.
CtSoP   Pequot Library, Southport, Conn.
CtWat   Watertown Library Association, Watertown, Conn.
CtY   Yale University Library, New Haven, Conn.
DLC   Library of Congress, Washington, D. C.
DLC-HW   Herndon-Weik Collection, Library of Congress
DLC-RTL   The Robert Todd Lincoln Collection of the Papers of Abraham Lincoln, Library of Congress
DLM   Lincoln Museum, Ford's Theatre, National Park Service, Washington, D. C.
DNA   National Archives, Washington, D. C. All additional abbreviations and numbers given with this symbol are those employed by the National Archives at the time the manuscript was located.
DNM   National Museum Library, Washington, D. C.

DeHi	Historical Society of Delaware Library, Wilmington, Del.
DeWI	Wilmington Institute Free Library, Wilmington, Del.
I-Ar	Archives Division, Illinois State Library, Springfield, Ill.
IBloHi	McLean County Historical Society, Bloomington, Ill.
ICHi	Chicago Historical Society, Chicago, Ill.
ICU	University of Chicago Library, Chicago, Ill.
IDecJ	James Millikin University Library, Decatur, Ill.
IFre	Freeport Public Library, Freeport, Ill.
lHi	Illinois State Historical Library, Springfield, Ill.
IJI	Illinois College Library, Jacksonville, Ill.
ISLA	The Abraham Lincoln Association, Springfield, Ill.
IU	University of Illinois Library, Urbana, Ill.
IaCrM	Iowa Masonic Library, Cedar Rapids, Iowa
IaDaM	Davenport Public Museum, Davenport, Iowa
IaHA	Iowa State Department of History and Archives, Des Moines, Iowa
In	Indiana State Library, Indianapolis, Ind.
InFtwL	Lincoln National Life Foundation, Fort Wayne, Ind.
InHi	Indiana Historical Society, Indianapolis, Ind.
InLTHi	Tippecanoe County Historical Association, Lafayette, Ind.
InU	Indiana University Library, Bloomington, Ind.
KyBC	Berea College Library, Berea, Ky.
KyU	University of Kentucky Library, Lexington, Ky.
LU	Louisiana State University Library, Baton Rouge, La.
MB	Boston Public Library, Boston, Mass.
MCon	Free Public Library, Concord, Mass.
MFai	Millicent Library, Fairhaven, Mass.
MH	Harvard University Library, Cambridge, Mass.
MHi	Massachusetts Historical Society, Boston, Mass.
MS	Springfield Library Association, Springfield, Mass.
MSHi	Connecticut Valley Historical Society, Springfield, Mass.
MdAA	Hall of Records, State of Maryland, Annapolis, Md.
MdHi	Maryland Historical Society, Baltimore, Md.
MeHi	Maine Historical Society, Portland, Me.
MiD	Detroit Public Library, Detroit, Mich.
MiK-M	Kalamazoo Public Library Museum, Kalamazoo, Mich.
MiU-C	William L. Clements Library, University of Michigan, Ann Arbor, Mich.

MiU-Hi	Michigan Historical Collection, University of Michigan, Ann Arbor, Mich.
MnHi	Minnesota Historical Society, St. Paul, Minn.
MnSM	Macalester College Library, St. Paul, Minn.
MoHi	State Historical Society of Missouri, Columbia, Mo.
MoSHi	Missouri Historical Society, St. Louis, Mo.
N	New York State Library, Albany, N. Y.
NAuE	Fred L. Emerson Foundation, Auburn, N. Y.
NBLiHi	Long Island Historical Society, Brooklyn, N. Y.
NBuG	Grosvenor Library, Buffalo, New York
NBuHi	Buffalo Historical Society, Buffalo, N. Y.
NDry	Southworth Library, Dryden, N. Y.
NHi	New-York Historical Society, New York City
NIC	Cornell University Library, Ithaca, N. Y.
NN	New York Public Library, New York City
NNC	Columbia University Library, New York City
NNP	Pierpont Morgan Library, New York City
NRU	University of Rochester Library, Rochester, N. Y.
NSh	John Jermain Memorial Library, Sag Harbor, N. Y.
NSk	Skaneateles Library Association, Skaneateles, N. Y.
NWM	U. S. Military Academy Library, West Point, N. Y.
NbO	Omaha Public Library, Omaha, Nebr.
NcGu	Guilford College Library, Guilford, N. C.
NhExP	Phillips Exeter Academy, Exeter, N. H.
NjP	Princeton University Library, Princeton, N. J.
OCHP	Historical and Philosophical Society of Ohio, Cincinnati, Ohio
OClCS	Case Institute of Technology, Cleveland, Ohio
OClWHi	Western Reserve Historical Society, Cleveland, Ohio
OFH	Hayes Memorial Library, Fremont, Ohio
OMC	Marietta College Library, Marietta, Ohio
ORB	Oliver R. Barrett Collection, Chicago, Ill.*
OSHi	Clark County Historical Society, Springfield, Ohio
OrHi	Oregon Historical Society, Portland, Ore.
PHC	Haverford College Library, Haverford, Pa.
PHi	Historical Society of Pennsylvania, Philadelphia, Pa.

* After the *Collected Works* was in press, the collection of the late Oliver R. Barrett was sold at auction by Parke-Bernet Galleries (Catalog 1315) on February 19-20, 1952. It has been impossible to trace all new owners of the more than two hundred items, and impracticable to change the source citations for those which are known, but many of the more important items went to such well-known collections as those in the Library of Congress (Debates Scrapbook, purchased for the Alfred Whital Stern Collection) and Illinois State Historical Library (letters to Joshua F. Speed, etc.).

PMA	Allegheny College Library, Meadville, Pa.
PP	Free Library of Philadelphia, Philadelphia, Pa.
PPDrop	Dropsie College Library, Philadelphia, Pa.
PSt	Pennsylvania State College Library, State College, Pa.
PU	University of Pennsylvania Library, Philadelphia, Pa.
RPAB	Annmary Brown Memorial Library, Providence, R. I.
RPB	Brown University Library, Providence, R. I.
THaroL	Lincoln Memorial University, Harrogate, Tenn.
THi	Tennessee Historical Society, Nashville, Tenn.
ViU	University of Virginia Library, Charlottesville, Va.
VtU	University of Vermont Library, Burlington, Vt.
WBeloHi	Beloit Historical Society, Beloit, Wis.
WHi	State Historical Society of Wisconsin, Madison, Wis.
WvU	West Virginia University Library, Morgantown, W. Va.

Courtesy of Frederick Hill Meserve

JUNE 3, 1860
By Alexander Hesler

THE COLLECTED WORKS OF
ABRAHAM LINCOLN

◄─◆─►

Notes for Speech at Hartford, Connecticut[1]

[March 5, 1860]

SIGNS OF DECAY — BUSHWHACKING —
IRREPRESSIBLE CONFLICT —

JOHN BROWN

SHOE-TRADE —
True, or not true.
If true, what?
Mason
Plasters.
If not true, what?

[Illegible] is the question.
We must deal with it.
Magnitude of question.
What prevents just now?
Right — wrong — indifference
Indifference unphilosophical
Because nobody is indifferent
Must be converted to
Can be, or can not be done.
I suppose can not.
But if can, what result?
Indifference, then, must be rejected.
And what supported?
Sectionalism
Conservatism
John Brown
Conclusion

[1] Angle, pp. 239-40. According to Angle's note a newspaper reporter found the sheet of notes lying on a table in the City Hall after the speech and preserved it.

[1]

Speech at Hartford, Connecticut[1]

March 5, 1860

[*Daily Courant* Version]

Whether we will have it so or not, the slave question is the pre-vailing question before the nation. Though it may be true, and probably *is* true, that all parties, factions and individuals desire it should be settled, it still goes on unsettled—the all-prevailing and all-pervading question of the day. Hardly any other great question, however important it may have appeared, has been before the country several years, that had the power so to excite the public mind as this question of slavery. It has been so for six years, and before this received considerable consideration. It is in reality, older. It was rife before the Revolution, even. But it was settled, apparently. It has been settled many times; but each time it has risen it has come higher and higher. It has been coming up and going down. Its last rise was in January, 1854; it rose then higher than any former time, but this has never subsided. Otherwise than this, it grows more and more in magnitude and importance.

Two years ago, I said in a speech in Illinois, "We are now in the fifth year of an inauguration of a policy which was to settle this question satisfactorily, but we have not seen the end." It may now be added that since the winter of 1857-8, when the Lecompton imbroglio was created, those who then brought up the question have never been able to see the end. It characterized all the speeches, that the policy they had adopted "was working well, and we were just at the end of it, notwithstanding the efforts of Abolitionists to continue it along. We are just getting rid of this vexed question; and the tail of this hideous creature is just going out of sight."

Now we hear no more of this; and the question arises, "Why can't this question which we all desire so much to be settled, be satisfactorily arranged?" The reason is, that while we all agree that we want it settled, one faction wants to settle it one way, a second has a different plan, and a third still another. Each pulls in a different direction. All desire its settlement, but differ in the method of doing it; and none of them being in a decided majority have ever been able to accomplish the object.

[1] Hartford *Daily Courant*, March 6, 1860; Hartford *Evening Press*, March 6, 1860. Both versions are reproduced. Neither is clearly superior to the other as a whole, and each contains passages not in the other. An attempt to collate the two versions proved to be so unwieldy and saved so little space that it has been abandoned in favor of reproduction of both sources. Typographical errors have been corrected by the editors, but the reports are otherwise unchanged.

I think one great mistake is made by them all. I think our wisest men have made this mistake. They underrate its importance, and a settlement can never be effected until its magnitude is properly estimated. Until we do this, the means of settlement will never be properly estimated. Now what is the difficulty? One-sixth of the population of the United States is slave. One man of every six, one woman of every six, one child of every six, is a slave. Those who own them look upon them as property, and nothing else. They contemplate them as property, and speak of them as such. The slaves have the same "property quality," in the minds of their owners, as any other property. The entire value of the slave population of the United States, is, at a moderate estimate, not less than $2,000,000,000. This amount of *property* has a vast influence upon the minds of those who own it. The same amount of property owned by Northern men has the same influence upon *their* minds. In this we do not assume that we are better than the people of the South—neither do we admit that they are better than we. We are not better, barring circumstances, than they. Public opinion is formed relative to a property basis. Therefore, the slaveholders battle any policy which depreciates their slaves as property. What increases the value of this property, they favor. When you tell them that slavery is immoral, they rebel, because they do not like to be told they are interested in an institution which is not a moral one. When you enter into a defence of slavery, they seize upon it, for they like justification. The result is, that public opinion is formed among them which insists upon the encouragement or protection, the enlargement or perpetuation of slavery—and secures them property in the slave.

Now this comes in conflict with this proposition that we at the North view slavery as a wrong. We understand that the "equality of man" principle which actuated our forefathers in the establishment of the government is right; and that slavery, being directly opposed to this, is morally wrong. I think that if anything can be proved by natural theology, it is that slavery is morally wrong. God gave man a mouth to receive bread, hands to feed it, and his hand has a right to carry bread to his mouth without controversy.

We suppose slavery is wrong, and that it endangers the perpetuity of the Union. Nothing else menaces it. Its effect on free labor makes it what Seward has been so roundly abused for calling, an irrepressible conflict. Almost every man has a sense of certain things being wrong, and at the same time, a sense of its pecuniary value. These conflict in the mind, and make a riddle of a man. If slavery is considered upon a property basis, public opinion must be forced to its support. The alternative is its settlement upon the basis of its being wrong. Some men think it is a question of neither right or wrong; that it is a question of dollars and cents, only; that the Almighty has drawn a line across the country, south of which the land is always to be cultivated by slave labor; when the question is between the white man and the nigger, they go in for the white man; when it is between the nigger and the crocodile, they take sides with the nigger. There is effort to make this feeling of indifference prevalent in the country, and this is one of the things, perhaps, that prevents the sudden settlement of the question. Is it possible that a national policy can be sustained because nobody opposes or favors it? It may answer to serve the ends of politicians for a while, but it falls at last. There may be one way, however, to make it stand, and that is to make the opinion of the people conform to it; must be made to conclude that those who want slavery shall have it, and that it is simply a matter of dollars and cents. I do not believe a majority of the people of this nation can be made to take this view of it.

Is there any man of the Democratic party, especially the "Douglas wing," but will say that in his opinion the Declaration of Independence has no application to the negro? I have asked this question many times during the past three years, and no Democrat has yet denied that this was his belief, though I have asked it always where people are in the habit of answering their speakers when they please. So I assume this to be their belief to-day; and I tell you, you are safe to offer a premium to any man who will show you a Democrat who said so five years ago. I avow I never heard it from any man until I heard it from the lips of Judge Douglas. I had, to be sure, in certain portions of the country, heard men say something to this effect, but they didn't sneak around it with any statement like this. *They* took the bull by the horns, and said the Declaration of Independence wasn't true! Judge Taney might have first broached the doctrine. Perhaps he did; but I heard it first from Judge Douglas, though it was after Taney's Dred Scott decision. If so, Douglas possibly got it from him. Here's half the people of this nation saying what they would not have said five years ago; taking man from his kind and placing him among the brutes. This is a long stride towards bringing about this feeling of indifference in the minds of the people of this country. One more such stride and the object would be reached.

The proposition that there is a struggle between the white man and the negro contains a falsehood. There is *no* struggle between them. It assumes that unless the white man enslaves the negro, the negro will enslave the white man. In that case, I think I would go for enslaving the black man, in preference to being enslaved myself. As the learned Judge of a certain Court is said to have decided—"When a ship is wrecked at sea, and two men seize upon one plank which is capable of sustaining but one of them, either of them can rightfully push the other off!" There is, however, no such controversy here. They say that between the nigger and the crocodile they go for the nigger. The proportion, therefore, is, that as the crocodile to the nigger so is the nigger to the white man.

They tell us that they desire the people of a territory to vote slavery out or in as they please. But who will form the opinion of the people there? The territories may be settled by emigrants from the free States, who will go there with this feeling of indifference. The question arises, "slavery or freedom?" Caring nothing about it, they let it come in, and that is the end of it. It is the surest way of nationalizing the institution. Just as certain, but more dangerous because more insidious; but it is leading us there just as certainly and as surely as Jeff. Davis himself would have us go.

If, then, we of the Republican party who think slavery is a wrong, and would mould public opinion to the fact that it is wrong, should get the control of the general government, I do not say we would or should meddle with it where it exists; but we could inaugurate a policy which would treat it as a wrong, and prevent its extension.

For instance, out in the street, or in the field, or on the prairie I find a rattlesnake. I take a stake and kill him. Everybody would applaud the act and say I did right. But suppose the snake was in a bed where children were sleeping. Would I do right to strike him there? I might hurt the children; or I might not kill, but only arouse and exasperate the snake, and he might bite the children. Thus, by meddling with him here, I would do more hurt than good. Slavery is like this. We dare not strike at it where it is. The manner in which our constitution is framed constrains us from making war upon it where it already exists. The question that we now have to deal with is, "Shall we be acting right to take this snake and carry it to a bed where there are children?" The Republican party insists upon keeping it out of the bed.

Again: I met Mr. Cassius M. Clay in the cars at New Haven one day last week, and it was my first opportunity to take him by the hand. There was an old gentleman in the car, seated in front of us, whose coat collar was turned far down upon the shoulders. I saw directly that he had a large wen on his neck. I said to Mr. Clay, That wen represents slavery; it bears the same relation to that man that slavery does to the country. That wen is a great evil; the man that bears it will say so. But he does not dare to cut it out. He bleeds to death if he does, directly. If he does *not* cut it out; it will shorten his life materially.

This is only applicable to men who think slavery is wrong. Those who think it right, of course will look upon the rattlesnake as a jewel, and call the wen an ornament. I suppose the only way to get rid of it is, for those who think it wrong, to work together, and to vote no longer with the Democracy who love it so well.

Do you who think slavery is wrong, but still vote with the Democracy, act towards it as you do towards any other thing you consider wrong? I think not; on the contrary, you find fault with those who denounce it. In your view of the case it must not be discussed at all. In your view it must not be spoken of in the free States, because slavery is *not* there; nor in the slave States, because it *is* there; you do not want it brought into politics because it stirs up agitation; you do not want to hear of it from the pulpit because it is not religion; you do not want to take it into your Tract Societies because it creates disturbance *there*.

Are you consistent in this? You say that if the South themselves desire to stir the question, you wish them God-speed in it. Are you certain of that? In 1858 Frank P. Blair of Missouri did just this thing for his State. He went into the fight, and was a candidate for Congress. He was beaten; and when you heard of his defeat did you hang your heads in sorrow? I *reckon* not! I *guess*, that you threw your hat into the air and shouted, "Hurrah! for Democracy!" (Mr. Lincoln then proceeded to speak of the provision in the constitution which permitted the slave trade to continue 20 years. Although it was not expressly so stated, it was understood by the framers of that instrument that it was to have been abolished at the end of that time. He argued that if they had not considered slavery a wrong, they would not have thus limited the time of supply.) He continued:

I think the Democracy are pretty generally getting into a system of bushwhackery in this controversy. You all know how Seward has been abused for his "irrepressible conflict" doctrine. The Democracy have repeated it over, and over, and over again; I call this bushwhackery because they have been reminded time after time, but could never be made to admit, that the old fathers said the same thing. They dare not deny it because they know the proof is ready at your hands to meet their denial. Jefferson said it; Washington said it. Before Seward said it, the same statement was made by Pryor of Virginia in his Richmond *Enquirer*, the leading paper of his State. Pryor is sent to Washington and Douglas hugs him to his bosom, but goes into fits of hydrophobia at Seward's enunciation of the same doctrine which was preached by his Virginia friend.

Another species of bushwhacking is exhibited in their treatment of the John Brown and Harper's Ferry affair. They insist upon it that the Republican party incites insurrections. Did they, *can* they ever prove their statement? They tried it in the Senate Investigation Committee and failed, but they keep saying it. We have not been fairly dealt with in this matter. We need not [have] expected that we would have been. There was some State elections to come off soon afterwards. They had just passed through elections in other States, and been whipped out. They were glad this occurred at Harper's Ferry. They said to each other—"Jump in—*now's* your chance!" They were sorry there were not more killed; but taking it as they found it, they howled over it. The elections came off, but they did not result as the Democracy had expected. Each Republican knew that the charge that his party had incited the insurrection was, so far as he was concerned, a slander upon *him*. That is my philosophy of the result of the elections which ensued. The Democracy is still at work upon John Brown and Harper's Ferry, charging the Republicans with the crime of instigating the proceedings there; and if they think they are able to slander a woman into loving them, or a man into voting with them, they will learn better presently.

Now they are going to work at the shoe strike. I don't know that it comes into Connecticut. It goes into New Hampshire. A Democratic Senator gets up in the Senate Chamber and pompously announces that "I cannot dawt thot this strike is the thresult of the onforchunit wahfar brought aboat boy this sucktional controvussy!" Now whether this is so or not, I know one thing—*there is a strike*! And I am glad to know that there is a system of labor where the laborer can strike if he wants to! I would to God that such a system prevailed all over the world.

Now this strike is caused by a withdrawal of Southern trade, or it is not. If it is, what can you do to help it? Have you ever made war upon the South? No. Then how can you help yourselves? They withdraw their trade on a false accusation, because you never warred upon them, and consequently cannot stop the war they charge you with. You can, however, conform to their idea that slavery is right. This will satisfy them, but what is the effect on you? Why *slavery comes in upon you*! Public opinion against it gives way. The barriers which protected you from it are down;

slavery comes in, and white free labor that *can* strike will give way to slave labor that *cannot*!

* * * * * * *

The Republicans want to see all parts of the Union in harmony with one another. Let us do our duty, but let us look to what our duty is, and do nothing except after due deliberation. Let us determine, if we can, what will satisfy the South. Will they be satisfied that we surrender the territories to them unconditionally? No. If we promise never to instigate an invasion upon slavery? No. Equally without avail is the fact that they have found nothing to detect us in doing them any wrong. What then? We must say that slavery is right; we must vote for Douglas's new Sedition laws; we must withdraw our statement that slavery is wrong. If a slave runs away, they overlook the natural causes which impelled him to the act; do not remember the oppression or the lashes he received, but charge us with instigating him to flight. If he screams when whipped, they say it is not caused by the pains he suffers, but he screams because we instigate him to outcrying. We do let them alone, to be sure, but they object to our saying anything against their system. They do not ask us to change our free State constitutions, but they will yet do that. After demanding *what* they do, and *as* they do, they cannot stop short of this. They may be justified in this, believing, as they do, that slavery is right, and a social blessing. We cannot act otherwise than we do, believing that slavery is wrong. If it is right, we may not contract its limits. If it is wrong, they cannot ask us to extend it. Upon these different views, hinges the whole controversy. Thinking it right, they are justified in asking its protection; thinking it wrong, we cannot consent to vote for it, or to let it extend itself. If our sense of duty forbids this extension, let us do that duty. This contrivance of a middle ground is such that he who occupies it is neither a dead or a living man. Their "Union" contrivances are not for us, for they reverse the scriptural order and call the righteous, not sinners to repentance. They ask men who never had an aspiration except for the Union, to swear fealty to the Union. Let us not be slandered from our duties, or intimidated from preserving our dignity and our rights by any menace; but let us have faith that Right, Eternal Right makes might, and as we understand our duty, so do it!

[*Evening Press* Version]

Slavery is *the* great political question of the nation. Though all desire its settlement, it still remains the all-pervading question of the day. It has been so especially for the past six years. It is indeed older than the revolution, rising, subsiding, then rising again, till '54, since which time it has been constantly augmenting. Those who occasioned the Lecompton imbroglio now admit that they see no end to it. It had been their cry that the vexed question was just about to be settled—"the tail of this hideous creature is just going out of sight." That cry is "played out," and has ceased.

Why, when *all* desire to have this controversy settled, can we not settle it satisfactorily? One reason is, we want it settled in different ways. Each faction has a different plan—they pull different ways, and neither has a decided majority. In my humble opinion, the importance and magnitude of the question is underrated, even by our wisest men. If I be right, the first thing is to get a just estimate of the evil—then we can provide a cure.

One-sixth, and a little more, of the population of the United States are slaves—looked upon as property, as nothing but property. The cash value of these slaves, at a moderate estimate, is $2,000,000,000. This amount of property value has a vast influence on the minds of its owners, very naturally. The same amount of property would have an equal influence upon us if owned in the North. Human nature is the same—people at the South are the same as those at the North, barring the difference in circumstances. Public opinion is founded, to a great extent, on a property basis. What lessens the value of property is opposed, what enhances its value is favored. Public opinion at the South regards slaves as property and insists upon treating them like other property.

On the other hand, the free states carry on their government on the principle of the equality of men. We think slavery is morally wrong, and a direct violation of that principle. We *all* think it wrong. It is clearly proved, I think, by natural theology, apart from revelation. Every man, black, white or yellow, has a mouth to be fed and two hands with which to feed it—and that bread should be allowed to go to that mouth without controversy. (Applause.)

Slavery is wrong in its effect upon white people and free labor; it is the only thing that threatens the Union. It makes what Senator Seward has been much abused for calling an "irrepressible conflict." When they get ready to settle it, we hope they will let us know. Public opinion settles every question here—any policy to be permanent must have public opinion at the bottom—something in accordance with the philosophy of the human mind as it is. The property basis will have its weight—the love of property and a consciousness of right or wrong have conflicting places in our organization, which often make a man's course seem crooked—his conduct a riddle.

Some men would make it a question of indifference—neither right nor wrong—merely a question of dollars and cents—the Almighty has drawn a line across the land, below which it must be cultivated by slave labor, above which by free labor. They would say: "If the question is between the white man and the negro, I am for the white man; if between the negro and the crocodile, I am for the negro." There is a strong effort to make this policy of indifference prevail, but it can not be a durable one. A "don't care" policy won't prevail, for every body *does* care.

Is there a Democrat, especially one of the Douglas wing, but will declare that the Declaration of Independence has no application to the negro? It would be safe to offer a moderate premium for such a man. I have asked this question in large audiences where they were in the habit of answering right out, but no one would say otherwise. Not one of them said it five years ago. I never heard it till I heard it from the lips of Judge Douglas. True, some men boldly took the bull by the horns and said the Declaration of Independence was not true! They didn't sneak around the question. I say I *heard* first from Douglas that the Declaration did not apply to black men. Not a man of them said it till then—they all say it now. This is a long stride towards establishing the policy of indifference—one more such stride, I think, would do it.

The proposition that there is a struggle between the white man and the negro contains a falsehood. There *is* no struggle. *If* there was, I should be for the white man. If two men are adrift at sea on a plank which will bear up but one, the law justifies either in pushing the other off. I never had to struggle to keep a negro from enslaving me, nor did a negro ever have to fight to keep me from enslaving him. They say, between the crocodile and the negro they go for the negro. The logical proportion is therefore; as a white man is to a negro, so is a negro to a crocodile; or, as the negro may treat the crocodile, so the white man may treat the negro. The don't care policy leads just as surely to nationalising slavery as Jeff. Davis himself, but the doctrine is more dangerous because more insidious.

If the Republicans, who think slavery *is* wrong, get possession of the general government, we may not root out the evil at once, but may at least prevent its extension. If I find a venomous snake lying on the open prairie, I seize the first stick and kill him at once. But if that snake is in bed with my children, I must be more cautious—I shall, in striking the snake, also strike the children, or arouse the reptile to bite the children. Slavery is the venomous snake in bed with the children. But if the question is whether to kill it on the prairie or *put it in bed with other children,* I think we'd *kill* it! (Cheers and laughter.)

Another illustration. When for the first time I met Mr. Clay, the other day in the cars, in front of us sat an old gentleman with an enormous wen upon his neck. Everybody would say the wen was a great evil, and would cause the man's death after a while—but you couldn't cut it out, for he'd bleed to death in a minute. But *would you engraft the seeds of that wen on the necks of sound and healthy men?* He must endure and be patient, hoping for possible relief. The wen represents slavery on the neck of this country. This only applies to those who think slavery is wrong. Those who think it right would consider the snake a jewel, and the wen an ornament.

We want those (democrats) who think slavery wrong to quit voting with those who think it right. They don't treat it as they do other wrongs—they won't oppose it in the free states for it isn't there, nor in the slave states for it *is* there; don't want it in politics, for it makes agitation; not in the pulpit, for it isn't religion; not in a Tract Society, for it makes a fuss—there is no place for its discussion. Are they quite consistent in this?

If those democrats really think slavery wrong they will be much pleased when earnest men in the slave states take up a plan of gradual emancipation and go to work energetically and very kindly to get rid of the evil. Now let us test them. Frank Blair tried it; and he ran for Congress in '58, and got beaten. Did the democracy feel bad about it? I *reckon* not—I *guess* you all flung up your hats and shouted "Hurrah for the Democracy!" (Laughter—three cheers for Blair and three for Clay.)

He went on to speak of the manner in which slavery was treated by the Constitution. The word "slave" is no where used; the supply of slaves was to be prohibited after 1808; they stopped the spread of it in the territories; seven of the states abolished it. He argued very conclusively that it was then regarded as an evil which would eventually be got rid of, and that they desired, once rid of it, to have nothing in the constitution to remind them of it. The Republicans go back to first principles and deal with it as a wrong. Mason,[2] of Va., said openly that the framers of our government were anti-slavery. Hammond[3] of S. C., said "Washington set this evil example." Bully Brooks[4] said: "At the time the Constitution

[2] James M. Mason.   [3] James H. Hammond.   [4] Preston S. Brooks.

[11]

was formed, no one supposed slavery would last till now." We stick to the policy of our fathers.

The Democracy are given to "bushwhacking." After having their errors and mis-statements continually thrust in their faces, they pay no heed, but go on howling about Seward and the "irrepressible conflict." That is "bushwhacking." So with John Brown and Harper's Ferry. They charge it upon the Republican party and ignominiously fail in all attempts to substantiate the charge. Yet they go on with their bushwhacking, the pack in full cry after John Brown.

The democrats had just been whipped in Ohio and Pennsylvania, and seized upon the unfortunate Harper's Ferry affair to influence other elections then pending. They said to each other, "Jump in—now's your chance;" and were sorry there were not more killed. But they didn't succeed well. Let them go on with their howling. They will succeed when by slandering women you get them to love you, and by slandering men you get them to vote for you. (Great applause.)

Mr. Lincoln then took up the Massachusetts shoemakers' strike, treating it in a humorous and philosophical manner, and exposing to ridicule the foolish pretence of Senator Douglas—that the strike arose from "this unfortunate sectional warfare." Mr. Lincoln thanked God that we have a system of labor where there *can* be a strike. Whatever the pressure, there is a point where the workman may stop. (Applause and cheers for free labor.)

He didn't pretend to be familiar with the subject of the shoe strike—probably knew as little about it as Senator Douglas himself. This strike has occurred *as* the Senator says, or it has not. Shall we stop making war upon the South? We never have made war upon them. If any one has, [he] better go and hang himself and save Virginia the trouble. If you give up your convictions and call slavery right as they do, you let slavery in upon you—instead of *white* laborers who *can* strike, you'll soon have *black* laborers who *can't* strike.

I have heard that in consequence of this "sectional warfare," as Douglas calls it, Senator Mason of Va., had appeared in a *suit of homespun*. Now up in New Hampshire, the woolen and cotton mills are all busy, and there is no strike—they are busy making the very goods Senator Mason has quit buying! To carry out his idea, he ought to go *barefoot*! If that's the plan, they should begin at the *foundation*, and adopt the well-known "Georgia costume" of a shirt-collar and pair of spurs! ("Irrepressible" laughter and applause.)

It reminded him of the man who had a poor old lean, bony, spav-
ined horse, with swelled legs. He was asked what he was going
to do with such a miserable beast—the poor creature would die.
"Do?" said he. "I'm going to fat him up; *don't you see that I have
got him seal fat as high as the knees?*" (Roars of laughter.) Well,
they've got the Union dissolved up to the ankle, but no farther!
(Applause and laughter.)

All portions of this confederacy should act in harmony and
with careful deliberation. The democrats cry John Brown invasion.
We are guiltless of it, but our denial does not satisfy them. Nothing will satisfy them but disinfecting the atmosphere entirely of
all opposition to slavery. They have not demanded of us to yield
the guards of liberty in our state constitutions, but it will naturally
come to that after a while. If we give up to them, we cannot refuse even their utmost request. If slavery is right, it ought to be
extended; if not, it ought to be restricted—there is no middle
ground. Wrong as we think it, we can afford to let it alone where
it of necessity now exists; but we *cannot* afford to extend it into
free territory and around our own homes. Let us stand against
it!

The "Union" arrangements are all a humbug—they reverse the
scriptural order, calling the righteous and not sinners to repentance. Let us not be slandered or intimidated to turn from our duty.
Eternal right makes might—as we understand our duty, let us do
it!

Speech at New Haven, Connecticut[1]

March 6, 1860

MR. PRESIDENT AND FELLOW-CITIZENS OF NEW HAVEN: If the
Republican party of this nation shall ever have the national house
entrusted to its keeping, it will be the duty of that party to attend
to all the affairs of national house-keeping. Whatever matters of
importance may come up, whatever difficulties may arise in the
way of its administration of the government, that party will then
have to attend to. It will then be compelled to attend to other ques-

---

[1] New Haven *Daily Palladium*, March 7, 1860. The editors have corrected a
few typographical errors in the remarkably well printed *Palladium* text. Brackets
are in the source unless otherwise noted. Newspaper comment on the speeches at
Meriden, Connecticut (March 7), Woonsocket, Rhode Island (March 8), Norwich
and Bridgeport, Connecticut (March 9 and 10), indicate that Lincoln repeated
this speech substantially at each place, and the only complete report of any of
them—the speech at Norwich printed in the Norwich *Weekly Courier*, March 15
—is admittedly a copy of the *Palladium's* report of the New Haven speech.

tions, besides this question which now assumes an overwhelming importance—the question of Slavery. It is true that in the organization of the Republican party this question of Slavery was more important than any other; indeed, so much more important has it become that no other national question can even get a hearing just at present. The old question of tariff—a matter that will remain one of the chief affairs of national housekeeping to all time—the question of the management of financial affairs; the question of the disposition of the public domain—how shall it be managed for the purpose of getting it well settled, and of making there the homes of a free and happy people—these will remain open and require attention for a great while yet, and these questions will have to be attended to by whatever party has the control of the government. Yet, just now, they cannot even obtain a hearing, and I do not purpose to detain you upon these topics, or what sort of hearing they should have when opportunity shall come.

For, whether we will or not, the question of Slavery is *the* question, the all absorbing topic of the day. It is true that all of us—and by that I mean, not the Republican party alone, but the whole American people, here and elsewhere—all of us wish this question settled—wish it out of the way. It stands in the way, and prevents the adjustment, and the giving of necessary attention to other questions of national house-keeping. The people of the whole nation agree that this question ought to be settled, and yet it is not settled. And the reason is that they are not yet agreed *how* it shall be settled. All wish it done, but some wish one way and some another, and some a third, or fourth, or fifth; different bodies are pulling in different directions, and none of them having a decided majority, are able to accomplish the common object.

In the beginning of the year 1854 a new policy was inaugurated with the avowed object and confident promise that it would entirely and forever put an end to the Slavery agitation. It was again and again declared that under this policy, when once successfully established, the country would be forever rid of this whole question. Yet under the operation of that policy this agitation has not only not ceased, but it has been constantly augmented. And this too, although, from the day of its introduction, its friends, who promised that it would wholly end all agitation, constantly insisted, down to the time that the Lecompton bill was introduced, that it was working admirably, and that its inevitable tendency was to remove the question forever from the politics of the country. Can you call to mind any Democratic speech, made after the repeal of the Missouri Compromise, down to the time of the Lecompton bill,

in which it was not predicted that the Slavery agitation was just
at an end; that "the abolition excitement was played out," "the
Kansas question was dead," "they have made the most they can
out of this question and it is now forever settled." But since the
Lecompton bill no Democrat, within my experience, has ever pretended that he could see the end. That cry has been dropped. They
themselves do not pretend, now, that the agitation of this subject
has come to an end yet. [Applause.]

The truth is, that this question is one of national importance,
and we cannot help dealing with it: we must do something about
it, whether we will or not. We cannot avoid it; the subject is one
we cannot avoid considering; we can no more avoid it than a man
can live without eating. It is upon us; it attaches to the body politic as much and as closely as the natural wants attach to our
natural bodies. Now I think it important that this matter should
be taken up in earnest, and really settled. And one way to bring
about a true settlement of the question is to understand its true
magnitude.

There have been many efforts to settle it. Again and again it has
been fondly hoped that it was settled, but every time it breaks out
afresh, and more violently than ever. It was settled, our fathers
hoped, by the Missouri Compromise, but it did not stay settled.
Then the compromises of 1850 were declared to be a full and final
settlement of the question. The two great parties, each in National Convention, adopted resolutions declaring that the settlement made by the Compromise of 1850 was a finality—that it
would last forever. Yet how long before it was unsettled again! It
broke out again in 1854, and blazed higher and raged more furi-
ously than ever before, and the agitation has not rested since.

These repeated settlements must have some fault about them.
There must be some inadequacy in their very nature to the purpose for which they were designed. We can only speculate as to
where that fault—that inadequacy, is, but we may perhaps profit by past experience.

I think that one of the causes of these repeated failures is that
our best and greatest men have greatly underestimated the size of
this question. They have constantly brought forward small cures
for great sores—plasters too small to cover the wound. That is one
reason that all settlements have proved so temporary—so evanes-
cent. [Applause.]

Look at the magnitude of this subject! One sixth of our population, in round numbers—not quite one sixth, and yet more than
a seventh,—about one sixth of the whole population of the United

States are slaves! The owners of these slaves consider them property. The effect upon the minds of the owners is that of property, and nothing else—it induces them to insist upon all that will favorably affect its value as property, to demand laws and institutions and a public policy that shall increase and secure its value, and make it durable, lasting and universal. The effect on the minds of the owners is to persuade them that there is no wrong in it. The slaveholder does not like to be considered a mean fellow, for holding that species of property, and hence he has to struggle within himself and sets about arguing himself into the belief that Slavery is right. The property influences his mind. The dissenting minister, who argued some theological point with one of the established church, was always met by the reply, "I can't see it so." He opened the Bible, and pointed him to a passage, but the orthodox minister replied, "I can't see it so." Then he showed him a single word— "Can you see that?" "Yes, I see it," was the reply. The dissenter laid a guinea over the word and asked, "Do you see it now?" [Great laughter.] So here. Whether the owners of this species of property do really see it as it is, it is not for me to say, but if they do, they see it as it is through 2,000,000,000 of dollars, and that is a pretty thick coating. [Laughter.] Certain it is, that they do not see it as we see it. Certain it is, that this two thousand million of dollars, invested in this species of property, all so concentrated that the mind can grasp it at once—this immense pecuniary interest, has its influence upon their minds.

But here in Connecticut and at the North Slavery does not exist, and we see it through no such medium. To us it appears natural to think that slaves are human beings; *men*, not property; that some of the things, at least, stated about men in the Declaration of Independence apply to them as well as to us. [Applause.] I say, we think, most of us, that this Charter of Freedom applies to the slave as well as to ourselves, that the class of arguments put forward to batter down that idea, are also calculated to break down the very idea of a free government, even for white men, and to undermine the very foundations of free society. [Continued applause.] We think Slavery a great moral wrong, and while we do not claim the right to touch it where it exists, we wish to treat it as a wrong in the Territories, where our votes will reach it. We think that a respect for ourselves, a regard for future generations and for the God that made us, require that we put down this wrong where our votes will properly reach it. We think that species of labor an injury to free white men—in short, we think Slavery a great moral, social and political evil, tolerable only because, and so far as its actual existence makes it necessary to tolerate it, and that beyond that, it ought to be treated as a wrong.

Now these two ideas, the property idea that Slavery is right, and the idea that it is wrong, come into collision, and do actually produce that irrepressible conflict which Mr. Seward has been so roundly abused for mentioning. The two ideas conflict, and must conflict.

Again, in its political aspect, does anything in any way endanger the perpetuity of this Union but that single thing, Slavery? Many of our adversaries are anxious to claim that they are specially devoted to the Union, and take pains to charge upon us hostility to the Union. Now we claim that we are the only true Union men, and we put to them this one proposition: What ever endangered this Union, save and except Slavery? Did any other thing ever cause a moment's fear? All men must agree that this thing alone has ever endangered the perpetuity of the Union. But if it was threatened by any other influence, would not all men say that the best thing that could be done, if we could not or ought not to destroy it, would be at least to keep it from growing any larger? Can any man believe that the way to save the Union is to extend and increase the only thing that threatens the Union, and to suffer it to grow bigger and bigger? [Great applause.]

Whenever this question shall be settled, it must be settled on some philosophical basis. No policy that does not rest upon some philosophical public opinion can be permanently maintained. And hence, there are but two policies in regard to Slavery that can be at all maintained. The first, based on the property view that Slavery is right, conforms to that idea throughout, and demands that we shall do everything for it that we ought to do if it were right. We must sweep away all opposition, for opposition to the right is wrong; we must agree that Slavery is right, and we must adopt the idea that property has persuaded the owner to believe—that Slavery is morally right and socially elevating. This gives a philosophical basis for a permanent policy of encouragement.

The other policy is one that squares with the idea that Slavery is wrong, and it consists in doing everything that we ought to do if it is wrong. Now, I don't wish to be misunderstood, nor to leave a gap down to be misrepresented, even. I don't mean that we ought to attack it where it exists. To me it seems that if we were to form a government anew, in view of the actual presence of Slavery we should find it necessary to frame just such a government as our fathers did; giving to the slaveholder the entire control where the system was established, while we possessed the power to restrain

it from going outside those limits. [Applause.] From the necessities
of the case we should be compelled to form just such a government as our blessed fathers gave us; and, surely, if they have so
made it, that adds another reason why we should let Slavery alone
where it exists.

If I saw a venomous snake crawling in the road, any man would
say I might seize the nearest stick and kill it; but if I found that
snake in bed with my children, that would be another question.
[Laughter.] I might hurt the children more than the snake, and
it might bite them. [Applause.] Much more, if I found it in bed
with my neighbor's children, and I had bound myself by a solemn
compact not to meddle with his children under any circumstances,
it would become me to let that particular mode of getting rid of
the gentleman alone. [Great laughter.] But if there was a bed
newly made up, to which the children were to be taken, and it
was proposed to take a batch of young snakes and put them there
with them, I take it no man would say there was any question how
I ought to decide! [Prolonged applause and cheers.]

That is just the case! The new Territories are the newly made
bed to which our children are to go, and it lies with the nation to
say whether they shall have snakes mixed up with them or not.
It does not seem as if there could be much hesitation what our
policy should be! [Applause.]

Now I have spoken of a policy based on the idea that Slavery is
wrong, and a policy based upon the idea that it is right. But an
effort has been made for a policy that shall treat it as neither right
or wrong. It is based upon utter indifference. Its leading advocate
has said "I don't care whether it be voted up or down."
[Laughter.] "It is merely a matter of dollars and cents." "The
Almighty has drawn a line across this continent, on one side of
which all soil must forever be cultivated by slave labor, and on the
other by free;" "when the struggle is between the white man and
the negro, I am for the white man; when it is between the negro and the crocodile, I am for the negro." Its central idea is
indifference. It holds that it makes no more difference to us
whether the Territories become free or slave States, than whether
my neighbor stocks his farm with horned cattle or puts it into to-
bacco. All recognize this policy, the plausible sugar-coated name
of which is *popular sovereignty.* [Laughter.]

This policy chiefly stands in the way of a permanent settlement
of the question. I believe there is no danger of its becoming the
permanent policy of the country, for it is based on a public indifference. There is nobody that "don't care." ALL THE PEOPLE DO

CARE! one way or the other. [Great applause.] I do not charge that its author, when he says he "don't care," states his individual opinion; he only expresses his policy for the government. I understand that he has never said, as an individual, whether he thought Slavery right or wrong—and he is the only man in the nation that has not! Now such a policy may have a temporary run; it may spring up as necessary to the political prospects of some gentleman; but it is utterly baseless; the people are not indifferent; and it can therefore have no durability or permanence.

But suppose it could! Then it could be maintained only by a public opinion that shall say "we don't care." There must be a change in public opinion, the public mind must be so far debauched as to square with this policy of caring not at all. The people must come to consider this as "merely a question of dollars and cents," and to believe that in some places the Almighty has made Slavery necessarily eternal. This policy can be brought to prevail if the people can be brought round to say honestly "we don't care;" if not, it can never be maintained. It is for you to say whether that can be done. [Applause.]

You are ready to say it cannot, but be not too fast! Remember what a long stride has been taken since the repeal of the Missouri Compromise! Do you know of any Democrat, of either branch of the party—do you know one who declares that he believes that the Declaration of Independence has any application to the negro? Judge Taney declares that it has not, and Judge Douglas even vilifies me personally and scolds me roundly for saying that the Declaration applies to all men, and that negroes are men. [Cheers.] Is there a Democrat here who does not deny that the Declaration applies to a negro? Do any of you know of one? Well, I have tried before perhaps fifty audiences, some larger and some smaller than this, to find one such Democrat, and never yet have I found one who said I did not place him right in that. I must assume that Democrats hold that, and now, *not one of these Democrats can show that he said that five years ago!* [Applause.] I venture to defy the whole party to produce one man that ever uttered the belief that the Declaration did not apply to negroes, before the repeal of the Missouri Compromise! Four or five years ago we all thought negroes were men, and that when *"all men"* were named, negroes were included. But *the whole Democratic party has deliberately taken negroes from the class of men and put them in the class of brutes.* [Applause.] Turn it as you will, it is simply the truth! Don't be too hasty then in saying that the people cannot be brought to this new doctrine, but note that long stride. One more as long completes the journey, from where negroes are estimated as men to where they are estimated as mere brutes—as rightful property!

That saying, "in the struggle between the white man and the negro," &c., which I know came from the same source as this policy—that saying marks another step. There is a falsehood wrapped up in that statement. "In the struggle between the white man and the negro" assumes that there is a struggle, in which either the white man must enslave the negro or the negro must enslave the white. There is no such struggle! It is merely an ingenious falsehood, to degrade and brutalize the negro. Let each let the other alone, and there is no struggle about it. If it was like two wrecked seamen on a narrow plank, when each must push the other off or drown himself, I would push the negro off or a white man either, but it is not; the plank is large enough for both. [Applause.] This good earth is plenty broad enough for white man and negro both, and there is no need of either pushing the other off. [Continued applause.]

So that saying, "in the struggle between the negro and the crocodile," &c., is made up from the idea that down where the crocodile inhabits a white man can't labor; it must be nothing else but crocodile or negro; if the negro does not the crocodile must possess the earth; [laughter;] in that case he declares for the negro. The meaning of the whole is just this: As a white man is to a negro, so is a negro to a crocodile; and as the negro may rightfully treat the crocodile, so may the white man rightfully treat the negro. This very dear phrase coined by its author, and so dear that he deliberately repeats it in many speeches, has a tendency to still further brutalize the negro, and to bring public opinion to the point of utter indifference whether men so brutalized are enslaved or not. When that time shall come, if ever, I think that policy to which I refer may prevail. But I hope the good freemen of this country will never allow it to come, and until then the policy can never be maintained.

Now consider the effect of this policy. We in the States are not to care whether Freedom or Slavery gets the better, but the people in the Territories may care. They are to decide, and they may think what they please; it is a matter of dollars and cents! But are not the people of the Territories detailed from the States? If this feeling of indifference—this absence of moral sense about the question—prevails in the States, will it not be carried into the Territories? Will not every man say, "I don't care, it is nothing to me?" If any one comes that wants Slavery, must they not say, "I don't care whether Freedom or Slavery be voted up or voted down?" It results at last in naturalizing [nationalizing?][2] the institution of Slavery. Even if fairly carried out, that policy is just as certain to naturalize [nationalize] Slavery as the doctrine of Jeff Davis himself. These are only two roads to the same goal, and "popular sovereignty" is just as sure and almost as short as the other. [Applause.]

What we want, and all we want, is to have with us the men who think slavery wrong. But those who say they hate slavery, and are opposed to it, but yet act with the Democratic party— where are they? Let us apply a few tests. You say that you think slavery is wrong, but you denounce all attempts to restrain it. Is there anything else that you think wrong, that you are not willing to deal with as a wrong? Why are you so careful, so tender of this one wrong and no other? [Laughter.] You will not let us *do* a single thing as if it was wrong; there is no place where you will allow it to be even *called* wrong! We must not call it wrong in the Free States, because it is *not* there, and we must not call it wrong in the Slave States because it *is* there; we must not call it wrong in politics because that is bringing morality into politics, and we must not call it wrong in the pulpit because that is bringing politics into religion; we must not bring it into the Tract Society or the other societies, because those are such unsuitable places, and there is no single place, according to you, where this wrong thing can properly be called wrong! [Continued laughter and applause.]

Perhaps you will plead that if the people of Slave States should themselves set on foot an effort for emancipation, you would wish them success, and bid them God-speed. Let us test that! In 1858, the emancipation party of Missouri, with Frank Blair at their head, tried to get up a movement for that purpose, and having started a party contested the State. Blair was beaten, apparently if not truly, and when the news came to Connecticut, you, who knew that Frank Blair was taking hold of this thing by the right end, and doing the only thing that you say can properly be done to remove this wrong—did you bow your heads in sorrow because of that defeat? Do you, any of you, know one single Democrat that showed sorrow over that result? Not one! On the contrary every man threw up his hat, and hallooed at the top of his lungs, "hooray for Democracy!" [Great laughter and applause.]

Now, gentlemen, *the Republicans desire to place this great question of slavery on the very basis on which our fathers placed it,*

[2] Brackets not in the source. The *Palladium* text is possible, but Lincoln probably said "nationalizing."

and no other. [Applause.] It is easy to demonstrate that "our Fathers, who framed this government under which we live," looked on Slavery as wrong, and so framed it and everything about it as to square with the idea that it was wrong, so far as the necessities arising from its existence permitted. In forming the Constitution they found the slave trade existing; capital invested in it; fields depending upon it for labor, and the whole system resting upon the importation of slave-labor. They therefore did not prohibit the slave trade at once, but they gave the power to prohibit it after twenty years. Why was this? What other foreign trade did they treat in that way? Would they have done this if they had not thought slavery wrong?

Another thing was done by some of the same men who framed the Constitution, and afterwards adopted as their own act by the first Congress held under that Constitution, of which many of the framers were members; they prohibited the spread of Slavery into Territories. Thus the same men, the framers of the Constitution, cut off the supply and prohibited the spread of Slavery, and both acts show conclusively that they considered that the thing was wrong.

If additional proof is wanting it can be found in the phraseology of the Constitution. When men are framing a supreme law and chart of government, to secure blessings and prosperity to untold generations yet to come, they use language as short and direct and plain as can be found, to express their meaning. In all matters but this of Slavery the framers of the Constitution used the very clearest, shortest, and most direct language. But the Constitution alludes to Slavery three times without mentioning it once! The language used becomes ambiguous, roundabout, and mystical. They speak of the "immigration of persons," and mean the importation of slaves, but do not say so. In establishing a basis of representation they say "all other persons," when they mean to say slaves—why did they not use the shortest phrase? In providing for the return of fugitives they say "persons held to service or labor." If they had said slaves it would have been plainer, and less liable to misconstruction. Why didn't they do it. We cannot doubt that it was done on purpose. Only one reason is possible, and that is supplied us by one of the framers of the Constitution—and it is not possible for man to conceive of any other—they expected and desired that the system would come to an end, and meant that when it did, the Constitution should not show that there ever had been a slave in this good free country of ours! [Great applause.]

I will dwell on that no longer. I see the signs of the approaching triumph of the Republicans in the bearing of their political adversaries. A great deal of their war with us now-a-days is mere bushwhacking. [Laughter.] At the battle of Waterloo, when Napoleon's cavalry had charged again and again upon the unbroken squares of British infantry, at last they were giving up the attempt, and going off in disorder, when some of the officers in mere vexation and complete despair fired their pistols at those solid squares. The Democrats are in that sort of extreme desperation; it is nothing else. [Laughter.] I will take up a few of these *arguments*.

There is "THE IRREPRESSIBLE CONFLICT." [Applause.] How they rail at Seward for that saying! They repeat it constantly; and although the proof has been thrust under their noses again and again, that almost every good man since the formation of our government has uttered that same sentiment, from Gen. Washington, who "trusted that we should yet have a confederacy of Free States," with Jefferson, Jay, Monroe, down to the latest days, yet they refuse to notice that at all, and persist in railing at Seward for saying it. Even Roger A. Pryor, editor of the Richmond Enquirer, uttered the same sentiment in almost the same language, and yet so little offence did it give the Democrats that he was sent for to Washington to edit the States—the Douglas organ there, while Douglas goes into hydrophobia and spasms of rage because Seward dared to repeat it. [Great applause.] This is what I call bushwhacking, a sort of argument that they must know any child can see through.

Another is JOHN BROWN! [Great laughter.] You stir up insurrections, you invade the South! John Brown! Harper's Ferry! Why, John Brown was not a Republican! You have never implicated a single Republican in that Harper's Ferry enterprise. We tell you that if any member of the Republican party is guilty in that matter, you know it or you do not know it. If you do know it, you are inexcusable not to designate man and prove the fact. If you do not know it, you are inexcusable to assert it, and especially to persist in the assertion after you have tried and failed to make the proof. You need not be told that persisting in a charge which one does not know to be true is simply malicious slander. Some of you admit that no Republican designedly aided or encouraged the Harper's Ferry affair; but still insist that our doctrines and declarations necessarily lead to such results. We do not believe it. We know we hold to no doctrines, and make no declarations, which were not held to and made by our fathers who framed the Government under which we live, and we cannot see how declarations that were patriotic when they made them are villainous when we make them. You never dealt fairly by us in relation to that affair—and I will say frankly that I know of nothing in your character that should lead us to suppose that you would. You had just been soundly thrashed in elections in several States, and others were soon to come. You rejoiced at the occasion, and only were troubled that there were not three times as many killed in the affair. You were in evident glee—there was no sorrow for the killed nor for the peace of Virginia disturbed—you were rejoicing that by charging Republicans with this thing you might get an advantage of us in New York, and the other States. You pulled that string as tightly as you could, but your very generous and worthy expectations were not quite fulfilled. [Laughter.] Each Republican knew that the charge was a slander as to himself at least, and was not inclined by it to cast his vote in your favor. It was mere bushwhacking, because you had nothing else to do. You are still on that track, and I say, go on! If you think you can slander a woman into loving you or a man into voting for you, try it till you are satisfied! [Tremendous applause.]

Another specimen of this bushwhacking, that "shoe strike." [Laughter.] Now be it understood that I do not pretend to know all about the matter. I am merely going to speculate a little about some of its phases. And at the outset, *I am glad to see that a system of labor prevails in New England under which laborers* CAN *strike* when they want to [Cheers,] where they are not obliged to work under all circumstances, and are not tied down and obliged to labor whether you pay them or not! [Cheers.] I *like* the system which lets a man quit when he wants to, and wish it might prevail everywhere. [Tremendous applause.] One of the reasons why I am opposed to Slavery is just here. What is the true condition of the laborer? I take it that it is best for all to leave each man free to acquire property as fast as he can. Some will get wealthy. I don't believe in a law to prevent a man from getting rich; it would do more harm than good. So while we do not propose any war upon capital, we do wish to allow the humblest man an equal chance to get rich with everybody else. [Applause.] When one starts poor, as most do in the race of life, free society is such that he knows he can better his condition; he knows that there is no fixed condition of labor, for his whole life. I am not ashamed to confess that twenty five years ago I was a hired laborer, mauling rails, at work on a flat-boat—just what might happen to any poor man's son! [Applause.] I want every man to have the chance—and I believe a black man is entitled to it—in which he *can* better his condition—when he may look forward and hope to be a hired laborer this year and the next, work for himself afterward, and finally to hire men to work for him! That is the true system. Up here in New England, you have a soil that scarcely sprouts black-eyed beans, and yet where will you find wealthy men so wealthy, and poverty so rarely in extremity? There is not another such place on earth! [Cheers.] I desire that if you get too thick here, and find it hard to better your condition on this soil, you may have a chance to strike and go somewhere else, where you may not be degraded, nor have your family corrupted by forced rivalry with negro slaves. I want you to have a clean bed, and no snakes in it! [Cheers.] Then you can better your condition, and so it may go on and on in one ceaseless round so long as man exists on the face of the earth! [Prolonged applause.]

Now, to come back to this shoe strike,—if, as the Senator from Illinois asserts, this is caused by withdrawal of Southern votes, consider briefly how you will meet the difficulty. You have done nothing, and have protested that you have done nothing, to injure the South. And yet, to get back the shoe trade, you must leave off doing something that you are now doing. What is it? You must stop thinking slavery wrong! Let your institutions be wholly changed; let your State Constitutions be subverted, glorify slavery, and so you will get back the shoe trade—for what? You have brought owned labor with it to compete with your own labor, to under-work you, and to degrade you! Are you ready to get back the trade on those terms?

But the statement is not correct. You have not lost that trade; orders were never better than now! Senator Mason, a Democrat, comes into the Senate in homespun, a proof that the dissolution of the Union has actually begun! but orders are the same. Your factories have not struck work, neither those where they make anything for coats, nor for pants, nor for shirts, nor for ladies' dresses. Mr. Mason has not reached the manufacturers who ought to have made him a coat and pants! To make his proof good for anything he should have come into the Senate barefoot! (Great laughter.)

Another bushwhacking contrivance; simply that, nothing else! I find a good many people who are very much concerned about the loss of Southern trade. Now either these people are sincere or they are not. (Laughter.) I will speculate a little about that. If they are sincere, and are moved by any real danger of the loss of Southern trade, they will simply get their names on the white list,[3]

---

[3] Lincoln refers to a movement on the part of certain business interests to take advantage of the Southern boycott of New England manufactures by preparing a list of "white" (Democrat) rather than "black" (Republican) manufacturing concerns for the guidance of Southern purchasers.

and then, instead of persuading Republicans to do likewise, they will be glad to keep you away! Don't you see they thus shut off competition? They would not be whispering around to Republicans to come in and share the profits with them. But if they are not sincere, and are merely trying to fool Republicans out of their votes, they will grow very anxious about *your* pecuniary prospects; they are afraid you are going to get broken up and ruined; they did not care about Democratic votes—*Oh no, no, no!* You must judge which class those belong to whom you meet; I leave it to you to determine from the facts.

Let us notice some more of the stale charges against Republicans. You say we are sectional. We deny it. That makes an issue; and the burden of proof is upon you. You produce your proof; and what is it? Why, that our party has no existence in your section— gets no votes in your section. The fact is substantially true; but does it prove the issue? If it does, then in case we should, without change of principle, begin to get votes in your section, we should thereby cease to be sectional. You cannot escape this conclusion; and yet, are you willing to abide by it? If you are, you will probably soon find that we have ceased to be sectional, for we shall get votes in your section this very year. [Applause.] The fact that we get no votes in your section is a fact of your making, and not of ours. And if there be fault in that fact, that fault is primarily yours, and remains so until you show that we repel you by some wrong principle or practice. If we do repel you by any wrong principle or practice, the fault is ours; but this brings you to where you ought to have started—to a discussion of the right or wrong of our principle. If our principle, put in practice, would wrong your section for the benefit of ours, or for any other object, then our principle, and we with it, are sectional, and are justly opposed and denounced as such. Meet us, then, on the question of whether our principle, put in practice, would wrong your section; and so meet it as if it were possible that something may be said on our side. Do you accept the challenge? No? Then you really believe that the principle which our fathers who framed the Government under which we live thought so clearly right as to adopt it, and indorse it again and again, upon their official oaths, is, in fact, so clearly wrong as to demand your condemnation without a moment's consideration.

Some of you delight to flaunt in our faces the warning against sectional parties given by Washington in his Farewell address. Less than eight years before Washington gave that warning, he had, as President of the United States, approved and signed an act of Congress, enforcing the prohibition of Slavery in the north-western Territory, which act embodied the policy of Government upon that subject, up to and at the very moment he penned that warning; and about one year after he penned it he wrote LaFayette that he considered that prohibition a wise measure, expressing in the same connection his hope that we should some time have a confederacy of Free States.

Bearing this in mind, and seeing that sectionalism has since arisen upon this same subject, is that warning a weapon in your hands against us, or in our hands against you? Could Washington himself speak, would he cast the blame of that sectionalism upon us, who sustain his policy, or upon you who repudiate it? We respect that warning of Washington, and we commend it to you, together with his example pointing to the right application of it. [Applause.]

But you say you are conservative—eminently conservative—while we are revolutionary, destructive, or something of the sort. What is conservatism? Is it not adherence to the old and tried, against the new and untried? We stick to, contend for, the identical old policy on the point in controversy which was adopted by our fathers who framed the Government under which we live; while you with one accord reject, and scout, and spit upon that old policy, and insist upon substituting something new. True, you disagree among yourselves as to what that substitute shall be. You have considerable variety of new propositions and plans, but you are unanimous in rejecting and denouncing the old policy of the fathers. Some of you are for reviving the foreign slave-trade; some for a Congressional Slave-Code for the Territories; some for Congress forbidding the Territories to prohibit Slavery within their limits; some for maintaining Slavery in the Territories through the Judiciary; some for the "gur-reat pur-rin-ciple" that "if one man would enslave another, no third man should object," fantastically called "Popular Sovereignty;" [great laughter,] but never a man among you in favor of Federal prohibition of Slavery in Federal Territories, according to the practice of our fathers who framed the Government under which we live. Not one of all your various plans can show a precedent or an advocate in the century within which our Government originated. And yet you draw yourselves up and say "We are eminently conservative!" [Great laughter.]

It is exceedingly desirable that all parts of this great Confederacy shall be at peace, and in harmony, one with another. Let us Republicans do our part to have it so. Even though much provoked, let us do nothing through passion and ill temper. Even though the Southern people will not so much as listen to us, let us calmly consider their demands, and yield to them if, in our deliberate view of our duty, we possibly can. Judging by all they say and do, and by the subject and nature of their controversy with us, let us determine, if we can, what will satisfy them?

Will they be satisfied if the Territories be unconditionally surrendered to them? We know they will not. In all their present complaints against us, the Territories are scarcely mentioned. Invasions and insurrections are the rage now. Will it satisfy them if, in the future, we have nothing to do with invasions and insurrections? We know it will not. We so know because we know we never had anything to do with invasions and insurrections; and yet this total abstaining does not exempt us from the charge and the denunciation.

The question recurs, what will satisfy them? Simply this: we must not only let them alone, but we must, somehow, convince them that we do let them alone. [Applause.] This, we know by experience, is no easy task. We have been so trying to convince them, from the very beginning of our organization, but with no success. In all our platforms and speeches, we have constantly protested our purpose to let them alone; but this has had no tendency to convince them. Alike unavailing to convince them is the fact that they have never detected a man of us in any attempt to disturb them.

These natural and apparently adequate means all failing, what will convince them? This, and this only; cease to call slavery *wrong*, and join them in calling it *right*. And this must be done thoroughly—done in *acts* as well as in *words*. Silence will not be tolerated—we must place ourselves avowedly with them. Douglas's new sedition law must be enacted and enforced, suppressing all declarations that Slavery is wrong, whether made in politics, in presses, in pulpits, or in private. We must arrest and return their fugitive slaves with greedy pleasure. We must pull down our Free State Constitutions. The whole atmosphere must be disinfected of all taint of opposition to Slavery, before they will cease to believe that all their troubles proceed from us. So long as we call Slavery wrong, whenever a slave runs away they will overlook the obvious fact that he ran because he was oppressed, and declare he was stolen off. Whenever a master cuts his slaves with the lash, and they cry out under it, he will overlook the obvious fact that the negroes cry out because they are hurt, and insist that they were *put up to it by some rascally abolitionist*. [Great laughter.]

I am quite aware that they do not state their case precisely in this way. Most of them would probably say to us, "Let us alone, do nothing to us, and say what you please about Slavery." But we do let them alone—have never disturbed them—so that, after all, it is what we say, which dissatisfies them. They will continue to accuse us of doing, until we cease saying.

I am also aware they have not, as yet, in terms, demanded the overthrow of our Free State Constitutions. Yet those Constitutions declare the wrong of Slavery, with more solemn emphasis than do all other sayings against it; and when all these other sayings shall have been silenced, the overthrow of these Constitutions will be demanded, and nothing be left to resist the demand. It is nothing to the contrary, that they do not demand the whole of this just now. Demanding what they do, and for the reason they do, they can voluntarily stop nowhere short of this consummation. Holding as they do, that Slavery is morally right, and socially elevating, they cannot cease to demand a full national recognition of it, as a legal right, and a social blessing.

Nor can we justifiably withhold this, on any ground save our conviction that Slavery is wrong. If Slavery is right, all words, acts, laws, and Constitutions against it, are themselves wrong, and should be silenced, and swept away. If it is right, we cannot justly object to its nationality—its universality; if it is wrong, they cannot justly insist upon its extension—its enlargement. All they ask, we could readily grant, if we thought Slavery right; all we ask, they could as readily grant, if they thought it wrong. Their thinking it right, and our thinking it wrong, is the precise fact upon which depends the whole controversy. Thinking it right as they do, they are not to blame for desiring its full recognition, as being right; but, thinking it wrong, as we do, can we yield to them? Can we cast our votes with their view, and against our own? In view of our moral, social, and political responsibilities, can we do this?

Wrong as we think Slavery is, we can yet afford to let it alone where it is, because that much is due to the necessity arising from its actual presence in the nation; but can we, while our votes will prevent it, allow it to spread into the National Territories, and to overrun us here in these Free States?

If our sense of duty forbids this, then let us stand by our duty, fearlessly and effectively. Let us be diverted by none of those sophistical contrivances wherewith we are so industriously plied and belabored—contrivances such as groping for some middle ground between the right and the wrong, vain as the search for a man who should be neither a living man nor a dead man—such as a policy of "don't care" on a question about which all true men do care—such as Union appeals beseeching true Union men to yield to Disunionists, reversing the divine rule, and calling, not the sinners, but the righteous to repentance—such as invocations of Washington, imploring men to unsay what Washington did.

Neither let us be slandered from our duty by false accusations against us, nor frightened from it by menaces of destruction to the Government, nor of dungeons to ourselves. Let us have faith that right makes might; and in that faith, let us, to the end, dare to do our duty, as we understand it.

To William A. Beers and Sereno Mansfield[1]

Messrs. Beers & Mansfield   Springfield, Ills. March 14, 1860

Gentlemen Your request to take a Photographic likeness of me, while in your City, was duly received; but at a time when my arrangements were so made that I could not call upon you before leaving. I would have written sooner, but the matter passed out of my mind; and is now recalled by the sight of your note. I beg you will believe me guilty of no intentional disrespect. Very Respectfully   A. LINCOLN

[1] ALS, OClWHi. Beers and Mansfield were photographers at New Haven, Connecticut.

To A. Chester[1]

A. Chester, Esq   Springfield Ills.

Dear Sir: March 14, 1860

Your very kind and flattering letter, inclosing an invitation to the Connecticut editors to accept the hospitalities of those giving the invitation, while attending the Chicago convention, was received by me at New-Haven. I was the guest of an editor at the time—Mr. Jas. F. Babcock[2]—and to whom I delivered to [the?] document, perceiving no better way to dispose of it. I suppose it was published at once   Yours truly   A. LINCOLN

[1] ALS, ICHi. The identity of A. Chester is somewhat obscure. The inference is that he was a newspaper man at Chicago, but Chicago directories list only "Augustine Chester" as a lawyer in 1858, "Augustus Chester" (at the same address) in 1860, and again the same as "Augustin Chester" in 1862. An "A. Chester" edited the Kankakee *Gazette* (1853-1856), but that he was Lincoln's correspondent has not been verified.

[2] James F. Babcock was editor of the New Haven *Palladium*.

To Alexander W. Harvey[1]

Alexr. W. Harvey, Esq   Springfield, Ills.
Dear Sir   March 14, 1860

Your despach of the 27th. ult. to Mr. Greely, asking if you could not have a speech from me on my return, was forwarded to me by Mr. G. reaching me at Exeter N.H.

The appointments I had then already made carried me so far beyond my allotted time that I could not consistently add another.

I hope I may yet be allowed to meet the good people of Buffalo before the close of the struggle in which we are engaged. Yours Respectfully   A. LINCOLN

[1] ALS, RPB. Alexander W. Harvey was an attorney at Buffalo, New York.

To Rufus W. Miles[1]

Rufus W. Miles, Esq   Springfield,
My dear Sir: March 15– 1860

Reaching home yesterday from the East, I found your letter urging the necessity of my making a speech of a particular sort; and while I was considering it, your second note came in the morning, telling me I had already made the speech you were wanting, and thus relieving me considerably.

Thanking you for your kind feelings towards me, and your good opinion of my late speech, allow me to subscribe myself. Yours very truly   A. LINCOLN

[1] ALS, owned by Joseph W. Miles, Gilson, Illinois. Rufus W. Miles was representative from Knox County in the Illinois House of Representatives.

To Mark W. Delahay[1]

Dear Delahay—   Springfield, Ills– Mar– 16, 1860

I have just returned from the East. Before leaving, I received your letter of Feb. 6; and on my return I find those of the 17th. & 19th. with Genl. Lane's[2] note inclosed in one of them.

I sincerely wish you could be elected one of the first Senators for Kansas; but how to help you I do not know. If it were permissable for me to interfere, I am not personally acquainted with a single member of your Legislature. If my known friendship for you could be of any advantage, that friendship was abundantly manifested by me last December while in Kansas. If any member had written me, as you say some have Trumbull, I would very readily answer him. I shall write Trumbull on the subject at this sitting.

I understood, while in Kansas, that the State Legislature will not meet until the State is admitted. Was that the right understanding?

As to your kind wishes for myself, allow me to say I can not enter the ring on the money basis—first, because, in the main, it is wrong; and secondly, I have not, and can not get, the money. I say, in the main, the use of money is wrong; but for certain objects, in a political contest, the use of some, is both right, and indispensable. With me, as with yourself, this long struggle has been one of great pecuniary loss. I now distinctly say this. If you shall be appointed a delegate to Chicago, I will furnish one hundred dollars to bear the expences of the trip.[3]

Present my respects to Genl. Lane; and say to him, I shall be pleased to hear from him at any time. Your friend, as ever

A. LINCOLN—

P.S. I have not yet taken the newspaper slip to the Journal. I shall do that to-morrow; and then send you the paper as requested.

A. L.

[1] ALS, DLC-HW.   [2] James H. Lane.
[3] See Lincoln to Delahay, April 14, *infra*.

To Lyman Trumbull[1]

Hon: L. Trumbull   Springfield, Mar– 16, 1860

My dear Sir: When I first saw by the despaches that Douglas had run from the Senate while you were speaking I did not quite understand it; but seeing by the report that you were cramming down his throat that infernal stereotyped lye of his about "negro equality" the thing became plain.

Another matter. Our friend Delahay wants to be one of the Senators from Kansas. Certainly it is not for outsiders to obtrude their interference. Delahay has suffered a great deal in our cause, and been very faithful to it, as I understand. He writes me that some of the members of the Kansas Legislature have written you in a way that your simple answer might help him. I wish you would consider whether you can not assist him that far, without impropriety. I know it is a delicate matter; and I do not wish to press you beyond your own judgment.[2] Yours as ever

A. LINCOLN—

[1] ALS, CSmH.
[2] Trumbull replied, March 26, that he would be glad to help "our friend Delahay, if I knew how to do it. . . ." but that the Kansans who had written him had not inquired about Delahay and that he could write something in his behalf only if they asked (DLC-RTL).

To James W. Somers[1]

James W. Somers, Esq   Springfield,
My dear Sir: March 17, 1860

Reaching home from the East three days ago, I found your letter of Feb. 26th.

Considering your difficulty of hearing I think you would better settle in Chicago, if as you say, a good many already in fair practice there will take you into partnership. If you had not that difficulty I still should think it an even ballance whether you would not better remain in Chicago, with such a chance for a co-partnership.

If I went West, I think I would go to Kansas—to Leavenworth, or Atchison. Both these are, and will continue to be fine growing places.

I believe I have said all I can, and I have said it with the deepest interest for your welfare   Yours truly   A. Lincoln

[1] ALS-F, Henry C. Whitney, *Life on the Circuit with Lincoln*, 1892, p. 266. Somers wrote that he wanted to leave Urbana, and asked Lincoln's advice as to going into partnership with Henry C. Whitney in Chicago, or going to Missouri or Kansas (DLC-RTL). See also Lincoln's letter of recommendation, March 28, *infra*.

To E. Stafford[1]

Springfield, Illinois, March 17, 1860.

Dear Sir: Reaching home on the 14th instant, I found yours of the 1st. Thanking you very sincerely for your kind purposes toward me, I am compelled to say the money part of the arrangement you propose is, with me, an impossibility. I could not raise ten thousand dollars if it would save me from the fate of John Brown. Nor have my friends, so far as I know, yet reached the point of staking any money on my chances of success. I wish I could tell you better things, but it is even so. Yours very truly,

A. Lincoln.

[1] NH, VI, 7. There are no letters from E. Stafford in the Lincoln Papers, and efforts to identify him have been unsuccessful.

To Samuel Galloway[1]

Hon. Samuel Galloway   Chicago, March 24, 1860

My dear Sir: I am here attending a trial in court. Before leaving home I received your kind letter of the 15th. Of course I am gratified to know I have friends in Ohio who are disposed to give me the highest evidence of their friendship and confidence. Mr Parrott[2] of the Legislature, had written me to the same effect. If I have any chance, it consists mainly in the fact that the *whole* opposition would vote for me if nominated. (I dont mean to include the pro-slavery opposition of the South, of course.) My name is new in the field; and I suppose I am not the *first* choice of a very great many. Our policy, then, is to give no offence to others —leave them in a mood to come to us, if they shall be compelled to give up their first love. This, too, is dealing justly with all, and leaving us in a mood to support heartily whoever shall be nominated. I believe I have once before told you that I especially wish to do no ungenerous thing towards Governor Chase, because he gave us his sympathy in 1858, when scarcely any other distinguished man did. Whatever you may do for me, consistently with these suggestions, will be appreciated, and gratefully remembered.

Please write me again. Yours very truly   A. LINCOLN

[1] Copy, DLC-RTL. The copy is in Nicolay's handwriting and bears his certification as being "From the original, in the possession of Dr. Guy Coulter, Columbus Ohio." The original is presumably extant but has not been located.

[2] Edwin A. Parrott, representative in the Ohio legislature from Montgomery County, who had met Lincoln at Dayton in September, 1859.

To Lyman Trumbull[1]

Hon: L. Trumbull   Chicago, March 26. 1860

My dear Sir: They are having a desperate struggle in Connecticut; and it would both please, and help our friends there, if you could be with them in the last days of the fight. Having been there, I know they are proud of you as a son of their own soil, and would be moved to greater exertion by your presence among them. Can you not go? Telegraph them, and go right along. The fiendish attempt now being made upon Connecticut, must not be allowed to succeed. Yours as ever   A. LINCOLN

[1] ALS, CSmH.

To Ward H. Lamon[1]

Hon: W. H. Lamon.   Chicago, March 28– 1860

My dear Sir: Yours about motion to quash an indictment, was received yesterday. I think I had no authority but the Statute when I wrote the Indictment. In fact, I remember but little about it. I think yet there is no necessity for setting out the letter in *haec verba.* Our Statute, as I think, relaxes the high degree of technical certainty formerly required.

I am so busy with our case on trial here,[2] that I can not examine authorities near as fully as you can there.

If, after all, the indictment shall be quashed, it will only prove that my *forte* is as a Statesman, rather than as a Prossecutor. Yours as ever   A. LINCOLN.

[1] ALS, CSmH. As prosecuting attorney, Lamon wrote from Lincoln, Illinois, on March 26, about Lincoln's motion to quash the indictment against his client for sending a threatening letter. On Lincoln's suggestion the indictment had not included the letter. The motion declared that the letter was not set out in the indictment, and Lamon wished Lincoln to investigate authorities and find reason to sustain the indictment, since "Quashing an Indct. written by a prominent candidate for the Presidency of the U.S. by a *little court* like Col. [David] Davis' will not sound well in history." Names of litigants are not given, and no other references to the case have been found (DLC-RTL).

[2] Johnston *v.* Jones and Marsh, the famous "Sandbar Case." See Lincoln to Robert A. Kinzie, January 5, 1858, *supra.*

Recommendation for James W. Somers[1]

Whom it may concern—   Chicago. March 28. 1860

My young friend James W. Somers, the bearer of this, I have known from boyhood, and I can truly say that in my opinion he is entirely faithful, and fully competent to the performance[2] of any business he will undertake.   A. LINCOLN

[1] ALS-F, Whitney, *The Lincoln Autographic Album* [c.1891], p. 44. See letter to Somers, March 17, *supra.*

[2] "Discharge" deleted and "performance" inserted by Lincoln.

Endorsement on an Express Company Envelope[1]

[April 1, 1860]

This brought me Fifteen dollars, without any intimation as to whom it came from. It probably came from Mr. Patterson to whom I loaned that amount a few weeks ago.   LINCOLN—

[1] AES, DLC-RTL. This endorsement is written on an envelope of the United States Express Company, sent from Homer, Illinois. The date April 1, 1860, is not in Lincoln's hand, but may be that of the agent. The date September 25, 1858, given to this endorsement by Helen Nicolay (*Personal Traits of Abraham Lincoln,* p. 110) and followed by Angle (*New Letters and Papers of Abraham Lincoln,* p. 196) is obviously an error of transposition—the date belonging with the preceding item concerning Henry Chew. "Mr. Patterson" was probably one of two brothers, William and Golden Patterson of Champaign County, Illinois. In April, 1859, Lincoln had defended a third brother, Thomas Patterson, in a murder trial. See Lincoln's endorsement, August 14, *infra.*

To Richard M. Corwine[1]

Hon. R. M. Corwine.   Springfield, Ill., April 6th. 1860.

My Dear Sir   Reaching home yesterday after an absence of more than two weeks, I found your letter of the 24th of March. Remembering that when not a very great man begins to be mentioned for a very great position, his head is very likely to be a little turned, I concluded I am not the fittest person to answer the questions you ask. Making due allowance for this, I think Mr. Seward is the very best candidate we could have for the North of Illinois, and the very *worst* for the South of it. The estimate of Gov. Chase here is neither better nor worse than that of Seward, except that he is a newer man. They are regarded as being almost the same, seniority giving Seward the inside track. Mr. Bates, I think, would be the best man for the South of our State, and the worst for the North of it. If Judge McLean was fifteen, or even ten years younger, I think he would be stronger than either, in our state, taken as a whole; but his great age, and the recollection of the deaths of Harrison and Taylor have, so far, prevented his being much spoken of here.

I really believe we can carry the state for either of them, or for any one who may be nominated; but doubtless it would be easier to do it with some than with others.

I feel myself disqualified to speak of myself in this matter. I feel this letter will be of little value to you; but I can make it no better, under the circumstances. Let it be strictly confidential, not that there is any thing really objectionable in it, but because it might be misconstrued. Yours very truly,   A. LINCOLN.

[1] Tracy, pp. 138-39. Richard M. Corwine, a lawyer at Cincinnati, wrote that the delegates from Ohio were divided on Chase, Bates, Seward, and McLean, and asked whether Illinois would support McLean, Bates or Seward. He added, "I am pretty sure we could unite more votes on you than on Seward" (DLC-RTL).

To William Gooding[1]

Wm. Gooding, Esq   Springfield, Ills.
My dear Sir: April 6, 1860

Reaching home yesterday, I found your very kind and complimentary letter of March 21st.; and for which, I sincerely thank you. Our down East friends did, indeed, treat me with great kindness, demonstrating what I before believed, that all good, inteligent people are very much alike. Yours very truly

A. LINCOLN

[1] ALS-P, ISLA. William Gooding was an old acquaintance at Lockport, Illinois, who had been chief engineer for the construction of the Illinois-Michigan Canal, and in 1860 was still connected with the canal as secretary.

To William C. Hobbs and William H. Hanna[1]

Dr. W. C. Hobbs, &   Springfield,
W. H. Hanna, Esq   April 6. 1860

Gentlemen   Your despach, requesting me to deliver a speech at Bloomington is received. I very much prefer to make no more speeches soon; but if, as friends of mine, you can not excuse me, it is not much odds when—say, the evening of Tuesday the 10th. Inst. Yours as ever   A. LINCOLN

[1] ALS, ICU. William C. Hobbs was a schoolteacher and county clerk at Bloomington, Illinois.

To Richard V. B. Lincoln[1]

Richd. V. B. Lincoln, Esq   Springfield, Ills.
My dear Sir   April 6. 1860

Owing to absence from home, yours of March 19th. was not received till yesterday. You are a little mistaken. My grand-father did not go from Berks Co. Pa; but, as I learn, his ancesters did, some time before his birth. He was born in Rockingham Co Va; went from there to Kentucky, and there was killed by indians about 1784. That the family originally came from Berks, I learned a dozen years ago, by letter, from one of them, then residing at Sparta, Rockingham Co. Va. His name was David Lincoln.[2] I rem[em]ber, long ago, seeing Austin Lincoln, & Davis Lincoln, said to be sons of Hannaniah, or Annaniah Lincoln, who was said to have been a cousin of my grand-father.[3] I have no doubt you and I are distantly related. I should think from what you say, that you and my father were second cousins.

I shall be glad to hear from you at any time. Yours very truly
           A. LINCOLN

[1] ALS-F, Ervin S. Chapman, *Latest Light on Abraham Lincoln and War-Time Memories* [c.1917], p. 510. Richard V. B. Lincoln was a farmer and county commissioner at Laurelton, Pennsylvania. His letter of March 19 is not in the Lincoln Papers. [2] *Vide supra*, March 24, 1848.

[3] Hannaniah Lincoln's sons Austin and Davis migrated from Kentucky to Perry County and Spencer County, Indiana, probably a year or two before Abraham's father took his family to Spencer County.

To Cornelius F. McNeill[1]

C. F. McNeill, Esq.–   Springfield, April 6, 1860.

Dear Sir: Reaching home yesterday, I found yours of the 23d. March, inclosing a slip from *The Middleport Press*. It is not true that I ever *charged* anything for a political speech in my life—but this much is true: Last October I was requested, by letter, to deliver some sort of speech in Mr. Beechers[2] church, in Brooklyn, $200 being offered in the first letter. I wrote that I could do it in February, provided they would take a political speech, if I could find time to get up no other. They agreed, and subsequently I informed them the speech would have to be a political one. When I reached New York, I, for the first [time], learned that the place was changed to "Cooper Institute." I made the speech, and left for New Hampshire, where I have a son at school, neither asking for pay nor having any offered me. Three days after, a check for $200– was sent to me, at N.H., and I took it, *and did not know it was wrong*. My understanding now is, though I knew nothing of it at the time, that they did charge for admittance, at the Cooper Institute, and that they took in more than twice $200.

I have made this explanation to you as a friend; but I wish no explanation made to our enemies. What they want is a squabble and a fuss; and that they can have if we explain; and they can not have if we don't.

When I returned through New York from New England I was told by the gentlemen who sent me the check, that a drunken vagabond in the Club, having learned something about the $200, made the exhibition out of which *The Herald* manufactured the article quoted by *The Press* of your town.

My judgment is, and therefore my request is, that you give no denial, and no explanations.

Thanking you for your kind interest in the matter, I remain,
Yours truly,   A. LINCOLN.

[1] Copy, CSmH-Lamon Papers; copy (incomplete), DLC-HW. Cornelius F. McNeill was editor of the Middleport *Press* and an attorney at Middleport, Iroquois County, Illinois—a town no longer in existence, having become a part of Watseka, Illinois.   [2] Henry W. Beecher.

To John Pickering[1]

John Pickering, Esq.   Springfield, Ills., April 6, 1860.

My Dear Sir: Reaching home yesterday after an absence of two weeks, I found your letter of March 24th. Pamphlet copies of my late speech at Cooper Institute, N.Y., can be had at the office of the

N.Y. Tribune; at the Republican Club Room at Washington, and at the office of the Illinois Journal at this place. At which place they are cheapest, I do not certainly know.

I have no difficulty in knowing who you are, by the fact that I knew your father so very well. I shall be glad to hear from you at any time. Yours truly,   A. LINCOLN.

[1] Printed in Walter Colyer, "Times When Lincoln Remembered Albion," *Journal of the Illinois State Historical Society*, IX (January, 1917), 494-95. John Pickering was the son of William Pickering, Whig state representative from Edwards County (1842-1852).

To John M. Carson[1]

John M. Carson, Esq.,
Chairman of the Committee of Lectures   Springfield,
Of the Harrison Literary Institute.   April 7, 1860

Dear Sir: Yours of March 14 addressed to me at Chicago seeking to arrange with me to lecture for the Harrison Literary Institute has been received. I regret that I cannot make such an arrangement. I am not a professional lecturer. Have never got up but one lecture, and that I think rather a poor one. Besides, what time I can spare from my own business this season I shall be compelled to give to politics. Respectfully yours,   A. LINCOLN.

[1] Tracy, p. 141. The Harrison Literary Institute was at Philadelphia. See also the almost identical letter to F. C. Herbruger, *infra*. The fact that there is no letter of invitation from Carson in the Lincoln Papers is strange, especially since Herbruger's letter is preserved. The original letter to Carson has not been located, and in view of the almost identical text in Tracy, the editors have wondered whether the letter to Carson actually exists. A letter from Carson, July 19, 1860 (DLC-RTL), in which he introduces himself, as if for the first time, and offers to deliver 150 or 200 votes which he claims to control, in consideration of his appointment to a job in the postoffice or customs, is so written as to suggest that he had never before written to or received a letter from Lincoln.

To Harvey G. Eastman[1]

H. G. Eastman, Esq   Springfield, Ills.
Dear Sir   April 7. 1860

Yours of March 18th. addressed to me at Chicago, and requesting my photograph is received. I have not a single one now at my control; but I think you can easily get one at New-York. While I was there I was taken to one of the places where they get up such things, and I suppose they got my shaddow, and can multiply copies indefinitely.[2] Any of the Republican Club men there can show you the place. Yours truly   A. LINCOLN

1 ALS, owned by Miss Mary Bowditch Forbes, Milton, Massachusetts. Harvey G. Eastman was an abolitionist operating a business college at Poughkeepsie, New York.
2 The photographs made by Mathew Brady, February 27, 1860.

To F. C. Herbruger[1]

F. C. Herbruger, Secy &c   Springfield, Ills.
Dear Sir   April 7. 1860

Yours of March 14th. addressed to me at Chicago, and seeking to arrange with me to Lecture for the Harrison Literary Institute, has been received. I regret to say I can not make such arrangement. I am not a professional lecturer—have never got up but one lecture; and that, I think, rather a poor one. Besides, what time I can spare from my own business this season, I shall be compelled to give to politics. Respectfully Yours   A. LINCOLN

1 ALS, ORB. Herbruger's letter is on the letterhead of the "Hall of Harrison Literary Institute," Philadelphia, Pennsylvania, and he signs himself as "Secretary of Committee on Lectures" (DLC-RTL). See also the almost identical letter to Carson, *supra*.

To Lyman Trumbull[1]

Hon: L. Trumbull   Springfield, Ills. April 7– 1860

My dear Sir: Reaching home from Chicago, where I have been engaged two weeks in the trial of a lawsuit, I found your letter of March 26th.

Of course you can do no better for Delahay than you promise.[2]

I am trying to keep out of the contest among our friends for the Gubernatorial nomination;[3] but from what I hear, the result is in considerable doubt.

We have just had a clear party victory in our city election; and our friends are more encouraged, and our enemies more cowed by it, than by anything since the organization of the Republican party. Last year we carried the city; but we did it, not by our own strength; but by an open feud among our enemies. This year their feud was healed; and we beat them fairly by main strength.

I can scarcely give an opinion as to what effect a nomination of Judge McLean, by the Union convention, would have.[4] I do not believe he would accept it; and if he did, that fact alone, I think, would shut him out of the Chicago convention. If he were ten years younger he would be our best candidate. Yours as ever
                                                          A. LINCOLN

1 ALS, CSmH.   2 *Vide supra*, Lincoln to Trumbull, March 16, n.2.
3 Richard Yates received the Republican nomination and was elected.
4 Trumbull had written March 26 that he had heard the Union Convention would nominate Judge John McLean (DLC-RTL).

Speech at Bloomington, Illinois[1]

April 10, 1860

On Tuesday evening last, Hon. Abram Lincoln delivered a speech at Phoenix Hall in this city, of which we took tolerably full note, and of which we should be pleased to give a fuller notice than the crowded state of our columns today will permit. We shall, however, endeavor to state his points distinctly, and in such a manner as to do him no injustice.

After a few apologetic remarks, the speaker proceeded to comment upon polygamy in Utah, and the recent action in the United States house of representatives on that subject.[2] He said his main object in doing so was to call attention to the views and action of gentlemen who held to the doctrine of popular sovereignty, as related to the suppression of polygamy. These gentlemen, he said, were less than half the democratic members of the house—southern democrats voting for the anti-polygamy bill, because it favored the doctrine that congress could control the subject of *slavery* in the territories. But the Illinois democrats, although as much opposed to polygamy as any body else, dare not vote for the bill, because it was opposed to Mr. Douglas.

Mr. McClernand, of Illinois, had proposed to suppress the evil of polygamy by dividing up the territory, and attaching the different portions to other territories. He admitted that he had not seen Col. McClernand's speech on the subject; but proceeded to comment upon his action, nevertheless. McClernand's proposition was in harmony with the views formerly suggested by Mr. Douglas in a speech at Springfield; and he gave him credit for consistency, at least. But, inquired the speaker, how much better was it to divide up the territory and attach its parts to others? It was effecting indirectly that which Mr. McClernand denied could be done directly. This inconsistency, Mr. Lincoln illustrated by a classic example of a similar inconsistency: "If I cannot rightfully murder a man, I may tie him to the tail of a kicking horse, and let him kick the man to death!"

But why divide up the territory at all? continued he. Something must be wrong there, or it would not be necessary to act at all. And if one mode of interference is wrong, why not the other? Why is not an act dividing the territory as much against popular sovereignty as one for prohibiting polygamy? If you can put down polygamy in that way, why may you not thus put down slavery?

Mr. Lincoln said he *supposed* that the friends of popular sovereignty would say—if they dared speak out—that *polygamy* was wrong and slavery right; and therefore one might thus be put down and the other not; and after *supposing* several other things of northern democrats, he proceeded to notice, what he called, Mr. Douglas's sedition law.[3]

On the subject of the proposed law, he began by reading Mr. Douglas's resolution as offered to the senate. Everything prohibited in the resolution, said he, is wrong, and ought to be prohibited and punished. There was now no such law against them, simply, as he supposed, because nobody had thought the crimes enumerated in the resolution would ever be committed. And, moreover, he declared, not one of them ever had been committed! He defied any one to point to a single instance where the authorities or the people of one state had invaded another: or where there had been a conspiracy or combination to interfere with the institutions or property of the people in one state by citizens of another! John Brown, to be sure, had made a raid into Virginia; but Virginia had been competent to deal with him and his confederates without a congressional law; and hence no such law was necessary. Insurrections had always been put down; hence no law was necessary against them. What, then, inquired the speaker, was the *real* object of Mr. Douglas's proposition? He then quoted from that gentleman's speech on the subject, in which he says that Brown's raid into Virginia, and similar outrages, were the legitimate and logical result of the abolition teachings of the day. Then, said Mr. Lincoln, I conceive the real object of the proposed bill was to put down republicanism; to prevent republican meetings, and to shut men's mouths! If, however, he added, the only object is to punish negro-dealers, he had no objection. But he denied that any body had ever conspired to steal negroes.

The speaker then went on to comment on the proposed law, as if it was only meant to suppress free speech; addressed his remarks chiefly to Mr. Douglas, and throughout the speech seemed to consider him as the only man in the democratic party who was worthy of attention. A few words on the question why, if states and territories may introduce slavery, McLean county, or any individual may not, according to popular sovereignty, do the same, concluded the speech.

[1] *Illinois State Register*, April 17, 1860, copied from Bloomington *Statesman* (undated).

[2] H.R. 7, introduced by Representative Justin S. Morrill of Vermont, to punish the practice of polygamy, etc., passed the House April 5, but died in the Senate.

[3] Douglas' resolution introduced in the Senate January 16, calling on the Committee on the Judiciary to introduce a bill to protect a state or territory against invasion, etc., was tabled February 1.

To James F. Babcock[1]

Jas. F. Babcock, Esq   Springfield, Ills.

My dear Sir: April 14. 1860

Reaching home, after a short absence, I find your obliging letter of the 8th. I was very anxious for the result in Connecticut, and am much gratified that it is all safe.

As to the Presidential nomination, claiming no greater exemption from selfishness than is common, I still feel that my whole aspiration should be, and therefore must be, to be placed anywhere, or nowhere, as may appear most likely to advance our cause.

As to the names of confidential friends here, with whom you might correspond, I give you David Davis, Bloomington, Ills.

Julius White,[2] Chicago,   "

Dr. I. A. W. Buck, Aurora, "

A. Sympson, Carthage   "

I will add that Hon J. W. Grimes & Hon. S. R. Curtis, Senator & Representative from Iowa, are very friendly to me, though I do not know that they favor my nomination. The following named gentlemen are probably for me—and would like to correspond with you.

Hon: Saml. Galloway, Columbus, O.

"   Robt. C. Schenck, Dayton, O

"   J. W. Gorden,[3] Indianapolis, Ia.

W. T. Page, Esq. Evansville, Ia.

Hawkins Taylor, Esq. Keokuk, Iowa

Please do not understand that I wish to task you with the opening of a correspondence with all these gentlemen; I mean no more than to furnish you the names, and leave the rest to your own pleasure.

Please make my respects to your family, and believe me Yours very truly   A. LINCOLN—

[1] ALS, IHi. Babcock's letter of April 8 asked for names of prominent Republicans "who are your confidential friends, to whom I can write. . . ." (DLC-RTL).

[2] Not previously identified, Julius White was an insurance agent at Chicago, and Ira A. W. Buck was in the real estate and insurance business at Aurora, Illinois.

³ Not previously identified, Jonathan W. Gordon, whose name Lincoln misspelled, was a lawyer and a doctor at Indianapolis, and William T. Page was cashier of the Canal Bank at Evansville, Indiana.

To Mark W. Delahay[1]

M. W. Delahay,   Springfield, Ills.
My dear Sir   April 14, 1860

Reaching home last night I find your letter of the 7th. You know I was in New-England. Some of the acquaintances I made while there, write me since the elections that the close vote in Conn. & the quasi defeat in R.I. are a drawback upon the prospects of Gov. Seward; and Trumbull writes Dubois to the same effect. Do not mention this as coming from me. Both those states are safe enough for us in the fall. I see by the despaches that since you wrote, Kansas has appointed Delegates and instructed them for Seward. Dont stir them up to anger, but come along to the convention, & I will do as I said about expenses.[2] Yours as ever

A. LINCOLN

[1] ALS, DLC-HW. Delahay wrote on April 9 that the Kansas delegates were not instructed, but that a resolution was passed declaring Seward first choice (DLC-RTL).

[2] See Lincoln to Delahay, March 16, *supra*. Delahay was not appointed delegate, but Lincoln took the hint that he should have "some discreet friends" at the convention early.

To Solomon Sturges[1]

Mr. Solomon Sturges   Springfield,
Dear Sir: April 14, 1860

Yours of the 9th. is received; and, allow me to say, I should not disagree with you in many of the opinions therein expressed.

Whether I shall be able to attend the Chicago convention, I have not yet determined; and so, of course, I can not yet say whether I can accept your very kindly proffered hospitality. Yours very truly

A. LINCOLN

[1] ALS, owned by Burton Sturges, Chicago, Illinois. Solomon Sturges, a Chicago banker, wrote his views on slavery and offered Lincoln a room in his home during the convention.

To Whom It May Concern[1]

Whom it may concern.   Springfield, April 14, 1860

The bearer of this, Dr. Theodore Canissius, is the editor and proprietor of the Republican newspaper, published in German here; and is a true and worthy man. Any kindness and attention shown him will be appreciated by me.   A. LINCOLN

[1] ALS, owned by M. L. Wilson, Chevy Chase, Maryland.

To Hawkins Taylor[1]

Hawkins Taylor, Esq   Springfield, Ills.
My dear Sir: April 21, 1860
    Yours of the 15th. is just received. It surprises me that you have written twice, without receiving an answer. I have answered all I ever received from you; and certainly one since my return from the East.
    Opinions here, as to the prospect of Douglas being nominated, are quite conflicting—some very confident he *will*, and others that he will *not* be. I think his nomination possible; but that the chances are against him.
    I am glad there is a prospect of your party passing this way to Chicago. Wishing to make your visit here as pleasant as we can, we wish you to notify us as soon as possible, whether you come this way, how many, and when you will arrive. Yours very truly
                                                          A. LINCOLN

    [1] ALS, IaHA. Taylor's letters dated February 15 and 25 and that of April 15 are in the Lincoln Papers, but there is no record of Lincoln's replying prior to April 21. Taylor's answer of April 25 states that since the railroads will not give half fare Keokuk will not send a full delegation, but that he himself will attend (DLC-RTL).

To Lyman Trumbull[1]

Hon: L. Trumbull: Springfield,
My dear Sir: April 29. 1860
    Yours of the 24th. was duly received; and I have postponed answering it, hoping by the result at Charleston, to know who is to lead our adversaries, before writing. But Charleston hangs fire, and I wait no longer.
    As you request, I will be entirely frank. The taste *is* in my mouth a little; and this, no doubt, disqualifies me, to some extent, to form correct opinions. You may confidently rely, however, that by no advice or consent of mine, shall my pretentions be pressed to the point of endangering our common cause.
    Now, as to my opinions about the chances of others in Illinois. I think neither Seward nor Bates can carry Illinois if Douglas shall be on the track; and that either of them can, if he shall not be. I rather think McLean could carry it with D. on or off—in

other words, I think McLean is stronger in Illinois, taking all sections of it, than either S. or B; and I think S. the weakest of the three. I hear no objection to McLean, except his age; but that objection seems to occur to every one; and it is possible it might leave him no stronger than the others. By the way, if we should nominate him, how would we save to ourselves the chance of filling his vacancy in the Court? Have him hold on up to the moment of his inaugeration? Would that course be no draw-back upon us in the canvass?

Recurring to Illinois, we want something here quite as much as, and which is harder to get than, the electoral vote—the Legislature. And it is exactly in this point that Seward's nomination would be hard upon us. Suppose he should gain us a thousand votes in Winnebago, it would not compensate for the loss of fifty in Edgar.

A word now for your own special benefit. You better write no letters which can possibly be distorted into opposition, or quasi opposition to me. There are men on the constant watch for such things out of which to prejudice my peculiar friends against you. While I have no more suspicion of you than I have of my best friend living, I am kept in a constant struggle against suggestions of this sort. I have hesitated some to write this paragraph, lest you should suspect I do it for my own benefit, and not for yours; but on reflection I conclude you will not suspect me.

Let no eye but your own see this—not that there is anything wrong, or even ungenerous, in it; but it would be misconstrued. Your friend as ever   A. LINCOLN

[1] ALS, CSmH.

To Cyrus M. Allen[1]

Hon: C. M. Allen: Springfield, Ills.
My dear Sir: May 1. 1860.

Your very kind letter of the 27th. was received yesterday. This writing being early in the morning, Douglas is not yet nominated; but we suppose he certainly will be before sun-set to-day, a few of the smaller Southern states having seceded from the convention —just enough to permit his nomination, and not enough to hurt him much at the election. This puts the case in the hardest shape for us. But fight we must; and conquer we shall; in the end.

Our friend Dubois, and Judge David Davis, of Bloomington, one or both, will meet you at Chicago on the 12th.

If you let Usher & Griswold[2] of Terre-Haute know, I think they will co-operate with you. Yours very truly   A. LINCOLN

[1] ALS-F, ISLA. Cyrus M. Allen was a lawyer at Vincennes, Indiana.

[2] John P. Usher, lawyer, who became Secretary of the Interior in 1862; and William D. Griswold, lawyer, and later president of the Ohio and Mississippi Railroad.

To Lyman Trumbull[1]

PRIVATE

Hon: L. Trumbull   Springfield, May 1. 1860

Dear Sir: In my last letter to you I believe I said I thought Mr. Seward would be weaker in Illinois than Mr. Bates. I write this to qualify that opinion so far as to say I think S. weaker than B. in our close Legislative districts; but probably not weaker taking the whole State over.

We now understand that Douglas will be nominated to-day by what is left of the Charleston convention. All parties here dislike it. Republicans and Danites, that he should be nominated at all; and Doug. Dem's that he should not be nominated by an undivided convention. Yours as ever   A. LINCOLN

[1] ALS, CSmH.

To Richard M. Corwine[1]

PRIVATE

Hon: R. M. Corwine   Springfield, Ills. May 2. 1860.

Dear Sir: Yours of the 30th. ult. is just received. After what you have said, it is perhaps proper I should post you, so far as I am able, as to the "lay of the land." First then, I think the Illinois delegation will be unanamous for me at the start; and no other delegation will. A few individuals in other delegations would like to go for me at the start, but may be restrained by their colleagues. It is represented to me, by men who ought to know, that the whole of Indiana might not be difficult to get. You know how it is in Ohio. I am certainly not the first choice there; and yet I have not heard that any one makes any positive objection to me. It is just so everywhere so far as I can perceive. Everywhere, except in Illinois, and possibly Indiana, one or another is prefered to me, but there is no positive objection. This is the ground as it now appears. I believe you personally know C. M. Allen, of Vincennes, Ia.[2] He is a delegate, and has notified me that the entire Ia. delegation will be in Chicago the same day you name—Saturday the 12th. My friends Jesse K. Dubois, our Auditor, & Judge David Davis, will probably be there ready to confer with friends from other States. Let me hear from you again when anything occurs. Yours very truly   A. LINCOLN

[1] ALS, owned by Mrs. Lewis S. Thompson, Red Bank, New Jersey. A copy of Corwine's letter of April 30 in Lincoln's handwriting is preserved in the Lincoln Papers, perhaps because Lincoln turned the original over to his campaign managers. Corwine states his positive preference for Lincoln and his belief that ". . . we can not elect extreme men. Moderation in their past life & their present views, must mark them, or we can not elect. . . ." (DLC-RTL).
[2] Abbreviation for Indiana.

To James G. Wilson[1]

Mr. James G. Wilson.   Springfield, May 2, 1860.

My Dear Friend: I am greatly obliged for the volume of your friend Fitz Greene Halleck's poems. Many a month has passed since I have met with anything more admirable than his beautiful lines on Burns. With Alnwick Castle, Marco Bozzaris, and Red Jacket, I am also much pleased.

It is wonderful that you should have seen and known a sister of Robert Burns. You must tell me something about her when we meet again. Yours very truly,   A. LINCOLN.

[1] Tracy, p. 147. James G. Wilson was editor of the Chicago *Record*, a monthly devoted to religion, literature, and fine arts.

Remarks to Republican State Convention, Decatur, Illinois[1]

May 9, 1860

He stated that, some thirty years ago, then just emigrating to the State, he stopped with his mother's family, for one season, in what is now Macon County; that he built a cabin, *split rails*, and cultivated a small farm down on the Sangamon River, some six or eight miles from Decatur. These, he was informed, were taken from that fence; but, whether they were or not, he had mauled many and many better ones since he had grown to manhood. The cheers were renewed with the same vigor when he concluded his remarks.

[1] New York *Tribune*, May 22, 1860. Lincoln's brief remarks were made in response to a spontaneous call which arose from the floor of the convention when John Hanks carried two rails into the convention hall, bearing the following inscription: "ABRAHAM LINCOLN. The Rail Candidate FOR PRESI-

DENT IN 1860. Two rails from a lot of 3,000 made in 1830 by Thos. Hanks and Abe Lincoln—whose father was the first pioneer of Macon County." (*Ibid.*) The *Tribune* report of the inscription is in error concerning Hanks' name.

To Mark W. Delahay[1]

Hon: M. W. Delahay   Springfield,
My dear Sir   May 12. 1860
    Yours informing me of your arrival in Chicago was duly received. Dubois, our A[uditor, goes] to Chicago to-day; and he will hand you $[?   . The] remainder will come before you leave the s[tate.][2]
Look to Minnesota and Iowa rather, esp[ecially Iowa. Be] careful to give no offence, and keep cool under all circumstances
Yours in haste   A. LINCOLN.

[1] ALS, RPB. The original is mutilated. Words restored in brackets follow Angle, p. 243.   [2] See Lincoln to Delahay, March 16 and April 14, *supra.*

To Edward Wallace[1]

Dr. Edward Wallace: Springfield, Ills. May 12. 1860
    My dear Sir Your brother, Dr. W. S. Wallace, shows me a letter of yours, in which you request him to inquire if you may use a letter of mine to you, in which something is said upon the Tariff question.[2] I do not precisely remember what I did say in that letter; but I presume I said nothing substantially different from what I shall say now.
    In the days of Henry Clay I was a Henry Clay-tariff-man; and my views have undergone no material change upon that subject. I now think the Tariff question ought not to be agitated in the Chicago convention; but that all should be satisfied on that point, with a presidential candidate, whose antecedents give assurance that he would neither seek to force a tariff-law by Executive influence; nor yet to arrest a reasonable one, by a veto, or otherwise. Just such a candidate I desire shall be put in nomination. I really have no objection to these views being publicly known; but I do wish to thrust no letter before the public now, upon any subject. Save me from the appearance of obtrusion; and I do not care who sees this, or my former letter. Yours very truly   A. LINCOLN.

[1] ALS copy, DLC-RTL. Lincoln preserved a copy in an envelope addressed to Dr. Wallace at Chicago, where Wallace was attending the convention.
[2] *Vide supra,* October 11, 1859.

To Carl Schurz[1]

Hon: Carl Schurz.   Springfield, Ills.
My dear Sir   May 14. 1860
    Allow me to introduce my friend, Jesse K. Dubois, our Illinois
State Auditor. Yours truly   A. LINCOLN

[1] ALS, DLC-Schurz Papers. Carl Schurz was at the time chairman of the
Wisconsin delegation at the Republican National Convention, pledged to vote
for the nomination of William H. Seward.

Endorsement on the Margin of
the *Missouri Democrat*[1]

[May 17, 1860]
    I agree with Seward in his "Irrepressible Conflict," but I do not
endorse his "Higher Law" doctrine. *Make no contracts that will
bind me.*

[1] Herndon, III, 462. According to Herndon, "The day before the nomination
the editor [Edward L. Baker] of the Springfield *Journal* arrived in Chicago
with a copy of the Missouri *Democrat,* in which Lincoln had marked three
passages referring to Seward's position on the slavery question. On the margin
of the paper he had written in pencil . . . . " the communication as above.

Response to a Serenade[1]

May 18, 1860
    Mr. Lincoln said that he did not suppose the honor of such a
visit was intended particularly for himself, as a private citizen,
but rather to the representative of a great party; and in reference
to his position on the political questions of the day, he referred his
numerous and enthusiastic hearers to his previous public letters
and speeches. His speech was a perfect model in its way, and the
loud applause with which it was greeted shows that it struck the
right place in the minds of his hearers. Just previous to the conclusion of his speech, Mr. Lincoln said he would invite the whole
crowd into his house if it was large enough to hold them, (A voice,
"We will give you a larger house on the fourth of next March")
but as it could not contain more than a fraction of those who were
in front of it, he would merely invite as many as could find room.[2]

[1] *Illinois State Journal,* May 19, 1860. The serenade concluded an enthusiastic Republican parade to the Lincoln home, following adjournment of a rally
in the State House at nine o'clock, P.M.
[2] The *Journal* continues, "Deafening cheers greeted the invitation, and in

less than a minute Mr. Lincoln's house was invaded by as many as could 'squeeze in!' . . . When the crowd had partially dispersed, a number of ladies called upon Mr. Lincoln and wished him success in the coming campaign."

Reply to Committee of the Republican National Convention[1]

May 19, 1860

Mr. Chairman and gentlemen of the committee, I tender [to] you, and through you [to] the Republican National Convention, and all the people represented in it, my profoundest thanks for the high honor done me, which you now formally announce.

Deeply, and even painfully sensible of the great responsibility which is inseparable from that [this high] honor—a responsibility which I could almost wish had fallen upon some one of the far more eminent men and experienced statesmen whose distinguished names were before the Convention, I shall, by your leave, consider more fully the resolutions of the Convention, denominated the platform, and without unseasonable [unnecessary or unreasonable] delay, respond to you, Mr. Chairman, in writing—not doubting now, that the platform will be found satisfactory, and the nomination [gratefully] accepted.

And now, I will not longer defer the pleasure of taking you, and each of you, by the hand.

[1] *Illinois State Journal*, May 21, 1860; New York *Tribune*, May 25, 1860. The *Tribune* variations in the text are bracketed. The committee consisting of the president of the convention George Ashmun of Massachusetts and the chairmen of the various state delegations arrived at the Lincoln home sometime after eight o'clock, P.M. Gathered in the "large north parlor," they heard a brief notification speech by Ashmun and Lincoln's reply. Afterwards Ashmun introduced the delegates personally to Lincoln.

To Joshua R. Giddings[1]

COPY.

Hon: J. R. Giddings:　　　　　Springfield, Ills. May 21. 1860

My good friend: Your very kind and acceptable letter of the 19th. was duly handed me by Mr. Tuck.[2] It is indeed, most grateful to my feelings, that the responsible position assigned me, comes without conditions, save only such honorable ones as are fairly implied. I am not wanting in the purpose, though I may fail in the strength, to maintain my freedom from bad influences. Your letter comes to my aid in this point, most opportunely. May the Almighty grant that the cause of truth, justice, and humanity, shall in no wise suffer at my hands.

[51]

Mrs. L. joins me in sincere wishes for your health, happiness, and long life.   A LINCOLN.

1 ALS copy, DLC-RTL. Although marked "copy" by Lincoln, the document appears because of a few transpositions and emendations to be the first draft. Giddings wrote from Chicago that Lincoln had been nominated because of his honesty and freedom from corrupt men and that he should place himself under obligations to no one.

2 Amos Tuck, former U.S. representative (1847-1853) from Exeter, New Hampshire, who filled a speaking engagement at Springfield on May 21.

To George Ashmun[1]

Hon: George Ashmun: Springfield, Ills. May 23. 1860
President of the Republican National Convention.

Sir: I accept the nomination tendered me by the Convention over which you presided, and of which I am formally apprized in the letter of yourself and others, acting as a committee of the convention, for that purpose.

The declaration of principles and sentiments, which accompanies your letter, meets my approval; and it shall be my care not to violate, or disregard it, in any part.

Imploring the assistance of Divine Providence, and with due regard to the views and feelings of all who were represented in the convention; to the rights of all the states, and territories, and people of the nation; to the inviolability of the constitution, and the perpetual union, harmony, and prosperity of all, I am most happy to co-operate for the practical success of the principles declared by the convention. Your obliged friend, and fellow citizen

A. LINCOLN

1 ALS-P, ISLA; ADfS, DLC-RTL. The letter is accompanied by a copy in Lincoln's handwriting of the letter of Ashmun and others to Lincoln, May 18, 1860, which copy Ashmun requested in a letter dated May 21, for purposes of publication (DLC-RTL). Apparently Ashmun had not preserved a complete copy of his letter written as chairman and bearing the signature of the other members of the convention committee, and therefore asked Lincoln to furnish a copy along with his answer. Lincoln to Ashmun, May 26, *infra*, indicates that both Lincoln's answering letter dated May 23 and his copy of Ashmun's letter dated May 18 were sent on May 26. Whether Lincoln had mailed an earlier copy of his letter of acceptance on May 23, the day it was written, is not certain, since no other original ALS is known. One infers, however, that Lincoln had composed the draft preserved in the Lincoln Papers on May 23, that in reply to Ashmun's request of May 21, he copied it, together with a copy of Ashmun's letter of notification, and mailed them on May 26. If so, the additional letter of May 23, *infra*, presents a further puzzle. The original has not been located, and there is some question of its authenticity, unless the original is forthcoming. It appears, however, to have a place and function only if Lincoln did not compose his final reply until May 26, and then dated it back to May 23 both in the draft and the letter sent. The brevity and haste apparent in the contents of the short letter (*infra*) may indicate this conclusion.

To George Ashmun[1]

Hon. George Ashmun: Springfield, Ills. May 23 1860

Sir: Your letter I have just received. The principles as represented has my approval. It is my purpose upon my nomination to issue a Statement.

I will be happy to co-operate for the practical success of the principles as put forth by the Convention. Yours very truly

A. LINCOLN.

[1] Hertz, II, 773. For discussion of this letter see the note to letter *supra*.

To George Ashmun[1]

Private

Hon: Geo. Ashmun Springfield, Ills.

My dear Sir: May 26. 1860

Herewith is a copy of the Committe's letter to me, as you requested; together with my answer. The answer, I hope, is sufficiently brief to do no harm. Yours very truly A. LINCOLN

[1] ALS-P, ISLA. The letter is written on the bottom of the page which bears Lincoln's transcription of Ashmun's letter of notification, May 18, 1860. For discussion of the letter, see the note, Lincoln to Ashmun, May 23, *supra*.

To Salmon P. Chase[1]

Hon. S. P. Chase. Springfield, Ills. May 26, 1860.

My dear Sir: It gave me great pleasure to receive yours, mistakenly dated, May 17. Holding myself the humblest of all whose names were before the convention, I feel in especial need of the assistance of all; and I am glad—very glad—of the indication that you stand ready. It is a great consolation that so nearly all—all except Mr. Bates & Mr. Clay,[2] I believe,—of those distinguished and able men, are already in high position to do service in the common cause. Your Obt Servt A. LINCOLN.

[1] Copy, DLC-RTL. Although Chase's letter is dated May 17, the envelope is postmarked May 19, indicating that it was not sent until the day following the nomination (DLC-RTL).

[2] Cassius M. Clay, the noted Kentucky abolitionist, had run second to Senator Hannibal Hamlin of Maine in the balloting for candidate for vice-president.

To Cassius M. Clay[1]

Hon. C. M. Clay. Springfield, Ills.

My dear Sir: May 26. 1860

Yours of the 21st. is received, and for which I sincerely thank you. The humblest of all whose names were before the convention,

I shall, in the canvass, and especially afterwards, if the result shall devolve the administration upon me, need the support of all the talent, popularity, and courage, North and South, which is in the party; and it is with sincere gratification that I receive this early indication of your unwavering purpose to stand for the right. Your Obt. Servt.   A. LINCOLN

[1] ALS-F, ISLA.

To Schuyler Colfax[1]

Private
Hon. Schuyler Colfax   Springfield, Ills.
My dear Sir: May 26. 1860
    Your very kind, and acceptable letter of the 18th. was received two or three days since.
    You distinguish between yourself and my *original* friends[2]—a distinction which, by your leave, I propose to forget.
    I have acted upon your suggestion, and also upon my own impulse, in relation to our old friend R. W. T.[3] Yours very truly
                                                               A. LINCOLN

[1] ALS-F, ISLA.
[2] A supporter of Edward Bates for the presidential nomination, Colfax had written, "I need not say how heartily I join with your *original* friends in their greetings to you" (DLC-RTL).
[3] Colfax had suggested that Lincoln write Richard W. Thompson, leader of the Union Party in Indiana, candidates of which were John Bell and Edward Everett. Lincoln's letter to Thompson is presumably not extant.

To S. Wells Cone[1]

S. Wells Cone, Esq   Springfield,
Dear Sir: May 26. 1860
    Yours of the 24th. with newspaper slips, is received; and in answer, I have to say I expect to be at home constantly for some weeks. Yours very truly   A. LINCOLN

[1] ALS, owned by R. A. Ramsdell, Wilmington, Delaware. Sylvester Wells Cone was associated with his brother David D. Cone in publishing the Sumner, Kansas, *Gazette.* His letter of May 24, 1860, is not in the Lincoln Papers.

To C. F. Mitchell[1]

C. F. Mitchell, Esq.   Springfield, Ill., May 26, 1860.
    Dear Sir—Yours of the 23 with your business card, and newspaper extracts, is received, and for which I have only time to say I thank you. Yours etc.,   A LINCOLN

1 Hertz, II, 774. The original letter has not been found, and there is no letter from Mitchell dated May 23, 1860, in the Lincoln Papers. There are, however, letters from C. F. Mitchell of Flemingsburg, Kentucky, November 15, 1860, and January 27, 1861. He describes himself as a Quaker and Republican, almost alone in his region.

To Caleb B. Smith[1]

Hon: C. B. Smith—   Springfield, Ills. May 26. 1860

My dear Sir: Yours of the 21st. was duly received; but I have found no time till now, to say a word in the way of answer. I am, indeed, much indebted to Indiana; and, as my home friends tell me, much to you personally. Your saying you no longer consider Ia.[2] a doubtful state, is very gratifying. The thing starts well everywhere—too well, I almost fear, to last. But we are in, and stick or go through, must be the word.

Let me hear from Indiana occasionally. Your friend, as ever

A. LINCOLN.

1 ALS, PMA.   2 Indiana.

To Leonard Swett[1]

Dear Swett   Springfield, May 26, 1860

I see no objection to the letter you have written to Shaffer. Send it to him, but do not let him know I have seen it; and, by a post-script, tell him to come down and see me. Yours as ever

A. LINCOLN

1 ALS, owned by David Davis IV, Bloomington, Illinois. Swett had written Lincoln (no date, but probably May 25) enclosing a letter from John W. Shaffer of Freeport and also the letter he intended to send in reply to Shaffer, concerning party jealousies. Swett had promised certain Illinois and Pennsylvania delegates who were for Seward and Cameron that if they went for Lincoln they would be treated fairly. Swett thought these delegates later worked for Lincoln (DLC-RTL).

To Lyman Trumbull[1]

Hon: L. Trumbull: Springfield, May 26, 1860

My dear Sir: I have received three letters from you since the nomination, for all which I sincerely thank you. As you say, if we can not get our state up now, I do not see when we can. The nominations start well here, and everywhere else, so far as I have heard. We may have a back-set yet. Give my respects to the Republican Senators; and especially to Mr. Hamlin, Mr. Seward, Gen. Cameron, and Mr. Wade.

Also to your good wife.

Write again; and do not write so short letters as I do. Your friend, as ever   A. LINCOLN

¹ ALS, CSmH.

To Elihu B. Washburne¹

Hon: E. B. Washburne   Springfield, Ills. May 26, 1860

My dear Sir: I have several letters from you written since the nomination; but, till now, have found no moment to say a word by way of answer. Of course I am glad that the nomination is well received by our friends, and I sincerely thank you for so informing me. So far as I can learn, the nominations start well everywhere; and, if they get no back-set, it would seem as if they are going through.

I hope you will write often; and as you write more rapidly than I do, dont make your letters so short as mine. Yours very truly   A. LINCOLN

¹ ALS, owned by Hempstead Washburne, Chicago, Illinois.

To Samuel Haycraft¹

Hon. Saml. Haycraft   Springfield, Ills.
Dear Sir: May 28. 1860

Your recent letter, without date, is received. Also the copy of your speech on the contemplated Daniel Boone monument, which I have not yet had time to read. In the main you are right about my history. My father was Thomas Lincoln, and Mrs. Sally Johnston, was his second wife. You are mistaken about my mother —her maiden name was Nancy Hanks.² I was not born at Elizabethtown; but my mother's first child, a daughter, two years older than myself, and now long since deceased, was. I was born Feb. 12. 1809, near where Hogginsville [Hodgenville] now is, then in Hardin county. I do not think I ever saw you, though I very well know who you are—so well that I recognized your hand-writing, on opening your letter, before I saw the signature. My recollection is that Ben. Helm was first Clerk, that you succeeded him, that Jack Thomas and William Farleigh³ graduated in the same office, and that your handwritings were all very similar. Am I right?

My father has been dead near ten years; but my step-mother, (Mrs. Johnson) is still living.

I am really very glad of your letter, and shall be pleased to receive another at any time. Yours very truly   A. LINCOLN

[1] ALS-P, ISLA. Samuel Haycraft was circuit clerk at Elizabethtown, Kentucky. The letter to which Lincoln replied is not in the Lincoln Papers, the earliest letter from Haycraft being the one of August 19, 1860.

[2] It is unfortunate that Haycraft's letter is not extant, for Lincoln scholars have long wondered about his mistake. His later testimony to Herndon about Nancy Hanks' identity seems not to have been clear. It has been assumed that Haycraft's letter referred to Sally Bush Johnston as Lincoln's mother, but the assumption is hardly tenable since Haycraft knew about Thomas Lincoln's early residence at Elizabethtown and could scarcely have identified her as the mother of Thomas Lincoln's first child, whom he supposed to have been Abraham instead of Sarah. Probably Haycraft did not know Nancy Hanks at all, and in common with others among his Kentucky contemporaries, who began cudgeling their brains after Lincoln's nomination, confused her, as well as her mother with another notorious "Nancy" whose reputation has survived the years because of its unsavory quality. In spite of diligent research and scholarly criticism of sources, the status of research on the lineage of Nancy Hanks must be summarized as inconclusive. The best sources are Louis A. Warren, *Lincoln's Parentage & Childhood* (c.1926) and William E. Barton, *The Lineage of Lincoln* (1929) and *The Paternity of Abraham Lincoln* (1920). See also Warren's excellent statement of the case for Nancy Hanks in *The Lincoln Kinsman*, No. 33.

[3] All three men were lawyers practicing in Hardin County, Kentucky.

To Leonard Swett[1]

Hon. L. Swett: Springfield, Ills.
My dear Sir   May 30. 1860

Your letter, written to go to N.Y. is long, but substantially right, I believe. You heard Weed converse with me,[2] and you now have Putnams letter. It can not have failed to strike you that these men ask for just, the same thing—*fairness,* and fairness only. This, so far as in my power, they, and all others, shall have. If this suggests any modification of, or addition to, your letter, make it accordingly. Burn this, not that there is any thing wrong in it; but because it is best not to be known that I write at all. Yours as ever

A. LINCOLN

[1] ALS, owned by David Davis IV, Bloomington, Illinois. Swett wrote to Lincoln May 27, enclosing his reply to James O. Putnam (postmaster at Buffalo, New York, under Fillmore, and several times member of the New York Senate) and commenting, "I am afraid my letter will be regarded as reflecting your sentiments &. . . thought it but prudent to let you peruse it" (DLC-RTL).

[2] Thurlow Weed, publisher of the Albany, New York, *Evening Journal* and Seward's political manager, visited Lincoln on May 24.

To Schuyler Colfax[1]

Hon. Schuyler Colfax.   Springfield, Ills,
My dear Sir: May 31. 1860

Yours of the 26th. is received; and so far from regarding it as presumptuous, I should be right glad to have one from you every mail. Bear this in mind, and act accordingly. You will readily understand and appreciate why I write only very short letters. Yours very truly   A. Lincoln

1 ALS, The Rosenbach Company, Philadelphia and New York. Colfax's letter of May 26, began "Although you may regard my writing you again as rather presumptious, when I do not know whether my letters are acceptable. . . ." and gave a summary of information gleaned from New York politicians, to the effect that the opposition's only hope in that state was for disaffection in Republican ranks resulting from Seward's failure (DLC-RTL).

To Charles C. Nott[1]

Charles C. Nott, Esq.   Springfield, Ills, May 31, 1860.

My Dear Sir: Yours of the 23rd, accompanied by a copy of the speech delivered by me at the Cooper Institute, and upon which you have made some notes for emendations, was received some days ago. Of course I would not object to, but would be pleased rather, with a more perfect edition of that speech.

I did not preserve memoranda of my investigations; and I could not now re-examine, and make notes, without an expenditure of time which I can not bestow upon it. Some of your notes I do not understand.

So far as it is intended merely to improve in grammar, and elegance of composition, I am quite agreed; but I do not wish the sense changed, or modified, to a hair's breadth. And you, not having studied the particular points so closely as I have, can not be quite sure that you do not change the sense when you do not intend it. For instance, in a note at bottom of first page, you proposed to substitute "Democrats" for "Douglas." But what I am saying there is *true* of Douglas, and is not true of "Democrats" generally; so that the proposed substitution would be a very considerable blunder. Your proposed insertion of "residences" though it would do little or no harm, is not at all necessary to the sense I was trying to convey. On page 5 your proposed grammatical change would certainly do no harm. The *"impudently absurd"* I stick to. The striking out *"he"* and inserting *"we"* turns the sense exactly wrong. The striking out *"upon it"* leaves the sense too general and incomplete. The sense is "act as they acted *upon that question"*—not as they acted generally.

After considering your proposed changes on page 7, I do not think them material, but I am willing to defer to you in relation to them.

On page 9, striking out *"to us"* is probably right. The word *"lawyer's"* I wish retained. The word *"Courts"* struck out twice, I

[58]

wish reduced to "Court" and retained. "Court" as a collection more² properly governs the plural "have" as I understand. "The" preceding "Court," in the latter case, must also be retained. The words "quite," "as," and "or" on the same page, I wish retained. The italicising, and quotation marking, I have no objection to.

As to the note at bottom, I do not think any too much is admitted. What you propose on page 11 is right. I return your copy of the speech, together with one printed here, under my own hasty supervising. That at New York was printed without any supervision by me. If you conclude to publish a new edition, allow me to see the proof-sheets.

And now thanking you for your very complimentary letter, and your interest for me generally, I subscribe myself. Your friend and servant,   A. LINCOLN.

¹ George H. Putnam, *Abraham Lincoln: The People's Leader* (1909), pp. 225-27. Nott's letter of May 23 is also given by Putnam, but the original is not among the Lincoln Papers. See also the note to Lincoln's address at Cooper Institute, February 27, *supra*.

² Tracy, p. 150, is probably incorrect in giving "collective noun" instead of "collection more."

To Lyman Trumbull¹

Hon. L. Trumbull.   Springfield, Ills. May 31. 1860.

My dear Sir: Yours of the 28th. inclosing that which I have carefully read, and now return, is received. Please say to Mr. Hamlin that my letter of acceptance is already written and forwarded to Mr. Ashmun, at Springfield, Mass; that I would send him, Mr. Hamlin, a copy, only that Mr. Ashmun, when here, sought and obtained a promise from me that I would furnish a copy to no one; that the letter is very short, and, I think, conflicts with none of Mr. Morey's suggestions, except that it may be published by Mr. Ashmun before the Baltimore convention. Perhaps it would be best for Mr. Hamlin and yourself not to communicate the fact that the letter of acceptance is already written. I am glad to learn the Philadelphia meeting had force enough to not be spoiled by the storm. I look with great interest for your letters now. Your friend as ever,   A. LINCOLN

¹ ALS, CSmH. Trumbull's letter of May 28 is in the Lincoln Papers, but the enclosure is not, and Trumbull's letter indicates nothing of its nature except that it had been handed to him by Hannibal Hamlin "with a request that I forward it to you. Mr. Hamlin tells me the writer of the letter is an eminent politician of Mass. . . ." (DLC-RTL). Probably the author was George Morey, a wealthy lawyer at Boston, Massachusetts.

Form Letter to Applicants for Biographical Data[1]

(Biography)

Dear Sir   Springfield, Ills [c. June] 1860

Your letter to Mr. Lincoln of [blank] and by which you seek his assistance in getting up a biographical sketch of him, is received. Applications of this class are so numerous that it is simply impossible for him to attend to them. Yours &c

J. G. NICOLAY—

[1] AD, DLC-RTL. Lincoln obviously prepared this form for Nicolay following the nomination.

Form Reply to Requests for Political Opinions[1]

(Doctrine)

Dear Sir   Springfield Ills. [c. June] 1860

Your letter to Mr. Lincoln of [blank] and by which you seek to obtain his opinions on certain political points, has been received by him. He has received others of a similar character; but he also has a greater number of the exactly opposite character. The latter class beseech him to write nothing whatever upon any point of political doctrine. They say his positions were well known when he was nominated, and that he must not now embarrass the canvass by undertaking to shift or modify them. He regrets that he can not oblige all, but you perceive it is impossible for him to do so. Yours &c   J. G. NICOLAY.

[1] AD, DLC-RTL.

Autobiography Written for John L. Scripps[1]

[c. June, 1860]

Abraham Lincoln was born Feb. 12, 1809, then in Hardin, now in the more recently formed county of Larue, Kentucky. His father, Thomas, & grand-father, Abraham, were born in Rockingham county Virginia, whither their ancestors had come from Berks county Pennsylvania. His lineage has been traced no farther back than this.[2] The family were originally quakers, though in later times they have fallen away from the peculiar habits of that

[1] AD, DLC-RTL. Lincoln prepared this sketch for the guidance of John L. Scripps, who was writing a campaign biography to be published by the Chicago *Press and Tribune*. Scripps' *Life* was also issued by Horace Greeley as *Tribune Tracts No. 6.*

[2] This sentence is inserted between lines. Several of Lincoln's correspondents had pointed out the possibility of connections with the Lincolns of Hingham, Massachusetts, but the links had not been fully established at the time.

people. The grand-father Abraham, had four brothers—Isaac, Jacob, John & Thomas. So far as known, the descendants of Jacob and John are still in Virginia. Isaac went to a place near where Virginia, North Carolina, and Tennessee, join; and his decendants are in that region. Thomas came to Kentucky, and after many years, died there, whence his decendants went to Missouri. Abraham, grandfather of the subject of this sketch, came to Kentucky, and was killed by indians about the year 1784. He left a widow, three sons and two daughters. The eldest son, Mordecai, remained in Kentucky till late in life, when he removed to Hancock county, Illinois, where soon after he died, and where several of his descendants still reside. The second son, Josiah, removed at an early day to a place on Blue River, now within Harrison [Hancock] county, Indiana; but no recent information of him, or his family, has been obtained. The eldest sister, Mary, married Ralph Crume and some of her descendants are now known to be in Breckenridge county Kentucky. The second sister, Nancy, married William Brumfield, and her family are not known to have left Kentucky, but there is no recent information from them. Thomas, the youngest son, and father of the present subject, by the early death of his father, and very narrow circumstances of his mother, even in childhood was a wandering laboring boy, and grew up litterally without education. He never did more in the way of writing than to bunglingly sign his own name. Before he was grown, he passed one year as a hired hand with his uncle Isaac on Wata[u]ga, a branch of the Holsteen [Holston] River. Getting back into Kentucky, and having reached his 28th. year, he married Nancy Hanks—mother of the present subject—in the year 1806. She also was born in Virginia; and relatives of hers of the name of Hanks, and of other names, now reside in Coles, in Macon, and in Adams counties, Illinois, and also in Iowa. The present subject has no brother or sister of the whole or half blood. He had a sister, older than himself, who was grown and married, but died many years ago, leaving no child. Also a brother, younger than himself, who died in infancy. Before leaving Kentucky he and his sister were sent for short periods, to A.B.C. schools, the first kept by Zachariah Riney, and the second by Caleb Hazel.

At this time his father resided on Knob-creek, on the road from Bardstown Ky. to Nashville Tenn. at a point three, or three and a half miles South or South-West of Atherton's ferry on the Rolling Fork. From this place he removed to what is now Spencer county Indiana, in the autumn of 1816, A. then being in his eigth year. This removal was partly on account of slavery; but chiefly on ac-

count of the difficulty in land titles in Ky.[3] He settled in an unbroken forest; and the clearing away of surplus wood was the
great task a head. A. though very young, was large of his age,
and had an axe put into his hands at once; and from that till
within his twentythird year, he was almost constantly handling
that most useful instrument—less, of course, in plowing and har-
vesting seasons. At this place A. took an early start as a hunter,
which was never much improved afterwards. (A few days before
the completion of his eigth year, in the absence of his father, a
flock of wild turkeys approached the new log-cabin, and A. with a
rifle gun, standing inside, shot through a crack, and killed one of
them. He has never since pulled a trigger on any larger game.) In
the autumn of 1818 his mother died; and a year afterwards his
father married Mrs. Sally Johnston, at Elizabeth-Town, Ky—a
widow, with three children of her first marriage. She proved a
good and kind mother to A. and is still living in Coles Co. Illinois.
There were no children of this second marriage. His father's residence continued at the same place in Indiana, till 1830. While
here A. went to A.B.C. schools by littles, kept successively by Andrew Crawford, ———— Sweeney,[4] and Azel W. Dorsey. He does
not remember any other. The family of Mr. Dorsey now reside in
Schuyler Co. Illinois. A. now thinks that the agregate of all his
schooling did not amount to one year. He was never in a college
or Academy as a student; and never inside of a college or accad-
emy building till since he had a law-license. What he has in the
way of education, he has picked up. After he was twentythree, and
had separated from his father, he studied English grammar, imperfectly of course, but so as to speak and write as well as he now
does. He studied and nearly mastered the Six-books of Euclid, since
he was a member of Congress. He regrets his want of education,
and does what he can to supply the want. In his tenth year he was
kicked by a horse, and apparantly killed for a time. When he was
nineteen, still residing in Indiana, he made his first trip upon a
flat-boat to New-Orleans. He was a hired hand merely; and he
and a son of the owner,[5] without other assistance, made the trip.
The nature of part of the cargo-load, as it was called—made it
necessary for them to linger and trade along the Sugar coast—and
one night they were attacked by seven negroes with intent to kill
and rob them. They were hurt some in the melee, but succeeded
in driving the negroes from the boat, and then "cut cable"
"weighed anchor" and left.

[3] This sentence is an insertion.   [4] James Swaney, not Sweeney.
[5] Allen Gentry, son of James Gentry.

March 1st. 1830—A. having just completed his 21st. year, his father and family, with the families of the two daughters and sons-in-law, of his step-mother, left the old homestead in Indiana, and came to Illinois. Their mode of conveyance was waggons drawn by ox-teams, or A. drove one of the teams. They reached the county of Macon, and stopped there some time within the same month of March. His father and family settled a new place on the North side of the Sangamon river, at the junction of the timber-land and prairie, about ten miles Westerly from Decatur. Here they built a log-cabin, into which they removed, and made sufficient of rails to fence ten acres of ground, fenced and broke the ground, and raised a crop of sow[n] corn upon it the same year. These are, or are supposed to be, the rails about which so much is being said just now, though they are far from being the first, or only rails ever made by A.

The sons-in-law, were temporarily settled at other places in the county. In the autumn all hands were greatly afflicted with augue and fever, to which they had not been used, and by which they were greatly discouraged—so much so that they determined on leaving the county. They remained however, through the succeeding winter, which was the winter of the very celebrated "deep snow" of Illinois. During that winter, A. together with his step-mother's son, John D. Johnston, and John Hanks, yet residing in Macon county, hired themselves to one Denton Offutt, to take a flat boat from Beardstown Illinois to New-Orleans; and for that purpose, were to join him—Offut—at Springfield, Ills so soon as the snow should go off. When it did go off which was about the 1st. of March 1831—the county was so flooded, as to make traveling by land impracticable; to obviate which difficulty the[y] purchased a large canoe and came down the Sangamon river in it. This is the time and the manner of A's first entrance into Sangamon County. They found Offutt at Springfield, but learned from him that he had failed in getting a boat at Beardstown. This lead to their hiring themselves to him at $12 per month, each; and getting the timber out of the trees and building a boat at old Sangamon Town on the Sangamon river, seven miles N.W. of Springfield, which boat they took to New-Orleans, substantially upon the old contract. It[6] was in connection with this boat that occurred

[6] The remainder of this paragraph was omitted by Nicolay and Hay from the *Complete Works* in deference to Robert Todd Lincoln. In the margin of Hay's manuscript of *Abraham Lincoln: A History*, which was sent to Robert for approval, there is written beside Hay's account of this episode the query "Leave out (?)" followed by "I say leave out— R. T. L." (Nicolay and Hay Papers, IHi).

the ludicrous incident of sewing up the hogs eyes. Offutt bought thirty odd large fat live hogs, but found difficulty in driving them from where [he] purchased them to the boat, and thereupon conceived the whim that he could sew up their eyes and drive them where he pleased. No sooner thought of than decided, he put his hands, including A. at the job, which they completed—all but the driving. In their blind condition they could not be driven out of the lot or field they were in. This expedient failing, they were tied and hauled on carts to the boat. It was near the Sangamon River, within what is now Menard county.

During this boat enterprize acquaintance with Offutt, who was previously an entire stranger, he conceved a liking for A. and believing he could turn him to account, he contracted with him to act as clerk for him, on his return from New-Orleans, in charge of a store and Mill at New-Salem, then in Sangamon, now in Menard county. Hanks had not gone to New-Orleans, but having a family, and being likely to be detained from home longer than at first expected, had turned back from St. Louis. He is the same John Hanks who now engineers the "rail enterprize" at Decatur; and is a first cousin to A's mother. A's father, with his own family & others mentioned, had, in pursuance of their intention, removed from Macon to Coles county. John D. Johnston, the step-mother's son, went to them; and A. stopped indefinitely, and, for the first time, as it were, by himself at New-Salem, before mentioned. This was in July 1831. Here he rapidly made acquaintances and friends. In less than a year Offutt's business was failing—had almost failed,—when the Black-Hawk war of 1832—broke out. A joined a volunteer company, and to his own surprize, was elected captain of it. He says he has not since had any success in life which gave him so much satisfaction. He went the campaign, served near three months, met the ordinary hardships of such an expedition, but was in no battle. He now owns in Iowa, the land upon which his own warrants for this service, were located. Returning from the campaign, and encouraged by his great popularity among his immediate neighbors, he, the same year, ran for the Legislature and was beaten—his own precinct, however, casting it's votes 277 for and 7, against him. And this too while he was an avowed Clay man, and the precinct the autumn afterwards, giving a majority of 115 to Genl. Jackson over Mr. Clay. This was the only time A was ever beaten on a direct vote of the people. He was now without means and out of business, but was anxious to remain with his friends who had treated him with so much generosity, especially as he had nothing elsewhere to go to. He studied what he should do—thought of learning the black-smith trade—thought of trying to study law—rather thought he could not succeed at that without a better education. Before long, strangely enough, a man offered to sell and did sell, to A. and another[7] as poor as himself, an old stock of goods, upon credit. They opened as merchants; and he says that was *the* store. Of course they did nothing but get deeper and deeper in debt. He was appointed Postmaster at New-Salem—the office being too insignificant, to make his politics an objection. The store winked out. The Surveyor of Sangamon,[8] offered to depute to A that portion of his work which was within his part of the county. He accepted, procured a compass and chain, studied Flint, and Gibson a little, and went at it. This procured bread, and kept soul and body together. The election of 1834 came, and he was then elected to the Legislature by the highest vote cast for any candidate. Major John T. Stuart, then in full practice of the law, was also elected. During the canvass, in a private conversation he encouraged A. [to] study law. After the election he borrowed books of Stuart, took them home with him, and went at it in good earnest. He studied with nobody. He still mixed in the surveying to pay board and clothing bills. When the Legislature met, the law books were dropped, but were taken up again at the end of the session. He was re-elected in 1836, 1838, and 1840. In the autumn of 1836 he obtained a law licence, and on April 15, 1837 removed to Springfield, and commenced the practice, his old friend, Stuart taking him into partnership. March 3rd. 1837, by a protest entered upon the Ills. House Journal of that date, at pages 817, 818, A. with Dan Stone, another representative of Sangamon, briefly defined his position on the slavery question; and so far as it goes, it was then the same that it is now. The protest is as follows—(Here insert it)[9] In 1838, & 1840 Mr. L's party in the Legislature voted for him as Speaker; but being in the minority, he was not elected. After 1840 he declined a re-election to the Legislature. He was on the Harrison electoral ticket in 1840, and on that of Clay in 1844, and spent much time and labor in both those canvasses. In Nov. 1842 he was married to Mary, daughter of Robert S. Todd, of Lexington, Kentucky. They have three living children, all sons—one born in 1843, one in 1850, and one in 1853. They lost one, who was born in 1846. In 1846, he was elected to the lower House of Congress, and served one term only,

[7] William F. Berry.   [8] John Calhoun.
[9] *Vide supra*, March 3, 1837.

commencing in Dec. 1847 and ending with the inaugeration of Gen. Taylor, in March 1849. All the battles of the Mexican war had been fought before Mr. L. took his seat in congress, but the American army was still in Mexico, and the treaty of peace was not fully and formally ratified till the June afterwards. Much has been said of his course in Congress in regard to this war. A careful examination of the Journals and Congressional Globe shows, that he voted for all the supply measures which came up, and for all the measures in any way favorable to the officers, soldiers, and their families, who conducted the war through; with this exception that some of these measures passed without yeas and nays, leaving no record as to how particular men voted. The Journals and Globe also show him voting that the war was unnecessarily and unconstitutionally begun by the President of the United States. This is the language of Mr. Ashmun's amendment, for which Mr. L. and nearly or quite all, other whigs of the H. R. voted.

Mr. L's reasons for the opinion expressed by this vote were briefly that the President had sent Genl. Taylor into an inhabited part of the country belonging to Mexico, and not to the U.S. and thereby had provoked the first act of hostility—in fact the commencement of the war; that the place, being the country bordering on the East bank of the Rio Grande, was inhabited by native Mexicans, born there under the Mexican government; and had never submitted to, nor been conquered by Texas, or the U.S. nor transferred to either by treaty—that although Texas claimed the Rio Grande as her boundary, Mexico had never recognized it, the people on the ground had never recognized it, and neither Texas nor the U.S. had ever enforced it—that there was a broad desert between that, and the country over which Texas had actual control—that the country where-hostilities commenced, having once belonged to Mexico, must remain so, until it was somehow legally transferred, which had never been done.

Mr. L. thought the act of sending an armed force among the Mexicans, was *unnecessary*, inasmuch as Mexico was in no way molesting, or menacing the U.S. or the people thereof; and that it was *unconstitutional*, because the power of levying war is vested in Congress, and not in the President. He thought the principal motive for the act, was to divert public attention from the surrender of "Fifty-four, forty, or fight" to Great Brittain, on the Oregon boundary question.

Mr. L. was not a candidate for re-election. This was determined upon, and declared before he went to Washington, in accordance with an understanding among whig friends, by which Col. Hardin, and Col. Baker had each previously served a single term in the same District.[10]

In 1848, during his term in congress, he advocated Gen. Taylor's nomination for the Presidency, in opposition to all others, and also took an active part for his election, after his nomination—speaking a few times in Maryland, near Washington, several times in Massachusetts, and canvassing quite fully his own district in Illinois, which was followed by a majority in the district of over 1500 for Gen. Taylor.

Upon his return from Congress he went to the practice of the law with greater earnestness than ever before. In 1852 he was upon the Scott electoral ticket, and did something in the way of canvassing, but owing to the hopelessness of the cause in Illinois, he did less than in previous presidential canvasses.

In 1854, his profession had almost superseded the thought of politics in his mind, when the repeal of the Missouri compromise aroused him as he had never been before.

In the autumn of that year he took the stump with no broader practical aim or object that [than?] to secure, if possible, the reelection of Hon Richard Yates to congress. His speeches at once attracted a more marked attention than they had ever before done. As the canvass proceeded, he was drawn to different parts of the state, outside of Mr. Yates' district. He did not abandon the law, but gave his attention, by turns, to that and politics. The State agricultural fair was at Springfield that year, and Douglas was announced to speak there.

In the canvass of 1856, Mr. L. made over fifty speeches, no one of which, so far as he remembers, was put in print. One of them was made at Galena, but Mr. L. has no recollection of any part of it being printed; nor does he remember whether in that speech he said anything about a Supreme court decision. He may have spoken upon that subject; and some of the newspapers may have reported him as saying what is now ascribed to him; but he thinks he could not have expressed himself as represented.[11]

[10] The manuscript is asterisked at this point for the insertion of the next paragraph, which appears on a separate page.

[11] *Vide supra*, July 23, 1856. The report of the Galena speech in the Galena *Weekly North-Western Gazette*, July 29, 1856, quotes Lincoln as saying, "The Supreme Court of the United States is the tribunal to decide such questions [the constitutionality of a law restricting slavery], and we will submit to its decisions. . . ." Lincoln may never have seen the *Gazette* report. His later position on the Dred Scott decision was that Republicans should abide by the decision until they could get a reversal by the court. Referring to Lincoln's earlier speech at Galena, the Democrats construed Lincoln's statement as a contradiction of his later position.

To F. A. Wood[1]

F. A. Wood, Esq.   Springfield, Ills,
Dear Sir   June 1. 1860
    Yours of May 24th. is received. You say you are not a Lincoln
man; "but still would like to have Mr. L's autograph." Well, here
it is. Yours with respect   A. LINCOLN.

[1] ALS, RPB. Wood's letter is not among the Lincoln Papers, and he has not
been identified.

To H. Buck, Jr.
Form Reply to Request for Autograph[1]

Lieut. H. Buck, Jr   Springfield, Ills.
Dear Sir   June 2. 1860
    You request an autograph, and here it is. Yours truly
                                              A. LINCOLN.

[1] ALS, CSmH. There is a similar letter of this date to Edward Herrick, Jr.
(ALS, MH-Nolen Collection), and numerous others of later date. Since the
wording in such letters is identical, or so similar as to make repetition super-
fluous, later examples have not been included in the body of *The Collected
Works*, but each will be found listed in the chronological index to these volumes.

To Joseph C. Abbott[1]

Joseph C. Abbott, Esq   Springfield, Ills. June 4. 1860
    My dear Sir: Yours of the 22nd. was duly received; but, till
now, I have not found leisure to so much as acknowledge the receipt of it. Of course I very well remember you; and I shall be
pleased to hear from you at any time. Yours very truly
                                              A. LINCOLN.

[1] ALS, CSmH. Joseph C. Abbott was editor of the Boston *Atlas and Bee*. His
letter of May 22 is not in the Lincoln Papers.

To George Ashmun[1]

Hon: George Ashmun   Springfield, Ills. June 4 1860
    My dear Sir   It seems as if the question whether my first name
is "Abraham" or "Abram" will never be settled. It is *"Abraham"*
and if the letter of acceptance is not yet in print, you may, if you
think fit, have my signature thereto printed *"Abraham Lincoln."*
Exercise your own judgment about this. Yours as ever,
                                              A. LINCOLN.

[1] AL-F, ISLA. The present location of the original letter is not known. The facsimile, printed from an electrotype plate some years ago, does not include the close and signature, but earlier printings [Tarbell (Appendix), p. 338; NH, VI, 38] have been followed. By accident this letter got into print before the official letter of acceptance. Ashmun wrote in explanation on June 18, that the official letters had been set in type awaiting Hamlin's reply and that upon receiving Lincoln's note of June 4 he had called at the newspaper office to authorize the change in the full name, leaving the note for an editor who wished an autograph. The senior editor, returning in the absence of his colleague and seeing the letter, had assumed it was to be published (DLC-RTL).

To William A. Buckingham[1]

Springfield, Illinois,
Hon. Wm. A. Buckingham   June 4, 1860.

My Dear Sir: Your kind letter of congratulation was duly received, and I beg you will believe that necessity alone has delayed the acknowledgement of its receipt so long. I am truly glad to learn that you have recovered your voice and that your general health is better.

Please present my respects to Mrs. B. and believe me, Very truly yours,   A. LINCOLN

[1] Tracy, p. 152. Governor Buckingham of Connecticut wrote a brief letter of congratulation and closed with the comment that he was a much better man than "when you were here and have fully recovered my voice" (DLC-RTL).

To John Eddy[1]

John Eddy, Esq   Springfield, Ills.
My dear Sir: June 4. 1860

Your very gratifying letter of the 29th. ult; and although you considerately I [sic] say I need not answer it, I will at least acknowledge it's receipt.

Present my respects to Mr. James,[2] to all friends, and to "Little Rhoda" generally. Yours very truly   A. LINCOLN

[1] ALS, The Rosenbach Company, Philadelphia and New York. Lincoln had met John Eddy of Providence, Rhode Island, during his visit of February 28. Eddy's letter of May 29 is not in the Lincoln Papers, but there are later ones.
[2] Charles T. James of Providence, owner of cotton mills and a member of the U.S. Senate 1851-1857, was Eddy's brother-in-law.

To Samuel Haycraft[1]

PRIVATE
Hon. Saml. Haycraft.   Springfield, Ills. June 4, 1860

Dear Sir: Your second letter, dated May 31st. is received. You suggest that a visit to the place of my nativity might be pleasant

[69]

to me. Indeed it would. But would it be safe? Would not the people Lynch me?

The place on Knob Creek, mentioned by Mr. Read,[2] I remember very well; but I was not born there. As my parents have told me, I was born on Nolin, very much nearer Hodgin's-Mill than the Knob Creek place is. My earliest recollection, however, is of the Knob Creek place.

Like yourself I belonged to the whig party from it's origin to it's close. I never belonged to the American party organization; nor ever to a party called a Union party; though I hope I neither am, or ever have been, less devoted to the Union than yourself, or any other patriotic man.

It may not be altogether without interest to let you know that my wife is a daughter of the late Robert S. Todd, of Lexington Ky —and that a half sister[3] of hers is the wife of Ben. Hardin Helm, born and raised at your town, but residing at Louisville now, as I believe. Yours very truly   A. LINCOLN.

[1] ALS, CSmH. Haycraft's letter of May 31 is not in the Lincoln Papers.
[2] In his letter of August 19, Haycraft mentions showing Lincoln's letter to W. B. Read, probably the same man (DLC-RTL).   [3] Emilie Todd.

To Mordecai Mobley[1]

Major M. Mobley   Springfield, Ills.
My dear Sir.   June 4. 1860

Your kind letter of May 30th. is received. I can not answer all I am receiving; but I can do no less than acknowledge the receipt of one from an old friend like yourself. Present my respects to Mrs. Mobley, & believe me, Sincerely your friend   A. LINCOLN

[1] ALS, owned by Mrs. R. M. LaDue, Sioux City, Iowa.

To Charles E. Troutman[1]

Chas. E. Troutman, Esq   Springfield, Ills. June 4. 1860

Dear Sir   The Washington Agricultural Litterary Society of the Farm School, Pennsylvania, will please accept my thanks for the honor done me in electing me an honorary member of the same. Very Respectfully   A. LINCOLN

[1] ALS, PSt. Charles E. Troutman was a member of the first class to enter Farmer's High School in 1859 and graduated in 1861. In 1862 the name of the school was changed to the Agricultural College of Pennsylvania and in 1874 it became Pennsylvania State College. President James Buchanan was also made an honorary member of the Washington Agricultural Literary Society.

To Digby V. Bell[1]

Judge D. V. Bell: Springfield, Ill.,
My dear Sir: June 5, 1860.

The chair which you designate as the "Chair of State," is duly
at hand and gratefully accepted. In view of what it symbolizes,
might it not be called the "Chair of State and the Union of
States?" The conception of the maker is a pretty, a patriotic, and
a national one.

Allow me to thank both you and him much, for the chair, and
more for the sentiment which pervades the structure. Your obedient servant,   A. LINCOLN.

[1] *Illinois State Journal,* June 11, 1860. According to Bell's presentation letter,
also printed in the *Journal,* the chair had been made by J. D. Meese of Osseo,
Michigan, expressly "for the person who should be nominated as a candidate
. . . by the National Republican Convention." It consisted of "thirty-four different kinds of wood . . . symbolizing the *union* of the several States, including
Kansas." During the convention the chair occupied a prominent place on the
platform and at the close was turned over to Bell for delivery. The Chicago Directory for 1860 lists Bell as professor of commercial science at the University
of Chicago.

To Lyman Trumbull[1]

Hon. L. Trumbull   Springfield, Ills. June 5, 1860
My dear Sir: Yours of May 31, inclosing Judge Read's letter, is
received.

I see by the papers this morning, that Mr. Fillmore refuses to
go with us. What do the New-Yorkers at Washington think of this?
Gov. Reeder[2] was here last evening direct from Pennsylvania. He
is entirely confident of that state, and of the general result. I do
not remember to have heard Gen. Cameron's opinion of Penn.
Weed was here, and saw me; but he showed no signs whatever of
the intriguer. He asked for nothing; and said N.Y. is safe, without
condition.

Remembering that Peter denied his Lord with an oath, after
most solemnly protesting that he never would, I will not swear I
will make no committals; but I do think I will not.

Write me often. I look with great interest for your letters now.
Yours as ever,   A. LINCOLN

[1] ALS, CSmH. Trumbull's letter of May 31 reported that Benjamin F. Wade
would speak for Lincoln, that Seward had returned to Washington looking and
talking right, and that some Republicans were disturbed by reports that Thurlow Weed had talked with Lincoln. Trumbull enclosed a letter from John M.
Read of Pennsylvania, which described prospects as good (DLC-RTL).
[2] Andrew H. Reeder of Kansas had returned to Easton, Pennsylvania, to practice law.

To William M. Dickson[1]

Hon: W. M. Dickson.   Springfield, Ills.

My dear Sir: June 7. 1860

Your telegraphic despatch, the day of the nomination, was received; as also was, in due course, your kind letter of May 21st.
with Cousin Annie's note at the end of it.[2]

I have just now received a letter from Cincinnati, of which the
following is a copy.

"Hon. A. Lincoln   Cincinnati, June 5. 1860

Dr. Sir: We are extremely sorry to be under the necessity of
calling your attention to the inclosed bill during your sojourn at
the "Burnet" in Sept. last; but it appears there is no remedy left
us other than to advise you of it's never having been paid. We relied upon the Republican committee, but as yet have not been able
to find any one being willing to take the responsibility of paying
same—consequently advise you in the premises. Very Respy.
Yours,   Johnson, Saunders & Co["]

The inclosed bill is as follows:

"Burnet House

Cincinnati, Sept. 19– 1859

Hon: A. Lincoln

To Johnson, Saunders & Co. Dr.

Board & Parlor self & family	37.50
Extra Suppers. 3.50. Wines, Liquors & cigars 7.50.	11.00
Occupancy of room No. 15. committee.	5.00
	$53.50"

Now this may be right, but I have a slight suspicion of it, for
two or three reasons. First, when I left, I called at the office of the
Hotel, and was there distinctly told the bill "was settled" "was all
right" or words to that effect. Secondly, it seems a little steep that
"Board & parlor["] from Saturday 7½ P.M. to Monday 10½ A.M.
for a man woman and one small child, should be $37.50. Thirdly,
we had no extra suppers, unless having tea at our room the first
evening, was such. We were in the house over the time of five
meals, three only of which we took in the house. We did not once
dine in the house. As to wines, liquors & cigars, we had none—
absolutely none. These last may have been in room 15, by order
of Committee, but I do not recollect them at all.

Please look into this, and write me. I can and will pay it if it is

[72]

right; but I do not wish to be "diddled![")] Please do what you do quietly, having no fuss about it.³ Yours very truly A. LINCOLN

¹ ALS-P, ISLA. Dickson's letter of congratulations enclosed clippings from the Cincinnati *Gazette* and warned Lincoln to beware of Ohio politicians.
² Dickson's wife, who was Mrs. Lincoln's cousin.
³ See Lincoln to Dickson, June 15, *infra.*

Endorsement: Recommendation for Pardon of Emanuel Fowler¹

Believing that Judge Emerson knows what is right in this case, I join in the recommendation he makes.   A. LINCOLN
June 8– 1860

¹ AES, I-Ar. Lincoln's endorsement follows the endorsement of Judge Charles Emerson. Governor John Wood, who had succeeded to the governorship upon the death of William H. Bissell, March 18, 1860, wrote Secretary of State Ozias M. Hatch on June 10, 1860, granting the pardon (ALS, I-Ar).

To John A. Jones¹

J. A. Jones, Esq   Springfield, Ills.
My dear Sir: June 8, 1860
I can only find time, just now, to gratefully acknowledge the receipt of your kind congratulatory note. Your friend, as ever
A. LINCOLN—

¹ ALS, owned by Mrs. Roy W. Ide, Springfield, Illinois. John A. Jones was an attorney at Tremont, Illinois.

To James E. Harvey¹

James E. Harvey, Esq   Springfield, Ills.
My dear Sir: June 9. 1860
Your very acceptable letter of the 5th. is received; and I repeat what I said before, that I am glad to have one from you as often as you can conveniently write. Yours truly   A. LINCOLN

¹ ALS, PHi. A native South Carolinian who had made a name in the North as editor of the Philadelphia *North American and United States Gazette* and correspondent of the New York *Tribune*, James E. Harvey was appointed by Lincoln in 1861 as minister to Portugal. His letters (May 21, 27, and June 5) contain reports on politics in Pennsylvania and general political advice (DLC-RTL). Lincoln's letter to Harvey of May 31 is presumably not extant.

To Charles Lanman[1]

Charles Lanman Esq   Springfield, Ills. June 9. 1860

My dear Sir: Yours of the 4th. is duly received; and I shall gratefully accept the book[2] when it arrives, as it has not yet done. I already have a copy, which I purchased near a year ago, and which I have found both interesting and valuable.

I thank you for both your letter and the book, and shall be pleased to meet you at any time. Yours respectfully

A. LINCOLN—

1 ALS, CSmH. Charles Lanman of Monroe, Michigan, was a newspaper man and writer who later served as librarian of the House of Representatives and librarian of the War Department. His letter of June 4 is not in the Lincoln Papers.
2 Probably Lanman's *Dictionary of the United States Congress* (1859).

To Mrs. Deziah Vance[1]

Mrs. Deziah Vance   Springfield,
Madam   June 9, 1860

Your letter of June 5th. is received. I have no money collected by me for Mr. Vance, and I had ceased trying to collect any for him long before his death. You speak of my letters to Mr. Vance; and if I remember, they will show that the charge of Mr. Vance's claim here was transferred to Mr. W. H. Herndon. I think his claim was against a man, or men, by the name of Vanmeter. I never keep any body's money, which I collect, an hour longer than I can find a chance to turn it over to him. If you doubt this, get some of the busy bodies who are imposing on you in this matter, to find somebody who will swear he paid me money for Mr. Vance. If there is any such man he can be found.

If, as you say, Mr. Trimble spoke to me, and I gave him no satisfaction, it was because the truth was not satisfactory. Let Mr. Trimble or any one else come here and see the man or men, of whom they or you, think I received money for Mr. Vance, and learn of them how the truth is. I have no papers in my hands, belonging to Mr. Vance. I do not certainly know, but my opinion is that nothing can be got on those old claims, or that old claim of Mr. Vance. Yours &c   A. LINCOLN

1 ALS, owned by William H. Townsend, Lexington, Kentucky. Since Mrs. Vance's letter of June 5 is not in the Lincoln Papers, it is not possible to clarify entirely the matter about which she wrote, but it probably concerned claims similar to those about which Lincoln wrote to her husband, John W. Vance, on July 7, 1844 (q.v., *supra*).

To J. Mason Haight[1]

PRIVATE & CONFIDENTIAL.

J. Mason Haight, Esq   Springfield, Ills.
My dear Sir—   June 11. 1860

I think it would be improper for me to write, or say anything to, or for, the public, upon the subject of which you inquire. I therefore wish the letter I do write to be held as strictly confidential. Having kept house sixteen years, and having never held the "cup" to the lips of my friends then, my judgment was that I should not, in my new position, change my habit in this respect. What actually occurred upon the occasion of the Committee visiting me, I think it would be better for others to say   Yours Respectfully

A. LINCOLN

[1] ALS-F, ISLA. John Mason Haight, a newspaper man at Madison, Wisconsin, was an active member of the temperance society named Good Templars. His letter to Lincoln is not in the Lincoln Papers. The facsimile of Lincoln's reply was first reproduced in the New York *Voice*, a prohibition publication, on October 10, 1889, and the Chicago *Voice*, reproduced it a few days later on October 16.

To J. E. Tilton[1]

To J. E. Tilton.   Springfield, Ill.,
Boston.   June 11, 1860.

Dear Sir: I have received your note . . . and also the book. . . .

I have not yet had time to examine the book, but when I shall have done so, I probably shall present it it [*sic*] to the younger Lincoln, as you request. Yours truly   A. LINCOLN.

[1] Tracy, pp. 154-55. In the absence of Lincoln's original letter, only the incomplete text from Tracy is available. J. E. Tilton and Company were publishers at Boston, Massachusetts. Since their letter is not in the Lincoln Papers the book cannot be positively identified, but letters from Tilton (March 4 and March 23, 1864) offering complimentary copies of John T. Trowbridge's *Cudjo's Cave* warrants the assumption that it was one of the same author's popular stories for boys.

Memorandum Concerning His Birthplace[1]

June 14, 1860

I was born Feb. 12. 1809 in then Hardin county Kentucky, at a point within the now recently formed county of Larue, a mile, or a mile & a half from where Hodgin'sville now is. My parents being dead and my own memory not serving, I know no means of identifying the precise locality. It was on Nolin Creek.

June 14. 1860.   A. LINCOLN

[1] ADS-F, Allen T. Rice, ed., *Reminiscences of Abraham Lincoln* (1888), p. 607. According to the artist Thomas Hicks, who had painted Lincoln's portrait in June, 1860, the memorandum was jotted down at his request as he was leaving Springfield.

To Charles Sumner[1]

Hon. C. Sumner   Springfield, Ills.
My dear Sir: June 14. 1860

Your note of the 8th., and the copy of your recent speech, are received; and for both of which, please accept my thanks. I have not yet found time to peruse the speech; but I anticipate much both of pleasure, and instruction from it. Your Obt. Servt.

A. LINCOLN.

[1] ALS, CSmH. Sumner presumably enclosed a copy of his speech in the Senate, June 4, "The Barbarism of Slavery," but there is no copy with his letter of June 8. He describes the speech as an endeavor "to expose the true character of the assumptions now made by the Slave-masters" (DLC-RTL).

To Jasper E. Brady[1]

Hon. J. E. Brady   Springfield, Ills.
My dear Sir: June 15, 1860

Your very kind letter of the 7th was duly received; and, until receiving it, I do not remember to have known of your being located at Pittsburgh. Your kind remembrance of me gratifies me, as well as the flattering prospect which you give of the old "Key Stone."

I shall be much pleased to hear from you again. Very truly your friend,   A. LINCOLN.

[1] Hertz, II, 778. Brady was a Whig member of the House of Representatives with Lincoln in 1847-1849 who afterwards practiced law at Pittsburgh and became a clerk in the Paymaster General's Office 1861-1869. His letter of June 7 is not in the Lincoln Papers.

To William M. Dickson[1]

Hon: W. M. Dickson   Springfield, Ills.
My dear Sir   June 15. 1860

Yours inclosing receipt of "Burnet House" is received; and I sincerely thank you for your attention to this business. Let it stand as it is for the present, with the distinct understanding that you are not to ultimately lose the money.

Give my love to Cousin Annie. Yours very truly

A. LINCOLN

[1] ALS, CSmH. Dickson's letter of June 9, replying to Lincoln's of June 7, *supra*, enclosed a receipt made out in Lincoln's name, and related the following: "It seems that Messrs. Corwine & Eggleston [Richard M. Corwine and Benjamin Eggleston, members of the Ohio State Republican Committee] ordered an extra parlor and bed room . . . dined or supped with you and they ordered the liquor and cigars for the musicians, the extra suppers were for some of.them. . . . Now the best course is to have it paid at once without a word so I have paid it, ... but dont you send me any money whatever. At a proper time and quietly some of my particular friends, republicans will share the matter with me. For the honor of our city dont send me the money. I would not have it said that we have invited you here & then made you pay the expenses not only of yourself but of the committee too. . . ." (DLC-RTL).

To John L. Scripps[1]

John L. Scripps, Esq.   Springfield,
My dear Sir   June 16. 1860

In the Peoria speech of 1854, I have said the prohibition of slavery in the N.W. Territory was made a condition in the Virginia deed of cession. That is an error. Such prohibition is not a condition of the deed; and in any reprint of the speech, the text should be preserved, but there should be a note stating the error. Yours truly   A. LINCOLN.

[1] ALS, IHi. In his letter of June 18, Scripps said he was working hard on his biography of Lincoln, but no mention of reprinting the Peoria speech is made in any of his letters (June 2, 18, and 20) in the Lincoln Papers (DLC-RTL).

To Elihu B. Washburne[1]

Hon. E. B. Washburne   Springfield, Ills.
My dear Sir: June 17. 1860

This will barely reach you before your leaving for the West; and I write it merely to say I received yours of the 13th.; that I expect to be at home all summer; and that I shall be glad to see you as soon as convenient to yourself. Yours very truly

A. LINCOLN—

[1] ALS, owned by Hempstead Washburne, Chicago, Illinois. Washburne's letter of June 13, related that he had "many things, including a hitch in N.Y." about which he wished to talk to Lincoln, and proposed that he come to Springfield after his return home (DLC-RTL). Congress was to adjourn June 25.

To Oran Follett[1]

PRIVATE

O. Follett, Esq   Springfield, Ills.
Dear Sir: June 18. 1860

Your long letter of the 9th. was received only this morning. I write this to acknowledge the receipt of yours; to thank you for the interest you take in the cause; and to say that I previously had had my attention turned in the same direction. Yours very truly

A LINCOLN

[1] ALS, OCHP. Oran Follett wrote from Sandusky, Ohio, detailing incidents in earlier campaigns which he believed indicated that William H. Seward was surrounded by friends who used politics to secure financial advantages to themselves (DLC-RTL).

To Carl Schurz[1]

Carl Schurz, Esq   Springfield, Ills.
My dear Sir: June 18. 1860

Yours of May 22nd. was duly received; and now, on a careful re-perusal of it, I am much mortified that I did not attend to it at once. I fear I have no sufficient apology. I received it with multitudes of others, glanced over it too hastily to properly appreciate its' importance, laid it by, and it passed from my mind, till Gov. Koerner mentioned it to-day. In a general bringing up of my correspondence, I perhaps should have reached it to-day.

The main object of the letter—time—so far as it depended on *me*, is lost. I hope you have gone forward on your plan without my advice. To me it appears an excellent plan; and I have no sufficient experience to suggest any improvement of it. I think it would be desireable to have the opinion of the National committee upon it, if it can be obtained without too much loss of time.

And now, upon this bad beginning, you must not determine to write me no more; for I promise you, that no letter of yours to me, shall ever again be neglected.

I beg you to be assured that your having supported Gov. Seward, in preference to myself in the convention, is not even remembered by me for any practical purpose, or the slightest u[n]pleasant feeling. I go not back of the convention, to make distinctions among its' members; and, to the extent of our limited acquaintance, no man stands nearer my heart than yourself. Very truly your friend

A. LINCOLN—

[1] ALS-P, ISLA. Schurz had written as a member of the National Republican Committee in charge of the foreign department, proposing a list of all "Ger-

mans, Norwegians, Hollanders, etc. who can serve our cause in the way of public speaking. . . ." His plan was to organize them into squads to send to doubtful states, in the belief that the foreign vote of 1856 could be doubled in the North, and he wished to consult with Lincoln before leaving for Pennsylvania during the first or second week in June (DLC-RTL).

To Richard W. Thompson[1]

PRIVATE

Hon: R. W. Thompson: Springfield, Ills.
My dear Sir: June 18. 1860
    Your long letter of the 12th. is just received, and read. I write this to thank you for it; and to say I would like for you to converse freely with Hon: Henry Winter Davis.[2] And lest he be compromitted, by inference from this, let me say that he and I never met, or corresponded. Very truly your friend.   A. LINCOLN

    [1] ALS, InFtwL. Thompson's letter of June 12, in reply to Lincoln's non-existant letter of May 26, expressed gratification at Lincoln's nomination and gave the opinion in regard to running a Bell ticket in Indiana that "We should by holding off in the doubtful states let you carry them. . . . You must not infer from the above that I shall vote for you, although if it should turn out that we have no electoral ticket . . . that I may do so is possible." (DLC-RTL).
    [2] Henry Winter Davis, a cousin of Lincoln's friend David Davis, was Republican representative in Congress from Baltimore, Maryland. A former Know-Nothing, and earlier a Whig, his Southern extraction as well as his marked ability gave him a considerable following and influence in the border states.

Endorsement: James W. Somers to Lincoln[1]

[June 19, 1860]
    Just got home and found this letter. You are abundantly welcome to use my name by way of reference; and I wish you great success besides. Yours truly   A. LINCOLN

    [1] AES-F, Henry C. Whitney, *The Lincoln Autographic Album* [c.1891], p. 43. Apparently Lincoln wrote the endorsement on Somers' letter of June 10 and returned it. Somers' letter of June 22 (DLC-RTL) thanks Lincoln for replying to a letter of June 10.

To Samuel Galloway[1]

Especially Confidential

Hon: Saml. Galloway: Springfield, Ills.
My dear Sir   June 19, 1860
    Your very kind letter of the 15th. is received. Messrs. Follett, Foster & Co's Life of me is *not* by my authority; and I have scarcely been so much astounded by anything, as by their public an-

nouncement that it is authorized by me. They have fallen into some strange misunderstanding. I certainly knew they contemplated publishing a biography, and I certainly did not object to their doing so, *upon their own responsibility*. I even took pains to facilitate them. But, at the same time, I made myself tiresome, if not hoarse, with repeating to Mr. Howard, their only agent seen by me, my protest that I *authorized nothing*—would be *responsible for nothing*. How, they could so misunderstand me, passes comprehension. As a matter, *wholly my own*, I would authorize no biography, without *time*, and *opertunity* to carefully examine and consider every word of it; and, in this case, in the nature of things, I can have no such time and opertunity. But, in my present position, when, by the lessons of the past, and the united voice of all discreet friends, I am neither [to] write or speak a word for the public, how dare I to send forth, by my authority, a volume of hundreds of pages, for adversaries to make points upon without end. Were I to do so, the convention would have a right to reassemble, and substitute another name for mine.

For these reasons, I would not look at the proof sheets. I am determined to maintain the position of truly saying I never saw the proof sheets, or any part of their work, before it's publication.

Now, do not mistake me. I feel great kindness for Messrs. F. F. & Co—do not think they have intentionally done wrong. There may be nothing wrong in their proposed book. I sincerely hope there will not. I barely suggest that you, or any of the friends there, on the party account, look it over, & exclude what you may think would embarrass the party—bearing in mind, at all times, that I *authorize nothing*—will be *responsible* for *nothing*. Your friend, as ever   A. LINCOLN

¹ ALS, IHi. Galloway had suggested that proof sheets of the biography being published by Follett, Foster, and Company should be looked over by some of Lincoln's friends because James Q. Howard was too radical in his anti-slavery views and might possibly write something offensive to conservative Republicans (DLC-RTL). Howard had visited Springfield in May following Lincoln's nomination, to collect material for the biography which William Dean Howells would write, but in addition to the Howells book the publishers decided to issue a biography by Howard.

To Joshua R. Giddings¹

Hon. J. R. Giddings.   Springfield, Ills. June 26. 1860.

My dear Sir   Yours of June 19th was received in due course, and its receipt would have been sooner acknowledged but for illness in my family. The suggestions you make are very important, and are duly appreciated by me. If I fail, it will be for lack of *ability*, and not of *purpose*.

Your note, sent by Mr. Tuck, was received, and answered;[2] but as you make no mention of my answer, I fear you did not receive it.

Mrs. L. joins me in remembrances and good wishes for you. Yours very truly,   A. LINCOLN

[1] Copy, DLC-HW. Giddings letter of June 19 suggested that Lincoln follow the example set by John Quincy Adams in not answering any questions upon which he was expected to act as President until he was elected, and further that he should say to applicants for office that at the proper time he would select his cabinet and leave each secretary responsible for appointments in his department (DLC-RTL).   [2] *Vide supra*, May 21.

To William C. Bryant[1]

Mr. Wm. C. Bryant: Springfield, Ills. June 28. 1860

My dear Sir: Please accept my thanks for the honor done me by your kind letter of the 16th. I appreciate the danger against which you would guard me; nor am I wanting in the *purpose* to avoid it. I thank you for the additional strength your words give me, to maintain that purpose. Your friend & servant   A. LINCOLN

[1] ALS, Bryant MSS. in custody of Conrad G. Goddard, Roslyn, Long Island, New York. Bryant's letter warned Lincoln against politicians interested only in their own advancement and, reminding him that the candidate who makes pledges most cautiously has the greatest chance for success, suggested that Lincoln make no speeches and write no letters for publication (DLC-RTL).

To Whom It May Concern: For David L. Phillips[1]

Whom it may concern   Springfield, Ills. July 2. 1860

The bearer of this, Mr. D. L. Phillips, is one of our most active and efficient republicans in Illinois. He is doing good service in our cause; and will ask nothing not needed, and misapply nothing received by him. Yours &c   A. LINCOLN

[1] ALS-F, Los Angeles *Times*, February 12, 1931.

To Anson G. Henry[1]

My dear Doctor: Springfield, Ills. July 4, 1860

Your very agreeable letter of May 15th. was received three days ago. We are just now receiving the first sprinkling of your Oregon election returns—not enough, I think, to indicate the result. We should be too happy if both Logan and Baker should triumph.[2]

[81]

Long before this you have learned who was nominated at Chicago. We know not what a day may bring forth; but, to-day, it looks as if the Chicago ticket will be elected. I think the chances were more than equal that we could have beaten the Democracy *united*. Divided, as it is, it's chance appears indeed very slim. But great is Democracy in resources; and it may yet give it's fortunes a turn. It is under great temptation to do something; but what can it do which was not thought of, and found impracticable, at Charleston and Baltimore?. The signs now are that Douglas and Breckenridge will each have a ticket in every state. They are driven to this to keep up their bombastic claims of *nationality*, and to avoid the charge of *sectionalism* which they have so much lavished upon us.

It is an amusing fact, after all Douglas has said about *nationality*, and *sectionalism*, that I had more votes from the Southern section at Chicago, than he had at Baltimore! In fact, there was more of the Southern section represented at Chicago, than in the Douglas rump concern at Baltimore!!

Our boy,[3] in his tenth year, (the baby when you left) has just had a hard and tedious spell of scarlet-fever; and he is not yet beyond all danger. I have a head-ache, and a sore throat upon me now, inducing me to suspect that I have an inferior type of the same thing.

Our eldest boy, Bob, has been away from us nearly a year at school, and will enter Harvard University this month. He promises very well, considering we never controlled him much.

Write again when you receive this. Mary joins in sending our kindest regards to Mrs. H. yourself, and all the family. Your friend, as ever   A. LINCOLN—

[1] ALS-P, ISLA.
[2] Edward D. Baker, candidate for the U.S. Senate, and David Logan (son of Stephen T. Logan), who was a candidate for the U.S. House of Representatives.
[3] William Wallace Lincoln.

To Richard W. Thompson[1]

PRIVATE

Hon. R. W. Thompson: Springfield, Ills,
Dear Sir: July 10. 1860

Yours of the 6th. is received, and for which I thank you. I write this to acknowledge the receipt of it, and to say I take time (only a little) before answering the main matter.

If my *record* would *hurt* any, there is no hope that it will be over-looked; so that if friends can *help* any with it, they may as well do so. Of course, due caution and circumspection, will be used.

With reference to the same matter, of which you write, I wish you would watch Chicago a little. They are getting up a movement for the 17th. Inst. I believe a line from you to John Wilson,[2] late of the Genl. Land Office (I guess you know him well) would fix the matter.

When I shall have reflected a little, you will hear from me again. Yours very truly   A. LINCOLN.

Burn this.

[1] ALS, InFtWL. Thompson's letter of July 6 recounted plans of the Indiana Constitutional Unionists to run a Bell electoral ticket, which he opposed, and said that one of his chief arguments was that Lincoln, if elected, would not be "led into ultraism by radical men, but your administration will be national. If I could succeed in fixing this influence upon their mind, I should have little difficulty." He added that he wished to see Lincoln and "talk about some things that you ought not to write about," but that if he came to Springfield it would "get into the papers." (DLC-RTL). Lincoln sent Nicolay to Terre Haute, Indiana, to interview Thompson a few days later. See Lincoln to Thompson and instructions to Nicolay, July 16, *infra*.

[2] John Wilson was appointed commissioner of the General Land Office under President Fillmore.

Instructions for John G. Nicolay[1]

[c. July 16, 1860]

Ascertain what he wants.

On what subjects he would converse with me.

And the particulars if he will give them.

Is an interview indispensable?

Tell him my motto is "Fairness to all,"

But commit me to nothing.

[1] Copy, DLC-Nicolay Papers. The copy is marked "Unpublished MS.," but Lincoln's autograph manuscript is not in the Nicolay Papers. Nicolay carried the instructions for his interview with Richard W. Thompson, introducing Nicolay, *infra*, and the letter of July 10, *supra*.

To Leonard Swett[1]

Dear Swett: Springfield, Ills. July 16. 1860

Herewith I return the letters of Messrs: Putnam & Casey.[2] I thank you for sending them—in the main, they bring good news. And yet that matter, mentioned by Mr. Casey, about want of confidence in their Centrl. Com. pains me. I am afraid there is a germ of difficulty in it. Will not the men thus suspected, and treated as proposed, rebel, and make a dangerous explosion?³ When you write Mr. Casey, suggest to him that great caution and delicacy of action, is necessary in that matter.

I would like to see you & the Judge,⁴ one or both, about that matter of your going to Pa. Yours as ever,   A. LINCOLN.

¹ ALS, owned by David Davis, IV, Bloomington, Illinois.

² James O. Putnam of Buffalo, New York, and Joseph Casey, representative in congress from Pennsylvania, 1849-1851, appointed by Lincoln, Judge of the Court of Claims, 1861. Putnam's letter pleased Lincoln so much that he copied the following extract and filed it in the envelope of Swett's letter: "They have had large meetings; and they begin to feel that 'Old Abe' is a great fellow. This opinion I share, as you see. Do you know, Swett, I think him one of the most remarkable speakers of English, living? In all that constitutes logical eloquence, straight-forwardness, clearness of statement, sincerity that commands your admiration and assent, and a compact stren[g]th of argument, he is infinitely superior to Douglas, I think. The truth is, I have read every thing I have been able to find he has written or said, and the ring of the best metal is in them all. I dont wonder at your admiration." (DLC-RTL).

³ The Pennsylvania State Central Committee was controlled by followers of Andrew G. Curtin, Republican candidate for governor, and the faction supporting Simon Cameron were suspicious of their loyalty. See Lincoln to John M. Pomeroy, August 31, *infra.*   ⁴ Judge David Davis.

To Richard W. Thompson¹

Hon. R. W. Thompson   Springfield, Ills.,
My dear Sir: July 16, 1860.
    This introduces my friend, J. G. Nicolay. Converse as freely with him as you would with me. Yours truly,   A. LINCOLN

¹ Copy, David W. Henry, "Richard Wigginton Thompson," MS., In. The original letter was formerly in the Thompson Papers, but has not been located among the manuscripts now at The Lincoln National Life Foundation, Fort Wayne, Indiana.

To Hannibal Hamlin¹

Springfield, Illinois, July 18, 1860.

My dear Sir: It appears to me that you and I ought to be acquainted, and accordingly I write this as a sort of introduction of myself to you. You first entered the Senate during the single term I was a member of the House of Representatives, but I have no recollection that we were introduced. I shall be pleased to receive a line from you.

    The prospect of Republican success now appears very flattering, so far as I can perceive. Do you see anything to the contrary? Yours truly,   A. LINCOLN.

¹ NH, VI, 44. Hamlin replied, July 23, that although he was not sure, his recollection was that they had been formally introduced. He reported that Maine would do her whole duty and that New England looked well (DLC-RTL).

To Cassius M. Clay¹

Hon: Cassius M. Clay: Springfield, Ills.
My dear Sir: July 20, 1860

I see by the papers, and also learn from Mr. Nicolay, who saw you at Terre-Haute, that you are filling a list of speaking appointments in Indiana. I sincerely thank you for this; and I shall be still further obliged if you will, at the close of the tour, drop me a line, giving your impression of our prospects in that state.

Still more will you oblige us if you will allow us to make a list of appointments in our State, commencing, say, at Marshall, in Clark county, and thence South and West, along our Wabash and Ohio river border.

In passing, let me say, that at Rockport you will be in the county within which I was brought up from my eigth year—having left Kentucky at that point of my life. Yours very truly

A. LINCOLN.

¹ ALS, THaroL. See also Lincoln to Clay, August 10, *infra*.

To Abraham Jonas¹

Confidential

Hon. A. Jonas: Springfield, Ills.
My dear Sir   July 21, 1860

Yours of the 20th. is received. I suppose as good, or even better, men than I may have been in American, or Know-Nothing lodges; but in point of fact, I never was in one, at Quincy, or elsewhere. I was never in Quincy but one day and two nights, while Know-Nothing lodges were in existence, and you were with me that day and both those nights. I had never been there before in my life; and never afterwards, till the joint debate with Douglas in 1858. It was in 1854, when I spoke in some Hall there,² and after the speaking, you, with others, took me to an oyster saloon, passed an hour there, and you walked with me to, and parted with me at, the Quincy-House, quite late at night. I left by stage for Naples before day-light in the morning, having come in by the same route, after dark, the evening previous to the speaking, when I found you waiting at the Quincy House to meet me. A few days after I was there, Richardson,[3] as I understood, started this same story about my having been in a Know-Nothing lodge. When I heard of the charge, as I did soon after, I taxed my recollection for some incident which could have suggested it; and I remembered that on parting with you the last night, I went to the Office of the Hotel to take my stage passage for the morning, was told that no stage office for that line was kept there, and that I must see the driver, before retiring, to insure his calling for me in the morning; and a servant was sent with me to find the driver, who after taking me a square or two, stopped me, and stepped perhaps a dozen steps farther, and in my hearing called to some one, who answered him apparantly from the upper part of a building, and promised to call with the stage for me at the Quincy House. I returned and went to bed; and before day the stage called and took me. This is all.

That I never was in a Know-Nothing lodge in Quincy, I should expect, could be easily proved, by respectable men, who were always in the lodges and never saw me there. An affidavit of one or two such would put the matter at rest.

And now, a word of caution. Our adversaries think they can gain a point, if they could force me to openly deny this charge, by which some degree of offence would be given to the Americans. For this reason, it must not publicly appear that I am paying any attention to the charge. Yours truly   A. LINCOLN

[1] ALS, IHi. Jonas' letter of July 20 (miscataloged under date of July 25, DLC-RTL) related that "Isaac N. Morris is engaged in obtaining affadavits and certificates of certain Irishmen that they saw you in Quincy come out of a Know Nothing Lodge—the intention is to send the affadavits to Washington for publication. . . ."

[2] Lincoln spoke at Quincy in Kendall's Hall, November 1, 1854. *Vide supra.*

[3] William A. Richardson.

To William H. Seward[1]

[July 21, 1860]

I join in the foregoing invitation; and if a compliance with it will be no inconvenience to Gov. Seward, I shall be personally much gratified to meet him here.   A. LINCOLN.

[1] AES, NAuE. Lincoln's endorsement is written on a letter of Governor John Wood and others to Seward, July 21, 1860:

"We notice this morning [in the Chciago *Press and Tribune*], with pleasure, your letter to the Hon Aaron Goodrich of Minnesota, in which you promise to address the People of that gallant State, at a future day.

"On the Eighth day of August— there will be a *State Convention*, held in this city, to nominate a candidate to be elected, to the office of Lieutenant Governor— together with a Mass Meeting of the Republicans of this state. We anticipate a very large gathering—probably as large as any that will be held in the state—upon that occasion, and we cordially and urgently invite you to be present, and address the assembled multitude.

"We feel assured that you will come, if you possibly can, and request you to answer, by *telegraph*, addressed to John Wood, this city—that you will come, so that proper measures may be taken to make all who may attend the meeting as comfortable as we can."

Seward spoke in St. Paul on September 18, then went to Kansas. On October 1, he passed through Springfield on his way to Chicago and spoke from the platform of the train to a crowd of two to three thousand (*Illinois State Journal*, October 2, 1860).

To George C. Latham[1]

My dear George   Springfield, Ills. July 22. 1860.

I have scarcely felt greater pain in my life than on learning yesterday from Bob's letter, that you had failed to enter Harvard University. And yet there is very little in it, if you will allow no feeling of *discouragement* to seize, and prey upon you. It is a *certain* truth, that you *can* enter, and graduate in, Harvard University; and having made the attempt, you *must* succeed in it. *"Must"* is the word.

I know not how to aid you, save in the assurance of one of mature age, and much severe experience, that you *can* not fail, if you resolutely determine, that you *will* not.

The President of the institution, can scarcely be other than a kind man; and doubtless he would grant you an interview, and point out the readiest way to remove, or overcome, the obstacles which have thwarted you.

In your temporary failure there is no evidence that you may not yet be a better scholar, and a more successful man in the great struggle of life, than many others, who have entered college more easily.

Again I say let no feeling of discouragement prey upon you, and in the end you are sure to succeed.

With more than a common interest I subscribe myself   Very truly your friend,   A. Lincoln.

[1] ALS, owned by Mrs. H. S. Dickerman, Springfield, Illinois. George C. Latham, who had attended Phillips Exeter Academy with Robert Todd Lincoln, was a Springfield boy, the son of Philip C. Latham.

To Caleb B. Smith[1]

Springfield, [July 23], 1860.

My dear Sir: Yours of the 20th was duly received, and for which I sincerely thank you. From present appearances we might succeed in the general result, without Indiana; but *with* it, failure is scarcely possible. Therefore put in your best efforts. I see by the despatches that Mr. Clay had a rousing meeting at Vincennes. Yours very truly, A. LINCOLN.

¹ NH, VI, 47. The date of this letter in Nicolay and Hay's *Complete Works* (August 10, 1860) seems to be incorrect. Lincoln's reference to newspaper reports of Cassius Clay's speech at Vincennes would put the date more than two weeks earlier. Smith's letter of July 20 also reports on Clay's Indiana tour (DLC-RTL). Although Lincoln's manuscript letter has not been located, auction records of its sale (Parke-Bernet Sale 493, November 3, 1943) give the date of the letter as July 23, 1860.

To Francis E. Spinner¹

Hon. F. E. Spinner. Springfield, Ills. July 27, 1860.

Dear Sir: You will perhaps be pleased, as I have been, to know that many good men have tendered me substantially the same advice that you do (excepting as to re-election) and that no single man of any mark has, so far, tempted me to a contrary course. . . . Yours very truly, A. LINCOLN.

¹ Tracy, pp. 156-57. Francis E. Spinner, banker at Mohawk, New York, congressman 1855-1861, and later treasurer of the U.S. (1861-1875), wrote Lincoln July 23 that administration men were joining the Republicans to assist in spoils distribution, and warned that Lincoln should even "resist the importunities of your own political and personal friends." Such a course would "compel your reelection." In a postscript he promised to send *Com. Perry's Expedition to Japan* (1854) and reported that he could also send the "Pacific Rail Road Survey Reports" and the "Mexican Boundary Survey Reports" (DLC-RTL). See Lincoln to Spinner, September 24, *infra*.

To Carl Schurz¹

Hon. Carl Schurz. Springfield, Ills.
My dear Sir July 28. 1860

By the hand of J. G. Nicolay, whom you know, I send you the Scrap-book, containing the New-Orleans speech you desire. It also contains the speeches made at Chicago, St. Louis, and Memphis, immediately after the election of 1858. If the Scrap-book will be of much further service to you, you can keep it, till oppertunity occurs to return it; otherwise, let Mr. Nicolay bring it with him. Yours very truly A. LINCOLN

¹ ALS, DLC-Schurz Papers. Schurz had visited Lincoln on July 24, and doubtless expressed his wish for a copy of Douglas' speech at New Orleans. On August 22 he wrote Lincoln from New Albany, Indiana, that he had been "for about three weeks . . . working the state of Ind. . . ." and that he was returning the scrapbook (DLC-RTL).

To James O. Putnam[1]

Hon. James O. Putnam   Springfield, Ills.
My dear Sir   July 29. 1860
    I have just read the speech you sent me, with your note of the
23rd. attached.[2] I do not mean to flatter you when I say it is, indeed, a very excellent one. The manner in which you point out to
Gov. Hunt that his objections to the election of the Republican
candidate apply with manifold force to the candidate he would
elect instead, is truly admirable.
    And now allow me to name one error. John Adams was not
elected over Jefferson by the H.R; but Jefferson was over Burr.
Such is my recollection.[3] Yours very truly   A. LINCOLN

[1] ALS-F, New York *Times*, February 12, 1928. Putnam's note of July 23 is
not in the Lincoln Papers.
[2] Putnam spoke at Lockport, New York, on July 19, in reply to ex-Governor
Washington Hunt, who was a Bell supporter.
[3] Putnam wrote Lincoln on September 8 that he had corrected the error in
the pamphlet edition of his speech. See Lincoln to Putnam, September 13, *infra*
(DLC-RTL).

To Thomas Doney[1]

Thomas Doney, Esq   Springfield, Ills.
My dear Sir: July 30, 1860
    The picture (I know not the artistic designation) was duly and
thankfully received. I consider it a very excellent one; though,
truth to say, I am a very indifferent judge.
    The receipt of it should have been acknowledged long ago; but
it had passed from my mind till reminded of it by the letter of
our friend, Dr. Dodson.[2] Yours very truly   A. LINCOLN

[1] ALS, ORB. Thomas Doney was an engraver at Elgin, Illinois.
[2] There is no letter from Dr. Dodson in the Lincoln Papers, but Lincoln probably referred to Dr. B. E. Dodson of Dundee, Illinois.

To Simeon Francis[1]

Friend Francis—   Springfield, Ills. Aug. 4. 1860
    I have had three letters from you—one, a long one, received in
February; one, telling me of the deputation of Mr. Greely to
cast the vote of Oregon, in the Chicago convention, received a few
days before that convention; and one written since you knew the
result of your Oregon election, received a few days ago. I have not,
till now, attempted an answer to any of them, because I disliked

to write you a mere note, and because I could not find time to write at length.

Your brother Allen has returned from California, and, I understand, intends remaining here. Josiah[2] is running his J. P. court, about as when you left. We had a storm here last night which did considerable damage, the largest single instance of which, was to the Withies.[3] A wall of their brick shop building was thrown in, and, it is said destroyed ten thousand dollars worth of carriages. I have heard of no personal injury done.

When you wrote, you had not learned of the doings of the democratic convention at Baltimore; but you will be in possession of it all long before this reaches you. I hesitate to say it, but it really appears now, as if the success of the Republican ticket is inevitable. We have no reason to doubt any of the states which voted for Fremont. Add to these, Minnesota, Pennsylvania, and New-Jersey, and the thing is done. Minnesota is as sure as such a thing can be; while the democracy are so divided between Douglas and Breckenridge in Penn. & N.J. that they are scarcely less sure. Our friends are also confident in Indiana and Illinois. I should expect the same division would give us a fair chance in Oregon. Write me what you think on that point.

We were very anxious here for David Logan's election. I think I will write him before long. If you see Col. Baker,[4] give him my respects. I do hope he may not be tricked out of what he has fairly earned.

Make my kindest regards to Mrs. Francis; and tell her I both hope and believe she is not so unhappy as when I saw her last. Your friend, as ever   A. LINCOLN

[1] ALS, OrHi. In 1859, Simeon Francis had removed from Springfield to Portland, Oregon, where he published *The Oregon Farmer*.

[2] Josiah Francis, brother of Simeon.

[3] William H. Withey and George Withey, carriage and wagon manufacturers.

[4] Lincoln's old friend Edward D. Baker. The *verso* of the last page of Lincoln's letter bears a note by Francis as follows: "Gave this letter to Col. Baker to be shown at Salem when the Senator was to be chosen to stop some foolish lies in circulation."

To Simon Cameron[1]

PRIVATE

Hon. Simon Cameron.   Springfield, Ills.
My dear Sir: Aug. 6. 1860
Yours of the 1st. is duly received, and for which I sincerely thank you. Good news, from a reliable source, is always welcome.

Before this reaches you, my very good friend, Judge Davis,[2] will have called upon you, and, perhaps, shown you the "scraps" mentioned to you by Mr. Leslie.[3] Nothing about these, must get into the news-papers. Yours very truly   A. LINCOLN.

[1] ALS, DLC-Cameron Papers. Cameron wrote on August 1 that Pennsylvania was safe and needed no help. "My young friend, Mr. Lesley, who saw you the other day says you showed him your notes of speeches made in 1844, on the subject of protection, and his account of them gratifies us, all, very much." (DLC-RTL).   [2] David Davis.

[3] James Lesley, Jr., of Philadelphia. The "scraps" were the same notes preserved in the Lincoln Papers. *Vide supra*, December 1, 1847. Although Cameron refers to them as written in 1844, Lincoln dated them as written between 1846 and December, 1847.

Remarks at a Republican Rally, Springfield, Illinois[1]

August 8, 1860

My Fellow Citizens:—I appear among you upon this occasion with no intention of making a speech.

It has been my purpose, since I have been placed in my present position, to make no speeches. This assemblage having been drawn together at the place of my residence, it appeared to be the wish of those constituting this vast assembly to see me; and it is certainly my wish to see all of you. I appear upon the ground here at this time only for the purpose of affording myself the best opportunity of seeing you, and enabling you to see me.

I confess with gratitude, be it understood, that I did not suppose my appearance among you would create the tumult which I now witness. I am profoundly gratified for this manifestation of your feelings. I am gratified, because it is a tribute such as can be paid to no man as a man. It is the evidence that four years from this time you will give a like manifestation to the next man who is the representative of the truth on the questions that now agitate the public. And it is because you will then fight for this cause as you do now, or with even greater ardor than now, though I be dead and gone. I most profoundly and sincerely thank you.

Having said this much, allow me now to say that it is my wish that you will hear this public discussion by others of our friends who are present for the purpose of addressing you, and that you will kindly let me be silent.

[1] *Illinois State Journal*, August 9, 1860. This speech is misdated by Nicolay and Hay in the *Complete Works* (VI, 49) on August 14. The *Journal* devoted more than three columns to the mammoth occasion at the Fair Grounds, heading the first column with an elephant bearing in its trunk a banner inscribed

"WE ARE COMING!" and caparisoned in another which announced "CLEAR THE TRACK!"—the first known use of the elephant as symbol of the Republican party. Headlines followed: "A Political Earthquake!" "THE PRAIRIES ON FIRE/FOR LINCOLN!" The rally was described in superlatives. Five speakers' stands (other papers said "six") were filled simultaneously. Lincoln's arrival on the grounds occasioned a stampede for his carriage, whence he was lifted and carried above the crowd to one of the stands. After his brief remarks he escaped by stratagem on horseback while the expectant crowd massed around the carriage. The Cincinnati *Gazette* reporter admitted that "Immense is the only word that describes to-day's demonstration. . . . The enthusiasm was beyond all bounds. . . . I never saw so dense and large a crowd. . . . Mr. Lincoln's bearing to-day, under such a tribute of personal popularity and admiration as I have never before seen paid to any human being, more and more convinces me of the real greatness of his character. . . ." (Peoria *Daily Transcript*, August 13, 1860, copied from the *Gazette*.)

Endorsement: Buckner S. Morris to John Wood
Concerning Pardon of Patrick Cunningham[1]

[August 8, 1860]

I think it is almost always safe to pardon a convict, when, as in this case, the Judge before whom he was convicted, recommends it.

A. LINCOLN

[1] AES, I-Ar. Judge Buckner S. Morris, who had presided over the Lake County Circuit Court which convicted one Patrick Cunningham of manslaughter, gave Mary Cunningham, a sister, a letter dated August 7, recommending pardon. An endorsement on the *verso* indicates that Mary Cunningham brought the letter to Springfield in person on August 8, at which time she probably secured Lincoln's endorsement also.

To Cassius M. Clay[1]

Springfield, Illinois, August 10, 1860.

My dear Sir: Your very kind letter of the 6th was received yesterday. It so happened that our State Central Committee was in session here at the time; and, thinking it proper to do so, I submitted the letter to them. They were delighted with the assurance of having your assistance. For what appear good reasons, they, however, propose a change in the program, starting you at the same place (Marshall in Clark County), and thence northward. This change, I suppose, will be agreeable to you, as it will give you larger audiences, and much easier travel—nearly all being by railroad. They will be governed by your time, and when they shall have fully designated the places, you will be duly notified.

As to the inaugural, I have not yet commenced getting it up; while it affords me great pleasure to be able to say the cliques have not yet commenced upon me. Yours very truly, A. LINCOLN.

[1] NH, VI, 47-48. In reply to Lincoln's letter of July 20, *supra*, Clay wrote on August 6, that he had been through Southern Indiana and found the Fillmore party dissolved, with "our ticket . . . *surely winner* in Indiana." He agreed to speak at Marshall on August 28 and "run on till Sept 9th when I must return. . . . I will advise you in two respects—put Andrew Jackson's 'union' speech in your inaugural address: and stay clear of all *cliques!*" His next letter of August 12, agrees to the appointments made for him by the Illinois State Central Committee (DLC-RTL).

To M. B. Miner[1]

M. B. Miner, Esq   Springfield, Ills—
Dear Sir   Aug. 11. 1860

Yours of the 7th. with newspaper slip attached, is received; and for which I thank you. Yours truly   A. LINCOLN

[1] ALS, IaHA. Miner's letter is not in the Lincoln Papers, and he cannot be positively identified. It seems probable, however, that Martin B. Miner, an attorney at Jerseyville, Illinois, was the man.

To T. Apolion Cheney[1]

T. A. Cheney, Esq   Springfield, Ills., Aug. 14, 1860

Dear Sir   Yours of the 10th. is received and for which I thank you. I would cheerfully answer your questions in regard to the Fugitive Slave law, were it not that I consider it would be both imprudent, and contrary to the reasonable expectation of friends for me to write, or speak anything upon doctrinal points now. Besides this, my published speeches contain nearly all I could willingly say. *Justice* and *fairness* to *all*, is the utmost I have said, or will say. Yours truly   A. LINCOLN

[1] ALS-P, ISLA. Cheney's letter of August 10 is not among the Lincoln Papers, but his reply of August 19, written from Cherry Creek, New York, indicates that he was probably an abolitionist.

Endorsement: David Davis to John Wood
Concerning Pardon of Thomas Patterson[1]

August 14, 1860[2]

Considering the absence of previous bad character of Patterson himself, the necessities of his family, the excellent character of all his family connections, and the very numerously signed petition of his neighbors, I recommend that he be pardoned at once.

A. LINCOLN—

[1] AES, I-Ar. Judge David Davis' letter to Governor Wood concerning the pardon of Thomas Patterson of Vermilion County, convicted of manslaughter, is dated June 12, 1860. Patterson was pardoned August 30, 1860.

[2] This date is not in Lincoln's handwriting.

To George G. Fogg[1]

George G. Fogg, Esq   Springfield, Ills.
My dear Sir: Aug. 14. 1860

According to a printed notice attached to a letter of Gov. Morgan,[2] I suppose you have been at New-York since the 23rd. of July. *"How does it look now?"*

I am invited to a horse-show, at Springfield, Mass. beginning, I believe, on the 4th. of September.

Would it *help,* or *hurt,* our cause, if I were to go?

I am not itching to go, and seeking to be advised thereto. Yours very truly   A. LINCOLN.

[1] ALS, owned by Elwin L. Page, Concord, New Hampshire. George G. Fogg, a lawyer of Concord, New Hampshire, secretary of the Republican National Committee, replied August 18 that a trip to Springfield, Massachusetts, would not help (DLC-RTL).   [2] Edwin D. Morgan of New York.

To Samuel Galloway[1]

Hon. Saml. Galloway   Springfield, Ills.
My dear Sir   Aug. 14. 1860

I should be very glad indeed to see you here; but if coming will lessen your chance of success in your own election, do not come.

Mr. *Dill Wiegand*[2] has not yet presented his letter; but when he shall do so, I shall show him the attention you request. Yours very truly   A. LINCOLN

[1] ALS, IHi. Galloway's letter is not in the Lincoln Papers. Although his personal campaign for a seat in Congress was intensive (he was defeated by a narrow margin), the *Illinois State Journal*, October 15, 1860, lists seven speaking engagements for him in Illinois, October 18-25.

[2] No person of this name has been identified, but the possibility seems to be that Lincoln misread Galloway's handwriting for "Dr. H. Wigand," a Chase supporter of Springfield, Ohio, who thus signed his name in a letter to Lincoln in November, 1860 (DLC-RTL).

To James E. Harvey[1]

Private.
James E. Harvey, Esq.,   Springfield, Ill.,
My dear Sir,   Aug. 14, 1860.

Yours of the 9th inclosing the Spalding letter, is received. As to our *uneasy* friends in New York, (if there be such) all that can be said is *"Justice and fairness to all."* More than this has not been, and can not be, said to any.

Whether you go to Tennessee must depend upon your own

judgment. I expect to be constantly here; and I shall be much pleased to see you at any time. Yours very truly,

A. LINCOLN.

[1] Hertz, II, 782. Neither Harvey's letter of August 9, nor the enclosure of Spalding (Elbridge G. Spaulding of Buffalo, New York?) is in the Lincoln Papers.

To William Fithian[1]

Dr. Wm. Fithian   Springfield,
My dear Sir,   Aug. 15, 1860

I understand there is trouble in Old Vermilion about it's next Representative to the Legislature. I have learned nothing as to the grounds of the difficulty; but I will be greatly obliged if you will find a way of so adjusting it, that we do not lose that member. To lose Trumbull's re-election next winter would be a great disaster. Please do not let it fall upon us. I appeal to you because I can to no other, with so much confidence. Yours as ever   A. LINCOLN

[1] ALS, IHi. There is no reply from Fithian in the Lincoln Papers. Apparently the "trouble in Old Vermilion" was not settled, for Samuel G. Craig, a Democrat, was elected representative from that county.

To John B. Fry[1]

Private

John B. Fry, Esq   Springfield, Ills. August 15. 1860

My dear Sir: Yours of the 9th. inclosing the letter of Hon. John M. Botts, was duly received. The latter is herewith returned according to your request. It contains one of the many assurances I receive from the South that in no probable event will there be any very formidable effort to break up the Union. The people of the South have too much of good sense, and good temper, to attempt the ruin of the government, rather than see it administered as it was administered by the men who made it. At least, so I hope and believe.

I thank you both for your own letter, and a sight of that of Mr. Botts. Yours, very truly   A. LINCOLN

[1] Copy, DLC-Jeremiah S. Black Papers. John B. Fry wrote from New York City, reminding Lincoln of his acquaintance in 1846 when he had been introduced to Lincoln by John J. Hardin. He would campaign for Lincoln in Pennsylvania and New York beginning September 10, and enclosed a letter which indicated "the wish of the writer [John M. Botts of Virginia who had been in Congress with Lincoln] that you may be elected, although situated as he is, it would not do for him to say so. . . ." (DLC-RTL).

To George G. Fogg[1]

PRIVATE

Hon. George G. Fogg—   Springfield, Ills.

My dear Sir: Aug. 16, 1860

I am annoyed some by the printed paragraph below, in relation to myself, taken from the N.Y. Herald's correspondence from this place of August 8th.

He had, he said, on one occasion been invited to go into Kentucky and revisit some of the scenes with whose history his father in his lifetime had been identified. On asking by letter whether Judge Lynch would be present, he received no response; and he therefore came to the conclusion that the invitation was a trap laid by some designing person to inveigle him into a slave State for the purpose of doing violence to his person.[2]

This is decidedly wrong. I did not say it. I do not impugn the correspondent. I suppose he misconceived the statement from the following incident. Soon after the Chicago nomination I was written to by a highly respectable gentleman of Hardin County, Ky, inquiring if I was a son of Thomas Lincoln, whom he had known long ago, in that county. I answered that I was, and that I was myself born there. He wrote again, and, among other things, (did not *invite* me but) simply *inquired* if it would not be agreeable to me to revisit the scenes of my childhood. I replied, among other things, "It would indeed; but would you not Lynch me?" He did not write again.

I have, *playfully*, (and never otherwise) related this incident several times; and I suppose I did so to the Herald correspondent, though I do not remember it. If I did, it is all that I did say, from which the correspondent could have inferred his statement.

Now, I dislike, exceedingly, for Kentuckians to understand that I am charging them with a purpose to inveigle me, and do violence to me. Yet I can not go into the newspapers. Would not the editor of the Herald, upon being shown this letter, insert the short correction, which you find upon the inclosed scrap?

Please try him, unless you perceive some sufficient reason to the contrary. In no event, let my name be publicly used. Yours very truly   A. LINCOLN

CORRECTION

We have such assurance as satisfies us that our correspondent writing from Springfield, Ills, under date of Aug. 8– was mistaken in representing Mr. Lincoln as expressing a suspicion of a design to inveigle him into Kentucky for the purpose of doing him violence.

Mr. Lincoln neither entertains, nor has intended to express any such suspicion.

¹ ALS, CSmH. For further discussion of the subject of this letter, see Lincoln to Fogg, August 29, and Lincoln to Haycraft, August 16 and 23, *infra.*
² The clipping is pasted on the letter.

To Samuel Haycraft[1]

Hon. Saml. Haycraft   Springfield, Ills. Aug. 16. 1860

My dear Sir: A correspondent of the New-York Herald, who was here a week ago, writing to that paper, represents me as saying I had been invited to visit Kentucky, but that I suspected it was a trap to inveigle me into Kentucky, in order to do violence to me.

This is wholly a mistake. I said no such thing. I do not remember, but possibly I did mention my correspondence with you. But very certainly I was not guilty of stating, or insinuating, a suspicion of any intended violence, deception, or other wrong, against me, by you, or any other Kentuckian. Thinking this Herald correspondence might fall under your eye, I think it due to myself to enter my protest against the correctness of this part of it. I scarcely think the correspondent was malicious; but rather that he misunderstood what was said. Yours very truly

A. LINCOLN.

¹ ALS, CSmH. See Lincoln to Haycraft, August 23, *infra.*

To James F. Simmons[1]

PRIVATE

Hon. J. F. Simmons   Springfield, Ills.
My dear Sir   Aug. 17. 1860

I had not heard a word from Rhode-Island for a long time, till this morning, when I received a letter intimating that Douglas is inlisting some rich men there, who know how to use money, and that it is endangering the State.[2] How is this? Please write me.

Yours truly   A. LINCOLN

¹ ALS, IHi. James F. Simmons was U.S. Senator from Rhode Island. There is no reply from Simmons in the Lincoln Papers.
² See Lincoln to Weed, *infra,* n.1.

To Thurlow Weed[1]

PRIVATE

Hon. T. Weed—   Springfield, Ills– Aug. 17, 1860.

My dear Sir—Yours of the 13th. was received this morning. Douglas is managing the Bell-element with great adroitness. He had his men, in Kentucky, to vote for the Bell candidate, producing a result which has badly alarmed and damaged Breckinridge, and, at the same time, has induced the Bell men to suppose that Bell will certainly be President, if they can keep a few of the Northern States away from us, by throwing them to Douglas. But you, better than I, understand all this.

I think there will be the most extraordinary effort ever made, to carry New-York for Douglas. You, and all others who write me from your state, think the effort can not succeed; and I hope you are right; still it will require close watching, and great effort on the other side.

Herewith I send you a copy of a letter,[2] written at New-York, which sufficiently explains itself, and which may, or may not, give you a valuable hint.

You have seen that Bell tickets have been put on the track, both here, and in Indiana. In both cases, the object has been, I think, the same as the Hunt[3] movement in N. Y—to throw the States to Douglas. In our state we know the thing is engineered by Douglas men; and we do not believe they can make a great deal out of it. Yours very truly   A. LINCOLN

[1] ALS, NRU-Thurlow Weed Papers on deposit. Weed wrote on August 13 that the fusion between the Douglas and Bell factions in New York would not affect the result, which would be the same "if *all* the factions were to unite against us." The Douglas men were absurdly confident because they believed Seward men would work against Lincoln. Fusion in Pennsylvania would fail. Rhode Island was in danger because Douglas had got hold of some rich manufacturers who "know how to use money." (DLC-RTL).

[2] The copy, not in Lincoln's handwriting, is without signature, but bears the heading "167 Broadway N.Y. 13th Aug./6o." The writer relayed information from John Hardy, secretary of the Democratic National Executive Committee, that the Douglas party in New York would attempt no union with Breckinridge forces and that Bell men would go for Douglas. He added that three-fourths of the Fillmore vote would go for Lincoln and that "if Hunt Brooks & Co. keep up [the]ir engineering, all the Bell voters in [the] State can be put in an omnibus. . . ." (NRU-Weed Papers).

[3] Washington Hunt and James Brooks were former Whigs and ex-representatives in Congress, actively leading the Bell movement in New York.

To Charles H. Fisher[1]

C. H Fisher, Esq   Springfield Ill Aug 18th 1860.

Dear Sir—Your letter of the 14th inst. came duly to hand, together with the book written by your brother which you are kind enough to send me. Please accept my thanks for the same. While I have not yet found time to examine it, I doubt not I shall find much pleasure in its perusal. Yours Truly   A. LINCOLN.

[1] LS, PHi. Fisher's letter of August 14 is not in the Lincoln Papers, but see Lincoln to Fisher, August 27, *infra.*

To George Bliss and Others[1]

Messrs. Geo. Bliss, & others.   Springfield, Ills.
    Man[a]gers &c.   Aug. 22, 1860

Gentlemen—Yours of the 8th. inviting my attendance at your National Exhibition of Imported Blood, & American breeds of Horses, on the 4th. 5th. 6th. & 7th. days of September, at Springfield, Mass. was received in due course, and should have been answered sooner.

For reasons not neccessary to be mentioned, I am constrained to decline the honor which you so kindly tender me. Your Obt. Servt.
                         A. LINCOLN

[1] ALS, IHi. See Lincoln to Fogg, August 14, *supra.* George Bliss was a lawyer at Springfield, Massachusetts, president of the Worcester and Albany Railroad, and for several terms a member of the Massachusetts legislature.

To Samuel Haycraft[1]

[Hon Sam Haycraft   [Springfield, Ill
My dear S]   Aug 23 1860]

Yours of the 19th. is just received. I now fear I may have given you some uneasiness by my last letter. I did not mean to intimate that I had, to any extent, been involved, or embarrassed, by you; nor yet, to draw from you anything to relieve myself from difficulty. My only object was to assure you that I had not, as represented by the Herald correspondent, charged you with an attempt to inveigle me into Kentucky to do me violence. I believe no such thing of you, or of Kentuckians generally; and I dislike to be represented to them as slandering them in that way. [Yours truly
                         A LINCOLN]

[1] AL, CSmH. The letter has been mutilated by cutting away the top of the page, the close, and signature, and the removed portions have been restored in another hand. The restored date is somewhat difficult to read, but appears to be "Aug. 23." The envelope is postmarked but the numeral "3" is not clear. Haycraft's endorsement on the envelope seems to establish the date, however, as follows: "Aug. 23. 1860/This not answrd/26. Aug. answrd." Haycraft had written on August 19, that he fully understood the playfulness of Lincoln's language in the letter of June 4, and that he wished to clear himself of any knowledge of the New York correspondent's statement. He had taken the fact that Lincoln's letter was marked "private" to mean "not for publication," but had showed it to a few friends. If Lincoln desired him to make a statement to the New York *Herald,* he would be pleased to do so (DLC-RTL).

To Robert C. Schenck[1]

Hon. Robert C. Schenck   Springfield, Ills.
My dear Sir   Aug. 23. 1860

Yours of the 16th. was received two days ago, and that of the 18th. inclosing Mr. Judd's note, was received, last evening. I am

[99]

LEE COUNTY LIBRARY
SANFORD, N. C.

very glad you are coming among us. The *time* we must fix according to your own suggestion; and the *places*, I wish to have a hand in fixing myself. My judgment is to have you in this old whig region. I shall consult with Judd, have the appointments made, and you duly notified. *We really want you*. Will notify you at Dayton. Yours very truly   A. LINCOLN

¹ ALS, IHi. Robert C. Schenck of Dayton, Ohio, representative in congress (1843-1851, 1863-1871), and also a major general in the Union army until he resigned to run for congress in 1863, had written August 16 and 18 of his willingness to take the stump in Illinois (DLC-RTL).

To John Hanks¹

John Hanks, Esq   Springfield, Ills.
My dear Sir: Aug. 24. 1860

Yours of the 23rd. is received. My recollection is that I never lived in the same neighborhood with Charles Hanks till I came to Macon county, Illinos, after I was twenty-one years of age. As I understand, he and I were born in different counties of Kentucky, and never saw each other in that State; that while I was a very small boy my father removed to Indiana, and your father with his family remained in Kentucky for many years. At length you, a young man grown, came to our neighborhood, and were at our house, off and on, a great deal for three, four, or five years; and during the time, your father, with his whole family, except William, Charles, and William Miller, who had married one of your sisters, came to the same neighborhood in Indiana, and remained a year or two, and then went to Illinois. William, Charles, and William Miller, had removed directly from Kentucky to Illinois, not even passing through our neighborhood in Indiana.

Once, a year or two before I came to Illinois, Charles, with some others, had been back to Kentucky, and returning to Illinois, passed through our neighborhood in Indiana. He stopped, I think, but one day, (certainly not as much as three); and this was the first time I ever saw him in my life, and the *only* time, till I came to Illinois, as before stated. The year I passed in Macon county I was with him a good deal—mostly on his own place, where I helped him at breaking prarie, with a joint team of his and ours, which in turn, broke some on the new place we were improving.

This is, as I remember it. Dont let this letter be made public by any means. Yours very truly   A. LINCOLN

¹ ALS-P, ISLA. John Hanks wrote on August 23 that he had been thinking about answering his brother Charles Hanks' letter and wished to know when and where Lincoln first saw Charles. He also promised not to use Lincoln's letter (DLC-RTL). Charles Hanks had published a letter in the Decatur *Mag-*

net (copied by the *Fulton County Ledger*, July 31, 1860), in which he disputed the authenticity of the rails brought into the Decatur convention on May 9 by John Hanks and posed as an intimate relation who was politically opposed to Lincoln's principles.

To Charles H. Fisher[1]

Private

C. H. Fisher   Springfield, Ills– Aug. 27, 1860

Dear Sir: Your second note, inclosing the *supposed* speech of Mr. Dallas to Lord Brougham, is received. I have read the speech quite through, together with the real author's introductory, and closing remarks. I have also looked through the long preface of the book to-day. Both seem to be well written, and contain many things with which I could agree, and some with which I could not. A specimen of the latter is the declaration, in the closing remarks upon the "speech" that the institution is a *necessity* imposed on us by the negro race. That the going many thousand miles, seizing a set of savages, bringing them here, and making slaves of them, is a *necessity* imposed on *us* by *them*, involves a species of logic to which my mind will scarcely assent.[2]

[1] ADf, DLC-RTL. Fisher wrote from Philadelphia, August 22, enclosing a clipping from the *North American and U.S. Gazette* "signed 'Cecil'—who is my brother, giving his idea of what Mr. Dallas [George M. Dallas, minister to Great Britain] might have replied to Lord Brougham." The clipping refers to a meeting of an international statistical congress in London attended by a Negro delegate from Canada. Henry Peter Brougham had made a speech chiding the United States for slavery, and Minister Dallas had said nothing in reply. The book referred to was probably one of two written by Sidney G. (pseudonym "Cecil") Fisher: *Law of the Territories* (1859) and *Kanzas and the Constitution* (1856).

[2] Lincoln did not finish the letter. The envelope containing Fisher's letter bears Nicolay's endorsement: "needs no answer"; but Lincoln apparently was tempted to reply.

To Amory Holbrook[1]

Amory Holbrook, Esq   Springfield, Ills.

My dear Sir   Aug. 27. 1860

Your very agreeable letter of July 21st. was duly received. It is matter of much regret here that Logan[2] failed of his election. He grew up and studied law in this place, and his parents and sisters still reside here. We are also anxious for the result of your two U.S. Senatorial elections.

I shall be pleased to hear from you again. Yours very truly

A. LINCOLN.

[1] ALS, OrHi. Amory Holbrook, who had met Lincoln in Massachusetts in September, 1848, wrote from Oregon City, Oregon, where he had migrated in 1849, concerning the political scene in Oregon. He was a member of the Oregon legislature (DLC-RTL).   [2] David Logan.

To John M. Read[1]

Hon. John M. Read: Springfield, Ills.
My dear Sir   Aug. 27. 1860

The miniature likeness of myself, taken by your friend, J. Henry Brown, is an excellent one, so far as I can judge. To my unpracticed eye, it is without fault. Yours very truly

A. LINCOLN—

[1] ALS, DLC-Read Papers. A similar letter from Mrs. Lincoln dated August 25 is in the Read Papers. Judge John M. Read of the Pennsylvania Supreme Court, a prominent Philadelphia Republican, had sent a young Philadelphia artist to paint a portrait of Lincoln to be engraved by John Sartain for use in the campaign. Read and other Eastern Republicans were dissatisfied with the photographs of Lincoln which were in circulation during the campaign (see Lincoln to Babcock, September 13, *infra*).

To George G. Fogg[1]

Hon. George G. Fogg.   Springfield, Ills.
My dear Sir   Aug. 29, 1860

Yours of the 23rd. was only received yesterday evening.

You have done precisely right in that matter with the Herald. Do nothing further about it. Although it wrongs me, and annoys me some, I prefer letting it run it's course, to getting into the papers over my own name. I regret the trouble it has given you, and thank you also for having performed your part so cheerfully and correctly.

What you say of the Empire state is of a piece with all the news I receive from there. The whole field appears reasonably well. Yours very truly   A. LINCOLN

[1] ALS, CSmH. On August 23, Fogg replied to Lincoln's letter of August 16, *supra*, that he had called on James G. Bennett of the *Herald* and found him well inclined to Lincoln personally. Bennett would permit the corrections to appear over Fogg's name, or any responsible name, or dated at Springfield without name, but would not allow it to appear editorially or by a correspondent, which would be admitting an error, unless he could say it was by Lincoln's request. Fogg thought the correction under such stipulations was not desirable, and Norman Judd, who was in New York, agreed. Fogg concluded by stating that in his opinion the Republican nomination of Edwin D. Morgan for governor of New York was the strongest that could be made (DLC-RTL).

To Zachariah Chandler[1]

Hon. Z. Chandler   Springfield, Ills.
My dear Sir   Aug. 31, 1860

Your kind letter of the 28th is duly received. I very well remember meeting you at Kalamazoo in 1856. I very well remember

the jovial elderly lady, and wife of an M. C. with whom we took tea, calling you "Zach Chandler."

Your kind invitation I suppose I must decline. It is the opinion of friends, backed by my own judgment, that I should not really, or apparently, be showing myself about the country.

Please accept my thanks for the kindness of your invitation. Yours very truly   A. LINCOLN

¹ Copy, ISLA. Chandler wrote from Detroit, August 28, inviting Mr. and Mrs. Lincoln to be his guests on October 2, at the time of the Michigan State Fair (DLC-RTL).

To Benjamin F. James¹

B. F. James, Esq.   Springfield, Ills.
My dear Sir: Aug. 31. 1860

Your kind letter of congratulation, dated the 27th. was duly received. How time gallops along with us! Look at these great big boys of yours and mine, when it is but yesterday that we and their mothers were unmarried.

Make my respects to Mrs. James & Louis, and believe me Yours as ever   A. LINCOLN—

¹ ALS, IHi. The Lincoln Papers contain no letters from Lincoln's old friend Benjamin F. James written in 1860. James was practicing law in Chicago at this time.

To John M. Pomeroy¹

Private

Hon. John ———,   Springfield, Ills.
My dear Sir: Aug. 31. 1860

Yours of the 27th. is duly received. It consists almost exclusively of a historical detail of some local troubles among some of our friends in Pennsylvania; and I suppose it's object is to guard me against forming a prejudice against Mr. McC———. I have not heard near so much upon that subject as you probably suppose; and I am slow to listen to criminations among friends, and never expouse their quarrels on either side. My sincere wish is that both sides will allow by-gones to be by-gones, and look to the present & future only. Yours very truly   A. LINCOLN

¹ ALS, PHC. Pomeroy's name and that of Alexander K. McClure, chairman of the Pennsylvania State Committee, have been eradicated from the letter and replaced by lines. Pomeroy's letter of August 27 (DLC-RTL) establishes the identity of both men, and traces the quarrel between Cameron and Curtin factions of Pennsylvania Republicans, which at the time of his writing centered in the effort of the Cameron faction to "get up a Committee ostensibly auxiliary to the State Committee but which was really intended to supersede & destroy

it. The . . . movement is now virtually broken up & henceforth cordial cooperation with the State Committee may be expected from all but Cameron & his
immediate friends. . . ." Pomeroy wrote as a member of the state committee
who had been a delegate to the Chicago convention.

To John Hill[1]

John Hill, Esq.   Springfield, Ills.

Petersburg, Ills.   Sep. 1860

Sir: A pamphlet, over name, bearing the title of "Opposing principles of Henry Clay, and Abraham Lincoln" is being circulated
among the people. I quote from it as follows, towit:

SLAVERY IN THE DISTRICT OF COLUMBIA.

In 1837, as a member of the Illinois Legislature, Mr. LINCOLN, with
only four others, voted against the following resolution:
"*Resolved,* That the Government cannot abolish slavery in the District of Columbia against the consent of the citizens of said District
without a manifest breach of good faith." [See House Jour., 1836-7, p.
240.]

In Congress, at the session of 1848-49, he voted to institute measures
for the abolition of slavery in the District. In 1839, in the Illinois Legislature, he voted against a resolution to the effect—
"That as the General Government cannot do, directly, what it is
clearly prohibited from doing indirectly, that it is the openly declared
design of the Abolitionist of this nation to abolish slavery in the District of Columbia, with a view to its ultimate abolishment in the
States; . . . . and that, therefore, Congress ought not to abolish slavery in the District of Columbia." [House Jour., 1838-9, p. 329.][2]

It is seen in this that you arraign Mr. Lincoln, first, for a vote in
the Illinois Legislature of 1836-7—secondly for a vote in Congress
in 1848-9, and thirdly for a vote in the Illinois Legislature of 1839.

1 AL, DLC-RTL. John Hill was the son of Samuel Hill, Lincoln's old friend
of New Salem days. John's pamphlet was reprinted from a signed article
printed in the *Missouri Republican*, July 24, 1860. Lincoln's letter seems not to
have been completed or sent. Its manner suggests his intention that it be published or copied as a communication from some one else than himself, and the
two fragments (*infra*) dealing with the charges made in Hill's pamphlet suggest that an article may have been prepared for publication in lieu of the letter.
Lincoln's resentment of Hill's lack of respect for truth is all the more interesting in view of the fact that Hill became the prime source of the Ann Rutledge
story, the tradition of Lincoln's infidelity, and a number of other spurious or
dubious traditions concerning Lincoln's New Salem years, when in the *Menard
Axis*, February 15, 1862, he published an article entitled "A Romance of
Reality," composed largely of family gossip. It was this article which led Herndon to elaborate on the Ann Rutledge episode when he began collecting material
for his biography of Lincoln in 1866, and Hill rather than Herndon deserves
recognition for primary irresponsibility in first publishing stories which have
been perpetuated in popular belief.
2 This excerpt, including bracketed references, appears in the source as a clipping from the pamphlet, pasted on the manuscript page.

As authority for the first arraignment, you say ("See House Jour. p 240"). Now, I have that Journal, at this moment open before me, at page 240– and there is, upon that page, absolutely nothing upon that subject. But on pages 243 & 244 there is a series of resolutions, four in number, the third of which is very nearly, but not quite, such as you set out. But they were not voted upon that day; on the contrary, as appears by the same Journal, at pages 248 & 249, they were referred to a select committee. Seven days afterwards, as shown by the same Journal, at pages 309-310 & 311. the committee reported the resolutions back to the House, with an amendment proposed to *each* one of them; which amendments were all adopted by the House; and then the series, as amended, passed the House by Yeas and Nays, Mr. Lincoln, and five others voting against them.

Now, the point is, John, that the Journal does not show in what *shape* any of those resolutions stood, when Mr. Lincoln voted against them. It does show that they were all amended—were all changed from their original form; but what new shape they took does nowhere appear in the Journal. And hence, John, in stating that Mr. Lincoln voted against a resolution, in the shape you alledge he did, you state what is almost certainly false, and certainly what you do not know to be true.

But, more than this, John: These resolutions went to the senate, and were passed by that body, as appears by the Senate Journal, of that session, at pages 277 & 297. They were not spread upon the Senate Journal either, so that their substance and form remains entirely uncertain.

But again, John, Mr. Lincoln, with his colleague, Dan Stone, at the same session, and with reference to these identical resolutions, defined his position in relation to Slavery in the District of Columbia, by a written protest, entered upon the same Journal of the House of Representatives, at pages 817-818, and which entry and protest is as follows, towit.

The following protest was presented to the House which was read and ordered to be spread on the Journals, to-wit:
Resolutions upon the subject of domestic slavery having passed both branches of the General Assembly at its present session, the undersigned hereby protest against the passage of the same.
They believe that the institution of slavery is founded on both injustice and bad policy; but that the promulgation of abolition doctrines tend rather to increase than to abate its evils.
They believe that the Congress of the United States has no power, under the constitution to interfere with the institution of slavery in the different States.

They believe that the Congress of the United States has the power under the constitution to abolish slavery in the District of Columbia; but that that power ought not to be exercised, unless at the request of the people of said District.

The difference between these opinions and those contained in the said resolutions, is their reason for entering this protest.

DAN. STONE

A. LINCOLN

Representatives from the County of Sangamon.[3]

And now, John, we know you had these Journals in your hands— were ransacking them, and know of all these things—and yet you suppressed them. Why did you suppress them?

Your second arraignment of Mr. Lincoln is seen to be in these words, towit.

"In Congress, at the session of 1848-49 he voted to institute measures for the abolition of slavery in the District."

For this arraignment, you refer to no authority whatever; and with the Congressional Globe, for that session, now before me, I venture to say Mr. Lincoln gave no such vote. At page 38 of that volume of the congressional Globe, I find that on the question of granting leave to Mr. Palfrey[4] to introduce a bill "to repeal all acts, or parts of acts, of congress, establishing or maintaining slavery, or the slave-trade in the District of Columbia" taken by yeas and nays, Mr. Lincoln voted *against* granting the leave. And further on, at pages 55 & 56 on the question of laying upon the table, a bill already before the House, "to authorize the people of the District of Columbia to express their desires as to the existence of slavery therein" taken by yeas and nays, Mr. Lincoln voted to lay the bill on the table. And these are the only instances of votes, on questions of abolishing slavery in the District of Columbia, being taken by yeas and nays, during that session.

You were not very prudent, John, in stating a falsehood in this instance: but you were as prudent as possible, under the circumstances, to quote no authority by which to prove it.

Although Mr. Lincoln gave no other *votes* on the question, it is true, that he drew up, and sought to get before the House of Representatives, at that session, a bill for the abolition of slavery in the District of Columbia, upon the conditions that the abolition should be gradual, and only upon a vote of the majority of the people of the District, and with compensation to unwilling owners, and also embracing a fugitive slave clause, and an exception in

[3] The protest, not in Lincoln's handwriting, is a separate page inserted in the manuscript. It appears in the present edition under date of March 3, 1837, *supra*.
[4] John G. Palfrey, representative from Massachusetts.

favor of Officers of the Government, while in the District on the public business; all which appears in the same volume of the congressional Globe, at pages 212-244.[5]

As to your third arraignment of Mr. Lincoln, referring to the Ills. House Journal of 1838-9. page 329, I find on pages 322 & 323 of that Journal, that to a "resolution from the Senate requiring the Engrossing clerks of the Senate and House, respectively to make out copies of memorials and resolutions to be transmitted to congress &c." Mr. Calhoun (Candle-box)[6] offered, as an amendment, a long preamble, and five resolutions about slavery, one of which resolutions contains language substantially as you have quoted; that on motion, the preamble and resolutions were laid on the table by yeas and nays, shown at page 329-330—Mr. Lincoln voting to lay them on the table. Whether they were thus laid upon the table, with any reference to their *merits*, or because of their *incongruity*, as an amendment to a resolution from the Senate, prescribing the duty of the Engrossing clerks, fair minded men will judge; or, perhaps N. W. Edwards, now a Douglas man, and Gen. *W. F. Thornton*, one of the Douglas delegates to the late Charleston and Baltimore conventions can tell—they being two of the fortyfour who with Mr. Lincoln—voted to lay them on the table.

August 27. 1858. In his joint debate with Senator Douglas at Freeport, in answer to certain questions which had been propounded by Douglass, Mr. Lincoln said: "The fourth one is in regard to slavery in the District of Columbia. In relation to that, I have my mind very distinctly made up. I should be exceedingly glad to see slavery abolished in the District of Columbia. I believe that congress possesses the constitutional power to abolish it. Yet as a member of congress I should not, with my present views, be in favor of endeavoring to abolish slavery in the District of Columbia, unless it would be upon these conditions: *First*, that the abolition should be gradual. *Second*, that it should be on a vote of the

[5] *Vide supra*, January 10, 1849.

[6] John Calhoun of Sangamon County was nicknamed "Candle-box" as the result of an episode during his later career as Surveyor General of Kansas. Elected president of the Lecompton Convention, Calhoun was charged with counting and reporting the vote on the Lecompton Constitution. Departing for Washington soon after the election, he left the papers in charge of the chief clerk in the surveyor general's office. In the investigation which ensued, the clerk refused access to the returns and falsely stated that Calhoun had carried them to Washington. After considerable intrigue and an investigation by a committee of the territorial legislature, the clerk, L. A. McLane, was revealed to have hidden the returns in a *candle-box* buried under a woodpile. When McLane fled from the territory, his superior, Calhoun, bore the chief odium of the episode.

majority of the qualified voters of the District; and *third* that compensation should be made to unwilling owners. With these three conditions, I confess I would be exceedingly glad to see congress abolish slavery in the District of Columbia, and, in the language of Henry Clay, "sweep from the capitol that foul blot upon our nation." (*Joint Debates*, page 89—[7]

[7] The manuscript ends abruptly before the bottom of the page, suggesting that it was never completed.

Fragments of an Answer to John Hill[1]

[September, 1860]

The protest, before mentioned, placed on the Journal of the Illinois House of Representatives more than twenty three years ago; the draft of a bill, spread on the Congressional Globe more than eleven years ago; and his declaration in the Freeport debate not quite two years ago, are all in harmony with each other, and show conclusively what Mr. Lincoln's views are in regard to Slavery in the District of Columbia. They show that he thinks congress has the constitutional power to abolish it; and that the power might properly be exercised, *with* substantially such conditions as set out in the bill drawn by himself; and that it ought not to be exercised without such conditions.

The foregoing is the whole (excepting the report as indicated) which, after full examination, can be found on the subject of slavery, in the Journals of the Illinois Senate and House of Representatives, for the session of 1836-7.

It is seen that the *form* in which the resolutions passed, and were voted against by Mr. Lincoln, nowhere appears—the Journal showing that all of them were changed from the original form, by amendments, without showing what they were in the amended form.

Nor is this of the least consequence in determining Mr. Lincoln's views upon the subject, at that time; since, by the protest, he placed upon the same Journal, his own views upon the subject, in his own well considered language, which stand of record for the inspection of all who choose

[1] AD, DLC-RTL. In the Lincoln Papers these two fragments are separated from the draft of a letter to John Hill (*supra*). They have been linked with the reply to Hill because of their obvious similarity of reference. Possibly the fragments were intended for an editorial in the *Illinois State Journal* which Lincoln changed his mind about writing. The *Journal* had already answered Hill in part in the issue of August 25, and in the issue of September 19 printed the extracts from the *House Journal*, 1836-1837, to which Lincoln referred.

To Henry Wilson[1]

Hon. Henry Wilson   Springfield, Ills.
My dear Sir: Sep. 1. 1860

Yours of August 25th. was received yesterday.

The point you press—the importance of thorough organization—
is felt, and appreciated by our friends everywhere. And yet it involves so much more of dry, and irksome labor, that most of them
shrink from it—preferring parades, and shows, and monster meetings. I know not how this can be helped. I do what I can in my
position, for organization; but it does not amount to so much as it
should.

I shall be pleased to hear from you at all times. Yours very truly
                                                    A. LINCOLN.

[1] ALS, owned by Edward C. Stone, Boston, Massachusetts. Henry Wilson,
shoe manufacturer and U.S. Senator from Massachusetts (1855-1873), wrote
that he feared Republicans were overconfident and were neglecting organization in New England and New York (DLC-RTL).

To John Coulter[1]

Private

John Coulter, Esq   Springfield, Ills–
Dear Sir: Sept. 4. 1860

Yours of the 29th. is received; and I presume I understand what
has prompted you to write it. In 1832 I was first a candidate for
the Legislature, with some ten or a dozen other candidates. *Peter
Cartwright*, and three others were elected, of whom I was *not* one.
In 1834 he, and I, and several others, again become candidates; he
declined before the election, I saw the race through, and, with
three others, was elected. In 1835 he became a candidate to fill a
vacancy in the State Senate, and his sole competitor, Job Fletcher,
beat him by near six hundred majority.

In 1836, 1838, & 1840, I was successively elected to the Legislature—he not being a candidate at either of those elections.

I then ceased to be a candidate for anything till 1846, when I
ran for Congress. Mr. Cartwright was my competitor, and I beat
him, as I recollect 1511 majority, being about double the party majority of the District.

I was never a candidate for congress at any other time, and
never had any contest with Mr. Cartwright other than as I have
stated.

Please do not make this public   Yours truly   A. LINCOLN

[1] ALS, CCamStJ-Doheny Collection. John Coulter was a resident of Niles,
Michigan. His letter of August 29 is not in the Lincoln Papers.

To Hannibal Hamlin[1]

Springfield, Illinois, September 4, 1860.

My dear Sir: I am annoyed some by a letter from a friend in Chicago, in which the following passage occurs: "Hamlin has written Colfax[2] that two members of Congress will, he fears, be lost in Maine—the first and sixth districts; and that Washburne's[3] majority for governor will not exceed six thousand."

I had heard something like this six weeks ago, but had been assured since that it was not so. Your secretary of state,—Mr. Smith,[4] I think,—whom you introduced to me by letter, gave this assurance; more recently, Mr. Fessenden,[5] our candidate for Congress in one of those districts, wrote a relative here that his election was sure by at least five thousand, and that Washburne's majority would be from 14,000 to 17,000; and still later, Mr. Fogg, of New Hampshire, now at New York serving on a national committee, wrote me that we were having a desperate fight in Maine, which would end in a splendid victory for us.

Such a result as you seem to have predicted in Maine, in your letter to Colfax, would, I fear, put us on the down-hill track, lose us the State elections in Pennsylvania and Indiana, and probably ruin us on the main turn in November.

You must not allow it. Yours very truly,   A. Lincoln.

[1] NH, VI, 54-55.
[2] See Lincoln to Medill, *infra*. Hamlin replied to Lincoln on September 8: "I have not wriitten to *Colfax at all*, nor to any one any thing like the extract in your letter. . . ." He explained, however, that the third and sixth congressional districts were doubtful, since the majority in both in the last election had been less than a hundred (DLC-RTL).
[3] Israel Washburn, Jr., who spelled his name without an "e."
[4] Noah Smith of Calais, Maine. Hamlin's letter introducing him is not in the Lincoln Papers.
[5] Samuel C. Fessenden, brother of Senator William P. Fessenden.

To Joseph Medill[1]

PRIVATE

J. Medill, Esq   Springfield,
My dear Sir   Sep. 4. 1860

Yours of Aug. 30th. for some cause, only reached me last night. As to Pennsylvania, I have a letter from Gen. Cameron,[2] dated Aug. 29th. in which, among other things, he says:

"You may as well be getting your inaugeral address ready, so as to have plenty time to make it short. If possible we are daily becoming stronger in Pennsylvania, and in New-Jersey all is right."

Last night, just as I had read your letter, Mr. David Taggart called upon me. He is a very intelligent gentleman, lately was Speaker of the Penn. Senate, and is now upon our electoral ticket, and residing at Northumberland. He left home Thursday the 30th.; and he is very confident that Penn. is abun[dan]tly safe, both for Curtin[3] in Oct– & the National ticket in Novr. This from Cameron & Taggart, constitute[s] my latest news from Penn.

I am more annoyed by what you write me of Maine. Long ago I had heard about danger of two members of congress there; but at least six weeks since Mr. Hamlin[4] wrote me "all *is* safe in New-England["]; and very recently Mr. Fogg[5] of N.H. wrote from N. York saying: "We are having a desperate fight in Maine; but it will end in a splendid triumph for us." He had just come from Maine.

What you say about the Northern 30 counties of Illinois pleases me. Keep good your promise that they will give as much majority as they did for Fremont, and we will let you off. We can not be beaten, nor even hard run, in the state, if that holds true. Yours as ever   A LINCOLN.

[1] ALS, owned by the Chicago *Tribune*, Chicago, Illinois. Medill's letter of August 30 expressed fear that "our folks are resting in false security as to Pa.," and reported that Hamlin had written Colfax the first and sixth congressional districts in Maine would be lost, but that "We are stirring up Northern Illinois, and will give you the Fremont majority in 30 Northern counties." He enclosed a letter from E. Ethridge to Schuyler Colfax expressing worry about Indiana (DLC-RTL).   [2] Simon Cameron.

[3] Andrew G. Curtin, candidate for governor.

[4] Hannibal Hamlin to Lincoln, July 23– "*All is* well in New England. . . ." (DLC-RTL).

[5] George G. Fogg to Lincoln, August 23– "Our friends in Maine are having a great fight which is to be followed by a great victory. . . ." (DLC-RTL).

To Anson G. Chester[1]

Private

Anson G. Chester, Esq.   Springfield, Ills., Sept 5, 1860

My dear Sir: Yours of the 1st is received. The extract upon a newspaper slip which you sent, and which I herewith return, is a base forgery, so far as its authorship is imputed to me. I never said anything like it, at any time or place. I do not recognize it as anything I have ever seen before, emanating from any source. I wish my name not to be used; but my friends will be entirely safe in denouncing the thing as a forgery, so far as it is ascribed to me. Yours very truly   A. LINCOLN

[1] Tracy, pp. 161-62. Anson G. Chester was editor of the Buffalo, New York, *Commercial Advertiser*. In 1864 he left journalism for a commission as major

and appointment as New York military agent at Buffalo, and in later life entered the Presbyterian ministry. His letter of September 1 is not in the Lincoln Papers. See the note, Lincoln to A. Chester, March 14, *supra*. The newspaper clipping was undoubtedly from the Chicago *Times and Herald*. The *Illinois State Journal*, September 6, 1860, denounced the forgery in the following article, which may have been written by Lincoln and was certainly authorized by him:

"In the Chicago *Times and Herald* of the 4th we find the following, purporting to be 'a quotation from a speech made by Mr. Lincoln in 1844,' as taken from the *Macomb Eagle*:

'Mr. Jefferson is a statesman whose praises are never out of the mouths of the Democratic party. Let us attend to this uncompromising friend of freedom whose name is continually invoked against the Whig party. The character of Jefferson was repulsive. Continually puling about liberty, equality, and the degrading curse of slavery, he brought his own children to the hammer, and made money of his debaucheries. Even at his death he did not manumit his numerous offspring, but left them soul and body to degradation and the cart whip. A daughter of this vaunted champion of Democracy was sold some years ago at public auction in New Orleans, and purchased by a society of gentlemen, who wished to testify by her liberation their admiration of the statesman, who

"Dreamt of freedom in a slave's embrace."

'This single line I have quoted gives more insight to the character of the man than whole volumes of panegyric. It will outlive his epitaph, write it who may.'

"This is a bold and deliberate forgery, whether originating with the Chicago *Times and Herald* or the Macomb *Eagle*. Mr. Lincoln never used any such language in any speech *at any time*. Throughout the whole of his political life, Mr. Lincoln has ever spoken of Mr. Jefferson in the most kindly and respectful manner, holding him up as one of the ablest statesmen of his own or any other age, and constantly referring to him as one of the greatest apostles of freedom and free labor. This is so well known that any attempt, by means of fraud or forgery, to create the contrary impression, can only react upon the desperate politicians who are parties to such disreputable tactics."

To George S. Lester[1]

George S. Lester, Esq   Springfield, Ills.
My dear Sir: Sep. 5. 1860

Your very kind letter of Aug. 31st. is duly received, and, for which, I sincerely thank you.

Please make my respects to Mr. Babcock & family. Yours truly
A. LINCOLN

[1] ALS-P, ISLA. George S. Lester was a resident of New Haven, Connecticut, whom Lincoln doubtless met while stopping at the home of James F. Babcock in the fall of 1860. Lester's letter is not in the Lincoln Papers.

To Alexander K. McClure[1]

A. K. McClure, Esq.,   Springfield, Ills., Sept. 6, 1860

My dear Sir: Inclosed I send you a copy of a letter from New York, stating a matter, which, if true, deeply concerns our interests in Pennsylvania. The writer does not wish to be known; but some revelations of his in a former letter have subsequently been verified. Yours truly, A. LINCOLN

1 Tracy, p. 162. McClure answered September 12 that he was aware of the danger indicated by Lincoln's unnamed correspondent—a change in Democratic policy which is not specified but which vaguely implies an effort to split the Republican vote, perhaps by means of a deal with the Cameron clique who were at odds with the Curtin faction led by McClure. (RTL-DLC). See Lincoln to John M. Pomeroy, August 31, *infra*.

To Charles C. Nott[1]

Charles C. Nott, Esq. Springfield Ills. Sep. 6. 1860
My dear Sir Your note of the 1st. with the accompanying sheets, reached me this morning. I have looked over the sheets hastily, and herewith return them. You perceive I have touched them only very lightly. The notes you add I have not attempted to compare with originals, leaving that entirely to you. I think the notes are exceedingly valuable.

Before this reaches you, you will have received my letter in relation to "Abraham Baldwin."[2]

And now please accept for yourself, and present to the "Young Men's Republican Union" my grateful acknowledgements, for your and their exceeding kindness towards me in this matter. Yours very truly A. LINCOLN.

1 ALS, IHi. Nott's letter of September 1 accompanied proof sheets of the new pamphlet printing of the address at Cooper Institute (DLC-RTL). See Lincoln to Nott, May 31, *supra*.

2 Lincoln seems to imply that he had already written a letter about Abraham Baldwin in reply to Nott's query of August 28, concerning Baldwin. But the letter is not extant, and Nott's letter of September 17 indicates that he had not received it. Lincoln to Nott, September 22, *infra*, gives the substance of his reply. On August 28 Nott had written as follows: ". . . I have made no alterations other than those you sanctioned, except—

"1. I do not find that Abraham Baldwin voted on the Ordinance of '87. On the contrary he appears *not* to have acted with Congress during the sitting of the Convention. Wm. Pierce seems to have taken his place then; and his name is recorded as voting for the Ordinance. . . . I will therefore (unless you write to the contrary) strike out his name in that place and reduce the number from 'four' to 'three' where you sum up the number of times he voted." (DLC-RTL). Nott's corrections were allowed to stand.

To Elihu B. Washburne[1]

Hon. E. B. Washburne— Springfield, Ills. Sep. 9, 1860
My dear Sir: Yours of the 5th. was received last evening. I was right glad to see it. It contains the freshest "posting" which I now

have. It relieved me some from a little anxiety I had about Maine. Jo. Medill, on Aug. 30th. wrote me that Colfax had a letter from Mr. Hamlin saying we were in great danger of losing two members of Congress in Maine, and that your brother would not have exceeding 6000 majority for Governor. I addressed you at once, at Galena, asking for your latest information. As you are at Washington, that letter you will receive some time after the Maine election. Yours very truly   A. LINCOLN

1 ALS, owned by Hempstead Washburne, Chicago, Illinois.

To Charles G. Wilson[1]

Charles G. Wilson, Esq   Springfield, Ills.
My dear Sir   Sep. 10. 1860
    Yours of the 6th. is just received. I have pleasure in assuring you that there is no great pressure upon me for the offices in prospect. If, as you say, the newspapers & leading politicians, are intent upon schemes for the obtaining of office, they do not bring themselves within the range of my power to discourage them. Yours truly   A. LINCOLN.

1 ALS-F, Stan. V. Henkels Catalog 1430, April 24, 1929. The original letter has not been located. In the collection of R. E. Burdick of New York City is what purports to be the original of this letter. Comparison of the catalog facsimile with a photostat of this manuscript, however, reveals that they cannot both be genuine. There is no letter from Wilson, September 10, 1860, in the Lincoln Papers, but the New York *Herald*, January 17, 1861, in a dispatch from Springfield dated January 12, lists Charles G. Wilson of New York City as among Lincoln's callers.

To James F. Babcock[1]

Hon James F. Babcock   Springfield, Ills.
My dear Sir: Sep. 13. 1860
    Your two letters of the 8th., with newspaper slips, containing the proceedings of the Conn. Republican State Convention, and a consideration of our prospects in ·New-York, are received.
    The original of the picture you inclose,[2] and which I return, was taken from life, and is, *I* think, a very true one; though my wife, and many others, do not. My impression is that their objection arises from the disordered condition of the hair. My judgment is worth nothing in these matters. If your friend could procure one of the "heads" "busts" or whatever you call it, by Volk[3] at Chicago, I should think it the thing for him. Yours truly
                                           A. LINCOLN.

2 The photograph preserved with the letter is one made by Alexander Hesler in Chicago, February, 1857 (Meserve No. 6).

3 Leonard W. Volk, a young sculptor at Chicago for whom Lincoln sat in his spare time while attending court at Chicago in March, 1860.

To James O. Putnam[1]

Hon. James O. Putnam   Springfield, Ills.

My dear Sir   Sep. 13. 1860

Your short letter, with the newspaper containing your late ex-cellent speech at Rochester, was duly received, and for which I thank you sincerely.

You must not lay much stress on the blunder about Mr. Adams; for I made a more mischievous one, in the first printed speech of mine, on the Slavery question—Oct. 1854—I stated that the prohi-bition of slavery in the North West Territory was made a condi-tion in the Virginia deed of cession—while, in fact, it was not. Like yourself, I have since done what I could to correct the error. Yours very truly   A. Lincoln.

1 ALS-P, ISLA. Putnam wrote on September 8, following his speech at Rochester on September 7. Referring to Lincoln's letter of July 29, *supra*, he said, "That mistake in my Lockport speech as to John Adams, was a great blun-der. After receiving your letter, a pamphlet edition of the speech was published & the error corrected." (DLC-RTL).

To John Pettit[1]

Private

Hon. John Pettit   Springfield, Ills.

My dear Sir: Sep. 14. 1860

Yours of the 10th. is received. I have a good deal of news from New-York; but, of course, it is from *friends,* and is one-sided. They declare that no combination can deprive of us of [*sic*] the Empire State. It would seem that assurances to this point could not be better than I have. And yet it *may* be delusive.

If it would not be dishonorable, of which you can best judge, I wish you would name the sources of your information. Yours truly

A. Lincoln

1 ALS, The Rosenbach Company, Philadelphia and New York. Chief Justice John Pettit of the U.S. Courts in Kansas Territory and former U.S. representa-tive (1843-1849) and senator (1853-1855) from Indiana, answered from Leav-enworth, Kansas, September 29, that he was much relieved about news from New York (DLC-RTL).

To Nathaniel Grigsby[1]

Nathaniel Grigsby, Esq   Springfield, Ills. Sep. 20, 1860

My dear Sir: Your letter of July 19th. was received only a few days ago, having been mailed by your brother[2] at Gentryville, Ia.[3] on the 12th. of this month. A few days ago, Gov. Wood, of Quincy told me he saw you, and that you said you had written me. I had not then received your letter.

Of our three families who removed from Indiana together, my father, Squire Hall, and John D. Johnston, are dead—and all the rest of us are yet living. Of course the younger ones are grown up, marriages contracted, and new ones born. I have three boys now, the oldest of which is seventeen years of age.

There is now a Republican electoral ticket in Missouri, so that you can vote for me if your neighbors will let you. I would advise you not to get into any trouble about it. Give my kindest regards to your brother Charles.[4]

Within the present year I have had two letters from John Gorden,[5] who is living somewhere in Missouri,—I forget exactly where—and he says his father and mother are both still living near him. Yours very truly   A. LINCOLN

[1] ALS-P, ISLA. Grigsby's letter of July 19 is not in the Lincoln Papers. He was a boyhood friend of Lincoln's in Spencer County, Indiana, who was living in Missouri at the time of the letter.   [2] William Grigsby?
[3] Abbreviation for Indiana.
[4] Charles Grigsby had bought Thomas Lincoln's farm in 1830 when the Lincolns left Indiana for Illinois.
[5] John Gorden wrote from Buffalo, Missouri, February 7 and June 15, 1860 (DLC-RTL).

To Edwin D. Morgan[1]

Hon. E. D. Morgan   Springfield, Ills.
My dear Sir   Sep. 20. 1860

Yours of the 17th. is just received. Here, in Illinois, we are precisely in the condition you seem to understand—safe, as we think, on the National and State tickets, but in danger as to the Legislature. How the National committee can do anything in the premises I do not quite understand; tho, on this point I would refer to Mr. Judd. I shall confer with some friends, and write you again soon—saying no more now thant [sic] that, in my opinion, no one thing will do us so much good in *Illinois*, as the carrying of *Indiana* at the October election. The whole surplus energy of the party throughout the nation, should be bent upon that object up to the close of that election. I should say the same of Pennsylvania, were it not that our assurances seem so abundant of Curtin's election there.

If I might advise, I would say, bend all your energies upon Indiana now. Yours very truly   A. LINCOLN.

[1] ALS, N. Morgan's letter of September 17 asked for advice as to the situation in Illinois. He had heard that the Republicans might not secure the legislature while carrying the electoral vote (DLC-RTL).

To Nathan Sargent[1]

My dear Sir: Springfield, Ills. Sep. 20– 1860
Your very kind letter of the 15th. was received yesterday; and I have just time to acknowledge it's receipt, and to say I thank you for it; and that I shall be pleased to hear from you again whenever it is convenient for you to write. Yours very truly
Hon. N. Sargent—   A LINCOLN

[1] ALS-P, ISLA. Sargent's letter of September 15 is not in the Lincoln Papers. He had been sergeant-at-arms of the House of Representatives during Lincoln's term in congress.

To John Chrisman[1]

John Chrisman, Esq   Springfield, Ills. Sep. 21 1860
My dear Sir Yours of the 13th. was duly received. I have no doubt that you and I are related. My grand-father's Christian name was "Abraham." He had four brothers—Isaac, Jacob, John & Thomas. They were born in Pennsylvania, and my grand-father, and some, if not all the others, in early life removed to Rockingham Co. Virginia. There my father—named Thomas—was born. From there my grand-father removed to Kentucky, and was killed by Indians, about the year 1784. His brother Thomas, who was my father's uncle—also removed to Kentucky—to Fayette Co. I think—where, as I understand he lived, and died. I close, by repeating, I have no doubt you and I are related. Yours very truly
                    A. LINCOLN

[1] ALS, DLC-RTL. There are no letters from Chrisman in the Lincoln Papers, but an envelope postmarked "Waverly, Mo., March 15," containing Lincoln's letter of September 21, 1860, bears the following endorsement: "John Chrisman Mo. encloses an autograph letter of the President to him, and asks that his brother Jos. Chrisman, banished as a rebel, be allowed to return to Mo." Chrisman's letter was probably referred to the proper authority, but no trace of it has been found. John Chrisman, born at Linville, Virginia, was the son of Joseph Chrisman and Elizabeth Lincoln (daughter of Jacob who was the brother of Lincoln's grandfather Abraham).

To Mrs. M. J. Green[1]

Mrs. M. J. Green   Springfield, Ills.
My dear Madam.   Sep. 22. 1860
   Your kind congratulatory letter, of August, was received in due
course—and should have been answered sooner. The truth is I
have never corresponded much with ladies; and hence I postpone
writing letters to them, as a business which I do not understand.
I can only say now I thank you for the good opinion you express
of me, fearing, at the same time, I may not be able to maintain it
through life. Yours very truly   A. LINCOLN.

[1] ALS, CSmH. There is no letter from Mrs. M. J. Green in the Lincoln
Papers, and efforts to identify her have been unsuccessful.

To Anson G. Henry[1]

                                     Springfield, Ills. Sep. 22. 1860
   Dear Doctor   Yours of July 18th. was received some time ago.
When you wrote, you had not learned the result of the Democratic
conventions at Charleston & [Ba]ltimore. With the two tickets in
the field I should think it possible for our friends to carry Oregon.
But the general result, I think, does not depend upon Oregon. No
one, this side of the mountains, pretends that any ticket can be
elected by the People, unless it be ours. Hence great efforts to combine against us, are being made, which, however, as yet, have not
had much success.
   Besides what we see in the newspapers, I have a good deal of
private correspondence; and, without giving details, I will only
say, it all looks very favorable to our success.
   Make my best respects to Mrs. H. and the rest of your family.
Your friend as ever   A. LINCOLN

[1] ALS-P, ISLA.

To Charles C. Nott[1]

Charles C. Nott, Esq.,   Springfield, Ills., Sept. 22, 1860.
   My Dear Sir: Yours of the 17th was duly received. The 250
copies have not yet arrived. I am greatly obliged to you for what
you have done, and what you propose to do.
   The "Abraham Baldwin letter" in substance was that I could
not find the Journal of the Confederation Congress for the session
at which was passed the Ordinance of 1787—and that in stating
Mr. Baldwin had voted for its passage, I had relied on a communi-

[118]

cation of Mr. Greeley, over his own signature, published in the New York *Weekly Tribune* of October 15, 1859. If you will turn to that paper, you will there see that Mr. Greeley apparently copies from the Journal, and places the name of Mr. Baldwin among those of the men who voted for the measure.

Still, if the Journal itself shows differently, of course it is right. Yours very truly,   A. LINCOLN.

[1] George H. Putnam, *Abraham Lincoln: The People's Leader* (1909), pp. 229-30. Nott's letter of September 17 specified that "the 'Abraham Baldwin letter' referred to in your last I regret to say has *not* arrived. From your not touching the proofs in that regard, I inferred (and hope) that the correction was not itself an error." (DLC-RTL). See Lincoln to Nott, September 6, *supra*.

To G. Yoke Tams[1]

Private & confidential

G. Yoke Tams, Esq   Springfield, Ills– Sep. 22. 1860

My dear Sir: Your letter asking me "Are you in favor of a Tariff & Protection to American Industry?" is received. The convention which nominated me, by the 12th. plank of their platform, selected their position on this question; and I have declared my approval of the platform, and accepted the nomination. Now, if I were to *publicly* shift this position, by adding or subtracting anything, the convention would have the right, and probably would be inclined, to displace me as their candidate. And I feel confident that you, on reflection, would not wish me to give *private* assurances to be seen by some, and kept secret from others.

I enjoin that this shall, by no means be made public. Yours Respectfully   A. LINCOLN

[1] ALS copy, DLC-RTL. Entirely in Lincoln's handwriting, the manuscript appears to be a copy retained by Lincoln for his file. G. Yoke Tams wrote from Manayunk, Pennsylvania, September 15, "I take the liberty of asking you one plain question. Are you in favour of a Tarriff & Protection to American Industry. . . ." (DLC-RTL).

To John Van Dyke[1]

Hon. John Van Dyke   Springfield, Ills.
My dear Sir: Sep. 22. 1860

Your very kind letter of the 17th. is duly received; and for which I sincerely thank you. Hon. Moses Hampton[2] has written me one under similar circumstances, he now being a Judge at Pittsburgh.

Please make my best respects to Mrs. V. D. of whom I have very pleasant recollections. Yours very truly   A. LINCOLN

1 ALS-P, ISLA. John Van Dyke was judge of the New Jersey Supreme Court. His letter of September 17 is not in the Lincoln Papers.

2 Moses Hampton, Whig congressman from Pennsylvania 1847-1851, and an admirer of Lincoln's abilities as raconteur during their acquaintance in Congress, wrote a letter of congratulations on May 23 (DLC-RTL), but no later letter is in the Lincoln Papers.

To John T. Hanks[1]

Dear John   Springfield, Ills. Sep. 24, 1860

Your letter of July 22– was received a few days ago. If your Father and Mother desire you to come home, it is a delicate matter for me to advise you not to do it. Still, as you ask my advice, it is that if you are doing well, you better stick to it. If you have a good start there, and should give it up, you might not get it again, here, or elsewhere. It can not be other than their first wish that you shall do well.

And now, as to politics, I am very much obliged to you for what you offer to do for me in Oregon. This side of the Rocky Mountains things appear reasonably well for the general result. In opposing David Logan, at the late congressional election in Oregon, I suppose you did what you thought was right; and when a man does what he thinks is right, he does the best he can. Still, I am sorry you did not think differently, as I knew David from his childhood, and he studied law in our office when his father and I were partners.

I heard from our relations over at Charleston, about three weeks ago, and they were well then.

Write me again when you receive this. Your Uncle

A. LINCOLN

1 ALS-P, ISLA. John T. Hanks, the son of Dennis F. Hanks, had migrated to California and later to Oregon. Writing from Canyonville, Oregon, July 22, he reviewed Oregon politics and his personal affairs (DLC-RTL).

To Francis E. Spinner[1]

Hon. F. E. Spinner   Springfield, Ills.
My dear Sir: Sep. 24. 1860

Yours of the 19th. was received in due course, the Bag of books having been received two days before. I am much obliged for both the books and the letter.

You are right in the suspicion that our foes are now driving at Pennsylvania; but our friends there are fully apprized of this, and say they can and will repulse them. Yours very truly

A. LINCOLN

To John M. Brockman[1]

J. M. Brockman, Esq   Springfield, Ills. Sep. 25. 1860

Dear Sir: Yours of the 24th. asking "the best mode of obtaining a thorough knowledge of the law" is received. The mode is very simple, though laborious, and tedious. It is only to get the books, and read, and study them carefully. Begin with Blackstone's Commentaries, and after reading it carefully through, say twice, take up Chitty's Pleading, Greenleaf's Evidence, & Story's Equity &c. in succession. Work, work, work, is the main thing. Yours very truly   A. LINCOLN

[1] ALS, owned by Mrs. Ida Brockman Cornelius, Humboldt, Nebraska. Brockman's letter is not in the Lincoln Papers. He was a young school teacher of Pleasant Plains, Illinois, whose plans for studying law were abandoned after he had moved to Brownville, Nebraska, and enlisted in the Fifth Iowa Cavalry. Following the Civil War he settled in Nebraska as a farmer and stockman and later served two terms in the state legislature.

To Benjamin F. James[1]

B. F. James, Esq   Springfield, Ills.
My dear Sir   Sep. 26. 1860

I have now had your kind letter for near a month, without answering it. Nor have I much to communicate, even now, beyond, what you know quite as well as I, by the public prints. So far as I have private information, the prospect for the election looks quite encouraging.

Please make my respects to Mrs. J. and Louis; and also to your Father. Your friend as ever   A. LINCOLN

[1] ALS, IHi. See Lincoln to James, August 31, *supra*. Lincoln may have forgotten that he had acknowledged James' letter of congratulation.

To Nehemiah D. Sperry[1]

N. D. Sperry, Esq   Springfield, Ills.
My dear Sir: Sep. 26. 1860

Yours of the 19th. is duly received; and for which I sincerely thank you.

My intelligence from Penn. & from the whole field, is very

much the same as you seem to have. As to my forgiving you for detaining me last Spring, I certainly do not hold you, and the Republicans of Connecticut, my debtors in anything. Yours very truly

A. LINCOLN

[1] ALS, CSmH. Sperry's letter of September 19 is not in the Lincoln Papers. A former Know-Nothing who had become a Republican, he was appointed postmaster at New Haven, Connecticut, in 1861 and remained in office until 1886. He was a member of the Republican National Committee during Lincoln's administration and served eight terms as U.S. representative beginning in 1886.

To James E. Harvey[1]

(Private.)

Springfield, Ill., September 27, 1860.

My dear Sir: Yesterday I was gratified by the receipt of yours of the 22d. There is no reality in that suspicion about Judge Kelley. Neither he nor any other man has obtained or sought such a relation with me. Yours very truly,   A. LINCOLN.

[1] NH, VI, 59. Harvey's letter of September 22 gave political news, including a rumor that Judge William D. Kelley, Democratic candidate for congress ". . . was represented to be the personal exponent of your views & wishes, & in the event of success would be so regarded." (DLC-RTL). See Lincoln to Kelley, October 13, *infra*.

To George B. Lincoln[1]

G. B. Lincoln, Esq.,   Springfield, Ill.,
My dear Sir: Sept 27, 1860

Yours of the 22nd with the accompanying presents, by the hand of Mr. Alvey, is received. They are all good and one is a great curiosity. Please accept my sincere thanks for them. Yours very truly   A. LINCOLN.

[1] Copy, ISLA. Specifying that he was not related, George B. Lincoln of New York City wrote on September 22 that he was sending "By the kindness of your worthy neighbour Mr. Alvey who is returning to Springfield . . . as a present to your Boys a few specimens the [campaign] medals . . . . a small *unique Photograph* . . . also for the Boys—and for *Mrs. Lincoln* the larger Photograph—under glass. . . ." (DLC-RTL). James W. Alvey was a traveling salesman living at Springfield.

To Daniel P. Gardner[1]

Professor Gardner   Springfield, Ills.
Dear Sir: Sep. 28. 1860

Some specimens of your Soap have been used at our house and Mrs. L. declares it is a superb article. She at the same time, protests that *I* have never given sufficient attention to the "soap question" to be a competent judge. Yours truly   A. LINCOLN

[1] ALS-F, *Genuine Autograph Letters from the Most Distinguished Men of Our Country, Presented to Prof. Gardner, the New England Soap Man* (1870). "Professor" Daniel Pierce Gardner was an itinerant soap manufacturer and vendor who distributed his wares by means of humorous lectures to which the purchase of a bar of soap was the price of admission. He claimed to be "a lineal descendant, in an air line, of that glorious Puritan, Awful Gardner, who landed on the everlasting hills of New England from a desolate fishing smack . . . ." presumably referring to Thomas Gardner (1592?-1677), one of a number of fishermen who established in 1624 a settlement at the mouth of the Naumkeag River which later became Salem, Massachusetts (see Frank A. Gardner, *Gardner Memorial; A Biographical and Genealogical Record* . . . . 1933; and Joseph B. Felts, *Annals of Salem*, 2 vols., 1845-1849). Although Daniel P. Gardner was announced in the *Illinois State Journal* (September 28, 1860) as a professor of Brown University, he is not of record at that institution.

Dialogue between Stephen A. Douglas and John C. Breckinridge[1]

Louisville, Ky– Sep. 29. 1860

Meeting & Dialogue of Douglas & Breckenridge—

DOUG— Well, you have succeeded in breaking up the Democratic party.

BRECK— Certainly, for the time being, the party is under a cloud, to say the least; but why you should say *I* did it, I do not comprehend.

DOUG— Perhaps I should charge it to your *supporters,* rather than to *you.*

BRECK— The blame, as I conceive, is neither upon my friends or me.

DOUG—They insisted on having a plat-form, upon which *I* could not stand.

BRECK— Aye, and *you* insisted on having a platform upon which *they* could not stand.

DOUG—But *mine* was the true *Democratic* platform.

BRECK— That presents the exact point in dispute; my friends insist that *theirs* is the true Democratic platform.

DOUG— Let us argue it, then.

BRECK— I conceive that argument is exhausted; *you* certainly could advance nothing new, and *I* know not that I could. There is, however, a colatteral point, upon which I would like the exchange of a few words.

DOUG—What is it?

BRECK— It is this: We insisted on Congressional protection of Slave property in the national teritories; and you broke with us professedly because of this.

DOUG— Exactly so; I insisted upon non-intervention.

BRECK— And yet you are forming coalitions, wherever you can, with Bell, who is for this very congressional protection of slavery—for the very thing which you pretend, drove you from us—for Bell, with all his Know-Nothingism, and anti-democracy of every sort.

DOUG— Bell is a good Union-man; and you, and your friends, are a set of disunionists.

BRECK— Bah! You have known us long, and intimately; why did you never denounce us as disunionists, till since our refusal to support *you* for the Presidency? Why have you never warned the North against our disunion schemes, till since the Charleston and Baltimore sessions of the National convention? Will you answer, Senator Douglas?

DOUG— The condition of my throat will not permit me to carry this conversation any further.

1 AD, DLC-RTL. Lincoln's *jeu d'esprit*, written in pencil, was probably suggested by Douglas' speech at Louisville, September 29, in which Douglas made the points included in Lincoln's imaginary dialogue.

To Moses Fowler[1]

Moses Fowler, Esq   Springfield, Ills.
My dear Sir   Oct. 1. 1860

This introduces our friend Hon. S. A. Hurlbut, one of our best Illinois Republican Speakers. It happens oppertunely that he can be with you, at Lafayette, on the 5th. Inst. Yours very truly

A. LINCOLN

1 ALS, owned by Cecil Fowler, Lafayette, Indiana. Moses Fowler was a prominent Republican in the mercantile and banking business at Lafayette, Indiana.

To James H. Reed[1]

J. H. Reed, Esq   Springfield, Ills. Oct. 1. 1860

My dear Sir   Yours of Sep. 21st. was received some time ago; but I could not, till now, find time to answer it. I never was in McDonough county till 1858. I never said anything derogatory of Mr. Jefferson, in McDonough county, or elsewhere. About three weeks ago,[2] for the first time in my life, did I ever see, or hear, the language, attributed to me, as having been, used towards Mr. Jefferson; and then it was sent to me, as you now send, in order that I might say whether it came from me. I never used any such language at any time. You may rely on the truth of this; although it is my wish that you do not publish it. Yours truly

A. LINCOLN

[1] ALS, ORB. Reed's letter of September 21, is not in the Lincoln Papers. He was co-publisher with Horace Bigelow of the Aledo, Illinois, *Record*.

[2] See Lincoln to Anson G. Chester, September 5, *supra*.

To James E. Harvey[1]

(*Private and confidential.*)

October 2, 1860.

My dear Sir: To comply with your request to furnish extracts from my tariff speeches is simply impossible, because none of those speeches were published. It was not fashionable here in those days to report one's public speeches. In 1844 I was on the Clay electoral ticket in this State (*i.e.*, Illinois) and, to the best of my ability, sustained, together, the tariff of 1842 and the tariff plank of the Clay platform.[2] This could be proven by hundreds—perhaps thousands—of living witnesses; still it is not in print, except by inference. The Whig papers of those years all show that I was upon the electoral ticket; even though I made speeches, among other things *about* the tariff, but they do not show *what* I said about it. The papers show that I was one of a committee which reported, among others, a resolution in these words:

"That we are in favor of an adequate revenue on duties from imports so levied as to afford ample protection to American industry."

But, after all, was it really any more than the tariff plank of our present platform? And does not my acceptance pledge me to that? And am I at liberty to do more, if I were inclined? Yours truly,

A. LINCOLN.

[1] NH, VI, 61-62. Harvey's letter of September 25 referred to the visit of James Leslie, Jr., as correspondent of Harvey's paper, the *North American and U.S. Gazette* (see Lincoln to Cameron, August 6, *supra*) and his search for newspaper reports of Lincoln's speeches of 1844: "It is of very great importance to us, to have extracts from these speeches, as pointed as possible, with the dates and attending circumstances. . . ." (DLC-RTL).

[2] *Vide supra*, June 19, 1844. See also the reports of Lincoln's speech at Sugar Creek, March 1, 1844, and his debates with John Calhoun and Alfred W. Cavarly, March 20-25, 1844, *supra*. These reports are so fragmentary and biased that even if Lincoln knew of them he would scarcely have used them.

To Jesse W. Fell[1]

[Hon. J. W. Fell.]   Springfield,
My dear Sir   Oct. 5. 1860

Yours, inclosing the letter I now return, was duly received, and
for which I sincerely thank you. Our friends all understand, as
you do, the importance of carrying one of the three Districts you
mention. Whatever can be will be done. [Yours very truly
                                                    A. LINCOLN]

1 ALS, DLC. The bracketed portions of this letter have been clipped and
pasted at the end of the autobiographical sketch sent to Fell with the letter
of December 20, 1859 (q.v., *supra*). Fell's letter is not in the Lincoln Papers.

To William H. Herndon[1]

Springfield Ills Oct. 10th 1860

Dear William: I cannot give you details, but it is entirely certain that Pennsylvania and Indiana have gone Republican very
largely, Penn 25,000 & Indiana 5 to 10. Ohio of course is safe.
Yours as ever   A. LINCOLN.

1 Copy, DLC-HW. Herndon sent the copy to Jesse W. Weik and added the
following explanation, here somewhat abridged: "The history of the letter is
as follows. I was making a speech for Lincoln in Petersburg on the evening
of Oct. 10th and had fairly got into the spirit of the hour when some one
rushed into the court room and handed me the letter. I, at first, thought that
it might contain sad news from my family. I opened the letter and read it
over to myself before reading to the people and then I read it aloud to the
crowd. I never finished that speech. The crowd yelled—screamed—threw up
their hats—ran out of doors—made bonfires—&c. &c. . . . I gave the letter
in '81 to a Mr. Parker, President of the Englewood soldiers memorial association near Chicago. . . ."

To William H. Seward[1]

Hon. W. H. Seward.   Springfield, Ills.
My dear Sir   Oct. 12. 1860

Your kind note of the 8th. is received. I am quite satisfied with
what you said, at Chicago, upon the point I mentioned to you;
and I am much obliged to you for saying it. I hope it did not give
you much trouble weaving it into the general web of your discourse.

I shall look up the speech made at DuBuque and published in
the N.Y. Times.

I have had no fears of New-York recently; though, of course,
I am glad to have the expression of your continued confidence. It
now really looks as if the Government is about to fall into our

hands. Pennsylvania, Ohio, and Indiana have surpassed all expectation, even the most extravagant. Most sincerely Your friend

A. LINCOLN—

[1] ALS, NAuE. On October 8, Seward wrote Lincoln from Auburn, New York:

"I do not know how successfully I met your wishes in what I said at Chicago on the point you indicated to me. I was less fully reported on that point than I spoke. But I find a report of my speech at Dubuque in the N. York Times in which the subject which had given you uneasiness was presented freely and strongly.

"We arrived here on Saturday night and I find no reason to doubt this State will redeem all the promises we have made. . . ." (DLC-RTL).

Seward spoke at Dubuque, Iowa, on September 21.

To William D. Kelley[1]

Private

Hon. William D. Kelly   Springfield, Ills.
My dear Sir: Oct– 13. 1860

Yours of the 6th. asking permission to inscribe your new legal work to me, is received. Gratefully accepting the proffered honor, I give the leave, begging only that the inscription may be in modest terms, not representing me as a man of great learning, or a very extraordinary one in any respect. Yours very truly

A. LINCOLN.

[1] ALS, owned by A. H. Greenly, Hoboken, New Jersey. William D. Kelley, judge of the Court of Common Pleas at Philadelphia (1846-1856) and later U.S. representative from Pennsylvania (1861-1890) asked Lincoln's permission to inscribe his two-volume work on international law.

To John M. Read[1]

Hon. John M. Read   Springfield Ill
Dear Sir—   Oct 13th 1860.

The box containing the two framed engravings, sent me by yourself, came safely to hand. Please to accept my thanks for the same.

We are indulging in much rejoicing over the late splendid victories in Pennsylvania, Indiana, and Ohio, which seem to foreshadow the certain success of the Republican cause in November.
Yours Truly   A. LINCOLN

[1] LS, DLC-Read Papers. The letter is in Nicolay's handwriting except for the signature. The engravings mentioned were by the artist John Sartain. See Lincoln to Read, August 27, *supra*.

To L. Montgomery Bond[1]

PRIVATE

L. Montgomery Bond, Esq   Springfield, Ills.

My dear Sir: Oct– 15. 1860

Yours of the 1st. has been at hand some days   You ask "In the event of your election to the Presidency, and of the election of a majority of Republicans to the next congress would you countenance radicalism to the extent of embittering the feelings of our Southern bretheren." I certainly am in no temper, and have no purpose, to embitter the feelings of the South; but whether I am inclined to such a course as would, in fact, embitter their feelings, you can better judge by my published speeches, than by anything I would say in a short letter, if I were inclined now, as I am not, to define my position anew. Yours truly   A. LINCOLN

[1] ALS-P, ISLA. Lewis Montgomery Bond was a tea merchant at Philadelphia who had formerly been in business in New Orleans. His letter is not in the Lincoln Papers.

The Canal-Scrip Fraud[1]

[c. October 16, 1860]

It is now less than three weeks to the election. For months we have been trying to get an unequivocal declaration from democratic newspaper's and democratic candidates for the Legislature, whether it is, or is not their purpose, at the next session, to release Gov Matteson from the payment of the money obtained by him through the canal script-fraud. But we have tried in vain. There is nothing left for us, but an appeal to the tax-payers. We say to them "it is your business." By your votes you can hold him to it, or you can release him." "Every year a part of the price of all you sell, from beef-cattle down to butter and eggs, is wrung from you in gold, to replenish a State Treasury" "To a certain extent, this is indispensable; but it is for you to say whether it shall be thus wrung from you to be litterally stolen, and applied to establishing banks, and building palaces for nabobs." "Will you attend to it?"

Several years ago, the Auditor sold certain state lands, receiving therefor, as the law required, certain internal improvement script. This script was deposited with the then Governor, not being cancelled, or destroyed. Recently it has been discovered that a portion of this script has found it's way out of the Governor's custody, to New-York, where it has been funded and State bonds issued for it payable to *Peter O Strang*. Thus this script was once paid for with state lands, and then again with State bonds. But this is not the end. The bonds are brought to the Treasury here, and bought in with the gold of the tax-payers. One Lowe brings them and gets the gold for them. It turns out that the bonds are filled up in this Lowe's handwriting, and then transferred from *Peter O Strang* to Lowe, also in Lowe's handwriting. Who is *Peter O. Strang*, and how he got the script out of the Governor's custody, to treat it as his own, get State bonds for it, nobody seems to know. But this much is known. Matteson was Governor when the script *may* have gone from the executive custody, and Lowe was his agent at New-York, to fill up state bonds in rightful cases. Only a few days ago Lowe was in Springfield, and a suit was commenced against him for the money obtained from the State on the bonds. For a time the Sheriff could not find him; but at last he was found concealed in Matteson's house. And this too, after the Sheriff had been once turned away from the house, by Matteson himself.

[1] ADf, DLC-RTL. The *Illinois State Journal* editorialized numerous times during the weeks prior to the election concerning the discovery of "redeemed coupons and canal scrip, in large quantities, funded fraudulently" (*Journal*, September 20, 1860). Although in July, 1859, a grand jury had failed to find a true bill against ex-Governor Joel A. Matteson in connection with the purported fraud, the discovery of further irregularities in September, 1860, was made a political issue by the Republican press. Perhaps the present manuscript was intended as an article for the *Journal* or another Republican organ. If so the editors have not been able to locate it in print. Quite likely Lincoln thought better of using it at all and merely filed it away. The date [Oct. 1854?] assigned to the document in the Lincoln Papers cannot be supported.

To Grace Bedell[1]

Private

Miss. Grace Bedell   Springfield, Ills.
My dear little Miss.   Oct 19. 1860

Your very agreeable letter of the 15th. is received.

I regret the necessity of saying I have no daughters. I have three sons—one seventeen, one nine, and one seven, years of age. They, with their mother, constitute my whole family.

As to the whiskers, having never worn any, do you not think people would call it a piece of silly affection if I were to begin it now? Your very sincere well-wisher   A. LINCOLN.

[1] ALS, owned by H. D. Billings, Delphos, Kansas. The original letter to which Lincoln replied, now owned by George Dondero, Royal Oak, Michigan, is an historic document that the editors can scarcely do otherwise than reproduce in full:

N Y

Hon A B Lincoln   Westfield Chatauque Co
        Dear Sir   Oct 15. 1860
                    My father has just home from the fair and
brought home your picture and Mr. Hamlin's. I am a little girl only eleven
years old, but want you should be President of the United States very much
so I hope you wont think me very bold to write to such a great man as you
are. Have you any little girls about as large as I am if so give them my love
and tell her to write to me if you cannot answer this letter. I have got 4
brother's and part of them will vote for you any way and if you will let your
whiskers grow I will try and get the rest of them to vote for you   you would
look a great deal better for your face is so thin. All the ladies like whiskers and
they would tease their husband's to vote for you and then you would be
President. My father is a going to vote for you and if I was a man I would
vote for you to but I will try and get every one to vote for you that I can
I think that rail fence around your picture makes it look very pretty   I have
got a little baby sister she is nine weeks old and is just as cunning as can be.
When you direct your letter dir[e]ct to Grace Bedell Westfield Chatauque
County New York
    I must not write any more   answer this letter right off   Good bye
                                                                Grace Bedell

To William S. Speer[1]

Confidential.

Wm. S. Speer Esq   Springfield, Ill. Oct 23d 1860.
    My dear Sir   Yours of the 13th was duly received. I appreciate
your motive when you suggest the propriety of my writing for
the public something disclaiming all intention to interfere with
slaves or slavery in the States; but in my judgment, it would do
no good. I have already done this many—many, times; and it is
in print, and open to all who will read. Those who will not read,
or heed, what I have already publicly said, would not read, or heed,
a repetition of it.
    "If they hear not Moses and the prophets, neither will they be
persuaded though one rose from the dead." Yours Truly
                                                            A. LINCOLN

[1] Copy, DLC-RTL. Speer's letter of October 13 is not in the Lincoln Papers,
but later letters from him are written from Shelbyville, Tennessee. He had
bought a printing press and ". . . for three months . . . worked day and night
to ascertain, to help form, and to correct public opinion." (Speer to Lincoln,
December 24, 1860, DLC-RTL).

To David Turnham[1]

David Turnham, Esq   Springfield, Ills.
My dear old friend: Oct. 23. 1860
    Your kind letter of the 17th. is received. I am indeed very glad
to learn you are still living and well. I well remember when you

and I last met, after a separation of fourteen years, at the cross-road voting place, in the fall of 1844. It is now sixteen years more and we are both no longer young men. I suppose you are a grand-father; and I, though married much later in life, have a son nearly grown.

I would much like to visit the old home, and old friends of my boyhood, but I fear the chance for doing so soon, is not very good. Your friend & sincere well-wisher   A. LINCOLN

[1] ALS, Evansville Public Museum, Evansville, Indiana. This letter is mis-dated November 19, 1860, in Hertz, II, 792. David Turnham was an old friend and neighbor of the Lincolns in Spencer County, Indiana, whom Lincoln had last seen, November 4, 1844, on his visit to Indiana. Turnham's letter is not in the Lincoln Papers.

Guarantee to Pay Freight Charges for a Lady[1]

Springfield, Oct. 24. 1860

The lady-bearer of this, says she has freight at the depot, which she can not get without four dollars. If this be correct, let her have the freight, and I will pay you any amount not exceeding four dollars on presentation of this note   A. LINCOLN.

[1] ADS, DLC-RTL. The document bears at bottom the receipt dated October 29 and signed by (Edward B.) Egbert, clerk at the Great Western Railroad freight office. There is no conjecture as to the lady's identity.

To J. C. Lee[1]

Confidential

J. C. Lee, Esq   Springfield, Ills.
Dear Sir   Oct. 24, 1860

Yours of the 14th. was received some days ago, and should have been answered sooner.

I never gave fifty dollars, nor one dollar, nor one cent, for the object you mention, or any such object.

I once *subscribed* twentyfive dollars, to be paid whenever Judge Logan would decide it was necessary to enable the people of Kansas to defend themselves against any force coming against them from without the Territory, and not by authority of the United States. Logan never made the decision, and I never paid a dollar on the subscription. The whole of this can be seen in the files of the Illinois Journal, since the first of June last. Yours truly

A. LINCOLN

[1] ALS, RPB. J. C. Lee's letter of October 14, 1860, is not in the Lincoln Papers, but it seems probable that he was John C. Lee, president of the Young Men's Republican Association of Jacksonville, Illinois. It also seems probable

that the subject of his letter to Lincoln was the charge that Lincoln had contributed money to John Brown's cause, which Democrats were using against Lincoln in the campaign.

To H. E. Hoelke[1]

H. E. Hoelke, Esq   Springfield, Ills.
My dear Sir   Oct. 26. 1860
    Yours of the 25th. accompanied by the likenesses of Hon: T. H. Benton, Hon. Edward Bates, and Hon. F. P. Blair, Jr, and also the Photograph of my residence, is duly to hand, and for all which, please accept my thanks. Yours very truly   A. LINCOLN.

[1] ALS, IHi. H. E. Hoelke was a photographer at St. Louis, Missouri.

To David Hunter[1]

Private & confidential

Maj. David Hunter: Springfield, Ills. Oct. 26. 1860
    My dear Sir: Your very kind letter of the 20th. was duly received, and for which, please accept my thanks.

    I have another letter from a writer unknown to me, saying the officers of the Army at Fort Kearney, have determined, in case of Republican success, at the approaching Presidential election, to take themselves, and the arms at that point, South, for the purpose of resistence to the government. While I think there are many chances to one that this is a hum-bug, it occurs to me that any real movement of this sort in the army would leak out and become known to you. In such case, if it would not be unprofessional, or dishonorable (of which you are to be judge) I shall be much obliged if you will apprize me of it. Yours very truly

A. LINCOLN

[1] ALS, CSmH. Major David Hunter, stationed at Fort Leavenworth, Kansas, wrote on October 20 that on a visit East he had received a report that a number of young men in Virginia had bound themselves "by oaths most solemn" to assassinate Lincoln if he were elected. Granting the absurdity of the report, he warned Lincoln to remember that "on 'the *institution*' these good people are most certainly demented. . . ." (DLC-RTL).

To George T. M. Davis[1]

Private & confidential.

Geo. T. M. Davis, Esq   Springfield, Ills.
My dear Sir: Oct. 27. 1860
    Mr. Dubois has shown me your letter of the 20th.; and I promised him to write you. What is it I could say which would quiet

alarm? Is it that no interference by the government, with slaves or slavery within the states, is intended? I have said this so often already, that a repetition of it is but mockery, bearing an appearance of weakness, and cowardice, which perhaps should be avoided. Why do not uneasy men *read* what I have already said? and what our *platform* says? If they will not read, or heed, then [these?], would they read, or heed, a repetition of them? Of course the declaration that there is no intention to interfere with slaves or slavery, in the states, with all that is fairly implied in such declaration, is true; and I should have no objection to make, and repeat the declaration a thousand times, if there were no danger of encouraging bold bad men to believe they are dealing with one who can be scared into anything.

I have some reason to believe the Sub-National committee, at the Astor House, may be considering this question; and if their judgment should be different from mine, mine might be modified by theirs. Yours very truly   A. LINCOLN.

[1] ALS, IHi. Davis was an old friend who had practiced law at Alton in the 1830's and following a distinguished career in the War with Mexico and later in the War department had become a prominent New York businessman. His letter to Jesse K. Dubois reported a plan hatching in New York and various Southern cities to cause a general money and stock panic in the event of Lincoln's election. He suggested that leading merchants write a public letter to Lincoln, who in his reply would give such assurances as would block the movement (DLC-RTL). His reply of October 31, admitted that Lincoln could say nothing more than he had already said, but insisted that repeating it as president-elect would carry weight and would not be regarded as cowardice or timidity (DLC-RTL). See also Lincoln to Truman Smith, November 10, *infra.*

To Richard W. Thompson[1]

Hon R. W. Thompson   Springfield, Ills.
My dear Sir   Oct. 28. 1860.

Your very acceptable letter of the 20th sent by Express, was received only yesterday. I am indeed grateful for your generous course towards me so far; and I doubt not what you are doing, and will do, to the end of the contest is, and will be, the most judicious.

Your suggestions are all worthy of consideration, and shall receive it. The eyes of some of our best sentinels are already upon that matter of forged naturalization papers to be issued as from your court; and, if possible, the use of such papers will be prevented. Yours very truly   A. LINCOLN.

[1] Hertz, II, 788. Thompson's letter of October 20 is not in the Lincoln Papers.

To Mrs. Eliza A. Hamilton[1]

Mrs. E. A. Hamilton   Springfield, Ills. Oct. 29. 1860

Your very kind letter of the 19th. was received a few days ago. Your Father[2] calls on me almost every day, and I have mentioned your letter to him, and presented your affectionate regards, as requested. Your sister, Mrs. Johnston,[3] I have not seen since receiving your letter.

The health of my family & self, for which you kindly inquire, is reasonably good. Please present my respects to your good husband. Yours very truly   A. LINCOLN

[1] ALS, IHi. Eliza Ann Hamilton was the wife of Reverend John A. Hamilton of Keene, New Hampshire.

[2] Erastus Wright, who was a land and general agent in partnership with his son-in-law, Robert P. Johnston, at Springfield.

[3] Mrs. Robert P. Johnston (Maria Jane Wright).

To Mrs. Stephen A. Hurlbut[1]

Mrs. S. A. Hurlbutt   Springfield, Ills.,
My dear Madam   Oct. 29, 1860

Your good husband, who is making speeches for us in this county, has desired me to write you that he is well, which I take great pleasure in doing. I will add, too, that he is rendering us very efficient service. Yours very truly   A. LINCOLN

[1] ALS, RPB.

To George D. Prentice[1]

(Copy)   Private & confidential

Geo. D. Prentice, Esq   Springfield, Ills. Oct. 29. 1860

My dear Sir: Yours of the 26th. is just received. Your suggestion that I, in a certain event, shall write a letter, setting forth my conservative views and intentions, is certainly a very worthy one. But would it do any good? If I were to labor a month, I could not express my conservative views and intentions more clearly and strongly, than they are expressed in our plat-form, and in my many speeches already in print, and before the public. And yet even you, who do occasionally speak of me in terms of personal kindness, give no prominence to these oft-repeated expressions of conservative views and intentions; but busy yourself with appeals to all conservative men, to vote for Douglas—to vote any way which can possibly defeat me—thus impressing your readers that you think, I am the very worst man living. If what I have already said has failed to convince you, no repetition of it would convince you. The writing of your letter, now before me, gives assurance that you would publish such a letter from me as you suggest; but, till now, what reason had I to suppose the Louisville Journal, even, would publish a *repe[ti]tion* of that which is already at it's command, and which it does not press upon the public attention?

And, now my friend—for such I esteem you personally—do not misunderstand me. I have not decided that I will not do substantially what you suggest. I will not forbear[2] doing so, merely on *punctilio* and pluck. If I do finally abstain, it will be because of apprehension that it would do harm. For the good men of the South—and I regard the majority of them as such—I have no objection to repeat seventy and seven times. But I have *bad* men also to deal with, both North and South—men who are eager for something new upon which to base new misrepresentations—men who would like to frighten me, or, at least, to fix upon me the character of timidity and cowardice. They would seize upon almost any letter I could write, as being an *"awful coming down."* I intend keeping my eye upon these gentlemen, and to not unnecessarily put any weapons in their hands. Yours very truly   A. LINCOLN

[The following endorsement appears on the back:]

Confidential

The within letter was written on the day of it's date, and, on reflection, withheld till now. It expresses the views I still entertain.

A. LINCOLN

[1] ALS copy, DLC-RTL. George D. Prentice, editor of the Louisville, Kentucky, *Journal* wrote October 26, that while he had no doubt of Lincoln's personal and political integrity he was opposed to his election. Recognizing that Lincoln would be elected, however, he would suggest that Lincoln ". . . prepare a letter . . . setting forth your conservative views . . . and therefore calculated to assure all the good citizens of the South and to take from the disunionists every excuse or pretext for treason." (DLC-RTL).

[2] Lincoln deleted "abstain from" and substituted "forbear."

To George G. Fogg[1]

George G. Fogg. Esq   Springfield, Ills. Oct. 31. 1860

My dear Sir: I sincerely thank you for yours of the 26th. It is the first I have had from any of our *knowing* friends at the City, for several days.

Allow me to beg that you will not live in much apprehension of my precipitating a letter upon the public. Yours very truly

A. LINCOLN

[1] ALS, CSmH. Fogg's letter of October 26 enclosed a clipping from the New York *Times* which stated that upon election Lincoln would, or should, issue a statement concerning the institutions of the South. Fogg urged that Lincoln be silent until inaugurated (DLC-RTL).

To John G. Nicolay[1]

November 3, [1860]

I wish Mr. Nicolay would invite the following gentlemen to tea at my house, at 5 P.M. to-morrow.

Mr. Schenck	Mr. Philips
Mr. Piatt	Mr. Hatch
Mr. Cartter	Mr. Dubois &
Mr. Ogden	Mr. Nicolay—himself—

Saturday, Nov. 3.   LINCOLN

[1] ALS, DLC-Nicolay Papers. Robert C. Schenck, Donn Piatt, and David K. Cartter, of Ohio, were being mentioned as possible appointees to the cabinet in the event of Chase's declination, and Lincoln probably wished to have them meet the Illinois party leaders William B. Ogden, David L. Phillips, Ozias M. Hatch, and Jesse K. Dubois. A check mark preceding each name, except Ogden's, probably indicates Nicolay's performance of instructions.

To David Chambers[1]

Hon. David Chambers   Springfield Ill Nov 5th 1860.

Dear Sir—Your kind letter of the 31st ult. came duly to hand. Please accept my thanks for the favor. Yours Truly

A. LINCOLN.

[1] LS, DLC. David Chambers of Zanesville, Ohio, was U.S. representative 1821-1823 and for several terms a member of the Ohio legislature. His letter of October 31 is not in the Lincoln Papers.

To Hannibal Hamlin[1]

Confidential

Hon. H. Hamlin.   Springfield, Ills. Nov. 8, 1860

My dear Sir. I am anxious for a personal interview with you at as early a day as possible. Can you, without much inconvenience, meet me at Chicago? If you can, please name as early a day as you conveniently can, and telegraph me; unless there be sufficient time, before the day named, to communicate by mail. Yours very truly   A. LINCOLN.

[1] ALS, IHi. Lincoln and Hamlin met at Chicago, November 21-26, to discuss the formation of Lincoln's cabinet.

To John Comstock[1]

John Comstock, Esq.   Springfield, Ill.,
My Dear Sir: Nov. 9, 1860.

The barrel of flour, mentioned in your letter of the 2d, was duly received, and for which Mr. Peterfish, Messrs. Geo. Field & Co., and yourself, will please accept my sincere thanks. Yours very truly,   A. LINCOLN.

[1] Peoria *Daily Transcript*, November 14, 1860. John Comstock was a land agent and president of the Republican Club at Peoria who had sent Lincoln a barrel of flour "manufactured in the procession at the dedication of the Wigwam in this city on the 31st Aug. last . . . . Mr. W. Peterfish made and presents the barrel & Messrs. George Field & Co. the flour. . . ." (DLC-RTL). The Peoria Directory lists William Petefish as a cooper and doubtless this is the correct spelling of his name.

To Nathan Sargent[1]

N. Sargent, Esq   Springfield Ill. Nov 9th 1860.

Dear Sir—I have duly received your letter of the 4th inst. Will you please to write to me by return mail and give me the name of the Republican whom Judge Campbell suggested for Secretary of State? Yours Truly   A. LINCOLN

[1] LS, IHi. Sargent's letter of November 4 is not in the Lincoln Papers, but his reply on November 12 states that Judge Campbell had suggested Thomas Ewing of Ohio. Writing from Washington, Sargent may have referred to Judge John A. Campbell of the United States Supreme Court, who was trying to assuage hostile feelings in the South, but in view of Sargent's Philadelphia connections, he may have meant the prominent Democrat James Campbell, who had been judge of the Philadelphia Court of Common Pleas, 1842-1850.

To Winfield Scott[1]

                                             Springfield, Ills. Nov. 9. 1860
For Lieut. Gen. Scott, with the respects of   A. LINCOLN.

Mr. Lincoln tenders his sincere thanks to Gen. Scott, for the copy of his "views &c," which is received; and especially for this renewed manifestation of his patriotic purposes as a citizen, connected, as it is, with his high official position, and most distinguished character, as a military captain.   A.L.

[1] ADfS, DLC-RTL. General Scott's memorandum "Views suggested by the imminent danger of a disruption of the Union by the secession of one or more Southern States," October 29, 1860, gave his opinion that secession would lead to four confederacies, that Lincoln should point out the unprofitable nature of slavery in the western territories, that seizure of Southern forts would precede secession, that a policy of moderation and firmness for the next twelve months would perhaps prevent secession, and that although he had no political interests he preferred the Bell-Everett ticket (DLC-RTL).

Views on Commercial and Financial Uneasiness[1]

[c. November 9, 1860]

I find Mr. Lincoln is not insensible to any uneasiness in the minds of candid men, nor to any commercial, or financial, depression, or disturbance, in the country if there be such; still he does not, so far as at present advised, deem it necessary, or proper for him to make, or authorize, any public declaration. He thinks candid men need only to examine his views already before the public.

[1] ADf, DLC-RTL. This document is obviously contemporary with the letters to Truman Smith, November 10, and Nathaniel P. Paschall, November 16, *infra.* Possibly Lincoln jotted down the statement for Henry S. Sanford to copy and take back with him (see letter to Smith). It is also possible that Lincoln jotted it down for the correspondent of the New York *Tribune*, whose dispatch of November 9 reads in part as follows: "I believe it is correct to say that, although he is not at all unmindful of the uneasiness which may exist in many parts of the country, nor of the unfortunate commercial troubles that may have been threatened, he still does not discover any cause for specially developing his policy, or offering any public expression of his views." (New York *Tribune*, November 10, 1860).

To Truman Smith[1]

Private & confidential.

Hon. Truman Smith   Springfield Ill Nov 10th 1860.

My dear Sir   This is intended as a strictly private letter to you, and not as an answer to yours brought me by Mr. Sanford.[2] It is with the most profound appreciation of your motive, and highest respect for your judgment too, that I feel constrained, for the present, at least, to make no declaration for the public.

First, I could say nothing which I have not already said, and which is in print, and open for the inspection of all. To press a repetition of this upon those who *have* listened, is useless; to press it upon those who have *refused* to listen, and still refuse, would be wanting in self-respect, and would have an appearance of sycophancy and timidity, which would excite the contempt of good men, and encourage bad ones to clamor the more loudly.

I am not insensible to any commercial or financial depression that may exist; but nothing is to be gained by fawning around the *"respectable scoundrels"* who got it up. Let them go to work and repair the mischief of their own making; and then perhaps they will be less greedy to do the like again. Yours very truly

A. LINCOLN.

[1] Copy, DLC-RTL. Ex-representative (1839-1843, 1845-1849) and Senator (1849-1854) Truman Smith of Stamford, Connecticut, wrote on November 7, urging Lincoln to make a public statement ". . . to disarm mischief makers, to

allay causeless anxiety, to compose the public mind and to induce all good citizens to . . . 'judge the tree by it's fruit'. . . ." (DLC-RTL). See also Lincoln to George T. M. Davis, October 27, *supra.*

[2] Henry S. Sanford of Derby, Connecticut, chargé d'affaires at Paris during President Taylor's administration, had carried a letter of introduction dated October 30, 1860 (DLC-RTL), but there is no other letter from Smith prior to that of November 7. Probably Sanford's mission was concerned with the same subject as Smith's letter of November 7.

To [Albert?] Hale[1]

Springfield, Nov. 12. 1860

Mr. Hale will oblige me, if he will send by the bearer, the Chicago Tribune we were looking at this morning. Yours truly

A. LINCOLN

[1] ALS, owned by the Chicago *Tribune,* Chicago, Illinois. Although "Mr. Hale" cannot be positively identified, the probability is that Reverend Albert Hale, pastor of Springfield's Second Presbyterian Church, was the possessor of the newspaper sought by Lincoln.

To Samuel Haycraft[1]

Private, and confidential

Hon. Samuel Haycraft   Springfield, Ills. Nov. 13. 1860

My dear Sir. Yours of the 9th. is just received. I can only answer briefly. Rest fully assured that the good people of the South who will put themselves in the same temper and mood towards me which you do, will find no cause to complain of me.

While I can not, as yet, make any committal as to offices, I sincerely hope I may find it in my power to oblige the friends of Mr. Wintersmith. [Yours very truly,   A. LINCOLN.]

[1] ALS, CSmH. The close and signature have been cut from the manuscript. Haycraft's letter of November 9 expressed hope for Lincoln's administration and the belief that ". . . our Southern fire eaters will find . . . you a conservative cheif of the nation in a national point of view. . . ." and noted that the people of Elizabethtown, Kentucky, hoped Robert L. Wintersmith, a Lincoln elector, would be "remembered while favours are being dispensed." (DLC-RTL).

To Nathaniel P. Paschall[1]

Private & confidential.

N. P. Paschall Esq   Springfield Nov 16th. 1860.

My dear Sir   Mr. Ridgely[2] showed me a letter of yours in which you manifest some anxiety that I should make some public declaration with a view to favorably affect the business of the country. I said to Mr. Ridgely I would write you to-day, which I now do.

I could say nothing which I have not already said, and which is in print and accessible to the public. Please pardon me for suggesting that if the papers, like yours, which heretofore have persistently garbled, and misrepresented what I have said, will now fully and fairly place it before their readers, there can be no further misunderstanding. I beg you to believe me sincere when I declare I do not say this in a spirit of complaint or resentment; but that I urge it as the true cure for any real uneasiness in the country that my course may be other than conservative. The Republican newspapers now, and for some time past, are and have been republishing copious extracts from my many published speeches, which would at once reach the whole public if your class of papers would also publish them.

I am not at liberty to shift my ground—that is out of the question. If I thought a *repetition* would do any good I would make it. But my judgment is it would do positive harm. The secessionists, *per se* believing they had alarmed me, would clamor all the louder.

Yours &c   A. LINCOLN.

1 Copy, DLC-RTL. Paschall, editor of the *Missouri Republican*, replied, November 18, that his paper had advocated that Lincoln, being elected, be given a fair trial, but he added that if Missouri was to be kept in the Union a statement from Lincoln would be needed. Lincoln's previous speeches had little effect in the South because they came from papers such as the New York *Tribune* and *Times* and the Chicago *Tribune* and *Democrat*, all enemies of the South. Paschall suggested that Lincoln authorize Herndon or some other friend to condense all his speeches of the past three years for publication (DLC-RTL).
2 Probably Nicholas H. Ridgely or Charles Ridgely, Springfield bankers.

To Henry Asbury[1]

Henry Asbury Esq   Springfield, Ills.
My dear Sir   Nov. 19. 1860

Yours of the 9th. was received in due course; but, till now, I have not found time to acknowledge the receipt of it.

It is a little curious, and not wholy uninteresting, to look over those old letters of yours and mine. I would like to indulge in some comments, but really I have not the time. Yours very truly

A. LINCOLN

1 ALS, RPB. Asbury's letter of November 9 is not in the Lincoln Papers.

To Park Benjamin[1]

Park Benjamin, Esq   Springfield, Ills.
My dear Sir.   Nov. 19. 1860

Your kind note of congratulation was received in due course; and you are not disappointed in the hope you express that I may set some value upon it.

That my political position, and personal history, are such as to meet the unselfish approval of one possessing your high literary fame and character, is matter of sincere pride with me. Yours very truly   A. LINCOLN—

[1] ALS, owned by Henry R. Benjamin, New York City. New York journalist and man of letters, Park Benjamin wrote on November 7 that he hoped Lincoln would set some value on the congratulations ". . . of a literary man and not a party-politician; but your firm, fast and constant friend during the contest. . . ." (DLC-RTL).

To Joshua F. Speed[1]

Dear Speed—   Springfield. Ills. Nov. 19. 1860

Yours of the 14th. is received. I shall be at Chicago Thursday the 22nd. Inst. and one or two succeeding days. Could you not meet me there?

Mary thinks of going with me; and therefore I suggest that Mrs. S. accompany you.

Please let this be private, as I prefer a very great crowd should not gather at Chicago.

Respects to Mrs. S. Your friend, as ever   A. LINCOLN

[1] ALS, ORB. Speed's letter written at Louisville, Kentucky, November 14, sent congratulations and offered ". . . . if it would be agreeable to you I will come & see you—and I think I can impart to you some information as to men and public sentiment here which may be valuable." (DLC-RTL). Speed met Lincoln at Chicago, more or less secretly at Speed's hotel, and according to Speed's later testimony, Lincoln led up to an offer of a place in the cabinet, which Speed forestalled by declaring that he wanted no appointment. Lincoln then asked Speed to sound out James Guthrie of Louisville, secretary of the treasury under Franklin Pierce, as a possible secretary of war (Herndon, III, 477).

Passage Written for Lyman Trumbull's Speech at Springfield, Illinois[1]

November 20, 1860

I have labored in, and for, the Republican organization with entire confidence that whenever it shall be in power, each and all of the States will be left in as complete control of their own affairs respectively, and at as perfect liberty to choose, and employ, their own means of protecting property, and preserving peace and order within their respective limits, as they have ever been under any administration. Those who have voted for Mr. Lincoln, have expected, and still expect this; and they would not have voted for him had they expected otherwise. I regard it as extremely fortunate for the peace of the whole country, that this point, upon which the Republicans have been so long, and so persistently misrepresented, is now to be brought to a practical test, and placed beyond the possibility of doubt.[2] Disunionists *per se*,[3] are now in hot haste to get out of the Union, precisely because they perceive they can not, much longer, maintain apprehension among the Southern people that their homes, and firesides, and lives, are to be endangered by the action of the Federal Government. With such *"Now, or never"* is the maxim.[4]

I am rather glad of this military preparation in the South. It will enable the people the more easily to suppress any uprisings there, which their misrepresentations of purposes may have encouraged.

[1] AD, IHi. Trumbull's note, written in pencil at the top of the page, is as follows: "Furnished by Mr. Lincoln & copied into my remarks . . . at Springfield, Ill. Nov. 20— 1860." Although Lincoln felt constrained not to express publicly in his own person the assurance which so many of his correspondents were demanding, he undertook by means of Trumbull's speech to try the effect of a quasi-official statement of his views. That his anticipation of failure for the effort did not lessen his disappointment is indicated in his letter to Henry J. Raymond, November 28, *infra*. As will be seen in the succeeding footnotes, Trumbull went even beyond Lincoln's assurance, and yet the secessionists ignored the statement.

[2] In Trumbull's speech as reported in the *Illinois State Journal*, November 21, 1860, the following passage is inserted at this point: "It should be a matter of rejoicing to all true Republicans, that they will now have an opportunity of demonstrating to their political adversaries and to the world, that they are not for interfering with the domestic institutions of any of the States, nor the advocates of negro-equality or amalgamation, with which political demagogues have so often charged them. When this is shown, a re-action will assuredly take place in favor of Republicanism, the Southern mind even will be satisfied, the rights of Northern men will be respected, and the fraternal feeling existing in olden times, when men from all parts of the country went forth together to battle for a common cause, against a common enemy, will be restored."

[3] Trumbull's speech inserted as follows: "of whom, unfortunately, there have been a few in the country for some years, ...'

[4] The next paragraph was not used by Trumbull.

Remarks at Springfield, Illinois[1]

November 20, 1860

FRIENDS AND FELLOW-CITIZENS:—Please excuse me, on this occasion, from making a speech. I thank you for the kindness and compliment of this call. I thank you, in common with all others, who have thought fit, by their votes, to indorse the Republican cause. I rejoice with you in the success which has, so far, attended that cause. Yet in all our rejoicing let us neither express, nor cherish, any harsh feeling towards any citizen who, by his vote, has differed with us. Let us at all times remember that all American citizens are brothers of a common country, and should dwell together in the bonds of fraternal feeling.

Let me again beg you to accept my thanks, and to excuse me from further speaking at this time.

¹ *Illinois State Journal*, November 21, 1860. Lincoln made his remarks when called out by a parade of Wide-Awakes which passed the Lincoln home on the way to the Wigwam where Senator Trumbull and others were to address a Republican victory celebration.

Remarks at Lincoln, Illinois¹

November 21, 1860

FELLOW CITIZENS:—I thank you for this mark of your kindness toward me. I have been shut up in Springfield for the last few months, and therefore have been unable to greet you, as I was formerly in the habit of doing. I am passing on my way to Chicago, and am happy in doing so to be able to meet so many of my friends in Logan County, and if to do no more, to exchange² with you the compliments of the season, and to thank you for the many kindnesses you have manifested toward me. I am not in the habit of making speeches now, and I would therefore ask to be excused from entering upon any discussion of the political topics of the day. I am glad to see so many happy faces, and to listen to so many pleasant expressions. Again thanking you for this honor, I will pass on my journey.

¹ New York *Tribune*, November 23, 1860. Lincoln's party, including Mrs. Lincoln, Senator and Mrs. Trumbull, and Mr. and Mrs. Donn Piatt of Ohio, left Springfield on the morning train for Chicago. Three short speeches were made en route, at Lincoln, Bloomington, and Lexington.

² The New York *Herald*, November 22, reported this phrase as follows: ". . . even if to do no more than exchange with you. . . ."

Remarks at Bloomington, Illinois¹

November 21, 1860

FELLOW-CITIZENS OF BLOOMINGTON AND MCLEAN COUNTY: I am glad to meet you after a longer separation than has been common between you and me. I thank you for the good report you made of the election in Old McLean. The people of the country have again fixed up their affairs for a constitutional period of time. By the way, I think very much of the people, as an old friend said he thought of woman. He said when he lost his first wife, who had been a great help to him in his business, he thought he was ruined

—that he could never find another to fill her place. At length, however, he married another, who he found did quite as well as the first, and that his opinion now was that any woman would do well who was well done by. So I think of the whole people of this nation—they will ever do well if well done by. We will try to do well by them in all parts of the country, North and South, with entire confidence that all will be well with all of us.

¹ New York *Tribune*, November 23, 1860. *The Illinois State Journal*, November 23, and the New York *Herald*, November 22, have identical wording.

Remarks at Lexington, Illinois¹

November 21, 1860

. . . . "Old Abe" came out, showed himself and made a little speech, thanking his fellow citizens for the honor of their presence, and reminding them that soon after the Sixth of November he heard good news from *this portion* of McLean County.

¹ Lexington *Weekly Globe*, November 22, 1860. The *Globe* further commented, "Old Abe looks as though the campaign had worn lightly upon him. He is commencing to raise a beautiful pair of whiskers, and looks younger than usual. Still there is no disguising the fact that he is homely. . . ."

Endorsement: Thomas B. Bryan to Lincoln¹

[November 22, 1860]

I now fear I can not find leisure to avail myself of this Mr. Bryan's kindness.   A. LINCOLN

¹ AES, ICHi. On November 22, 1860, Thomas B. Bryan, proprietor of Bryan Hall, Chicago, invited President-elect and Mrs. Lincoln to visit his establishment to view the "Gallery of the Presidential Portraits from Washington to Lincoln inclusive. . . ." Lincoln's reply is written in pencil on the back of Bryan's invitation.

Endorsement: Caspar Butz to Lincoln¹

[November 23, 1860]

We expect to leave for home on the morning of the 24th. I therefore regret to say I can not see Mr. Schurz here to-morrow.

A LINCOLN

¹ AES, DLC-RTL. Caspar Butz's letter dated November 23, 1860, requests an interview for Carl Schurz who will come to Chicago on the 24th on his way East "in passing through this city. . . ." Butz was a prominent Chicago Republican, former representative in the state legislature from Cook County.

To Henry C. Whitney[1]

H. C. Whitney, Esq   Chicago,
My dear Sir.   Nov. 26. 1860
   Your note in behalf of Mr. Alshuler was received. I gave him a sitting.
   I regret not having an oppertunity to see more of you.
   Please present my respects to Mrs. W. & to your good Father & Mother   Yours very truly   A LINCOLN

[1] ALS, IHI. The letter is written on stationery of the Tremont House. Whitney had requested Lincoln to allow his friend Samuel G. Alschuler, a photographer formerly at Urbana, Illinois, to take a photograph. The resulting photograph is unique in showing Lincoln with half-whiskers.

To Hannibal Hamlin[1]

Springfield, Illinois, November 27, 1860.
   My dear Sir: On reaching home I find I have in charge for you the inclosed letter.
   I deem it proper to advise you that I also find letters here from very strong and unexpected quarters in Pennsylvania, urging the appointment of General Cameron to a place in the cabinet.
   Let this be a profound secret, even though I do think best to let you know it. Yours very sincerely,   A. LINCOLN.

[1] NH, VI, 72-73. Lincoln and Hamlin had discussed cabinet appointments at Chicago. There is nothing in Hamlin's letter of December 4, to indicate the nature of Lincoln's enclosure. See Lincoln to Hamlin, December 8, *infra*.

To Fred R. Jackson[1]

Fred R. Jackson, Esq   Springfield, Ills. Nov. 27. 1860
   My dear Sir   Your kind letter of congratulation is received, and for which, please accept my thanks. Below is my autograph, according to your request. Yours truly   A. LINCOLN.

[1] ALS, RPB. Jackson's letter is not in the Lincoln Papers. He was a resident of Stillwater, New York.

To Henry J. Raymond[1]

Private & confidential

Hon. H. J. Raymond   Springfield, Ills.
My dear Sir   Nov. 28. 1860
   Yours of the 14th. was received in due course. I have delayed so long to answer it, because my reasons for not coming before the

public in any form just now, had substantially appeared in your paper (The Times), and hence I feared they were not deemed sufficient by you, else you would not have written me as you did.

I now think we have a demonstration in favor of my view. On the 20th. Inst. Senator Trumbull made a short speech which I suppose you have both seen and approved.[2] Has a single newspaper, heretofore against us, urged that speech [upon its readers] with a purpose to quiet public anxiety? Not one, so far as I know. On the contrary the Boston Courier, and its' class, hold me responsible for the speech, and endeavor to inflame the North with the belief that it foreshadows an abandonment of Republican ground by the incoming administration; while the Washington Constitution, and its' class hold the same speech up to the South as an open declaration of war against them.

This is just as I expected, and just what would happen with any declaration I could make. These political fiends are not half sick enough yet. "Party malice" and not "public good" possesses them entirely. "They seek a sign, and no sign shall be given them." At least such is my present feeling and purpose. [Yours very truly

A. LINCOLN]

[1] ALS, IHi. An accompanying note by Raymond explains that he had cut off the signature to oblige a friend with Lincoln's autograph.

[2] See Lincoln's statement incorporated in Trumbull's speech, November 20, *supra.*

Note for John H. Littlefield[1]

Springfield, Nov– 30. 1860

I will pay five dollars to whomever will loan that sum to the bearer, Mr. Littlefield. A. LINCOLN–

[1] ADS, CSmH. John H. Littlefield was a law student in the Lincoln & Herndon office.

To Alexander H. Stephens[1]

Hon. A. H. Stephens Springfield, Ills.
My dear Sir. Nov. 30, 1860

I have read, in the newspapers, your speech recently delivered (I think) before the Georgia Legislature, or it's assembled members. If you have revised it, as is probable, I shall be much obliged if you will send me a copy. Yours very truly A. LINCOLN.

[1] ALS, CSmH. Stephens replied, December 14, that he had not revised the speech but that the newspaper reports were substantially correct (*ibid.*).

Certified Transcript of Passage from the House Divided Speech[1]

December 7, 1860

"We are now far into the fifth year since a policy was initiated, with the avowed object, and confident promise, of putting an end to slavery agitation. Under the operation of that policy, that agitation has not only not ceased, but has continually augmented. I believe it will not cease till a crisis shall have been reached and passed. A house divided against itself cannot stand. I believe this government cannot endure permanently half slave and half free. I do not expect the Union to be dissolved. I do not expect the house to fall; but I do expect it will cease to be divided. It will become all one thing or all the other. Either the opponents of slavery will arrest the further spread of it, and place it where the public mind shall rest in the belief that it is in course of ultimate extinction; or its advocates will push it forward till it will become alike lawful in all the States old as well as new—North as well as South."

The foregoing, in pencil, in my own hand, is a copy of an extract of a speech of mine delivered June 16. 1858, which I now state at the request of Mr. E. B. Pease.[2]   A. LINCOLN
Dec. 7. 1860.

[1] The Rosenbach Company, *The History of America in Documents* (1951), III, 15. According to the catalog description this is an autograph document signed.   [2] Edward B. Pease was a hardware dealer at Springfield.

To Hannibal Hamlin[1]

(Private.)

Springfield, Illinois, December 8, 1860.

My dear Sir: Yours of the 4th was duly received. The inclosed to Governor Seward covers two notes to him, copies of which you find open for your inspection.[2] Consult with Judge Trumbull; and if you and he see no reason to the contrary, deliver the letter to Governor Seward at once. If you see reason to the contrary, write me at once.

I have had an intimation that Governor Banks would yet accept a place in the cabinet. Please ascertain and write me how this is. Yours very truly,   A. LINCOLN.

[1] NH, VI, 75-76. Hamlin's letter of December 4 concerns his going to Seward to learn his wishes about a cabinet post (DLC-RTL). Hamlin replied December 14 that he had consulted with Trumbull and then delivered the letters to

Seward. He answered Lincoln's question regarding Nathaniel P. Banks by saying that Gideon Welles or John A. Andrew, governor-elect of Massachusetts,
would be a better appointment: "Mr. B. is a man of decided ability, but he *is*
wonderfully cold and selfish. I do not hear him talked of by our N. E. friends."
(DLC-RTL).   [2] *Vide infra.*

To William H. Seward[1]

Springfield, Ills. Dec. 8 1860

My dear Sir: With your permission, I shall, at the proper time,
nominate you to the Senate, for confirmation, as Secretary of State,
for the United States.

Please let me hear from you at your own earliest convenience.
Your friend and obedient servant   A. LINCOLN.

Hon. William H. Seward,
  Washington   D.C.

[1] ALS, NAuE; ALS copy, MeHi. Hamlin wrote on the bottom of the copy:
"The above letter with another in the same words, which I was to deliver to
Mr Seward were recd by me from Mr Lincoln   The one to Mr Seward was
duly delivered, and that was the first information he had that the position of
Secy of State would be offered to him   The letters were both in the hand writ-
ing of Mr Lincoln   H. HAMLIN."

To William H. Seward[1]

Private & Confidential

Springfield Ills. Dec. 8. 1860

My dear Sir: In addition to the accompanying, and more formal
note, inviting you to take charge of the State Department, I deem
it proper to address you this. Rumors have got into the newspapers
to the effect that the Department, named above, would be tendered
you, as a compliment, and with the expectation that you would
decline it. I beg you to be assured that I have said nothing to justify
these rumors. On the contrary, it has been my purpose, from the
day of the nomination at Chicago, to assign you, by your leave,
this place in the administration. I have delayed so long to communicate that purpose, in deference to what appeared to me to be
a proper caution in the case. Nothing has been developed to change
my view in the premises; and I now offer you the place, in the
hope that you will accept it, and with the belief that your position
in the public eye, your integrity, ability, learning, and great experience, all combine to render it an appointment pre-eminently
fit to be made.

One word more. In regard to the patronage, sought with so much eagerness and jealousy, I have prescribed for myself the maxim, "Justice to all"; and I earnestly beseech your co-operation in keeping the maxim good. Your friend, and obedient servant

Hon. William H. Seward   A. LINCOLN—
Washington   D.C.

¹ ALS, NAuE. Seward replied to Lincoln's longer and more informal letter on December 13, asking ". . . a little time to consider whether I possess the qualifications and temper of a minister and whether it is in such a capacity that my friends would prefer that I should act if I am to continue at all in the public service. . . . Whatever may be my conclusion you may rest assured of my hearty concurrence in your views in regard to the distribution of the public offices as you have communicated them. . . ." (DLC-RTL). On December 28 Seward sent a brief, formal letter of acceptance.

To Lyman Trumbull¹

Private

Hon. Lyman Trumbull—   Springfield, Ills. Dec. 8. 1860.

My dear Sir: Yours of the 2nd. is received. I regret exceedingly the anxiety of our friends in New-York, of whom you write; but it seems to me the sentiment in that state which sent a united delegation to Chicago in favor of Gov. S. ought not, and must not be snubbed, as it would be by the omission to offer Gov. S. a place in the cabinet. I will, myself, take care of the question of "corrupt jobs" and see that justice is done to all, our friends, of whom you write, as well as others. I have written Mr. Hamlin, on this very subject of Gov. S. and requested him to consult fully with you. He will show you my note, and inclosures to him; and then please act as therein requested. Yours as ever   A. LINCOLN

¹ ALS, ICHi. Trumbull wrote on December 2 that a committee headed by William C. Bryant had called on him with reports of corruption in the New York legislature which might lose the next state elections if not repudiated, and that since Seward's friends were implicated the committee ". . . did not think it advisable for Gov. S. to go into the cabinet, lest his going should bring with it a set of dishonest men." (DLC-RTL).

To Lyman Trumbull¹

Private, & confidential

Hon. L. Trumbull.   Springfield, Ills. Dec. 10. 1860

My dear Sir: Let there be no compromise on the question of *extending* slavery. If there be, all our labor is lost, and, ere long, must be done again. The dangerous ground—that into which some of our friends have a hankering to run—is Pop. Sov. Have none

of it. Stand firm. The tug has to come, & better now, than any
time hereafter. Yours as ever   A. LINCOLN.

1 ALS, CSmH. Trumbull's letter of December 4 voiced surprise "that the
House voted to raise a committee on the State of the Union. It seems to me
that for Republicans to take steps towards getting up committees on proposing
new compromises . . . would be wrong. . . ." (DLC-RTL). See Lincoln to
Kellogg, December 11, *infra*.

To William Kellogg[1]

Private & confidential.

Hon. William Kellogg.   Springfield, Ills.
My dear Sir—   Dec. 11. 1860

Entertain no proposition for a compromise in regard to the *extension* of slavery. The instant you do, they have us under again;
all our labor is lost, and sooner or later must be done over. Douglas
is sure to be again trying to bring in his "Pop. Sov." Have none of
it. The tug has to come & better now than later.

You know I think the fugitive slave clause of the constitution
ought to be enforced—to put it on the mildest form, ought not to
be resisted. In haste   Yours as ever   A. LINCOLN

1 ALS, ORB. Kellogg wrote on December 6, advising Lincoln of the action of
the House in raising a committee, of which he was a member, ". . . to consider
that part of the President's Message in relation to the secession of the Cotton
States. . . ." and asking Lincoln's suggestions ". . . in relation to the remedy
for the present difficulties. . . ." (DLC-RTL).

Editorial in the *Illinois State Journal*[1]

December 12, 1860

We see such frequent allusion to a supposed purpose on the part
of Mr. Lincoln to call into his cabinet two or three Southern gentlemen, from the parties opposed to him politically, that we are
prompted to ask a few questions.

1st. Is it known that any such gentleman of character, would accept a place in the cabinet?

2— If yea, on what terms? Does he surrender to Mr. Lincoln, or
Mr. Lincoln to him, on the political difference between them? Or
do they enter upon the administration in open opposition to each
other?

What is the understanding on these questions?

1 AD, DLC-RTL. The editorial appeared in the *Journal* on December 12,
1860.

To Elihu B. Washburne[1]

Private & confidential

Hon. E. B. Washburne   Springfield, Ills. Dec. 13. 1860

My dear Sir. Your long letter received. Prevent, as far as possible, any of our friends from demoralizing themselves, and our cause, by entertaining propositions for compromise of any sort, on "*slavery extention*" There is no possible compromise upon it, but which puts us under again, and leaves all our work to do over again. Whether it be a Mo. line, or Eli Thayer's Pop. Sov. it is all the same. Let either be done, & immediately filibustering and extending slavery recommences. On that point hold firm, as with a chain of steel. Yours as ever   A. LINCOLN

[1] ALS, owned by Clarke Washburne, Winnetka, Illinois. Washburne wrote on December 9 of the imminent peril of secession, his fear that President Buchanan would let Charleston forts go by not sending a defending force, and his belief that Republicans should stay out of the debate in Congress and that in particular the Committee of Thirty-three would do little good, but would result ". . . in distracting our friends. . . ." (DLC-RTL).

Endorsement: Richard M. Corwine to Lincoln[1]

[c. December 14, 1860]

See if there is anything in this.

[1] AE, DLC-Nicolay Papers. Lincoln's endorsement is on the envelope of Corwine's long letter of December 14, 1860, expressing the opinion that the South will quiet down if handled firmly.

To John A. Gilmer[1]

Strictly confidential.

Hon. John A. Gilmer: Springfield, Ill. Dec 15, 1860.

My dear Sir— Yours of the 10th is received. I am greatly disinclined to write a letter on the subject embraced in yours; and I would not do so, even privately as I do, were it not that I fear you might misconstrue my silence. Is it desired that I shall shift the ground upon which I have been elected? I can not do it. You need only to acquaint yourself with that ground, and press it on the attention of the South. It is all in print and easy of access. May I be pardoned if I ask whether even you have ever attempted to procure the reading of the Republican platform, or my speeches, by the Southern people? If not, what reason have I to expect that any additional production of mine would meet a better fate? It would make me appear as if I repented for the crime of having been elected, and was anxious to apologize and beg forgiveness. To so represent me, would be the principal use made of any letter I might now thrust upon the public. My old record cannot be so used; and that is precisely the reason that some new declaration is so much sought.

Now, my dear sir, be assured, that I am not questioning *your* candor; I am only pointing out, that, while a new letter would hurt the cause which I think a just one, you can quite as well effect every patriotic object with the old record. Carefully read pages 18, 19, 74, 75, 88, 89, & 267 of the volume of Joint Debates between Senator Douglas and myself, with the Republican Platform adopted at Chicago, and all your questions will be substantially answered. I have no thought of recommending the abolition of slavery in the District of Columbia, nor the slave trade among the slave states, even on the conditions indicated; and if I were to make such recommendation, it is quite clear Congress would not follow it.

As to employing slaves in Arsenals and Dockyards, it is a thing I never thought of in my life, to my recollection, till I saw your letter; and I may say of it, precisely as I have said of the two points above.

As to the use of patronage in the slave states, where there are few or no Republicans, I do not expect to inquire for the politics of the appointee, or whether he does or not own slaves. I intend in that matter to accommodate the people in the several localities, if they themselves will allow me to accommodate them. In one word, I never have been, am not now, and probably never shall be, in a mood of harassing the people, either North or South.

On the territorial question,[2] I am inflexible, as you see my position in the book. On that, there is a difference between you and us; and it is the only substantial difference. You think slavery is right and ought to be extended; we think it is wrong and ought to be restricted. For this, neither has any just occasion to be angry with the other.

As to the state laws, mentioned in your sixth question, I really know very little of them. I never have read one. If any of them are in conflict with the fugitive slave clause, or any other part of the constitution, I certainly should be glad of their repeal; but I could hardly be justified, as a citizen of Illinois, or as President of the United States, to recommend the repeal of a statute of Vermont, or South Carolina.

With the assurance of my highest regards I subscribe myself Your obt. Servt.,   A. LINCOLN

P.S. The documents referred to, I suppose you will readily find
in Washington. A. L.

[1] Copy, DLC-RTL. Gilmer's letter of December 10, enclosed with Corwin's
letter of December 11 (DLC-RTL), asked Lincoln to make a public statement
answering specific questions, the nature of which is indicated by Lincoln's replies. Although Lincoln marked his letter "strictly confidential," an article appeared shortly afterward in the *Missouri Democrat* (copied by Cincinnati *Daily
Commercial,* January 10, 1861), which recounted an interview in the parlor of
Lincoln's home while he was in the midst of writing "to some Southern gentlemen." In the interview the identical points are made in almost identical language. Probably Francis P. Blair, Jr., wrote the article. See Lincoln to Blair,
December 18, *infra.* Lincoln to Trumbull and to Weed, December 17, *infra,*
indicate that the letter to Gilmer was enclosed to Thomas Corwin for delivery
to Gilmer. A second letter to Gilmer broaching the question of his accepting a
place in the cabinet, written on or after December 21, is presumably not extant.
Gilmer to Lincoln, December 29, refers to receipt of a telegram dated December 21, and a letter received December 26, requesting Gilmer to come to Springfield. Gilmer replied that such a visit ". . . would not be useful. . . ." (DLC-
RTL).

[2] Gilmer's question read ". . . whether, on the application of any new State
for admission into the Union, you would veto an act of Congress admitting the
same because slavery was tolerated in her constitution . . . also indicate the
policy . . . to settle . . . the disturbing question of slavery in the Territories."
(DLC-RTL).

To Lyman Trumbull[1]

Confidential

Hon. Lyman Trumbull   Springfield, Ills. Dec. 17. 1860

My dear Sir: Yours inclosing Mr. Wade's letter, which I herewith return, is received.

If any of our friends do prove false, and fix up a compromise on
the territorial question, I am for fighting again—that is all. (It is
but repetition for me to say I am for an honest inforcement of the
constitution—fugitive slave clause included.) Mr. Gilmer of N.C.
wrote me; and I answered confidentially, inclosing my letter to
Gov. Corwin,[2] to be delivered or not, as he might deem prudent. I
now inclose you a copy of it.

[The signature has been cut off.]

[1] ALS, CSmH. Trumbull wrote on December 14, enclosing an "old letter"
from Benjamin F. Wade, ". . . but you will see from it, what his views are."
He added that he understood some people "high up" in the South were to write
Lincoln for a statement and that if they were sufficiently prominent Lincoln's
answer might do good (DLC-RTL).

[2] No letter of this period to Thomas Corwin seems to be extant, but Lincoln
here implies that his letter to John A. Gilmer (December 15, *supra*) was sent
to Corwin, and Corwin's letter of December 11 enclosing Gilmer's letter of December 10 requested that Lincoln's reply be enclosed in care of Corwin.

To Thurlow Weed[1]

Private & confidential.

Hon. Thurlow Weed   Springfield, Ills– Dec. 17– 1860

My dear Sir Yours of the 11th. was received two days ago. Should the convocation of Governors, of which you speak, seem desirous to know my views on the present aspect of things, tell them you judge from my speeches that I will be inflexible on the territorial question; that I probably think either the Missouri line extended, or Douglas' and Eli Thayer's Pop. Sov. would lose us every thing we gained by the election; that filibustering for all South of us, and making slave states of it, would follow in spite of us, under either plan.

Also, that I probably think all opposition, real and apparant, to the fugitive slave [clause] of the constitution ought to be withdrawn.

I believe you can pretend to find but little, if any thing, in my speeches, about secession; but my opinion is that no state can, in any way lawfully, get out of the Union, without the consent of the others; and that it is the duty of the President, and other government functionaries to run the machine as it is. Yours very truly

A. LINCOLN—

[1] ALS, NRU-Thurlow Weed Papers on deposit. Weed wrote on December 11 that he and others had thought it a good plan to invite the governors to meet at New York City on Thursday, December 20, so that ". . . if possible, there should be harmony of views and action between them." (DLC-RTL).

To Edward Bates[1]

Confidential.

Springfield, Ill Dec 18th 1860.

My dear sir: Yours of to-day is just received. Let a little editorial appear in the Missouri Democrat, in about these words:

"We have the permission of both Mr. Lincoln and Mr. Bates to say that the latter will be offered, and will accept, a place in the new Cabinet, subject of course to the action of the Senate. It is not yet definitely settled which Department will be assigned to Mr. Bates."

Let it go just as above, or with any modification which may seem proper to you. Yours very truly   A. LINCOLN

Hon. Edward Bates

[1] Copy, DLC-RTL. Bates wrote on December 18 that upon returning to St. Louis from his conference with Lincoln he and judicious friends had concluded

that "a good effect might be produced on the public mind—especially in the border Slave States—by letting the people know (substantially) the relations which now subsist between us. . . ." (DLC-RTL).

To Montgomery Blair[1]

Hon. M. Blair   Springfield, Ills.
My dear Sir   Dec. 18. 1860

Yours of the 14th. is just received. I have just sent a confidential letter to Hon. Mr. Gilmer[2] of N.C. a copy of which I have inclosed to Senator Trumbull. In order that you may see why I think a public letter from me would do harm, and how all proper objects which could be effected by it, can be as well effected without, I authorize Judge Trumbull to show you the copy,—confidentially, of course. Yours truly   A. LINCOLN

[1] ALS, DLC-Blair Papers.
[2] See letter to John A. Gilmer, December 15, *supra*.

To John D. Defrees[1]

Confidential

Hon. Jno. D. Defrees.   Springfield Ills.
My dear Sir   Dec. 18. 1860

Yours of the 15th. is received. I am sorry any republican inclines to dally with Pop. Sov. of any sort. It acknowledges that slavery has equal rights with liberty, and surrenders all we have contended for. Once fastened on us as a settled policy, filibustering for all South of us, and making slave states of it, follows in spite of us, with an early Supreme court decision, holding our free-state constitutions to be unconstitutional.

Would Scott or Stephens go into the cabinet? And if yea, on what terms? Do they come to me? or I go to them? or are we to lead off in open hostility to each other? Yours truly

A. LINCOLN

[1] ALS, IHi. John D. Defrees, chairman of the Indiana State Republican Committee, wrote from Washington, December 15, that the threat of secession was greater than the West realized: "The fartherest any of our Republicans are willing to go is to secure genuine popular sovereignty to the people of our Territories—not the Douglas sham. . . ." He added that many Republicans thought Scott of Virginia should be secretary of war and Stephens of Georgia should be secretary of the navy (DLC-RTL). Both Robert E. Scott and General Winfield Scott were being mentioned for the cabinet.

To Henry J. Raymond[1]

Confidential

Hon. H. J. Raymond   Springfield, Ills.
My dear Sir   Dec. 18, 1860

Yours of the 14th. is received. What a very mad-man your correspondent, Smedes is. Mr. Lincoln is not pledged to the ultimate extinctinction [*sic*] of slavery; does not hold the black man to be the equal of the white, unqualifiedly as Mr. S. states it; and never did stigmatize their white people as immoral & unchristian; and Mr. S. can not prove one of his assertions true.

Mr. S. seems sensitive on the questions of morals and christianity. What does he think of a man who makes charges against another which he does not know to be true, and could easily learn to be false?

As to the pitcher story, it is a forgery out and out. I never made but one speech in Cincinnati—the last speech in the volume containing the Joint Debates between Senator Douglas and myself.[2] I have never yet seen Gov. Chase. I was never in a meeting of negroes in my life; and never saw a pitcher presented by anybody to anybody.

I am much obliged by your letter, and shall be glad to hear from you again when you have anything of interest. Yours truly

A. LINCOLN

[1] ALS-P, ISLA. Raymond's letter of December 14 enclosed a rabid communication from William C. Smedes, Vicksburg, Mississippi, December 8, 1860, in which that member of the Mississippi legislature vowed he ". . . would regard death by a stroke of lightning to Mr Lincoln as but a just punishment from an offended deity. . . ." Smedes was particularly aroused by a speech purported to have been made by Lincoln when some free negroes presented a pitcher to Salmon P. Chase at Cincinnati (DLC-RTL). The speech has appeared in collections of Lincoln's works (Hertz, II, 531), as purportedly delivered at Cincinnati, Ohio, May 6, 1842. Raymond's letter mentioned his having read it recently in the New York *Herald*, and asked whether it was authentic. According to biographies of Chase the occasion was authentic, but Lincoln was not present; the speech in question having been made by Chase himself.

[2] *Vide supra*, September 17, 1859. Governor Chase was not present on any occasion during Lincoln's Ohio trip in September, 1859. See Lincoln to Chase, September 21, 1859, *supra*.

Resolutions Drawn up for Republican Members of Senate Committee of Thirteen[1]

Resolved: [December 20, 1860]

That the fugitive slave clause of the Constitution ought to be enforced by a law of Congress, with efficient provisions for that object, not obliging private persons to assist in it's execution, but punishing all who resist it, and with the usual safeguards to liberty, securing free men against being surrendered as slaves—

That all state laws, if there be such, really, or apparantly, in conflict with such law of Congress, ought to be repealed; and no opposition to the execution of such law of Congress ought to be made—

That the Federal Union must be preserved.

[1] AD, NAuE. See Bancroft, *Life of William H. Seward* (1900) II, 10. See letter to Trumbull, December 21, *infra*, for circumstances under which the resolutions were composed. Seward wrote on December 26 that on December 24 he had offered first to the Republican members of the Committee of Thirteen, and afterwards the whole Committee, ". . . three propositions which seemed to me to cover the ground of the suggestion made by you through Mr Weed as I understood it. First. That the constitution should never be altered so as to authorize Congress to abolish or interfere with slavery in the states. This was accepted. Second. That the Fugitive slave law should be amended by granting a jury trial to the fugitive. . . ." This was amended so as to name the jury from the state which the fugitive had fled, and was voted down by the Republicans. The third resolution—that Congress should recommend that the states revise legislation concerning persons recently resident in the state and repeal all in conflict with the constitution—was rejected. At another meeting on December 26, Seward continued, he had offered a fourth proposition to the effect that Congress should pass a law to prevent invasion of a state, which was amended and rejected. Whereupon the Republican members of the committee, together with Trumbull and Fessenden, met to consider Lincoln's resolutions: "While we think the ground has already been covered we find that in the form you give it it would divide our friends not only in the Committee but in Congress, a portion being unwilling to give up their old opinion that the duty of executing the constitutional provisions concerning fugitives from service belongs to the States, and not at all to Congress. But we shall confer—and act wisely as we can." (DLC-RTL).

To Francis P. Blair, Sr.[1]

Confidential

Hon. F. P. Blair, Ser.   Springfield, Ills.
My dear Sir   Dec. 21. 1860

Yours giving an account of an interview with Gen. Scott, is received, and for which I thank you. According to my present view, if the forts shall be given up before the inaugeration, the General must retake them afterwards. Yours truly   A. LINCOLN

[1] ALS, owned by Blair Lee, Philadelphia, Pennsylvania. Blair wrote on December 18 of his interview with James H. Van Alen of New York, who was on his way to Springfield with a letter from General Winfield Scott to Lincoln. Blair thought Lincoln might assure the country through Scott that he meant to defend the country against conspirators. The letter which Van Alen carried to Lincoln was probably the copy of Scott to President Buchanan, December 15,

1860, endorsed by Scott with a note supplying what he omitted to say "this morning at the interview with . . . the President. . . ." The gist of this was that President Jackson had caused reinforcements to be sent to Fort Moultrie and Charleston Harbor, and had remarked that he was not making war on South Carolina, but that if South Carolina attacked, she would be warring on the United States (DLC-RTL).

To Andrew G. Curtin[1]

Confidential

Hon. A. G. Curtin   Springfield, Ills.
My dear Sir   Dec. 21. 1860

Yours of the 14th. was only received last night. I am much obliged by your kindness in asking my views in advance of preparing your inaugeral. I think of nothing proper for me to suggest except a word about this secession and disunion movement. On that subject, I think you would do well to express, without passion, threat, or appearance of boasting, but nevertheless, with firmness, the purpose of yourself, and your state to maintain the Union at all hazzards. Also, if you can, procure the Legislature to pass resolutions to that effect. As [*sic*] [I] shall be very glad to see your friend, the Attorney General,[2] that is to be; but I think he need scarcely make a trip merely to confer with me on the subject you mention. Yours very truly   A. LINCOLN

[1] ALS-P, ISLA. Curtin's letter of December 14 is in the Nicolay Papers (DLC).   [2] Samuel A. Purviance.

To Lyman Trumbull[1]

Confidential

Hon. Lyman Trumbull   Springfield, Ills.
My dear Sir.   Dec. 21, 1860

Thurlow Weed was with me nearly all day yesterday, & left at night with three short resolutions which I drew up,[2] and which, or the substance of which, I think would do much good, if introduced, and unanamously supported by our friends. They do not touch the territorial question. Mr. Weed goes to Washington with them; and says he will, first of all, confer with you and Mr. Hamlin.[3] I think it would be best for Mr. Seward to introduce them, & Mr. Weed will let him know that I think so. Show this to Mr. Hamlin; but beyond him, do not let my name be known in the matter. Yours as ever   A. LINCOLN

[1] ALS, ICHi. Trumbull's letters of December 24 and 31 do not mention the resolutions, probably because he knew of Seward's detailed letter of December 26. [2] *Vide supra*.

[3] Hamlin wrote on December 27 that Weed had showed him the resolutions and that he approved them, excepting the word "apparently" in the second paragraph, which should be omitted (DLC-RTL).

To Elihu B. Washburne[1]

Confidential

Hon. E. B. Washburne   Springfield, Ills.
My dear Sir: Dec. 21. 1860

Last night I received your letter giving an account of your interview with Gen. Scott, and for which I thank you. Please present my respects to the General, and tell him, confidentially, I shall be obliged to him to be as well prepared as he can to either *hold*, or *retake*, the forts, as the case may require, at, and after the inaugeration. Yours as ever   A. LINCOLN

[1] ALS, IHi. Washburne wrote on December 17 summarizing an interview with General Winfield Scott to the effect that Scott had recommended reinforcement of the Charleston forts in October, that Fort Moultrie was practically defenseless, and that Fort Sumter with only five workmen in it was the key to the harbor.

To David Hunter[1]

Confidential

Major David Hunter,   Springfield, Ills., Dec. 22, 1860.

My dear Sir: I am much obliged by the receipt of yours of the 18th. The most we can do now is to watch events, and be as well prepared as possible for any turn things may take. If the forts fall, my judgment is that they are to be retaken. When I shall determine definitely my time of starting to Washington, I will notify you. Yours truly,   A. LINCOLN.

[1] Copy, DLC-Nicolay Papers. Major Hunter wrote again (*vide supra*, October 26) on December 18 from Fort Leavenworth, Kansas, recounting the purported scheme of Governor Henry A. Wise of Virginia in 1856 to prevent the inauguration of John C. Frémont in the event of his election, and suggesting the likelihood of a similar plan to employ force to prevent Lincoln's inauguration. As a precaution he recommended that 100,000 Wide-Awakes be assembled in Washington to prevent such an incident. He also thanked Lincoln for an invitation to attend the inaugural.

To Peter H. Silvester[1]

Confidential

Hon. P. H. Silvester   Springfield, Ills.
My dear Sir   Dec. 22. 1860

Your kind letter of Nov. 16th. was duly received. Want of time has delayed me so long before acknowledging the receipt of it. This, even now, is the most I can do.

The political horizon looks dark and lowering; but the people, under Providence, will set all right.

If Mr. B. surrenders the forts, I think they must be retaken.
Yours truly   A. LINCOLN

[1] ALS, owned by Mrs. Townsend Morey, Albany, New York. Silvester was a lawyer of Coxsackie, New York, and Whig congressman from New York, 1847-1851.

To Alexander H. Stephens[1]

For your own eye only.

Hon. A. H. Stephens—   Springfield, Ills.
My dear Sir   Dec. 22, 1860

Your obliging answer to my short note is just received, and for which please accept my thanks. I fully appreciate the present peril the country is in, and the weight of responsibility on me.

Do the people of the South really entertain fears that a Republican administration would, *directly*, or *indirectly*, interfere with their slaves, or with them, about their slaves? If they do, I wish to assure you, as once a friend, and still, I hope, not an enemy, that there is no cause for such fears.

The South would be in no more danger in this respect, than it was in the days of Washington. I suppose, however, this does not meet the case. You think slavery is *right* and ought to be extended; while we think it is *wrong* and ought to be restricted. That I suppose is the rub. It certainly is the only substantial difference between us. Yours very truly   A. LINCOLN

[1] ALS, CSmH. Stephens' reply of December 30 is not in the Lincoln Papers, but a portion of it is given in *Recollections of Alexander H. Stephens*, edited by Myrta L. Avary (1910), p. 60, as follows: "Personally, I am not your enemy— far from it; and however widely we may differ politically, yet I trust we both have an earnest desire to preserve and maintain the Union. . . . When men come under the influence of fanaticism, there is no telling where their impulses or passions may drive them. This is what creates our discontent and apprehensions, not unreasonable when we see . . . such reckless exhibitions of madness

as the John Brown raid into Virginia, which has received so much sympathy from many, and no open condemnation from any of the leading members of the dominant party. . . . In addressing you thus, I would have you understand me as being not a personal enemy, but as one who would have you do what you can to save our common country. A word fitly spoken by you now would be like 'apples of gold in pictures of silver.' "

To Hannibal Hamlin[1]

Springfield, Illinois, December 24, 1860.

My dear Sir: I need a man of Democratic antecedents from New England. I cannot get a fair share of that element in without. This stands in the way of Mr. Adams.[2] I think of Governor Banks, Mr. Welles, and Mr. Tuck.[3] Which of them do the New England delegation prefer? Or shall I decide for myself? Yours as ever,

A. LINCOLN.

[1] NH, VI, 86-87. Hamlin replied December 29 that he had ". . . no hesitation in saying that . . . Mr. Wells is the better man for New England. . . ." (DLC-RTL).

[2] Charles Francis Adams, member of congress from Massachusetts.

[3] Amos Tuck, member of congress from New Hampshire, 1847-1853, who had been chairman of the New Hampshire delegation at the Chicago convention.

To Isaac N. Morris[1]

Confidential

Hon. I. N. Morris   Springfield, Ills.
My dear Sir: Dec. 24, 1860

Without supposing that you and I are any nearer together, politically, than heretofore, allow me to tender you my sincere thanks for your Union resolution, expressive of views upon which we never were, and, I trust, never will be at variance. Yours very truly   A. LINCOLN.

[1] ALS, owned by Edward C. Stone, Boston, Massachusetts. On December 17, Isaac N. Morris, Democratic member of congress from Quincy, Illinois, had offered a resolution in the House of Representatives, reading in part as follows: ". . . That we properly estimate the immense value of our national Union to our collective and individual happiness . . . cherish a cordial . . . attachment to it . . . will watch its preservation with jealous anxiety . . . that we have seen nothing in the past, nor . . . present, either in the election of Abraham Lincoln to the Presidency . . . or from any other existing cause, to justify its dissolution; that we regard its perpetuity as of more value than the temporary triumph of any party or any man. . . ." (*Illinois State Journal*, December 19, 1860). The resolution passed 115 to 44.

To Lyman Trumbull[1]

Hon. Lyman Trumbull   Springfield, Ills. Dec. 24, 1860

My dear Sir   I expect to be able to offer Mr. Blair a place in the cabinet; but I can not, as yet, be committed on the matter, to any extent whatever.

Despaches have come here two days in succession, that the Forts in South Carolina, will be surrendered by the order, or consent at least, of the President.

I can scarcely believe this; but if it prove true, I will, if our friends at Washington concur, announce publicly at once that they are to be retaken after the inauguration. This will give the Union men a rallying cry, and preparation will proceed somewhat on their side, as well as on the other. Yours as ever

A. LINCOLN.

[1] ALS, CSmH. Trumbull wrote December 18, proposing that Montgomery Blair be made secretary of war (DLC-RTL).

To Duff Green[1]

Gen. Duff Green.   Springfield, Ill. Dec 28th 1860.

My dear Sir— I do not desire any amendment of the Constitution. Recognizing, however, that questions of such amendment rightfully belong to the American People, I should not feel justified, nor inclined, to withhold from them, if I could, a fair opportunity of expressing their will thereon, through either of the modes prescribed in the instrument.

In addition I declare that the maintainance inviolate of the rights of the States, and especially the right of each state to order and control its own domestic institutions according to its own judgment exclusively, is essential to that balance of powers on which the perfection, and endurance of our political fabric depends —and I denounce the lawless invasion, by armed force, of the soil of any State or Territory, no matter under what pretext, as the gravest of crimes.

I am greatly averse to writing anything for the public at this time; and I consent to the publication of this, only upon the condition that six of the twelve United States Senators for the States of Georgia, Alabama, Mississippi, Louisiana, Florida, and Texas shall sign their names to what is written on this sheet below my name, and allow the whole to be published together. Yours truly

A. LINCOLN.

We recommend to the people of the States we represent respectively, to suspend all action for dismemberment of the Union, at least, until some act, deemed to be violative of our rights, shall be done by the incoming administration

[1] Copy, DLC-RTL. This letter was enclosed with the letter to Trumbull, *infra*. It was never made public, and Trumbull's letters in the Lincoln Papers (December 31, 1860, January 3, 7, and 16, 1861) make no mention of it. Green came to Springfield as an emissary of President Buchanan. The fact that his visit went unnoticed in the press suggests that great secrecy was observed by both sides. According to his later account given to the New York *Herald* (January 8, 1861), he was satisfied that Lincoln sincerely wished "to administer the government in such a manner as to satisfy the South. . . ." Green wrote Lincoln on January 7, 1861, that he had received ". . . your letter of the 31st Dec. I regret your unwillingness to recommend an amendment to the constitution which will arrest the progress of secession. . . ." (DLC-RTL). Undoubtedly Green refers to this letter. Perhaps Trumbull handed him a copy under the later date.

To Lyman Trumbull[1]

Hon. Lyman Trumbull   Springfield Ill Dec 28th 1860.

My dear Sir— Gen. Duff Green is out here endeavoring to draw a letter out of me. I have written one, which herewith I inclose to you, and which I believe could not be used to our disadvantage. Still, if, on consultation with our discreet friends, you conclude that it may do us harm, do not deliver it.

You need not mention that the second clause of the letter is copied from the Chicago Platform. If, on consultation, our friends, including yourself, think it can do no harm, keep a copy and deliver the letter to Gen. Green. Yours as ever   A. LINCOLN.

[1] Copy, DLC-RTL. See note to Green letter, *supra*.

To William C. Bryant[1]

Springfield, Illinois, December 29, 1860.

My dear Sir: Yours of the 25th is duly received. The "well-known politician" to whom I understand you to allude did write me, but not press upon me any such compromise as you seem to suppose, or, in fact, any compromise at all.

As to the matter of the cabinet, mentioned by you, I can only say I shall have a great deal of trouble, do the best I can.

I promise you that I shall unselfishly try to deal fairly with all men and all shades of opinion among our friends. Yours very truly,

A. LINCOLN.

¹ NH, VI, 89. Bryant wrote on December 25: "The rumor having got abroad
that you have been visited by a well known politician of New York who has a
good deal to do with the stock market and who took with him a plan of compromise manufactured in Wall Street, it has occurred to me that you might
like to be assured of the manner in which those Republicans who have no connections with Wall Street regard a compromise on the slavery question. . . .
The restoration of the Missouri Compromise would disband the Republican
party. . . ." Bryant added that he was glad the cabinet would have some Republicans of Democratic antecedents (DLC-RTL). The "well known politician"
was probably Thurlow Weed, who conferred with Lincoln on December 20.

To William H. Seward¹

Private

Hon. W. H. Seward: Springfield, Ills.

My dear Sir Dec. 29. 1860

Yours of the 25th. suggesting the names of Col. Fremont, and
Messrs. Hunt, Raynor, and Gilmer for places in the Cabinet is received. I had thought of all of them before, but not very definitely
of any except Mr. Gilmer. I wrote him, requesting him to visit me
here; and my object was that if, on full understanding of my position, he would accept a place in the cabinet, to give it to him. He
has neither come, nor answered me. If you will ascertain his feelings, and write me, I shall be obliged. Our german friends might
not be quite satisfied with his appointment, but I think we could
appease them. Yours very truly A. LINCOLN

¹ ALS, NAuE. On December 25, Seward wrote Lincoln: "I feel it my duty
to submit for your consideration the names of Col. Fremont for Secretary of
War, Randall Hunt of Louisiana— and John A Gilmer or Kenneth Raynor of
North Carolina for other places. Should you think that any of these gentlemen
would be likely to be desirable in the Administration, I should find no difficulty I think in ascertaining whether they would accept, without making the
matter public. . . ." (DLC-RTL).

See Lincoln to Gilmer, December 15, *supra*, and to Seward, January 3 and
12, 1861, *infra*.

To James W. Webb¹

Private

Col. J. W. Webb. Springfield, Ills.

My dear Sir: Dec. 29. 1860

Yours kindly seeking my view as to the proper mode of dealing
with secession, was received several days ago, but, for want of
time I could not answer it till now. I think we should hold the
forts, or retake them, as the case may be, and collect the revenue.
We shall have to forego the use of the federal courts, and *they* that
of the mails, for a while. We can not fight them in to holding
courts, or receiving the mails.

This is an outline of my view; and perhaps suggests sufficiently, the whole of it. Yours very truly   A. LINCOLN

¹ ALS, CtY. James W. Webb wrote from New York, December 24, seeking Lincoln's views and stating that he was editor of the New York *Courier and Enquirer* (DLC-RTL).

Memorandum on the Charges against Simon Cameron¹

[c. December 31, 1860]

At the election of Senator in Pennsylvania in 1857 General C. *bribed* three members of the Legislature *Lebo, Mancer,* and *Wagonsella;* and part of the consideration paid is now in the hands of William B. Mann of Philadelphia. Bonds—A Mr. Mc-*Aber,* received the Bonds from General C. for the purpose of corrupting the Legislature. The bonds in Mann's hands were either paid to members, or or [*sic*] retained by McAber, for compensation as a go between. McAber will swear to all this. The witness was afterward bribed by General C. through John B. Beck, brother-in-law of the witness. A Mr. Johns, a member at the next session, moved to investigate this matter, and was bribed out of it by General C.
Witness J. C. *Bonbager—Cashiered.*

If Pollock will give his word that he believes General C. to be personally and politically an honest man and whether he believes his ? is the result of honest dealing,²

Look to report of investigation of 1855—and Protest—Winnebago matter.
In 1849, in a Democratic Convention, he attempted to bribe a *convention.*

¹ Copy, DLC-Nicolay Papers. Nicolay's copy of this memorandum is, together with the copy of the memorandum summarizing the recommendations in Cameron's favor (*infra*) labeled "aut. MS.," and given a headnote as follows: "Orig. in envelope 'Presidential Dec. 1860.' (Written in pencil and endorsed on back, 'In regard to Cameron') (Pinned to other sheets.)" Written in the left-hand margin of the first page is an additional note, "W. B. Mann and C. C. Cary know of this/also Dr. Eckart." Whether this notation was Nicolay's or a copy of Lincoln's notation is uncertain. Although Lincoln's autograph memorandum of the favorable recommendations as reproduced *infra*, is still in the Lincoln Papers, the original from which Nicolay made his copy of the unfavorable memorandum has disappeared and may have been destroyed by Robert Todd Lincoln.
² The sentence is left incomplete, followed by a vacant line. The question mark is in the source.

Memorandum on the Appointment
of Simon Cameron[1]

[c. December 31, 1860]

J. K. Moorhead—M.C.

"I have no hesitation in saying that if Penna. receives the honor, it should be in the person of Genl. Cameron."

Wm. Nichols.	1st. Sen. Dist	
G. Rush Smith.	2nd. " "	Joint letter from Philada.
Jno. H. Parker	3rd. " "	
Geo. Conwell	4th. " "	

"He (Cameron) is the universally acknowledged head and representative man of the 'Peoples Party' of the State; and it is not only the desire of the people of the State, in view of the position he thus occupies, as well as his practical business qualifications and life devotion to the material interests of the state, that he should be at the head of the Treasury Department under your administration, but also of the great body of your friends in this city"

F. W. Thomas	Joint letter from, Germans, Propri[e]tor, Editor & President of Rep. Assoc[i]ation at Philada.
Theodore Kell	
F. T. Loes	
Peter Ford	

"Feeling assured as we do that the appointment of the Hon Simon Cameron would be hailed with joy by the citizens of this state, and that it would secure to our city and our state future triumphs for the Republican party, we respectfully present his name for your kind and favorable consideration.

Jos. Casey—Harrisburg—Ex. M.C. & Del. to Chicago.
Many letters from him.

J. S. Haldeman—Fairview. Former Pa. Pres. of State Ag. Soc. & Del. to Chicago. Long letter.

J. P. Sanderson—Philada.

Wm. F. Small—Philada. Long Letter.

John Z. Goodrich—Stockbridge, Mass. Long letter

Charles T. Jones—Philada. Letter.

Russell Essett—Pittsburgh. Letter.

Francis Blackburne, Philada.—Del. to Chicago. Long letter.

Levi Kline—Lebanon, Pa. Del to C. & Com-man. Long letter.

Hazelhurst, Philada. Letter.

Isaac. G. Gordon—Brookville, Pa. Rep in Leg. Letter

David Wilmot. Towanda. Pa. Letter.
A. H. Reeder—Easton, Pa. Letters & visit.
Leonard Ulmer. Williamsport, Pa. Letter
J. W. Killinger, M.C. Lebanon, Pa. Letter
John M. Butler, M.C. almost, Philada. Letter
Henry D. Moore. State. Treasurer, that is to be. Phil. Letter.
J. L. Rightmyer
Jesse Hillman
L. Ulmer — Williamsport, *Pa.* Joint letter.
S. H. Walters
Jno. A Hiestand. Editor—Lancaster, Pa. Letter.
Geo. A. Coffey—Phil—   Letter
A. R. McIlvaine. Ex. M.C. Brandywine Manor Pa. Letter.
Geo. R. Hendrickson—Mountjoy—Lancaster Co. Pa. Letter.
John M. Butler
Wm. Elliott
Joseph S. Morey — Joint letter from Phil.
E. Ward
John W. Wallace. New Castle, Pa. Letter
G. L. Vliet. Woodbury N.J. Letter.
Robert M. Palmer
Jacob G. Frick
S. A. Bergstresser — Dels. to Chicago. Letter from Pottsville Pa.
Wm. C. Lawson
G. Rush Smith—Phil—Letter.
John C. Myers. Editor—Reading Pa. Letter
John Strohm, Ex. M.C. Lancaster Co. Pa. Letter
B. Rush Petrikin.   Pa. Letter
Wm. B. Thomas—Pres. of Rep. Cent Club, Phil. Letter.
Wm. H. Kerr. Sheriff of Phil. City & Co. Letter—
Daniel G. Thomas. Rep. in Leg. Phil. Letter
R. P. King—Elector—Phil. Letter.
James M. Moore. Phil—Letter.
David Taggart, Elector—Northumberland, Pa. Letter
Joseph Buffington. Kittaning Pa. Letter
John F. Long—Lancaster Pa. Letter.
Hon. F. P. Stanton.   Letter.
James Pollock. Ex. MC. & Ex. Gov. Milton, Pa. Letter.
David Mumma. Jr. Head elector, Harrisburg, Pa. Letter.

[1] AD, DLC-RTL. The approximate date of this memorandum, like that of the preceding one, is supplied on the basis of Lincoln's letter to Cameron (*infra*) and of the fact that during December he had considered the *pros* and *cons* of the appointment as summarized in the memoranda themselves.

To Simon Cameron[1]

Hon. Simon Cameron   Springfield, Ills.
My dear Sir: Dec. 31, 1860
  I think fit to notify you now, that by your permission, I shall, at the proper time, nominate you to the U.S. Senate, for confirmation as Secretary of the Treasury, or as Secretary of War—which of the two, I have not yet definitely decided. Please answer at your own earliest convenience. Your Obt. Servt.   A. Lincoln—

[1] ALS, DLC-Cameron Papers. There is no reply to this in the Lincoln Papers. Cameron had visited Lincoln together with Edward Bates the day before. See Lincoln to Cameron, January 3, 1861, for Lincoln's withdrawal of his offer.

To Salmon P. Chase[1]

Hon. S. P. Chase   Springfield, Ill., December 31, 1860.
  My dear Sir: In these troublous times, I would [much][2] like a conference with you. Please visit me here at once. Yours very truly,   A. Lincoln.

[1] NH, VI, 90; Robert B. Warden, *Account of the Private Life and Public Services of Salmon Portland Chase* (1874), p. 364. Chase replied January 2 that he would come to Springfield the next day (DLC-RTL). On January 5, he conferred with Lincoln about his appointment to the cabinet, and left without accepting or rejecting the offer.   [2] Not in Warden.

Endorsement:
Jesse K. Dubois and William Butler to Lincoln[1]

[January ? 1861]
  Do not think any objection to Turner of enough importance to have a squabble over.   A. Lincoln

[1] AES, IHi. Dubois' undated letter, signed also by Butler, recommended Stephen T. Logan, John Wood, John M. Palmer, Burton C. Cook, and David Davis as the Illinois delegates to the Peace Convention to be held in Washington in February, but noted that Governor Richard Yates wanted "to select [Thomas J.] Turner in place of Davis. . . . We want your personal friends on the commission and not men opposed to you." (ALS, IHi). Thomas J. Turner of Freeport, Illinois, was a Democrat, U.S. representative 1847-1849 and speaker of the Illinois House of Representatives 1854-1856.

Fragment on the Constitution and the Union[1]

[c. January, 1861]
  All this is not the result of accident. It has a philosophical cause. Without the *Constitution* and the *Union*, we could not have at-

tained the result; but even these, are not the primary cause of our great prosperity. There is something back of these, entwining itself more closely about the human heart. That something, is the principle of "Liberty to all"—the principle that clears the *path* for all—gives *hope* to all—and, by consequence, *enterprize,* and *industry* to all.

The *expression* of that principle, in our Declaration of Independence, was most happy, and fortunate. *Without* this, as well as *with* it, we could have declared our independence of Great Brittain; but *without* it, we could not, I think, have secured our free government, and consequent prosperity. No oppressed, people will *fight,* and *endure,* as our fathers did, without the promise of something better, than a mere change of masters.

The assertion of that *principle,* at *that time,* was *the* word, *"fitly spoken"* which has proved an "apple of gold" to us. The *Union,* and the *Constitution,* are the *picture* of *silver,* subsequently framed around it. The picture was made, not to *conceal,* or *destroy* the apple; but to *adorn,* and *preserve* it. The *picture* was made *for* the apple—*not* the apple for the picture.

So let us act, that neither *picture,* or *apple* shall ever be blurred, or bruised or broken.

That we may so act, we must study, and understand the points of danger.

1 AD, ORB. This fragment may have been written earlier than January, 1861. The only clue in the context as to a date is Lincoln's allusion to the metaphor in *Proverbs* 25:11, which Alexander Stephens had used in his letter to Lincoln of December 30, 1860 (*vide supra,* Lincoln to Stephens, December 22, note). No speech which employs the language of the fragment has been found, but it seems probable that Lincoln wrote the passage some time prior to or during the preparation of his First Inaugural Address.

To Simon Cameron[1]

Private   (Copy)

Hon. Simon Cameron   Springfield, Ills. Jan. 3, 1861
    My dear Sir   Since seeing you things have developed which make it impossible for me to take you into the cabinet. You will say this comes of an interview with McClure; and this is partly, but not wholly true. The more potent matter is wholly outside of Pennsylvania; and yet I am not at liberty to specify it. Enough that it appears to me to be sufficient. And now I suggest that you write me declining the appointment, in which case I do not object

to its being known that it was tendered you. Better do this at once, before things so change, that you can not honorably decline, and I be compelled to openly recall the tender. No person living knows, or has an intimation that I write this letter. Yours truly

A. LINCOLN

P.S. Telegraph, me instantly, on receipt of this, saying "All right"   A. L.

1 ALS copy, DLC-RTL. Lincoln apparently sent a telegram at the time he wrote the letter, for Cameron replied January 5 that he had received the dispatch and was awaiting the letter (DLC-RTL). There are no further letters from Cameron in the Lincoln Papers prior to March 4, 1861. See Lincoln's second letter under date of January 3, which was actually written on January 13 and enclosed with Lincoln's letter to Cameron of January 13, infra.

To William H. Seward[1]

Private

Hon. W. H. Seward   Springfield, Ills. Jan. 3. 1861

My dear Sir: Yours without signature was received last night. I have been considering your suggestions as to my reaching Washington somewhat earlier than is usual. It seems to me the inaugeration is not the most dangerous point for us. Our adversaries have us more clearly at disadvantage, on the second Wednesday of February, when the votes should be officially counted. If the two Houses refuse to meet at all, or meet without a quorum of each, where shall we be? I do not think that this counting is constitutionally essential to the election; but how are we to proceed in absence of it?

In view of this, I think it is best for me not to attempt appearing in Washington till the result of that ceremony is known.

It certainly would be of some advantage if you could know who are to be at the heads of the War and Navy Departments; but until I can ascertain definitely whether I can get any suitable men from the South? and who?.and how many? I can not well decide. As yet, I have no word from Mr. Gilmer, in answer to my request for an interview with him. I look for something on the subject, through you, before long. Yours very truly   A. LINCOLN.

1 ALS, NAuE. Seward's letter of December 29, without signature, informed Lincoln of a plot to seize the capital on or before March 4, and added ". . . I am not giving you opinions and rumors. Believe that I know what I write. . . . I therefore renew my suggestion of your coming here earlier than you otherwise would—and coming in by surprise—without announcement." Seward further suggested that he be informed of Lincoln's choice of secretaries for War and

Navy and that they be advised to come to Washington as soon as possible. On January 1, he wrote that Gilmer had gone home but that he would see him ". . . as soon as he returns." (DLC-RTL).

To Lyman Trumbull[1]
Very Confidential

Hon. Lyman Trumbull   Springfield, Ills.
My dear Sir   Jan. 7. 1861

Yours of the 3rd. is just received. The democrats of our H.R. refused to make a quorum today, trying, as I understand, to prevent your re-election. I trust that before this reaches you, the telegraph will have informed you that they have failed, and you have triumphed.

Gen. C. has not been offered the Treasury, and, I think, will not be. It seems to me not only highly proper, but a *necessity*, that Gov. Chase shall take that place. His ability, firmness, and purity of character, produce the propriety; and that he alone can reconcile Mr. Bryant, and his class, to the appointment of Gov. S. to the State Department produces the necessity. But then comes the danger that the protectionists of Pennsylvania will be dissatisfied; and, to clear this difficulty, Gen. C. must be brought to co-operate. He would readily do this for the War Department. But then comes the fierce opposition to his having any Department, threatening even to send charges into the Senate to procure his rejection by that body. Now, what I would most like, and what I think he should prefer too, under the circumstances, would be to retain his place in the Senate; and if that place has been promised to another, let that other take a respectable, and reasonably lucrative place abroad. Also let Gen. C's friends be, with entire fairness, cared for in Pennsylvania, and elsewhere.

I may mention before closing that besides the very fierce opposition to Gen. C. he is more amply recommended for a place in the cabinet, than any other man.

I have a great notion to post Judd fully in this matter, and get him to visit Washington, and in his quiet way, try to adjust it satisfactorily. Yours as ever   A. LINCOLN.

[1] ALS, ICHi. Trumbull wrote on December 31 that the probable appointment of Cameron as ". . . Sec. of Treasury meets with the decided opposition of our truest friends in the Senate. . . ." On January 3, he wrote that the appointment of Cameron was regarded as an accomplished fact, but that ". . . I shall not be surprised if a very strong protest against it reaches you from Pa. . . ." (DLC-RTL).

To James T. Hale[1]

Confidential.

Hon. J. T. Hale   Springfield, Ill. Jan'y. 11th 1861.

My dear Sir—Yours of the 6th is received. I answer it only because I fear you would misconstrue my silence. What is our present condition? We have just carried an election on principles fairly stated to the people. Now we are told in advance, the government shall be broken up, unless we surrender to those we have beaten, before we take the offices. In this they are either attempting to play upon us, or they are in dead earnest. Either way, if we surrender, it is the end of us, and of the government. They will repeat the experiment upon us *ad libitum*. A year will not pass, till we shall have to take Cuba as a condition upon which they will stay in the Union. They now have the Constitution, under which we have lived over seventy years, and acts of Congress of their own framing, with no prospect of their being changed; and they can never have a more shallow pretext for breaking up the government, or extorting a compromise, than now. There is, in my judgment, but one compromise which would really settle the slavery question, and that would be a prohibition against acquiring any more territory. Yours very truly,   A. LINCOLN.

[1] Copy, DLC-RTL. James T. Hale, Republican congressman from Bellefonte, Pennsylvania, wrote January 6 as a member of a committee of congressmen from the border states, recommending an amendment to the Constitution denying the right of Congress to abolish slavery in the states, a joint resolution declaring that abolition could not take place in the District of Columbia without consent of Maryland and citizens of the District, an amendment of the fugitive slave law and that states repeal all personal liberty bills, and that the U.S. be divided at 36° 30′, all territories north of that line to be free and all those south of it to be free or slave as they chose (DLC-RTL).

To Winfield Scott[1]

         Springfield, Ill.

Lieutenant General Winfield Scott: Jany 11th 1861.

My dear Sir—I herewith beg leave to acknowledge the receipt of your communication of the 4th inst. enclosing (documents Nos. 1, 2, 3, 4, 5, and 6) copies of correspondence and notes of conversation with the President of the United States and the Secretary of War, concerning various military movements, suggested by yourself, for the better protection of the Government and the maintainance of public order.

Permit me to renew to you the assurance of my high appreciation of the many past services you have rendered the Union, and
of my deep gratification at this evidence of your present active
exertions to maintain the integrity and honor of the nation.

I shall be highly pleased to receive from time to time, such communications from yourself as you may deem it proper to make to
me. Very truly your obt. servt. A. LINCOLN

¹ Copy, DLC-RTL. General Scott's letter of January 4 is not in the Lincoln
Papers. The numbered documents referred to in Lincoln's letter are copies of
communications (No. 1) to President Buchanan, December 15, 1860; (No. 2)
to the Secretary of War, December 28, 1860; (No. 3) Buchanan to Scott, December 30, 1860; (No. 4) Scott to Buchanan, December 31, 1860; (No. 5)
Scott to Buchanan, December 30, 1860; (No. 6) Buchanan to Scott, December
31, 1860—all cataloged by date and dealing with the holding of Fort Sumter
(DLC-RTL).

To William H. Seward¹

Private

Hon. W. H. Seward   Springfield, Ills. Jan. 12. 1861

My dear Sir Yours of the 8th received. I still hope Mr. Gilmer
will, on a fair understanding with us, consent to take a place in the
Cabinet. The preference for him over Mr. Hunt or Mr. Gentry,² is
that, up to date, he has a *living* position in the South, while they
have not. He is only better than Winter Davis in that he is *farther*
South. I fear if we could get, we could not safely take more
than one such man—that is, not more than one who opposed us in
the election—the danger being to lose the confidence of our own
friends.

Your selection for the State Department having become public,
I am happy to find scarcely any objection to it. I shall have trouble
with every other Northern cabinet appointment—so much so that
I shall have to defer them as long as possible, to avoid being teased
to insanity to make changes. Your obt. servt A. LINCOLN—

¹ ALS, NAuE. Seward had written on January 4: "Mr G. of N.C. says he
will consider of the proposition and that he trusts that before giving an answer
he will be able to name a person better calculated than himself for the purpose
indicated. . . . He will not reply further until required to do so by you directly
or indirectly. . . ." Again on January 8 Seward wrote: "Mr. Gilmer has
written home confidentially and will give me an answer in a few days. . . ."
(DLC-RTL).
² Randall Hunt, a New Orleans attorney who later became President of the
University of Louisiana (1867-1884) and Meredith P. Gentry, Whig ex-congressman (1839-1843; 1845-1853) from Tennessee.

To Simon Cameron[1]

Private & confidential.

Hon. Simon Cameron   Springfield, Ills.
My dear Sir: Jan. 13. 1861

At the suggestion of Mr. Sanderson,[2] and with hearty good-will besides, I herewith send you a letter dated Jan. 3rd.—the same in date, as the last you received from me. I thought best to give it that date, as it is, in some sort, to take the place of that letter. I learn, both, by a letter of Mr. Swett, and from Mr. Sanderson, that your feelings were wounded by the *terms* of my letter really of the 3rd. I wrote that letter under great anxiety, and perhaps I was not as guarded in it's terms as I should have been; but I beg you to be assured, I intended no offence. My great object was to have you act quickly—if possible, before the matter should be complicated with the Penn. Senatorial election. Destroy the offensive letter,[3] or return it to me.

I say to you now I have not doubted that you would perform the duties of a Department ably and faithfully. Nor have I for a moment intended to ostracise your friends. If I should make a cabinet appointment for Penn. before I reach Washington, I will not do so without consulting you, and giving all the weight to your views and wishes which I consistently can. This I have always intended. Yours truly   A. LINCOLN.

[*Enclosure*]

Hon. Simon Cameron   Springfield, Ills.
My dear Sir: Jan. 3. 1861

When you were here about the last of December, I handed you a letter saying I should at the proper time, nominate you to the Senate for a place in the cabinet. It is due to you, and to truth, for me to say you were here by my invitation, and not upon any suggestion of your own. You have not, as yet, signified to me, whether you would accept the appointment; and, with much pain, I now say to you, that you will relieve me from great embarrassment by allowing me to recall the offer. This springs from an unexpected complication; and not from any change of my view as to the ability or faithfulness with which you would discharge the duties of the place.

I now think I will not definitely fix upon any appointment for Pennsylvania until I reach Washington. Your Obt. Servt.

A. LINCOLN.

[1] ALS, DLC-Cameron Papers.
[2] John P. Sanderson, state senator and one of Cameron's confidential friends,

who had visited Lincoln on January 12 to reinforce Cameron's claim to an appointment.

³ Apparently Cameron did destroy this letter, but Lincoln had preserved a copy (q.v., January 3, *supra*).

To John E. Wool[1]

General John E. Wool   Springfield, Ills. Jany. 14. 1861

My dear Sir: Many thanks for your patriotic and generous letter of the 11th. Inst. As to how far the military force of the government may become necessary to the preservation of the Union; and, more particularly, how that force can best be directed to the object, I must rely chiefly upon Gen. Scott and yourself. It affords me the profoundest satisfaction to know, that with both of you, judgment and feeling, go heartily with your sense of professional and official duty, to the work.

It is true that I have given but little attention to the Military Department of government; but, be assured, I can not be ignorant as to who is Gen. Wool, or what he has done.

With my highest esteem and gratitude, I subscribe myself Your Obt. Servt.   A. LINCOLN

[1] ALS, IHi; copy, DLC-RTL. General Wool wrote on January 11 enclosing two printed letters containing his views, and added ". . . with me the preservation of the Union is paramount; and . . . I am prepared against all threats to see you safely placed in the Presidential chair . . . if my services as military commander . . . be deemed necessary." He added in a postscript, "Lest you may not know the part I have acted in behalf of my country, I send you . . . a pamphlet. . . ." (DLC-RTL).

To John G. Nicolay[1]

[January 14, 1861]

Mr. Nicolay will please make two copies of Gen. Wool's letter, and one copy of my answer to it.   LINCOLN

[1] AES, DLC-RTL.

Remarks Concerning Concessions to Secession[1]

[c. January 19-21, 1861]

I learn from a gentleman who had an interview with Mr. Lincoln, at Springfield, within the past week that the latter in discussing the existing state of affairs expressed himself as follows: —"I will suffer death before I will consent or will advise my friends to consent to any concession or compromise which looks like buying the privilege of taking possession of this government to which we have a constitutional right; because, whatever I might think of the merit of the various propositions before Congress, I should regard any concession in the face of menace the destruction of the government itself, and a consent on all hands that our system shall be brought down to a level with the existing disorganized state of affairs in Mexico. But this thing will hereafter be as it is now, in the hands of the people; and if they desire to call a Convention to remove any grievances complained of, or to give new guarantees for the permanence of vested rights, it is not mine to oppose."

[1] New York *Herald*, January 28, 1861. Although not a public pronouncement, these remarks, dated at Washington, January 27, were given such prominence in the press that they assumed the proportions of a public statement. Both the New York *Tribune* (February 4-28) and Chicago *Tribune* (February 9-21) carried the opening statement under "Mottoes for the Day" as a more or less official pronouncement. Representative William Kellogg who had conferred with Lincoln on compromise, January 19-21, was probably the "gentleman" who gave the text of Lincoln's remarks to the *Herald*.

To William H. Seward[1]

Private

Hon. W. H. Seward   Springfield, Ills.
My dear Sir   Jan. 19. 1861

Your two letters in relation to Gen. Cameron, are received. I have written him, by the hand of a confidential friend of his, in a way which I suppose will be satisfactory to him.

Your recent speech[2] is well received here; and, I think, is doing good all over the country.

I am glad of the opinion, expressed in your letter that the secessionists are already in danger of reaction. Yours truly

A. LINCOLN

[1] ALS, NAuE. Seward had written on January 13 that Cameron—"very much grieved by the result of the proposition to him of a Cabinet place. . . ." —would now insist that neither New Jersey nor Pennsylvania have a place in the cabinet, and that "by some explanation to be made to him he shall . . . be put before the public in a position as strong as he was before he was invited to go to Springfield. . . ." Again on January 15, Seward wrote, ". . . I now learn that there is a movement to satisfy you that it would be wise to appoint a gentleman in N Jersey . . . desired also by Pennsylvania. . . . I should dread exceedingly the army of Camerons friends in hostility. . . ." (DLC-RTL).

[2] Seward's speech in the Senate on January 12, outlining his conciliatory views on enforcement of the Fugitive Slave Law, the admission of territories, and the passing of laws to prevent invasion of states.

To Simon Cameron[1]

Hon. Simon Cameron.   Springfield, Ills.
My dear Sir   Jan. 21. 1861
   I shall be obliged if you will visit me again at this place. Your
Obt. Servt.   A. LINCOLN

[1] ALS, DLC-RTL. Evidently this letter was not sent. The envelope bears
Nicolay's notation: "Found sealed and opened/by me Sept 26th 1878/Jno.G.
Nicolay."

To Peter Page[1]

Private

Peter Page, Esq.   Springfield, Jany. 21st, 1861.
   Dear Sir: While an almost overwhelming amount of business
and correspondence has prevented my sooner answering your letter of the 3d inst., you may rest assured that it has neither been
forgotten nor overlooked. Permit me now to return you my heartfelt thanks for your very generous offer of both personal service
and pecuniary aid, to secure my inauguration. While it is a very
gratifying personal compliment to myself, I prize it more highly
as an evidence of the public loyalty and devotion to our Government which I am confident almost unanimously pervades the people of this state. Happily, I think there is no immediate necessity
for employing the proffered help, and while I hope the ten thousand dollars you propose to give may always be employed in the
peaceful channels of business or commerce, I am pleased to have
the assurance that in the event of trouble or danger, you and others
stand ready to give both your lives and your fortunes to the defense and maintenance of the government and the Union. Your
obedient Servant,   A. LINCOLN.

[1] Hertz, II, 802. Peter Page, a real estate dealer in Chicago, wrote January
3 to offer his personal services as a bodyguard and to be "one of one hundred
in Chicago to raise ten thousand dollars each rather than to submit to the hu-
miliating demands of the South. . . ." (DLC-RTL).

To Matias Romero[1]

Mr. Matias Romero.   Springfield, Ills.
My dear Sir: Jan. 21. 1861
   Allow me to thank you for your polite call, as Charge d'Affaires
of Mexico. While, as yet I can do no official act on behalf of the
United States, as one of it's citizens, I tender the expression of my

[177]

sincere wishes for the happiness, prosperity, and liberty of yourself, your government, and its people. Your Obt. Servt

A. LINCOLN

[1] ALS, IHi. Upon instructions from President Benito P. Juarez to ". . . proceed to the place of residence of President-elect Lincoln and in the name of this government . . . to make clear . . . the desire which animates President Juarez, of entering into the most cordial relations. . . .", Romero made a trip from Washington to Springfield and conferred with Lincoln on January 19 and 21 (Ocampo to Romero, December 22, 1860, Reservada, Numero 17, Archivo de Relationes Esteriores, Mexico, D.F.).

To S. Austin Allibone[1]

S. Austin Allibone, Esq   Springfield, Ills.
My dear Sir   Jan. 22/61

Yours of the 18th. with the manuscript letter of Genl. Wool, herewith returned, and newspaper slips, is received; and for all which, please accept my thanks. A few days since I received a highly valued letter from Gen. Wool himself, which, being marked *"private"* perhaps it were better not to speak of publicly. Yours truly   A. LINCOLN—

[1] ALS, MH-Nolen Collection. Samuel Austin Allibone, author and merchant at Philadelphia, wrote January 8 quoting recent letters from General John E. Wool and enclosing clippings. Since there is no letter of January 18, Lincoln was probably in error as to the date (DLC-RTL).

To Diplomatic Agents of the United States[1]

United States of America
State of Illinois
Springfield, Jany. 22, 1861

To all Diplomatic Agents of the United States of America in Europe.

Gentlemen: This will introduce to you C. M. Hardy Esq, a citizen of the State of Illinois, and United States of America, who goes on a tour of travel through Europe during the coming summer.

Mr. Hardy is reliably recommended to me as a highly intelligent, worthy and honorable gentleman; and any assistance or favor you may render him will be kindly remembered by himself and give me much gratification.

With high consideration I subscribe myself   Your obt. Servt.

A. LINCOLN

[1] ALS-P, ISLA. Charles M. Hardy of Rock Island, Illinois, wished to spend a summer in Europe (Hardy to Lincoln, January 1, 1861, DLC-RTL).

To Isaac Fenno[1]

Private

Isaac Fenno Esq   Springfield Ill.
Dear Sir   Jany 22 1861

Your note of the 1st inst., together with a very substantial and handsome overcoat which accompanied it by Express, were duly received by me, and would both have been acknowledged sooner but for the multifarious demands upon my time and attention.

Permit me now to thank you sincerely for your elegant and valuable New Year's Gift, and the many kind expressions of personal confidence and regard contained in your letter. Your obt Servt.   A. LINCOLN.

[1] LS, ICU. No correspondence from Fenno is in the Lincoln Papers, but he has been identified as a wholesale clothing dealer at Boston, Massachusetts.

Remarks to an Indiana Delegation[1]

January 22, 1861

Another Indiana delegation made their appearance this morning, consisting of a legislative committee, appointed under a joint resolution, to invite Mr. Lincoln to pass through the capital of the Hoosier State while on his way to Washington. They were received by the President elect in the course of the forenoon. In reply to their invitation, he stated that circumstances had as yet prevented him from definitely selecting any particular route; that he had seriously thought of going via Indianapolis, and would let them know his final decision in the course of the next fortnight.

[1] New York *Herald*, January 28, 1861.

Remarks to a Pennsylvania Delegation[1]

January 24, 1861

Dr. SMITH, Chairman of the Committee,[2] stated to Mr. LINCOLN the purpose of the resolutions intrusted to the care of the Committee, and had reached the point where it was stated that Pennsylvania desired to have in the Cabinet one who had ever been true to her interests, when Mr. LINCOLN interrupted him by saying:

"Yes, I know who you allude to—Gen. CAMERON. This subject has already engaged a large share of my attention, and I have every reason to hope that your wishes will be gratified. I feel a strong desire to do something for your big State, and I am determined she shall be satisfied, if I can do it."

The resolutions were read to him, when he continued, nearly in this language:

"Gentlemen, in the formation of my Cabinet, I shall aim as nearly as possible at perfection. Any man whom I may appoint to such a position, must be, as far as possible, like Caesar's wife, pure and above suspicion, of unblemished reputation, and undoubted integrity. I have already appointed Senator SEWARD and Mr. BATES, of Missouri, and they are men whose characters I think the breath of calumny cannot impeach. In regard to Gen. CAMERON, I have received assurances without limit from gentlemen whose word is entitled to credit, that he is eminently fitted for the position which his friends desire him to fill, and that his appointment would give great satisfaction to Pennsylvania. I have a great desire to appoint Gen. CAMERON, for the reason that he was formerly a Democrat, and I wish to give that element a fair representation in the distribution of the offices. Both Mr. SEWARD and Mr. BATES were formerly old line Whigs, and, for this reason, I feel a disposition to appoint Gen. CAMERON. But on the other hand, there is a strong opposition to him; not from his own State, it is true, for the opposition to him there is so slight that it is scarcely worth mentioning. The feeling against him appears to come from Ohio, and one or two of the other Western States. His opponents charge him with corruption in obtaining contracts, and contend that if he is appointed he will use the patronage of his office for his own private gain. I have no knowledge of the acts charged against him, but I intend to make an investigation of the whole matter, by allowing his opponents to submit their proof, and I shall give him an opportunity of explaining any part he may have had in the transactions alleged against him. For my own part, I can see no impropriety in his taking contracts, or making money out of them, as that is mere matter of business. There is nothing wrong in this, unless some unfairness or dishonesty is shown, which supposition I have no doubt Gen. CAMERON will be able to disprove. I shall deal fairly with him, but I say to you, gentlemen, frankly, that if the charges against him are proven, he cannot have a seat in my Cabinet, as I will not have any man associated with me whose character is impeached. I will say further, that if he vindicates himself, I have the strongest desire to place him in the position you wish him to fill, and which you think the interests of your State demand. If, after he has been appointed, I should be deceived by subsequent transactions of a disreputable character, the *responsibility will rest*

upon you gentlemen of Pennsylvania who have so strongly pre-
sented his claims to my consideration. But this is supposing a state
of things which may never occur."

[1] New York *Times*, February 7, 1861, copied from the Philadelphia *Mercury*.
[2] H. G. Smith, O. H. P. Parker, Peter Ford, and Charles Adams were the
committee representing the Republican Club of Philadelphia.

To R. A. Cameron, Walter March, and David C. Branham[1]

Springfield Jany 26th 1861.

Messrs Cameron, Marsh & Branham   Committee

Gentlemen—I have the honor to acknowledge the receipt, by
your hands, of a copy of a Joint Resolution, adopted by the Legislature of the State of Indiana, on the 15th. inst inviting me to visit
that honorable body on my way to the Federal Capital.

Expressing my profound graitude for this flattering testimonial
of their regard and esteem, be pleased to bear to them my acceptance of their kind invitation, and inform them that I will endeavor to visit them, in accordance with their expressed desire, on
the 12th of February next.

With feelings of high consideration, I remain   Your humble
servant   A LINCOLN

[1] Copy, DLC-RTL. The letter from the committee asking to see Lincoln, dated
at Springfield, January 22, bears the names "D. C. Branam" and "W. Marsh."
Other sources give the spelling as Branham and March.

To John Hanks[1]

Dear John   Springfield, Jan. 28. 1861

I now think I will pass Decatur, going to Coles, on the day after
to-morrow—Wednesday, the 30th. of the month. Be ready, and go
along. Yours as ever   A. LINCOLN

[1] ALS-F, ISLA. Lincoln spent January 31 with his stepmother in Coles
County.

To James Sulgrove, Eric Locke, William Wallace, and John F. Wood[1]

Springfield Ill. Jan. 28, 1861.

Messrs. James Sulgrove, Eric Locke, William Wallace, and John
F. Wood Committee

Gentlemen: I received to-day from the hands of Mr. Locke, a

transcript of the Resolutions passed at a meeting of the citizens of Indianapolis, inviting me to visit that city on my route to Washington.

Permit me to express to the citizens of Indianapolis, through you, their committee, my cordial thanks for the honor shown me. I accept with great pleasure the invitation so kindly tendered, and will be in your city on the 12th day of February next. Your obt. Servt.

A. LINCOLN

[1] LS copy, DLC-RTL.

Endorsement: Thomas Reynolds to Lincoln[1]

[c. January 29, 1861]

Answer this respectfully.

[1] AE, DLC-RTL. Reynolds' letter of January 29 invited Lincoln to use the Great Western Railway in Illinois on his trip to Washington.

Remarks at Charleston, Illinois[1]

January 31, 1861

He held a public reception in the town hall at Charleston, attended by hundreds of people. Being called upon to make a speech, he stated that the time for a public definition of the policy of his administration had not come, and that he could but express his gratification at seeing so many of his friends and give them a hearty greeting. Most of those in attendance then shook hands with him and dispersed, amidst enthusiastic cheering.

[1] New York *Herald*, February 4, 1861.

To Benjamin Eggleston, Charles L. Moore and A. McAlpin[1]

Springfield, Ill., Feb. 1, 1861.

Messrs. Benj. Eggleston, Charles L. Moore and A. McAlpin:

Gentlemen: Yours of to-day, communicating two resolutions— one of a Citizens' Meeting, and the other [of] the City Council, both of the City of Cincinnati, and inviting me to make that city a [stopping] point on my way to Washington—is received. With my grateful acknowledgments to the citizens, City Council and yourselves, gentlemen, I accept the kind invitation, with the understanding, however, that all ceremonies which would occupy much time, must be dispensed with. Your obedient servant,

A. LINCOLN.

[1] New York *Times*, February 8, 1861.

To William H. Seward[1]

Private & confidential.

Hon. W. H. Seward   Springfield, Ills. Feb. 1. 1861

My dear Sir On the 21st. ult. Hon. W. Kellogg, a Republican M.C of this state whom you probably know, was here, in a good deal of anxiety, seeking to ascertain to what extent I would be consenting for our friends to go in the way of compromise on the now vexed question. While he was with me I received a despatch from Senator Trumbull, at Washington, alluding to the same question, and telling me to await letters. I thereupon told Mr. Kellogg that when I should receive these letters, posting me as to the state of affairs at Washington, I would write you, requesting you to let him see my letter. To my surprise when the letters mentioned by Judge Trumbull came, they made no allusion to the "vexed question" This baffled me so much that I was near not writing you at all, in compliance with what I had said to Judge Kellogg.

I say now, however, as I have all the while said, that on the territorial question—that is, the question of extending slavery under the national auspices,—I am inflexible. I am for no compromise which *assists* or *permits* the extension of the institution on soil owned by the nation. And any trick by which the nation is to acquire territory, and then allow some local authority to spread slavery over it, is as obnoxious as any other.

I take it that to effect some such result as this, and to put us again on the high-road to a slave empire is the object of all these proposed compromises. I am against it.

As to fugitive slaves, District of Columbia, slave trade among the slave states, and whatever springs of necessity from the fact that the institution is amongst us, I care but little, so that what is done be comely, and not altogether outrageous. Nor do I care much about New-Mexico, if further extension were hedged against.
Yours very truly   A. LINCOLN—

[1] ALS, NAuE.

To Daniel Ullmann[1]

Hon. Daniel Ullmann: Springfield, Ill., Feb. 1, 1861.

Dear Sir:—Your kind letter of the 25th ult., and the express package containing the bronze medal of Mr. Clay, both came safely to hand this morning.

Permit me, in the first place, to return you my heartfelt thanks for your goodness in sending me this valuable present; and secondly, to express the extreme gratification I feel in possessing so beautiful a memento of him whom, during my whole political life, I have loved and revered as a teacher and leader. Your ob't servant,

A. LINCOLN.

[1] Chicago *Tribune*, February 14, 1861. Daniel Ullmann, a New York attorney who had been the Know-Nothing candidate for governor in 1854, wrote on January 25, that he was sending a bronze medal of Henry Clay—one of 150 which had been made some years before—which he had reserved ". . . with the intention . . . of presenting it to the citizen of the school of Henry Clay, who should first be elected to the Presidency of the United States. . . ." (DLC-RTL).

To George D. Prentice[1]

Private

Geo. D. Prentice, Esq   Springfield, Ills. Feb. 2, 1861

My dear Sir   Yours of the 31st. ult. requesting a copy of the inaugeral is received. I have the document already blocked out; but in the now rapidly shifting scenes, I shall have to hold it subject to revision up to near the time of delivery. So soon as it shall take what I can regard as it's final shape, I shall remember, if I can, to send you a copy. Yours very truly   A. LINCOLN

[1] ALS, CSmH.

To Andrew G. Curtin[1]

Hon. Andrew G. Curtin   Springfield, Ills.

My dear Sir.   Feb. 4. 1861

Mr. S. Newton Pettis[2] handed me your letter introducing him, to-day. He tells me he thinks you suspect that an impression unfavorable to you, has somehow been made upon me. I beg you to be assured this is a mistake. When I have friends who disagree with each other, I am very slow to take sides in their quarrel. I expect, on my winding way to Washington, to make brief stops at Pittsburgh, Philadelphia, and Harrisburg; and I shall be glad to meet you at any or all those places; or in fact, at any other place. Yours very truly   A. LINCOLN

[1] ALS, IHi.

[2] Solomon Newton Pettis was an attorney at Meadville, Pennsylvania, whom Lincoln appointed associate justice for Colorado Territory in 1861.

Endorsement: Geza Mihalotzy to Lincoln[1]

[c. February 4, 1861]

I cheerfully grant the request above made.   A. LINCOLN

[1] AES, ICHi. Captain Geza Mihalotzy of a newly organized company of militia in Chicago wrote on February 4 asking permission to ". . . entitle ourselves 'Lincoln Riflemen,' of Slavonic Origin."

To Edwin D. Morgan[1]

Springfield Ill Feby 4th 1861.

Sir: Your letter of the 30th ult. inviting me on behalf of the Legislature of New York to pass through that State on my route to Washington, and tendering me the hospitalities of her authorities and people, has been duly received.

With feelings of deep gratitude to you and them, for this testimonial of regard and esteem, I beg you to notify them that I accept the invitation so kindly extended. Your obt. Servt.

His Excellency E. D. Morgan   A. LINCOLN
Governor of New York

P.S.—Please let ceremonies be only such as to take the least time possible. A. L.

[1] LS, N. The letter is in Nicolay's handwriting and probably was composed by him, but the postscript was added by Lincoln. Nicolay had written Morgan on Lincoln's instruction, February 1, 1861, that Lincoln had not replied to Morgan's invitation of January 19 only because he had thought the legislature might pass a resolution inviting him and wished to reply to both at the same time (DLC-RTL).

To Thurlow Weed[1]

Private

Thurlow Weed, Esq   Springfield, Ills. Feb. 4, 1861

My dear Sir. I have both your letter to myself, and that to Judge Davis, in relation to a certain gentleman in your state claiming to dispense patronage in my name, and also to be authorized to use my name to advance the chances of Mr. Greely for an election to the U.S. Senate. It is very strange that such things should be said by any one. The gentleman you mention, did speak to me of Mr. Greely, in connection with the Senatorial election, and I replied in terms of kindness towards Mr. Greely which I really feel, but always with an express protest that my name *must* not be used in the Senatorial election, in favor of, or against any one. Any other representation of me, is a misrepresentation.

As to the matter of dispensing patronage, it perhaps will surprise you to learn, that I have information that *you* claim to have my authority to arrange that matter in N.Y. I do not believe you have so claimed; but still so some men say. On that subject you know all I have said to you is "justice to all," and I beg you to believe I have said nothing more particular to any one. I say this to re-assure you that I have not changed my purpose; in the hope however, that you will not use my name in the matter. Yours truly

A. LINCOLN.

[185]

1 ALS, NRU-Weed Papers on deposit. Weed wrote both Lincoln and David Davis on January 28 that New York *Tribune* stockholder and state representative from Westchester, Benjamin F. Camp, was representing that Lincoln favored Greeley's election to the Senate, and that he (Camp) would, in the event of Greeley's election, have the disposal of New York patronage. Davis enclosed Weed's letter with one of his own, February 2, suggesting that it might be wise to telegraph or write Weed ". . . to set yourself right." (DLC-RTL).

To Charles S. Olden[1]

Springfield Ill Feby 6th 1861.

Sir: Your letter of the 1st inst. inviting me, in compliance with the request of the Legislature of New Jersey, to visit your State Capital while on my journey to Washington, has been duly received.

I accept the invitation, with much gratitude to you and them for the kindness and honor thus offered. Your obt. Servt.

His Excellency Chas. S Olden   A. LINCOLN
Governor of New Jersey

P.S. Please arrange no ceremonies that will waste time.

1 Copy, DLC-RTL.

To John A. Andrew and the Senate and House of Representatives of Massachusetts[1]

Springfield, Ills. Feb. 7, 1861

His Excellency, the Governor, the President of the Senate, and the Speaker of the House of Representatives, for the Commonwealth of Massachusetts—

Gentlemen Your kind letter of Feb. 1st., with a copy of the resolution of the General Court, inviting me, in the name of the government and People of Massachusetts, to visit the State, and accept its hospitality, previous to the time of the Presidential inaugeration, is gratefully received by the hand of Col. Horace Binney Sargent; and, in answer, I am constrained to say want of time, denies me the pleasure of accepting the invitation so generously tendered. Your Obedient Servant   A. LINCOLN.

1 ALS copy, DLC-RTL; LS, CSmH. The letter sent is copied in Nicolay's hand and signed by Lincoln.

To William Dennison[1]

Springfield Ill Feb 7th 1861.

Sir: Your letter of the 31st ult. inviting me, on behalf of the Legislature of Ohio, to visit Columbus, on my way to Washington, has been duly received.

With profound gratitude for the mark of respect and honor thus cordially tendered me by you and them, I accept the invitation. Your obt Servt.   A LINCOLN

His Excellency W. Dennison
Governor of Ohio
Please arrange no ceremonies which will waste time.

¹ Copy, DLC-RTL.

To Norman B. Judd[1]

Hon. N. B. Judd—   Springfield, Ills.
My dear Sir   Feb. 7, 1861
If it shall not incommode you, your company, on the whole, or any part of my journey to Washington, will be very agreeable to me. Yours as ever   A. LINCOLN.

¹ ALS, owned by Verne Miners, Chicago, Illinois.

To John G. Lowe, Thomas A. Phillips, and W. H. Gillespie[1]

Springfield Ill. Feby 7th 1861.
Gentlemen: Your note of to-day, inviting me while on my way to Washington, to pass through the town and accept the hospitalities of the citizens of Dayton, Ohio, is before me.

A want of the necessary time makes it impossible for me to stop in your town. If it will not retard my arrival at or departure from the city of Columbus, I will endeavor to pass through and at least bow to the friends there; if, however it would in any wise delay me, they must not even expect this, but be content instead to receive through you, my warmest thanks for the kindness and cordiality with which they have tendered this invitation. Your obt Servt.   A. LINCOLN

Messrs. J. G. Lowe, T A. Phillips & W H Gillespie
committee.

¹ Copy, DLC-RTL. That Nicolay composed Lincoln's reply is indicated by Lincoln's autograph note on the verso of the letter of invitation from Lowe, Phillips, and Gillespie: "Mr. Nicolay will answer this that I will pass through Dayton, and bow to the friends there, if I can get to and from Columbus just as soon; otherwise not. Lincoln." John G. Lowe was an attorney; Thomas A. Phillips, a cotton manufacturer; and W. H. Gillespie, the mayor, of Dayton, Ohio.

To Darwin A. Finney and Others[1]

Hon. D. A. Finly & others   Springfield, Ills.
  Committee.   Feb. 8, 1861

Gentlemen: Yours of the 4th., inviting me, on behalf of the Legislature of Pennsylvania, to visit Harrisburg on my way to the Federal Capital, is received; and, in answer, allow me to say, I gratefully accept the tendered honor.

The time of arrival, and other details, are subject to future arrangement Your Obt. Servt.   A. LINCOLN—

[1] ALS copy, DLC-RTL. Darwin A. Finney, whose name Lincoln misspelled, was state senator from Crawford County, Pennsylvania.

To George B. Senter and Others[1]

Geo. B. Senter & others,   Springfield, Ills.
  Committee   Feb. 8, 1861

Gentlemen Yours of the 6th. inviting me, in compliance with a resolution of the city council, of the City of Cleveland, Ohio, to visit that city on my contemplated journey to Washington, is duly to hand; and, in answer, I have the honor to accept the invitation. The time of arrival, and other details, are subject to future arrangement. Your Obt. Servt.   A. LINCOLN—

[1] ALS copy, DLC-RTL; LS, OClWHi. George B. Senter was mayor of Cleveland, Ohio.

Receipt for Notes Left with Robert Irwin for Collection[1]

[February 9? 1861]

Abraham Lincoln leaves with the under-signed for safe-keeping, and to receive interest, the following papers—

One note of A. J. Van Deren, J. M. Vanderen, Cyrus W. Van Deren, security, and Lewis Johnson, for one thousand dollars, ballance due, interest at ten per cent, paid up to March 18– 1861.

Two notes of N. W. Edwards, together amounting to fifteen hundred and eighty seven dollars and ninety cents, interest at ten per cent due from Jan 16. 1860.

Two notes of Smith, Edwards & Co, for aggregate ballance of one thousand dollars, and interest at ten per cent from Jan. 16. 1861.

One note of J. K. Lewis and Thomas Lewis, for one hundred and fifty dollars, interest at ten per cent due from April 22, 1860.

One note, and mortgage of Isaac Lindsay, for six hundred dollars, interest at [te]n per cent, due from August 28. 1860.

One note & mortgage, of William Cline, for Seven hundred and fifty dollars, interest at ten per cent from Nov. 22. 1859.

One note & mortgage of J. Ruckel, for five hundred dollars, interest at ten per cent, due from Sep 28– 1860.

One note of John Cook, for seven hundred and fifty dollars, interest due, from April 17, 1860.

One Springfield City bond, for one thousand dollars reduced by two payments to $666.67.

One Certificate of Six shares of Alton & Sangamon Railroad stock

One certificate of Scholarship in Illinois State University.

One note of N. B. Judd, for three thousand dollars, with interest at ten per cent from Sep 1. 1859.

    Policy of Insurance

    Lease of house

    Notes on Haines,[2]   Rob. Irwin

[1] AD, owned by Springfield Marine Bank, Springfield, Illinois. Only the signature is not in Lincoln's hand. With the receipt is a certification by David Davis, administrator of Lincoln's estate, that all the notes were collected in the amount of $9,044.41, ". . . except the note on N B. Judd, & the shares in the Alton & Sangamon R R. . . ." The notes represented loans to residents of Sangamon County, with the exception of Norman B. Judd's of Chicago. Previously unidentified are Archibald J., John M., and Cyrus W. Van Deren, brothers, and their brother-in-law, Lewis Johnson; Joseph K. Lewis and William Cline, Sangamon County farmers; and Thomas Lewis, brother of Joseph, a Springfield banker. Smith, Edwards & Company was John T. Smith and Ninian W. Edwards (later Smith, Wickersham & Company), dry goods merchants.

[2] A. and Jonathan Haines of Pekin, Illinois, for legal fees.

Receipt to Samuel H. Melvin[1]

S. H. Melvin.   February 9, 1861

              Bot. of A. Lincoln.

6 Chairs	2 00	12 00
1 Spring Mattress		26 00
1 Wardrobe		20 00
1 Whatnot		10 00
1 Stand		1 50
9½ yds Stair Carpet	50	4 75
4 Comforters	2 00	8 00
		$82.25

              Recd payment

Springfield   A. Lincoln

Feby 9th 1861

[1] DS, owned by E. P. Melvin, Pasadena, California. Samuel H. Melvin was a wholesale and retail dealer in drugs and medical supplies in Springfield.

Farewell Address at Springfield, Illinois[1]

[A. Version]

February 11, 1861

My friends—No one, not in my situation, can appreciate my feeling of sadness at this parting. To this place, and the kindness of these people, I owe every thing. Here I have lived a quarter of a century, and have passed from a young to an old man. Here my children have been born, and one is buried. I now[2] leave, not knowing when, or whether ever, I may return, with a task before me greater than that which rested upon Washington. Without the assistance of that Divine Being, who ever attended him, I cannot succeed. With that assistance I cannot fail. Trusting in Him, who can go with me, and remain with you and be every where for good,[3] let us confidently hope that all will yet be well. To His care commending you, as I hope in your prayers you will commend me, I bid you an affectionate farewell

[B. Version][4]

My Friends:

No one not in my position can appreciate the sadness I feel at this parting. To this people I owe all that I am. Here I have lived more than a quarter of a century; here my children were born, and here one of them lies buried. I know not how soon I shall see you again. A duty devolves upon me which is, perhaps, greater than that which has devolved upon any other man since the days of Washington. He never would have succeeded except for the aid of Divine Providence, upon which he at all times relied. I feel that I cannot succeed without the same Divine aid which sustained him, and on the same Almighty Being I place my reliance for support, and I hope you, my friends, will all pray that I may receive that Divine assistance without which I cannot succeed, but with which success is certain. Again I bid you an affectionate farewell.

[C. Version][5]

Friends,

No one who has never been placed in a like position, can understand my feelings at this hour, nor the oppressive sadness I feel at this parting. For more than a quarter of a century I have lived among you, and during all that time I have received nothing but kindness at your hands. Here I have lived from my youth until now I am an old man. Here the most sacred ties of earth were assumed; here all my children were born; and here one of them lies buried. To you, dear friends, I owe all that I have, all that I am.

All the strange, chequered past seems to crowd now upon my mind. To-day I leave you; I go to assume a task more difficult than that which devolved upon General Washington. Unless the great God who assisted him, shall be with and aid me, I must fail. But if the same omniscient mind, and Almighty arm that directed and protected him, shall guide and support me, I shall not fail, I shall succeed. Let us all pray that the God of our fathers may not forsake us now. To him I commend you all—permit me to ask that with equal security and faith, you all will invoke His wisdom and guidance for me. With these few words I must leave you—for how long I know not. Friends, one and all, I must now bid you an affectionate farewell.

[1] AD, DLC-RTL. Written down in pencil after the event, as the train was leaving Springfield, the manuscript begins in Lincoln's handwriting and concludes in Nicolay's. Both Lincoln's and Nicolay's portions are, though cramped and irregular, very legibly and deliberately written. Henry Villard's story that he at one time had the pencilled manuscript and lost it, may or may not be true. His statement that John Hay took notes and that a stenographer was present, may also be true, but these documents have not been found. The other versions given below may stem from these sources. For Villard's account see *Lincoln on the Eve of '61, A Journalist's Story,* edited by Harold G. and Oswald Garrison Villard (1941) and *Memoirs of Henry Villard* (1904).

[2] Lincoln's handwriting ends and Nicolay's begins.

[3] The remainder of this sentence is in Lincoln's handwriting.

[4] This version is from a broadside distributed in April, 1865, by The American News Company of New York (PHi; IHi). It is in all but a few marks of punctuation identical with that which appeared in *Harper's Weekly* and various eastern newspapers on February 12, 1861.

[5] *Illinois State Journal,* February 12, 1861. Some authorities, beginning with Herndon, regard this text as the most accurate one. If this version was taken down as Lincoln spoke, this may be so. Unfortunately, however, no verification of this possibility, earlier than Villard's, exists, and his account contains too many discrepancies to be accepted verbatim.

Remarks at Tolono, Illinois[1]

February 11, 1861

I am leaving you on an errand of national importance, attended, as you are aware, with considerable difficulties. Let us believe, as some poet has expressed it:—

Behind the cloud the sun is still shining.

I bid you an affectionate farewell.

[1] New York *Tribune* and New York *Herald,* February 12, 1861.

Remarks at Danville, Illinois[1]

February 11, 1861

Mr. Lincoln again stepped out, and addressing himself to the enthusiastic gathering, remarked, that if he had any blessings to dispense, he would certainly dispense the largest and roundest to his good old friends of Vermillion county.

1 New York *Herald*, February 12, 1861.

Remarks at Indiana State Line[1]

February 11, 1861

Gentlemen of Indiana; I am happy to meet you on this occasion, and enter again the state of my early life, and almost of maturity. I am under many obligations to you for your kind reception, and to Indiana for the aid she rendered our cause which, I think, a just one. Gentlemen, I shall address you at greater length at Indianapolis, but not much greater. Again gentlemen, I thank you for your warm hearted reception.

1 *The Courier*, Lafayette, Indiana, February 12, 1861.

Speech at Lafayette, Indiana[1]

February 11, 1861

FELLOW CITIZENS:—We have seen great changes within the recollection of some of us who are the older. When I first came to the west, some 44 or 45 years ago, at sundown you had completed a journey of some 30 miles which you had commenced at sunrise, and thought you had done well. Now only six hours have elapsed since I left my home in Illinois where I was surrounded by a large concourse of my fellow citizens, almost all of whom I could recognize, and I find myself far from home surrounded by the thousands I now see before me, who are strangers to me. Still we are bound together, I trust in christianity, civilization and patriotism, and are attached to our country and our whole country. While some of us may differ in political opinions, still we are all united in one feeling for the Union. We all believe in the maintainance of the Union, of every star and every stripe of the glorious flag, and permit me to express the sentiment that upon the union of the States, there shall be between us no difference. My friends, I meet many friends at every place on my journey, and I should weary myself should I talk at length, therefore permit me to bid you an affectionate farewell.

1 *The Courier*, Lafayette, Indiana, February 12, 1861.

Remarks at Thorntown and Lebanon, Indiana[1]

February 11, 1861

At Thorntown he was betrayed into an anecdote to illustrate a point, and the train started before he got to the place where the laugh came in, and the people were left to wonder what the meaning might be. He was apologizing for not making a speech. He had heard of a man who was a candidate for a county office, who owned a horse that he set great store by, but he was a slow animal and sure footed. He had canvassed extensively with a good chance for the nomination. On the morning of the day of the convention, he mounted his favorite to go to the county seat, but in spite of whip and spur, his horse lagged on the road, biting at every bush, and when he arrived late in the evening, the convention was over and he was defeated. So of him, if he stopped at every station to make a stump speech he would not arrive at Washington until the inauguration was over. The Thorntown folks only heard the first part of the story, where the candidate was urging his steed to pass the juicy bushes. He laughed over the cutting short of his yarn, and when the train arrived at Lebanon he was jocularly told that some of the Thorntown folks had followed the train on foot, and were panting outside to hear the conclusion of the story. He told it over good-humoredly to the crowd at Lebanon. Every station along the road had its crowd—all anxious to see the man whose election to the first office in the gift of a free people has been the cause (whether with reason or not) of the distracted state of the country.

1 Indianapolis *Daily Sentinel*, February 12, 1861.

Reply to Oliver P. Morton
at Indianapolis, Indiana[1]

February 11, 1861

Gov. Morton and Fellow Citizens of the State of Indiana:

Most heartily do I thank you for this magnificent reception, and while I cannot take to myself any share of the compliment thus paid, more than that which pertains to a mere instrument, an accidental instrument, perhaps I should say, of a great cause, I yet must look upon it as a most magnificent reception, and as such, most heartily do I thank you for it.

You have been pleased to address yourselves to me chiefly[2] in behalf of this glorious Union in which we live, in all of which you have my hearty sympathy, and, as far as may be within my power, will have, one[3] and inseparably, my hearty consideration. While I do not expect, upon this occasion, or on any occasion, till after[4] I get to Washington, to attempt any lengthy speech, I will only say that to the salvation of this Union there needs but one single thing—the hearts of a people like yours. [Applause.] When the people[5] rise in masses in behalf of the Union and the liberties of their country, truly may it be said, "The gates of hell shall not prevail against them." [Renewed applause.]

In all the trying positions in which I shall be placed, and doubtless I shall be placed in many trying ones,[6] my reliance will be placed upon you and the people of the United States—and I wish you to remember now and forever, that it is your business, and not mine; that if the union of these States, and the liberties of this people, shall be lost, it is but little to any one man of fifty-two years of age, but a great deal to the thirty millions of people who inhabit these United States, and to their posterity in all coming time. It is your business to rise up and preserve the Union and liberty, for yourselves, and not for me. I desire they shall be constitutionally preserved.

I, as already intimated, am but an accidental instrument, temporary, and to serve but for a limited time, but I appeal to you again to constantly[7] bear in mind that with you, and not with politicians, not with Presidents, not with office-seekers, but with you, is the question, "Shall the Union and shall the liberties of this country be preserved to the latest generation?" [Loud and prolonged applause.]

[1] Indianapolis *Journal* and Cincinnati *Daily Gazette*, February 12; and Cincinnati *Daily Commercial*, February 13, 1861. These papers report the speech better than the Indianapolis *Daily Sentinel*, but no one of the three reports is wholly reliable. Our text is a collation of all three. Although we have chosen the most probable reading, in instances where the variant word or phrase may have some claim, it is given in a footnote. Lincoln spoke from the rear platform in reply to Governor Morton, who welcomed him from an open barouche drawn up beside the train.   [2] *Gazette* has "cheerily."

[3] *Commercial* has "now."

[4] *Journal* and *Commercial* have "or until" and omit the preceding "or on any occasion."

[5] *Journal* and *Commercial* have "The people, when they rise. . . ."

[6] *Journal* and *Commercial* have "such" instead of "trying ones."

[7] *Gazette* has "continue to" instead of "constantly."

Speech from the Balcony of the Bates House at Indianapolis, Indiana[1]

February 11, 1861

It is not possible, in my journey to the national capital, to address assemblies like this which may do me the great honor to meet me as you have done, but very briefly. I should be entirely worn out if I were to attempt it. I appear before you now to thank you for this very magnificent welcome which you have given me, and still more for the very generous support which your State recently gave to the political cause of the whole country, and the whole world. [Applause.] Solomon has said, that there is a time to keep silence. [Renewed and deafening applause.] * * * * *2 We know certain that they mean the same thing while using the same words now, and it perhaps would be as well if they would keep silence.

The words "coercion" and "invasion" are in great use about these days. Suppose we were simply to try if we can, and ascertain what, is the meaning of these words. Let us get, if we can, the exact definitions of these words—not from dictionaries, but from the men who constantly repeat them—what things they mean to express by the words. What, then, is "coercion"? What is "invasion"? Would the marching of an army into South Carolina, for instance, without the consent of her people, and in hostility against them, be coercion or invasion? I very frankly say, I think it would be invasion, and it would be coercion too, if the people of that country were forced to submit. But if the Government, for instance, but simply insists upon holding its own forts, or retaking those forts which belong to it,—[cheers,]—or the enforcement of the laws of the United States in the collection of duties upon foreign importations,—[renewed cheers,]—or even the withdrawal of the mails from those portions of the country where the mails themselves are habitually violated; would any or all of these things be coercion? Do the lovers of the Union contend that they will resist coercion or invasion of any State, understanding that any or all of these would be coercing or invading a State? If they do, then it occurs to me that the means for the preservation of the Union they so greatly love, in their own estimation, is of a very thin and airy character. [Applause.] If sick, they would consider the little pills of the homoepathist as already too large for them to swallow. In their view, the Union, as a family relation, would not be anything like a regular marriage at all, but only as a sort of free-love arrangement,—[laughter,]—to be maintained on what that sect calls passionate attraction. [Continued laughter.] But, my friends, enough of this.

What is the particular sacredness of a State? I speak not of that position which is given to a State in and by the Constitution of the United States, for that all of us agree to—we abide by; but that position assumed, that a State can carry with it out of the Union that which it holds in sacredness by virtue of its connection with the Union. I am speaking of that assumed right of a State, as a primary principle, that the Constitution should rule all that is less than itself, and ruin all that is bigger than itself. [Laughter.] But,

I ask, wherein does consist that right? If a State, in one instance, and a county in another, should be equal in extent of territory, and equal in the number of people, wherein is that State any better than the county? Can a change of name change the right? By what principle of original right is it that one-fiftieth or one-ninetieth of a great nation, by calling themselves a State, have the right to break up and ruin that nation as a matter of original principle? Now, I ask the question—I am not deciding anything—[laughter,] —and with the request that you will think somewhat upon that subject and decide for yourselves, if you choose, when you get ready,—where is the mysterious, original right, from principle, for a certain district of country with inhabitants, by merely being called a State, to play tyrant over all its own citizens, and deny the authority of everything greater than itself. [Laughter.] I say I am deciding nothing, but simply giving something for you to reflect upon; and, with having said this much, and having declared, in the start, that I will make no long speeches, I thank you again for this magnificent welcome, and bid you an affectionate farewell. [Cheers.]

1 Indianapolis *Daily Sentinel*, February 12, 1861. Although the text printed in the Indianapolis *Journal*, February 12, Cincinnati *Daily Commercial* and New York *Tribune*, February 13, purports to have been revised by Lincoln, it omits colorful sentences and even necessary phrases undoubtedly spoken by Lincoln. Space scarcely justifies inclusion of both versions, and on the ground that Lincoln's revision, if made, must have been exceedingly hurried, the editors have chosen the *Sentinel* text as the better of the two.

2 Asterisks are in the original. No other report supplies the omitted passage, which was apparently lost by the reporter in the cheering.

Remarks from the Balcony at Bates House, Indianapolis, Indiana[1]

February 11, 1861

Last night, previous to Mr. Lincoln's departure from the Bates House, he was again introduced from the balcony, by the Hon. Sol. Meredith. Mr. Lincoln said he had no speech to make. If he made speeches whenever his friends desired, he would not be able to reach the National Capital at the appointed time. He once more thanked the assemblage for the reception, and trusted we all might meet again under one flag of one Union. He bade them affectionate farewell.

1 New York *Tribune*, February 13, 1861. The next morning prior to his departure from the Bates House, Lincoln was introduced again from the balcony and made practically the same remarks (Cincinnati *Daily Commercial*, February 13, 1861).

Remarks at Lawrenceburg, Indiana[1]

February 12, 1861

My fellow-countrymen. You call upon me for a speech; I have none to give to you, and have not sufficient time to devote to it if I had. I suppose you are all Union men here, (cheers and cries of "Right") and I suppose that you are in favor of doing full justice to all, whether on that side of the river (pointing to the Kentucky shore), or on your own. (Loud cheering and cries of "We are.") If the politicians and leaders of parties were as true as the PEOPLE, there would be little fear that the peace of the country would be disturbed. I have been selected to fill an important office for a brief period, and am now, in your eyes, invested with an influence which will soon pass away; but should my administration prove to be a very wicked one, or what is more probable, a very foolish one, if you, the PEOPLE, are but true to yourselves and to the Constitution, there is but little harm I can do, *thank God!*

[1] Cincinnati *Daily Commercial*, February 13, 1861. Of the several newspaper reports of this speech, this seems to be the only attempt at a complete verbatim report.

Reply to Robert Hosea, Cincinnati, Ohio[1]

February 12, 1861

Mr. CHAIRMAN:—I thank you, citizens of Cincinnati, Ohio, and Kentucky, for this reception. As I understand it is a part of the programme that I will address you a little more at length at the Burnet House, I will, for the present, postpone the making of any remarks. I will proceed at once from here. I remark here that it is not my purpose to make a lengthy speech.

[1] Cincinnati *Daily Commercial*, February 13, 1861. Robert Hosea, chairman of the reception committee, made a speech of welcome at the station where an immense throng had gathered.

Speech at Cincinnati, Ohio[1]

February 12, 1861

Mr. Mayor, ladies and gentlemen: Twenty-four hours ago, at the Capital of Indiana, I said to myself I have never seen so many people assembled together in winter weather. I am no longer able to say that. But it is what might reasonably have been expected— that this great city of Cincinnati would thus acquit herself on such an occasion. My friends, I am entirely overwhelmed by the magnificence of the reception which has been given, I will not say to

me, but to the President elect of the United States of America.
[Loud cheering.] Most heartily do I thank you, one and all for
it. [Applause.]

I am reminded by the address of your worthy Mayor, that this
reception is given not by any one political party, and even if I
had not been so reminded by His Honor I could not have failed to
know the fact by the extent of the multitude I see before me now.
I could not look upon this vast assemblage without being made
aware that all parties were united in this reception. [Applause.]
This is as it should be. It is as it should have been if Senator Douglas had been elected. It is as it should have been if Mr. Bell had
been elected—as it should have been if Mr. Breckinridge had been
elected—as it should ever be when any citizen of the United
States is constitutionally elected President of the United States.
(Great applause.) Allow me to say that I think what has occurred
here to-day could not have occurred in any other country on the
face of the globe, without the influence of the free institutions
which we have unceasingly enjoyed for three-quarters of a century. (Applause.) There is no country where the people can turn
out and enjoy this day precisely as they please, save under the
benign influence of the free institutions of our land. [Applause.]

I hope that, although we have some threatening National difficulties now—I hope that while these free institutions shall continue to be in the enjoyment of millions of free people of the
United States, we will see repeated every four years what we now
witness. [Applause.]

In a few short years, I and every other individual man who is
now living will pass away. I hope that our national difficulties will
also pass away, and I hope we shall see in the streets of Cincinnati
—good old Cincinnati—for centuries to come, once every four
years her people give such a reception as this to the constitutionally
elected President of the whole United States. [Applause.] I hope
you shall all join in that reception, and that you shall also welcome
your brethren far across the river to participate in it. We will welcome them in every State of the Union, no matter where they are
from. From away South we shall extend them a cordial good will
when our present differences shall have been forgotten and blown
to the winds forever. [Applause.]

I[2] have spoken but once, before this, in Cincinnati. That was
a year previous to the late Presidential election. On that occasion, in a playful manner, but with sincere words, I addressed
much of what I said, to the Kentuckians. I gave my opinion that
we, as Republicans, would ultimately beat them as democrats; but

that they could postpone that result longer by nominating Senator Douglas for the Presidency than they could in any other way. They did not, in any true sense of the word, nominate Douglas, and the result has come certainly as soon as even I expected. I also told them how I expected they would be treated, after they should have been beaten; and I now wish to re-call their attention to what I then said upon that subject. I then said: "When we do, as we say, beat you, you perhaps want to know what we will do with you. I will tell you, so far as I am authorized to speak for the opposition, what we mean to do with you. We mean to treat you, as near as we possibly can, as Washington, Jefferson, and Madison treated you. We mean to leave you alone, and in no way to interfere with your institution; to abide by all and every compromise of the constitution, and, in a word, coming back to the original proposition, to treat you, so far as degenerated men (if we have degenerated) may, according to the examples of those noble fathers —Washington, Jefferson and Madison. We mean to remember that you are as good as we; that there is no difference between us, other than the difference of circumstances. We mean to recognize, and bear in mind always, that you have as good hearts in your bosoms as other people, or as we claim to have, and treat you accordingly."

Fellow citizens of Kentucky—friends—bretheren, may I call you —in my new position, I see no occasion, and feel no inclination, to retract a word of this. [Applause.] If it shall not be made good, be assured, the fault shall not be mine. [Applause.]

And now, fellow citizens of Ohio, have you, who agree with him who now addresses you, in political sentiment—have you ever entertained other sentiments towards our brethren of Kentucky than those I have expressed to you. [Loud and continued cries of "No."] If not, then why shall we not, as heretofore, be recognized and acknowledged as brethren again, living in peace and harmony one with another? [Cries of "We will."] I take your response as the most reliable evidence that it may be so, along with other evidence, trusting that the good sense of the American people, on all sides of all rivers in America, under the Providence of God, who has never deserted us, that we shall again be brethren, forgetting all parties —ignoring all parties. My friends I now bid you farewell. [Long continued applause.]

1 Cincinnati *Daily Gazette*, February 13, 1861; AD, DLC-RTL. The Cincinnati *Daily Commercial*, February 13, reports the speech with considerable verbal variation from the *Gazette*, but without substantial difference. Collation being impossible because of the wide differences and there being little to justify printing both texts, the editors have chosen the *Gazette* as the better because it adheres closely to the three extant manuscript pages of the speech. Lincoln

spoke from the balcony of the Burnet House in reply to an introduction by Mayor Richard M. Bishop.

2 This and the next paragraph follow the autograph manuscript.

Fragment of Speech Intended for Kentuckians[1]

[c. February 12, 1861]

I am grateful, for the oppertunity your invitation affords me to appear before an audience of my native state. During the present winter it has been greatly pressed upon me by many patriotic citizens, Kentuckians among others, that I could in my position, by a word, restore peace to the country. But what word? I have many words already before the public; and my position was given me on the faith of those words. Is the desired word to be confirmatory of these; or must it be contradictory to them? If the former, it is useless repe[ti]tion; if the latter, it is dishonorable and treacherous.

Again, it is urged as if the word must be spoken before the fourth of March. Why? Is the speaking the word a *"sine qua non"* to the inauguration? Is there a Bell-man, a Breckinridge-man, or a Douglas man, who would tolerate his own candidate to make such terms, had he been elected? Who amongst you would not die by the proposition, that your candidate, being elected, should be inaugerated, solely on the conditions of the constitution, and laws, or not at all. What Kentuckian, worthy of his birth place, would not do this? Gentlemen, I too, am a Kentuckian.

Nor is this a matter of mere personal honor.[2] No man can be elected President without some opponents, as well as supporters; and if when elected, he can not be installed, till he first appeases his enemies, by breaking his pledges, and and [*sic*] betraying his friends, this government, and all popular government, is already at an end. Demands for such surrender, once recognized, and yielded to, are without limit, as to nature, extent, or repetition. They break the only bond of faith between public, and public servant; and they distinctly set the minority over the majority. Such demands acquiesced in, would not merely be the ruin of a man, or a party; but as a precedent they would ruin the government itself.

I do not deny the possibility that the people may err in an election; but if they do, the true [remedy] is in the next election, and not in the treachery of the person elected.

During[3] the winter just closed, I have been greatly urged, by many patriotic men, to lend the influence of my position to some compromise, by which I was, to some extent, to shift the ground

upon which I had been elected. This I steadily refused. I so refused, not from any party wantonness, nor from any indifference
to the troubles of the country. I thought such refusal was demanded
by the view that if, when a Chief Magistrate is constitutionally
elected, he cannot be inaugurated till he betrays those who elected
him, by breaking his pledges, and surrendering to those who tried
and failed to defeat him at the polls, this government and all popular government is already at an end. Demands for such surrender,
once recognized, are without limit, as to nature, extent and repetition. They break the only bond of faith between public and public servant; and they distinctly set the minority over the majority.

I presume there is not a man in America, (and there ought not
to be one) who opposed my election, who would, for a moment,
tolerate his own candidate in such surrender, had he been successful in the election. In such case they would all see, that such surrender would not be merely the ruin of a man, or a party; but, as a
precedent, would be the ruin of the government itself.

I do not deny the possibility that the people may err in an election; but if they do, the true cure is in the next election; and not
in the treachery of the party elected.

[1] AD, DLC-RTL. The five small pages of this manuscript and the three
pages of manuscript of the Cincinnati speech (*supra*) in which Lincoln speaks
to the Kentuckians, are written on the same lined note paper. On the back of
the fifth page is pasted a clipping from the first edition of the First Inaugural
Address (*vide infra*, p. 259, n. 77) which was printed in Springfield before Lincoln's departure for Washington. This indicates that Lincoln prepared the fragment prior to February 12, and that he contemplated a brief visit to his native
state while at Cincinnati, the nearest point in his itinerary.

[2] Lincoln revised this sentence to the form given. As first written it read: "If
when a Chief Magistrate is constitutionally elected, he can not be installed,
till he betrays those who elected him, by breaking his pledges, and surrendering
to his opponents, this government, and all popular government, is already at
an end."

[3] The remainder of the fragment is a clipping from the First Inaugural as
printed in Springfield, pasted on the back of the last page.

Speech to Germans at Cincinnati, Ohio[1]

February 12, 1861

[*Commercial* Version]

MR. CHAIRMAN: I thank you and those whom you represent, for
the compliment you have paid me, by tendering me this address.
In so far as there is an allusion to our present national difficulties,
which expresses, as you have said, the views of the gentlemen
present, I shall have to beg pardon for not entering fully upon
the questions, which the address you have now read, suggests.

[201]

I deem it my duty—a duty which I owe to my constituents—to you, gentlemen, that I should wait until the last moment, for a development of the present national difficulties, before I express myself decidedly what course I shall pursue. I hope, then, not to be false to anything that you have to expect of me.

I agree with you, Mr. Chairman, that the working men are the basis of all governments, for the plain reason that they are the most numerous, and as you added that those were the sentiments of the gentlemen present, representing not only the working class, but citizens of other callings than those of the mechanic, I am happy to concur with you in these sentiments, not only of the native born citizens, but also of the Germans and foreigners from other countries.

Mr. Chairman, I hold that while man exists, it is his duty to improve not only his own condition, but to assist in ameliorating mankind; and therefore, without entering upon the details of the question, I will simply say, that I am for those means which will give the greatest good to the greatest number.

In regard to the Homestead Law, I have to say that in so far as the Government lands can be disposed of, I am in favor of cutting up the wild lands into parcels, so that every poor man may have a home.

In regard to the Germans and foreigners, I esteem them no better than other people, nor any worse. [Cries of good.] It is not my nature, when I see a people borne down by the weight of their shackles—the oppression of tyranny—to make their life more bitter by heaping upon them greater burdens; but rather would I do all in my power to raise the yoke, than to add anything that would tend to crush them.

Inasmuch as our country is extensive and new, and the countries of Europe are densely populated, if there are any abroad who desire to make this the land of their adoption, it is not in my heart to throw aught in their way, to prevent them from coming to the United States.

Mr. Chairman, and Gentlemen, I will bid you an affectionate farewell.

[*Gazette* Version]

Mr. Chairman: I thank you and those you represent, for the compliment paid me by the tender of this address. In so far as there is an allusion to our present national difficulties, and the suggestion of the views of the gentlemen who present this address, I beg you will excuse me from entering particularly upon it. I deem it due to myself and the whole country, in the present extraordi-

nary condition of the country and of public opinion, that I should
wait and see the last development of public opinion before I give
my views or express myself at the time of the inauguration.
[Cheers.] I hope at that time to be false to nothing you have been
taught to expect of me. [Cheers.]

I agree with you, Mr. Chairman, and with the address of your
constituents, in the declaration that working men are the basis of
all governments. That remark is due to them more than to any
other class, for the reason that there are more of them than of
any other class. And as your address is presented to me not only
on behalf of workingmen, but especially of Germans, I may say
a word as to classes. I hold the value of life is to improve one's
condition. Whatever is calculated to advance the condition of the
honest, struggling laboring man, so far as my judgment will enable me to judge of a correct thing, I am for that thing.

An allusion has been made to the Homestead Law. I think it
worthy of consideration, and that the wild lands of the country
should be distributed so that every man should have the means
and opportunity of benefitting his condition. [Cheers.] I have
said I do not desire to enter into details, nor will I.

In regard to Germans and foreigners, I esteem foreigners no
better than other people, nor any worse. [Laughter and cheers.]
They are all of the great family of men, and if there is one shackle
upon any of them, it would be far better to lift the load from them
than to pile additional loads upon them. [Cheers.] And inasmuch
as the continent of America is comparatively a new country, and
the other countries of the world are old countries, there is more
room here, comparatively speaking, than there is there; and if
they can better their condition by leaving their old homes, there is
nothing in my heart to forbid them coming; and I bid them all
God speed. [Cheers.]

Again, gentlemen, thanking you for your address, I bid you
good night.

¹ Cincinnati *Daily Commercial* and *Daily Gazette*, February 13, 1861. Since
the two versions vary considerably, both are reproduced. Brackets in the text
are from the sources. Lincoln spoke in reply to a speech by Frederick Oberkline
(the *Gazette* gives "Oberkleine"), chairman of a committee representing eighteen German industrial associations that called in a body to pay their respects.

Remarks at London, Ohio¹

February 13, 1861

Fellow citizens, I do not appear before you to make a speech, and
have not strength nor time to do so. If I were to undertake to make

a speech at every station, I should be completely tuckered out (not Mr. L's term, but its equivalent) before I reached the capital.

I perceive a band of music present, and while the iron horse stops to water himself, I would prefer they should discourse in their more eloquent music than I am capable of.

1 London, Ohio, *National Democrat*, February 14, 1861. Although Lincoln made similar short speeches at other stops between Cincinnati and Columbus, Ohio, this is the only text which has been located in a contemporary newspaper.

Address to the Ohio Legislature, Columbus, Ohio[1]

February 13, 1861

MR. PRESIDENT AND MR. SPEAKER AND GENTLEMEN OF THE GENERAL ASSEMBLY:—It is true, as has been said by the President of the Senate, that very great responsibility rests upon me in the position to which the votes of the American people have called me. I am deeply sensible of that weighty responsibility. I cannot but know what you all know, that, without a name, perhaps without a reason why I should have a name, there has fallen upon me a task such as did not rest even upon the Father of his country, and so feeling I cannot but turn and look for the support without which it will be impossible for me to perform that great task. I turn, then, and look to the American people and to that God who has never forsaken them. Allusion has been made to the interest felt in relation to the policy of the new administration. In this I have received from some a degree of credit for having kept silence, and from others some deprecation. I still think that I was right. In the varying and repeatedly shifting scenes of the present, and without a precedent which could enable me to judge by the past, it has seemed fitting that before speaking upon the difficulties of the country, I should have gained a view of the whole field, to be sure, after all, being at liberty to modify and change the course of policy, as future events may make a change necessary. I have not maintained silence from any want of real anxiety. It is a good thing that there is no more than anxiety, for there is nothing going wrong. It is a consoling circumstance that when we look out there is nothing that really hurts anybody. We entertain different views upon political questions, but nobody is suffering anything. This is a most consoling circumstance, and from it we may conclude that all we want is time, patience and a reliance on that God who has never forsaken this people. Fellow citizens, what I have said, I have said altogether extemporaneously, and I will now come to a close.

¹ New York *Herald*, February 14, 1861. Other papers reported this speech without substantial variation from this text. Lincoln was introduced by Lieutenant Governor Robert C. Kirk.

Speech from the Steps of the Capitol at Columbus, Ohio¹

February 13, 1861

LADIES AND GENTLEMEN:—I appear before you only to address you briefly. I shall do little else than to thank you for this very kind reception, to greet you and bid you farewell. I should not find strength, if I were otherwise inclined, to repeat speeches of very great length, upon every occasion similar to this—although few so large—which will occur on my way to the Federal Capitol. The General Assembly of the great State of Ohio has just done me the honor to receive me, and to hear a few broken remarks from myself. Judging from what I see, I infer that that reception was one without party distinction, and one of entire kindness—one that had nothing in it beyond a feeling of the citizenship of the United States of America. Knowing, as I do, that any crowd, drawn together as this has been, is made up of the citizens near about, and that in this county of Franklin there is great difference of political sentiment, and those agreeing with me having a little the shortest row, (laughter,) from this, and the circumstances I have mentioned, I infer that you do me the honor to meet me here without distinction of party. I think this is as it should be. Many of you who were not favorable to the election of myself to the Presidency were favorable to the election of the distinguished Senator from the State in which I reside. If Senator Douglas had been elected to the Presidency in the late contest, I think my friends would have joined heartily in meeting and greeting him on his passage through your Capital, as you have me to-day. If any of the other candidates had been elected, I think it would have been altogether becoming and proper for all to have joined in showing honor, quite as well to the office, and the country, as to the man. The people are themselves honored by such a concentration. I am doubly thankful that you have appeared here to give me this greeting. It is not much to me, for I shall very soon pass away from you; but we have a large country and a large future before us, and the manifestations of good-will towards the government, and affection for the Union which you may exhibit are of immense value to you and your posterity forever. (Applause.) In this point of view it is that I thank you most heartily for the exhibition you have given me, and with this allow me to bid you an affectionate farewell. (Deafening applause and cheers.)

[1] *The Crisis* (Columbus), February 21, 1861. Lincoln addressed the crowd in front of the Capitol following his appearance before the legislature.

Remarks at Newark, Ohio[1]

February 14, 1861

I understand that arrangements were made for something of a speech from me here, when the train moved down, but it has gone so far that it has deprived me of addressing the many fair ladies assembled, while it has deprived them of observing my very interesting countenance. It is impossible for me to make you a speech: there is not time, so I bid you farewell.

[1] Newark *North American*, February 14, 1861.

Remarks at Cadiz Junction, Ohio[1]

February 14, 1861

After the tumult had subsided he spoke a few words to the people, thanking them for their kind reception, and stated that there were a great many stopping places between his home and Washington, and if he stopped at every one he would not get to Washington until after the Inauguration and that would not suit him. He had but time to thank them heartily for this kind and cordial farewell, when he was ushered into the dining room of the Parks House . . . .

 . . . .After dinner, Mr. Lincoln appeared on the platform of the car, and told the people that he could not make a speech, "as he was too full for utterance," but if they had time they would organize the train, and pass a vote of thanks to the people of Harrison County for the excellent dinner they had received, and especially to the lady of the house.

[1] Cadiz *Republican*, February 20, 1861; Cadiz *Sentinel*, February 20, 1861.

Speech at Steubenville, Ohio[1]

February 14, 1861

Mr. Chairman and Fellow-Citizens:—The subject of the short address which has been made to me, though not an unfamiliar one, involves so many points, that in the short time allotted to me, I shall not be able to make a full and proper response. Though the people have made me by electing me, the instrument to carry out the wishes expressed in the address, I greatly fear that I shall not be the repository of the ability to do so. Indeed I know I shall not, more than in purpose, unless sustained by the great body of the people, and by the Divine Power, without whose aid we can do nothing. We everywhere express devotion to the Constitution. I believe there is no difference in this respect, whether on this or on the other side of this majestic stream. I understand that on the other side, among our dissatisfied brethren, they are satisfied with the Constitution of the United States, if they can have their rights under the Constitution. The question is, as to what the Constitution means—"What are their rights under the Constitution?" That is all. To decide that, who shall be the judge? Can you think of any other, than the voice of the people? If the majority does not control, the minority must—would that be right? Would that be just or generous? Assuredly not! Though the majority may be wrong, and I will not undertake to say that they were not wrong in electing me, yet we must adhere to the principle that the majority shall rule. By your Constitution you have another chance in four years. No great harm can be done by us in that time—in that time there can be nobody hurt. If anything goes wrong, however, and you find you have made a mistake, elect a better man next time. There are plenty of them.

(Here the Engine whistled.) These points involve the discussion of many questions which I have not time to consider. I merely give them to you for your reflection. I almost regret that I alluded to it at all.

Ladies, gentlemen and friends, I thank you for this kind and overwhelming reception, and bid you farewell.

[1] *The American Union* (Steubenville), February 20, 1861.

Remarks at Wellsville, Ohio[1]

February 14, 1861

Mr. Lincoln came out on the hind platform of the rear car and, after the cheering had ceased, said that he made his appearance merely to pass a word of greeting, and then to bid farewell, as he said he had been informed that the train would halt just a minute and a half, consequently he would not be able to make a speech even if he were prepared to do so; that if he should make a speech at every station stopped at, he would not be able to reach Washington until after the 4th of March. Here some old, drunken chap rushed up with his paw extended, and asked if he would shake hands with him, saying at the same time, that he had not voted for him but for Douglas—a sad representative by the way—of Douglas Democracy. Mr. Lincoln shook hands with him and said if he and the other friends of Mr. Douglas would assist in keeping the ship of state afloat, that perhaps Mr. Douglas might be selected to pilot it sometime in the future, but if it were allowed to go to pieces now, Mr. Douglas would, of course, stand no chance hereafter. He said he would do what he could to preserve the Union and if the people would do the same, the thing would be accomplished.

1 New Lisbon, Ohio, *The Buckeye State,* February 21, 1861.

Remarks at Rochester, Pennsylvania[1]

February 14, 1861

He remarked that he had no speech to make, as it was impossible to speak at every point where his fellow citizens greeted him, and thanked them for this expression of their wishes toward him. He was now on his way to Washington, and about the 4th of March he would speak to all who chose to hear him. A voice in the crowd enquired "What will you do with the secessionists then?" Turning toward the direction of the voice, Mr. Lincoln replied, "My friend, that is a matter which I have under very grave consideration."

1 Beaver, Pennsylvania, *Argus,* February 20, 1861.

Remarks at the Monongahela House, Pittsburgh, Pennsylvania[1]

February 14, 1861

Fellow Citizens: We had an accident upon the road to-day, and were delayed till this late hour. I am sorry for this, inasmuch as it was my desire and intention to address the citizens of Pennsylvania, briefly, this evening, on what is properly styled their peculiar interest. And I still hope that some arrangement may be made to-morrow morning which will afford me the pleasure of talking to a larger number of my friends than can assemble in this hall. ["Go on now; there's enough here."] I have a great regard for Allegheny county. It is "the banner county of the Union," [cheers,] and rolled up an immense majority for what I, at least, consider a good cause. By a mere accident, and not through any merit of mine, it happened that I was the representative of that cause, and I acknowledge with all sincerity the high honor you have conferred on me. ["Three cheers for Honest Abe," and a voice saying, "It was no accident that elected you, but your own merits, and the worth of the cause."] I thank you, my fellow citizen, for your kind remark, and trust that I feel a becoming sense of the responsibility resting upon me. ["We know you do."]

I could not help thinking, my friends, as I traveled in the rain through your crowded streets, on my way here, that if all that people were in favor of the Union, it can certainly be in no great danger—it will be preserved. [A voice—"We are all Union men." Another voice—"That's so." A third voice—"No compromise." A fourth—"Three cheers for the Union."] But I am talking too long, longer than I ought. ["Oh, no! go on; split another rail." Laughter.] You know that it has not been my custom, since I started on the route to Washington, to make long speeches; I am rather inclined to silence, ["That's right"] and whether that be wise or not, it is at least more unusual now-a-days to find a man who can hold his tongue than to find one who cannot. [Laughter, and a voice—"No *rail*ery Abe."] I thank you, sincerely, for the warm reception I have received, and in the morning, if an arrangement can be made, of which I am not yet certain, I may have something to say to you of that "peculiar interest of Pennsylvania" before mentioned. ["Say it now, we are all attention."] Well, my friends, as it is not much I have to say, and as there may be some uncertainty of another opportunity, I will utter it now, if you will permit me to procure a few notes that are in my overcoat pocket. ["Certainly we will," and cheers.][2]

[1] Pittsburgh *Dispatch*, February 15, 1861. Lincoln spoke standing on a chair to the crowd assembled in the lobby.

[2] According to the *Dispatch*, Lincoln retired to get his notes and later appeared on the balcony outside the hotel to make the brief remarks (*infra*) announcing postponement of the speech until the next morning.

Remarks from Balcony of the Monongahela House, Pittsburgh, Pennsylvania[1]

February 14, 1861

Fellow-citizens, I have been prevailed upon by your committee to postpone my intended remarks to you until to-morrow, when we hope for more favorable weather, and I have made my appearance now only to afford you an opportunity of seeing, as clearly as may be, my beautiful countenance! [Loud laughter, and cheers.] In the morning at half-past eight o'clock I purpose speaking to you from this place. Until then, I bid you all good night.

1 Pittsburgh *Dispatch*, February 15, 1861.

Speech at Pittsburgh, Pennsylvania[1]

February 15, 1861

Mayor Wilson and Citizens of Pennsylvania: I most cordially thank his Honor Mayor Wilson, and the citizens of Pittsburg generally for this flattering reception. It is[2] the more grateful, because I know that, while it is not given to me alone, but to the cause which I represent, yet it is given under circumstances which clearly prove to me that there is good will and sincere feeling at the bottom of it.

And here, fellow citizens, I may remark that in every short address I have made to the people, and in every crowd through which I have passed of late, some allusion has been made to the present distracted condition of the country. It is naturally expected that I should say something upon this subject, but to touch upon it at all would involve an elaborate discussion of a great many questions and circumstances, would require more time than I can at present command, and would perhaps unnecessarily commit me upon matters which have not yet fully developed themselves. [Immense cheering, and cries of "good!" "that's right!"]

The condition of the country, fellow-citizens, is an extraordinary one, and fills the mind of every patriot with anxiety and solicitude. My intention is to give this subject all the consideration which I possibly can before I speak fully and definitely in regard to it— so that, when I do speak, I may be as nearly right as possible. And when I do speak, fellow-citizens, I hope to say nothing in opposition to the spirit of the Constitution, contrary to the integrity of the Union, or which will in any way prove inimical to the liberties of the people or to the peace of the whole country. And, fur-

1 Pittsburgh *Dispatch*, February 16, 1861. The *Dispatch* version has been selected in preference to that of the New York *Tribune* of the same date because it more closely parallels the incomplete manuscript in that portion of the speech and because it sounds more like Lincoln throughout. In some instances, however, where the *Dispatch* reporter seems to have missed a phrase, the *Tribune* variant is given in a footnote. The New York *Herald*, February 16, gives the same version as the *Tribune* and follows it with a shorter version taken from Lincoln's manuscript. The manuscript, preserved in the Lincoln Papers, is here printed following the *Dispatch* version. All brackets are in the source. Lincoln was introduced by Mayor George Wilson.

2 *Tribune* reads "I am," probably correctly.

thermore, when the time arrives for me to speak on this great subject, I hope to say nothing which will disappoint the reasonable expectations of any man, or disappoint the people generally throughout the country, especially if their expectations have been based upon anything which I may have heretofore said.

Notwithstanding the troubles across the river, [the speaker pointing southwardly, and smiling] there is really no crisis, springing from anything in the government itself. In plain words, there is really no crisis except an *artificial one!* What is there now to warrant the condition of affairs presented by our friends "over the river?" Take even their own view of the questions involved, and there is nothing to justify the course which they are pursuing. I repeat it, then—*there is no crisis,* excepting such a one as may be gotten up at any time by designing politicians.[3] My advice, then, under such circumstances, is to keep cool. If the great American people will only keep their temper, on both sides of the line, the troubles will come to an end, and the question which now distracts the country will be settled just as surely as all other difficulties of like character which have originated in this government have been adjusted. Let the people on both sides keep their self-possession, and just as other clouds have cleared away in due time, so will this, and this great nation shall continue to prosper as heretofore. But, fellow citizens, I have spoken longer on this subject than I had intended in the outset—and I shall say no more at present.

Fellow citizens, as this is the first opportunity[4] which I have had to address a Pennsylvania assemblage, it seems a fitting time to indulge in a few remarks upon the important question of a tariff—a subject of great magnitude, and one which is attended with many difficulties, owing to the great variety of interests which it involves. So long as direct taxation for the support of government is not resorted to, a tariff is necessary. The tariff is to the government what a meal is to the family; but, while this is admitted, it still becomes necessary to modify and change its operations according to new interests and new circumstances. So far there is little difference of opinion among politicians, but the question as to how far imposts may be adjusted for the protection of home industry, gives rise to various views and objections. I must confess that I do not understand this subject in all its multiform bearings, but I promise you that I will give it my closest attention, and endeavor to comprehend it more fully. And here I may remark that the Chicago

---

[3] *Tribune* reads "by turbulent men, aided by designing politicians."

[4] Compare the remainder of the speech with the prepared manuscript, *infra.*

platform contains a plank upon this subject, which I think should be regarded as law for the incoming administration. In fact, this question, as well as all other subjects embodied in that platform, should not be varied from what we gave the people to understand would be our policy when we obtained their votes. Permit me, fellow citizens, to read the tariff plank of the Chicago platform, or rather, to have it read in your hearing by one who has younger eyes than I have.

Mr. Lincoln's private Secretary then read section twelfth of the Chicago platform, as follows:

That, while providing revenue for the support of the General Government by duties upon imposts, sound policy requires such an adjustment of the imposts as to encourage the development of the industrial interest of the whole country, and we commend that policy of national exchanges which secures to the working men liberal wages, to agriculture remunerating prices, to mechanics and manufacturers an adequate reward for their skill, labor and enterprise, and to the nation commercial prosperity and independence.

Mr. Lincoln continued—Now, fellow-citizens, I must confess that there are shades of difference in construing even this plank of the platform. But I am not now intending to discuss these differences, but merely to give you some general ideas upon this subject. I have long thought that if there be any article of necessity which can be produced at home with as little or nearly the same labor as abroad, it would be better to protect that article. Labor is the true standard of value. If a bar of iron, got out of the mines of England, and a bar of iron taken from the mines of Pennsylvania, be produced at the same cost, it follows that if the English bar be shipped from Manchester to Pittsburg, and the American bar from Pittsburg to Manchester, the cost of carriage is appreciably lost. [Laughter.] If we had no iron here, then we should encourage its shipment from foreign countries; but not when we can make it as cheaply in our own country. This brings us back to our first proposition, that if any article can be produced at home with nearly the same cost as abroad, the carriage is lost labor.

The treasury of the nation is in such a low condition at present that this subject now demands the attention of Congress, and will demand the immediate consideration of the new Administration. The tariff bill now before Congress may or may not pass at the present session. I confess I do not understand the precise provisions of this bill, and I do not know whether it can be passed by the present Congress or not. It may or may not become the law of the land—but if it does, that will be an end of the matter until a modification can be effected, should it be deemed necessary. If it does not pass (and the latest advices I have are to the effect that it is still pending) the next Congress will have to give it their earliest attention.

According to my political education, I am inclined to believe that the people in the various sections of the country should have their own views carried out through their representatives in Congress, and if the consideration of the Tariff bill should be postponed until the next session of the National Legislature, no subject should engage your representatives more closely than that of a tariff. And if I have any recommendation to make, it will be that every man who is called upon to serve the people in a representative capacity, should study this whole subject thoroughly, as I intend to do myself, looking to all the varied interests of our common country, so that when the time for action arrives adequate protection can be extended to the coal and iron of Pennsylvania, the corn of Illinois, and the "reapers of Chicago." Permit me to express the hope that this important subject may receive such consideration at the hands of your representatives, that the interests of no part of the country may be overlooked, but that all sections may share in common the benefits of a just and equitable tariff. [Applause.]

But I am trespassing upon your patience—[cries of "no!" "no!" "Go on—we'll listen!"] and must bring my remarks to a close. Thanking you most cordially for the kind reception which you have extended me, I bid you all adieu. [Enthusiastic applause.]

[Manuscript Prepared for the Pittsburgh Speech][5]

For the first time I now have the honor to appear before a Pennsylvania audience.[6]

It is often said that the tariff is the specialty of Pennsylvania. Assuming that direct taxation is not to be adopted, the tariff question must be as durable as the government itself. It is a question of national house-keeping. It is to the government what replenishing the meal-tub is to the family. Ever-varying circumstances will require frequent modifications, as to amounts needed, and sources of supply. So far there is little difference of opinion among the people. It is as to whether, and how far, duties on imports, shall be adjusted to favor home production in the home market, that controversy begins. One party insists that such adjustment oppresses one class for the advantage of another; while the other party ar-

---

[5] AD, DLC-RTL.

[6] This sentence has been crossed out, but the *Dispatch* version corroborates its inclusion.

gues that with all its incidents, and in the long run, all classes are benefitted. In the Chicago Platform there is a plank upon this subject, which should be a general law, to the incoming administration. We should do neither more nor less than we gave the people reason to believe we would, when they gave us their votes. That plank is as I now read.

[The 12th plank of the Chicago platform was here read.][7]

As with all general propositions, doubtless there will be shades of difference in construing this. I have, by no means, a thoroughly matured judgment upon this subject—especially as to details. Some general ideas are about all. I have long thought that to produce any necessary article at home, which can be made of as good quality, and with as little labor at home as abroad, would better be made at home, at least by the difference of the carrying from abroad. In such case, the carrying is demonstrably a dead loss of labor. For instance, labor being the true standard of value, is it not plain, that if equal labor get a bar of rail-road iron out of a mine in England, and another out of a mine in Pennsylvania, each can be laid down in a track at home, cheaper than they could exchange countries, at least by the cost of carriage. If there be a present cause why one can be both made and carried, cheaper, in *money price*, than the other can be made without carrying, that cause is an unnatural, and injurious one, and ought, gradually, if not rapidly, to be removed.[8]

The condition of the Treasury at this time would seem to render an early revision of the tariff indispensable. The Morrill bill, now pending before congress, may, or may not become a law. I am not posted as to it's particular provisions; but if they are generally satisfactory, and the bill shall now pass, there will be an end for the present. If, however, it shall not pass, I suppose the whole subject will be one of the most pressing and important, for the next congress. By the constitution, the executive may recommend measures which he may think proper; and he may veto those he thinks improper; and it is supposed he may add to these, certain indirect influences to affect the action of congress. My political education strongly inclines me against a very free use of any of these means, by the Executive, to control the legislation of the country. As a rule, I think it better that congress should originate, as well as perfect its measures, without external bias. I therefore would rather recommend to every gentleman who knows he is to

[7] Not in Lincoln's handwriting.
[8] The remainder of the manuscript is in pencil and was probably written later than the first portion.

be a member of the next congress, to take an enlarged view, and post himself thoroughly so as to contribute his part to such an adjustment of the tariff, as shall produce a sufficient revenue, and in in [sic] its other bearings, so far as possible, be just and equal to all sections of the country & classes of the people.

Remarks at Alliance, Ohio[1]

February 15, 1861

LADIES AND GENTLEMEN: I appear before you merely to greet you and say farewell. I have no time for long speeches, and could not make them at every stopping place without wearing myself out. If I should make a speech at every town, I would not get to Washington until some time after the inauguration. [Laughter.] But as I am somewhat interested in the inauguration, I would like to get there a few days before the 4th of March.

[1] Salem, Ohio, *Republican*, February 20, 1861. Substantially the same as the resumé given in the Canton, Ohio, *Stark County Democrat*, February 20, 1861.

Speech at Cleveland, Ohio[1]

February 15, 1861

MR. CHAIRMAN AND FELLOW CITIZENS OF CLEVELAND:—We have been marching about two miles through snow, rain and deep mud. The large numbers that have turned out under these circumstances testify that you are in earnest about something or other. But do I think so meanly of you as to suppose that that earnestness is about me personally? I would be doing you injustice to suppose you did. You have assembled to testify your respect to the Union, the constitution and the laws, and here let me say that it is with you, the people, to advance the great cause of the Union and the constitution, and not with any one man. It rests with you alone. This fact is strongly impressed on my mind at present. In a community like this, whose appearance testifies to their intelligence, I am convinced that the cause of liberty and the Union can never be in danger. Frequent allusion is made to the excitement at present existing in our national politics, and it is as well that I should also allude to it here. I think that there is no occasion for any excitement. The crisis, as it is called, is altogether an artificial crisis. In all parts of the nation there are differences of opinion and politics. There are differences of opinion even here. You did not all vote for the person who now addresses you. What is happening now will not hurt those who are farther away from here. Have they not all their rights now as they ever have had? Do they not have their fugitive slaves returned now as ever? Have they not the same constitution that they have lived under for seventy odd years? Have they not a position as citizens of this common country, and have we any power to change that position? (Cries of "No.") What then is the matter with them? Why all this excitement? Why all these complaints? As I said before, this crisis is all artificial. It has no foundation in facts. It was not argued up, as the saying is, and cannot, therefore, be argued down. Let it alone and it will go down of itself (Laughter). Mr. Lincoln said they must be content with but a few words from him. He was very much fatigued, and had spoken so frequently that he was already hoarse. He thanked them for the cordial and magnificent reception they had given him. Not less did he thank them for the votes they gave him last fall, and quite as much he thanked them for the efficient aid they had given the cause which he represented—a cause which he would say was a good one. He had one more word to say. He was given to understand that this reception was not tendered by his own party supporters, but by men of all parties. This is as it should be. If Judge Douglas had been elected and had been here on his way to Washington, as I am to-night, the republicans should have joined his supporters in welcoming him, just as his friends have joined with mine to-night. If all do not join now to save the good old ship of the Union this voyage nobody will have a chance to pilot her on another voyage. He concluded by thanking all present for the devotion they have shown to the cause of the Union.

[1] New York *Herald*, February 16, 1861. The text of this speech as printed in the Cleveland *Commercial* differs verbally to some degree, but is substantially the same as that reproduced here. Other New York papers and the Cincinnati *Gazette* have the same text as the *Herald*.

To William P. Hacker and Others[1]

Cleveland, Ohio, Feb. 15, 1861.

Gentlemen:—I have to-day received the invitation you extend to me on behalf of the Select and Common Councils of the City of Philadelphia, to visit the same and partake of its hospitalities, while on my way to the Federal capital.

I accept with much gratitude the proffered honor, and hope to arrive in your society on Thursday, the 21st instant, at four o'clock, P.M. Your obedient servant,   A. LINCOLN.

Wm. P. Hacker, Esq., Chairman, and members of the Committee, &c.

[1] Philadelphia *Inquirer*, February 18, 1861. William P. Hacker was chairman of the committee to make arrangements for the reception at Philadelphia.

To Elihu B. Washburne[1]

Hon. E. B. Washburne   Cleveland, O.
My dear Sir   Feb 15th 1861.

I have decided to stop at a public, rather than a private house, when I reach Washington; and Mrs. L. objects to the National on account of the sickness four years ago.[2] With this to guide you, please call to your assistance all our Republican members from Illinois, and select and engage quarters for us. Yours as ever

A. LINCOLN

[1] LS, IHi.

[2] At the time of President Buchanan's inauguration, a severe intestinal malady afflicted guests at the National Hotel. Buchanan himself became ill, and in pro-Southern circles there were rumors of a Republican plot to poison Democratic leaders.

Remarks at Ravenna, Ohio[1]

February 15, 1861

LADIES AND GENTLEMEN:—I appear before you merely to greet you and say farewell. I have no time for long speeches, and could not make them at every stopping place without wearing myself out. If I should make a speech at every town, I should not get to Washington until some time *after the inauguration.* (Laughter.) I am, however, all the time sensible of the deepest gratitude to the people of Ohio for their large contribution to the cause which I think is the just one. There are doubtless those here who did not vote for me, but I believe we make common cause for the Union ("That's so." "We are with you there," &c.) But let me tell to those who did not vote for me, an anecdote of a certain Irish friend that I met yesterday. He said he did not vote for me, but went for Douglas. "Now," said I to him, "I will tell you what you ought to do in that case. If we all turn in and keep the ship from sinking this voyage, there may be a chance for Douglas on the next; but if we let it go down now, neither he nor anybody else will have an opportunity of sailing in it again." Now, was not that good advice? ("Yes, yes," "that's the talk.") Once more, let me say good-bye.

[1] Portage, Ohio, *Sentinel,* February 20, 1861.

Remarks at Hudson, Ohio[1]

February 15, 1861

Ladies and Gentlemen:—I stepped upon this platform to see you, and to give you an opportunity of seeing me, which I suppose you desire to do. You see by my voice that I am quite hoarse. You will not, therefore, expect a speech from me.

1 Akron, Ohio, *Summit County Beacon*, February 21, 1861.

Remarks at Painesville, Ohio[1]

February 16, 1861

LADIES AND GENTLEMEN—I have stepped out upon this platform that I may see you and that you may see me, and in the arrangement I have the best of the bargain. The train only stops for a few minutes, so that I have time to make but few remarks, and the condition of my voice is such that I could not do more if there were time. We are met by large crowds of people at almost every ten miles, but in few instances where there are so many as here, or where there are so many (turning towards them and bowing) good-looking ladies. I can only say now that I bid you good morning and farewell.

Then turning towards it he said, "let us have the better music from the Band."

1 Painesville *Telegraph*, February 21, 1861. The Cleveland *Plain Dealer*, February 16, gives a shorter but similar report.

Remarks at Ashtabula, Ohio[1]

February 16, 1861

. . . . "I can only say how do you do, and farewell, as my voice you perceive will warrant nothing more. I am happy to see so many pleasant faces around me and to be able to greet you as friends."

As he bowed in conclusion, some one on behalf of the ladies, called for Mrs. Lincoln, to which the president replied that "he should hardly hope to induce her to appear, as he had always found it very difficult to make her do what she did not want to."

1 Ashtabula *Weekly Telegraph*, February 23, 1861.

Remarks at Conneaut, Ohio[1]

February 16, 1861

I have lost my voice and cannot make a speech, but my intentions are good. He then thanked the people for the kindly demonstration, and as the cars commenced to move slowly forward through the crowd which lined both sides of the track, Capt. Appleby, our fellow-townsman, called out to him, "Don't give up the ship!" To which Mr. Lincoln responded "with your aid I never will as long as life lasts."

[1] Conneaut *Reporter*, February 21, 1861.

Remarks at Erie, Pennsylvania[1]

February 16, 1861

Being hoarse and fatigued, he excused himself from speaking at any length or expressing his opinions on the exciting questions of the day. He trusted that when the time for speaking, fully and plainly, should come, he would say nothing not in accordance with the Constitution and the Laws and the manifest interests of the whole country. Counselling all to firmness, forbearance, and patriotic adherence to the Constitution and the Union, he retired amidst applause.

[1] Erie *Weekly Gazette*, February 21, 1861.

Remarks at Westfield, New York[1]

February 16, 1861

At Westfield, Mr. LINCOLN greeted a large crowd of ladies, and several thousand of the sterner sex. Addressing the ladies, he said, "I am glad to see you; I suppose you are to see me; but I certainly think I have the best of the bargain. (Applause.) Some three months ago, I received a letter from a young lady here; it was a very pretty letter, and she advised me to let my whiskers grow, as it would improve my personal appearance; acting partly upon her suggestion, I have done so; and now, if she is here, I would like to see her; I think her name was Miss BARLLY."[2] A small boy, mounted on a post, with his mouth and eyes both wide open, cried out, "there she is, Mr. LINCOLN," pointing to a beautiful girl, with black eyes, who was blushing all over her fair face. The President left the car, and the crowd making way for him, he reached her, and gave her several hearty kisses, and amid the yells of delight from the excited crowd, he bade her good-bye, and on we rushed.

[1] Philadelphia *Inquirer*, February 20, 1861.
[2] Grace Bedell. See Lincoln's letter, October 19, 1860, *supra*.

Remarks at Dunkirk, New York[1]

February 16, 1861

At Dunkirk, at least 12,000 or 15,000 were assembled, a triumphal arch was erected over the track, with Union mottoes upon it, music and military surrounded us, fair ladies waved their handkerchiefs, and a platform around a flag staff, covered with velvet carpet, was prepared for Mr. LINCOLN to speak from. He stepped from the cars upon it, and as the tumult subsided, said, "I am glad to meet you all; I regret I cannot stop to speak to you, but were I to stop and make a speech at every station, I would not reach Washington until after the inauguration. *Standing as I do, with my hand upon this staff, and under the folds of the American flag,* I ASK YOU TO STAND BY ME SO LONG AS I STAND BY IT.

1 Philadelphia *Inquirer*, February 20, 1861.

Speech at Buffalo, New York[1]

February 16, 1861

Mr. Mayor, and Fellow Citizens of Buffalo and the State of New York:—I am here to thank you briefly for this grand reception given to me, not personally, but as the representative of our great and beloved country. (Cheers.) Your worthy Mayor has been pleased to mention in his address to me, the fortunate and agreeable journey which I have had from home, on my rather circuitous route to the Federal Capital. I am very happy that he was enabled in truth to congratulate myself and companions [company] on that fact. It is true we have had nothing, thus far, to mar the pleasure of the trip. We have not been met alone by those who assisted in giving the election to me—I say not alone—but by the whole population of the country through which we have passed. This is as it should be.

Had the election fallen to any other of the distinguished candidates instead of myself, under the peculiar circumstances, to say the least, it would have been proper for all citizens to have greeted him as you now greet me. It is evidence of the devotion of the whole people to the Constitution, the Union, and the perpetuity of the liberties of this country. (Cheers.) I am unwilling, on any occasion, that I should be so meanly thought of, as to have it supposed for a moment that I regard these demonstrations as tendered to me personally. They should be tendered to no individual man. They are tendered to the country, to the institutions of the country, and to the perpetuity of the [liberties of the] country for which these institutions were made and created.

Your worthy Mayor has thought fit to express the hope that I may be able to relieve the country from its present—or I should say, its threatened difficulties. I am sure I bring a heart true to the work. (Tremendous applause.) For the ability to perform it, I must trust in that Supreme Being who has never forsaken this favored land, through the instrumentality of this great and intelligent people. Without that assistance I shall surely fail. With it I cannot fail.

When we speak of threatened difficulties to the country, it is natural that there should be expected from me something with regard to particular measures. Upon more mature reflection, however, others will agree with me that when it is considered that these difficulties are without precedent, and have never been acted upon by any individual situated as I am, it is most proper I should wait, see the developments, and get all the light I can, so that when I do speak authoritatively I may be as near right as possible. (Cheers.) When I shall speak authoritatively, I hope to say nothing inconsistent with the Constitution, the Union, the rights of all the States, of each State, and of each section of the country, and not to disappoint the reasonable expectations of those who have confided to me their votes.

In this connection allow me to say that you, as a portion of the great American people, need only to maintain your composure. Stand up to your sober convictions of right, to your obligations to the Constitution, act in accordance with those sober convictions, and the clouds which now arise in the horizon will be dispelled, and we shall have a bright and glorious future; and when this generation has passed away, tens of thousands will inhabit this country where only thousands inhabit [it] now.

I do not propose to address you at length—I have no voice for it. Allow me again to thank you for this magnificent reception, and bid you farewell.

[1] Buffalo *Morning Express*, February 18, 1861; New York *Herald*, February 17, 1861. The *Express* and *Herald* texts are substantially the same. At a few points important variations in the *Herald* are given in brackets.

Remarks at Batavia, New York[1]

February 18, 1861

At Batavia, gray as was the light and deep as was the snow, there was a very large gathering of people, who saluted Mr. LINCOLN with cheers and with the firing of cannon. Of course they wanted to hear him speak, but to their calls he replied that he did not appear before them or the country as a talker, nor did he desire to obtain a reputation as such. He thanked them for the kind attention manifested by their rising at so inconvenient an hour, and bade them farewell amidst a burst of genuine enthusiasm.

[1] New York *Times*, February 19, 1861.

Remarks at Rochester, New York[1]

February 18, 1861

I confess myself, after having seen large audiences since leaving home, overwhelmed with this vast number of faces at this hour of the morning. I am not vain enough to believe that you are here from any wish to see me as an individual, but because I am, for the time being, the representative of the American people. I could not, if I would, address you at any length. I have not the strength, even if I had the time, for a speech at these many interviews that are afforded me on my way to Washington. I appear merely to see you, and to let you see me, and to bid you farewell. I hope it will be understood that it is from no disposition to disoblige anybody, that I do not address you at greater length.

[1] New York *Times, Tribune,* and *Herald,* February 19, 1861.

Remarks at Clyde, New York[1]

February 18, 1861

At Clyde an enthusiastic crowd was gathered, who welcomed Mr. Lincoln with a salute and cheers. He thanked the people for the welcome, but had no speech to make, and no time to make it in. He was glad to see them, and bade them good morning.

[1] New York *Tribune,* February 19, 1861.

Remarks at Syracuse, New York[1]

February 18, 1861

LADIES AND GENTLEMEN: I see you have erected a very fine and handsome platform here for me, and I presume you expected me to speak from it. If I should go upon it you would imagine that I was about to deliver you a much longer speech than I am. I wish you to understand that I mean no discourtesy to you by thus declining. I intend discourtesy to no one. But I wish you to understand that though I am unwilling to go upon this platform, you are not at liberty to draw any inferences concerning any other platform with which my name has been or is connected. [Laughter and applause.] I wish you a long life and prosperity individually, and pray that with the perpetuity of those institutions under which we have all so long lived and prospered, our happiness may be secured, our future made brilliant, and the glorious destiny of our country established forever. I bid you a kind farewell.

[1] New York *Times,* February 19, 1861.

Remarks at Utica, New York[1]

February 18, 1861

Ladies and Gentlemen—I have but a short speech to make you. I have no time to make remarks of any length. I appear before you to bid you farewell—to see you, and to allow you all to see me. At the same time I acknowledge, ladies, that I think I have the best of the bargain in the sight. I only appear to greet you, and to say farewell. I will come out again on the platform before the train leaves, so that you may see me.

(Mr. Lincoln was then introduced to a number of gentlemen on the car, passing around at the same time, until he reached the north side, when he made the following remarks):

Gentlemen—I come around to say to you what I did to those on the other side, which was but a few words, and little more than good morning, as it were, and farewell. I can't however say here, exactly what I did on the other side, as there are no ladies on this side. I said that there were so many ladies present that I had the best part of the sight, but bear in mind I don't make any such admission now. Farewell!

[1] Utica *Evening Telegraph*, February 18, 1861.

Remarks at Little Falls, New York[1]

February 18, 1861

Ladies and Gentlemen: I appear before you merely for the purpose of greeting you, saying a few words and bidding you farewell. I have no speech to make, and no sufficient time to make one if I had; nor have I the strength to repeat a speech, at all the places at which I stop, even if all the other circumstances were favorable. I have come to see you and allow you to see me (Applause) and in this so far [as] regards the Ladies, I have the best of the bargain on my side. I don't make that acknowledgement to the gentlemen, (Increased laughter) and now I believe I have really made my speech and am ready to bid you farewell when the cars move on.

[1] Herkimer, New York, *Democrat*, February 20, 1861.

Remarks at Fonda, New York[1]

February 18, 1861

At Fonda, in response to enthusiastic greetings, Mr. Lincoln made a short speech, and, in declining to mount a platform prepared for him, said that, though he would not get upon *it*, he wished it to be distinctly understood that he would never shrink from a platform on which he properly belonged.

¹ New York *Times*, February 19, 1861.

Remarks at Schenectady, New York[1]

February 18, 1861

Mr. Lincoln, appearing at the rear end of the car, being introduced by Hon. Judge Potter,[2] said that he saw they had done him the honor of erecting a very handsome platform here, but he should be obliged to decline using it, not that he repudiated platforms, but because he had refused to speak on one at other places. He really had no speech to make, no time to make one, and no sufficient strength to make one. You are all here to see and to be seen, but where there are so many assembled he thought that he obtained the best view. And now he must bid them all farewell as the train would soon start. We were only able to obtain a few disjointed sentences of what the President said.

¹ Schenectady *Daily Evening Star*, February 19, 1861.
² Platt Potter, judge of the Supreme Court of New York (1856-1873).

Reply to Mayor George H. Thacher
at Albany, New York[1]

February 18, 1861

MR. MAYOR: I can hardly appropriate to myself the flattering terms in which you communicate the tender of this reception, as personal to myself. I most gratefully accept the hospitalities tendered to me, and will not detain you or the audience with any extended remarks at this time. I presume that in the two or three courses through which I shall have to go, I shall have to repeat somewhat, and I will therefore only repeat[2] to you my thanks for this kind reception.

¹ New York *Herald* and *Times*, February 19, 1861.
² New York *Tribune*, February 19, 1861, reads "express."

Reply to Governor Edwin D. Morgan
at Albany, New York[1]

February 18, 1861

MR. GOVERNOR—I was pleased to receive an invitation to visit the capital of the great Empire State of this nation on my way to the federal capital, and I now thank you, Mr. Governor, and the people of this capital and the people of the State of New York, for this most hearty and magnificent welcome. If I am not at fault, the great Empire State at this time contains a greater population than did the United States of America at the time she achieved her national independence. I am proud to be invited to pass through your capital and meet them, as I now have the honor to do. I am notified by your Governor that this reception is given without distinction of party. I accept it more gladly because it is so. Almost all men in this country, and in any country where freedom of thought is tolerated, attach themselves to political parties. It is but ordinary charity to attribute this to the fact that in so attaching himself to the party which his judgment prefers, the citizen believes he thereby promotes the best interests of the whole country; and when an election is passed, it is altogether befitting a free people, that until the next election, they should be as one people. The reception you have extended to me to-day is not given to me personally. It should not be so, but as the representative for the time being of the majority of the nation. If the election had resulted in the selection of either of the other candidates, the same cordiality should have been extended him, as is extended to me this day, in their testimony of the devotion of the whole people to the Constitution and to the whole Union, and of their desire to perpetuate our institutions, and to hand them down in their perfection to succeeding generations. I have neither the voice nor the strength to address you at any greater length. I beg you will accept my most grateful thanks for this devotion, not to me, but to this great and glorious free country.

1 New York *Herald* and *Times*, February 19, 1861. The New York *Tribune* text, same date, is at considerable verbal variance, but the variations are not sufficiently significant to merit collation.

Address to the Legislature at Albany, New York[1]

February 18, 1861

MR. PRESIDENT AND GENTLEMEN OF THE LEGISLATURE OF THE STATE OF NEW YORK: It is with feelings of great diffidence, and I may say with feelings of awe, perhaps greater than I have recently experienced, that I meet you here in this place. The history of this great State, the renown of those great men who have stood here, and spoke here, and been heard here, all crowd around my fancy, and incline me to shrink from any attempt to address you.

Yet I have some confidence given me by the generous manner in which you have invited me, and by the still more generous manner in which you have received me to speak further. You have invited and received me without distinction of party. I cannot for a moment suppose that this has been done in any considerable degree with reference to my personal services, but that it is done in so far as I am regarded at this time as the representative of the majesty [majority] of this great nation. I doubt not this is the truth and the whole truth of the case, and this is as it should be. It is much more gratifying to me that this reception has been given to me as the representative of a free people than it could possibly be if tendered me [merely] as an evidence of devotion to me, or to any one man personally, and now I think it were more fitting that I should close these hasty remarks. It is true that while I hold myself without mock modesty, the humblest of all individuals that have ever been elevated to the Presidency, I have a more difficult task to perform than any one of them. You have generously tendered me the united support of the great Empire State. For this, in behalf of the nation, in behalf of the present and future of the nation, in behalf of the civil and religious liberty for all time to come, most gratefully do I thank you. I do not propose to enter into an explanation of any particular line of policy as to our present difficulties to be adopted by the incoming administration. I deem it just to you, to myself and to all that I should see everything, that I should hear everything, that I should have every light that can be brought within my reach, in order that when I do so speak, I shall have enjoyed every opportunity to take correct and true ground; and for this reason I don't propose to speak at this time of the policy of the Government; but when the time comes I shall speak as well as I am able for the good of the present and future of this country—for the good both of the North and the South of this country—for the good of the one and the other, and of all sections of the country. [Rounds of applause.] In the mean time, if we have patience; if we restrain ourselves; if we allow ourselves not to run off in a passion, I still have confidence that the Almighty, the Maker of the Universe will, through the instrumentality of this great and intelligent people, bring us through this as He has through all the other difficulties of our country. Relying on this, I again thank you for this generous reception. [Applause and cheers.]

---

1 New York *Times, Herald,* and *Tribune,* February 19, 1861. The *Times* and *Herald* have practically the same text. Bracketed words are variants in the *Herald* or *Tribune.*

Reply to M. I. Townsend and Committee[1]

February 18, 1861

I shall be obliged to go by way of Troy in pursuing my journey to-morrow morning. It is with pleasure, therefore, that I accept your invitation. I shall only be able to remain a few moments with you. But I appreciate the compliment of the invitation. I will spend just as much time with you as the train permits. In this, as in other matters, it is my intention as it shall be my purpose to do everything possible to gratify my friends.

[1] Troy, New York, *Daily Times*, February 19, 1861. Townsend and members of a committee from Troy called upon Lincoln at the Delavan House, Albany, New York, to invite him to visit Troy the next day.

Remarks at Troy, New York[1]

February 19, 1861

Mr. Mayor and Fellow Citizens of Troy, New York:—I am here to thank you for this noble demonstration of the citizens of Troy, and I accept this flattering reception with feelings of profound gratefulness. Since having left home, I confess, sir, having seen large assemblages of the people, but this immense gathering more than exceeds anything I have ever seen before. Still, fellow citizens, I am not so vain as to suppose that you have gathered to do me honor as an individual, but rather as the representative for the fleeting time of the American people. I have appeared only that you might see me and I you, and I am not sure but that I have the best of the sight.

Again thanking you, fellow citizens, I bid you an affectionate farewell.

[1] Troy *Daily Budget*, February 19, 1861. The New York *Herald* and *Tribune*, February 20, report Lincoln's remarks at Troy with considerable verbal variance from the *Budget*, and between themselves. The import is the same, however, and the variations are scarcely worth collating. Lincoln was welcomed by Mayor Isaac McConihe.

Remarks at Hudson, New York[1]

February 19, 1861

FELLOW CITIZENS: I see that you have provided a platform, but I shall have to decline standing on it. (Laughter and applause.) The Superintendent tells me I have not time during our brief stay here to leave the train. I had to decline standing on some

[227]

very handsome platforms prepared for me yesterday. But I say to you, as I said to them, you must not on this account draw the inference that I have any intention to desert any platform I have a legitimate right to stand on. I do not appear before you for the purpose of making a speech. I come only to see you and to give you the opportunity to see me; and I say to you, as I have before said to crowds where there were so many handsome ladies as there are here, I have decidedly the best of the bargain. I have only, therefore, to thank you most cordially for this kind reception, and bid you all farewell.

¹ New York *Herald*, February 20, 1861. The New York *Tribune* version is shorter but substantially the same.

Remarks at Poughkeepsie, New York¹

February 19, 1861

I cannot expect to make myself heard by any considerable number of you, my friends, but I appear here rather for the purpose of seeing you and being seen by you. (Laughter.) I do not believe that you extend this welcome—one of the finest I have ever received—to the individual man who now addresses you but rather to the person who represents for the time being the majesty of the constitution and the government. (Cheers.) I suppose that here, as everywhere, you meet me without distinction of party, but as the people. (Cries of "yes," "yes.") It is with your aid, as the people, that I think we shall be able to preserve—not the country, for the country will preserve itself, (cheers), but the institutions of the country—(great cheering); those institutions which have made us free, intelligent and happy—the most free, the most intelligent and the happiest people on the globe. (Tremendous applause.) I see that some, at least, of you are of those who believe that an election being decided against them is no reason why they should sink the ship. ("Hurrah.") I believe with you, I believe in sticking to it, and carrying it through; and, if defeated at one election, I believe in taking the chances next time. (Great laughter and applause.) I do not think that they have chosen the best man to conduct our affairs, now—I am sure they did not—(here the speaker was interrupted by noise and confusion in another part of the crowd)—but acting honestly and sincerely, and with your aid, I think we shall be able to get through the storm. (Here Mr. Sloan caught hold of Mr. Lincoln's arm and pulled him around to see the locomotives—the Union and Constitution—which passed gaily dressed with flags. Turning hastily, Mr. Lincoln continued)—In addition to what I have said, I have only to bid you farewell. (Cheers and a salute, amid which the train moved on.)

1 New York *Herald*, February 20, 1861. The New York *Tribune* version is considerably more verbose, but substantially the same.

Remarks at Fishkill, New York[1]

LADIES AND GENTLEMEN: February 19, 1861

I appear before you not to make a speech. I have no sufficient time, if I had the strength, to repeat speeches at every station where the people kindly gather to welcome me as we go along. If I had the strength, and should take the time, I should not get to Washington until after inauguration, which you must be aware would not fit exactly. (Laughter.) That such an untoward event might not transpire, I know you will readily forego any further remarks; and I close by bidding you farewell. (Loud cheers.)

1 New York *Tribune*, February 20, 1861.

Remarks at Peekskill, New York[1]

February 19, 1861

LADIES AND GENTLEMEN: I have but a moment to stand before you to listen to and return your kind greeting. I thank you for this reception and for the pleasant manner in which it is tendered to me by our mutual friends. I will say in a single sentence, in regard to the difficulties that lie before me and our beloved country, that if I can only be as generously and unanimously sustained as the demonstrations I have witnessed indicate I shall be, I shall not fail; but without your sustaining hands I am sure that neither I nor any other man can hope to surmount those difficulties. I trust that in the course I shall pursue I shall be sustained, not only by the party that elected me, but by the patriotic people of the whole country.

1 New York *Herald*, February 20, 1861. The New York *Tribune* version differs verbally, but is substantially the same.

Remarks upon Arriving at the Astor House, New York City[1]

February 19, 1861

FELLOW CITIZENS—I have stepped before you merely in compliance with what appeared to be your wish, and with no purpose of making a speech. In fact, I do not propose making a speech this afternoon. I could not be heard by any but a very small fraction of you at best; but what is still worse than that is, that I have nothing just now to say worth your hearing. (Loud applause.) I beg you to believe that I do not now refuse to address you through any disposition to disoblige you, but the contrary. But at the same time I beg of you to excuse me for the present.

¹ New York *Herald*, February 20, 1861. The New York *Tribune* version is substantially the same.

Speech at the Astor House, New York City¹

February 19, 1861

Mr. CHAIRMAN AND GENTLEMEN:—I am rather an old man to avail myself of such an excuse as I am now about to do, yet the truth is so distinct and presses itself so distinctly upon me that I cannot well avoid it, and that is that I did not understand when I was brought into this room that I was brought here to make a speech. It was not intimated to me that I was brought into the room where Daniel Webster and Henry Clay had made speeches,² and where one in my position might be expected to do something like those men, or do something unworthy of myself or my audience. I therefore will beg you to make very great allowance for the circumstances under which I have been by surprise brought before you. Now, I have been in the habit of thinking and speaking for some time upon political questions that have for some years past agitated the country, and if I were disposed to do so, and we could take up some one of the issues as the lawyers call them, and I were called upon to make an argument about it to the best of my ability, I could do that without much preparation. But that is not what you desire to be done here to-night. I have been occupying a position, since the Presidential election, of silence, of avoiding public speaking, of avoiding public writing. I have been doing so because I thought, upon full consideration, that was the proper course for me to take. (Great applause.) I am brought before you now and required to make a speech, when you all approve, more than anything else, of the fact that I have been silent—(loud laughter, cries of "Good—good," and applause)—and now it seems to me from the response you give to that remark it ought to justify me in closing just here. (Great laughter.) I have not kept silent since the Presidential election from any party wantonness, or from any indifference to the anxiety that pervades the minds of men about the aspect of the political affairs of this country. I have kept si-

lence for the reason that I supposed it was peculiarly proper that
I should do so until the time came when, according to the customs
of the country, I should speak officially. (Voice, partially inter-
rogative, partially sarcastic, "Custom of the country?") I heard
some gentleman say, "According to the custom of the country;" I
alluded to the custom of the President elect at the time of taking
his oath of office. That is what I meant by the custom of the
country. I do suppose that while the political drama being enacted
in this country at this time is rapidly shifting in its scenes, forbidding an anticipation with any degree of certainty to-day what
we shall see to-morrow, that it was peculiarly fitting that I should
see it all up to the last minute before I should take ground, that
I might be disposed by the shifting of the scenes afterwards again
to shift. (Applause.) I said several times upon this journey, and I
now repeat it to you, that when the time does come I shall then
take the ground that I think is right—(interruption by cries of
"Good," "good," and applause)—the ground I think is right for
the North, for the South, for the East, for the West, for the whole
country—(cries of "Good," "Hurrah for Lincoln," and great applause). And in doing so I hope to feel no necessity pressing upon
me to say anything in conflict with the constitution, in conflict
with the continued union of these States—(applause)—in conflict
with the perpetuation of the liberties of these people—(cheers)—
or anything in conflict with anything whatever that I have ever
given you reason to expect from me. (Loud cheers.) And now, my
friends, have I said enough. (Cries of "No, no," "Go on," &c.)
Now, my friends, there appears to be a difference of opinion between you and me, and I feel called upon to insist upon deciding
the question myself. (Enthusiastic cheers.)

[1] New York *Herald*, February 20, 1861. The New York *Tribune* text is substantially the same, but omits some phrases and sentences. The reception at
which Lincoln spoke was held on the night of February 19.
[2] In introducing Lincoln, E. Delafield Smith had alluded to the fact that
the reception room at the Astor House had been the scene of receptions
honoring Webster and Clay.

To the People of Newark, New Jersey[1]

[February 19, 1861]
I shall be able to do no more than to bow to the people of New
Ark from the train   A LINCOLN

[1] ALS-F, ISLA. This brief note was written at the Astor House, probably
in response to an inquiry from Newark Republicans.

Reply to the Brooklyn Common Council Committee, New York City[1]

February 19, 1861

. . . . Mr. Lincoln thanked the authorities of Brooklyn for their kind attention, and regretted that his engagements, during his brief stay in New York, would not permit him to visit the city of churches, though it would have afforded him much pleasure to have done so, had circumstances permitted.

[1] Philadelphia *Inquirer*, February 21, 1861.

Announcement in the *Illinois State Journal*[1]

February 20, 1861

The notes and papers of Mr. LINCOLN are left with Mr. ROBERT IRWIN, where persons interested can find them. If any of his accounts are left unpaid, Mr. IRWIN will pay them on being satisfied of their correctness. A. LINCOLN.

Feb. 20, 1861.

[1] *Illinois State Journal*, February 21, 1861.

Reply to Mayor Fernando Wood at New York City[1]

February 20, 1861

Mr. MAYOR—It is with feelings of deep gratitude that I make my acknowledgment for this reception which has been given me in the great commercial city of New York. I cannot but remember that this is done by a people who do not by a majority agree with me in political sentiments. It is the more grateful [to me] because in this reception I see that, in regard to the great principles of our government, the people are very nearly or quite unanimous.

In reference to the difficulties that confront us at this time, and of which your Honor thought fit to speak so becomingly, and so justly as I suppose, I can only say that I fully concur in the sentiments expressed by the Mayor. In my devotion to the Union I hope I am behind no man in the Union; but as to the wisdom with which to conduct affairs tending to the preservation of the Union, I fear

[232]

that even too great confidence may have been reposed [placed] in me. I am sure I bring a heart devoted to the work.

There is nothing that can ever bring me willingly to consent to the destruction of this Union, under which not only the commercial city of New York, but the whole country has acquired its greatness, unless it were to be that thing for which the Union itself was made. I understand a ship to be made for the carrying and preservation of the cargo, and so long as the ship can be saved, with the cargo, it should never be abandoned. This Union should likewise never be abandoned unless it fails and the probability of its preservation shall cease to exist without throwing the passengers and cargo overboard. So long, then, as it is possible that the prosperity and the liberties of the people can be preserved in the Union, it shall be my purpose at all times to preserve it. Thanking you for the reception given me, allow me to come to a close.

[1] New York *Herald*, February 21, 1861. The significant verbal variations in the New York *Tribune* report have been inserted in brackets. Lincoln spoke at City Hall.

Remarks from the Balcony of City Hall, New York City[1]

February 20, 1861

FRIENDS: I do not appear for the purpose of making a speech. I design to make no speech. I came merely to see you, and allow you to see me. [Cheers.] And I have to say to you, as I have said frequently to audiences on my journey, that, in the sight, I have the best of the bargain. [Tremendous cheers.] Assuming that you are all for the Constitution, the Union [renewed cheering], and the perpetual liberties of this people, I bid you farewell. [Cheers.]

[1] New York *Tribune* and *Herald*, February 21, 1861. The texts are practically identical.

Remarks at Jersey City, New Jersey[1]

February 21, 1861

Ladies and gentlemen of the State of New-Jersey, I shall only thank you briefly for this very kind and cordial reception—not as given to me individually, but as to the representative of the chief magistracy of this great nation. I cannot make any speech now to you, as I shall be met frequently to-day in the same manner as you have received me here, and, therefore, have not the strength to address you at length. I am here before you care-worn, for little else than to greet you, and to say farewell. You have done me the very high honor to present your reception of me through your own great man—a man with whom it is an honor to be associated anywhere—a man with whom no State could be poor. [Applause, long continued.] His remarks of welcome, though brief, deserve an hour's well-considered reply; but time, and the obligations before me, render it necessary for me to close my remarks—allow me to bid you a kind and grateful farewell.

Mr. Lincoln's remarks were received with demonstrations of applause, and the waving of handkerchiefs.

Loud calls were then made for Vice-President Hamlin; but it was announced that he was not present, and would be detained in New-York till to-morrow.

Then followed a rush to shake hands with Mr. Lincoln, and in the rush and crush the policemen and reporters were nearly annihilated. Loud cries were kept up for "Lincoln, Lincoln," and to quiet the crowd Mr. Lincoln once more came to the front of the platform and said:

There appears to be a desire to see more of me, and I can only say that from my position, especially when I look around the gallery (bowing to the ladies), I feel that I have decidedly the best of the bargain, and in this matter I am for no compromises here. [Applause and much laughter.]

[1] New York *Tribune*, February 22, 1861. William L. Dayton, attorney general of New Jersey, introduced Lincoln.

Remarks at Newark, New Jersey[1]

February 21, 1861

MR. MAYOR: I thank you for the reception to your city, and would say in response, that I bring a heart sincerely devoted to the work you desire I should do. With my own ability I cannot succeed, without the sustenance of Divine Providence, and of this great, free, happy, and intelligent people. Without these I cannot hope to succeed; with them I cannot fail. Again I return you my thanks. [Cheers.]

[1] New York *Tribune*, February 22, 1861. Other papers reported the speech with wide latitude of verbal differences, but the substance is the same. Follow-

ing the remarks, Lincoln was driven through town in an open barouche to the "upper depot" where the train had proceeded, and where he was again introduced and "made a few remarks, thanking the townspeople for their complimentary turnout. . . ." (New York *World*, February 22).

Remarks at New Brunswick, New Jersey[1]

February 21, 1861

Mr. L. then made a few remarks, saying substantially that "he was gratified with the manifestations of respect and kind feelings which his fellow-citizens were pleased to give so frequently; that he did not appear before them to make a speech, because he had none to make, and didn't know that it would be proper to make a speech even if he had one to make and the disposition to make it. He appeared to see them and give them an opportunity to see him; to say good morning to them, and, when the cars started off, to say farewell."

[1] New Brunswick *Fredonian*, February 21, 1861. Lincoln was introduced from the rear platform of the last car by Judge John Van Dyke.

Address to the New Jersey Senate at Trenton, New Jersey[1]

February 21, 1861

MR. PRESIDENT AND GENTLEMEN OF THE SENATE OF THE STATE OF NEW-JERSEY: I am very grateful to you for the honorable reception of which I have been the object. I cannot but remember the place that New-Jersey holds in our early history. In the early Revolutionary struggle, few of the States among the old Thirteen had more of the battle-fields of the country within their limits than old New-Jersey. May I be pardoned if, upon this occasion, I mention that away back in my childhood, the earliest days of my being able to read, I got hold of a small book, such a one as few of the younger members have ever seen, "Weem's Life of Washington." I remember all the accounts there given of the battle fields and struggles for the liberties of the country, and none fixed themselves upon my imagination so deeply as the struggle here at Trenton, New-Jersey. The crossing of the river; the contest with the Hessians; the great hardships endured at that time, all fixed themselves on my memory more than any single revolutionary event; and you all know, for you have all been boys, how these early impressions last longer than any others. I recollect thinking then, boy even though I was, that there must have been something more than common that those men struggled for. I am exceedingly anxious that that thing which they struggled for; that something even more than National Independence; that something that held out a great promise to all the people of the world to all time to come; I am exceedingly anxious that this Union, the Constitution, and the liberties of the people shall be perpetuated in accordance with the original idea for which that struggle was made, and I shall be most happy indeed if I shall be an humble instrument in the hands of the Almighty, and of this, his almost chosen people, for perpetuating the object of that great struggle. You give me this reception, as I understand, without distinction of party. I learn that this body is composed of a majority of gentlemen who, in the exercise of their best judgment in the choice of a Chief Magistrate, did not think I was the man. I understand, nevertheless, that they came forward here to greet me as the constitutional President of the United States—as citizens of the United States, to meet the man who, for the time being, is the representative man of the nation, united by a purpose to perpetuate the Union and liberties of the people. As such, I accept this reception more gratefully than I could do did I believe it was tendered to me as an individual.

[1] New York *Tribune*, February 22, 1861.

Address to the New Jersey General Assembly at Trenton, New Jersey[1]

February 21, 1861

MR. SPEAKER AND GENTLEMEN: I have just enjoyed the honor of a reception by the other branch of this Legislature, and I return to you and them my thanks for the reception which the people of New-Jersey have given, through their chosen representatives, to me, as the representative, for the time being, of the majesty of the people of the United States. I appropriate to myself very little of the demonstrations of respect with which I have been greeted. I think little should be given to any man, but that it should be a manifestation of adherence to the Union and the Constitution. I understand myself to be received here by the representatives of the people of New-Jersey, a majority of whom differ in opinion from those with whom I have acted. This manifestation is therefore to be regarded by me as expressing their devotion to the

Union, the Constitution and the liberties of the people. You, Mr. Speaker, have well said that this is a time when the bravest and wisest look with doubt and awe upon the aspect presented by our national affairs. Under these circumstances, you will readily see why I should not speak in detail of the course I shall deem it best to pursue. It is proper that I should avail myself of all the information and all the time at my command, in order that when the time arrives in which I must speak officially, I shall be able to take the ground which I deem the best and safest, and from which I may have no occasion to swerve. I shall endeavor to take the ground I deem most just to the North, the East, the West, the South, and the whole country. I take it, I hope, in good temper—certainly no malice toward any section. I shall do all that may be in my power to promote a peaceful settlement of all our difficulties. The man does not live who is more devoted to peace than I am. [Cheers.] None who would do more to preserve it. But it may be necessary to put the foot down firmly. [Here the audience broke out into cheers so loud and long that for some moments it was impossible to hear Mr. L.'s voice.] He continued: And if I do my duty, and do right, you will sustain me, will you not? [Loud cheers, and cries of "Yes," "Yes," "We will."] Received, as I am, by the members of a Legislature the majority of whom do not agree with me in political sentiments, I trust that I may have their assistance in piloting the ship of State through this voyage, surrounded by perils as it is; for, if it should suffer attack now, there will be no pilot ever needed for another voyage.

Gentlemen, I have already spoken longer than I intended, and must beg leave to stop here.

¹ New York *Tribune*, February 22, 1861.

Remarks at Trenton House, Trenton, New Jersey¹

February 21, 1861

I have been invited by your representatives to the Legislature, to visit this, the capital of your honored State, and in acknowledging their kind invitation, compelled to respond to the welcome of the presiding officers of each body, and I suppose they intended I should speak to you through them, as they are the representatives of all of you; and if I was to speak again here, I should only have to repeat in a great measure much that I have said, which would be disgusting to my friends around me who have met here. I have no speech to make ["that's right"], but merely appear to see you and let you look at me; and as to the latter, I think I have greatly the best of the bargain. [Laughter.] My friends, allow me to bid you farewell.

¹ New York *Tribune* and *World*, February 22, 1861. The texts are similar.

Reply to Mayor Alexander Henry
at Philadelphia, Pennsylvania¹

February 21, 1861

Mr. Mayor and Fellow Citizens of Philadelphia—I appear before you to make no lengthy speech. I appear before you to thank you for the reception. The reception you have given me to-night is not to me, the man, the individual, but to the man who temporarily represents, or should represent, the majesty of the nation. (Applause.) It is true, as your worthy Mayor has said, that there is great anxiety amongst the citizens of the United States at this time. I say I deem it a happy circumstance that the dissatisfied portion of our fellow citizens do not point us to anything in which they are being injured, or about to be injured, from which I have felt all the while justified in concluding that the crisis, the panic, the anxiety of the country at this time is artificial. If there be those who differ with me upon this subject, they have not pointed out the substantial difficulty that exists. (Tremendous cheering.)

I do not mean to say that this artificial panic has not done harm. That it has done much harm I do not deny. The hope that has been expressed by your worthy Mayor, that I may be able to restore peace and harmony and prosperity to the country, is most worthy in him; and most happy indeed shall I be if I shall be able to fulfill and verify that hope. (Cheers.)

I promise you in all sincerity, that I bring to the work a sincere heart. Whether I will bring a head equal to that heart, will be for future time to determine. It were useless for me to speak of the details of the plans now. I shall speak officially on next Monday week, if ever. If I should not speak, then it were useless for me to do so now. [If I do speak, then it is useless for me to do so now.]² When I do speak, as your worthy Mayor has expressed the hope, I will take such grounds as I shall deem best calculated to restore peace, harmony and prosperity to the country, and tend to the perpetuity of the nation, and the liberty of these States and all these people. (Applause.)

[238]

Your worthy Mayor has expressed the wish, in which I join with him, that if it were convenient for me to remain with you in your city long enough to consult, [your merchants and manufacturers;][3] or, as it were, to listen to those breathings rising within the consecrated walls where the Constitution of the United States, and, I will add, the Declaration of American Independence was originally framed, I would do so.

I assure you and your Mayor that I had hoped on this occasion, and upon all occasions during my life, that I shall do nothing inconsistent with the teachings of those holy and most sacred walls.

I have never asked anything that does not breathe from those walls. All my political warfare has been in favor of the teachings coming forth from that sacred hall. May my right hand forget its cunning and my tongue cleave to the roof of my mouth, if ever I prove false to those teachings.

Fellow citizens, I have addressed you longer than I expected to do, and allow me now to bid you good night.

[1] Philadelphia *Inquirer*, February 22, 1861. The New York *Tribune* and other papers give similar texts. Lincoln spoke from the balcony of the Continental Hotel upon arrival.

[2] Bracketed words are in the New York *Tribune* but not in the *Inquirer*.

[3] Bracketed words are in the New York *Tribune* and *World* but not in the *Inquirer*.

Reply to a Delegation from Wilmington, Delaware[1]

February 21, 1861

Mr. CHAIRMAN:—I feel highly flattered by the encomiums you have seen fit to bestow upon me. Soon after the nomination of Gen. TAYLOR I attended a political meeting in the city of Wilmington, and have since carried with me a fond remembrance of the hospitalities of the city on that occasion.[2] The programme established provides for my presence in Harrisburg in twenty-four hours from this time.

I expect to be in Washington on Saturday. It is, therefore, an impossibility that I should accept your kind invitation. There are no people whom I would more gladly accommodate than those of Delaware; but circumstances forbid, gentlemen. With many regrets for the character of the reply I am compelled to give you, I bid you adieu.

[1] Philadelphia *Inquirer*, February 22, 1861. Lincoln replied to a speech of invitation by William S. McCaulley, chairman of the delegation from Wilmington, in the reception parlor of the Continental Hotel. This speech has appeared in other editions (Lapsley) of Lincoln's works, incorrectly dated February 22. [2] See June 10, 1848, *supra*.

Speech in Independence Hall,
Philadelphia, Pennsylvania[1]

February 22, 1861

Mr. CUYLER:—I am filled with deep emotion at finding myself standing here in the place where were collected together the wisdom, the patriotism, the devotion to principle, from which sprang the institutions under which we live. You have kindly suggested to me that in my hands is the task of restoring peace to our distracted country. I can say in return, sir, that all the political sentiments I entertain have been drawn, so far as I have been able to draw them, from the sentiments which originated, and were given to the world from this hall in which we stand. I have never had a feeling politically that did not spring from the sentiments embodied in the Declaration of Independence. (Great cheering.) I have often pondered over the dangers which were incurred by the men who assembled here and adopted[2] that Declaration of Independence— I have pondered over the toils that were endured by the officers and soldiers of the army, who achieved that Independence. (Applause.) I have often inquired of myself, what great principle or idea it was that kept this Confederacy so long together. It was not the mere matter of the separation of the colonies from the mother land; but something in that Declaration giving liberty,[3] not alone to the people of this country, but hope to the world for all future time. (Great applause.) It was that which gave promise that in due time the weights should be lifted from the shoulders of all men, and that *all* should have an equal chance. (Cheers.) This is the sentiment embodied in that Declaration of Independence.

Now, my friends, can this country be saved upon that basis? If it can, I will consider myself one of the happiest men in the world if I can help to save it. If it can't be saved upon that principle, it will be truly awful. But, if this country cannot be saved without giving up that principle—I was about to say I would rather be assassinated on this spot than to surrender it.[4] (Applause.)

Now, in my view of the present aspect of affairs, there is no need of bloodshed and war. There is no necessity for it. I am not in favor of such a course, and I may say in advance, there will be no blood shed unless it be forced upon the Government. The Government will not use force unless force is used against it.[5] (Prolonged applause and cries of "That's the proper sentiment.")

My friends, this is a wholly unprepared speech. I did not expect to be called upon to say a word when I came here—I supposed I was merely to do something towards raising a flag. I may, therefore, have said something indiscreet, (cries of "no, no"), but I have said nothing but what I am willing to live by, and, in[6] the pleasure of Almighty God, die by.

1 Philadelphia *Inquirer*, February 23, 1861. Important variations of the text in the New York *Tribune* are given in footnotes. Lincoln was welcomed by Theodore L. Cuyler, president of the Select Council of Philadelphia.

2 New York *Tribune* reads, "and framed and adopted."

3 *Tribune* reads, "but that sentiment in the Declaration of Independence which gave liberty."

4 Lincoln's allusion may have been suggested by the warning which he had received of a plot to assassinate him when the presidential train passed through Baltimore.

5 *Tribune* reads in place of this sentence, ". . . , and then it will be compelled to act in self-defense."   6 *Tribune* reads, "and if it be the pleasure."

Speech at the Flag-raising before Independence Hall, Philadelphia, Pennsylvania[1]

February 22, 1861

FELLOW CITIZENS:— I am invited and called before you to participate in raising above Independence Hall the flag of our country, with an additional star upon it. (Cheers.) I propose now, in advance of performing this very pleasant and complimentary duty, to say a few words. I propose to say that when that flag was originally raised here it had but thirteen stars. I wish to call your attention to the fact, that, under the blessing of God, each additional star added to that flag has given additional prosperity and happiness to this country until it has advanced to its present condition; and its welfare in the future, as well as in the past, is in your hands. (Cheers.) Cultivating the spirit that animated our fathers, who gave renown and celebrity to this Hall, cherishing that fraternal feeling which has so long characterized us as a nation, excluding passion, ill-temper and precipitate action on all occasions, I think we may promise ourselves that not only the new star placed upon that flag shall be permitted to remain there to our permanent prosperity for years to come, but additional ones shall from time to time be placed there, until we shall number as was anticipated by the great historian, five hundred millions of happy and prosperous people. (Great applause.) With these few remarks, I proceed to the very agreeable duty assigned me.

¹ Philadelphia *Inquirer*, February 23, 1861. Immediately following the speech in Independence Hall, Lincoln was accompanied to a platform outside where he was introduced to the assembled crowd by Stephen Benton, chairman of the Committee on City Property, in charge of the ceremonies. The new flag contained thirty-four stars, the thirty-fourth representing Kansas, admitted into the Union on January 29, 1861.

Remarks at Leaman Place, Pennsylvania¹

February 22, 1861

Mr. Lincoln appeared and said he was too unwell to say much to them. He expressed his pleasure on entering the great county of Lancaster, and thanked them for their friendly greeting, concluding by saying that he had merely come out to see them and let them see him, *in which he thought he had the best of the bargain!* To this the crowd responded "no you haven't!"

Loud calls being made for Mrs. Lincoln, Mr. L. brought her out, and said he had concluded to give them "the long and the short of it!" This remark—with the disparity between the *length* of himself and wife—produced a loud burst of laughter, followed by enthusiastic cheers as the train moved off.

¹ Lancaster, Pennsylvania, *Evening Express*, February 22, 1861.

Remarks at Lancaster, Pennsylvania¹

February 22, 1861

LADIES AND GENTLEMEN OF OLD LANCASTER: I appear not to make a speech. I have not time to make them at length, and not strength to make them on every occasion, and, worse than all, I have none to make. I come before you to see and be seen and, as regards the ladies, I have the best of the bargain; but, as to the gentlemen, I cannot say as much. There is plenty of matter to speak about in these times, but it is well known that the more a man speaks the less he is understood—the more he says one thing, his adversaries contend he meant something else. I shall soon have occasion to speak officially, and then I will endeavor to put my thoughts just as plain as I can express myself, true to the Constitution and Union of all the States, and to the perpetual liberty of all the people. Until I so speak, there is no need to enter upon details. In conclusion, I greet you most heartily, and bid you an affectionate farewell.

1 New York *Tribune* and *Times*, February 23, 1861. Other versions are substantially the same.

Reply to Governor Andrew J. Curtin at Harrisburg, Pennsylvania[1]

February 22, 1861

Gov. Curtin and citizens of the State of Pennsylvania: Perhaps the best thing that I could do would be simply to endorse the patriotic and eloquent speech which your Governor has just made in your hearing. [Applause.] I am quite sure that I am unable to address to you anything so appropriate as that which he has uttered.

Reference has been made by him to the distraction of the public mind at this time and to the great task that lies before me in entering upon the administration of the General Government. With all the eloquence and ability that your Governor brings to this theme, I am quite sure he does not—in his situation he cannot—appreciate as I do the weight of that great responsibility. I feel that, under God, in the strength of the arms and wisdom of the heads of these masses, after all, must be my support. [Immense cheering.] As I have often had occasion to say, I repeat to you— I am quite sure I do not deceive myself when I tell you I bring to the work an honest heart; I dare not tell you that I bring a head sufficient for it. [A voice—"we are sure of that."] If my own strength should fail, I shall at least fall back upon these masses, who, I think, under any circumstances will not fail.

Allusion has been made to the peaceful principles upon which this great Commonwealth was originally settled. Allow me to add my meed of praise to those peaceful principles. I hope no one of the Friends who originally settled here, or who lived here since that time, or who live here now, has been or is a more devoted lover of peace, harmony and concord than my humble self.

While I have been proud to see to-day the finest military array, I think, that I have ever seen, allow me to say in regard to those men that they give hope of what may be done when war is inevitable. But, at the same time, allow me to express the hope that in the shedding of blood their services may never be needed, especially in the shedding of fraternal blood. It shall be my endeavor to preserve the peace of this country so far as it can possibly be done, consistently with the maintenance of the institutions of the country. With my consent, or without my great displeasure, this country shall never witness the shedding of one drop of blood in fraternal strife.

And now, my fellow-citizens, as I have made many speeches, will you allow me to bid you farewell?

¹ Harrisburg, *Pennsylvania Daily Telegraph,* February 22, 1861. Variant texts in New York *Tribune* and New York *Times,* February 23, 1861. Lincoln spoke from the balcony of the Jones House.

Address to the Pennsylvania General Assembly at Harrisburg¹

February 22, 1861

Mr. Speaker of the Senate and also Mr. Speaker of the House of Representatives, and Gentlemen of the General Assembly of the State of Pennsylvania, I appear before you only for a very few brief remarks in response to what has been said to me. I thank you most sincerely for this reception, and the generous words in which support has been promised me upon this occasion. I thank your great Commonwealth for the overwhelming support it recently gave—not me personally—but the cause which I think a just one, in the late election. [Loud applause.]

Allusion has been made to the fact—the interesting fact perhaps we should say—that I for the first time appear at the Capitol of the great Commonwealth of Pennsylvania, upon the birthday of the Father of his Country. In connection with that beloved anniversary connected with the history of this country, I have already gone through one exceedingly interesting scene this morning in the ceremonies at Philadelphia. Under the kind conduct of gentlemen there, I was for the first time allowed the privilege of standing in old Independence Hall, [enthusiastic cheering], to have a few words addressed to me there and opening up to me an opportunity of expressing with much regret that I had not more time to express something of my own feelings excited by the occasion—somewhat to harmonize and give shape to the feelings that had been really the feelings of my whole life.

Besides this, our friends there had provided a magnificent flag of the country. They had arranged it so that I was given the honor of raising it to the head of its staff [applause]; and when it went up, I was pleased that it went to its place by the strength of my own feeble arm. When, according to the arrangement, the cord was pulled and it flaunted gloriously to the wind without an accident, in the light [bright]² glowing sun-shine of the morning, I could not help hoping that there was in the entire success of that beautiful ceremony, at least something of an omen of what is to come. [Loud applause.] Nor could I help, feeling then as I often have felt, that in the whole of that proceeding I was a very humble instrument. I had not provided the flag; I had not made the arrangement for elevating it to its place; I had applied but a very small portion of even my feeble strength in raising it. In the whole transaction, I was in the hands of the people who had arranged it, and if I can have the same generous co-operation of the people of this nation, I think the flag of our country may yet be kept flaunting gloriously. [Enthusiastic, long continued cheering.]

I recur for a moment but to repeat some words uttered at the hotel in regard to what has been said about the military support which the general government may expect from the Commonwealth of Pennsylvania, in a proper emergency. To guard against any possible mistake do I recur to this. It is not with any pleasure that I contemplate the possibility that a necessity may arise in this country for the use of the military arm. [Applause.] While I am exceedingly gratified to see the manifestation upon your streets of your military force here, and exceedingly gratified at your promise here to use that force upon a proper emergency, while I make these acknowledgments, I desire to repeat, in order to preclude any possible misconstruction, that I do most sincerely hope that we shall have no use for them—[loud applause]—that it will never become their duty to shed blood, and most especially never to shed fraternal blood. I promise that, (in so far as I may have wisdom to direct,) if so painful a result shall in any wise be brought about, it shall be through no fault of mine. [Cheers.]

Allusion has also been made, by one of your honored Speakers, to some remarks recently made by myself at Pittsburgh, in regard to what is supposed to be the especial interest of this great Commonwealth of Pennsylvania. I now wish only to say, in regard to that matter, that the few remarks which I uttered on that occasion were rather carefully worded. I took pains that they should be so. I have seen no occasion since to add to them or subtract from them. I leave them precisely as they stand; [applause] adding only now that I am pleased to have an expression from you, gentlemen of Pennsylvania, significant that they are satisfactory to you.

And now, gentlemen of the General Assembly of the Commonwealth of Pennsylvania, allow me again to return to you my most sincere thanks.

[Mr. Lincoln took his seat amid rapturous and prolonged cheering.]

1 Harrisburg, *Pennsylvania Daily Telegraph*, February 22, 1861. Variant
texts in New York *Tribune* and New York *Times*, February 23, 1861.
2 "Bright" appears in *Tribune*.

Reply to Committee of Congress Reporting the Electoral Count[1]

February 26, 1861

With deep gratitude to my countrymen for this mark of their confidence; with a distrust of my own ability to perform the required duty under the most favorable circumstances, now rendered doubly difficult by existing national perils; yet with a firm reliance on the strength of our free government, and the ultimate loyalty of the people to the just principles upon which it is founded, and above all an unshaken faith in the Supreme Ruler of nations, I accept this trust. Be pleased to signify my acceptance to the respective Houses of Congress.

1 Copy, DLC-RTL. The copy is in Nicolay's handwriting, but bears the incorrect date "Feb. 9, 1864," in another hand. There is also in the Lincoln Papers a rough copy or draft in another hand, which may be the transcript made at the time of Lincoln's reply, and revised by Nicolay for the press. The text in the New York *Herald*, February 27, 1861, is verbally the same.

Reply to Mayor James G. Berret at Washington, D.C.[1]

February 27, 1861

Mr. Mayor—I thank you, and through you the municipal authorities of this city by whom you are accompanied for this welcome; and as it is the first time in my life, since the present phase of politics has presented itself in this country, that I have said anything publicly within a region of country where the institution of slavery exists, I will take this occasion to say, that I think very much of the ill feeling that has existed and still exists between the people of the section from whence I came and the people here, is owing to a misunderstanding between each other which unhappily prevails. I therefore avail myself of this opportunity to assure you, Mr. Mayor, and all the gentlemen present, that I have not now, and never have had, any other than as kindly feelings towards you as to the people of my own section. I have not now, and never have had, any disposition to treat you in any respect otherwise than as my own neighbors. I have not now any purpose to withhold from you any of the benefits of the constitution, under any circumstances, that I would not feel myself constrained to withhold from my own neighbors; and I hope, in a word, when we shall become

[246]

better acquainted—and I say it with great confidence—we shall like each other the more. Again I thank you for the kindness of this reception.

¹ New York *Herald*, February 28, 1861. Mayor Berret and the Common Council of Washington visited President Buchanan at the White House and then called to welcome President-elect Lincoln at Willard's Hotel.

Response to a Serenade¹

February 28, 1861

MY FRIENDS—I suppose that I may take this as a compliment paid to me, and as such please accept my thanks for it. I have reached this city of Washington under circumstances considerably differing from those under which any other man has ever reached it. I have reached it for the purpose of taking an official position amongst the people, almost all of whom were opposed to me, and are yet opposed to me, as I suppose. (Several voices, "No, no." Other voices "Go on, sir; you are mistaken in that, indeed you are.") I propose no lengthy address to you now. I only propose to say, as I did say on yesterday, I believe, when your worthy Mayor and Board of Aldermen called upon me, that I thought much of the ill feeling that has existed between you and the people of your surroundings and that people from amongst whom I come, has depended, and now depends, upon a misunderstanding. (Several voices—"That's so;" and applause.) I hope that if things shall go along as prosperously as I believe we all desire they may, I may have it in my power to remove something of this misunderstanding—(cries of "Good," "Good," and loud applause)—that I may be enabled to convince you, and the people of your section of the country, that we regard you as in all things being our equals—in all things entitled to the same respect and to the same treatment that we claim for ourselves—(cries of "Good," and applause)—that we are in no wise disposed, if it were in our power, to oppress you or deprive you of any of your rights under the constitution of the United States or even narrowly to split hairs with you in regard to these rights. (Loud and prolonged cheering.) But are determined to give you, so far as lies in our hands, all your rights under the constitution, not grudgingly, but fully and fairly. (Cries of "Good," and applause.) I hope that by thus dealing with you we will become better acquainted and be better friends. (Cries of "Good," and applause.) And now my friends with these very few remarks, I again return my thanks for this compliment, and expressing my desire to hear a little more of your good music, I bid you good night.

[1] New York *Herald*, March 1, 1861. The U.S. Marine Band and a great crowd had gathered outside Willard's Hotel while President and Mrs. Lincoln were holding a levee in the hotel parlors. Lincoln responded to "Hail to the Chief."

To Gideon Welles[1]

[March, 1861?]

Sec. of the Navy, please see Mr. Williams, who can give some information about the defences [of Charleston.   A. LINCOLN]

[1] ALS, owned by Stephen V. Feeley, Washington, D.C. Mr. Williams has not been identified. The card on which this note is written has been burned, and the date is illegible, but the conclusion and signature are legible in part.

List of Senators' Preferences for Cabinet Appointment[1]

[March 1? 1861]

Trumbull– [Lyman B.]	Chase	x
Anthony [Henry B.]	Simmons	
Baker [Edward D.]	Cameron	
Bingham [Kinsley S.]	Chase–	
Chandler [Zachariah]	Cameron	
Clark [Daniel]	Chase– Simmons	x
Collamer [Jacob]	Simmons	
Dixon [James]	Cameron	
Doolittle [James R.]	Chase– Fessenden– Sherman–	
Durkee [Charles]	Chase	
Fessenden [William P.]	Chase–	x
Foote [Solomon Foot]	Dayton	x
Foster [Lafayette S.]	Dayton. Against Chase & Cameron x	
Grimes [James W.]	Dayton	
Hale [John P.]	Chase	x
Morrell [Lot M. Morrill]	Chase	
Harlin [James Harlan]	Chase–	
King [Preston]	Chase & Sherman	x
Simmons [James F.]	Chase	

[1] AD, DLC-RTL.

To William H. Seward[1]

Private

Hon. W. H. Seward   Willard's. Feb. [*sic*] March 1. 1861

Dear Sir   If a successor to Gen. Twiggs is attempted to be appointed, do not allow it to be done. Yours in haste

A. LINCOLN.

[1] ALS, NAuE. General David E. Twiggs in command of the Department of Texas, disbanded his forces in February, 1861, and accepted a major general's commission from Georgia.

First Inaugural Address—First Edition and Revisions[1]

March 4, 1861

In[2] compliance with a custom as old as the government itself, I appear before you to address you briefly, and to take, in your presence, the oath prescribed by the Constitution of the United States, to be taken by the President "before he enters on the execution of his office."[3]

[1] Documents, DLC-RTL. The original manuscript was composed during January, 1861, but, with the exception noted below (note 2) is presumably not extant. It was set in type at the office of the *Illinois State Journal* and printed in eight numbered pages. How many copies were struck off is not known, but there are two extant copies in the Lincoln Papers, both labeled "First Edition" by Lincoln. One of these copies, which bears no corrections, is herein reproduced. The revisions in Lincoln's hand on the second copy, as well as subsequent revisions, by Lincoln, Seward, and Browning, are indicated by means of footnotes. For the final text, see First Inaugural Address—Final Text, *infra*.

Lincoln must have made further revisions in proof sheets of the First Edition before the printing of the Second Edition, for the Second Edition omits some paragraphs and shows verbal changes from his corrected First Edition. No source of these corrections has been found.

There are five extant copies of the Second Edition: one copy (in the Lincoln Papers) bears further corrections in Lincoln's handwriting, some of which, at least, were adopted after Lincoln had studied Seward's suggestions for revision in late February; a second copy (in the Henry E. Huntington Library) which was given to Orville H. Browning bears his single suggestion for revision; a third copy (in the Lincoln Papers) with lines numbered by Seward is accompanied by six pages (including a verso) of Seward's manuscript suggestions for revision keyed to the line numbering (footnotes herein show Seward's suggestions relegated to their appropriate places in text); a fourth copy (in the Lincoln Papers) bears Nicolay's transcription of Seward's suggestions; and a fifth copy was cut up into clippings which were used in the preparation of the final text (*infra*).

In addition to the clippings from the fifth copy of the second edition, the final text (*infra*) includes passages inserted in Lincoln's handwriting, incorporating but not closely following the preceding revisions and suggestions; many passages were completely rewritten. Two other copies of this final text were made up. One (in the Harvard Library) with Lincoln's rewritten portions copied in Nicolay's hand, was prepared by Nicolay for the press; the other (owned by Crosby N. Boyd of Washington, D.C.) was prepared by an unidentified hand specifically for the Washington *Star* as the earliest paper to go to press after the inaugural ceremonies.

Footnotes 3-99 indicate the revisions which were made or suggested up to the draft of the final text. Sources of revisions are indicated as follows: (L-1ST) indicates Lincoln's revision of the First Edition, and (L-2ND) his revision of the second edition; (S-2ND) indicates Seward's suggestions for revision of the second edition; and (B-2ND) indicates Browning's one suggestion.

[2] The autograph manuscript of what appears to be an earlier draft of this paragraph is as follows: "In compliance with a custom as old as the government, I appear before you to address you briefly, and, in your presence, to take the oath prescribed by the Constitution and laws to be taken by whomever ["enters upon" deleted] assumes to perform the ["discharge" deleted] duties of our national chief magistrate." (DLC-RTL).

[3] (S-2ND) "Omit the inverted commas."

The more modern custom of electing[4] a Chief Magistrate upon a previously declared platform[5] of principles, supercedes, in a great measure, the necessity of repeating[6] those principles in an inaugural address.[7] Upon the plainest grounds of good faith, one so elected is not at liberty to shift his position.[8] It is necessarily implied, if not expressed, that, in his judgment, the platform which he thus accepts,[9] binds him to nothing either unconstitutional or inexpedient.

Having[10] been so elected upon the Chicago Platform, and while I would repeat nothing in it, of aspersion or epithet or question of motive against any man or party, I hold myself bound by duty, as well as impelled by inclination to follow, within the executive sphere, the principles therein declared. By no other course could I meet the reasonable expectations of the country.[11]

I do not consider it necessary at present for me to[12] say more than I have, in relation to those matters of administration, about which there is no special excitement.

Apprehension seems to exist among the people of the Southern States, that by the accession of a Republican Administration, their property, and their peace, and personal security, are to be endangered. There has never been any reasonable cause for such apprehension. Indeed, the most ample evidence to the contrary has all the while existed, and been open to their inspection. It is found in nearly all the published speeches of him who now addresses you. I do but quote from one of those speeches when I declare that "I have no purpose, directly or indirectly, to interfere with the institution of slavery in the States where it exists. I believe I have no lawful right to do so, and I have no inclination to do so." Those who nominated and elected me did so with full knowledge that I had made this and many other similar declarations, and had never recanted them. And more than this, they placed in the platform, for my acceptance, and as a law to themselves, and to me, the clear and emphatic resolution which I now read:

4 (S-2ND) "Instead of [']electing['] write 'nominating.' "

5 (S-2ND) "Instead of [']platform['] write 'summary.' "

6 (L-1ST) "Repeating" deleted, "re-stating" inserted.

7 (L-1ST) "Inaugural" deleted, "of this character" inserted following "address."

8 (S-2ND) "Strike out all between 'Upon' and 'position' both included."

9 (S-2ND) "After the word 'that' strike out 'in his judgment the platform which he thus accepts['] and insert [']the summary binds the officer elected.[']"

10 (S-2ND) "Strike out all these lines [paragraph beginning with "Having"] and write 'With this explanation I deem it my duty as I am disposed in feeling to follow so far as they apply to the Executive sphere the principles on which I was brought before the American People.' "

11 (L-2ND) Paragraphs two and three are marked for deletion.

12 (L-2ND) "Say more than I have, in relation to" deleted, "discuss" inserted.

"*Resolved*, That the maintenance inviolate of the rights of the States, and especially the right of each State to order and control its own domestic institutions according to its own judgment exclusively, is essential to that balance of power on which the perfection and endurance of our political fabric depend; and we denounce the lawless invasion by armed force of the soil of any State or Territory, no matter under what pretext, as among the gravest of crimes."

I now reiterate these sentiments: and in doing so, I only press upon the public attention the most conclusive evidence of which the case is susceptible, that the property, peace and security of no section are to be in anywise endangered by the now incoming Administration. I add too, that all the protection which, consistently with the Constitution and the laws, can be given, will be cheerfully given[13] to all the States—as cheerfully to one section as to another.

There is much controversy about the delivering up of fugitives from service or labor. The clause I now read is as plainly written in the Constitution as any other of its provisions:

"No person held to service or labor in one State, under the laws thereof, escaping into another, shall, in consequence of any law or regulation therein, be discharged from such service or labor, but shall be delivered up on claim of the party to whom such service or labor may be due."

It is scarcely questioned that this provision was intended by those who made it, for the reclaiming of what we call fugitive slaves; and the intention of the law-giver is the law. All members of Congress swear their support to the whole Constitution—to this provision as much as to any other. To the proposition, then, that slaves whose cases come within the terms of this clause, "shall be delivered up," their oaths are unanimous. Now, if they would all begin[14] in good temper, could they not, with something like[15] nearly equal unanimity, frame and pass a law,[16] through which to keep good that unanimous oath?

There is some difference of opinion whether this clause should be enforced by national or by state authority; but surely that difference is not a very material one. If the slave is to be surrendered, it can be of but little consequence to him, or to others, by which authority it is done. And should any one, in any case, be content

---

[13] (S-2ND) "After the words 'cheerfully given' insert 'in every case and under all circumstances.' "

(L-2ND) "When lawfully demanded, for whatever cause" inserted.

[14] (L-1ST) "All begin" deleted, "make the effort" inserted.

[15] (L-1ST) "Something like" deleted.

[16] (L-1ST) "Through" deleted, "by means of" inserted.

that his oath shall go unkept, on a merely unsubstantial controversy as to *how* it shall be kept?

Again, in any law upon this subject, ought not all the safeguards of liberty known in human and[17] civilized jurisprudence to be introduced, so that a free man be not, in any case, surrendered as a slave?

I take the official oath to-day, with no mental reservations, and with no purpose to construe the Constitution or laws, by any hypercritical rules. And while I do not think proper[18] now to specify particular acts of Congress as proper to be enforced, I do suggest that it will be much safer for all, both in official and private stations, to conform to and abide by all those acts which stand unrepealed, than to violate any of them, trusting to find impunity in having them held to be unconstitutional.

It is now[19] seventy-two years since the first inauguration of a President under our national Constitution. During the[20] period between then and now,[21] fifteen different and greatly distinguished citizens, have in succession, administered the executive branch of the government. They have conducted it through many perils; and, on the whole,[22] with great success. Yet, with all this scope for precedent, I now enter upon the same task for the brief constitutional term of four years, under great and peculiar difficulty. A disruption of the Federal Union[23] is menaced, and, so far as can be on paper, is already effected. The particulars of what has been done are so familiar and so fresh, that I need[24] to waste no[25] time in recounting them.

I hold, that in contemplation of universal law, and of the Constitution, the Union of these States is perpetual. Perpetuity is implied, if not expressed, in the fundamental law of all national governments. It is safe to assert that no government proper, ever had a provision in its organic law for its own termination. Continue to execute all the express provisions of our national Constitution, and the Union will endure forever—it being impossible to destroy it, except by some action not provided for in the instrument itself.

---

[17] (L-1ST) "Human and" deleted, "and humane" inserted after "civilized."
[18] (L-2ND) "Think proper" deleted, "choose" inserted.
[19] (S-2ND) "Strike out 'now.'"
    (L-2ND) Deletion adopted.
[20] (L-1ST) "The" deleted, "that" inserted.
[21] (L-1ST) "Between then and now" deleted.
[22] (S-2ND) "Strike out 'on the whole' and write 'generally.'"
    (L-2ND) Substitution adopted.
[23] (S-2ND) "After the word 'Union' strike out the rest of the sentence, and insert, 'heretofore only menaced is now formidably attempted.'"
[24] (L-1ST) "Not" inserted.   [25] (L-1ST) "No" deleted, "any" inserted.

Again, if the United States be not a government proper, but an association of States in the nature of contract merely, can it, as a contract, be peaceably unmade, by less than all the parties who made it? One party to a contract may violate it—break it, so to speak; but does it not require all to[26] rescind it?

Descending from these general principles, we find the proposition that, in legal contemplation, the Union is perpetual, confirmed by the history of the Union itself. The Union is much older than the Constitution. It was formed in fact, by the Articles of Association in 1774. It was matured and continued by the Declaration of Independence in 1776. It was further matured and expressly declared and pledged,[27] to be perpetual, by the Articles of Confederation in 1778. And finally, in 1787, one of the declared objects for ordaining and establishing the Constitution, was *"to form a more perfect union."*

But if destruction of the Union, by one, or by a part only, of the States, be lawfully possible, the Union is *less* perfect than before, which[28] contradicts the Constitution, and therefore is absurd.[29]

It follows from these views that no State, upon its own mere motion, can lawfully get out of the Union,—that *resolves* and *ordinances* to that effect are legally nothing;[30] and that acts of violence, within any State or States,[31] are insurrectionary or treasonable,[32] according to circumstances.

I therefore consider that[33] the Union is unbroken; and, to the extent of my ability, I shall take care[34] that the laws of the Union be faithfully executed in all the States. Doing this I deem to be only a simple duty on my part; and I shall perform it,[35] unless my rightful masters, the American people, shall withhold the requisite means, or, in some tangible way,[36] direct the contrary. I trust this will not be regarded as a menace, but only as the declared purpose

[26] (L-1ST) "Lawfully" inserted.

[27] (L-2ND) "And pledged" deleted, "plighted, and engaged," inserted.

[28] (L-2ND) "Which contradicts the" deleted [deletion of "the" was obviously unintentional], "and therefore is absurd" deleted, "having lost the vital element of perpetuity" inserted.

[29] (S-2ND) "Strike out the whole line [*i.e.*, "therefore is absurd."]."

[30] (S-2ND) "For 'nothing' write 'void.'" (L-2ND) Substitution adopted.

[31] (L-1ST) "Against the [deletion] authority, of the United States" inserted.

[32] (S-2ND) "For [']treasonable,['] write 'revolutionary.'"

(L-2ND) Substitution adopted.

[33] (S-2ND) "After the word 'that' write [']in the view of the constitution and the laws.[']" (L-2ND) Insertion adopted.

[34] (S-2ND) "After the word [']care['] insert 'as the constitution itself expressly enjoins upon me.[']" (L-2ND) Insertion adopted.

[35] (L-1ST) "So far as practicable" inserted.

[36] (S-2ND) "Instead of 'tangible way' write 'authoritative manner.[']"

(L-2ND) Substitution adopted.

of the Union that it will[37] have its own, and defend itself.[38]

In doing this there needs to be no bloodshed or violence; and there shall be none, unless[39] forced upon the national authority. All[40] the power at my disposal will be used to reclaim[41] the public property and places which have fallen; to hold, occupy and possess these,[42] and all other property and places belonging to the government, and to collect the duties on imports;[43] but beyond what may be necessary for these,[44] there will be no invasion of any State.[45]

[37] (L-1ST) "Will" and "defend" underlined.

[38] (S-2ND) "Instead of 'will have its own, and defend itself' write [']will constitutionally defend and maintain itself.' "   [39] (L-1ST) "It be" inserted.

[40] (S-2ND) "Strike out the whole [sentence] and insert, 'The power confided to me shall be used indeed with efficacy but also with discretion in every case and exigency according to the circumstances actually existing and with a view and a hope of a peaceful solution of the national troubles and the restoration of fraternal sympathies and affections.[']"

[41] (B-2ND) Orville H. Browning suggested revision of this sentence to omit "to reclaim the public property and places which have fallen" and to continue ". . . to hold, occupy and possess the property and places belonging to the government. . . ."   (L-2ND) Deletion adopted.

Browning to Lincoln February 17, 1861, explained that "On principle the passage is right as it now stands. The fallen places ought to be reclaimed. But cannot that be accomplished as well, or even better without announcing the purpose in your inaugural?" (DLC-RTL). On the back of Browning's letter Lincoln wrote the following sentence, probably as a tentative insertion to be made in the Address: "Americans, all, we are not enemies, but friends. We have sacred ties of affection which, though strained by passion, let us hope can never be broken." (DLC-RTL). Part of this phrasing went into Lincoln's concluding paragraph added to the final copy following Seward's suggestion. See note 99 and compare Lincoln's last paragraph in the final text *infra*.

[42] (L-2ND) "These" changed to "the," "and all other" deleted.

[43] (L-1ST) "Imports" deleted, "imposts" inserted.

[44] (L-1ST) "Objects" inserted.

[45] (L-2ND) "State" deleted, "part of the country—no using of force against, or among the people" inserted.

(L-1ST) Passages inserted as follows: "Where hostility to the government [United States], in any interior locality shall be so great and so universal, as to forbid [prevent] competent citizens of their own, to hold, and exercise [resident citizens from holding] the federal offices, there will be no attempt to force obnoxious strangers among them [the people] for that object. While the strict. legal right, may exist in the government to enforce the exercise of the [these] offices under such circumstances, ["under . . . circumstances" deleted] the attempt [to do so] would be so irritating, and so nearly impracticable, with all, that I deem it better to forego, for the time, the uses of such offices." Bracketed variants represent further changes which appear in the second edition as finally struck off.

(S-2ND) "Strike out the whole sentence [*i.e.*, Lincoln's insertion actually including two sentences] and insert 'There are in this government as in every other emergencies when the exercise of power lawful in itself is less certain to secure the just ends of administration, than a temporary forbearance from it with reliance on the voluntary though delayed acquiescence of the people in the laws which have been made by themselves and for their own benefit. I shall not lose sight of this obvious maxim.' " Suggestion not adopted.

The mails, unless refused, will continue to be furnished in all parts of the Union. So far as possible, the people everywhere shall have that sense of perfect security which is most favorable to calm thought and reflection.[46]

That there are persons[47] who seek to destroy the Union at all events, and are glad of any pretext to do it, I will neither affirm or deny; but if there be such, I need address no word to them.[48] To those, however, who really love the Union, may I not speak?

Before entering upon so grave a matter as the destruction of our national Union,[49] would it not be wise to ascertain precisely why we do it? Will you hazard so desperate a step, while there is any possibility that any portion of the ills you fly from have no real existence? Will you while the certain ills you fly to, are greater than all the real ones you fly from? Will you risk the commission of so fearful a mistake?

All profess to be content in the Union, if all constitutional rights can be maintained. Is it true, then, that any[50] right, plainly written in the Constitution, has been denied? I think not. Happily the human mind is so constructed, that no party can reach to the audacity of doing this. Think, if you can, of a single instance in which a plainly written provision of the Constitution has ever been denied. If, by the mere force of numbers, a majority should deprive a minority of any clearly written constitutional right, it might, in a moral point of view, justify revolution—certainly would, if such right were a vital one;[51]—but such is not our case. All the vital rights of minorities, and of individuals, are so plainly assured to them, by affirmations and negations[52] in the Constitution, that controversies never arise concerning them. But no organic law can ever be framed with a provision specifically applicable to every[53] question which may occur in practical admin-

46 (L-1ST) "This course will be pursued, unless current experience shall show a modification, or change to be proper" inserted.

47 (S-2ND) "After the word [']persons['] insert 'in one section as well as in the other.'" (L-2ND) "Either North or South" inserted.

48 (S-2ND) "After the word 'them' insert 'because I am sure they must be few in number and of little influence when their pernicious principles are fully understood.[']"

49 (L-1ST) "Union" deleted, "fabric" inserted.
   (L-2ND) "Union" deleted, and "fabric, with all its benefits, it's memories, and it's hopes," inserted.

50 (S-2ND) "After the word 'any' write 'distinct.'"

51 (L-1ST) Punctuation changed to period and "but" capitalized.

52 (S-2ND) "After the word 'negations' write [']guarantees and prohibitions.[']" (L-2ND) Insertion adopted.

53 (S-2ND) "After the word 'every' write 'possible.'"
   (L-2ND) Insertion adopted.

istration. No foresight can anticipate, nor any document of reasonable length contain express provisions for all possible questions. Shall fugitives from labor be surrendered by national or by State authority? The Constitution does not expressly say. *May* Congress prohibit slavery in the territories? The Constitution does not expressly say. *Must* Congress protect slavery in the territories? The Constitution does not expressly say.

From questions of this class spring all our constitutional controversies, and we divide upon them into majorities and minorities. If the minority will not submit,[54] the majority must, or the government must cease. There is no other alternative; for continuing the government, is submission[55] on one side or the other. If a minority, in such case, will secede rather than submit,[56] they make a precedent which, in turn, will divide and ruin them; for a minority of their own number[57] will secede from them whenever a majority refuses to be controlled by such minority.[58] For instance, why may not South Carolina,[59] a year or two hence, arbitrarily, secede from[60] a new Southern Confederacy, just as she[61] now claims to secede from the present Union? Her people, and, indeed, all secession people,[62] are now being educated to the precise temper of doing this. Is there such perfect identity of interests among the States to compose a Southern Union, as to produce harmony only, and prevent renewed secession? Will[63] South Carolina be found lacking in either the restlessness or the ingenuity to pick a quarrel with Kentucky?

Plainly, the central idea of secession, is the essence of anarchy.[64] A constitutional[65] majority is the only true sovereign of a free

54 (S-2ND) "Strike out 'submit' and insert 'acquiesce.' "

  (L-2ND) Substitution adopted.

55 (S-2ND) "Strike out 'submission' & insert 'acquiescence.' "

  (L-2ND) Substitution adopted.

56 (S-2ND) "For 'submit' write 'acquiesce.' "

  (L-2ND) Substitution adopted.   57 (L-2ND) "Number" deleted.

58 (L-2ND) "Such minority" deleted, "them" inserted.

59 (S-2ND) "For 'South Carolina' write 'Alabama or Florida.' "

  (L-2ND) "South Carolina" deleted, "any portion of a new confederacy" inserted.

60 (L-2ND) "From a new Southern Confederacy" deleted, "again" inserted.

61 (L-2ND) "She now claims" changed to "the larger number now claim."

62 (S-2ND) "For [']People['] write 'communities.' "

  (L-2ND) "Her people, and, indeed, all secession people," deleted, "All who cherish secession ideas" inserted.   63 (L-1ST) This sentence deleted.

64 (S-2ND) "After the word 'anarchy' strike out the next sentence and write [']A majority held in restraint by constitutional checks and limitations and always changing easily with deliberate changes of popular opinions and sentiments is &c.[']"

  (L-2ND) "—of disintegration" inserted following "anarchy."

65 (L-2ND) "Constitutional" changed to "constitutionally expressed."

people. Whoever rejects it, does, of necessity, fly to anarchy or to despotism. Unanimity is impossible; the rule of a minority, as a permanent arrangement, is wholly inadmissable; so that, rejecting the majority principle, anarchy or despotism[66] is all that is left.[67]

Some, if not all of the States which claim to have withdrawn from the Union, have declared the supposed grievances which impelled them to the separation. Most prominent among these is the charge, in substance, that the Republican party have *avowed* the purpose to destroy the property of the Southern people. With all due deference and respect, allow me to declare that the Republican party have made no such avowal. The Republican party of the nation have spoken but twice; and in both instances they expressly avowed what necessarily implies the exact contrary—in 1860, as

[66] (L-1ST) "In some form" inserted.

[67] (L-1ST) The following paragraph is inserted at this point (variants enclosed in brackets are from the second edition as printed, and superior italic letters are the key to further revisions which immediately follow the text): "I do not forget the position assumed by some, that constitutional questions are to be decided by the Supreme Court; nor do I question [deny] that such decisions must be binding and conclusive ["and conclusive" deleted, "in any case," inserted] upon the parties to a suit as to the subject [object] of that [the][a] suit.[b] And, while it is obviously possible, that such decision may be erroneous in any given case, still the evil effect following it, being limited to the [that] particular case, with the chances [chance] that it may be over-ruled, and never become a precedent for other cases, can better be borne, than could the greater evils of a different rule.[c] But[d] if the whole ["whole" deleted] policy of the government upon vital questions, extending to [affecting] the whole people, is to be irrevocably fixed by decisions of the Supreme court,[e] it is plain that the people will have ceased to be their own rulers, having[f] turned their government over to the despotism[g] of the few men [life-officers] composing the court. Nor is there, in this view, any assault upon the court, or the judges. It is a duty from which they may not shrink, to decide cases, when ["when" deleted] properly brought before them; and, it is no fault of theirs, if others seek to turn their decisions to political purposes."

[a] (L-2ND) "The" deleted, "that" inserted.

[b] (S-2ND) "After the words 'the suit,' [*i.e.*, at the end of the first sentence of Lincoln's insertion] insert [']while they are entitled to very high respect and consideration in all parallel cases by all other departments of the government.[']"

[c] (S-2ND) "Strike out 'rule' [*i.e.*, at end of second sentence in Lincoln's insertion] and insert 'practice.'" (L-2ND) "Rule" deleted, "practice" inserted.

[d] (S-2ND) "Strike out 'But' [*i.e.*, first word in third sentence of Lincoln's insertion] and insert [']At the same time the candid citizen must confess that.[']"

[e] (S-2ND) "After the word [']Court,['] [*i.e.*, in the third sentence of Lincoln's insertion] strike out the words 'it is plain that' and insert 'made in the ordinary course of litigation between parties in personal actions.'"

[f] (S-2ND) "After the word [']having['] [*i.e.*, in the third sentence of Lincoln's insertion] strike out the rest of the sentence and write [']practically resigned their government into the hands of that eminent tribunal.'" (L-2ND) "Pro tanto" inserted after "having."

[g] (L-2ND) "Despotism" deleted, "arbitrary control" inserted.

already quoted in this discourse; and, in 1856, in their National Convention at Philadelphia, as I now read:

"*Resolved,* That the maintenance of the principles promulgated in the Declaration of Independence, and embodied in the Federal Constitution, is essential to the preservation of Republican institutions, and that the Federal Constitution, *the rights of the States,* and the Union of the States, shall be preserved."

In addition to this, I aver that, to my knowledge, no sub-division, or individual, of the Republican party has ever avowed, or entertained, a purpose to destroy or to interfere with the property of the Southern people. For myself, I can declare, with perfect certainty, that I have never avowed, or entertained any such purpose; and I have never used any expression intended to convey such a meaning.[68]

The[69] Republican party, as I understand, have avowed the purpose to prevent, if they can, the extension of slavery, under the national auspices; and upon this arises the only[70] dispute between the sections.

One section[71] believes slavery is *right,* and ought to be extended, while the other believes it is *wrong,* and ought not to be extended. This is the only substantial dispute. The fugitive slave clause of the Constitution, and the law for the suppression of the foreign slave trade, are each as well enforced,[72] as any law can ever be in a community where the moral sense of the people is against[73] the law itself. The great body of the people abide by the dry legal obligation in both cases, and a few break over in each. This, I think, cannot be perfectly cured; and it would be worse in both cases *after* the separation of the sections, than before. The foreign slave trade, now imperfectly suppressed, would be[74] revived without

---

68 (L-1ST) The following passage is inserted at this point: "The supposed purpose, then, of one section to destroy the property of the other, has no real existence; and to break up the government for that imaginary cause, would be a most melancholy mistake." At some point after his revision of the first edition, and before the printing of his second edition, Lincoln decided to omit this paragraph, as well as the preceding quotation from the Republican resolution of 1856, and the sentence which introduced it. Neither they nor Lincoln's further insertion appear in the second edition.
69 (S-2ND) "Strike out the whole paragraph."
70 (L-2ND) "Material" inserted.
71 (S-2ND) "After the word 'section' insert [']of our country.[']"
72 (S-2ND) "After the word 'enforced' write 'perhaps.' "
   (L-2ND) Insertion adopted.
73 (S-2ND) "Strike out the words 'is against' and insert 'imperfectly supports.[']"
74 (S-2ND) "After the word 'be' insert 'ultimately.' "
   (L-2ND) Insertion adopted.

restriction, in one section; while fugitive slaves, now only partially surrendered, would not be surrendered at all, by the other.

Physically speaking, we cannot separate. We cannot remove our respective sections from each other, nor build an impassable wall between them. A husband and wife may be divorced, and go out of the presence, and beyond the reach of each other; but the different parts of our country cannot do this. They cannot but remain face to face; and intercourse, either amicable or hostile, must continue between them. Is it possible[75] to make that intercourse more advantageous or[76] satisfactory, *after* separation than *before?* Can aliens make treaties easier than friends can make laws? Can treaties be more faithfully enforced between aliens than laws can among friends? Suppose you go to war, you cannot fight always; and when, after much loss on both sides, and no gain on either, you cease fighting, the identical old questions, as to terms of intercourse, are again upon you.

During[77] the winter just closed, I have been greatly urged, by many patriotic men, to lend the influence of my position to some compromise, by which I was, to some extent, to shift the ground upon which I had been elected. This I steadily refused. I so refused, not from any party wantonness, nor from any indifference to the troubles of the country. I thought such refusal was demanded by the view that if, when a Chief Magistrate is constitutionally elected, he cannot be inaugurated till he betrays those who elected him, by breaking his pledges, and surrendering to those who tried and failed to defeat him at the polls, this government and all popular government is already at an end. Demands for such surrender, once recognized, are without limit, as to nature, extent and repetition. They break the only bond of faith between public and public servant; and they distinctly set the minority over the majority.

I presume there is not a man in America, (and there ought not to be one) who opposed my election, who would, for a moment, tolerate his own candidate in such surrender, had he been successful in the election. In such case they would all see, that such surrender would not be merely the ruin of a man, or a party; but, as a precedent, would be the ruin of the government itself.

I do not deny the possibility that the people may err in an election; but if they do, the true cure is in the next election; and not in the treachery of the party elected.

---

[75] (L-2ND) "Then," inserted.   [76] (L-2ND) "More" inserted.
[77] (L-1ST) The next three paragraphs have been deleted by clipping them out of the revised first edition.

Why[78] should there not be a patient confidence in the ultimate justice of the people? Is there any better or equal hope, in the world? In our present differences, is either party without faith[79] in the right? If the Almighty Ruler of nations, with his eternal truth and justice, be[80] on our[81] side, or on yours, that truth and that justice will surely prevail, by the judgment of this great tribunal, the American people.

By the frame of the government under which we live, this same people have widely given their public servants but little power for mischief; and have, with equal wisdom, provided for the return of that little to their own hands at very short intervals.

While[82] the people remain patient, and true to themselves, no man, even in the presidential chair, by any extreme of wickedness or folly, can[83] very seriously injure the government in the short space of four years.

This[84] country, with its institutions, belongs to the people who inhabit it. Whenever they shall grow weary of the existing government, they can exercise their *constitutional* right of amending it, or their *revolutionary* right to dismember or overthrow it. As[85] I am not much impressed with the belief that the present Constitution can be improved, I make no recommendations of amendments. I am, rather, for the old ship, and the chart of the old pilots. If, however, the people desire a new, or[86] an altered vessel, the matter is exclusively their own, and they can move in the premises, as well without as with an executive recommendation.[87] I shall place no obstacle in the way of what may appear to be their wishes.

The Chief Magistrate derives all his authority from the people, and they have conferred none upon him to fix terms for the sepa-

---

[78] (L-1st) The next three paragraphs have been clipped and inserted two paragraphs later.   [79] (L-2nd) "Of being" inserted.

[80] (S-2nd) "Strike out the words 'be on our side or on yours' and insert 'be on the side of the North, or of the South, of the East or of the West.'"

[81] (L-2nd) "Our" deleted, "your" inserted; probably this is an error.

[82] (S-2nd) "Strike out all the words to and including 'chair' and insert 'While the people retain their virtue and vigilance no legislature and no administration can.[']"   [83] (S-2nd) "Strike out 'can.'"

[84] (L-1st) The next two paragraphs have been clipped and moved up three paragraphs to follow the sentence ending "are again upon you."

[85] (S-2nd) "Strike out the whole sentence and insert 'While so great a diversity of opinion exists on the question what amendments, if, indeed any would be effective in restoring peace and safety, it would only tend to aggravate the dispute if I were to attempt to give direction to the public mind in that respect.[']"   [86] (L-2nd) "A new or" deleted.

[87] (L-2nd) "The constitution itself prescribes two distinct modes, either of which they can pursue" inserted.

ration of the States. The people themselves can do this[88] if they choose; but the executive, as such, has nothing to do with it. His duty is to administer the present government, as it came to his hands, and to transmit it,[89] unimpaired by him, to his successor.

My countrymen, one and all, take *time*[90] and think *well*, upon this whole subject. Nothing[91] valuable can be lost by taking time. Nothing[92] worth preserving is either breaking or burning. If there be an object to *hurry* any of you, in hot haste, to a point where[93] you would never go[94] *deliberately*, that object will be frustrated by taking time; but no good object can be frustrated by it. Such of you as are now dissatisfied, still have the old Constitution unimpaired, and, on the sensitive point, the laws of your own framing under it; while the new administration will have no immediate power, if it would, to change either. If it were admitted that you who are dissatisfied, hold the right side in the dispute, there still is no single good reason for precipitate action. Intelligence, patriotism, Christianity, and a firm reliance on Him, who has never yet forsaken this favored land, are still competent to adjust, in the best way, all our present difficulty.

In *your* hands, my dissatisfied fellow countrymen, and not in *mine*, is the momentous issue of civil war. The government will not assail *you*, unless[95] you *first* assail *it*. You can have no conflict, without being yourselves the aggressors. *You* have no oath registered in Heaven to destroy the government, while *I* shall have the most solemn one to "preserve, protect, and defend" it. *You* can forbear the *assault* upon it;[96] *I* can *not* shrink from the *defense* of it.[97] With *you*, and not with *me*, is the solemn question of[98] "Shall it be peace, or a sword?"[99]

<hr>

[88] (L-2ND) "Too" inserted.

[89] (S-2ND) "After the words 'transmit it' insert 'if possible.'"

[90] (S-2ND) "Strike out the words 'take time' and insert 'think calmly.'"

[91] (S-2ND) "Strike out all from 'Nothing valuable['] to [']burning['] both inclusive.   [92] (L-2ND) This sentence deleted.

[93] (L-1ST) "Point where" deleted, "step which" inserted.

[94] (L-1ST) "Go" deleted, "take" inserted.

[95] (S-2ND) "Strike out the words 'unless you first assail it.[']"

[96] (L-1ST) "Upon it" deleted.

[97] (L-1ST) "Of it" deleted.

(S-2ND) "Strike out all after the word 'defense.'"

[98] (L-2ND) "Of" deleted.

[99] (S-2ND) On the back of the fourth page of Seward's list of suggestions appears the following suggestion for a closing paragraph: "I close. We are not we must not be aliens or enemies but ["countrym" deleted] fellow countrymen and brethren. Although passion has strained our bonds of affection too hardly they must not ["be broken they will not" deleted], I am sure they will not be broken. The mystic chords which proceeding from ["every ba" deleted] so many battle fields and ["patriot" deleted] so many patriot graves ["bind" deleted] pass

through all the hearts and ["hearths" deleted] all the hearths in this broad continent of ours will yet ["harmon" deleted] again harmonize in their ancient music when ["touched as they surely" deleted] breathed upon ["again" deleted] by the ["better angel" deleted] guardian angel of the nation."

In addition to this suggestion, a manuscript page in the handwriting of Frederick W. Seward, who was his father's secretary, headed "Suggestions for a closing paragraph," reads as follows:

"However unusual it may be at such a time to speak of sections or to sections, yet in view of the misconception & agitations which have strained the ties of brotherhood so far, I hope it will not be deemed a departure from propriety, whatever it may be from custom, to say that if in the criminations and misconstructions which too often imbue our political contests, any man south of this capital has been led to believe that I regard with a less friendly eye, his rights, his interests or his domestic safety and happiness, or those of his State, than I do those of any other portion of my country or that I would invade or disturb any legal right or domestic institution in the South, he mistakes both my principles and feelings, and does not know me. I aspire to come in the spirit, however far below the ability and the wisdom, of Washington, of Madison, of Jackson and of Clay. In that spirit I here declare that in my administration I shall know no rule but the Constitution, no guide but the laws, and no sentiment but that of equal devotion to my whole country, east, west, north and south."

First Inaugural Address—Final Text[1]

March 4, 1861

Fellow citizens of the United States:[2]

In compliance with a custom as old as the government itself, I appear before you to address you briefly, and to take, in your presence, the oath prescribed by the Constitution of the United States, to be taken by the President "before he enters on the execution of his office."

I do not consider it necessary, at present, for me to discuss those matters of administration about which there is no special anxiety, or excitement.[3]

Apprehension seems to exist among the people of the Southern States, that by the accession of a Republican Administration, their property, and their peace, and personal security, are to be endangered. There has never been any reasonable cause for such apprehension. Indeed, the most ample evidence to the contrary has all the while existed, and been open to their inspection. It is found in nearly all the published speeches of him who now addresses you.

[1] D and AD, DLC-RTL. The text is reproduced from Lincoln's final copy. All insertions and revised passages in Lincoln's handwriting are indicated in footnotes. Lincoln's capitalization and use of the apostrophe have been made to conform, in Lincoln's insertions, with the usage in the printed portions, otherwise Lincoln's usage is preserved.

[2] The salutation does not appear in Lincoln's final copy, but was written in by Nicolay on the press copy.

[3] Paragraph in Lincoln's handwriting, replacing paragraphs 2, 3, and 4 of the preceding drafts.

I do but quote from one of those speeches when I declare that "I have no purpose, directly or indirectly, to interfere with the institution of slavery in the States where it exists. I believe I have no lawful right to do so, and I have no inclination to do so." Those who nominated and elected me did so with full knowledge that I had made this, and many similar declarations, and had never recanted them. And more than this, they placed in the platform, for my acceptance, and as a law to themselves, and to me, the clear and emphatic resolution which I now read:

"*Resolved*, That the maintenance inviolate of the rights of the States, and especially the right of each State to order and control its own domestic institutions according to its own judgment exclusively, is essential to that balance of power on which the perfection and endurance of our political fabric depend; and we denounce the lawless invasion by armed force of the soil of any State or Territory, no matter under what pretext, as among the gravest of crimes."

I now reiterate these sentiments: and in doing so, I only press upon the public attention the most conclusive evidence of which the case is susceptible, that the property, peace and security of no section are to be in anywise endangered by the now incoming Administration. I add too, that all the protection which, consistently with the Constitution and the laws, can be given, will be cheerfully given to all the States[4] when lawfully demanded, for whatever cause—as cheerfully to one section,[5] as to another.

There is much controversy about the delivering up of fugitives from service or labor. The clause I now read is as plainly written in the Constitution as any other of its provisions:

"No person held to service or labor in one State, under the laws thereof, escaping into another, shall, in consequence of any law or regulation therein, be discharged from such service or labor, but shall be delivered up on claim of the party to whom such service or labor may be due."

It is scarcely questioned that this provision was intended by those who made it, for the reclaiming of what we call fugitive slaves; and the intention of the law-giver is the law. All members of Congress swear their support to the whole Constitution—to this provision as much as to any other. To the proposition, then, that slaves whose cases come within the terms of this clause, "shall be delivered up," their oaths are unanimous. Now, if they would make the effort in good temper, could they not, with nearly equal

[4] "When lawfully demanded, for whatever cause" inserted.
[5] Comma inserted.

unanimity, frame and pass a law, by means of which to keep good that unanimous oath?

There is some difference of opinion whether this clause should be enforced by national or by state authority; but surely that difference is not a very material one. If the slave is to be surrendered, it can be of but little consequence to him, or to others, by which authority it is done. And should any one, in any case, be content that his oath shall go unkept, on a merely unsubstantial controversy as to *how* it shall be kept?

Again, in any law upon this subject, ought not all the safeguards of liberty known in civilized and humane jurisprudence to be introduced, so that a free man be not, in any case, surrendered as a slave? And[6] might it not be well, at the same time, to provide by law for the enforcement of that clause in the Constitution which guarranties that "The citizens of each State shall be entitled to all previleges and immunities of citizens in the several States?"

I take the official oath to-day, with no mental reservations, and with no purpose to construe the Constitution or laws, by any hypercritical rules. And while I do not choose[7] now to specify particular acts of Congress as proper to be enforced, I do suggest,[8] that it will be much safer for all, both in official and private stations, to conform to, and abide by, all those acts which stand unrepealed, than to violate any of them, trusting to find impunity in having them held to be unconstitutional.

It is[9] seventy-two years since the first inauguration of a President under our national Constitution. During that period fifteen different and greatly distinguished citizens, have, in succession, administered the executive branch of the government. They have conducted it through many perils; and, generally,[10] with great success. Yet, with all this scope for precedent, I now enter upon the same task for the brief constitutional term of four years, under great and peculiar difficulty. A disruption of the Federal Union[11] heretofore only menaced, is now formidably attempted.

I hold, that in contemplation of universal law, and of the Constitution, the Union of these States is perpetual. Perpetuity is implied, if not expressed, in the fundamental law of all national governments. It is safe to assert that no government proper, ever had a provision in its organic law for its own termination. Continue to

6 The rest of this paragraph inserted.
7 "Think proper" deleted, "choose" inserted.   8 Comma inserted.
9 "Now" deleted.   10 "On the whole" deleted, "generally" inserted.
11 "Is menaced, and, so far as can be on paper, is already effected. The particulars of what has been done are so familiar, and so fresh, that I need not to waste any time in recounting them." deleted, and revision inserted as above.

execute all the express provisions of our national Constitution, and the Union will endure forever—it being impossible to destroy it, except by some action not provided for in the instrument itself.

Again, if the United States be not a government proper, but an association of States in the nature of contract merely, can it, as a contract, be peaceably unmade, by less than all the parties who made it? One party to a contract may violate it—break it, so to speak; but does it not require all to lawfully rescind it?

Descending from these general principles, we find the proposition that, in legal contemplation, the Union is perpetual, confirmed by the history of the Union itself. The Union is much older than the Constitution. It was formed in fact, by the Articles of Association in 1774. It was matured and continued by the Declaration of Independence in 1776. It was further matured[12] and the faith of all the then thirteen States expressly plighted and engaged that it should be perpetual, by the Articles of Confederation in 1778. And finally, in 1787, one of the declared objects for ordaining and establishing the Constitution, was *to form a more perfect union.*

But if destruction of the Union, by one, or by a part only, of the States, be lawfully possible, the Union is *less* perfect than before[13] the Constitution,[14] having lost the vital element of perpetuity.

It follows from these views that no State, upon its own mere motion, can lawfully get out of the Union,—that *resolves* and *ordinances* to that effect are legally void;[15] and that acts of violence, within any State or States, against the authority of the United States, are insurrectionary or revolutionary,[16] according to circumstances.

I[17] therefore consider that, in view of the Constitution and the laws, the Union is unbroken; and, to the extent of my ability, I shall take care, as the Constitution itself expressly enjoins upon me, that the laws of the Union be faithfully executed in all the States. Doing this I deem to be only a simple duty on my part; and I shall perform it, so far as practicable, unless my rightful masters, the American people, shall withhold the requisite means, or, in some authoritative manner,[18] direct the contrary. I trust this

[12] "And expressly declared and pledged, to be" deleted, "and the faith of all the then thirteen States expressly plighted and engaged that it should be" inserted. [13] "Which contradicts" deleted.

[14] "And therefore is absurd" deleted, "having lost the vital element of perpetuity" inserted. [15] "Nothing" deleted, "void" inserted.

[16] "Treasonable" deleted, "revolutionary" inserted.

[17] This sentence written on a slip pasted on the verso, replaces the sentence in preceding drafts.

[18] "Tangible way" deleted, "authoritative manner" inserted.

will not be regarded as a menace, but only as the declared purpose of the Union that it *will*[19] constitutionally defend, and maintain itself.

In doing this there needs to be no bloodshed or violence; and there shall be none, unless it be forced upon the national authority. The[20] power confided to me, will be used to hold, occupy, and possess the property, and places belonging to the government, and to collect the duties and imposts; but beyond what may be necessary for these objects, there will be no invasion—no using of force against, or among the people anywhere. Where hostility to the United States, in any interior locality, shall be so great and so universal, as to prevent competent resident citizens from holding the Federal offices, there will be no attempt to force obnoxious strangers among the people for that object. While the strict legal right may exist in the government to enforce the exercise of these offices, the attempt to do so would be so irritating, and so nearly impracticable with all, that I deem it better to forego, for the time, the uses of such offices.

The mails, unless repelled,[21] will continue to be furnished in all parts of the Union. So far as possible, the people everywhere shall have that sense of perfect security which is most favorable to calm thought and reflection. The[22] course here indicated will be followed, unless current events, and experience, shall show a modification, or change, to be proper; and in every case and exigency, my best discretion will be exercised, according to circumstances actually existing, and with a view and a hope of a peaceful solution of the national troubles, and the restoration of fraternal sympathies and affections.

That there are persons in one section, or another[23] who seek to destroy the Union at all events, and are glad of any pretext to do it, I will neither affirm or deny; but if there be such, I need address no word to them. To those, however, who really love the Union, may I not speak?

Before entering upon so grave a matter as the destruction of our national fabric,[24] with all its benefits, its memories, and its hopes, would it not be wise to ascertain precisely why we do it? Will you

[19] "Have its own, and *defend* itself" deleted, "constitutionally defend, and maintain itself" inserted.
[20] This sentence inserted on a slip replacing the sentence in the preceding drafts. [21] "Refused" deleted, "repelled" inserted.
[22] The rest of this paragraph is inserted, replacing the sentence in preceding drafts. [23] "In one section, or another" inserted.
[24] "Union" deleted, "fabric, with all its benefits, it's memories, and it's hopes," inserted.

hazard so desperate a step, while there is any possibility that any portion of the ills you fly from, have no real existence? Will you, while the certain ills you fly to, are greater than all the real ones you fly from? Will you risk the commission of so fearful a mistake?

All profess to be content in the Union, if all constitutional rights can be maintained. Is it true, then, that any[25] right, plainly written in the Constitution, has been denied? I think not. Happily the human mind is so constituted,[26] that no party can reach to the audacity of doing this. Think, if you can, of a single instance in which a plainly written provision of the Constitution has ever been denied. If, by the mere force of numbers, a majority should deprive a minority of any clearly written constitutional right, it might, in a moral point of view, justify revolution—certainly would, if such right were a vital one.[27] But such is not our case. All the vital rights of minorities, and of individuals, are so plainly assured to them, by affirmations and negations, guarranties and prohibitions,[28] in the Constitution, that controversies never arise concerning them. But no organic law can ever be framed with a provision specifically applicable to every[29] question which may occur in practical administration. No foresight can anticipate, nor any document of reasonable length contain express provisions for all possible questions. Shall fugitives from labor be surrendered by national or by State authority? The Constitution does not expressly say. *May* Congress prohibit slavery in the territories? The Constitution does not expressly say. *Must* Congress protect slavery in the territories? The Constitution does not expressly say.

From questions of this class spring all our constitutional controversies, and we divide upon them into majorities and minorities. If the minority will not acquiesce,[30] the majority must, or the government must cease. There is no other alternative; for continuing the government, is acquiescence[31] on one side or the other. If a minority, in such case, will secede rather than acquiesce,[32] they make a precedent which, in turn, will divide and ruin them; for a minority of their own[33] will secede from them, whenever a majority refuses to be controlled by such minority. For instance,[34]

25 "Distinct" inserted and deleted.
26 "Constructed" deleted, "constituted" inserted.
27 Punctuation and capital inserted to begin a new sentence.
28 "Guarranties and prohibitions," inserted.
29 "Possible" inserted and deleted.
30 "Submit" deleted, "acquiesce" inserted.
31 "Submission" deleted, "acquiescence" inserted.
32 "Submit" deleted, "acquiesce" inserted.   33 "Number" deleted.
34 This sentence and the next are inserted on a slip replacing two sentences in the preceding drafts.

why may not any portion of a new confederacy, a year or two hence, arbitrarily secede again, precisely as portions of the present Union now claim to secede from it. All who cherish disunion sentiments, are now being educated to the exact temper of doing this. Is there such perfect identity of interests among the States to compose a new[35] Union, as to produce harmony only, and prevent renewed secession?

Plainly, the central idea of secession, is the essence of anarchy. A[36] majority, held in restraint by constitutional checks, and limitations, and always changing easily, with deliberate changes of popular opinions and sentiments, is the only true sovereign of a free people. Whoever rejects it, does, of necessity, fly to anarchy or to despotism. Unanimity is impossible; the rule of a minority, as a permanent arrangement, is wholly inadmissable; so that, rejecting the majority principle, anarchy, or despotism in some form, is all that is left.

I do not forget the position assumed by some, that constitutional questions are to be decided by the Supreme Court; nor do I deny that such decisions must be binding in any case, upon the parties to a suit, as to the object of that[37] suit, while[38] they are also entitled to very high respect and consideration, in all paralel cases, by all other departments of the government. And while it is obviously possible that such decision may be erroneous in any given case, still the evil effect following it, being limited to that particular case, with the chance that it may be over-ruled, and never become a precedent for other cases, can better be borne than[39] could the evils of a different practice. At the same time the candid citizen must confess that if the policy of the government, upon vital questions, affecting the whole people, is to be irrevocably fixed by decisions of the Supreme Court, the instant they are made, in ordinary litigation between parties, in personal actions, the people will have ceased, to be their own rulers, having, to that extent, practically resigned their government, into the hands of that eminent tribunal. Nor is there, in this view, any assault upon the court, or the judges. It is a duty, from which they may not shrink, to decide cases properly brought before them; and it is no fault of theirs, if others seek to turn their decisions to political purposes.

One section of our country[40] believes slavery is *right*, and ought

[35] "Southern" deleted, "new" inserted.
[36] This sentence inserted in place of the sentence in preceding drafts.
[37] "The" deleted, "that" inserted.   [38] The rest of this sentence is inserted.
[39] The rest of this paragraph is written on a slip laid over the remainder of the paragraph and the next short paragraph [The Republican party, as I understand. . . .] in the preceding drafts.   [40] "Of our country" inserted.

to be extended, while the other believes it is *wrong,* and ought not to be extended. This is the only substantial dispute. The fugitive slave clause of the Constitution, and the law for the suppression of the foreign slave trade, are each as well enforced, perhaps,[41] as any law can ever be in a community where the moral sense of the people imperfectly supports[42] the law itself. The great body of the people abide by the dry legal obligation in both cases, and a few break over in each. This, I think, cannot be perfectly cured; and it would be worse in both cases *after* the separation of the sections, than before. The foreign slave trade, now imperfectly suppressed, would be ultimately[43] revived without restriction, in one section; while fugitive slaves, now only partially surrendered, would not be surrendered at all, by the other.

Physically speaking, we cannot separate. We cannot remove our respective sections from each other, nor build an impassable wall between them. A husband and wife may be divorced, and go out of the presence, and beyond the reach of each other; but the different parts of our country cannot do this. They cannot but remain face to face; and intercourse, either amicable or hostile, must continue between them. Is it possible then[44] to make that intercourse more advantageous, or more[45] satisfactory, *after* separation than *before?* Can aliens make treaties easier than friends can make laws? Can treaties be more faithfully enforced between aliens, than laws can among friends? Suppose you go to war, you cannot fight always; and when, after much loss on both sides, and no gain on either, you cease fighting, the identical old questions, as to terms of intercourse, are again upon you.

This country, with its institutions, belongs to the people who inhabit it. Whenever they shall grow weary of the existing government, they can exercise their *constitutional* right of amending it, or their *revolutionary* right to dismember, or overthrow it. I[46] can not be ignorant of the fact that many worthy, and patriotic citizens are desirous of having the national constitution amended. While I make no recommendation of amendments, I fully recognize the rightful authority of the people over the whole subject, to be exercised in either of the modes prescribed in the instrument itself; and I should, under existing circumstances, favor, rather than oppose, a fair oppertunity being afforded the people to act upon it.

[41] "Perhaps" inserted.
[42] "Is against" deleted, "imperfectly supports" inserted.
[43] "Ultimately" inserted.   [44] "Then" inserted.   [45] "More" inserted.
[46] The rest of this paragraph and the next two paragraphs are written on slips replacing the remainder of the paragraph in the preceding drafts.

I will venture to add that, to me, the convention mode seems preferable, in that it allows amendments to originate with the people themselves, instead of only permitting them to take, or reject, propositions, originated by others, not especially chosen for the purpose, and which might not be precisely such, as they would wish to either accept or refuse. I understand a proposed amendment to the Constitution—which amendment, however, I have not seen, has passed Congress, to the effect that the federal government, shall never interfere with the domestic institutions of the States, including that of persons held to service. To avoid misconstruction of what I have said, I depart from my purpose not to speak of particular amendments, so far as to say that, holding such a provision to now be implied constitutional law, I have no objection to its being made express, and irrevocable.

The Chief Magistrate derives all his authority from the people, and they have conferred none upon him to fix terms for the separation of the States. The people themselves can do this also[47] if they choose; but the executive, as such, has nothing to do with it. His duty is to administer the present government, as it came to his hands, and to transmit it, unimpaired by him, to his successor.

Why should there not be a patient confidence in the ultimate justice of the people? Is there any better, or equal hope, in the world? In our present differences, is either party without faith of being[48] in the right? If the Almighty Ruler of nations, with his eternal truth and justice, be on your side of the North, or on yours of the South,[49] that truth, and that justice, will surely prevail, by the judgment of this great tribunal, the American people.

By the frame of the government under which we live, this same people have wisely given their public servants but little power for mischief; and have, with equal wisdom, provided for the return of that little to their own hands at very short intervals.

While the people[50] retain their virtue, and vigilence, no administration, by any extreme of wickedness or folly, can very seriously injure the government, in the short space of four years.

My countrymen, one and all,[51] think calmly and *well*, upon this whole subject. Nothing valuable can be lost by taking time.[52] If there be an object to *hurry* any of you, in hot haste, to a step which

---

[47] "Also" inserted.   [48] "Of being" inserted.

[49] "Our side, or on yours" deleted, "your side of the North, or on yours of the South" inserted.

[50] "Remain patient, and true to themselves, no man, even in the presidential chair" deleted, "retain their virtue, and vigilence, no administration" inserted.

[51] "Take *time* and think" deleted, "think calmly and" inserted.

[52] "Nothing worth preserving is either breaking or burning" deleted.

you would never take *deliberately*, that object will be frustrated by taking time; but no good object can be frustrated by it. Such of you as are now dissatisfied, still have the old Constitution unimpaired, and, on the sensitive point, the laws of your own framing under it; while the new administration will have no immediate power, if it would, to change either. If it were admitted that you who are dissatisfied, hold the right side in the dispute, there still is no single good reason for precipitate action. Intelligence, patriotism, Christianity, and a firm reliance on Him, who has never yet forsaken this favored land, are still competent to adjust, in the best way, all our present difficulty.

In *your* hands, my dissatisfied fellow countrymen, and not in *mine*, is the momentous issue of civil war. The government will not assail *you*.[53] You can have no conflict, without being yourselves the aggressors. *You* have no oath registered in Heaven to destroy the government, while *I* shall have the most solemn one to "preserve, protect and defend" it.[54]

I am loth to close. We are not enemies, but friends. We must not be enemies. Though passion may have strained, it must not break our bonds of affection. The mystic chords of memory, streching from every battle-field, and patriot grave, to every living heart and hearthstone, all over this broad land, will yet swell the chorus of the Union, when again touched, as surely they will be, by the better angels of our nature.

[53] "Unless you *first* assail *it*" deleted.

[54] Last two sentences of preceding drafts deleted, and the final paragraph written on the bottom of the page. See Seward's suggestion for the final paragraph (note 99) of the revisions of the first edition *supra*, which furnished the basis for Lincoln's final paragraph. See also note 41 of the revisions of the first edition, for the sentence which Lincoln jotted down on the back of Browning's letter of February 17, 1861.

Appointment of John G. Nicolay[1]

March 4, 1861

Pursuant to the authority vested in me by the second Section of the Act of Congress of the third of March 1857, I hereby appoint John G. Nicolay, of Illinois, Private Secretary to the President of the United States.   ABRAHAM LINCOLN

Washington,
    4th. March 1861.

[1] DS, DLC-Nicolay Papers.

Reply to a New York Delegation[1]

March 4, 1861

[*Times* Version]

FELLOW CITIZENS: I thank you for this visit. I thank you that you call upon me, not in any sectional spirit, but that you come, without distinction of party, to pay your respects to the President of the United States. I am informed that you are mostly citizens of New-York. [Cries of "All," "all."] You all appear to be very happy. May I hope that the public expression which I have this day given to my sentiments, may have contributed in some degree to your happiness. [Emphatic exclamations of assent.] As far as I am concerned, the loyal citizens of every State, and of every section, shall have no cause to feel any other sentiment. [Cries of "Good," "Good."] As towards the disaffected portion of our fellow-citizens, I will say, as every good man throughout the country must feel, that there will be more rejoicing over one sheep that is lost, and is found, than over the ninety-and-nine which have gone not astray. [Great cheering.] And now, my friends, as I have risen from the dinner-table to see you, you will excuse me for the brevity of my remarks, and permit me again to thank you heartily, and cordially, for this pleasant visit, as I rejoin those who await my return.

[*Star* Version]

Friends and Fellow-Citizens:—I understood, both before I appeared from your committee and by the introduction of my friend,[2] that you were from New York. You seem to be in good humor after the proceedings of the day. If I have been fortunate enough to contribute to your good feeling I am glad, and I shall rejoice if what I have said may cause the friends of the Union South to feel good when they hear it. I made it as near right as I could, in my poor humble judgment, and in accordance with the principles of the Constitution and the perpetuity of freedom. [Cheers.] I made it as well for the good of those who lived south of Mason and Dixon's line as you who live north of that line. [Cheers.] As I rise from the dinner table to speak to you, I hope it will not be amiss to bid you good night.

---

[1] New York *Times*, March 5, 1861; Washington *Evening Star*, March 6, 1861. The *Times* reports the delegation as "numbering at least five hundred," and the *Star* "nearly a thousand strong." Brackets are in the sources.

[2] According to the *Star* Lincoln was introduced by William H. Ferry, state senator from Oneida County; according to the *Times* Stewart L. Wadford introduced the delegation to Lincoln.

To William H. Seward[1]

Executive Mansion. March 4 1861.

My dear Sir: Your note of the 2nd. Inst. asking to withdraw your acceptance of my invitation to take charge of the State Department, was duly received.

It is the subject of most painful solicitude with me; and I feel constrained to beg that you will countermand the withdrawal. The public interest, I think, demands that you should; and my personal feelings are deeply inlisted in the same direction. Please consider, and answer by 9 o'clock, A.M. to-morrow. Your Obt. Servt.

Hon. W. H. Seward.   A. LINCOLN

[1] ALS, NAuE. Seward's brief letter of March 2 stipulates that "Circumstances which have occurred since I expressed to you in December last my willingness to accept the office of Secretary of State seem to me to render it my duty to ask leave to withdraw that consent." (DLC-RTL).

To Simon Cameron[1]

Dear Sir: Executive Chamber March 5. 1861

If the public service admits of a change, without injury, in the office of chief clerk of the War Department, I shall be pleased of [sic] my friend, E. Elmer Ellsworth,[2] who presents you this, shall be appointed. Of course, if you see good reason to the contrary, this is not intended to be arbitrary. Yours truly   A LINCOLN

Hon. Simon Cameron.

[1] ALS, DLC-Cameron Papers.
[2] Colonel Elmer Ephraim Ellsworth was a young law student of Chicago who in 1860 had raised and trained a company of Zouaves which became famous for drill exhibitions. On Lincoln's invitation he accompanied the presidential party to Washington. Being inclined to active military service instead of a clerkship, he proceeded to New York to organize a Zouave regiment. His spectacular death at Alexandria, Virginia, occurred May 24, 1861, when he was shot by the proprietor of a hotel from the roof of which he was removing a Confederate flag. He is usually credited with being the first casualty of the Civil War. See Lincoln's letter to Ellsworth's parents, May 25, *infra*. Although there is considerable confusion of Ellsworth's first and second names, the *Dictionary of American Biography* accepts "Elmer Ephraim" on the basis of a manuscript account written by Ellsworth's mother.

Reply to Pennsylvania Delegation[1]

March 5, 1861

Mr. Chairman and Gentlemen of the Pennsylvania Delegation:

—As I have so frequently said[2] heretofore, when I have had occasion to address the people of the Keystone, in my visits to that

State, I can now but repeat the assurance of my gratification at the support you gave me at the late election, and at the promise of a continuation of that support which is now tendered to me.

Allusion has been made to the hope that you entertain that you have a President and a Government. In respect to that I wish to say to you, that in the position I have assumed I wish to do no more than I have ever given reason to believe I would do. I do not wish you to believe that I assume to be any better than others who have gone before me. I prefer rather to have it understood that if we ever have a Government on the principles we prefer, we should remember while we exercise our opinion, that others have also rights to the exercise of their opinions, and we should endeavor to allow these rights, and act in such a manner as to create no bad feeling. I hope we have a Government and a President. I hope and wish it to be understood that there may be allusion to no unpleasant differences.

We must remember that the people of all the States are entitled to all the privileges and immunities of the citizens of the several States. We should bear this in mind, and act in such a way as to say nothing insulting or irritating. I would inculcate this idea, so that we may not, like Pharisees, set ourselves up to be better than other people.

Now my friends, my public duties are pressing today, and will prevent my giving more time to you. Indeed, I should not have left them now, but I could not well deny myself to so large and respectable a body.

1 Philadelphia *Inquirer*, March 6, 1861. Lincoln responded to a speech by Winthrop W. Ketchum of Luzerne, Pennsylvania. The order in which Lincoln received the various state delegations on March 5 has been deduced from the press reports, but may not be entirely accurate. In addition to delegations from Pennsylvania, Massachusetts, and Illinois, a delegation from Michigan "some 150 strong headed by Senator Chandler, paid a visit of respect. . . ." (Washington *Evening Star*, March 6, 1861), but no speech was reported.

2 *Inquirer* has "heard" instead of "said."

Reply to Massachusetts Delegation[1]

March 5, 1861

I am thankful for this renewed assurance of kind feeling, and confidence, and support of the Old Bay State, in so far as you, Mr. Chairman, have expressed, in behalf of those whom you represent, your sanction of what I have enunciated in my inaugural address. This is very grateful to my feelings. The subject was one of great delicacy, in presenting views at the opening of an administration under the peculiar circumstances attending my entrance upon the official duties connected with the Government. I studied all the points with great anxiety, and have presented them with whatever of ability and sense of justice I could bring to bear.

If it meet the approbation of our good friends in Massachusetts, I shall be exceedingly gratified; while I hope it will meet the approbation of friends everywhere. I am thankful for the expressions of those who have voted with us; and like every other man of you, I like them certainly as I do others. [Laughter.] As President, in the administration of the Government, I hope to be man enough not to know one citizen of the United States from another, [cries of "Good!"] nor one section from another. I shall be gratified to have the good friends of Massachusetts and others, who have thus far supported me in these national views, still to support me in carrying them out.

1 Washington *National Republican* and New York *Tribune*, March 6; and Washington *Evening Star*, March 5, 1861. Lincoln replied to a speech by Charles R. Train, congressman from Framingham, Massachusetts.

Reply to Illinois Delegation[1]

March 5, 1861

Mr. Arnold, and fellow citizens of my own State of Illinois: I am obliged to you for this renewed mark of your kindness and confidence in my humble self. I have so often addressed the people of Illinois, and so frequently in their hearing said all that I know how to say, that I am a little more troubled to know what not to say upon this occasion than I ever have been. [Laughter.] We are all rejoiced, doubtless, at the success so far of the principles of Government which we have regarded as being just and right; which, as I hope, we have contended for only because we so regarded them, not because of any selfishness or sectionalism, or anything calculated to wrong any other of our citizens or section of the country. I certainly can say for myself, and I think for the rest of you, that these are the sentiments which have actuated all of us. And having advanced as far as we have in this cause, I have to request of you, which I think I need hardly do, either, that you will sustain me in trying to do ample and full justice to all the people of the different sections of this great Confederacy. [Applause.] In saying this, I think I have said as much as I know how to say upon this occasion. [Laughter and applause.]

1 Washington *National Republican* and *Evening Star*, March 6, 1861. Lincoln responded to a speech by Isaac N. Arnold, congressman from Chicago. According to the *Star* the delegation numbered "several hundred." Brackets are in the sources.

To William H. Seward[1]

Hon. W. H. Seward.   Executive Chamber
My dear Sir   March 5, 1861
    Please give me an interview at once Yours truly
                                    A. LINCOLN
    [1] ALS, NAuE.

To William H. Seward[1]

My dear Sir: Executive Mansion   March 6. 1861
    Will you please send me the blank nominations of Mr. Judd &
Mr. Kreismann as spoken of by us?
    I wish to send them in to-day. Yours truly   A LINCOLN
Hon. Sec. of State.

    [1] ALS, NAuE. On March 8, Lincoln appointed Norman B. Judd envoy
and minister at Berlin, and Herman Kreismann secretary of the legation.

Reply to Minnesota Delegation[1]

March 6, 1861

    Mr. Senator, members and gentlemen: I am very glad to meet
you this evening, and thank you for the compliment of this visit.
I have no time to make a speech, even if I desired to do so, but I
wish to express the pleasure I have experienced in contemplating
your enterprising people, and watching the rapid advance of
everything desirable in that young sister in the Republic-Minne-
sota. You may some of you differ from me, and I may be wrong,
but, according to my judgment, the people up your way have very
correct political views, and so in that particular, also, I give them
my approbation. (Laughter.) And while their political sentiments
accord with mine, I have no reason to doubt that they look upon
the rights of their brethren further South, as being entirely equal
to their own. (Applause.) and that while Minnesota will maintain
her principles, she will require and permit nothing to be done, that
does not favor the maintenance of the Constitution and fidelity to
the Union. (Cheers.)

    [1] Cincinnati *Daily Commercial*, March 11, 1861. Lincoln replied to a speech
by Senator Morton S. Wilkinson. Following the speech, the reporter (Henry
Villard) added: "The President then shook hands, and bowed himself out with
less grace than Beau Brummel or Chesterfield, excusing himself by informing
his guests that "a great man of my own making" (some Cabinet Officer—probably CALEB SMITH!)—"is waiting for me upstairs." Delegations from Indiana,
Maine, Ohio, California, and Vermont, also paid their respects on this date,
but no reports of speeches made by Lincoln have been discovered.

To William H. Seward[1]

Executive Chamber. March 7. 1861
My dear Sir Herewith is the Diplomatic address and my reply.[2]
To whom the reply should be addressed—that is, by what title, or
style, I do not quite understand; and therefore I have left it blank.

Will you please bring with you to-day the Message from the
War Department, with Gen. Scott's note upon it, which we had
here yesterday?[3] I wish to examine the General's opinion, which
I have not yet done. Yours very truly   A. LINCOLN
Hon. W. H. Seward.

[1] ALS, NAuE.   [2] *Vide infra.*
[3] See Lincoln to General Scott, March 9, *infra.* Probably the letter was the
one, referred to there, from Joseph Holt.

Reply to Diplomatic Corps[1]

March 7, 1861
Mr. Figaniere and Gentlemen of the Diplomatic Body:

Please accept my sincere thanks for your kind congratulations.

It affords me pleasure to confirm the confidence you so generously express in the friendly disposition of the United States,
through me, towards the Sovreigns, and Governments you respectively represent. With equal satisfaction I accept the assurance
you are pleased to give, that the same disposition is reciprocated
by your Sovereigns, your Governments, and yourselves.

Allow me to express the hope that these friendly relations may
remain undisturbed; and also my fervent wishes for the health
and happiness of yourselves personally.

[1] AD, DLC-RTL. The manuscript is in Lincoln's handwriting except for
the salutation, which was presumably supplied by an official in the State Department. See Lincoln to Seward, *supra.* J. C. de Figaniere é Moraô, minister
from Portugal, as the senior minister in service from a foreign country at
Washington, gave "an address in French, a translation of which had previously been furnished to Mr. Lincoln." (New York *Tribune,* March 8, 1861).

To Whom It May Concern[1]

Whom it may concern.   Executive Mansion   March 7. 1861

William Johnson, a colored boy, and bearer of this, has been
with me about twelve months; and has been, so far, as I believe,
honest, faithful, sober, industrious, and handy as a servant.

A. LINCOLN

[1] ALS, NN. The *Register of Officers and Agents, Civil, Military, and Naval,
in the Service of the U.S.* (hereafter cited as *U.S. Official Register*), 1861, lists
"W. H. Johnson, Fireman, President's House, $600 per annum." See also Lin-
coln to Welles, March 16, *infra.*

To Schuyler Colfax[1]

Hon. Schuyler Colfax   Executive Mansion March 8. 1861
My dear Sir: Your letter of the 6th. has just been handed me by Mr. Baker[2] of Minnesota. When I said to you, the other day, that I wished to write you a letter, I had reference, of course, to my not having offered you a cabinet appointment. I meant to say, and now do say, you were most honorably and amply recommended; and a tender of the appointment was not withheld on any ground disparaging to you. Nor was it withheld, in any part, because of anything happening in 1858—indeed, I should have decided as I did, easier than I did, had that matter never existed. I had partly made up my mind in favor of Mr. Smith—not conclusively of course—before your name was mentioned in that connection. When you were brought forward I said "Colfax is a young man—is already in position—is running a brilliant career, and is sure of a bright future in any event." "With Smith, it is now or never." I considered either abundantly competent, and decided on the ground I have stated. I now have to beg that you will not do me the injustice to suppose, for a moment, that I remembered any thing against you in malice. Yours very truly   A. LINCOLN

[1] ALS-P, ISLA. After calling on Lincoln with the Indiana delegation on March 6, Colfax had written "The very kindly remarks you made to me this morning were specially gratifying. . . . What has pained me *more than any thing else* was the rumor that your action was governed by 'prejudice on account of alleged Douglas proclivities in 1858'. . . ." (DLC-RTL).
[2] Probably James H. Baker, secretary of state for Minnesota.

Endorsement: Benjamin F. Wade to Lincoln[1]

[c. March 8, 1861]

If Mr. Anderson is better recommended in the Department than any other, for consul to Hamburg let him be appointed,

A. LINCOLN

[1] AES, DNA FS RG 59, Appointments, Box 216. Wade to Lincoln, March 8, 1861, recommended "James H. Anderson, Esqr., the bearer, of Marion, Ohio," for a German consulship, preferably at Hamburg. Anderson received the consulship at Hamburg.

To Edward Bates[1]

March 9, 1861

Please let Senator Wade name the man to be District Attorney for the Northern District of Ohio. . . .

[1] American Art Association Anderson Galleries Catalog 3955, March 4, 1932, No. 118. This fragmentary text is all that is available. According to the catalog description, a note by Senator Benjamin F. Wade, written on the bottom of Lincoln's letter, makes the appointment. Robert F. Paine of Cleveland received the appointment.

To Winfield Scott[1]

Lieutenant General Scott: Executive Mansion, March 9, 1861.

My dear Sir: On the 5th inst. I received from the Hon. Joseph Holt,[2] the then faithful and vigilant Secretary of War, a letter of that date, inclosing a letter and accompanying documents received by him on the 4th inst. from Major Robert Anderson commanding at Fort Sumpter South Carolina; and copies of all which I now transmit. Immediately on the receipt of them by me, I transmitted the whole to you for your consideration; and the same day you returned the package to me with your opinion endorsed upon it,[3] a copy of which opinion I now also transmit to you. Learning from you verbally that since then you have given the subject a more full and thorough consideration, you will much oblige me by giving answers, in writing, to the following interrogatories:

1st To what point of time can Major Anderson maintain his position at Fort Sumpter, without fresh supplies or reinforcement?

2d. Can you, with all the means now in your control, supply or re-inforce Fort Sumpter within that time?

3d If not, what amount of means and of what description, in addition to that already at your control, would enable you to supply and reinforce that fortress within the time?

Please answer these, adding such statements, information, and counsel as your great skill and experience may suggest.[4] Your obedient Servant   A. LINCOLN.

[1] Copy, DLC-RTL.
[2] Postmaster General Holt (1859-1861) had assumed charge of the War Department upon John B. Floyd's withdrawal from the cabinet, and remained as secretary under Lincoln until Simon Cameron took over on March 5.
[3] Holt's letter to Lincoln, March 5, bears Scott's endorsement: ". . . I now see no alternative but a surrender . . . as . . . we cannot send the third of the men in several months, necessary to give them relief. . . ." (DLC-RTL).
[4] Scott to Lincoln, March 11, 1861, answers Lincoln's three questions as follows: (1) ". . . he has hard bread, flour & rice for about 26 days, & salt meat . . . for about 48 . . . . how long he could hold out . . . cannot be answered with absolute accuracy. . . ." (2) "No: Not within many months. . . ." (3) ". . . a fleet of war vessels & transports, 5,000 additional regular troops & 20,000 volunteers . . . . would require new acts of Congress & from six to eight months." (DLC-RTL).

To Winfield Scott[1]

War Department, March 9, 1861.

My dear Sir: I am directed by the President to say he desires you to exercise all possible vigilance for the maintenance of all the places within the military department of the United States, and to promptly call upon all the departments of the government for the means necessary to that end. [SIMON CAMERON.]

1 NH, VI, 188. Although the original has not been located, Nicolay and Hay describe it as *"drafted by President Lincoln and Signed by the Secretary of War."* Brackets are in the source.

To William H. Seward[1]

My dear Sir   Executive Mansion March 9. 1861

I wish you would give Mr. Schurz[2] a full interview. Your Obt. Servt.   A. LINCOLN

Hon. W. H. Seward.

1 ALS, NAuE.
2 Carl Schurz, who was appointed minister to Spain, March 28.

To Gideon Welles[1]

Executive Mansion   March 9, 1861

Will the Sec. of Navy please call on me at once. Yours &c.

A. LINCOLN

1 ALS, The Rosenbach Company, Philadelphia and New York.

Remarks to Oregon Delegation[1]

March 9, 1861

A gentleman of the party remarked "that Oregon was a large State, and would soon wield a powerful influence upon the affairs of Government."

"Oh, yes," said Mr. Lincoln; "it's rather larger than Maryland and Rhode Island, which a man can hurry across in a few hours."

Some one remarked that "they had heard of a man who was not long getting across one of those States."

Mr. Lincoln, with a comical twist of his face, responded: "Gentlemen, if you please we won't say anything more on that subject;" and it was "drapped."[2]

¹ Washington *Evening Star*, March 12, 1861.

² The reference, of course, is to Lincoln's secret passage from Philadelphia to Washington on the night of February 22, which was heartily lampooned in the Democratic press.

To Truman Smith¹

Executive Mansion   March 10. 1861

Mr. L. will see Mr. Truman Smith at 8 o'clock this evening.

¹ AL, DLC-HW.

To Edward Bates¹

Hon. E. Bates   Executive Mansion

My dear Sir: March 11. 1861

This introduces Hon. I. N. Morris, with whom I wish you would converse in relation to the Russell fraud. I think it may subserve the public interest Yours truly   A. LINCOLN

¹ ALS, MoSHi. William Hepburn Russell of New York City, a member of the firm of Russell, Majors & Company was involved in a financial scandal too complicated for brief summary. The *Dictionary of American Biography* may be consulted for an adequate account.

To William H. Seward¹

Hon. Sec. of State.   Executive Mansion

My dear Sir   March 11, 1861

What think you of sending ministers at once as follows.

Dayton to England.

Fremont to France

Clay to Spain.

Corwin to Mexico?

We need to have these points guarded as strongly and quickly as possible.

This is suggestion merely, and not dictation. Your Obt. Servt.

A. LINCOLN

¹ ALS, NAuE. Seward replied the same day that he approved Cassius M. Clay for Spain and Thomas Corwin for Mexico, but "As to Fremont and France—the prestige is good. But I *think* that is all. If as I have heard, he is to be engaged in raising money there for his estates, it would be a serious complication. Beside this he is by birth and education a South Carolinian. . . . I would rather send Dayton there.

"For England I am sure Mr [Charles F.] Adams [is?] far above all others adapted to British Court &, society and infinitely more watchful capable . . . —every thing. New England is an important point. What better can we do for her. N. Jersey gives us little, and that grudgingly. I think Daytons appointment would be as much too large for her as any thing else we are likely to do for New England would be too small for her. . . ." (DLC-RTL).

To Montgomery Blair[1]

Hon. Post-Master General   Executive Mansion.
My dear Sir   March 12. 1861

I understand that the outgoing and incoming Representatives for the Cleveland District, unite in recommending Edwin Cowles[2] for P.M. in that City; that Senator Wade has considered the case & declines to interfere; & that no other M.C. interferes. Under these circumstances, if correct, I think Mr. Cowles better be appointed. Yours truly   A LINCOLN

[1] ALS, IaHA.
[2] Edwin Cowles, editor of the Cleveland *Leader*, received the appointment.

To Jacob Collamer[1]

Hon. Jacob Colamer.   Executive Mansion.
My dear Sir: March 12. 1861

God help me! It is said I have offended you. Please tell me how.
Yours very truly   A. LINCOLN

[1] ALS, owned by Charles W. Olsen, Chicago, Illinois. See Lincoln to Collamer, March 15, *infra*.

To Joseph Holt[1]

Hon. Joseph Holt: Executive Mansion
My dear Sir: March 12. 1861

I will be much obliged, if you will give me a private interview, to-day, say at 11 o'clock, A.M. Your Obt. Servt.   A. LINCOLN

[1] ALS, DLC-Holt Papers.

To Montgomery Blair[1]

Hon. P.M.G.   Executive Mansion
Dear Sir   March 13. 1861

The bearer of this, Mr. C. T. Hempston,[2] is a Virginian who wishes to get, for his son, a small place in your Dept. I think Virginia should be heard, in such cases.   LINCOLN

[1] ALS, IaHA.
[2] Lincoln's spelling seems to be "Hempston," but may be "Hempstow." In either case no appointment seems to have been made.

To Mark W. Delahay[1]

M. W. Delahay, Esq.   Executive Mansion
My dear Sir   March 13. 1861
 You will start for Kansas before I see you again; and when I
saw you a moment this morning, I forgot to ask you about some
of the Kansas appointments, which I intended to do. If you care
much about them, you can write, as I think I shall not make the
appointments just yet. Yours in haste   A. LINCOLN

[1] ALS, DLC-HW. Delahay to Lincoln March 29 expressed hope that ". . .
the appointment of Surveyor General for Kansas . . ." would not be made "until I can see you. . . ." (DLC-RTL). Delahay himself received the appointment.

To James R. Doolittle[1]

                                                  [c. March 13, 1861?]
 Please do not report on case of J. M. Richardson till you hear
from me. Yours truly.   A LINCOLN
 Hon. J. R. Doolittle.

[1] ALS, InFtWL. J. M. Richardson may have been John M. Richardson of
Missouri, nominated by Lincoln as agent for the Choctaw and Chickasaw In-
dians on March 13, 1861, whose appointment was never confirmed by the
Senate.

To William H. Seward[1]

Hon. W. H. Seward   Executive Mansion March 13. 1861
 Dear Sir   Gen. Cameron desires that Jacob S. Haldeman may
be appointed Minister Resident, at Sweden & Norway; and I am
willing to oblige him, if you see no objection. Your Obt. Servt.
                                                  A. LINCOLN

[1] ALS, NAuE. Jacob S. Haldeman, president of the Harrisburg National
Bank and formerly a member of the Pennsylvania legislature, received the appointment.

To William H. Seward[1]

Hon. W. H. Seward   Executive Mansion. March 14. 1861
 My dear Sir   Allow me to introduce Mr. F. Hassaurek, one of
our best german Republican workers in America; residing at Cincinnati, and of whose character you can not be ignorant. Please
give him an interview. Yours truly   A. LINCOLN

[1] ALS, NAuE. Frederick Hassaurek, editor of the Cincinnati *Hochwach-
ter* and sub-editor of the Ohio *Staats Zeitung*, was appointed minister to Ecua-
dor.

To Jacob Collamer[1]

Hon. Jacob Collamer.   March 15. 1861
My dear Sir   I am much relieved to learn that I have been mis-
informed as to your having been offended. Yours very truly

A LINCOLN

[1] ALS, owned by Charles W. Olsen, Chicago, Illinois. On March 14, Collamer replied to Lincoln's note of March 12, *supra*, "I am entirely insensible
that you have, in any way, offended me. I cherish no sentiment towards you
but that of kindness & confidence. . . ." (ALS, *ibid.*).

Memoranda:
Appointment of Mark H. Dunnell[1]

[c. March 15, 1861]

Mr. Senator Fessenden, is anxious that Maine shall have the
consul general of Canada & that Mark H. Dunnell shall be the
man.

The Vice President, and the United congressional delegation of
Maine urge the appointment of Mark H. Dunnell as Consul General for Canada, always bearing in mind that Mr. Fessenden, first
of all, wishes Mr. Morse to be Consul to London

[1] AD, DNA FS RG 59, Appointments, Box 277. Each memorandum is on a
separate page. Lincoln nominated Mark H. Dunnell to be consul at Vera Cruz,
March 22, 1861.

Memorandum:
Appointment of Freeman H. Morse[1]

[c. March 15, 1861]

Mr. Senator Fessenden is exceedingly anxious that that [*sic*]
Hon: Freeman H. Morse shall be consul to London—& he says
when he first mentioned Mr. Morse's name for that place, I said it
was the first application.

[1] AD, DNA FS RG 59, Appointments, Box 349. Lincoln nominated Morse
for the consulship at London, March 20, 1861.

To William H. Seward[1]

The Hon. Secretary of State   Executive Mansion
My dear Sir   March 15. 1861
   Assuming it to be possible to now provision Fort-Sumpter, under
all the circumstances, is it wise to attempt it?

Please give me your opinion, in writing, on this question. Your
Obt. Servt.   A. LINCOLN.

[1] ALS copy, DLC-RTL. This letter, copied by Nicolay and signed by Lincoln, was sent to each member of the cabinet. The several copies which have been located are: to Bates, IHi; to Blair, DLC-Blair Collection; to Seward, NAuE; to Smith, MH; to Welles, A. Conger Goodyear, New York City. The lengthy replies in the Lincoln Papers are abridged as follows: (1) Seward, March 15– "If it were possible to peacefully provision Fort Sumter, of course I should answer, that it would be both unwise and inhuman not to attempt it. But the facts of the case are known to be, that the attempt must be made with the employment of military and marine force, which would provoke combat, and probably initiate a civil war. . . . I would not provoke war in any way *now*. . . ." (2) Chase, March 16– ". . . . If the attempt will so inflame civil war as to involve an immediate necessity for the enlistment of armies . . . I cannot advise it. . . . But it seems to me highly improbable that the attempt . . . will produce such consequences. . . . I return, therefore, an affirmative answer. . . ." (3) Cameron, March 16– ". . . it would be unwise now to make such an attempt. . . . I am greatly influenced by the opinions of the Army officers who have expressed themselves on the subject, and who seem to concur that it is, perhaps, now impossible to succor that fort, substantially, if at all. . . . All the officers within Fort Sumter, together with Generals Scott and Totten, express this opinion. . . ." (4) Welles, March 15– "The question has two aspects, one military, the other political. The military gentlemen . . . represent that it would be unwise . . . and I am not disposed to controvert their opinions. . . . In a political view, I entertain doubts of the wisdom of the measure. . . . I do not . . . think it wise. . . ." (5) Smith, March 16– "After a careful consideration of the opinions of Gens. Scott and Totten, and also those of Commodore String[h]am and Mr. Fox . . . I have arrived at the conclusion that the probabilities are in favor of the success of the proposed enterprise, so far as to secure the landing of the vessels at the Fort, but . . . . it would not be wise under all the circumstances. . . ." (6) Blair, March 15– ". . . I submit the following considerations in favor of provisioning that Fort. The ambitious leaders of the late Democratic party have availed themselves . . . to found a Military Government in the Seceding States. To the connivance of the late administration it is due alone that this Rebellion has been enabled to attain its present proportions. . . . I . . . agree that we must look to the people in these States for the overthrow of this rebellion. . . . How is this to be carried into effect? That it is by measures which will inspire respect for the power of the Government and the firmness of those who administer it does not admit of debate. . . . The evacuation of Fort Sumpter . . . will convince the rebels that the administration lacks firmness and will therefore, . . . so far from tending to prevent collision, will ensure it unless . . . all attempts are given up to maintain the authority of the United States. . . ." (7) Bates, [March 16]– "This is not a question of lawful right nor physical power, but of prudence & patriotism only. The right is . . . unquestionable . . . the Government has the power and the means. . . . The wisdom of the act must be tested by the value of the object to be gained, & by the hazards to be encountered. . . . I am willing to evacuate Fort Sumter, rather than be an active party in the beginning of civil war. . . . If Fort Sumter *must* be evacuated . . . the more Southern forts,—Pickens, Key West &c—should, without delay, be put in condition of easy defence. . . . Upon the whole, I do not think it *wise now* to attempt to provision Fort Sumter. . . ."

Reply to Luis Molina, Minister from Nicaragua[1]

March 16, 1861

Mr. MOLINA: I am happy to receive the letters you present, and to recognize you, sir, as Envoy Extraordinary and Minister Plenipotentiary of Nicaragua near the United States.

In conferring a higher rank upon you as a token of regard on the part of the Government and people of Nicaragua towards this country, they have done our Government and people an honor for which we are duly grateful, while they have also manifested an increased confidence in you, which we can attest is deserved, and thereby have done you a distinguished honor, upon which we congratulate you.

On behalf of the United States I fully reciprocate towards your Government and people the kind wishes and friendly purposes you so generously express towards ours.

Please communicate to his excellency the President of Nicaragua my high esteem and consideration, and my earnest wish for his health, happiness, and long life.

Be assured, sir, I do not allow myself to doubt that your public duties and social intercourse here will be so conducted as to be entirely acceptable to the Government and people of the United States.

[1] Washington *Daily National Intelligencer*, March 18, 1861. The same text, except for variations in punctuation, appeared in the New York *Tribune* and other papers. Luis Molina, who had represented both Nicaragua and Costa Rica at Washington for several years, made a brief speech upon presenting the credentials accrediting him as envoy extraordinary and minister plenipotentiary. Hertz, II, 823, misdates Lincoln's reply as of March 17.

To Winfield Scott[1]

[March 16, 1861]

If Lieut. Genl. Scott perceives no impropriety in my granting Mr. Hamilton's request, made within, I should be gratified to do it. Will Genl. Scott please answer? Your Obt. Servt. A. LINCOLN

[1] ALS, DLC-Nicolay Papers. Lincoln's note is written on the back of a letter from Andrew J. Hamilton, retiring Union congressman from Texas, who requested that Lieutenant John C. Howard, suspended by court-martial in Washington Territory, be restored to his post. General Scott's answer is written below Lincoln's note: "The sentence was disapproved by the late President (without assigning a reason) & Lieut. Howard released from arrest—that is, restored to duty. . . ." Howard resigned his commission, September 6, 1861. Hamilton was appointed brigadier general of volunteers and military governor of Texas in 1862.

To Winfield Scott[1]

Executive Mansion   March 16. 1861

I have examined, to some extent, this case of Major Henshaw, and have been brought to deeply sympathize with him. He wishes to be appointed a Paymaster; and if, in the opinion of Gen. Scott, this can be done without impropriety, it would gratify me to do it. Your Obt. Servt.   A. LINCOLN.

[1] ALS, RPB-Henshaw Papers. The note is written on the end leaf of the pamphlet, *Proceedings of a General Court Martial . . . for the Trial of Brevet Major John C. Henshaw* (New York, 1858). Leonard Swett to Lincoln, December 26, 1860, endorsed by David Davis, sets forth John C. Henshaw's wish for reinstatement as paymaster. Major Henshaw had been court-martialed while stationed in Arkansas, on charges growing out of his refusal to use his troops to catch runaway slaves. Army regulations prevented his restoration to line service. Although no record of Scott's action in the case has been found, Henshaw was eventually appointed captain and assistant adjutant general, August 7, 1862, and became major and judge advocate February 29, 1864. See also Lincoln's memorandum, April 3, *infra*.

To the Senate[1]

To the Senate: March 16, 1861

The Senate has transmitted to me a copy of the Message sent by my predecessor to that Body on the 21st. day of February last, proposing to take its advice on the subject of a proposition made by the British Government through its Minister here to refer the matter in controversy between that Government and the Government of the United States to the arbitrament of the King of Sweden and Norway, the King of the Netherlands, or the Republic of the Swiss Confederation.

In that Message, my predecessor stated that he wished to submit to the Senate the precise questions following, namely:

"Will the Senate approve a treaty referring to either of the Sovereign Powers above named the dispute now existing between the Governments of the United States and Great Britain concerning the boundary line between Vancouver's Island and the American Continent? In case the referee shall find himself unable to decide where the line is by the description of it in the Treaty of 15th. June, 1846, shall he be authorized to establish a line according to the treaty as nearly as possible? Which of the three Powers named by Great Britain as an arbiter shall be chosen by the United States?"

I find no reason to disapprove of the course of my predecessor in this important matter, but, on the contrary, I not only shall

receive the advice of the Senate thereon cheerfully, but I respectfully ask the Senate for their advice on the two [three?] questions before recited.   ABRAHAM LINCOLN.
Washington, 16th March, 1861.

1 DS, DNA RG 46, Senate 37B B6. This message was referred to the committee on foreign relations, and on March 19, Senator Sumner submitted a resolution that the dispute be submitted to the Republic of Switzerland as arbiter. On March 27, further consideration of the resolution was postponed to "the 2d Monday of December next." (*Executive Journal*, XI, 357).

To Gideon Welles[1]

Hon. Gideon Welles   Executive Mansion
Dear Sir   March 16/61
    The bearer (William) is a servant who has been with me for some time & in whom I have confidence as to his integrity and faithfulness. He wishes to enter your service. The difference of color between him & the other servants is the cause of our seperation. If you can give him employment you will confer a favour on   Yours truly   A. LINCOLN

1 LS-F, ISLA. See Lincoln to "Whom it may concern," March 7, *supra*.

Endorsement: Jesse K. Dubois to Lincoln[1]

[c. March 17, 1861]
    Dubois, who writes this, is my particular friend; and while, possibly, *the* thing he wishes, can not be done, something else may.
                                                                    LINCOLN.

1 AES, DNA RG 48, Applications, Indian Agencies, Superintendent of Indian Affairs (Northern), Box 1266. The endorsement seems to have been clipped from the envelope and pasted on the back of Dubois' letter of March 17, 1861, requesting appointment of his son-in-law, James P. Luse, editor of the Lafayette, Indiana, *Journal*, as superintendent of Indian affairs for the Northern Superintendency. Clark W. Thompson of Minnesota received the appointment, however, and Luse later received the postmastership of Lafayette. See also Lincoln to Dubois, March 30, *infra*.

Memorandum on Fort Sumter[1]

March 18[?] 1861
    Some considerations in favor of withdrawing the Troops from Fort Sumpter, by President Lincoln.

1st. The Fort cannot be permanently held without reinforcement.

This point is too apparent too [*sic*] need proof

The cutting off supplies and consequent starvation, not to mention disease, would compel surrender in a few months at farthest, without firing a gun

2 The Fort cannot now be re-inforced without a large armament, involving of course a bloody conflict and great exasperation on both sides, and when re-inforced can only be held by sufficient number to garrison the post and to keep open communication with it by means of the harbor.

3. The Fort in the present condition of affairs is of inconsiderable military value, for: It is not necessary for the Federal Government to hold it in order to protect the City of Charleston from foreign invasion, nor: Is it available under existing circumstances for the purpose of collecting the revenue: and, It is difficult to see how the possession of the Fort by the Secessionists can be rendered a means of annoyance to the Federal Government. Every purpose for which the fort can now be made available would be better subserved by Ships of War, outside the harbor.

4 The abandonment of the Post would remove a source of irritation to the Southern people and deprive the secession movement of one of its most powerful stimulants.

5 It would indicate both an independent and a conservative position on part of the new administration, and would gratify and encourage those, who while friendly to the Union are yet reluctant to see extreme measures pursued.

6 It would tend to confound and embarrass those enemies of the Union both at the North and South who have relied on the cry of "Coercion" as a means of keeping up the excitement against the Republican Party.

7 If the garrison should, while in an enfeebled condition be successfully attacked, or from want of proper supplies should be cut off by disuse the administration would be held responsible for it and this fact would be used by their opponents with great effect.

8 The moral advantage to the Secessionists of a successful attack would be very great.

Objections

1st The danger of demoralizing the Republican Party by a measure which might seem to many to indicate timidity or in common parlance, "want of pluck."

That this may be the first impression is probable but if the measure is justified upon the double ground of the small importance of the post in a military point of view and the desire to conciliate wherever this can be safely done a second thought will discover the wisdom of the course, and increase rather than diminish the confidence of the party in its leaders.

2d The danger of the movement being construed by the Secessionists as a yielding from necessity, and in so far a victory on their part

[1] Copy, DLC-Welles Papers. There is some uncertainty about this three-page manuscript. It is not in Lincoln's handwriting. It may be a copy of a memorandum submitted to the cabinet, or a resumé of conflicting views as Lincoln orally presented them to the cabinet. Although the first and third pages are dated March 18, 1861, this date seems to have been added later. There is no Lincoln autograph in the Lincoln Papers that resembles the manuscript, but its presence in the Welles Papers seems to justify its inclusion here. Presumably Lincoln was recapitulating the opinions of the several members of the cabinet submitted on March 15 and 16 in response to Lincoln's letter of March 15, *supra*.

To Edward Bates[1]

Hon. Attorney Genl.　　Executive Mansion　March 18, 1861

A marshal for Kansas is needed at once; and unless the papers in your office show the appointment of some other person to be more proper, make out and send me a blank for James L. McDowell. Yours &c　　　　　　　　　　　　　　A. LINCOLN

[1] ALS, owned by Mrs. R. T. Kellogg, Silver City, New Mexico. James L. McDowell, mayor of Leavenworth (1859), received the appointment.

To Edward Bates[1]

Executive Mansion March 18. 1861.

Sir: I shall be obliged if you will give me your opinion in writing whether under the Constitution and existing laws, the Executive has power to collect duties on ship-board, off-shore, in cases where their collection in the ordinary way is, by any cause, rendered impracticable. This would include the question of lawful power to prevent the landing of dutiable goods, unless the duties were paid. Your Obt. Servt.　　　　　　　　　A. LINCOLN

The Honourable
　　Attorney General

[1] LS, DLC-RTL. See the similar letters to Chase and Welles, *infra*. Bates' reply is not in the Lincoln Papers.

Draft of a Proposed Order to Establish a Militia Bureau[1]

Executive Mansion
To the Secretary of War: March 18th 1861.

Sir: You will favor me by issuing an order detailing Lieut. Ephraim E Ellsworth, of the First Dragoons, for special duty as Adjutant and Inspector General of Militia for the United States, and in so far as existing laws will admit, charge him with the transaction, under your direction, of all business pertaining to the Militia, to be conducted as a separate bureau, of which Lieut. Ellsworth will be chief, with instructions to take measures for promoting a uniform system of organization, drill, equipment, &c. &c. of the U. S. Militia, and to prepare a system of[2] drill for Light troops, adapted for self-instruction, for distribution to the Militia of the several States. You will please assign him suitable office rooms, furniture &c. and provide him with a clerk and messenger, and furnish him such facilities in the way of printing, stationery, access to public records, &c. as he may desire for the successful prosecution of his duties; and also provide[3] in such manner as[4] may be most convenient and proper, for a monthly payment to Lieut Ellsworth, for this extra duty, sufficient to make his pay[5] equal that of a Major of Cavalry. Your obt. Servt.

[1] Copy, DLC-RTL. The order was submitted with Lincoln to Bates, *infra*. The original of this proposed order is not in the Lincoln Papers and has not been located elsewhere. The text given by Tracy, pp. 177-78, may have been prepared from Lincoln's original, and major variations as printed there are given in the succeeding footnotes. Presumably this order was not sent to the War Department after Bates' unfavorable report.

[2] Tracy prints the remainder of this sentence as follows: "instruction for the militia, to be distributed to the several states."

[3] Tracy prints "if you please" after "provide."

[4] Tracy prints "will best answer the purpose," instead of "may be most convenient and proper."

[5] Tracy prints "pay and emoluments" instead of "pay."

To Edward Bates[1]

Executive Mansion   March 18. 1861

Will the Attorney General please give his opinion in writing whether the Executive has any lawful authority to make such an order as the foregoing, and return this paper, with the answer, to me?   A. LINCOLN

[1] ALS, DLC-RTL. The draft of Lincoln's order, *supra*, was enclosed with this letter. Bates replied on April 18 that in his opinion the president had not the

power to establish the bureau "without Congressional enactment" and "an explicit appropriation by Congress . . . to provide the compensation proposed. . . ." (Copy, DLC-RTL). Apparently the order was never sent to Cameron. The original of Bates' reply is not in the Lincoln Papers.

To Salmon P. Chase[1]

Executive Mansion March 18, 1861

Sir   I shall be obliged if you will inform me whether any goods, wares and merchandize, subject by law to the payment of duties, are now being imported into the United States without such duties being paid, or secured according to law. And if yea, at what place or places? and for what cause do such duties remain unpaid, or [un]secured?

I will also thank you for your opinion whether, as a matter of fact, vessels off shore could be effectively used to prevent such importation, or to enforce the payment or securing of the duties.

If yea, what number, and description of vessels, in addition to those already in the Revenue service would be requisite? Your Obt. Servt.   A. LINCOLN

Hon: Sec. of Treasury—

[1] ALS, CSmH; LS copy, DLC-RTL. Chase replied under date of March — 1861, that he had no official information of illegal importations, but that there were no customs officers south of North Carolina, Tennessee, and Arkansas, and consequently no reports. He thought that offshore vessels could execute the revenue laws, but that all of the eleven vessels in service would have to be rearmed, and since only one was a steamer, at least three of the others should be replaced by steam vessels. In addition six storage ships and naval protection would be needed (DLC-RTL).

To William H. Seward[1]

Hon. Sec. of State   Executive Mansion March 18. 1861

My dear Sir—I believe it is a necessity with us to make the appointments I mentioned last night—that is, Charles F. Adams to England, William L. Dayton to France, George P. Marsh to Sardinia, and Anson Burlingame to Austria. These gentlemen all have my highest esteem, but no one of them is originally suggested by me except Mr. Dayton. Mr. Adams I take because you suggested him, coupled with his eminent fitness for the place. Mr. Marsh and Mr. Burlingame I take because of the intense pressure of their respective states, and their fitness also.

The objection to this card is that, locally they are so huddled up—three being in New England, and two from a single state. I have considered this, and will not shrink from the responsibility. This being done leaves but five full missions undisposed of—

Russia, China, Brazil, Peru, & Chili. And then, what about Carl Schurz? or, in other words, what about our german friends?

Shall we put the card through, and arrange the rest afterwards? What say you? Your Obt. Servt. A. LINCOLN

[1] ALS, NAuE. There is no reply from Seward in the Lincoln Papers, but the appointments of Charles Francis Adams, William L. Dayton, George P. Marsh, and Carl Schurz were made as Lincoln lists them. Anson Burlingame, being unacceptable to the Austrian government because of his opinions on Hungary and Sardinia, was appointed to China instead.

Memorandum to William H. Seward[1]

[March 18, 1861]

By some omission I failed to send the inclosed recommendations to the State Department. Would a consideration of them affect the conclusion of the Secretary, as to who shall be Secretary in Colorado, or Nevada? LINCOLN.

[1] ADS, DNA RG 59, Appointments, Box 355. The recommendations were for James W. Nye, who was appointed governor of Nevada.

To Gideon Welles[1]

Executive Mansion March 18, 1861

Sir I shall be obliged if you will inform me what amount of Naval force you could at once place at the control of the Revenue service. And also, whether at some distance of time you could so place an additional force; and how much? and at what time? Your Obt. Servt. A. LINCOLN

Hon. Sec. of Navy.

[1] ALS, DNA WR NB RG 45, Executive letters, No. 47; LS, DLC-RTL. Welles replied March 20 that twelve vessels would be put at control of the revenue service, but that the amount of force which could be so disposed in the future would depend on the number of men legally allowed to the Navy. Four vessels could be withdrawn from foreign service within three months. There were fifteen vessels not in commission. Seven vessels could be made available for west coast service (DLC-RTL). See Lincoln's letters to Chase and Bates of this date, *supra*.

To William H. Seward[1]

Executive Mansion March 19. 1861

Messrs Senators Simmons & Anthony wish John R Bartlett to be Minister to Rome. They are anxious on behalf of Rhode Island.

[1] AL, DNA FS RG 59, Appointments, Box 224. Senators from Rhode Island, James F. Simmons and Henry B. Anthony, had recommended John R. Bartlett of Providence, secretary of state for Rhode Island. Bartlett remained in office as secretary of state until 1872.

To Whom It May Concern[1]

Whom it may concern   Executive Mansion   March 19. 1861

I did see and talk with Master George Evans Patten, last May, at Springfield, Illinois. Respectfully   A LINCOLN

[1] ALS-F, ISLA. No letter from George Evans Patten is in the Lincoln Papers, and he has not been identified. One infers from Lincoln's note, however, that the boy wanted proof of his acquaintance, perhaps to silence skeptical friends.

Memorandum on Appointments to Territories[1]

March 20, 1861

Titus C. Wetmore,[2] informal delegate from Colorado, and Copeland Townsend,[3] of Colorado, formerly of Wisconsin, call this 20th. March and recommend for

> Governor — William Larrimer,[4] Col.
> Secretary — D. M. Kelsey[5]—
> C.[hief] J.[ustice]—
> 1 asso. T. C. Wetmore — Col.
> 2 do   ———
> Atty.   ———
> Marshall, Copeland Townsend, Col.
>   (ought to have been P.M. at Denver.)
> Surveyor. ———

Colorado Terrtory

State { Governor.	William Gilpin, of Colorado		
Secretary	Lewis L. Weld, " "		
Surveyor Genl.	David P. Holloway[6]	Ia.	
	Francis M. Case,	O.	
Chief Justice	Benjamin F. Hall	N. Y.	*Sew.*
Associate J.	S. Newton Pettis	Pa.	Cam.
Do. Do	Charles Lee Armour—	Md.	Bliss
Attorney	Theodore D. Edwards.	Ky.	
Marshal	Copeland Townsend.	Col.	

Dacota

Governor.	William Jayne[7]	of Ills.	
Secretary	John Hutchinson	of Kan.	
Surv. Genl.	George D. Hill[8]	Mich.	
C. J.	Philemon Bliss	O. Wade, Chase.	
1 Asso.	Allen A. Burton	Ky.	Speed & Clay
			Anderson
			Adams
			Harlan
2 D.	L. P. Williston[9]	Pa.	
Atty	H. M. Vaile	Kan — Gilpin	
			& [illegible]
Marshal.	W. F. Shaffer	Ter.	

[294]

[John K. Hord][10] Asks now to be Judge of either Territory, where not yet filled. March 27, 1861

Nevada.

Governor	James W. Nye[11]	N. Y.
Secretary	Orion Clemens[12]	Mo — *Bates*
Surveyor General.	J. W. North	*Min.*

Interior—no application[13]

C. J.	George Turner.[14]	O.
1 Asso.	Gorden N. Mott	California, Baker.
2 Asso.	Horatio Jones	Mo.
Atty	Benjamin Browker—	N. H — Hale.
Marshal.	David Bayles.	Mo.

Board of Pattent Appeal.

John M. Hodges	Vermont
George Harding	Pa
Thomas C. Theaper	O.

Judges in Nebraska

C. J.	William Pitt Kellogg	Ills.
x	Sam Milligan	Tenn — Johns. Eth.[15]

[1] AD, DLC-RTL. These three pages in Lincoln's autograph and one page of recommendations (not reproduced) for John K. Hord, bearing Lincoln's endorsement as reproduced, were apparently Lincoln's summary of territorial offices and prospective appointees, as of March 20-27.

[2] Titus C. Wetmore, formerly a hotel keeper at Malta, Illinois, had migrated to Colorado in 1860. His letter in the Lincoln Papers, written from Washington, January 17, 1861, indicates that he was a delegate of the United Mining District, Rocky Mountains.

[3] Copeland Townsend, formerly of Oconomowoc, Wisconsin, received the appointment as marshal of Colorado.

[4] William Larimer, a native of Pennsylvania and one of the founders of Denver, Colorado.

[5] D. M. Kelsey has not been identified, but did not receive the appointment.

[6] The names of Holloway of Indiana and Case were crossed out by Lincoln.

[7] "J. M. North   Minn–" and "Nathaniel G. Wilson" were deleted and "William Jayne" inserted.

[8] "Francis M. Case" and Lysander Cutler   Wisc" were deleted and "George D. Hill Mich." inserted.

[9] "James E. M[echen?] Mich." was deleted and "L. P. Williston Pa." inserted.

[10] A page, not in Lincoln's handwriting, listing the numerous public officials of Ohio who recommended John K. Hord, bears Lincoln's endorsement as reproduced.

[11] "Rufus King Wisc" deleted and "James W. Nye N. Y." inserted.

[12] "W. L. Brown. Ia." deleted and "Orion Clemens—Mo—*Bates*" inserted.

[13] This line has been crossed out.

[14] "Sam Milligan Tenn. Johnson & Eth" deleted and "George Turner. O" inserted.   [15] Senator Andrew Johnson and Representative Emerson Etheridge.

To Robert Irwin[1]

Private

Robert Irwin, Esq   Washington D. C.
My dear Sir: March 20. 1861

I am scared about your friend Dennison. The place is so fiercely sought by, and for, others, while, except what has come through you, his name is not mentioned at all, that I fear appointing him will appear too arbitrary on my part. I have made no appointments at the city as yet; but it has pained me that among the scores of names urged, his has not occurred once. Your tired friend   A. LINCOLN

[1] ALS, IHi. Robert Irwin to Lincoln, February 27, 1861, asked for the appointment of attorney George Denison of New York as naval officer of the port of New York, and an undated note requests "for the last time . . . cannot you consistently give my Friend Denison the appointment he has solicited. . . ." (DLC-RTL). For further developments in this appointment, see Lincoln to Chase, May 16 and 18, *infra*.

To Donald McClennan[1]

Donald McClennan Esq   Executive Mansion
Dear Sir: March 20. 1861

I have the honor to acknowledge the receipt of your favour of Jan 31st and the accompanying shawles and blankets presented by you through the Hon John Satterlee.

Permit me to express my sincere gratitude for the kind feelings that prompted your present & my gratification at the forward state of California manufactures which those articles exhibit. Your obt Ser

[1] Df, DLC-RTL. The draft is in John Hay's handwriting. Donald McClennan wrote, January 31, 1861, "I desire to present . . . an union grey shawl, made of California wool and the first manufactured in this State, together with a pair of family blankets of our manufacture, at the Chrysopolis Mills, Mission Dolores San Francisco. . . ." (DLC-RTL).

To Caleb B. Smith[1]

Hon. Sec. of Interior   Executive Mansion   March 20. 1861

Please make out and send blank appointments for all Indian places, to serve in Wisconsin, in favor of the persons unitedly recommended by the Wisconsin Congressional delegation.

And in like manner, all in Minnesota, in favor of the persons

unitedly recommended by the Minnesota Republican delegation in congress. Of course these relate to Executive appointments. Yours truly   A. LINCOLN

¹ ALS, DNA NR RG 48, Appointments, Indian Agencies, Miscellaneous, Box 1268.

To Simon Cameron¹

Hon. Sec. of War   Executive Mansion
My dear Sir   March 21. 1861
    Thomas J. Pickett, the bearer of this, and an Illinois State Senator, resides at the City of Rock-Island, in that State, and in the immediate vicinity of the Island of that name. The Island belongs to the U.S; and Mr. Pickett thinks there is an agency for it, in charge of your Department, worth some $700. If this be true, I wish Mr. Pickett could have the agency. Yours very truly
                                                                            A LINCOLN

¹ALS, IHi. Pickett received the agency of the Island of Rock Island.

To William H. Seward¹

[March 21, 1861?]
What says Gov. Seward to making the appointment mentioned within.   LINCOLN

¹ AES, NAuE. Lincoln's undated endorsement is written on the back of a letter from Winfield Scott and Joseph G. Totten to Montgomery Blair, March 21, 1861, recommending appointment of General Joseph G. Swift as postmaster at Geneva, New York. William Johnson, rather than Swift, received the appointment.

To Gideon Welles¹

Hon. Sec. of Navy   Executive Mansion   March 22. 1861
    Sir: I understand there is a vacancy in the office of Engineer in Chief of the Navy, which I shall have to fill by appointment. Will you please avail yourself of all the means in your power for determin[ing] and present me the name of [the] best man for the service [?] of other circumstances. Yours &c   A. LINCOLN

¹ ALS-P, ISLA. The manuscript is burned at the edges. Restorations are by the editors. There is no reply from Welles in the Lincoln Papers, but Benjamin F. Isherwood of New York was appointed.

Endorsement: Meredith Helm to Lincoln[1]

I wish Mr. Thomas Mustin, and Mr. Jones, named within, may retain their places, for the present, at least. A LINCOLN
March 25. 1861.

[1] AES, RPB. Dr. Meredith Helm of Springfield, Ilinois, wrote a letter on March 20, 1861, introducing "Thomas Mustin, and Mr. Thos. Jones, the former my brother in law, the latter his son in law," and asking that they be permitted to retain their respective offices. Mustin held a clerkship in the fifth auditor's office and Jones a clerkship in the census office.

Endorsements: Caleb B. Smith to Lincoln[1]

We demand that the appointment named within be made at once. EDGAR COWAN
March 25, 1861. JOHN COVODE

Let it be done. LINCOLN

[1] AES, DNA RG 48, Appointments, Indian Agencies, Box 1274. Both endorsements are in Lincoln's handwriting, the first bearing signatures of Senator Edgar Cowan and Representative John Covode of Pennsylvania. Smith's letter concerned the appointment of Walter A. Burleigh of Pennsylvania to the Yankton Sioux Indian Agency. Burleigh was appointed.

To William H. Seward[1]

[March 25, 1861]
Senator Grimes wishes A. L. Wolff made consul to Basle in Switzerland.

[1] AL, DNA FS RG 59, Appointments, Box 406. August L. Wolff of Iowa received the appointment.

To James W. Grimes and James Harlan[1]

[c. March 26, 1861?]
Messrs. Grimes & Harlan. Would your friend, Sanders be Surveyor General of Nevada? Yours truly A. LINCOLN
P. S answer at once.

[1] ALS, DLC. Lincoln's note is undated, and no reply has been found. On March 26, 1861, Alvin Saunders of Iowa was nominated by Lincoln to be Governor of Nebraska. The Senate confirmed the nomination on March 27.

To the Senate[1]

March 26, 1861

To the Senate of the United States. I have received a copy of a resolution of the Senate passed on the 25th instant requesting me, if in my opinion not incompatible with the public interest to communicate to the Senate the despatches of Major Robert Anderson to the War Department during the time he has been in command at Fort Sumter.

On examining the correspondence thus called for I have with the highest respect for the Senate come to the conclusion that at the present moment the publication of it would be inexpedient.

Washington, 26th. March, 1861.   [ABRAHAM LINCOLN.]

[1] Copy, DLC-RTL. Labeled "(Copy)" in Lincoln's autograph, the document is otherwise in Seward's handwriting and is without signature. The original has not been found, and the text does not appear in the Senate *Executive Journal*. The *Congressional Globe*, March 29, 1861, prints the same text as in the copy, under proceedings of March 27, 1861 (p. 1512). The text printed by Nicolay and Hay (VI, 225-26) contains minor verbal variations ("the resolution," "of Fort Sumter," "On examination of"), which may represent the wording of the original.

To Edward Bates[1]

Hon. Atty. General   Executive Mansion
My dear Sir   March 27, 1861

Senator Foote sends me word that the Vermont delegation desires George Howe to be District Attorney; and C C. P. Baldwin to be Marshal for Vermont. The initials I can not help. I send them as sent to me. Send me the blank appointments. Yours &c

A. LINCOLN

[1] ALS owned by Mrs. R. T. Kellogg, Silver City, New Mexico. C. C. P. Baldwin of Bradford, and George Howe of Brattleboro, Vermont, received their respective appointments.

To Edward Bates[1]

[c. March 27, 1861]

Will the Attorney General give the bearers of this, an audience, and examine this petition as soon as possible.   A. LINCOLN

[1] AES, DNA RG 204, U. S. Pardon Attorney, A 361. Endorsement on a petition March 27, 1861, from a delegation of the Chickasaw Tribe of Indians, asking a respite of six months in the execution of Reyburn Porter and Billy Jimmy of the Chickasaw Tribe, convicted in November, 1860, of the murder of two white men.

Memorandum:
Appointment of Thomas P. Campbell[1]

March 27, 1861

On this 27th. of March 1861 Hon. Mr. Blair of Pa. calls and presses that Thomas P. Campbell Esq. of his District shall be consul to Glasgow, or have some other eligible appointment. Mr. Blair says his District does a large share of the voting, and never receives any thing. Therefore he is very anxious in this matter.

[1] AD, DLC-RTL. Representative Samuel S. Blair's recommendation of Thomas P. Campbell of Huntington, Pennsylvania, was not followed. James S. Prettyman of Delaware received the appointment.

Reply to Joseph Bertinatti[1]

March 27, 1861

CHEVALIER BERTINATTI: With a degree of pleasure no less than that which you express in presenting it, I receive and accept the letter of his Majesty, your august Sovereign, which accredits you as his Minister Resident near this Government.

While I hold it to be the duty of the United States not to interfere with the differences of foreign Governments and countries, I trust I may, without offence to any, congratulate your Sovereign and yourself upon the high position which Sardinia holds in the scale of nations. I hope, too, that whatever has been or shall be done may result in the augmented prosperity and happiness of the people concerned.

Please assure your august Sovereign that his good wishes for our country are reciprocated by us for his, and that it shall be our constant care to maintain the friendly relations now happily existing between the two.

Chevalier Bertinatti, your personal promotion is a subject of satisfaction to the Government of the United States.

[1] Washington *Daily National Intelligencer*, March 28, 1861. Lincoln replied to a brief speech by Chevalier Bertinatti of Sardinia on presenting his credentials of promotion from consul to minister.

To Hiram Barney[1]

Hon. Hiram Barney   Washington
My dear Sir: March 29, 1861

Please come here. I think I can make up the New-York card better after having a talk with you. Yours truly   A. LINCOLN

[1] ALS-P, ISLA. Barney was a prominent New York City attorney who was appointed collector of the Port of New York.

Memorandum: Edward D. Baker's Recommendations for California Appointments[1]

March 29, 1861

It is stated that Col. Baker's recommendations for California would be judicious and satisfactory, by,

Thomas Fitch	Walter S. Denio	Rod. Matthewson
Geo W. Wright	Wm. H. Stevens	[Roderick Matheson]
Chas W. Rand	Capt. [Frank] Folger	S[amuel] H. Parker
D. J. Staples	J. C. Birsaye [Birdsye]	A. J. Butler

[1] AD, DLC-RTL. The envelope endorsed by Lincoln *"California/* Baker's backers & Cand./ (Partial only)" also contains a small slip, not in Lincoln's handwriting, listing "California/ Collecter Naval agent, Sam Bell. Naval officer Willard B. Farwell. Superintendent of the Mint, Robt. I Stevens."

To Gideon Welles and Simon Cameron[1]

Executive Mansion

Honorable Secretary of the Navy [War],   March 29, 1861

Sir: I desire that an expedition, to move by sea, be got ready to sail as early as the 6th. of April next, the whole according to memorandum attached; and that you co-operate with the Secretary of War [the Navy] for that object. Your Obedient Servant

A. LINCOLN.

[Enclosure][2]

Navy Dept.

Stmrs Pocahontas at Norfolk, Pawnee at Washington, and Revenue Cutter Harriet Lane at N. York to be ready [under sailing orders] for sea with one months stores [stores, etc. for one month]. Three hundred seamen [men] to be [kept] ready for leaving the [departure from on board] receiving ship at N. York [for departure from on board the receiving-ships at New York].

War Dept.

Two hundred men at N. York ready to leave garrison—one years stores to be put in a portable form. [Two hundred men to be ready to leave Governor's Island in New York. Supplies for twelve months for one hundred men to be put in portable shape, ready for instant shipping. A large steamer and three tugs conditionally engaged.]

[1] ALS-P, ISLA; NH, VI, 226-27. Although the original manuscript of the copy to Cameron as printed by Nicolay and Hay has not been located, the copy to Welles, with enclosure, is available. The variations in wording in the

Cameron copy as printed by Nicolay and Hay are given in brackets. At the cabinet meeting on March 29, Lincoln requested written opinions on the expedition. Seward and Smith opposed, while Welles, Chase, Bates, and Blair concurred. The written opinions of Seward, Welles, Smith, Chase, and Bates are in the Lincoln Papers, but the opinion of Blair (printed in NH, VI, 230) is not, and no opinion of Cameron is of record on this date.

² The enclosure with the Welles letter is not in Lincoln's handwriting.

To Jesse K. Dubois[1]

Hon. J. K. Dubois: Washington,
My dear Sir   March 30. 1861

I was nearly as sorry as you can be at not being able to give Mr. Luce the appointment you desired for him. Of course I *could* have done it; but it would have been against the united, earnest, and, I add, angry protest of the republican delegation of Minnesota, in which state the office is located. So far as I understand, it is unprecedented, [to] send an officer into a *state* against the wishes of the members of congress of the State, and of the same party. Your friend as ever   A. LINCOLN

¹ ALS, IHi. Dubois to Lincoln, March 27, 1861, expressed disappointment that John P. Luse, his son-in-law, failed to receive the appointment as Northern superintendent of Indian affairs for Minnesota: *"My heart was set* on this *application* for him, as in his appointment I could have transferred my dying daughter from the Wabash Valley to the healthy climate of Minessotta and perhaps prolonged her life. . . ." (DLC-RTL). See Lincoln's endorsement on letter from Dubois, (c. March 17, 1861), *supra.*

Endorsement on Petition
Concerning California Appointments[1]

March 30, 1861

This paper is presented the 30th. of March 1861, by Mr. Jos. A. Nunes, as spokesman of about fiftyfive Californians, being present, stating it to be the expression of a majority of California Republicans now in Washington.

¹ AE, DLC-RTL. Signed by Joseph A. Nunes, president of the California Republican conventions of 1856 and 1860, and fifty-four other California Republicans, the petition of March 28, 1861, requests that the president consult Leland Stanford, Gordon N. Mott, J. W. Simonton, Charles Watrous, and John Satterlee in regard to federal appointments in California. Lincoln's envelope endorsement reads: "California/ Document of the 55."

To Honorable Secretary[1]

Hon: Secretary   Executive Mansion   March 30. 1861

The bearer of this, Alexander R. McKee, is a brother-in-law, of the late Col. John Hardin of Illinois, and is an out, and out Republican. He resides in Kentucky, as he ever has done. I think I am not mistaken in saying he is popular with all Kentuckians. He desires a place in one of the Departments, and I wish he could have it. Yours truly   A. LINCOLN

[1] ALS, owned by William H. Townsend, Lexington, Kentucky. This letter of introduction produced an appointment for McKee to the consulship at Panama. Alexander R. McKee had served for many years as clerk of court at Lancaster, Kentucky.

To Caleb B. Smith[1]

[c. March 30, 1861]

Comodore Gregory, Comd. by Mr. Jefferson, Jany. 16. 1861[2]— presents himself and presses that his son, named within, be retained as agent for the Poncas tribe, in Dakota.

[1] AE, DNA NR RG 48, Applications, Indian Agencies, Box 1272. Captain Francis H. Gregory to Lincoln, March 30, 1861, requests the retention of his son John S. Gregory as agent for the Ponca Tribe.
[2] Lincoln's inadvertent error; Gregory was commissioned January 16, 1809.

To John T. Stuart[1]

PRIVATE

Dear Stuart: . Washington, March 30, 1861

Cousin Lizzie[2] shows me your letter of the 27th. The question of giving her the Springfield Post-office troubles me. You see I have already appointed William Jayne a territorial governor, and Judge Trumbulls brother[3] to a Land-office. Will it do for me to go on and justify the declaration that Trumbull and I have divided out all the offices among our relatives? Dr. Wallace, you know, is needy, and looks to me; and I personally owe him much.

I see by the papers, a vote is to be taken as to the Post-office.[4] Could you not set up Lizzie and beat them all? She, being here, need know nothing of it, & therefore there would be no indelicacy on her part. Yours as ever   A. LINCOLN

[1] ALS, owned by heirs of Stuart Brown, Springfield, Illinois. Stuart replied April 3, ". . . I would not let the case of Cousin Lizzie trouble me if I were you. . . ." and William Butler and Jesse K. Dubois advised on March 25, that the president should do nothing until after the city election and that he not sanction election by the people at all (DLC-RTL). The incumbent John M. Lindsay continued in office until August 16, when John Armstrong was installed.
[2] Elizabeth Todd Grimsley.
[3] Benjamin M. Trumbull was appointed receiver of the land office at Omaha, Nebraska.
[4] Although the advisability of an election was discussed in the *Illinois State Journal*, none was held.

Memorandum: California Appointments[1]

[c. April 1, 1861]

Rabe thinks we should ask the advice of Col. Keys (Gen. Scott's Sec) about appointments.

[1] AE, DLC-RTL. Lincoln's endorsement is written on an undated note from William Rabé, enclosed with a letter from Rabé dated April 1, 1861, listing appointments which Rabé recommended in California. Dr. William Rabé, appointed marshal for the northern district of California, was a druggist at San Francisco and secretary of the California state Republican committee.

Memoranda on Federal Appointments[1]

[c. April 1, 1861]

Baltimore—Maryland.[2]

Collector — Henry W. Hoffman.
Dep.
Surveyor of P — William L. Marshall
Naval Officer — Francis S. Cockran [Corkran].
Dep.
Appraiser Genl. Frederick Schley.
1. Appraiser — Charles P. Montague
2. Do.   — Joseph F. Meredith
Navy Agent — Wm. Pinckney Ewing
Post-Master — William H. Purnell.
Attorney —
Marshal — Washington Bonifant.

About appointments in California.[3]
Consult Leland Stanford & Eugene L. Sullivan.

California[4]

Sacramento —			
	Collector —	L. H. Foote	$3430.00
Monterey.			
	Collector —	John F. Porter	"3055.52
Sonoma.			
	Collector	Seth M. Swain.	"3165.71
Santa Barbara			
	Collector	Samuel B. Brinkerhoff[5]	
San Joaquin			
	Collector	S. W. Sperry.	"3174.55

[1] AD, DLC-RTL. These memoranda are scattered among the Lincoln Papers, but seem to be contemporary and have been grouped together for convenience. The number of the document in the RTL is given in a footnote to each.
[2] RTL, 9523.
[3] RTL, 9532.   [4] RTL, 13639-13641.
[5] The omitted Santa Barbara item is written in the left-hand margin.

San Diego
	Collector	Joshua Sloan.	$2250.00
San Pedro			
	Surveyor —	Oscar Macy.	"3000.00

San Francisco
	Collector —	Ira P. Rankin	"7900.00
	Dep. & Aud.		"3125.00
	Dep.		"3125.00
	Dep.		"3125.00
	Appraiser Genl.	Samuel J. Bridge.	"3125.00
	Appraiser.	Benj. W. Mudge.	"3125.00
	do.	John P. Zane.	"3125.00
	Naval Officer		"6250.00
	Surveyor		"5625.00

Mint
	Superintendent —	Robert J. Stevens	"4500.00
	Treasurer	David W. Cheeseman[6]	"4500.00
	Melter &	Walter S. Denio	"3000.00
	Assayer.	Conrad Wiegand	"3000.00
	Comr	William Schmolz	"3000.00

Navy
Navy Agent —

Judicial Department —

Northern District.
| | Attorney. | William H. Sharp | |
| | Marshal. | William Rabe. | |

Southern District
| | Attorney. | [Kimball H.] Dimmick | |
| | Marshal. | Henry D. Barrows | |

| 83 | Surveyor General — | | $4500.00 |

85-86 San Francisco L. O
| | Register. | George B. Tingley | "3000.00 |
| | Receiver. | Royal H. Waller. | "3000.00 |

Los Angeles L. O
| | Register | Antonio Maria Pico. | "3000.00 |
| | Receiver. | Lewis Sperry. | "3000.00 |

Maryville L. O.
| | Register. | A. J. Snyder. | "3000.00 |
| | Receiver. | J. Compton. | "3000.00 |

Humboldt L. O
| | Register. | John M. Eddy. | "3000.00 |
| | Receiver. | William H. Pratt. | "3000.00 |

Stockton L. O
| | Register. | George D. Webster | "3000.00 |
| | Receiver. | G. C. Havens. | "3000.00 |

Visalia L. O
| | Register. | Henry W. Briggs. | "3000.00 |
| | Receiver. | George M. Gerrish. | "3000.00 |

[6] The name has been written over another name which is illegible.

95 California Indian Dept.

North. Superintendency (S.F). Geo. M. Hanson		$4000.00
South — do Miner Frisby, Jr.		
Klamath. Sub-Agency.		"1500.00
Cal. Agency (Norm Lecker)		"3000.00
Sub– do– (Mendocino)		"1500.00
Sub– do —		"1500.00

California Indian Dept. cont.

Tejon Agency	$3000.00
Klamath Agency	"3000.00

Nebraska & Kansas[7]

Land Dept. cont.

Dakota City L. O
Register
Receiver

91 Indian Dept.

Superintendent (St. L)	2000.00
Blackfeet Agency	1500.00
Upper Mo. Agency	1500.00
Yancton Sioux Agency	1500.00
Upper Platte Agency	1500.00
Omaha Agency	1500.00
Ottoe & Mo. A	1500.00
Pawnee A	1500.00
Kickapoo A	1500.00
Delaware A	1500.00
Shaw. & Wy. A	1500.00
Pottawatamie A	1500.00
Great Nemaha A.	1500.00
Sac & Fox A	1500.00
Kansas A	1500.00
Osage R. A.	1500.00

Nebraska —[8]

Governor Nebraskan
Secretary
C. J.
Ass. J.
Ass. J.
Attorney
Marshal

84 Land Dept. (Kansas & Nebraska)

Surveyor General	$2000.00
Lecompton L. O	
Register	
Receiver	
Kickapoo L. O	
Register	
Receiver	

[7] RTL, 13646.   [8] RTL, 13645.

[306]

Fort Scott L. O
    Register
    Receiver
Ogden L. O
    Register
    Receiver
Omaha L. O
    Register
    Receiver
Brownville L. O
    Register
    Receiver
Nebraska City L. O
    Register
    Receiver

New-Mexico[9]

Governor
Secretary
C. J.
Ass. J.
Ass. J.
Attorney
Marshal-
Land Dept
84. Surveyor-Genl. $3000.00
85-6 Santa Fe L. O.
    Register   "3000.00
    Receiver   "3000.00
94 Indian Dept.
    Superintendent — Santa-Fe   "2000.00
    Utah Agency   "1550.00
    Apache Agency   "1550.00
    Abiqun Agency   "1550.00
    Santa Fe Agency   "1550.00
    Navajo Agency   "1550.00
    do   "1550.00

Hon——Conkling's card for N. Y. city.[10]
    Collector   Hiram Barney
    Surveyor   Henry B. Stanton
    Naval Officer   Abraham [Abram] Wakeman—Thinks
        Mr. Denison preferable to either Mr. Dorsheimer,
        Draper, or Welch, partly because they all at present
        hold offices.
    District Attorney   Wm. Curtis Noyes
    Marshal   Jedediah W. Hartt
    Navy Agent   D. D. T. Marshall
    Superintendent of the Assay Office   Alfred Wells
    Assistant Treasurer   George Opdyke

[9] RTL, 13642.
[10] RTL, 9550. The heading and marginal note following "Wakeman" are in Lincoln's autograph; the list is Roscoe Conkling's.

Utah[11]

Governor		
Secretary		
C. J.		
Ass. J		
Ass. J.		
Attorney		
Marshal		
84 Land Dept		
Surveyor General		$3000.00
Salt Lake L. O		
Register		"3000.00
Receiver		"3000.00
94 Indian Dept.		
Superintendent (S.L.C)		"2500.00
Agent		"1550.00
Agent		"1000.00
Agent		"1000.00

Washington & Oregon[12]

Governor—	William H. Wallace	
Secretary	Leander J. S. Turney	
C J.	C. C. Hewitt	
Ass. J.	James E. Wyche	
Ass. J.		
Attorney	John J. McGilvra	
Marshal		
84 Land Dept.		
Surveyor Gener		$3000.00
Olympia L. O		
Register.	Arthur A. Denny,	2500.00
Receiver.	Joseph Cushman,	2500.00
94 Indian Dept.		
Superintendent		2500.00
Puget Sound Agency		1500.00
Squakson Agency		1000.00
Siletz Agency		1500.00
Umpqua Agency		1000.00
Grand Ronde Agency		1500.00
E. Oregon Agency		1500.00
Cayuse Agency		1000.00
Col. River Agency		1500.00
Local do		1000.00
Flathead Agency		1500.00
Astoria Agency		1000.00

Collector at Fort-Townsend.
          Victor Smith
Collector at Nesqually.
          Henry C. Wilson.

[11] RTL, 13643.   [12] RTL, 13644.

Memorandum on Federal Appointments[1]

[c. April 1, 1861]

Andrew J. Atkinson.	Pa.	28. papers
Presley G Athey	Ills.	1.
A. J. Barker	Pa.	1
E W. Beckwith	Conn.	1
Hiram Beckwith	Wis.	7
J. A. Berry	O	3
Geo. M. Brinkerhoff	Ills	1
C. S. Broderick	Ia.	1
T. C. Buntin	Ia	19
M. G. Birvies	Mo.	1
I. N. Burket	Pa	2
C. B. Campbell		2
T. A. Cheney	N.Y	1
Levi Clark.	Kan	1
Samuel F. Fletcher	Ia	1
H. W. Cobb	Ills.	1
Silas Colgrove	Ia	4
Frank M. Cooley	Pa	4
G. E. H. Day	Minn.	1
J. M. Craddock	Ills.	3
A. Denny		1
J. Nevin Dickinson	Pa	2
John S. Dill	Ills	1
H. S. Dodd	Iowa	1
Chas. B. Dorrence	Pa.	7
Chas. B. Dienkhard	Ark.	1
David M. Dunn	Ia	1
Joseph Eldridge	N.Y	1
Abraham Ellis	Kan	1
H. N. Farnham	N.Y.	2
Benjamin Fenn		1
Joseph Froskett	Iowa	1 Paper
John A. Filbert	Md.	5
Chas. W. Fribley	Pa.	1
B. C. Gillam	Ills	4

[1] AD, DLC-RTL. This document appears to be an incomplete list of persons
recommended for office and the number of recommendations for each.

Memorandum on Foreign Appointments[1]

[c. April 1, 1861]

Vacancy—

Dip.

Sec.   to China
Sec.   to Russia.
Min. & Sec. Argentine Con.
             Consuls
             Havanna —   Schufeldt — Seward.
             Odessa —   John D. Arnold, of Ills.
             Marseilles.   J.   C. Van Horn. (See
                                   papers filed for Glasgow)
             Lyons.   James Lesley.
             Messina.   Mark Howard.   Conn.
                                   Welles.

             Monrovia.
             Gabboon.
             Ning Po.   Willie P. Mangum.   N.C.
             Foo. Choo.   W. H. Carpenter.   N.Y.
             Apia   Daniel Ketcham   N.Y.
             Rio —   Parsons — Chase
             Montevideo.
             Guakil [Guayaquil?]
             Florence.   T. Bigelow Lawrence — no pay.

[1] AD, DLC-RTL.

Memorandum: Appointment of Oliver G. Abell[1]

[c. April 1, 1861]

Oliver G. Abell is an applicant for a Land-Office on the Pacific.
Mr. Abell is the child of very intimate friends of mine, and I
would like, if possible, to oblige him.

[1] AD, DNA NR RG 48, Applications, Registers and Receivers, General Land
Office, California, 1852-1868, Box 1276. Oliver G. Abell is listed as a clerk in the
General Land Office in Washington in 1863. He was the son of Lincoln's old
friend at New Salem, Illinois, Bennett Abell. His letter of April, 1861, is in the
Lincoln Papers.

Memorandum: Appointments of John C. Baum and Adolphus Carnes[1]

[c. April 1, 1861]

Hon. John A. Gurley, recommends for P.M. at Cin. John C.
Baum. For Collector—Adolphus Carnes.

[1] AD, DLC-RTL.

Memorandum: Appointment of Edward F. Beale[1]

[c. April 1, 1861]

Hon. John Hickman, and Hon. John W. Forney, think that Edward F. Beale, now resident of California, ought, by all means, to be Surveyor General of Cal.

[1] AD, DNA NR RG 48, Appointments, Surveyors General, Box 2, 1861.

Memorandum: Appointment of Postmaster at Binghamton, New York[1]

[c. April 1, 1861]

I appointed P.M. at Binghampton, on special request of Gov. Seward.

[1] AD, DLC-Nicolay Papers. Lincoln appointed William Stuart postmaster at Binghamton, New York.

Memorandum: Appointment of James S. Boal[1]

[c. April 1, 1861]

Dr. Robert Boal of Lacon, Ills, wishes his son, James St. C. Boal, to be Assistant Sec. of Leg. to Paris—& I want him to be obliged.

[1] AD, DNA FS RG 59, Appointments, Box 277. There is no record of Boal's appointment.

Memorandum: Appointment of George Dwight[1]

[c. April 1, 1861]

Mr. Samuel Bowles, introduced by Hon. Geo. Ashmun, joins the Mass. del. in recommending George Dwight to be Sup. of Armory at Springfield, Mass.

[1] AD, DLC-RTL.

Memorandum:
Appointment of John W. Griffiths[1]

[c. April 1, 1861]

"Ichabod" wants John W. Griffiths to be a constructor in the Philadelphia Navy Yard. He has an interest in it.

[1] AD, DLC-RTL. "Ichabod" was probably Lincoln's boyhood friend Israel S. Smith. See Lincoln to Welles about this appointment, April 19, *infra*. Griffiths was the naval architect who first suggested the famous "clipper" ships and was editor of the *Nautical Magazine and Naval Journal*. He had built the gunboat *Pawnee* in 1858.

Memorandum:
Appointment of John P. Hatterscheidt[1]

[c. April 1, 1861]

When we come to act again upon consulships, I wish John P. Hatterscheidt to be appointed to Antwerp, unless some reason to the contrary, not now known to me, shall appear.   A. LINCOLN

[1] AD, DLC-RTL. The memorandum is with an undated letter recommending Hatterscheidt, "a citizen of Kansas," signed by James H. Lane and Samuel C. Pomeroy. Hatterscheidt was appointed to the consulship at Moscow during the recess of the Senate and confirmed by the Senate, July 26.

Memorandum:
Appointment of James H. Holmes[1]

[c. April 1, 1861]

James H. Holmes, for Surveyor General, of New-Mexico. Recommended by known men.

[1] AD, DNA NR RG 48, Applications, Surveyors General, New Mexico, Box 1261.

Memorandum:
Appointment of John L. Mansfield[1]

[c. April 1, 1861]

Mr. John L. Mansfield, Elector, of Madison, Ia. is an applicant for consul at Havre; but being in easy circumstances, would accept a different one with smaller emolument.

[1] AD, DNA FS RG 59, Appointments, Box 341. James O. Putnam was appointed consul at Havre, and there is no record of an appointment for John L. Mansfield of Madison, Indiana (not Iowa).

Memorandum: Appointment of Amasa Mason[1]

[c. April 1, 1861]

Amasa Mason, of Buffalo, N.Y. is urgently pressed by Gov. Corwin, of Ohio, for consul at Melbourne, Gov. Corwin declaring that the Mercantile community of N.Y. city very much desire his appointment.

[1] AD, DNA FS RG 59, Appointments, Box 342. Corwin to Lincoln, April 1, 1861, recommended Mason (DLC-RTL), but William Blanchard of Maryland was consul at Melbourne as of September 30, 1861.

Memorandum:
Appointment of John H. Peters[1]

[c. April 1, 1861]

It is proposed that Judge John H. Peters, of S.C. be Consul to Tunis, with an eye to the Cotten culture.

[1] AD, DLC-RTL. Lincoln appointed Peters during the recess of the Senate and sent his nomination on July 9, but the *Executive Journal* does not record confirmation of the appointment after referral to the committee on commerce.

Memoranda:
Appointment of William B. Richmond[1]

[c. April 1, 1861]

Mr. Richmond resides in Tenn. and is recommended by Messrs Bell, Johnson, Maynard & Nelson. Also by Senator Simmons & other Rhode Islanders.

App. Consul at Paris or Havre. Recommended by Senator Simmons & also Messrs Bell & Johnson.

[1] AD, DNA FS RG 59, Appointments, Box 370. William B. Richmond was not appointed to either post, but on December 23, Lincoln nominated him for the consulship at Tunis upon John H. Peters' failure (*supra*) to be confirmed. On March 24, 1862, Lincoln withdrew William B. Richmond's nomination in favor of Amos Perry of Rhode Island, who was confirmed April 15 (*Executive Journal*). The persons listed as recommending Richmond were Senator James F. Simmons of Rhode Island, Andrew Johnson, John Bell, Representative Horace Maynard, and Representative Thomas A. R. Nelson—all of Tennessee. Lincoln was in error in listing Senator Simmons among William B. Richmond's supporters, having confused the latter with William W. Richmond, also an applicant for the Paris consulship. Both William B. of Tennessee and William W. of New Orleans had resided abroad for some years. Both were well recommended, loyal, and apparently of unusual competence. But neither was appointed because of the confusion of identity. See Lincoln to Seward, June 8 and August 7, and Lincoln's memorandum concerning William W. Richmond, August 25, *infra*.

To Andrew H. Foote[1]

Washington, April 1, 1861.

Fit out *Powhatan* to go to sea at the earliest possible moment under sealed orders. Orders by a confidential messenger go forward to-morrow.   ABRAHAM LINCOLN.

Commandant Navy Yard,
    Brooklyn, N.Y.

[1] *Naval Records*, Series I, IV, 109. The several communications addressed to Foote, Mercer, and Porter on April 1, as printed in various sources are all in

general agreement, but our failure to locate the original documents issued in connection with the *Powhatan* episode leaves much to be desired in clarifying the circumstances which occasioned the several communications. The fact that the text of these communications as printed in Hertz, II, 825-28, is either badly garbled or derived from an unknown if authentic source, further complicates the matter. It seems scarcely probable that Lincoln would have written two different letters in each case, at once so verbally different, yet substantially the same. Hence the editors have relied on the *Official Records* for the texts here reproduced. Lincoln's secret orders to Foote, Mercer, and Porter were issued on Seward's advice, unknown to the Navy Department. Hence there developed a sad confusion which deprived the Sumter expedition of the *Powhatan*, Gustavus V. Fox, in command of the expedition, did not learn of the *Powhatan's* withdrawal until April 13 while awaiting its arrival at Charleston harbor. See Lincoln's letter exonerating Fox, May 1, *infra*.

To Andrew H. Foote[1]

Sir: Executive Mansion, April 1, 1861.

You will fit out the *Powhatan* without delay. Lieutenant Porter will relieve Captain Mercer in command of her. She is bound on secret service, and you will under no circumstances communicate to the Navy Department the fact that she is fitting out.

Commandant Navy Yard,   ABRAHAM LINCOLN.
New York.

[1] *Naval Records*, Series I, IV, 109. David D. Porter, *Naval History of the Civil War* (New York, 1886), p. 102, gives the same text. This is the order sent by messenger, referred to above.

To Samuel Mercer[1]

Washington City, April 1, 1861.

Sir: Circumstances render it necessary to place in command of your ship, and for a special purpose, an officer who is duly informed and instructed in relation to the wishes of the Government, and you will therefore consider yourself detached; but in taking this step the Government does not intend in the least to reflect upon your efficiency or patriotism; on the contrary, have the fullest confidence in your ability to perform any duty required of you.

Hoping soon to be able to give you a better command than the one you now enjoy, and trusting that you will have full confidence in the disposition of the Government toward you, I remain,

Captain Samuel Mercer, U.S. Navy.   ABRAHAM LINCOLN.

[1] *Naval Records*, Series I, IV, 109. Nicolay and Hay (VI, 238) date this letter April 2, on what grounds the editors cannot determine.

To Officers of the Army and Navy[1]

Executive Mansion, Washington, April 1, 1861.

All officers of the Army and Navy, to whom this order may be exhibited, will aid by every means in their power the expedition under the command of Col. Harvey Brown, supplying him with men and material and cooperating with him as he may desire.

ABRAHAM LINCOLN.

[1] OR, I, I, 367. The source designates this as an enclosure to General Scott's order to Colonel Harvey Brown of April 1, which was approved by Lincoln April 2, 1861. Colonel Brown was placed in command of the expedition to reinforce Fort Pickens.

To David D. Porter[1]

Executive Mansion, April 1, 1861.

Lieutenant D. D. Porter will take command of the steamer *Powhatan*, or any other United States steamer ready for sea which he may deem most fit for the service to which he has been assigned by confidential instructions of this date.

All officers are commanded to afford him all such facilities as he may deem necessary for getting to sea as soon as possible. He will select the officers who are to accompany him.

Recommended: WM. H. SEWARD.   ABRAHAM LINCOLN.

[1] *Naval Records*, Series I, IV, 108.

To David D. Porter[1]

Executive Mansion, April 1, 1861.

Sir: You will proceed to New York, and with the least possible delay assume command of any naval steamer available. Proceed to Pensacola Harbor, and at any cost or risk prevent any expedition from the mainland reaching Fort Pickens or Santa Rosa [Island].

You will exhibit this order to any naval officer at Pensacola if you deem it necessary after you have established yourself within the harbor, and will request cooperation by the entrance of at least one other vessel.

This order, its object, and your destination will be communicated to no person whatever until you reach the harbor of Pensacola.   ABRAHAM LINCOLN.

Lieutenant D. D. Porter, U.S. Navy.

Recommended: WM. H. SEWARD.

[1] *Naval Records*, Series I, IV, 108-109.

To Winfield Scott[1]

Lieut General Scott: Executive Mansion April 1st 1861.

Would it impose too much labor on General Scott to make short, comprehensive daily reports to me of what occurs in his Department, including movements by himself, and under his orders, and the receipt of intelligence? If not I will thank him to do so. Your Obedient Servant   A. LINCOLN

[1] Copy, DLC-RTL. General Scott reported April 1, and with fair regularity thereafter. These daily reports, together with Lincoln's memoranda on the days Scott failed to report ("No report from Gen. Scott this 19. April 1861.") are in the Lincoln Papers.

To William H. Seward[1]

Hon: W. H. Seward: Executive Mansion April 1, 1861

My dear Sir: Since parting with you I have been considering your paper dated this day, and entitled "Some thoughts for the President's consideration." The first proposition in it is, "1st. We are at the end of a month's administration, and yet without a policy, either domestic or foreign."

At the *beginning* of that month, in the inaugeral, I said "The power confided to me will be used to hold, occupy and possess the property and places belonging to the government, and to collect the duties, and imposts." This had your distinct approval at the time; and, taken in connection with the order I immediately gave General Scott, directing him to employ every means in his power to strengthen and hold the forts, comprises the exact domestic policy you now urge, with the single exception, that it does not propose to abandon Fort Sumpter.

Again, I do not perceive how the re-inforcement of Fort Sumpter would be done on a slavery, or party issue, while that of Fort Pickens would be on a more national, and patriotic one.

The news received yesterday in regard to St. Domingo, certainly brings a new item within the range of our foreign policy;[2] but up to that time we have been preparing circulars, and instructions to ministers, and the like, all in perfect harmony, without even a suggestion that we had no foreign policy.

Upon your closing propositions, that "whatever policy we adopt, there must be an energetic prossecution of it"

"For this purpose it must be somebody's business to pursue and direct it incessantly"

"Either the President must do it himself, and be all the while active in it, or"

[316]

"Devolve it on some member of his cabinet"

"Once adopted, debates on it must end, and all agree and abide"
I remark that if this must be done, *I* must do it. When a general
line of policy is adopted, I apprehend there is no danger of its being changed without good reason, or continuing to be a subject of
unnecessary debate; still, upon points arising in its progress, I
wish, and suppose I am entitled to have the advice of all the cabinet. Your Obt. Servt.   A. LINCOLN

1 ALS, DLC-RTL. The envelope with the letter is addressed by Lincoln
"Hon. W. H. Seward/Present." There is no reply in the Lincoln Papers. Lincoln may have handed the letter to Seward personally or sent it by messenger.
If so, he must have requested its return. The fact that no biography of Seward
mentions such a letter among the Seward Papers indicates that the document in
the Lincoln Papers is probably the original which was never sent. The
editors have doubts that the letter was presented to Seward at all. Having written it, Lincoln may have thought better of rebuking his secretary in writing
and handled the matter orally. The memorandum to which Lincoln replied is in
the handwriting of Frederick W. Seward, as follows:

"Some thoughts for the President's consideration

April 1. 1861.

"1st. We are at the end of a month's administration and yet without a policy
either domestic or foreign.

"2d This, however, is not culpable, and it has been unavoidable. The presence
of the Senate, with the need to meet applications for patronage have prevented
attention to other and more grave matters.

"3d. But further delay to adopt and prosecute our policies for both domestic
and foreign affairs would not only bring scandal on the Administration, but danger upon the country.

"4th. To do this we must dismiss the applicants for office. But how? I suggest
that we make the local appointments forthwith, leaving foreign or general ones
for ulterior and occasional action.

"5th. The policy—at home. I am aware that my views are singular, and perhaps not sufficiently explained. My system is built upon this *idea* as a ruling
one, namely that we must

"*Change the question before the Public from one upon Slavery, or about
Slavery*

"for a question upon *Union or Disunion.*

"In other words, from what would be regarded as a Party question to one of
Patriotism or *Union*

"The occupation or evacuation of Fort Sumter, although not in fact a slavery,
or a party question is so *regarded.* Witness, the temper manifested by the Republicans in the Free States, and even by Union men in the South.

"I would therefore terminate it as a safe means for changing the issue. I
deem it fortunate that the last Administration created the necessity.

"For the rest. I would simultaneously defend and reinforce all the Forts in
the Gulf, and have the Navy recalled from foreign stations to be prepared for
a blockade. Put the Island of Key West under Martial Law

"This will raise distinctly the question of *Union* or *Disunion.* I would maintain every fort and possession in the South.

For *Foreign Nations.*

"I would demand explanations from *Spain* and France, categorically, at once.

"I would seek explanations from Great Britain and Russia, and send agents into *Canada, Mexico* and *Central America,* to rouse a vigorous continental *spirit of independence* on this continent against European intervention.

"And if satisfactory explanations are not received from Spain and France,
"Would convene Congress and declare war against them
"But whatever policy we adopt, there must be an energetic prosecution of it.
"For this purpose it must be somebody's business to pursue and direct it incessantly.
"Either the President must do it himself, and be all the while active in it; or
"Devolve it on some member of his Cabinet. Once adopted, debates on it must end, and all agree and abide.
"It is not in my especial province.
"But I neither seek to evade nor assume responsibility" (DLC-RTL).

[2] The Spanish colonists in San Domingo had hoisted the Spanish flag on March 16, and the Spanish ship *Blanca* had been sent from Havana with troops to assist in annexation of the country.

To Gideon Welles[1]

(Confidential.)

To the Secretary of the Navy.   Executive Mansion,
Dear Sir: April 1, 1861.

You will issue instructions to Captain Pendergrast,[2] commanding the home squadron, to remain in observation at Vera Cruz—important complications in our foreign relations rendering the presence of an officer of rank there of great importance.

Captain Stringham[3] will be directed to proceed to Pensacola with all possible despatch, and assume command of that portion of the home squadron stationed off Pensacola. He will have confidential instructions to cooperate in every way with the commander of the land forces of the United States in that neighborhood.

The instructions to the army officers, which are strictly confidential, will be communicated to Captain Stringham after he arrives at Pensacola.

Captain Samuel Barron will relieve Captain Stringham in charge of the Bureau of detail.   ABRAHAM LINCOLN.

P.S. As it is very necessary at this time to have a perfect knowledge of the personnel of the navy, and to be able to detail such officers for special purposes as the exigencies of the service may require. I request that you will instruct Captain Barron to proceed and organize the Bureau of detail in the manner best adapted to meet the wants of the navy, taking cognizance of the discipline of the navy generally, detailing all officers for duty, taking charge of the recruiting of seamen, supervising charges made against officers, and all matters relating to duties which must be best understood by a sea officer. You will please afford Captain Barron any facility for accomplishing this duty, transferring to his department the clerical force heretofore used for the purposes specified. It is to be understood that this officer will act by authority of Secretary of the Navy, who will exercise such supervision as he may deem necessary. ABRAHAM LINCOLN.

[1] Gideon Welles, "Fort Sumter," *The Galaxy*, November, 1870, X, 624. Welles describes the letter as being in the handwriting of Montgomery C. Meigs and the postscript in the handwriting of David D. Porter and comments that "the President expressed as much surprise as I felt that he had signed and sent me such a document." He adds: "Pendergrast did not go to Vera Cruz nor Stringham to Pensacola." (p. 626). [2] Garrett J. Pendergrast. [3] Silas H. Stringham.

To Mrs. Mary Hancock Colyer[1]

Executive Mansion April 2. 1861

My Dear Madam   I have the honour to acknowledge the receipt of your favour of the 22nd of March.

Permit me to express my cordial thanks for the interesting relic you were so kind as to send me, as well as for the flattering sentiment with which it was accompanied. I am with great respect Your Obdt Servt.   A. LINCOLN

Mary Hancock Colyer 105 Bleeker St New York

[1] LS, owned by Richard F. Lufkin, Boston, Massachusetts. Mrs. Colyer wrote March 22, 1861, ". . . As niece of John Hancock, I take pleasure in presenting . . . a share ticket issued by the province of Massachusetts Bay, 1765, for the rebuilding of Faneuil Hall, signed by John Hancock, and endorsed on the back by Abraham Lincoln . . . one of your ancestors. . . ." (DLC-RTL).

Memorandum:
Appointment of Ward H. Lamon[1]

April 2, 1861

This April 2, 1861, these papers were presented in person to me, by John Van Riswick, Samuel Norment, Benedict Milburn, William Wise, George Mattingly, Thomas Lewis, W. Krzyzanowski— J. J. Coombs, Amos Duvall, George Feaman & William P. Wood, & James A. Wise.

[1] AE, DLC-RTL. The endorsement is written on a petition of Washington, D.C., citizens for appointment of Lamon as marshal of the District. See Lincoln to Bates, April 6, *infra*.

Memorandum: Appointment of Simeon Smith[1]

April 2, 1861

This 2nd. day of April 1861 Mr. Senator Preston King appears in person, and presses that *Simeon Smith*, of Minnesota be appointed

Commissioner of Pensions. Mr. King makes a personal appeal in the case.

1 DNA NR RG 48, Applications, Secretary of the Interior, Box 1293. Simeon Smith, a native of New York, was commissioned major in the Second Minnesota Infantry, July 23, 1861, and resigned to accept a commission as paymaster, August 29, 1861.

To William H. Seward[1]

Executive Mansion   2d April 1861.

I direct that ten thousand dollars be paid to Captain M. C. Meigs, by the Secretary of State[2]—from the secret service fund.

ABRAHAM LINCOLN

1 DS, RPB. Captain Montgomery C. Meigs accompanied Colonel Harvey Brown as chief engineer on the expedition to reinforce Fort Pickens.
2 "By the Secretary of State" inserted by Lincoln.

To Gideon Welles[1]

April 2, 1861

Mr. G. H. Heap will if summoned by Capt. D. D. Porter U.S. Navy, join him instantly in New York, temporarily vacating his desk at the Navy department.

1 Stan. V. Henkels Catalog 1342, January 4, 1924, No. 8. Gwinn H. Heap, a clerk in the Navy Department, sailed on the *Powhatan* as acting paymaster.

To Erasmus D. Keyes[1]

Executive Mansion,
Lieutenant-Colonel E. D. Keyes,   Washington,
United States Army, Military Secretary: April 3, 1861.

You will proceed forthwith to the city of New York to carry out the instructions which you have received here. All requisitions made upon officers of the staff by your authority, and all orders given by you to any officer of the Army in my name, will be instantly obeyed.   ABRAHAM LINCOLN.

1 Erasmus D. Keyes, *Fifty Years Observation of Men and Events* (New York, 1884), p. 387. Lieutenant Colonel Keyes, military secretary to General Scott, was authorized to prepare plans for reinforcement of Fort Pickens (Order of General Scott to Colonel Harvey Brown, April 1, OR, I, I, 366).

Memorandum:
Appointment of John C. Henshaw[1]

[c. April 3, 1861][2]

Mr. Kellogg does me great injustice to write in this strain. He has had more favors than any other Illinois member, not excepting, I think, Judge Trumbull. Is it really in his heart to add to my perplexities now?   A. LINCOLN.

[1] AES, ORB. The endorsement is written on the back of William Kellogg to Lincoln: "Mansion of Prst Lincoln Wdnsdy April 3 1861. . . . I desire to withdraw, the pamphlet and papers I left with you this morning relating to the appointment of Major Henshaw . . . I regret to again trouble you, and hope never again to feel the humiliation I did in our interview of this morning—or again to solicit patronage, that I may not demand as the right of a representative of the people and a citizen of the Republic. . . ."
[2] This endorsement is dated April 5, 1861 in Hertz, II, 828.

To Gideon Welles[1]

(Confidential)

Executive Mansion   3d April 1861.

The secretary of the Navy will please cause three complete sets of signal books telegraphic & common to be delivered to the bearer.
                                                 ABRAHAM LINCOLN

[1] LS, DNA WR NB RG 45, Executive Letters, 57. No record has been found identifying the bearer. The signal books may have been intended for Major Anderson at Fort Sumter. If so, their failure to arrive was a contributing factor to the failure of the expedition to relieve the fort, for the Army could not understand Navy signals.

To Robert Anderson[1]

[War Department] Washington, April 4. 1861

Sir: Your letter of the 1st. inst. occasions some anxiety to the President.[2]

On the information of Capt. Fox,[3] he had supposed you could hold out till the 15th. inst. without any great inconvenience; and had prepared an expedition to relieve you before that period.

Hoping still that you will be able to sustain yourself till the 11th. or 12th. inst. the expedition will go forward; and, finding your flag flying, will attempt to provision you, and, in case the effort is resisted, will endeavor also to reinforce you.

You will therefore hold out if possible till the arrival of the expedition.

It is not, however, the intention of the President to subject your command to any danger or hardship beyond what, in your judgment, would be usual in military life; and he has entire confidence that you will act as becomes a patriot and a soldier, under all circumstances.

Whenever, if at all, in your judgment, to save yourself and command, a capitulation becomes a necessity, you are authorized to make it. [Respectfully   SIMON CAMERON.]
[To Major Robert Anderson
  U.S. Army]

This was sent by Capt. Talbot, on April 6, 1861, to be delivered to Maj. Anderson, if permitted. On reaching Charleston, he was refused permission to deliver it to Major Anderson.

[1] ADf and AE, DLC-RTL. In addition to Lincoln's draft, the letter signed by Cameron and sent by Captain Theodore Talbot, assistant adjutant general, is in the Lincoln Papers. Bracketed portions are from Cameron's letter and are not in Lincoln's draft. Lincoln's endorsement is written on the envelope containing Cameron's letter.

[2] Anderson to Lorenzo Thomas indicated that because of scarcity of rations he had discharged laborers working on the fort, but that the secretary of war for South Carolina had not given authority for their removal. ". . . . If the Governor permits me to send off the laborers we will have rations enough to last us about a week." (OR, I, I, 230).

[3] Gustavus V. Fox, assistant secretary of the Navy, in command of the Sumter expedition.

Memorandum:
Appointment of Ethelbert P. Oliphant[1]

[c. April 5, 1861]

Ethelbert P. Oliphant, of Uniontown, Pa. is an old acquaintance of mine; and I wish, if I can make it reasonably convenient to give him a place. He prefers a Judgeship in Nebraska; but I am to try to find something for him, either in the Departments here, or elsewhere.

Swamp-land matter.

[1] AD, DLC-RTL. Oliphant to Lincoln, July 28, 1859, recalled that ". . . our first acquaintance and interview, took place in the Spring of 1832 at 'Salem'. . . . Our next meeting was in the *'bloody Fourth'* . . . where we were *'fratres miles'* in the Black Hawk War. . . ." Oliphant's letter of April 5, 1861, asked for a judgeship in the swamp land division of the General Land Office: "Allow me however just *modestly* to remark, that I think I am deserving of something better. . . ." (DLC-RTL). Lincoln appointed Oliphant associate justice of Washington Territory.

To Ira P. Rankin[1]

April 5, 1861

Lockwood M. Todd, above named, is a cousin of Mrs. L. and she and I will be much obliged if the collector can give him the place he seeks.

[1] Parke-Bernet Catalog 130, October 18-19, 1939, No. 213. Ira P. Rankin, collector of customs at San Francisco, wrote Lincoln, May 31, 1861, "I feel compelled to write to you in regard to the appointment of L. M. Todd as Custom House Drayman . . . a formal protest has been sent to me against it, signed by the county Committee, and a large number of the Republicans of Solano County, where he resides, representing that he has been a most bitter and violent opponent of the Republican party. . . ." (DLC-RTL). No record of Todd's appointment has been found prior to March 25, 1864, when he was made commissary of subsistence with rank of captain. He was the son of Dr. John Todd of Springfield, Illinois.

To Edward Bates[1]

Hon. Attorney General   Executive Mansion
Dear Sir: April 6. 1861

Please make out and send me the proper document, for appointing Ward H. Lamon, to be Marshal for the District of Columbia.
Yours truly   A. LINCOLN

[1] ALS, ORB. See memorandum concerning Lamon's appointment, April 2, *supra*.

To Robert S. Chew[1]

[War Department.] Washington, April 6. 1861

Sir—You will proceed directly to Charleston, South Carolina; and if, on your arrival there, the flag of the United States shall be flying over Fort-Sumpter, and the Fort shall not have been attacked, you will procure an interview with Gov. Pickens, and read to him as follows:

"I am directed by the President of the United States to notify you to expect an attempt will be made to supply Fort-Sumpter with provisions only; and that, if such attempt be not resisted, no effort to throw in men, arms, or amunition, will be made, without further notice, or in case of an attack upon the Fort"

After you shall have read this to Governor Pickens, deliver to him the copy of it herein inclosed, and retain this letter yourself.

But if, on your arrival at Charleston, you shall ascertain that Fort Sumpter shall have been already evacuated, or surrendered, by the United States force; or, shall have been attacked by an opposing force, you will seek no interview with Gov. Pickens, but return here forthwith. [Respectfully   SIMON CAMERON

Secy of War]

[Endorsement]

Notice carried by R. S. Chew to Gov. Pickens, and his report as to how he gave the notice.

¹ ADf, AD, AE; DLC-RTL. In addition to Lincoln's autograph draft of the letter, the paragraph quoted in the letter, and the endorsement on the envelope, Cameron's LS copied from Lincoln's draft and Chew's report to the President on April 8, are in the Lincoln Papers. Bracketed portions are not in Lincoln's draft, but are reproduced from Cameron's LS. Robert S. Chew was a clerk in the State Department. His report is as follows:

"To the President   Charleston S.C. April 8th 1861
"Under the foregoing orders I left Washington at 6 P.M. Saturday April 6th, 1861, in company with Capt. Theodore Talbot, U.S. Army, and arrived at Charleston, S.C. on Monday at the same hour. Finding that Fort Sumter had neither been surrendered, evacuated nor attacked, I immediately thro' Capt. Talbot, requested an interview with Governor Pickens, which was at once accorded to me, and I then read to him the portion of said orders in italics [quotation marks], and delivered to him the copy of the same which was furnished to me for that purpose, in the presence of Capt Talbot. Govr. Pickens received the Copy and said he would submit it to General Beauregard, he having, since the ratification of the Constitution of the Confederate States by South Carolina, been placed in charge of the Military operations in this vicinity. Genl. Beauregard was accordingly sent for, and the Governor read the paper to him.
"In reply to a remark made by Governor Pickens in reference to an answer I informed him that I was not authorised to receive any communication from him in reply. Respectfully submitted   R. S. CHEW"

To Gideon Welles¹

April 6, 1861

I have a letter [here from Fort] Sumter which Commodore [Stri]ngham ought to see before he leaves. Yours truly

A. LINCOLN.

¹ Stan. V. Henkels Catalog 1342, January 4, 1924, No. 48E. Brackets are in the catalog which describes the item as damaged by fire. Lincoln probably wanted to show Silas H. Stringham the report of Captain Theodore Talbot who returned from Fort Sumter on April 6.

To Andrew G. Curtin¹

Gov. A. G. Curtin   Executive Mansion
My dear Sir: April 8. 1861
I think the necessity of being *ready* increases. Look to it. Yours truly   A. LINCOLN

¹ ALS-P, ISLA.

To James M. Edmunds[1]

Executive Mansion,

Commissioner of the General Land Office.   April 8. 1861

Sir—In pursuance of the 18th. and 19th. sections of the Act mentioned in the foregoing letter,[2] I direct that the Yancton Land District be now formed with the boundaries described in said section 18, and that the Land Office for said District be located at the town of Vermilion in said District. I also name Jesse Wherry, of Virginia to be Receiver of Public Monies, and Henry A. Kennerly of Missouri, to be Register of said Land Office

ABRAHAM LINCOLN

[1] ALS, South Dakota Historical Society.
[2] A letter from Commissioner James M. Edmunds.

Memorandum: Appointment of Surveyor and Collector of the Port of New York[1]

[c. April 8, 1861]

Greely, Opdycke, Field & Wadsworth, in favor of having the two big puddings on the same side of the board.

[1] AE, DLC-RTL. The endorsement is written on the envelope enclosing letters from Horace Greeley, George Opdyke, David D. Field, and James S. Wadsworth, April 8, 1861. Greeley asked ". . . the selection of a Surveyor of the Port who shall be in full accord and sympathy with the Collector already appointed. . . . The appointments made for this state . . . have generally been made from the other wing of the party. . . ." (DLC-RTL). The surveyorship went to Rufus F. Andrews, whom Greeley had recommended on February 6 for district attorney for New York (*ibid.*).

Memorandum:
Appointment of Commissioner of Pensions[1]

April 9, 1861

Joseph H. Barrett, for Comr. of Pensions. Mention to Cabinet today—April 9, 1861.

[1] AE, DLC-RTL. The endorsement is written on a letter of William Helmick's to Lincoln, April 6, 1861, withdrawing his application in favor of Joseph H. Barrett of Cincinnati.

Memorandum: Appointment of Christian Metz[1]

[c. April 9, 1861]

When I received these notes the commission in the case mentioned, had been signed and sent away.   LINCOLN

[325]

[1] AES, NBuHi. The endorsement is written on a letter of Salmon P. Chase's to Preston King, April 8, 1861, forwarded to Lincoln in recommendation of Christian Metz for collector at Buffalo, New York. Metz received the appointment.

To James Short[1]

James Short   Washington,
Petersburg, Ills.   April 9. 1861
 Go to Charleston, Ills. and see Geo. M. Hanson. A. LINCOLN

[1] ALS copy, DLC-RTL. George M. Hanson of Charleston, Illinois, was appointed to the Northern superintendency of Indian agencies in California. Lincoln's old friend James Short was appointed supervisor of the Round Valley, California, reservation.

To Simon Cameron[1]

Hon. Sec. of War   Executive Mansion April 10. 1861
 Dear Sir: Gov. Curtin telegraphs us to send him a drill-officer. Better send one at once.
 I have talked with Col. Smith[2] about it. Your Obt. Servt.
              A. LINCOLN

[1] ALS, RPB.
[2] Lieutenant Colonel Charles F. Smith, in command of the Department of Washington.

To Salmon P. Chase[1]

Hon. Sec. of Treasury   Executive Mansion
Dear Sir   April 10. 1861
 Mr. Wood thinks that possibly he can save you something in the matter of engraving Treasury Notes. Please give him an interview, & see what there is of it. Yours truly A. LINCOLN

[1] ALS-P, ISLA. There is no reply from Chase or other documents related to the subject of this letter in the Lincoln Papers. William S. Wood of New York was engaged in soliciting business for the American Bank Note Company of New York. A letter of Tracy R. Edson, President, American Bank Note Company, to William S. Wood, June 6, 1861, contains a memorandum on the printing of defense bonds for the State of Missouri, which Edson asked Wood to bring "to the notice of the President." (DLC-RTL). Wood was nominated to the Senate as commissioner of public buildings on July 5, but failed to be confirmed, one of the objections to his appointment being his activities in connection with the printing of government securities.

To Montgomery Blair[1]

Hon. P.M.G.   Executive Mansion.
Sir—   April 11. 1861.
 Has a Post-Master been appointed, as yet, at Covington, Ky. Col. Carpenter, wishes John S. Scott to be appointed. He says

Scott, is a Douglas Union-man. I know nothing as to the propriety of this; but write to keep a promise. LINCOLN

[1] ALS, DLC-Nicolay Papers. Blair's reply is written on the bottom of the letter as follows: "The incumbent of this office is a Mr. [W.D.] Holt in whose behalf the Hon Mr. [Joseph] Holt is interested & applied *indirectly* to me for his retention. MB"

To Simon Cameron[1]

[c. April 11, 1861]
What says the Sec. of War to this? LINCOLN

[1] AES, DLC-RTL. The endorsement is written on a letter from John Pope to Ward H. Lamon, April 11, 1861. Captain John Pope, son of Nathaniel Pope, serving as topographical engineer building lighthouses on the Great Lakes, suggested that ". . . it would be well for Mr Lincoln to have near him some Army friend interested in him personally. . . . I would be gratified therefore if the President would order me to Washington . . . as his aid & military Secretary. . . ." Cameron's endorsement reads: "The Secretary of War thinks this a *very* modest request." (DLC-RTL). See also, Lincoln to Cameron, April 26, *infra.*

To Salmon P. Chase[1]

Hon. S. P. Chase: Executive Mansion April 11. 1861.

Dear Sir: W. W. Danenhower, is the only marked representative of the American organization in Ills. who co-operated with us in 1858 & 1860, and who is now asking any thing here. He was very serviceable to us then, and is very needy now. Can any thing be found for him—permanent, or temporary? Please try. Yours very truly A. LINCOLN

[1] ALS, CSmH. William W. Danenhower, an attorney of Chicago, was appointed chief clerk in the fourth auditor's office.

Memorandum: Appointment of Mahlon Yardley[1]

April 11, 1861

This 11th. day of April 1861, Mr. Caleb N. Taylor, personally appears and urges, in behalf of the 7th. Congressional District, that Mahlon Yardley, be appointed Deputy Surveyor at Philadelphia. In this Hon. D. Wilmot & Hon. Jno. Covode, back Mr. Taylor.

[1] AD-P, ISLA. Caleb N. Taylor of Bristol, Pennsylvania, had been a delegate to the Chicago convention in 1860 and was elected representative in congress 1867-1871. Yardley did not receive the appointment and was commissioned first lieutenant, Company K, One Hundred and Fourth Pennsylvania Volunteers. He was promoted to captain and provost marshal of the Fifth District, Pennsylvania, April 29, 1863.

Memorandum: Appointments at Boston[1]

April 11, 1861

Isaac Clark wants two weeks delay of appointments at Boston.

[1] AE, DLC-RTL. Isaac Clark, candidate for surveyor of the port of Boston, wrote April 10, 1861, asking "two weeks delay . . . for the purpose of coming to some satisfactory arrangement among ourselves. . . ." (DLC-RTL).

Memorandum: Maryland Appointments[1]

April 11, 1861

Gov. Hicks, on the 11th. of April 1861, advises that Maryland appointments be delayed 8 or 10 days. He also recommends that, as to such appointments, I take the advice of H. W. Davis, Thomas Swann, J. Bond Chaplin, and W. H. Purnell.[2]

I wish French S. Evans to be deputy collector, or deputy Naval officer.[3]

[1] AD, DLC-RTL.
[2] Representative Henry Winter Davis, President Thomas Swann of the Baltimore and Ohio Railroad, and William H. Purnell, whom Lincoln appointed postmaster at Baltimore. J. Bond Chaplin has not been identified.
[3] This is written on the verso. Evans was appointed deputy naval officer.

Order Designating the *National Republican*[1]

Executive Department, Washington   April 11th 1861.

In virtue of his authority to designate at discretion one newspaper in the city of Washington for the publication of notices and advertisements from the Executive departments, in addition to the two entitled to such publication, by having the largest permanent subscription, (U.S. Statutes, Vol. 5, page 795,) the President designates the "National Republican," and his private secretary will communicate this order to the several Executive departments.[2]

ABRAHAM LINCOLN

Although[3] I do not perceive the necessity of it, I have no objection to say the above designation is to stand, until further order, notwithstanding any change of proprietors which may have occurred.   A. LINCOLN

Feb. 16. 1863.

[1] DS and AES, RPB.   [2] Nicolay wrote the letters on April 19.
[3] This endorsement appears on the bottom of the page and is reproduced here rather than under its chronological date. William J. Murtaugh became publisher of the *Republican* in 1863.

To Edward Bates[1]

Hon. Atty. General   Executive Mansion
My dear Sir: April 12, 1861
   On examination of papers, and full consideration, I have con-
cluded to appoint Earl Bill, Marshal for the Northern District of
Ohio. Please send me the commission. Yours truly   A. LINCOLN

  [1] ALS-P, ISLA. Earl Bill of Tiffin, Ohio, had served one term (1850-1851) in
the Ohio Senate and was a delegate to the Chicago convention in 1860.

To Edward Bates[1]

Hon. Atty. General.   Executive Mansion
My dear Sir: April 12, 1861
   The two Senators of Penn. with the brief before them recommend Alexander Murdoch for Marshall of the Western District,
and Robert B. Carnahan, for Attorney of the same District. Send
me the Commissions. Yours truly   A. LINCOLN

  [1] Copy, ISLA. Alexander Murdoch of Washington, Pennsylvania, and Robert
B. Carnahan of Pittsburgh received the appointments designated.

Memorandum:
Appointment of Thomas Webster, Jr.[1]

April 12, 1861
   The above named gentlemen appear in person and press for the
appointment of Thomas Webster Jr. as Collector of the Port at
Philadelphia.
   They say his appointment will give general satisfaction, while
that of no other person will.
   April 12, 1861.

  [1] AE, DLC-RTL. The endorsement is written on the bottom of a list of sixteen
names headed "Delegation of Philadelphia Merchants." Thomas Webster was
not appointed, Chase's selection being William B. Thomas, wealthy flour manufacturer and abolitionist.

Reply to a Committee
from the Virginia Convention[1]

[April 13, 1861]
Hon: William Ballard Preston, Alexander H. H. Stuart,
& George W. Randolph, Esq—
   Gentlemen: As a committee of the Virginia convention, now in
session, you present me a preamble and resolution, in these words:
   Whereas,[2] in the opinion of this Convention the uncertainty which
prevails in the public mind as to the policy which the Federal Execu-

[329]

tive intends to pursue toward the seceded States is extremely injurious to the industrial and commercial interests of the country; tends to keep up an excitement which is unfavorable to the adjustment of pending difficulties, and threatens a disturbance of the public peace; therefore

Resolved, that a committee of three delegates be appointed by this Convention to wait upon the President of the United States, present to him this preamble and resolution, and respectfully ask of him to communicate to this Convention the policy which the Federal Executive intends to pursue in regard to the Confederate States.

Adopted by the Convention of the State of Virginia, Richmond, April 8th 1861

In pursuance of the foregoing resolution, the following delegates were appointed to constitute said committee.

> Hon. William Ballard Preston.
> Hon. Alexander H. H. Stuart.
> George W. Randolph Esq.

JOHN JANNEY PRESIDENT

JNO. L. EUBANK SECRETARY.

In answer I have to say, that having, at the beginning of my official term, expressed my intended policy, as plainly as I was able, it is with deep regret, and some mortification, I now learn, that there is great, and injurious uncertainty, in the public mind, as to what that policy is, and what course I intend to pursue. Not having, as yet, seen occasion to change, it is now my purpose to pursue the course marked out in the inaugeral address. I commend a careful consideration of the whole document, as the best expression I can give of my purposes. As I then, and therein, said, I now repeat:

"The power confided to me will be used to hold, occupy, and possess, the property, and places belonging to the Government, and to collect the duties, and imposts; but, beyond what is necessary for these objects, there will be no invasion—no using of force against, or among the people anywhere"

By the words "property, and places, belonging to the Government" I chiefly allude to the military posts, and property, which were in the possession of the Government when it came to my hands. But[3] if, as now appears to be true, in pursuit of a purpose to drive the United States authority from these places, an unprovoked assault, has been made upon Fort-Sumpter, I shall hold myself at liberty to re-possess, if I can, like places which had been seized before the Government was devolved upon me.

And, in every event, I shall, to the extent of my ability, repel force by force.

In case it proves true, that Fort-Sumpter has been assaulted, as is reported, I shall perhaps, cause the United [States] mails to be withdrawn from all the States which claim to have seceded—believing that the commencement of actual war against the Government, justifies and possibly demands this.

I scarcely need to say that I consider the Military posts and property situated within the states, which claim to have seceded, as yet belonging to the Government of the United States, as much as they did before the supposed secession.

Whatever else I may do for the purpose, I shall not attempt to collect the duties, and imposts, by any armed invasion of any part of the country—not meaning by this, however, that I may not land a force, deemed necessary, to relieve a fort upon a border of the country. From the fact, that I have quoted a part of the inaugeral address, it must not be infered that I repudiate any other part, the whole of which I re-affirm, except so far as what I now say of the mails, may be regarded as a modification.

[1] ADf, DLC-RTL. William B. Preston was elected to the Confederate Congress in 1861, and Alexander H. H. Stuart was a member of the Virginia Senate; General George W. Randolph, later secretary of war for the Confederacy (1862-1863), represented Virginia's military forces.

[2] The single page preamble and resolution is attached to Lincoln's reply.

[3] The remainder of this paragraph and the next two are inserted replacing the following: "But if, by efforts to drive the United States forces from these places, either by assault or starvation, a collision of arms shall be occasioned, I shall hold myself at liberty to re-possess, if I can, like places which had been seized before the Government was devolved upon me." Fort Sumter had been attacked on April 12.

To Winfield Scott(?)[1]

[April 14, 1861]

Please send over the Ft. Sumpter Messenger at once.

LINCOLN.

[1] ALS, DLC-RTL. The date of this note is that assigned to it in the Lincoln Papers.

Proclamation Calling Militia and Convening Congress[1]

April 15, 1861

By the President of the United States

A Proclamation.

Whereas the laws of the United States have been for some time past, and now are opposed, and the execution thereof obstructed, in the States of South Carolina, Georgia, Alabama, Florida, Mississippi, Louisiana and Texas, by combinations too powerful to be suppressed by the ordinary course of judicial proceedings, or by the powers vested in the Marshals by law,

Now therefore, I, Abraham Lincoln, President of the United States, in virtue of the power in me vested by the Constitution, and the laws, have thought fit to call forth, and hereby do call forth, the militia of the several States of the Union, to the aggregate number of seventy-five thousand, in order to suppress said combinations, and to cause the laws to be duly executed. The details, for this object, will be immediately communicated to the State authorities through the War Department.

I appeal to all loyal citizens to favor, facilitate and aid this effort to maintain the honor, the integrity, and the existence of our National Union, and the perpetuity of popular government; and to redress[2] wrongs already long enough endured.

I deem it proper to say that the first service assigned to the forces hereby called forth will probably be to re-possess the forts, places, and property which have been seized from the Union; and in every event, the utmost care will be observed, consistently with the objects aforesaid, to avoid any devastation, any destruction of, or interference with, property, or any disturbance of peaceful citizens in any part of the country.

And I hereby command the persons composing the combinations aforesaid to disperse, and retire peaceably to their respective abodes within twenty days from this date.

Deeming that the present condition of public affairs presents an extraordinary occasion, I[3] do hereby, in virtue of the power in me vested by the Constitution,[4] convene both Houses of Congress. Senators and Representatives are therefore summoned to assemble at their respective chambers, at 12 o'clock, noon, on Thursday, the fourth day of July, next, then and there to consider and determine, such measures, as, in their wisdom, the public safety, and interest may seem to demand.

In Witness Whereof I have hereunto set my hand, and caused the Seal of the United States to be affixed.

Done at the city of Washington this fifteenth day of April in the year of our Lord One thousand, Eight [L.S.] hundred and Sixty-one, and of the Independence of the United States the Eighty-fifth.

ABRAHAM LINCOLN

By the President
WILLIAM H. SEWARD, Secretary of State.

1 DS, DNA FS RG 11, Proclamations; ADf, DLC-RTL. The official copy in the Archives is not in Lincoln's handwriting but bears emendations in his handwriting as indicated in footnotes.
2 "Redress its wrongs already too long endured" emended by Lincoln as reproduced.   3 "I do hereby," inserted by Lincoln.
4 "I do hereby" deleted at this point by Lincoln.

To William Dennison[1]

April 15, 1861
Thirteen Regiments.

1 OR, III, I, 73. Governor Dennison telegraphed "What portion of the 75,000 militia . . . do you give to Ohio? Great rejoicing here over your proclamation. . . ." (*Ibid.*).

To Elmer E. Ellsworth[1]

Col. E. E. Ellsworth
My dear Sir:

Washington,
April 15. 1861

Ever since the beginning of our acquaintance, I have valued you highly as a person[al] friend, and at the same time (without much capacity of judging) have had a very high estimate of your military talent. Accordingly I have been, and still am anxious for you to have the best position in the military which can be given you, consistently with justice and proper courtesy towards the older officers of the army. I can not incur the risk of doing them injustice, or a discourtesy; but I do say they would personally oblige me, if they could, and would place you in some position, or in some service, satisfactory to yourself. Your Obt. Servt.

A. LINCOLN

1 ALS-F, ISLA. Concerning Ellsworth's appointment see Lincoln to Cameron, March 5, *supra* and note.

To Henry W. Hoffman[1]

[c. April 15, 1861]

If there is any secessionist in your department, I wish you would remove him, and give the place to Mr. S. C. Atkinson; or, if, in any way you can give him a place, I shall be obliged.

Mr. Huffman, Collector.   A. LINCOLN

1 ALS, The Rosenbach Company, Philadelphia and New York. Henry W. Hoffman was appointed April 15, 1861, and this communication seems to have been written near that date. S. C. Atkinson has not been identified.

Memorandum:
Appointment of Newell A. Thompson[1]

[c. April 15, 1861]

Hon. George Ashmun, especially desires Newell A. Thompson to be Navy Agent at Boston.

[1] AE, DLC-RTL. The endorsement is written on the back of Ashmun to Lincoln, April 15, 1861, recommending Colonel Thompson. Eugene L. Norton of Boston received the appointment instead of Thompson.

Memorandum: New York Appointments[1]

[c. April 15, 1861]

Collector —	Hiram Barney —	R.D.
Surveyor —	[Abram] Wakeman —	S.W.
Naval O.	George Dennison [sic]	— W.
Apr. Genl.	Tho. McElrath —	S.W.
Navy A.	[D.D.T.] Marshall —	R.D.
	[Isaac] Henderson	
Mint. — —	[Daniel?] Ullmann[2]	Am.
Sub. Treas.	[Richard M.] Blatchford—	S.W.
Attorney —	E. Del. Smith —	S.W.
Marshall.	Henry B. Stanton	R.D.
P. Master.	James Taylor.[3]	S.W.

[1] AD, NAuE; copy, DLC-RTL. The copy is dated by Nicolay, April 30, 1861, but Chase to Lincoln, April 15, indicates a conference on the New York appointments on this date (DLC-RTL), and other references confirm April 15 as the date of this particular slate of New York appointments. The designation "S.W." probably meant "Seward-Weed" and "Am" following "Ullmann" would suggest "American or Know-Nothing," and "R.D." was perhaps "Reformed Democrat."

[2] This may have been John J. Ullmann rather than Daniel Ullmann.

[3] Probably an error for William B. Taylor, Seward's choice, who received the appointment.

To Winfield Scott[1]

Lieut. General Scott: Executive Mansion
My dear Sir: April 15. 1861

Col. Peter G. Washington tells me it is my duty to call an officer to the command of the District of Columbia militia now in the U.S. service, and that he, by rank in the District of militia, is entitled to the place.

Is it my duty to call, or designate, such officer? and if yea, is

Col. Washington, by military law usage, or courtesy, entitled to the place?

Please investigate & inform me   Your Obt. Servt.

A. LINCOLN

[1] ALS, DLC-RTL. Charles P. Stone, inspector general, endorsed the letter as follows: "Col Washington was an officer of the old Organization . . . but that organization has been legally broken up and replaced by a new one. . . ." Scott's endorsement specified that ". . . we do not want him or any other field officer, with the District Volunteers mustered into the service of the U.S.—because those volunteers are doing duty as separate & independent companies, & require no field officer. . . ." (*Ibid.*).

To Gideon Welles[1]

Hon. Sec. of Navy,   Executive Mansion.
My dear Sir:—   April 15, 1861.

I must relieve myself of the remaining California appointments. The charge against Samuel Bell is unsustained, and, in fact, in a good degree, disproved. I therefore request that you send me a Commission for him as Navy Agent   Very truly,

A. LINCOLN.

[1] Angle, pp. 267-68. Samuel Bell had served as comptroller of California and was a delegate to the Chicago convention in 1860. Eugene L. Sullivan to Welles, March 15, 1861, asks that his previous letter of recommendation for Bell be withdrawn: ". . . I have learned . . . his record as Comptroller of the State of California is not altogether clear." (DLC-RTL). See also Lincoln to Welles, May 8, *infra*, concerning Bell's appointment.

To Simon Cameron[1]

Hon. Sec. of War: Executive Mansion
My dear Sir   April 16. 1861

Some time ago I requested that Ben. Hardin Helm, might be appointed a Pay-Master, which I still desire.[2]

Next to this, for the sake of my friend, Major Hunter, I especially wish Robert A. Kinzie[3] to be appointed a Pay-Master. This is not a formality, but an earnest reality. Your Obt. Servt.

A. LINCOLN

[1] ALS, DLC-Cameron Papers.
[2] Mrs. Lincoln's brother-in-law accepted a commission in the Confederate Army, was promoted to brigadier general, and died of wounds received at Chickamauga, September 21, 1863.
[3] Robert A. Kinzie, David Hunter's brother-in-law, had migrated to Kansas in 1847. He was appointed paymaster with rank of major, May 2.

Memorandum: Retention of Fletcher Webster[1]

[c. April 16, 1861]

Hon. Geo. Ashmun, especially wishes that Fletcher Webster may be allowed to serve out his term.

[1] AE, DLC-RTL. Ashmun to Lincoln, April 16, 1861, requested retention of Daniel Webster's son Fletcher as surveyor of Port of Boston. Fletcher Webster became colonel of the Twelfth Massachusetts, June 26, 1861, and was killed at the second battle of Bull Run in August, 1862.

To Edward Bates[1]

Hon. Atty. Gen.   Executive Mansion

My dear Sir: April 17, 1861

Two of the Judges for Nebraska have been appointed.[2] Please send me your Briefs as to the remaining Judge and the Attorney & Marshal. Yours truly,   A. LINCOLN.

[1] ALS, owned by Ashley T. Cole, New York City.

[2] See memorandum on appointments to territories, March 20, *supra*. Lincoln appointed William F. Lockwood of Dakota City to the remaining judgeship, David L. Collier of Omaha as attorney, and Phineas W. Hitchcock of Omaha as marshal.

Memorandum: Appointment of Albert G. Enos[1]

April 17, 1861

I have but very slight acquaintance with Mr. Enos, but, Col. Gridly who writes the accompanying letter, is my intimate political & personal friend, whom I would like to obliged [*sic*].

April 17, 1861.   A. LINCOLN.

[1] Parke-Bernet Catalog 905, December 1-2, 1947, No. 275. Gridley was undoubtedly Lincoln's friend Asahel Gridley of Bloomington, Illinois. Albert G. Enos, on the back of whose letter the endorsement is written, was commissioned major of the Eighth Pennsylvania regiment, September 18, 1861, resigned October 15, 1862.

To William H. Seward[1]

Hon. Sec. of State—   Executive Mansion

Dear Sir   April 17– 1861

The Gov. of Nebraska has been appointed. Will you please send me your Brief for *Secretary* of that Territory? Yours truly

A. LINCOLN

[1] ALS, NAuE. Alvin Saunders of Mount Pleasant, Iowa, had been appointed Governor. See Lincoln to Seward, April 27, *infra*, for Lincoln's appointment of Algernon S. Paddock as secretary.

To Gideon Welles[1]

Hon. Gideon Welles.   Executive Mansion
My dear Sir: April 17. 1861

I have no reason to doubt that Mr. James S. Chalker, the bearer of this, is, as he says, the author of the "Wide Awake," order. As he is your townsman, you will know; and if it is all straight, please add your recommendation to mine, that he have some suitable appointment in the Army, which he desires. When you shall [have] added your word, send the whole to the War Department. Yours truly   A. LINCOLN

[1] ALS, The Rosenbach Company, Philadelphia and New York. No record of James S. Chalker's appointment has been found.

To William H. Seward[1]

Hon. W. H. Seward.   Executive Mansion
My dear Sir   April 18. 1861

You astonish me by saying Mr. Weed understands there is some alienation, or enmity of feeling, on my part towards him. Nothing like it. I shall be glad to see him any time, & have wondered at not have [*sic*] seen [him] here already. Yours very truly

A. LINCOLN

[1] ALS, NN.

To Edward Wallace[1]

Dr. Edward Wallace   Executive Mansion
Dear Sir   April 18. 1861

Having, to-day concluded to appoint you Naval Officer at Philadelphia, I now, at the request of Dr. Luther,[2] a strong and honorable competitor of yours, and at the urgent request of Gen. Cameron also, earnestly solicit you to appoint Col. John C. Meyers, of your own city, the deputy Naval officer. You will personally oblige me by doing this, besides smoothing things which otherwise might be a little rough[3]   Yours very truly   A LINCOLN

[1] ALS, IHi.   [2] Dr. Diller Luther of Reading, Pennsylvania.

[3] John C. Myers was not appointed. Deputy naval officer of Philadelphia as of September 30, 1861, was David F. Williams.

To Gideon Welles[1]

Hon. Sec. of Navy   Executive Mansion
Dear Sir   April 18. 1861
    Be here on Philadelphia appointments, at 12. o'clock to-day.
Yours truly   A. LINCOLN

[1] ALS, Ct. See Lincoln to Wallace, *supra.*

Memorandum[1]

No report from Gen. Scott this 19. April 1861.

[1] AE, DLC-RTL. Beginning April 1, on General Scott's reports Lincoln endorsed "Genl. Scott's daily report—No. 1," etc. The reports continued until May 4, the last being No. 24.

Proclamation of a Blockade[1]

April 19, 1861

By the President of the United States of America:

A Proclamation.

Whereas an insurrection against the Government of the United States has broken out in the States of South Carolina, Georgia, Alabama, Florida, Mississippi, Louisiana, and Texas, and the laws of the United States for the collection of the revenue cannot be effectually executed therein conformably to that provision of the Constitution which requires duties to be uniform throughout the United States:

And whereas a combination of persons engaged in such insurrection, have threatened to grant pretended letters of marque to authorize the bearers thereof to commit assaults on the lives, vessels, and property of good citizens of the country lawfully engaged in commerce on the high seas, and in waters of the United States: And whereas an Executive Proclamation has been already issued, requiring the persons engaged in these disorderly proceedings to desist therefrom, calling out a militia force for the purpose of repressing the same, and convening Congress in extraordinary session, to deliberate and determine thereon:

Now, therefore, I, Abraham Lincoln, President of the United States, with a view to the same purposes before mentioned, and to the protection of the public peace, and the lives and property of quiet and orderly citizens pursuing their lawful occupations, until Congress shall have assembled and deliberated on the said unlawful proceedings, or until the same shall have ceased, have further deemed it advisable to set on foot a blockade of the ports within the States aforesaid, in pursuance of the laws of the United States, and of the law of Nations, in such case provided. For this purpose a competent force will be posted so as to prevent entrance and exit of vessels from the ports aforesaid. If, therefore, with a view to violate such blockade, a vessel shall approach, or shall attempt to leave either of the said ports, she will be duly warned by the Commander of one of the blockading vessels, who will endorse on her register the fact and date of such warning, and if the same vessel shall again attempt to enter or leave the blockaded port, she will be captured and sent to the nearest convenient port, for such proceedings against her and her cargo as prize, as may be deemed advisable.

And I hereby proclaim and declare that if any person, under the pretended authority of the said States, or under any other pretense, shall molest a vessel of the United States, or the persons or cargo on board of her, such person will be held amenable to the laws of the United States for the prevention and punishment of piracy.

In witness whereof, I have hereunto set my hand, and caused the seal of the United States to be affixed.

[L.S.] Done at the City of Washington, this nineteenth day of April, in the year of our Lord one thousand eight hundred and sixty-one, and of the Independence of the United States the eighty-fifth.

ABRAHAM LINCOLN

By the President:
WILLIAM H. SEWARD, Secretary of State

[1] DS, DNA FS RG 11, Proclamations.

Inscription in Album
of Mary Rebecca Darby Smith[1]

White House, April 19, 1861.

Whoever in later-times shall see this, and look at the date, will readily excuse the writer for not having indulged in sentiment, or poetry. With all kind regards for Miss Smith.   A. LINCOLN.

[1] Parke-Bernet Catalog 1026, January 10-11, 1949, No. 56. According to the source Miss Smith was a friend of President Buchanan's who attended Lincoln's inaugural and called on the new president on April 19.

To Gideon Welles[1]

Hon. Sec. of Navy   Executive Mansion
My dear Sir   April 19, 1861
I find on page 99 of the Navy Register that there is an officer called "Naval Constructor," whom it is said, you are to appoint.
The bearer of this, Israel S. Smith, a man now residing at Philadelphia, but whom I knew in boyhood, and whom I would like to oblige, is anxious and interested to have John W. Griffiths, appointed to that office. Please examine, and appoint him, if it can properly be done. Yours truly   A. LINCOLN

[1] ALS, The Rosenbach Company, Philadelphia and New York. See memorandum on appointment of Griffiths, c. April 1, *supra.*

To Thomas H. Hicks and George W. Brown[1]

Gov. Hicks, & Mayor Brown   Washington, April 20. 1861
Gentlemen: Your letter by Messrs. Bond, Dobbin & Brune, is received. I tender you both my sincere thanks for your efforts to keep the peace in the trying situation in which you are placed. For the future, troops *must* be brought here, but I make no point of bringing them *through* Baltimore. Without any military knowledge myself, of course I must leave details to Gen. Scott. He hastily said, this morning, in presence of these gentlemen, "March them *around* Baltimore, and not through it." I sincerely hope the General, on fuller reflection, will consider this practical and proper, and that you will not object to it. By this, a collision of the people of Baltimore with the troops will be avoided, unless they go out of their way to seek it. I hope you will exert your influence to prevent this.
Now, and ever, I shall do all in my power for peace, consistently with the maintainance of government. Your Obt. Servt.
                                                          A. LINCOLN

[1] ALS, Carnegie Institute Museum, Pittsburgh, Pennsylvania. Mayor Brown of Baltimore sent Hugh L. Bond, George W. Dobbin, and John C. Brune with a letter dated April 18, 1861, ". . . to explain fully the fearful condition of affairs in this city. The people are exasperated . . . by the passage of troops, and . . . are decided in the opinion that no more should be ordered to come. . . . It is my solemn duty to inform you that it is not possible for more soldiers to pass through Baltimore unless they fight their way at every step. . . ." On April 19, a telegram signed by Governor Hicks and Mayor Brown notified Lincoln of a collision between citizens of Baltimore and troops. On April 20, Brown acknowledged receipt of Lincoln's letter carried by Bond, Dobbin, and Brune, and promised to preserve the peace if ". . . no more troops will be brought through the city. . . ." (DLC-RTL). A secessionist mob of Baltimore

had fired into Massachusetts troops forced to march through the city because of obstructions placed on the track by the mob. Approximately four soldiers and nine citizens were killed and rioting continued for several days.

To Thomas H. Hicks and George W. Brown[1]

Washington, April 20, 1861

Gov. Hicks, I desire to consult with you and the Mayor of Baltimore relative to preserving the peace of Maryland. Please come immediately by special train, which you can take at Baltimore, or if necessary one can be sent from hence. Answer forthwith.

LINCOLN

[1] Copy, MdAA-Executive Letter Book (1854-1866), p. 195. The same telegram was sent to both Governor Hicks and Mayor Brown after the dispatch of the letter *supra*. Governor Hicks was not in Baltimore, but Brown telegraphed that he was "coming immediately." (DLC-RTL). According to *The* (Baltimore) *South*, April 22, and New York *Tribune*, April 24, George W. Dobbin, John C. Brune and S. T. Wallis accompanied Mayor Brown. Governor Hicks wrote Lincoln April 22, protesting further landing of troops at Annapolis and suggesting that the British minister, Lord Lyons ". . . be requested to act as mediator between the contending parties of our country." (DLC-RTL). Seward replied at Lincoln's direction that ". . . the national highway thus selected by the Lieutenant General has been chosen by him upon consultation with prominent magistrates and citizens of Maryland, as the one which, while a route is absolutely necessary, is further removed from the populous cities of the State, and with the expectation that it would, therefore, be the least objectionable one." He added that ". . . no domestic contention . . . ought, in any case, to be referred to any foreign arbitrament. . . ." (New York *Tribune*, April 24, 1861). A statement issued by Mayor Brown, April 21, as printed in *The South*, April 22, reported Lincoln's remarks during the interview on April 20 in substantial agreement with Lincoln's letter dispatched earlier on the same day, *supra*.

Reply to Baltimore Committee[1]

April 22, 1861

You, gentlemen, come here to me and ask for peace on any terms, and yet have no word of condemnation for those who are making war on us. You express great horror of bloodshed, and yet would not lay a straw in the way of those who are organizing in Virginia and elsewhere to capture this city. The rebels attack Fort Sumter, and your citizens attack troops sent to the defense of the Government, and the lives and property in Washington, and yet you would have me break my oath and surrender the Government without a blow. There is no Washington in that—no Jackson in that—no manhood nor honor in that. I have no desire to invade the South; but I must have troops to defend this Capital. Geographically it lies surrounded by the soil of Maryland; and mathematically the necessity exists that they should come over her territory. Our men are not moles, and can't dig under the earth; they are not birds, and can't fly through the air. There is no way but to march across, and that they must do. But in doing this there is no need of collision. Keep your rowdies in Baltimore, and there will be no bloodshed. Go home and tell your people that if they will not attack us, we will not attack them; but if they do attack us, we will return it, and that severely.

1 Hertz, II, 830-31. Although the source of Lincoln's remarks as printed by Hertz is probably a newspaper, the editors have been unable to locate it. Hertz dates the event April 28, 1861, but reports in the Baltimore *Daily Exchange* and *The South*, April 23, 1861, indicate conclusively that this reply was made to a committee of fifty representing the Young Men's Christian Associations of Baltimore on Monday, April 22. Reports in the Philadelphia and New York papers as well as the Baltimore papers give only fragments of Lincoln's remarks as printed by Hertz, and the editors have reproduced the Hertz text for want of a satisfactory contemporary source.

To Gideon Welles[1]

Hon. Secretary of Navy,   Executive Mansion, April 23, 1861.

Dear Sir: I think I saw three vessels go up to the Navy Yard just now. Will you please send down and learn what they are? Yours truly   A. LINCOLN

1 Tracy, p. 180. There is no reply in the Lincoln Papers.

To Montgomery Blair[1]

Hon. P.M. General,   Executive Mansion, April 24, 1861.

My dear Sir: Near a week ago, it was settled for Cornelius Walborn to be Post-Master at Philadelphia. Has the actual appointment been made? I have the papers in the case from your Department lying by me, and will sign and send them over, if you say so. Your obed't Serv't,   A. LINCOLN

1 Tracy, p. 181. Cornelius Walborn had been appointed April 20, on Simon Cameron's personal recommendation.

To Reverdy Johnson[1]

Confidential.

Hon. Reverdy Johnson   Executive Mansion, April 24th 1861.

My dear Sir: Your note of this morning is just received. I forebore to answer yours of the 22d because of my aversion (which I thought you understood,) to getting on paper, and furnishing new grounds for misunderstanding.

I *do* say the sole purpose of bringing troops *here* is to defend this capital.

I *do* say I have no purpose to *invade* Virginia, with them or any other troops, as I understand the word *invasion*. But suppose Virginia sends her troops, or admits others through her borders, to assail this capital, am I not to repel them, even to the crossing of the Potomac if I can?

Suppose Virginia erects, or permits to be erected, batteries on the opposite shore, to bombard the city, are we to stand still and see it done? In a word, if Virginia strikes us, are we not to strike back, and as effectively as we can?

Again, are we not to hold Fort Monroe (for instance) if we can? I have no objection to declare a thousand times that I have no purpose to *invade* Virginia or any other State, but I do not mean to let them invade us without striking back. Yours truly

A. LINCOLN

[1] Copy, DLC-RTL. Maryland's ex-senator (1845-1849) and recent delegate to the Peace Conference wrote on April 24 that he desired an answer to his letter of April 22 before he left Washington. A contemporary copy of the earlier letter made by Joseph Holt, in the Lincoln Papers, reads in part as follows: ". . . . The existing excitement and alarm . . . of my own State and of Virginia are owing . . . to an apprehension that it is your purpose to use the military force you are assembling in this District for the invasion of . . . these States. . . ." (DLC-RTL).

Memorandum: Retirement of John H. Wright and William H. Swift[1]

April 24, 1861

Let Surgeon [John] H. Wright and Surgeon William Swift be placed on the retired list, as within recommended by the Secretary of the Navy. A. LINCOLN.

April 24, 1861

[1] AES, DNA WR NB RG 45, Executive Letters, No. 75. Welles to Lincoln, April 24, on which Lincoln's endorsement is written, recommends the action taken. Wright had served from December 9, 1839; Swift, from July 24, 1813.

Memorandum:
Operation of the Chicopee Works[1]

[c. April 25, 1861]

Let the suggestion of the Vice-President as to putting the Chicopee works into operation be duly considered by the War Department. A. LINCOLN.

1 OR, III, I, 106. Lincoln's endorsement is on Hamlin's letter of April 23, written from New York, which reads in part, ". . . We are sadly deficient, and we want and need and should have rifled cannon. Let me urge earnestly and frankly that the works at Chicopee [Massachusetts] be put in operation to their utmost capacity to furnish them."

To Winfield Scott[1]

Lieutenant General Scott   Washington, April 25– 1861.

My dear Sir: The Maryland Legislature assembles to-morrow at Anapolis; and, not improbably, will take action to arm the people of that State against the United States. The question has been submitted to, and considered by me, whether it would not be justifiable, upon the ground of necessary defence, for you, as commander in Chief of the United States Army, to arrest, or disperse the members of that body. I think it would *not* be justifiable; nor, efficient for the desired object.

First, they have a clearly legal right to assemble; and, we can not know in advance, that their action will not be lawful, and peaceful. And if we wait until they shall *have* acted, their arrest, or dispersion, will not lessen the effect of their action.

Secondly, we *can* not permanently prevent their action. If we arrest them, we can not long hold them as prisoners; and when liberated, they will immediately re-assemble, and take their action. And, precisely the same if we simply disperse them. They will immediately re-assemble in some other place.

I therefore conclude that it is only left to the commanding General to watch, and await their action, which, if it shall be to arm their people against the United States, he is to adopt the most prompt, and efficient means to counteract, even, if necessary, to the bombardment of their cities—and in the extremest necessity, the suspension of the writ of habeas corpus. Your Obedient Servant

ABRAHAM LINCOLN.

1 ALS copy, DLC-RTL. Endorsed by Lincoln on envelope "Copy of letter to Genl. Scott." Upon assembling, the Maryland legislature appointed a committee to confer with the president. See Lincoln's reply, May 4, *infra*.

To Simon Cameron[1]

Hon. Sec. of War: Executive Mansion April 26. 1861

I learn that the Gov. of Illinois, who is acquainted with Capt. John Pope, now at Cincinnati, desires to have Capt. Pope sent to Illinois to assist in the organization & equipment of the military forces of the State.

Are his present duties such that he could not properly be ordered to report himself to Gov. Yates? If not, please direct him to report to Gov. Yates for duty. Yours truly   A. LINCOLN

(over)

P.S. Capt. Todd[2] leaves for the West to-morrow afternoon; and, being an experienced military man, would bear and deliver any despaches confided to him.   A. L.

[1] ALS, IHi. Pope wrote Lincoln, April 20, "The Governor of Illinois has telegraphed me to go on to Springfield at once to assist in the organization & equipment of the military forces of the State. . . . I have therefore applied by this mail . . . for leave of absence for one year. . . ." (DLC-RTL). Pope's nomination as brigadier general of volunteers, May 17, was confirmed by the Senate August 5, 1861.

[2] Lockwood M. Todd. See Lincoln to Ira P. Rankin, April 5, *supra*.

Reply to the Frontier Guard[1]

April 26, 1861

I have desired as sincerely as any man—I sometimes think more than any other man—that our present difficulties might be settled without the shedding of blood. I will not say that all hope is yet gone. But if the alternative is presented, whether the Union is to be broken in fragments and the liberties of the people lost, or blood be shed, you will probably make the choice, with which I shall not be dissatisfied.

[1] New York *Tribune*, May 1, 1861. "The Frontier Guard, under the command of Senator Lane of Kansas, numbering 150, and composed mostly of Kansas men, called on Mr. Lincoln on Friday. . . . Mr. Lincoln responded briefly, concluding as follows:" (*ibid.*). This item is misdated by Hertz (II, 830) April 28, and by Lapsley (V, 292) April 27.

To Edward Bates[1]

Executive Mansion,
Hon. Attorney General,   April 27, 1861

My dear Sir: I have concluded to appoint Lockwood, (I think you have his Christian name) to the remaining Judgeship in Nebraska Territory. He resides there. Please send the commission. Yours truly,   A. LINCOLN.

[1] Thomas F. Madigan, *A Catalogue of Lincolniana* (1929), p. 11. Lincoln appointed William F. Lockwood of Dakota City, Nebraska Territory, a native of Ohio who had migrated to the territory in 1857.

Memorandum: Appointment of John T. Burris[1]

Let the commission be made out according to the within recommendation.   A LINCOLN

April 27, 1861

[1] AES, DNA RG 60, Papers of the Attorney General, Appointments, Kansas, Box 465. The endorsement is written on the back of Samuel C. Pomeroy and James H. Lane to Lincoln, April 15, 1861, recommending appointment of John T. Burris as United States district attorney for Kansas.

To Timothy Munroe[1]

Col. T. Monroe   Executive Mansion
Comr. 8th. Reg. Mass. V. M.   April 27. 1861

Sir: Yours in regard to fatigue dress for your command, has been received and sent to the War Department, with the expression of my wish that your request be complied with.

Allow me now to tender you, and through you, the officers and men under your command, my sincere thanks for the zeal, energy and gallantry generally, and especially for the great efficiency, in opening the communication between the North and this city, displayed by you and them   Yours truly   A. LINCOLN

[1] ALS-P, ISLA. Colonel Timothy Munroe, commander of the Eighth Massachusetts Volunteer Militia, resigned May 5, 1861, on account of age. His regiment had worn out their uniforms in repairing railroad track on their march from Annapolis to Washington.

Proclamation of Blockade[1]

April 27, 1861
By the President of the United States of America,

A Proclamation.

Whereas, for the reasons assigned in my Proclamation of the 19th. instant, a blockade of the ports of the States of South Carolina, Georgia, Florida, Alabama, Louisiana, Mississippi and Texas, was ordered to be established:

And whereas, since that date, public property of the United States has been seized, the collection of the revenue obstructed, and duly commissioned officers of the United States while engaged in executing the orders of their superiors have been arrested and held in custody as prisoners or have been impeded in the discharge of their official duties without due legal process, by persons claiming to act under authorities of the States of[2] Virginia and North Carolina, an efficient blockade of the ports of those States will also be established.

In witness whereof, I have hereunto set my hand, and caused the seal of the United States to be affixed.

    Done at the City of Washington, this twenty-seventh day of April, in the year of our Lord one thousand eight [L.S.] hundred and sixty one, and of the Independence of the United States the eighty-fifth. ABRAHAM LINCOLN

By the President:
  WILLIAM H. SEWARD, Secretary of State.

[1] DS, DNA FS RG 11, Proclamations.
[2] "Maryland" deleted at this point.

To Winfield Scott[1]

          April 27, 1861

To the Commanding General of the Army of the United States:

 You are engaged in repressing an insurrection against the laws of the United States. If at any point on or in the vicinity of the [any] military line, which is now [or which shall be] used between the City of Philadelphia and the City of Washington, via Perryville, Annapolis City, and Annapolis Junction, you find resistance which renders it necessary to suspend the writ of Habeas Corpus for the public safety, you, personally or through the officer in command at the point where the [at which] resistance occurs, are authorized to suspend that writ. ABRAHAM LINCOLN

 April 27 1861

[1] LS, is owned by Foreman M. Lebold, Chicago, Illinois. In addition to the signature the number "27" in the date line is in Lincoln's handwriting. As printed by Nicolay and Hay (VI, 258) this order lacks the phrase "via Perryville, Annapolis City, and Annapolis Junction," and differs in having the variant phrases which are bracketed in the text.

To William H. Seward[1]

Hon. Secretary of State,   Executive Mansion
Dear Sir: April 27, 1861

 I have concluded to appoint A. S. Paddock of Nebraska Territory to be secretary of the territory. Please send the commission. Yours truly,   A. LINCOLN

[1] Lincoln, Nebraska, *Sunday Star*, October 11, 1931. According to the accompanying article in the *Star*, the original letter ". . . for some strange and unknown reason today is found among other old and significant documents in the Russian soviet government's public library in Leningrad. . . . Walter L. Locke, former editor of the Dayton, Ohio, News . . . chanced to see the letter. . . ."

To Whom It May Concern[1]

Whom it may concern   Washington D.C.   April 27. 1861

The bearer of this, Hon. H. V. Sullivan resides, and for a long time has resided at Quincy, Illinois, and is a most respectable, and trust-worthy gentleman.   A. LINCOLN

[1] ALS, CSmH. Henry V. Sullivan was a former editor of the Quincy, Illinois, *Republican* and proprietor of a mill at Quincy.

To William H. Seward[1]

Hon. W. H. Seward: Executive Mansion

Dear Sir   April 29. 1861

If you have no objection to Timothy C. Smith having one of the $2000 consulships remaining open in Russia, I have none. Yours truly   A. LINCOLN

[1] ALS, NAuE. Timothy C. Smith of Vermont was appointed consul at Odessa.

To Caleb B. Smith[1]

Hon. Sec. of Interior   Executive Mansion

Dear Sir   April 29, 1861

If the Pawnee Indian Agency has not already been disposed of, send a commission for it, in favor of Henry W. DePuy, of Nebraska Yours truly   A. LINCOLN.

[1] ALS, RPB. A forged tracing of this letter is in the Huntington Library. Henry W. DePuy was a resident of Fontenelle, Dodge County, Nebraska Territory.

To Gideon Welles[1]

Hon. Secretary of the Navy,   Executive Mansion,

Sir: April 29. 1861

You will please to have as strong a War Steamer as you can conveniently put on that duty, to cruise upon the Potomac, and to look in upon, and, if practicable, examine the Bluff and vicinity, at what is called the White House, once or twice per day; and, in case of any attempt to erect a battery there, to drive away the party attempting it, if practicable; and, in every event to report daily to your Department, and to me. Your Obt. Servt.   A. LINCOLN

Private note. The above order I make at the suggestion of General Scott,[2] though the execution of it, I believe is substantially what you are already doing   A. L.

¹ ALS-P, ISLA. A forgery of this letter, addressed to General A. H. Terry, dated October 1, 1863, is in the New York Public Library.
² The suggestion is contained in Scott's daily report, No. 20, April 26, 1861 (DLC-RTL).

Memorandum:
Appointment of Stephen A. Hurlbut¹

The writer of this letter is especially worthy of attention. In anything further done for Illinois, let him not be neglected.

April 30, 1861.   A. LINCOLN

¹ AES, DLC-Nicolay Papers. Hurlbut wrote April 23, ". . . The Six Regiments of Illinois are more than full. *Seventy Companies* are rejected—mine among them. . . . We will relieve the Regulars from the frontier, or act any where else, but we must *act* or spoil. . . ." (*Ibid.*). Hurlbut was commissioned brigadier general of volunteers, May 17, 1861.

To Caleb B. Smith¹

Executive Mansion,

Secretary of the Interior.   Washington April 30, 1861.

Dear Sir: Send Commissions as follows: Register of Land Office at Sante Fé, N.M., Joel Houghton, in place of O. H. Perry Richardson, removed.

Indian Agent at Sante Fé, John Ward, in place of Silas Kendrick,² removed.

Indian Agent, Ramon Luna, in place of John L. Russell,³ removed.

Indian Agent, José Antonio Maurinares,⁴ in place of Diego Archuletta, removed.

If you and Mr. Dole⁵ approve the above, let the Commissions be sent. Yours truly,   A. LINCOLN.

¹ Tracy, p. 180; Hertz, II, 832; Parke-Bernet Catalog 1352, May 27, 1952, No. 166. Tracy misdates April 13; others give April 30. John S. Watts to Lincoln, April 2, 1861, listed the New Mexico appointments, for which Lincoln ordered commissions in this letter, as ". . . agreed upon between Mr. Otero the Delegate of New Mexico and myself. . . ." (DLC-RTL). Smith to Lincoln, April 29, indicated that "Judge Watts is anxious to return home & I shall be pleased if you will make some local appointments upon his recommendation. . . ." (DLC-RTL).
² Watts lists "Silas F. Kendrick."
³ Watts lists "John T. Russell."
⁴ Watts lists the name as "Mausinaries," and the *U. S. Official Register*, 1861, gives it as "Mausinares."
⁵ William P. Dole, commissioner of Indian affairs.

To Joseph G. Totten[1]

Executive Mansion April 30. 1861

The President will thank Gen. Totten for a brief interview with him here.

[1] AL, RPB. Joseph G. Totten was chief of engineers of the U. S. Army and held *ex-officio* supervision of the U. S. Military Academy at West Point.

To Robert Anderson[1]

Major Robert Anderson   Washington, D.C.

My dear Sir   May 1. 1861

A few days ago I caused an official letter to be written you through the War Department,[2] expressive of the approbation and gratitude I considered due you and your command from this Government.

I now write this, as a purely private and social letter, to say I shall be much gratified to see you here at your earliest convenience, when and where I can personally testify my appreciation of your services and fidelity; and, perhaps, explain some things on my part, which you may not have understood.

I shall also be very glad to see any of the officers who served with you at Fort Sumpter, and whom it might be convenient and agreeable for you to invite to accompany you here. Your Obt. Servt.

A. LINCOLN

[1] ALS, DLC-Anderson Papers.
[2] Cameron to Anderson, April 20, 1861 (OR, I, I, 16).

To Gustavus V. Fox[1]

Capt. G. V. Fox   Washington, D.C.

My dear Sir   May 1, 1861

I sincerely regret that the failure of the late attempt to provision Fort-Sumpter, should be the source of any annoyance to you. The practicability of your plan was not, in fact, brought to a test. By reason of a gale, well known in advance to be possible, and not improbable, the tugs, an essential part of the plan, never reached the ground; while, by an accident, for which you were in no wise responsible, and possibly I, to some extent was, you were deprived of a war vessel with her men, which you deemed of great importance to the enterprize.[2]

I most cheerfully and truly declare that the failure of the undertaking has not lowered you a particle, while the qualities you developed in the effort, have greatly heightened you, in my estimation. For a daring and dangerous enterprize, of a similar character, you would, to-day, be the man, of all my acquaintances, whom I would select.

You and I both anticipated that the cause of the country would be advanced by making the attempt to provision Fort-Sumpter, even if it should fail; and it is no small consolation now to feel that our anticipation is justified by the result. Very truly your friend   A LINCOLN

¹ ALS, MHi.
² The *Powhatan* had been placed under command of David D. Porter on secret orders (q.v., April 1, *supra*). Fox's report, April 19, 1861, on the failure of the Sumter expedition, emphasized the storm of April 12-13 and the expectation of the arrival of the *Powhatan*, which was to play a leading role in the attempt to relieve the fort. Fox commented with understandable bitterness, "I learned on the 13th instant that the Powhatan was withdrawn from duty off Charleston on the 7th instant, yet I was permitted to sail on the 9th, the Pawnee on the 9th, and the Pocahontas on the 10th, without intimation that the main portion— the fighting portion—of our expedition was taken away." (OR, I, I, 11).

To Isham G. Harris¹

To His Excellency the Governor   Executive Department
    of the State of Tennessee—   Washington, D.C.
      Nashville Tenn.   May [1 ?] 1861

Sir: Yours of the 29th. ultimo, calling my attention to the supposed seizure, near Cairo, Illinois, of the Steamboat C. E. Hillman, and claiming that the said boat and it's cargo are the property of the State of Tennessee and her citizens; and demanding to know whether the seizure was made by the authority of this Government, or is approved by it, is duly received.

In answer I have to say this Government has no official information of such seizure;² but assuming that the seizure was made, and that the cargo consisted chiefly of munitions of War owned by the State of Tennessee, and passing into the control of it's Governor, this Government avows the seizure, for the following reasons.

A legal call was recently made upon the said Governor of Tennessee to furnish a quota of militia to suppress an insurrection against the United States, which call said Governor responded to by a refusal, couched in disrespectful and malicious language.³ This Government therefore infers that munitions of War passing into the hands of said Governor, are intended to be used against the United States; and the government will not indulge the weakness of allowing it, so long as it is in it's power to prevent. This Government will not, at present, question, but that the State of Tennessee, by a majority of it's citizens, is loyal to the Federal Union, and the government holds itself responsible in damages for all injuries it may do to any who may prove to be such.

[1] ADf, DLC-RTL. Governor Harris' letter of April 29 complained that "On the 26th inst. the Steamboat C. E. Hillman . . . was seized . . . by an armed force on the Steamboat Swallow. . . . The boat Hillman was owned by citizens of Tennessee and its cargo was the property of this State. . . . It becomes my . . . duty . . . to request that the President shall inform me whether the same was done by or under the instructions of the Federal Government, or is approved by said Government. . . ." (DLC-RTL).

[2] Governor Richard Yates of Illinois had telegraphed on April 24 to the officer in command at Cairo to stop the *C. E. Hillman* and *John D. Perry* and seize all arms and munitions. The action was taken without orders from Washington.

[3] Harris to Cameron, April 17, 1861: "Tennessee will not furnish a single man for purpose of coercion, but 50,000, if necessary, for the defense of our rights and those of our Southern brethren." (OR, III, I, 81).

Remarks at a Band Concert[1]

May 1, 1861

Upon the President's making his appearance on the portico of the White House, he was greeted with the most enthusiastic applause from the vast throng present; in response to which, the President made a few remarks, in which he congratulated them upon the prospects of a happy termination of the present difficulties, but assuring them that the people were more powerful in that than he himself was.

[1] Washington *National Republican*, May 2, 1861. Lincoln's remarks followed the performance by the Seventh New York regimental band.

Endorsement:
Simon Cameron to Cassius M. Clay[1]

I cheerfully concur in the foregoing testimonial given by the Hon. Secretary of War.   A. LINCOLN,
                                             President of the United States.
Executive Mansion, May 2, 1861.

[1] Cassius M. Clay, *The Life of Cassius Marcellus Clay: Memoirs, Writings, and Speeches,* . . . (Cincinnati, 1886), p. 269. Cameron extended appreciation ". . . of the very prompt and patriotic manner in which your Battalion was organized for the defense of the capital. . . ."

Remarks to Rhode Island Marine Battery[1]

May 2, 1861

The magnificent Providence marine corps artillery . . . passed in review before President Lincoln, who expressed himself as much pleased with the completeness of the battery, and with the patriotism of the noble little State which has come out so nobly in defence of the Union.

1 Washington *Daily National Intelligencer*, May 3, 1861.

To William H. Seward[1]

Hon. Sec. of State   Executive Mansion
My dear Sir   May 2, 1861
Our Chicago detective has arrived; and I have promised to have you meet him and me here at 8. o'clock this evening. Yours truly
                                                                A. LINCOLN

1 ALS, NAuE. Allan Pinkerton in a letter from Chicago, April 21, 1861, offered his services and sent a cipher code to be used in communicating with him. "In the present disturbed state of affairs I dare not trust this to the mails so send by one of my force who was with me at Baltimore. . . ." (DLC-RTL). Whether Pinkerton, or his operative Timothy Webster who carried his messages, was to meet Seward, is uncertain.

Proclamation Calling for 42,034 Volunteers[1]

May 3, 1861
By the President of the United States

A Proclamation.

Whereas existing exigencies demand immediate and adequate measures for the protection of the National Constitution and the preservation of the National Union by the suppression of the insurrectionary combinations now existing in several States for opposing the laws of the Union and obstructing the execution thereof, to which end a military force in addition to that called forth by my proclamation of the fifteenth day of April in the present year, appears to be indispensably necessary,

Now, therefore, I, Abraham Lincoln President of the United States, and Commander-in-Chief[2] of the Army and Navy thereof, and of the Militia of the several States, when called into actual service, do hereby call into the service of the United States, forty-two thousand and thirty four volunteers, to serve for the period of three years, unless sooner discharged, and to be mustered into service as Infantry and cavalry. The proportions of each arm, and the details of enrollment and organization will be made known, through the Department of War.

And I also direct that the regular army of the United States be increased by the addition of eight regiments of infantry, one regiment of cavalry, and one regiment of artillery, making altogether a maximum aggregate increase of twenty-two thousand, seven hundred and fourteen officers and enlisted men; the details of which increase will also be made known through the Department of War.

And I further direct the enlistment for not less than one or more than three years, of eighteen thousand seamen, in addition to the present force, for the naval service of the United States. The details of the enlistment and organization will be made known through the Department of the Navy.

The call for volunteers hereby made, and the direction for the increase of the regular army, and for the enlistment of seamen hereby given, together with the plan of organization adopted for the volunteer and for the regular forces hereby authorized, will be submitted to Congress as soon as assembled.

In the meantime I earnestly invoke the coöperation of all good citizens in the measures hereby adopted, for the effectual suppression of unlawful violence, for the impartial enforcement of constitutional laws, and for the speediest possible restoration of peace and order and, with these, of happiness and prosperity throughout our country.

[L.S.]   In testimony whereof I have hereunto set my hand and caused the seal of the United States to be affixed. Done at the City of Washington this third day of May, in the year of our Lord one thousand eight hundred and sixty-one, and of the independence of the United States the eighty-fifth.   ABRAHAM LINCOLN

By the President:
WILLIAM H. SEWARD, Secretary of State.

[1] DS, DNA FS RG 11, Proclamations; DfS, DLC-RTL.
[2] The draft in the Lincoln Papers shows Lincoln's emendation of the remainder of this sentence to its final form. The original reading was: ". . . of the Army and Navy forces do hereby call into service of the United States . . ."

Memorandum:
Appointment of Andrew W. Evans[1]

The appointment within requested ought to be made if practicable   A. LINCOLN
May 4, 1861

[1] AES, IHi. The endorsement appears on the letter dated May 3, 1861, from Alexander Evans, ex-congressman (1847-1853) of Elkton, Maryland, asking that his brother, Lieutenant Andrew W. Evans, stationed at Fort Buchanan, New Mexico, be promoted to a colonelcy in one of the new regular regiments. Andrew W. Evans was promoted to captain May 14, 1861, becoming colonel of the First Maryland Volunteers, April 15, 1864.

To Charles S. Olden[1]

His Excellency Charles S. Olden   Washington D.C.
Govr. of the State of New-Jersey   May 4, 1861
  My dear Sir: Yours of the 29th. ult. covering copy of a letter of E. R. V. Wright Major General of 2nd. Div. N.J.S. Militia, tendering the services of said Division to the United States, to continue as long as the President may require such services" has been duly received.

  I lose no time in tendering you, and through you, General Wright and all the officers and men of his Division, my sincere and hearty thanks for the part each takes in this patriotic effort.

  I shall send the papers immediately to the War Department with the recommendation that Gen. Wright's Division be at once received into the new corp's of Volunteers, for which a call, by Proclamation appears to-day. Your Obt. Servt.   A. LINCOLN

[1] ALS-P, ISLA. See Lincoln's endorsement, *infra.*

Endorsement: Charles S. Olden to Lincoln[1]

  I recommend that the Division named within be admitted into the new Corps of Volunteers just called for.   A. LINCOLN.
May 4, 1861.

[1] Stan. V. Henkels Catalog 1379, October 15, 1925, No. 31. Governor Olden's letter of April 29, 1861, enclosed a communication from Major General Edwin R. V. Wright, ". . . the object of which is to inform you through me that the officers of the division have unanimously resolved to tender to you the services of the said division." (OR, III, I, 130).

To Winfield Scott[1]

  Col. Lander is a valuable man to us. Will Genl. Scott see him a few minutes, and consider the feasability of his plan?
May 4, 1861.   A. LINCOLN

[1] AES, IHi. Lincoln's endorsement is on the back of Seward's letter of May 2, 1861, recommending Colonel Frederick W. Lander's project of raising a regiment of Virginia volunteers. Lander was appointed brigadier general of volunteers, May 17, 1861.

To William H. Seward[1]

Hon. Sec. of State   Executive Mansion
Dear Sir   May 4. 1861
  The Maryland Committee men, or Commissioners, are to be here at ten o'clock this morning. Yours truly   A. LINCOLN

[1] ALS, NAuE.

Reply to Committee from Maryland Legislature[1]

May 4, 1861

The President replied that their suggestions and representations should be duly considered; but that he should now say no more than [that] the public interest and not any spirit of revenge should actuate his measures.

[1] Washington *Daily National Intelligencer*, May 7, 1861. The committee had ". . . expressed their belief that no immediate effort at secession or resistance . . . would be attempted . . . and asked that . . . the State . . . be spared the evils of a military occupation or a revengeful chastisement for former transgressions." See Lincoln to Otho Scott, Robert M. McLane, and William J. Ross, May 6, *infra*.

To Gideon Welles[1]

My dear Sir.   May 4, 1861

I understand there is a vacancy in the Staff of Marine Corps, Adjutant and Inspector, and that Lieut. Nicholson of the Marine Corps, is well recommended for the place, by Genl. Scott, among others. If all this be true, let him be appointed. Yours truly

A. LINCOLN.

[1] Stan. V. Henkels Catalog 1342, January 4, 1924, No. 13. Augustus S. Nicholson was appointed adjutant and inspector of the Marine Corps with rank of major, May 6, 1861.

To Joseph H. Barrett[1]

Hon. Com. of Pensions   Executive Mansion
My dear Sir   May 6, 1861

I understand there is a clerkship vacant by the resignation of a Mr. Woodley.[2] If so, I will be personally obliged if you will give it to the bearer of this—Albert I. Brooks,[3] formerly of Ill. now of Ky. I am an . . . . on this; and if Mr. Smith[4] has to make the appointment, procure him to make it for me   Yours truly

A. LINCOLN

[1] Copy, ISLA. The copy is obviously inaccurate, but efforts to procure a photostat have failed.   [2] W. H. Woodley of Virginia.
[3] Albert I. Brooks formerly of Petersburg, Illinois, received the appointment.
[4] The pension office was under Caleb B. Smith, secretary of Interior.

To Salmon P. Chase[1]

Executive Mansion, May 6, 1861.

My dear Sir: Mr. French S. Evans, the bearer of this, thinks there is an appraisership still vacant at Baltimore, and if so, I very sincerely wish you would give it to him. I have been greatly—I

may say grievously—disappointed and disobliged by Mr. Corkran's[2] refusal to make Mr. Evans deputy naval officer, as I requested him to do.

A point must be strained to give Mr. Evans a situation. Yours
very truly,   A. LINCOLN.

[1] NH, VI, 266. On April 13, Chase had recommended French S. Evans, formerly editor of the Baltimore *Patriot,* who had been driven out of Baltimore
because of his Union sympathy (DLC-RTL). Evans is listed as deputy naval
officer at Baltimore as of September 30, 1861.

[2] Francis S. Corkran, appointed naval officer at Baltimore, April 15, 1861. See
Lincoln to Corkran, *infra.*

To Salmon P. Chase[1]

Hon. Sec. of Treasury[2]   Executive Department
Dear Sir   May 6, 1861

The Secretary of State this moment introduces to me Mr. James
Gordon Bennett, Jr. who tenders to the U.S. service, a fine Yacht
of 160 tons burthen. If you allow him an interview, which I ask
for him, he will talk with you about putting some other vessels of
the same class, into the service. We send this subject to you because we believe these vessels may be made most available in the
Revenue service. Yours truly,   A. LINCOLN

[1] ALS, DNA FI RG 26, General Records, U.S. Coast Guard. The son of the
editor of the New York *Herald* was commissioned third lieutenant in the revenue
cutter service, May 15, 1861, and resigned his commission when his yacht
Henrietta was taken out of the service after a year.

[2] "Navy" as first written, and "Treasury" substituted by Lincoln.

To Francis S. Corkran[1]

Hon. F. S. Corkran   Washington D.C.
My dear Sir   May 6, 1861

I am quite sure you are not aware how much I am disobliged by
the refusal to give Mr. F. S. Evans a place in the Custom-House. I
had no thought that the men to whom I had given the higher officers [*sic*] would be so ready to disoblige me. I still wish you
would give Mr. Evans the place of Deputy Naval Officer. Yours &c.
                                                      A. LINCOLN

[1] ALS, IHi. See Lincoln to Chase, *supra.*

To Hannibal Hamlin[1]

Hon. H. Hamlin   Washington, D.C. May 6, 1861
My dear Sir   Please advise me at the close of each day what
troops left during the day, where going, and by what route; what

remaining at N.Y, and what expected in the next day. Give the
numbers, as near as convenient, and what corps they are. This information, reaching us daily, will be very useful, as well as satisfactory. [Yours very truly,   A. LINCOLN.]

¹ ALS, CSmH. The letter bears Hamlin's endorsement, April, 1889, that he
had cut off the close and signature. Hamlin to Lincoln, Hampden, Maine, May
11, 1861, explained that he had remained in New York two weeks without
hearing from Lincoln. "I left there and reached home last eve, where I recd
your note of the 6th. . . . I will *at once* repair to N.Y. or to *any place* . . .
and perform as well as I can that or any other service you may require. . . ."
(DLC-RTL).

To Otho Scott, Robert M. McLane,
and William J. Ross¹

Messrs. Otho Scott   R. M. McLane &   Washington D.C.
Wm. J. Ross. Commissioners of the Legislature   May 6, 1861.
of the State of Maryland.

Gentlemen   On presenting me the resolution of the Legislature
of your State, and addressing me verbally, two days ago, you had
the kindness to say you did not expect an immediate answer. Ap-
preciating what you said orally, I, however, attempt no answer except to what is written in the resolution.

The resolution is as follows (Here insert it)²

To the question "in regard to the present and any proposed prospective Military use or occupation of the soil and property of the
State, by the General Government &c" the answer must necessarily
be contingent.

¹ ADf, DLC-RTL. The letter was apparently never completed. See the re-
port of Lincoln's oral reply, May 4, *supra.*
² The resolution in the Lincoln Papers reads in part as follows: ". . . to com-
municate immediately, in person, with the President of the United States in
regard to the present and any proposed prospective Military use or occupation
of the soil and property of the State by the General Government; and they are
directed to ascertain and report to the General assembly . . . whether any becoming arrangements with the General Government are practicable in that
connexion, for the maintenance of the peace and honor of the State, and the
security of its inhabitants."

To William H. Seward¹

Hon. Sec. of State   Executive Mansion May 6. 1861
My dear Sir   Gen. Cameron is anxious that E. Joy Morris shall
be Minister to Constantinople; and if Gen. Webb has definitely declined it, why might not Mr Morris be appointed? Pennsylvania

is well entitled to the place, and Gen. C. thinks there is political reason for the appointment being made at once. Your Obt. Servt.

A. LINCOLN

[1] ALS, NAuE. Representative Edward Joy Morris of Philadelphia was appointed minister to Turkey, June 8, 1861. James W. Webb of New York became minister to Brazil.

Order to Robert Anderson[1]

May 7, 1861

To all who shall see these presents greeting:

Know Ye, That reposing special trust and confidence in the patriotism, valor, fidelity, and abilities of Colonel ROBERT ANDERSON, U.S. Army, I have empowered him and do hereby empower him to receive into the Service of the United States, as many regiments of volunteer troops from the State of Kentucky and from the Western part of the State of Virginia, as shall be willing to engage in the service of the United States for the period of three years, upon the terms and according to the plan proposed by the Proclamation of May 3, 1861, and General Order, No. 15, from the War Department of May 4, 1861.

The troops whom he may receive shall be on the same footing in every respect as those of the like kind called for in the proclamation above cited, except that the officers thereof shall be commissioned by the United States.

He is, therefore, carefully and diligently to discharge the duty hereby devolved upon him by doing and performing all manner of things thereunto belonging.

Given under my hand at the City of Washington, this seventh day of May, in the year of our Lord one thousand eight hundred and sixty-one, and in the eighty-fifth year of the Independence of the United States.   ABRAHAM LINCOLN

By the President,
    SIMON CAMERON   Secretary of War.

[1] DS, DLC-Anderson Papers. Major Robert Anderson was promoted to brigadier general, June 17, 1861. His designation as colonel in this order may refer to his brevet rank.

To Salmon P. Chase[1]

Hon. Secretary of Treasury.   Executive Mansion, May 7, 1861.

My dear Sir: You may remember that John S. Gallaher, a worthy Virginia gentleman, has been and is an applicant for an

Auditorship in your Department. He now writes a friend here that he understands that the place of 5th Auditor has been made vacant by the resignation of a North Carolinian. If this is true, might not Mr. Gallaher have the place? Yours truly, A. LINCOLN

[1] Tracy, p. 182. John C. Underwood of Virginia received the appointment. John S. Gallaher is not of record as a federal employee until the *U.S. Official Register* lists him as a clerk in the quartermaster general's office, September 30, 1863.

To the Regent Captains
of the Republic of San Marino[1]

May 7, 1861

Abraham Lincoln,
President of the United States of America.

To the Regent Captains of the Republic of San Marino
Great and Good Friends

I have received and read with great sensibility the letter which as Regent Captains of the Republic of San Marino you addressed to me on the 29th of March last. I thank the Council of San Marino for the honor of citizenship they have conferred upon me.

Although your dominion is small, your State is nevertheless one of the most honored, in all history. It has by its experience demonstrated the truth, so full of encouragement to the friends of Humanity, that Government founded on Republican principles is capable of being so administered as to be secure and enduring.

You have kindly adverted to the trial through which this Republic is now passing. It is one of deep import. It involves the question whether a Representative republic, extended and aggrandized so much as to be safe against foreign enemies can save itself from the dangers of domestic faction. I have faith in a good result.

Wishing that your interesting State may endure and flourish forever, and that you may live long and enjoy the confidence and secure the gratitude of your fellow citizens, I pray God to have you in his holy keeping. Your Good Friend

Washington, May 7 1861 ABRAHAM LINCOLN

By the President

WILLIAM H. SEWARD Secretary of State

[1] LS-P, ISLA; copy, DNA FS RG 59, Communications to Foreign Sovereigns and States, III, 173. The original is presumably still in the archives of San Marino.

To Gideon Welles[1]

Hon. Sec. of Navy   Executive Mansion
Dear Sir   May 7, 1861

Lieut. McLaughlin, of the Navy calls upon me saying he tendered you his resignation, which has not yet been accepted, and which he now wishes to withdraw, and that you refer him to me. I can not take the lead in the case. You know the circumstances, which I do not; and if you think fit to allow him to withdraw the resignation, I make no objection; but I can not take the lead. Yours truly   A. LINCOLN

[1] ALS, The Rosenbach Company, Philadelphia and New York. Augustus McLaughlin, a native of Maryland and appointed from Arkansas, was not permitted to withdraw his resignation. The *Naval Records* have him at a later date in the Confederate Navy.

To Joseph H. Barrett[1]

                              Executive Mansion
Hon. Comr. of Pensions,   May 8. 1861

My dear Sir   Once more I ask you to find a clerkship for a man of your own name—O. D. Barret, of Oswego Co New-York. Yours truly   A. LINCOLN

[1] ALS-F, *Munsey's Magazine*, March, 1895, XII, 591. Oliver D. Barrett is listed as clerk in the Pension office as of September 30, 1861.

To Salmon P. Chase[1]

                    Executive Mansion, May 8, 1861.

My dear Sir: I am told there is an office in your department called "The Superintending Architect of the Treasury Department, connected with the Bureau of Construction," which is now held by a man of the name of Young,[2] and wanted by a gentleman of the name of Christopher Adams.

Ought Mr. Young to be removed, and if yea, ought Mr. Adams to be appointed? Mr. Adams is magnificently recommended; but the great point in his favor is that Thurlow Weed and Horace Greeley join in recommending him. I suppose the like never happened before, and never will again; so that it is now or never. What say you? Yours truly,   A. LINCOLN.

[1] NH, VI, 268-69. Lincoln's endorsement on envelope reads "Christopher Adams, of/N.Y. for/Bureau of Construction." A scrap of envelope endorsed, not in Lincoln's hand, "Christopher Adams./Architect & Builder/ of New York. Bureau of Construction" and bearing on the verso, Lincoln's endorsement "Rec-

ommended by both/Weed & Greely" is in the Lincoln Papers, but the letters of Greeley and Weed are not.

² Ammi B. Young, supervising architect, still held the office as of September 30, 1861.

To James W. Ripley[1]

Col. Ripley: Executive Mansion
My dear Sir: May 8, 1861

Hon. Mr. Colfax impresses me with the necessity of very early attention to placing arms, artillery &c, along the Ohio River, particularly on the borders of Indiana and Illinois. Of course you understand this subject better than I; and therefore this is to be taken as a general suggestion, and, in no sense as dictation. Yours truly

A. LINCOLN

[1] ALS, IHi. Colonel James W. Ripley was chief of ordnance, U.S. Army, promoted to brigadier general by brevet, July 2, 1861.

To William H. Seward[1]

I understand the consulship named within has fees only, & if so, I think the appointment might be made.   A. LINCOLN
May 8, 1861.

[1] AES, DNA FS RG 59, Appointments, Box 329. The endorsement is written on the back of Roderick W. Cameron to Lincoln, May 8, 1861, endorsed also by Winfield Scott, asking the consulship at Sydney, Australia, for Edward Leavenworth, secretary of Columbia College, New York City. Roderick W. Cameron was a Canadian merchant at New York, operating a line of ships to Australia.

To William B. Thomas[1]

Hon. W. B. Thomas.   Washington, D.C.
Collector   May 8. 1861

My dear Sir   I do not *demand*, or *insist*, even, that you shall make any appointment in your office; but I would be much obliged if you could give a place to [blank] Ridgeway,[2] or to such person as a widow sister of his—a Mrs. Corneau[3]—would name. It is for her sake I make this request, she being an acquaintance and very highly valued friend of mine. Yours very truly   A. LINCOLN

[1] ALS, PHi. William B. Thomas, was collector of the customs office at Philadelphia.
[2] Charles S. Ridgeway was clerk in the custom house at Philadelphia as of September 30, 1861.
[3] Mrs. Charles S. Corneau (Elizabeth Ridgeway), of Springfield, Illinois.

To Gideon Welles[1]

Hon. Gideon Welles.   Executive Mansion,
My dear Sir   May 8, 1861.
I understand that there is some opposition to the appointment of
Capt. G. V. Fox to the clerkship we talked of. My wish, and advice
is, that you do not allow any ordinary obstacle prevent his appointment. He is a live man, whose services we cannot well dispense
with. Yours very truly   A. LINCOLN.

[1] Hertz, II, 834. Gustavus V. Fox was appointed chief clerk of the Navy Department, May 8, 1861, and became assistant secretary of the Navy by a bill
introduced in the Senate creating the office, July 16.

To Gideon Welles[1]

May 8, 1861.
Please send up papers (Commission I believe) for Samuel Bell as
Navy Agent, at San Francisco. Yours truly   A. LINCOLN.

[1] Stan. V. Henkels Catalog 1342, January 4, 1924, No. 9. See Lincoln to
Welles, April 15, *supra*, concerning Bell's appointment. Bell's appointment was
not made.

To Salmon P. Chase[1]

Executive Mansion, May 9, 1861.
My dear Sir: Mr. James N. Muller wishes to be supervising inspector of steamboats for the district of Baltimore. I am somewhat
interested for him, and as the place is in your department, if you
will look into the question of his qualification for the place, and
shall be satisfied with him, I will appoint him,—no matter how
soon. Yours truly,   A. LINCOLN.

[1] NH, VI, 269. Chase replied May 9, "The inquiries necessary to ascertain
the fitness of Mr. Muller . . . shall be immediately made." (DLC-RTL). See
Lincoln to Chase, May 31, *infra*. Muller received the appointment, was confirmed by the Senate, reconsidered, and then rejected on August 6, 1861. Nominated again January 16, 1862, he was confirmed March 19, 1862.

To Salmon P. Chase[1]

Executive Mansion, May 10, 1861.
My dear Sir: I have felt myself obliged to refuse the post-office
at this place to my old friend Nathan Sargent, which wounds him,
and consequently me, very deeply. He now says there is an office
in your department, called the "Commissioner of Customs," which

the incumbent, a Mr. Ingham, wishes to vacate. I will be much obliged if you agree for me to appoint Mr. Sargent to this place. Yours very truly,   A. LINCOLN.

1 NH, VI, 269. Sargent received the place of commissioner of customs vacated by Samuel Ingham of Connecticut.

Endorsement: Mark W. Delahay to Lincoln[1]

[May 10, 1861]
Come at 8. Saturday evening.   LINCOLN

1 AES, The Rosenbach Company, Philadelphia and New York. Written on the back of a note from Delahay, May 10, 1861, requesting an interview on matters "of great importance to our People and myself."

To Thomas H. Hicks[1]

His Excellency   Washington, D.C.
T. H. Hicks   May 10. 1861
    My dear Sir   Yours of the 8th. is received, and shall have the best attention I can bestow upon it. Yours very truly
                                                          A. LINCOLN

1 ALS, IHi. Governor Hicks' letter of May 8, 1861, asked federal intervention in the seizure of the customs house at Oxford, Maryland, and of canal boats with produce for Georgetown and Maryland (DLC-Nicolay Papers). Apparently there was another letter from Hicks on May 10, which Lincoln endorsed and sent to the Treasury Department. Although the Register of Miscellaneous Letters, Vol. 32, P6 (DNA RG 56), lists the letter from Hicks, May 10, endorsed by Lincoln, the letter is missing from the file.

Proclamation
Suspending Writ of Habeas Corpus in Florida[1]

May 10, 1861
By the President of the United States of America.

A Proclamation.

Whereas, an insurrection exists in the State of Florida, by which the lives, liberty and property of loyal citizens of the United States are endangered:

And whereas it is deemed proper that all needful measures should be taken for the protection of such citizens, and all officers of the United States in the discharge of their public duties, in the State aforesaid:

Now therefore be it known that I, Abraham Lincoln, President of the United States, do hereby direct the Commander of the Forces of the United States on the Florida coast, to permit no person to exercise any office or authority upon the Islands of Key West, the Tortugas and Santa Rosa, which may be inconsistent with the laws & constitution of the United States, authorizing him at the same time, if he shall find it necessary, to suspend there the writ of *Habeas Corpus* and to remove from the vicinity of the United States fortresses all dangerous or suspected persons.

In witness whereof, I have hereunto set my hand, and caused the seal of the United States to be affixed.

Done at the City of Washington, this tenth day of May in the year of our Lord one thousand eight hundred and [L.S.] sixty-one, and of the Independence of the United States the eighty-fifth. ABRAHAM LINCOLN

By the President:

WILLIAM H. SEWARD, Secretary of State.

[1] DS, DNA FS RG 11, Proclamations.

To William Sprague[1]

Executive Mansion May 10. 1861

His Excellency Gov. Wm. Sprague

My dear Sir: I think I had a letter from you some time ago naming a person whom you would like to have appointed P.M. at Providence, R.I. and day-before yesterday, a gentleman urged the name of Thomas A. Doyle, as being the man whom you would like to have appointed. I write this now to assure you that while your wishes in this respect, are entitled to, and have received the highest consideration, there is a difficulty, such as I have not surmounted in any other case. It is that a different man—Walter C. Simmons[2]— is recommended by both the Senators, and both the old Representatives of the State, and also by one of the new Representatives.

In these cases the Executive is obliged to be greatly dependent upon members of Congress; and while, under peculiar circumstances, a single member or two, may be occasionally over-ruled, I believe as strong a combination as the present never has been.

I therefore beg you to be assured that if I follow the rule in this case, as it appears to me I must, it will be with pain and not with pleasure, that you are not obliged.

[1] ADf, DLC-RTL. Governor Sprague of Rhode Island was in Washington on May 10 and answered the same day that his letter recommending Thomas A. Doyle, who later married Sprague's sister, ". . . was written long before the present crisis. I have refused since then, to interfere with any appointments . . . . I beg you to feel no unpleasantness for the course which your duty compels you to take. . . ." (DLC-RTL).

[2] Walter C. Simmons was the son of Senator James F. Simmons.

To Lorenzo Thomas[1]

Adjutant General   Executive Mansion
My Dear Sir: May 10, 1861
     Mr. O. Pullizi,[2] as I understand, was once in the regular Army, and resigned under some charges, of which you probably know more than I do. He now wishes to re-enter the Army; and if it violates no rule of law or propriety I shall be glad for him to be obliged in that respect. Yours truly,   A. LINCOLN

[1] Copy, CSmH. Lorenzo Thomas was promoted to adjutant general March 7, 1861.

[2] The source is probably in error as to the initial. The only Pullizi of record in the Army Registers is Venerando Pulizzi, who was reinstated with rank of first lieutenant, May 14, 1861, and resigned again September 9, 1861.

To Edward Bates[1]

Hon. Attorney General   Executive Mansion
My dear Sir   May 11, 1861
     Please send me a commission for Phineas W. Hitchcock, as Marshal of Nebraska. Yours very truly   A. LINCOLN

[1] ALS, DNA GE RG 60, Papers of Attorney General, Segregated Lincoln Material.

To Gideon Welles[1]

Hon. Gideon Welles.   Executive Mansion,
My dear Sir   May 11, 1861.
     Some time ago, at the request of Commander E. B. Boutwell, I asked you to look into the case of his suspension, and ascertain whether he might not, without inconsistency, be relieved from the remainder of his suspension. I am now informed that his case is not yet acted upon. I make no complaint of this, knowing you are overwhelmed with business; but I will be obliged if you will attend to it as soon as possible. Yours very truly   A. LINCOLN.

[1] Hertz, II, 834. In June, 1858, Edward B. Boutwell of Virginia had been found guilty of disobedience to lawful orders, neglect of duty, and scandalous conduct. The court sentenced him to be dismissed, but the sentence was commuted to "five years Furlough Pay." Welles replied, May 16, 1861, ". . . I am not in possession of any fact which calls upon me to advise a further mitigation. . . ." (DLC-RTL). Boutwell was dismissed from the service, July 31, 1861.

To Gideon Welles[1]

Executive Mansion, May 11, 1861.
     Sir: Lieutenant D. D. Porter was placed in command of the steamer *Powhatan* and Captain Samuel Mercer was detached there-

from by my special order, and neither of them is responsible for any apparent or real irregularity on their part or in connection with that vessel.

Hereafter Captain Porter is relieved from that special service and placed under the direction of the Navy Department, from which he will receive instructions and to which he will report. Very respectfully,   ABRAHAM LINCOLN.

The Secretary of the Navy.

1 *Naval Records*, Series I, IV, 128.

To Hiram Barney[1]

Hon. Hiram Barney   Washington, D.C.
My dear Sir   May 13. 1861

Two or three days ago I wrote in behalf of Mr. William Ward, of your City, inclosing Mr. Greeley's letter introducing him to me. Since then I have been more deeply interested for Mr. Ward, by conversations with him, and with others who know him, and his history. If you can do something for him I shall be obliged. Yours very truly   A LINCOLN

1 ALS, owned by Mrs. Joseph Brady, Pasadena, California. Lincoln's letter to Barney of May 9 is presumably not extant. Barney's letter of May 11, acknowledged its receipt ". . . enclosing Mr. Greeley's letter on behalf of Mr. William Ward of this city. I understand you to desire Mr. Ward's application considered on its merits. . . ." (DLC-RTL). William Ward is not listed in the New York customs house as of September 30, 1861.

To Simon Cameron[1]

Hon. Sec. of War   Executive Mansion, May 13, 1861

Dear Sir—You see on the other side of this sheet that four german Regiments already raised in New-York, wish to form a Brigade, and have Carl Schurz for their Brigadier General. Why should it not be done at once? By the Plan of organization, I see I am to appoint the generals.

Schurz says he would, if allowed, go immediately to Fortress Monroe; and if it would be an objection that, by rank, he would command the garrison there, he would, of choice, waive that.

I am for it, unless there be some valid reason against it. Answer soon. Yours truly   A. LINCOLN.

1 ALS copy, DLC-RTL. On the bottom of the sheet is a note not in Lincoln's hand: "C.S. will be at 445 North 5th Str. Philadelphia on Monday 13th. and at the Prescott-house corner of Spring Str. & Broadway, New-York on Tuesday

14th. and Wednesday 15th." See Lincoln to Schurz, *infra*. Lincoln's letter is written on the back of a "Duplicate" copy of a petition to Governor Morgan signed by field officers of the Seventh and Eighth Regiments, United Turner Rifles, and DeKalb Regiment, requesting him to unite the four regiments into one brigade and to tender its command to Carl Schurz.

To Carl Schurz[1]

[May 13, 1861 ?]

Get the german Brigade in shape, and, at their request, you shall be Brigadier General. Will write you at New-York.

A. LINCOLN

[1] ADfS, DLC-RTL. A line has been drawn through the signature. This is probably the draft of a telegram intended for Carl Schurz at Philadelphia. See Lincoln to Cameron and note, *supra*. See also Lincoln to Schurz, May 16, *infra*.

To Whom It May Concern[1]

To Whom it May Concern   May 13, 1861

James A. Sheehan, 3rd Sergeant of the Washington Light Infantry Batallion, inquires whether the U.S. will accept a regiment of loyal Baltimoreans, if he will raise and teach one, [to w]hich I answer, I suppose [such] a Regiment would be accepted; but to avoid confusion, the approval of the Secretary of War must first be had.

[1] American Art Association Catalog, December 3, 1923, No. 541. Brackets are in the source. There is no record of a commission for James A. Sheehan.

To Robert Anderson[1]

Col. Robert Anderson   Washington, D.C.
My dear Sir   May 14. 1861

Some time ago, and before it was arranged for you to go West, as now, the question was upon us how arms sent to Cincinnati for Kentuckians, could surely be put in the hands of friends, and not of enemies; and, for this purpose, and without their knowledge, Messrs Crittenden, Guthrie, and Joshua F. Speed, bearer of this, or any one of them, were designated to distribute the arms, in their discretion. After you left here last week it occurred to us that you could perform this service as safely, and perhaps more expeditiously, by reason that you will be on the spot, and will not have to wait for the co-operation of any one; and a direction was accordingly sent to the parties forwarding the arms to Cincinnati. It now occurs further that the kind assistance of these gentlemen may still be valuable to you in this, and perhaps other matters; and when it shall so appear to you it is hoped you will avail yourself of it. Mr. Speed, though less known to the world than the other gentlemen, is far better known to me than either of them; and I have the utmost confidence in his loyalty and integrity, and also in his judgment on any subject which he professes to understand. I think you will find him a most agreeable companion, and at the same time a most valuable assistant in our common cause. Yours very truly

A. LINCOLN

¹ ALS, NWM. On the back of the letter appears the following list of names, probably representing the men recommended to Anderson by Speed for supervision of the distribution of arms at the designated places: James Harlan, Frankfort; James Speed, Louisville; Garrett Davis, Paris; Samuel Lusk, Lancaster; John H. Ward, Bowling Green; Thornton F. Marshall, Augusta; James H. [Lord?], Frankfort; Charles A. Wickliffe, Bowling Green. On May 19, Anderson acknowledged receipt of Lincoln's letter ". . . introducing Mr. Joshua F. Speed and giving me instructions about issuing arms to our friends in Ky. I will carefully attend to the performance of that duty. . . . Mr. Speed and other gentlemen . . . advise that I should not, at present, have any thing to do with the raising of troops in Ky. . . . Many of our friends think that it would be advisable for me to take command of New Port Barracks. . . ." (DLC-RTL). On May 28, the Department of Kentucky was constituted, with Anderson in command.

To Simon Cameron¹

Hon. Sec. of War—   Executive Mansion
My dear Sir—   May 14. 1861

After you left here to-day, Mr. Blair came in; and, being told what we had been doing in relation to generals and colonels, he seemed to be dissatisfied. Would it not be better for you to see Mr. Blair, and ascertain what is the trouble with him? We should take some pains to avoid dissatisfaction among ourselves. Yours very truly   A. LINCOLN

¹ ALS, DLC-Cameron Papers. Although the circumstances of mobilization were so complex, not to say chaotic, that any succinct statement of the conflict between the War Department and other branches of the government is open to criticism, the basic difficulty seems to have been that the Army wished to keep, logically enough, some semblance of an orderly promotion of regular officers and integration of troops, while Montgomery Blair, as well as the governors of the loyal states and numerous individual politicians were demanding wholesale acceptance of volunteer regiments and elected officers. Cameron repeatedly refused to accept volunteer regiments, and there was much opposition to the appointment of "political" generals. Also, in the border states, the conflict between the War Department's view of military rule and the political insistence upon subordination of the military to loyal local political exigencies brought about near chaos in such trouble spots as St. Louis. For further comment on Blair's opposition to the War Department policy see Lincoln to Cameron, May 16, *infra*, and note.

Memorandum:
Appointments of Major Generals[1]

[c. May 14, 1861]

McClellan ⎫
Mansfield[2] ⎬ Major Generals in the Regular Army.

Butler— Major General in the 3 year corps.

[1] AD, IHi.

[2] Mansfield's name is crossed out. George B. McClellan's appointment as major general and Joseph K. F. Mansfield's appointment as brigadier general, May 14, were sent to the Senate on July 13, along with many other promotions and appointments in the U.S. Army. Benjamin F. Butler's appointment as major general of volunteers, May 16, went to the Senate, July 29.

To Gideon Welles[1]

Hon. Sec. of Navy   Executive Mansion
My dear Sir: May 14. 1861

I know but little about ships; but I feel a good deal of interest for George W. Lawrence, of Maine, who is a proficient in that line. I believe it is settled that the Govt. has large use for all barches [sic] of Maine; and I shall be glad if Mr. Lawrence can be engaged in it on fair terms to himself and to us. Yours very truly

A. LINCOLN

[1] ALS, IHi. George W. Lawrence, of Warren, Maine, had been a delegate to the Chicago convention in 1860.

To Simon Cameron[1]

Hon. Sec. of War.   Executive Mansion
My dear Sir—   May 16. 1861

If possible, take the six Regiments now offered by Massachusetts. By their peculiar talent for taking care of themselves, they will give us less trouble in supplying them, than will most other troops. At all events give these gentlemen a hearing   Yours truly

A. LINCOLN

[1] ALS, IHi. On the bottom of the page is written, "Not agreed to for the present. Simon Cameron." The Massachusetts First, Second, Seventh, Ninth, Tenth, and Eleventh Regiments were later accepted. On May 6, Governor John A. Andrew had written Montgomery Blair ". . . I pray you claim and secure to us . . . the right to furnish six regiments . . . to march with the advancing column over the streets where our brothers poured out their blood. . . ." (William Schouler, *A History of Massachusetts in the Civil War*, I, 166). Blair to Lincoln, May 16, reads in part as follows: "The error in Meig's programme is common to the whole army and this is the reason why I have been so persistent

[370]

in seeking an outsider for a leader. The military look upon the contest as one between the whole people of the South and the people of the North. This is a fundamental and fatal error. . . . Nor do I think there is any disrespect to Genl. Scott involved in the President's adopting his own policy instead of Scott's in the management of the war. . . ." (DLC-RTL). See also Lincoln to Cameron, May 14, 1861, *supra*.

To Salmon P. Chase[1]

Executive Mansion, May 16, 1861.

My dear Sir: I have not at all considered the qualifications of applicants for appraiserships at New York. Mr. David Webb seems to understand that he has no opposition for one of the places.[2] If this is so, or, in any event, if you wish to appoint him, send me the commission.

Also send me a commission for Mr. George Dennison[3] as naval officer. This last I shall have to do, and I may as well do it at once. Yours truly,   A. LINCOLN.

[1] NH, VI, 273.   [2] David Webb was not appointed.
[3] Chase replied May 16, "Agreeably to your direction I send a Commission for Mr. Dennison; but I shall not fulfill my duty to you if I do not say that I fear, if you make this appointment, you will regret it.

"When it was first proposed . . . I felt that setting aside so many prominent men for a gentleman so little known . . . was of questionable expediency. . . . many of the most eminent and influential gentlemen of New York have expressed . . . such unfavorable opinions of Mr. Dn . . . that were the responsibility of decision mine, I should not put my name to the commission. . . . If Mr. Dn. is unjustly censured and your kindness prompts you to place him . . . is there not some other, less conspicuous, in which he may receive equal benefits & have the opportunity of proving himself now undervalued?" (DLC-RTL). See Lincoln to Chase, May 18, *infra*, for further developments in this case.

To Carl Schurz[1]

Hon. Carl Schurz   Washington, D.C.
My dear Sir: May 16. 1861

I have delayed so long to either Telegraph or write you, hoping to get the matter of which we spoke, into a satisfactory shape; but at last I have not succeeded. On Monday I was about to Telegraph you to proceed, but was arrested in it on the question of rank—that it would put you in command at Fortress Monroe.

Yesterday the New-York Committee were here; and their mission ended in their getting an order to move forward, from N.Y. city fourteen Regiments said to be there now—five to this city, and nine to Fortress Monroe. It did not occur to me till after I parted with the Committee, that probably your four german Regiments are included in this same fourteen. If so, they will either come here, or go to Fortress Monroe at once. I still hope you may be made Brig. Gen. of them; but I can not make it move smoothly just yet. Write, or Telegraph me when you receive this. Yours as ever

A. LINCOLN

[1] ALS, DLC-Schurz Papers. Schurz replied May 19, "I have just received your kind letter of the 16th instant. . . . The brigade is formed by the State board and consists of the 7th, 8th and 20th, all German regiments, and Ellsworth's Zouaves. The field-officers of the three German regiments have resolved to vote for me . . . and have addressed a letter to Colonel Ellsworth, informing him of their desire. . . . As far as Fortress Monroe is concerned, the difficulty about the rank seems to be removed by General Butler's promotion . . . ." (DLC-Nicolay Papers). Butler was promoted to major general of volunteers, May 16, 1861.

Memorandum: Military Arrests[1]

[c. May 17, 1861]

Unless the *necessity* for these arbitrary arrests is *manifest*, and *urgent*, I prefer they should cease. A. LINCOLN

[1] Copy, IHi-Nicolay and Hay Papers, IV, 5. The copy of U.S. Attorney Edward C. Carrington's letter, May— 1861, complaining that the military authorities were arresting, trying, and imprisoning citizens in the District of Columbia, bears also the copies of Lincoln's endorsement, General Joseph K. F. Mansfield's remarks, May 17, that he had ordered only two men into confinement, and General Scott's endorsement, May 18, stating that he had ordered only one Erastus Wood confined, as a spy.

To Francis P. Blair, Jr.[1]

Private

Hon. F. P. Blair   Washington D.C. May 18. 1861

My Dear Sir. We have a good deal of anxiety here about St. Louis. I understand an order has gone from the War Department to you, to be delivered or withheld in your discretion, relieving Gen. Harney from his command. I was not quite satisfied with the order when it was made, though on the whole I thought it best to make it; but since then I have become more doubtful of its propriety. I do not write now to countermand it; but to say I wish you would withhold it, unless in your judgement the necessity to the contrary is very urgent.

There are several reasons for this. We better have him a *friend* than an *enemy*. It will dissatisfy a good many who otherwise would be quiet. More than all, we first relieved him, then restored him, & now if we relieve him again, the public will ask, "why all this vacillation."

Still if, in your judgment, it is *indispensable* let it be so. Yours very truly   A LINCOLN

1 Copy, DLC-Nicolay Papers. On April 21, Brigadier General William S. Harney was relieved from command of the Department of the West. AGO *Special Orders No. 128*, May 8, revoked the previous order. On May 16, Lincoln approved General Scott's recommendation that Harney be placed on an indefinite leave of absence, and AGO *Special Orders No. 135*, again relieved Harney of command and granted the leave recommended. Further developments brought the letter signed by Lorenzo Thomas, May 27, *infra*.

To Salmon P. Chase[1]

Executive Mansion, May 18, 1861.

My dear Sir: The suggestions of your note accompanying the commission for Mr. Dennison[2] as naval officer at New York have been considered in the same spirit of kindness in which I know they were offered. They present the very difficulty which has embarrassed me from the first in the case: that Mr. Dennison has not the position in the public eye which would lead to the expectation of his receiving so high an office. I believe I have told you fully what it was, and is, that pressed me to appoint him: the urgent solicitation of an old friend[3] who has served me all my life, and who has never before received or asked anything in return. His (Mr. Dennison's) good character was vouched for from the start by many at New York, including Mr. Opdyke.

At length, when I was, as it were, in the very act of appointing him, Mr.——[4] made a general charge of dishonesty against him. I pressed him for particulars, and it turned out that Mr. Dennison in his business as a lawyer had got some printing done for his clients, becoming personally responsible for the work, and had not paid for it when dunned.[5] While this, if true, is certainly not to be commended, I believe the like might, in some cases, be proven upon me. They are a class of debts which our clients ought to pay, and when we are personally dunned for them we sometimes hang fire. Besides, Mr. Dennison went far toward a satisfactory explanation of one case; and while Mr. —— intimated that there were other cases, he did not specify them.

I consider that the charge of dishonesty has failed; and it now seems to me more difficult to change my purpose than if the charge had never been made. Yours as ever,   A. LINCOLN.

1 NH, VI, 274-75.
2 George Denison. See Lincoln to Chase, May 16, *supra*, n. 3.
3 See Lincoln to Robert Irwin, March 20, *supra*.
4 Parke Godwin to Lincoln, April 16: "It is exceedingly important that the

MAY 1 8, 1 8 6 1

appointment of Mr. Denison as Naval Officer at New York should be delayed. I think I can show that he is a dishonest man. . . ." (DLC-RTL).

⁵ Godwin to Lincoln, April 20: ". . . there has been upon the Ledger of Wm. C. Bryant Co. various charges for Job Printing ordered by Mr. Denison and delivered to him for which he has steadily refused to pay." (DLC-RTL).

Memorandum: Appointment of —— Monroe[1]

May 18, 1861

Let Mr. Monroe be appointed when it can be done consistently with previous committals. A. LINCOLN

[1] ADS, owned by John W. Wholihan, Jackson, Michigan. There is no record of appointment for "Mr. Monroe."

To Simon Cameron[1]

Hon. Sec. of War: Executive Mansion
My dear Sir: May 20, 1861
Col. Julian Allen, a Polish gentleman, naturalized, proposes raising a Regiment of our citizens of his nationality, to serve in our Army. He proposes getting them from the different States, without particular order, as can be most conveniently done, and organizing them here, so that they, as a Regiment, will hail from no particular State. Mr. Allen is highly recommended, as you will see by his testimonials. If he so raises and tenders a Regiment, I am in favor of accepting it, unless there be some objection which does not occur to me. Yours truly, A. LINCOLN.

[1] ALS, CSmH. Julian Allen was a Polish merchant of New York City. He received authority July 22, to raise a regiment of infantry, which was subsequently merged into the Morgan Rifles. There is no record of Allen's service in the Union army. This letter is misdated May 30 in Tracy, p. 185.

To Simon Cameron[1]

May 20, 1861

Please have the Regiments named within, mustered, and received; and orders given as to where they shall go. Please answer as to what you do. Also, please say whether any heavy guns are going forward to Cairo? A. LINCOLN
May 20. 1861.

[1] AES, IHi. Lincoln's note is written on the back of a telegram from Governor Richard Yates to Colonel John A. McClernand, May 18, 1861, which reported ". . . Six additional Regiments for three years or the war called for from Illi-

nois are ready. It is important they should be received immediately. . . ." There
is no reply from Cameron or any other official in the War Department, but see
Lincoln to McClernand, May 21, *infra*.

To Edwin D. Morgan[1]

His Excellency   Washington, D.C.
Gov. E. D. Morgan   May 20. 1861

My dear Sir: Yours of the 19th. is received. Your letter to the
Secretary of War I have not seen.

To not shirk just responsibility, I suppose I ought to admit that
I had much to do with the matter of which you complain.

The committee came here some time last week,[2] saying there
were fourteen Regiments in N.Y. city, not within the 38 you were
organizing; that *something must* be done with them,—that they
could not safely keep them longer, nor safely disband them. I could
not see—can not yet—how it could wrong you, or the Regiments
you were raising, for these 14 to move forward at once, provided
yours, too, should be received when ready. But aware of my own
ignorance in military matters, I sent to Genl. Scott to get his
opinion whether the thing could be safely done, both as to the
question of confusion, and also whether the Govt. could advan-
tageously keep and use the *whole*. His answer was that the *whole*
should come—of the 14[,]5 to come here, & 9 to Fortress Monroe. I
thought the whole difficulty was solved, and directed an order to be
made accordingly. I was even pleased with it; because I had been
trying for two weeks to begin the collecting of a force at Fortress
Monroe, and it now appeared as if this would begin.

Next day & after the committee had gone, I was brought to fear
that a squabble was to arise between you and the committee, by
which neither your Regiments nor theirs, would move in any
reasonable time; to avoid which, I wrote one of the committee—
Mr. Russell—to send them at once.[3]

I am very loth to do any wrong; but I do not see yet wherein
this was a wrong.

I certainly did not know that any Regiments especially under
your control were to be sent forward by the committee; but I do
not perceive the *substantial* wrong, even in such a case. That it may
be a *technical* wrong, I can readily understand—but we are in no
condition to waste time on technicalities.

The enthusiastic uprising of the people in our cause, is our great
reliance; and we can not safely give it any check, even though it
overflows, and runs in channels not laid down in any chart.

In ordering the 14 Regiments forward, no intimation was intended, that you were failing in activity, or in any duty. On the contrary, I acknowledge you have done, & are doing nobly; and for which I tender you my sincere thanks. Yours very truly

A. LINCOLN

1 ALS, N. Governor Morgan wrote May 19, 1861: ". . . the authority which has been given to the 'Union Defense Committee' to send fourteen Regiments from the city of New York . . . quite independent and irrespective of authority from the Executive of New York cannot fail to result in confusion and serious disaster. . . . (DLC-RTL). Hamilton Fish, chairman of the Union Defense Committee of New York, had been authorized by Cameron on May 15 to send ". . . to this city [Washington] five regiments and to Fort Monroe nine regiments. . . . Should the Governor decline to do so. . . ." (OR, III, I, 206). On May 20, Cameron wrote Simeon Draper: "The concluding words of my order to your committee were not intended to confer authority to send on troops independent of Governor Morgan, but . . . only in case of Governor Morgan's refusal. . . ." (*Ibid.*, p. 217).

2 The committee called on Lincoln May 15.

3 Lincoln's letter to Charles H. Russell, May 17, 1861, is presumably not extant.

Revision of William H. Seward to Charles Francis Adams[1]

Department of State,
Sir: Washington, May 21st 1861

Mr. Dallas in a brief dispatch of May 2d. (No. 333) tells us that Lord John Russell recently requested an interview with him on account of the solicitude which His Lordship felt concerning the effect of certain measures represented as likely to be adopted by the President. In that conversation the British Secretary told Mr. Dallas that the three Representatives of the Southern Confederacy were then in London, that Lord John Russell had not yet seen them, but that he was not unwilling to see them unofficially. He farther informed Mr. Dallas that an understanding exists between the British and French Governments which would lead both to take one and the same course as to recognition. His Lordship then referred to the rumor of a meditated blockade by us of Southern ports and a discontinuance of them as ports, of entry. Mr. Dallas answered that he knew nothing on those topics and therefore could say nothing. He added that you were expected to arrive in two weeks. Upon this statement Lord John Russell acquiesced in the

1 ALS-F, ISLA. Seward's draft bears Lincoln's suggestions for revision and Seward's own later revisions. No effort has been made to show all Seward's revisions. Passages or words deleted by Lincoln have been bracketed, and comments and insertions in Lincoln's hand have been italicized either in the text or in the footnote.

expediency of waiting for the full knowledge you were expected to bring.

Mr. Dallas transmitted to us some newspaper reports of Ministerial explanations made in Parliament.

You will base no proceedings on parliamentary debates farther than to seek explanations when necessary and communicate them to this Department. We intend to have a clear and simple record of whatever issue may arise between us and Great Britain.[2]

The President [is surprised and grieved] *regrets* that Mr. Dallas did not protest against the proposed unofficial intercourse between the British Government and the missionaries of the insurgents, [as well as against the demand for explanations made by the British Government].[3] It is due however to Mr. Dallas to say that our instructions had been given only to you and not to him, and that his loyalty and fidelity, too rare in these times, [among our late representatives abroad, are confessed and][4] *are* appreciated.

Intercourse of any kind with the so-called Commissioners is liable to be construed as a recognition of the authority which appointed them. Such intercourse would be none the less [wrongful] *hurtful* to us, for being called unofficial, and it might be even more injurious, because we should have no means of knowing what points might be resolved by it. Moreover, unofficial intercourse is useless and meaningless, if it is not expected to ripen into official intercourse and direct recognition. It is left doubtful here whether the proposed unofficial intercourse has yet actually begun. Your own [present] *antecedent* instructions are deemed explicit enough, and it is hoped that you have not misunderstood them. You will in any event desist from all intercourse whatever, unofficial as well as official with the British Government, so long as it shall continue intercourse of either kind with the domestic enemies of this country; [confining yourself simply to a delivery of a copy of this paper to the Secretary of State. After doing this][5] *when intercourse shall have been arrested for this cause,* you will communicate with this Department and receive further directions.

Lord John Russell has informed us of an understanding between the British and French Governments that they will act together in regard to our affairs. This communication however loses something of its value from the circumstance that the communication was withheld until after knowledge of the fact had been acquired by us from other sources. We know also another fact that has not yet

[2] *Leave out.*
[3] *Leave out, because it does not appear that such explanations were demanded.*
[4] *Leave out.*   [5] *Leave out.*

been officially communicated to us namely that other European States are apprized by France and England of their agreement and are expected to concur with or follow them in whatever measures they adopt on the subject of recognition. The United States have been impartial and just in all their conduct towards the several nations of Europe. They will not complain however of the combination now announced by the two leading powers, although they think they had a right to expect a more independent if not a more friendly course from each of them. You will take no notice of that or any other alliance. Whenever the European governments shall see fit to communicate directly with us we shall be as heretofore frank and explicit in our reply.

As to the blockade, you will say that by [the] *our own* laws [of nature] and *the laws [of nature and the laws]*[6] of nations this government has a clear right to suppress insurrection. An exclusion of commerce from national ports which have been seized by the insurgents, in the equitable form of blockade, is a proper means to that end. You will not insist[7] that our blockade is to be respected if it be not maintained by a competent force—but passing by *any immaterial question*[8] that question as not now a practical or at least an urgent one you will add that the blockade is now and it will continue to be so maintained, and therefore we expect it to be respected by Great Britain. You will add that we have already revoked the exequatur of a Russian Consul who had enlisted in the Military service of the insurgents and we shall dismiss or demand the recall of every foreign agent, Consular or Diplomatic who shall either disobey the Federal laws or disown the Federal authority.

As to the recognition of the so called Southern Confederacy it is not to be made a subject of technical definition. It is of course direct[9] recognition to publish an acknowledgment of the sovereignty and independence of a new power. It is direct recognition to receive its ambassadors Ministers agents or commissioners officially. A concession of belligerent rights is liable to be construed as a recognition of them. No one of these proceedings will [be borne] *pass unnoticed*[10] by the United States in this case.

Hitherto recognition has been moved only on the assumption that the so-called Confederate States are de facto a self sustaining

[6] The latter part of the insertion—"of nature and the laws"—has been crossed out, whether by Lincoln or Seward is uncertain.

[7] "Admit" is deleted and "not insist" inserted, by Seward.

[8] Seward deleted Lincoln's "any immaterial question" and added "that question as not now a practical or at least an urgent one."

[9] Lincoln's *"quasi"* changed by Seward to "direct" in both instances.

[10] Seward changed Lincoln's "unnoticed" to "unquestioned."

power. Now after long forbearance, designed to soothe discontent and avert the need of civil war, the land and naval forces of the United States have been put in motion to repress the insurrection. The true character of the pretended new State is at once revealed. It is seen to be a Power existing in pronunciamento only. It has never won a field. It has obtained no forts that were not virtually betrayed into its hands or seized in breach of trust. It commands not a single port on the coast nor any highway out from its pretended Capital by Land. Under these circumstances Great Britain is called upon to intervene and give it body and independence by resisting our measures of suppression. British recognition would be British intervention to create within our own territory a hostile State by overthrowing this Republic itself. [When this act of intervention is distinctly performed, we, from that hour, shall cease to be friends and (become once more, as we have twice before been), be forced to [become] enemies of Great Britain.][11]

As to the treatment of privateers in the insurgent service you will say that this is a question exclusively our own. We treat them as pirates. They are our own citizens, or persons employed by our citizens, preying on the commerce of our country. If Great Britain shall choose to recognise them as lawful belligerents, and give them shelter from our pursuit and punishment, the law of nations afford an adequate and proper remedy [and we shall avail ourselves of it.][12] *And while you need not to say this in advance, be sure that you say nothing inconsistent with it.*[13]

Happily, however Her Britannic Majesty's Government can avoid all these difficulties. It invited us in 1856 to accede to the declaration of the Congress of Paris, of which body Great Britain was herself a member, abolishing privateering everywhere in all cases and for ever. You *already* have our authority to propose to her our accession to that declaration. If she refuse to receive it it can only be because she is willing to become the patron of privateering when aimed at our devastation.

These positions are not elaborately defended now, because to vindicate them would imply a possibility of our waiving them.

[14] We are not insensible of the grave importance of this occasion.

[11] *Leave out.* Lincoln's "leave out" is also deleted and parentheses inserted to suggest a lesser deletion rather than the whole sentence.　　　[12] *Omit.*

[13] Lincoln's insertion has been crossed out.

[14] *Drop all from this line to the end, and in lieu of it, write "This paper is for your own guidance only, and not to be read, or shown to any one.["]* This suggestion was crossed out, presumably by Seward, and the remaining paragraphs remained in the communication. Seward incorporated Lincoln's "for your own guidance only," however, in two introductory paragraphs inserted at the beginning of the letter.

We see how upon the result of the debate in which we are engaged, a war may ensue, between the United States and one, two, or even more European nations. War in any case is as exceptionable from the habits as it is revolting from the sentiments of the American people. But if it come it will be fully seen that it results from the action of Great Britain, not our own, that Great Britain will have decided to fraternize with our domestic enemy either without waiting to hear from you our remonstrances and our warnings or after having heard them. War in defence of national life is not immoral, and war in defence of independence is an inevitable part of the discipline of nations.

The dispute will be between the European and the American branches of the British race. All who belong to that race will especially deprecate it; as they ought. It may well be believed that men of every race and kindred will deplore it. A war not unlike it between the same parties occurred at the close of the last century. Europe atoned by forty years of suffering for the error that Great Britain committed in provoking that contest. If that nation shall now repeat the same great error, the social convulsions which will follow may not be so long but they will be more general. When they shall have ceased it will, we think, be seen, whatever may have been the fortunes of other nations that it is not the United States that will have come out of them with its precious constitution altered or its honestly obtained dominion in any degree abridged. Great Britain has but to wait a few months and all her present inconveniences will cease with all our own troubles. If she take a different course she will calculate for herself the ultimate as well as the immediate consequences, and will consider what position she will hold when she shall have forever lost the sympathies and the affections of the only nation on whose sympathies and affections she has a natural claim. In making that calculation she will do well to remember that in the controversy she proposes to open we shall be actuated by neither pride, nor passion, nor cupidity, nor ambition; but we shall stand simply on the principle of self preservation and that our cause will involve the independence of nations and the rights of human nature.

I am, sir, respectfully your obedient servant,   W.H.S.

To Simon Cameron[1]

Hon. Sec. of War   Executive Mansion May 21. 1861
    My dear Sir   Why can not Col. Small's Philadelphia Regiment be received? I sincerely wish it could. There is something strange

about it. Give these gentlemen an interview, and take their Regiment. Yours truly   A. LINCOLN

¹ ALS, IHi. Colonel William F. Small's regiment was the Twenty-sixth Pennsylvania, organized shortly after Lincoln's election in 1860, accepted April 18, 1861, to report to Washington through Baltimore. Attacked by the mob at Baltimore, the regiment returned to Philadelphia. Maintained by private funds from April 20 to May 25, it was ordered into federal service with the muster dating back to May 5.

To John A. McClernand[1]

Hon. J. A. McClernand   Executive Mansion
My dear Sir: May 21. 1861
    I have just had the interview with Gen. Cameron. He says the six Illinois Regiments shall be received at once, and probably sent to Cairo—that he does not know, but will ascertain, whether heavy guns have gone to Cairo—that he thinks well of the proposition to buy the surplus produce on the Ohio[2]—and that he wishes to see you, and will admit you whenever you will send in your card.
    I wish you to go. Your Obt. Servt.   A. LINCOLN

¹ ALS, RPB. See Lincoln to Cameron, May 20, *supra*, in regard to the Illinois regiments.
² McClernand suggested that the government devise a plan to purchase surplus produce which the blockade deprived of its normal Southern outlets.

To Gideon Welles[1]

Hon. Sec. of Navy   Executive Mansion
My dear Sir   May 21, 1861
    The bearer of this—master Walter Trumbull—is a son of our Illinois Senator Trumbull. He wishes to be admitted into the Naval school, and I wish you may be able to oblige him. Please give him an interview, at all events. Yours very truly   A. LINCOLN

¹ ALS, owned by Charles W. Olsen, Chicago, Illinois. Walter Trumbull is listed as midshipman on probation at the Naval Academy as of September 30, 1863.

Approval of American Tract Society's Program of Distributing Books to Soldiers[1]

                                    Executive Mansion, May 22. 1861
    I approve Mr. Broughton's object as indicated by the within letter of Gov. Andrew.   A. LINCOLN

[1] ALS-F, THarol. Printed in facsimile on a broadside distributed by the American Tract Society, Lincoln's note is described as written upon the back of a letter from Governor John A. Andrew to Lincoln, May 18, 1861, introducing N. Broughton, Jr., of Boston, who wished to make arrangements for systematic distribution of religious books to the troops.

Memoranda:
Appointment of Charles H. Tillinghast[1]

Gen. James, of Rhode Island, wishes Charles H. Tillinghast, of N.Y. nephew of the Genl. to be a cadet at West-Point.
May 22d 1861.

Charles H. Tillinghast, already on the list for West-Point appointments, to be marked, as from Rhode-Island.
Gen. James, wants this.

[1] AD, DNA WR RG 94, U.S. Military Academy, 1861, No. 846, Box 79. The first memorandum is dated May 22, 1861, by a hand not Lincoln's. The second is undated. Charles T. James was an ex-senator from Rhode Island (1851-1857) and major general of the Rhode Island militia.

To Edwin D. Morgan[1]

Washington, May 22, 1861.
Governor E. D. Morgan, Albany, N.Y.: I wish to see you face to face to clear these difficulties about forwarding troops from New York.　　　　　　　　　　　　　　　　　　　　　A. LINCOLN.

[1] Tarbell (Appendix), p. 341. Governor Morgan replied May 24, 1861, that he had planned to visit Lincoln, but ". . . learning that Colonel [William B.] Franklin of the 12th Infy had been charged with duties at New York in relation to the movement of troops, I deemed it unnecessary." (DLC-RTL).

Remarks at Raising of the Flag
over the General Post Office Building[1]

May 22, 1861
The President, having advanced to the front of the platform, was enthusiastically greeted from the crowd. He said:—

SIR—Permit me to say, in response to your invitation, that I am very happy, upon this, as upon all occasions, to be an humble instrument in forwarding the very worthy object which you have expressed. I therefore shall take pleasure in performing the part assigned me upon this occasion, and I hope in a satisfactory manner. I suppose that extended remarks are not expected of me at this time, but that it is desired by all that we shall proceed at once to the work in hand, of raising our glorious national ensign to the proud and lofty eminence from which it is designed to have it wave. I am now ready to perform my part.

The ropes attached to the staff, and on which the flag was fastened, were then placed in the hands of the President, when, amid the most deafening applause from the crowd below, the flag was raised to its prominent position. There being but a slight breeze at the time of its reaching its place at the top of the staff, it remained for a moment or two motionless, when suddenly, a gentle wind rising from the north, its ample folds were extended to the breeze in a most graceful and beautiful manner, eliciting one universal outburst of applause from the assembled multitude, which was kept up for some time, as the flag continued waving its folds, extending in the direction of the South, as if offering to ensure protection to the advocates and upholders of the government and principles of which it was emblematical in that section of the country. This happy incident had the effect of eliciting the following appropriate remarks from the President:—

LADIES AND GENTLEMEN—I had not thought to say a word, but it has occurred to me that a few weeks ago the "Stars and Stripes" hung rather languidly about the staff all over the nation. So, too, with this flag, when it was elevated to its place. At first it hung rather languidly, but the glorious breeze came, and it now floats as it should. (Cries of "Good," and applause) And we hope that the same breeze is swelling the glorious flag throughout the whole nation.

¹ New York *Herald*, May 23, 1861. The report in the Washington *National Republican*, May 23, 1861, has slight verbal differences but is substantially the same.

To Edward Bates[1]

Hon. Attorney General.   Executive Mansion
My dear Sir: May 23. 1861
Please send me a commission for Joseph Casey, of Penn. as Judge of the court of claims, to fill the vacancy now existing. Yours truly
A. LINCOLN

¹ ALS, DNA GE RG 60, Papers of Attorney General, Segregated Lincoln Material.

To John A. Dahlgren[1]

Capt. Dahlgren.   Executive Mansion, May 23. 1861
My dear Sir   Allow me to introduce Col. J. A. McClernand, M. C. of my own District in Illinois. If he should desire to visit Fortress

Monroe, please introduce him to the Captain of one of the vessel[s] in our service, and pass him down and back. Yours very truly

A. LINCOLN

[1] ALS, ORB. Captain John A. Dahlgren was in command of the Washington Navy Yard and later became chief of ordnance for the Navy.

Memorandum: Appointment of —— Lewis[1]

May 23, 1861

Mr. Lewis, besides the recommendation of Mr. Barney, within, is introduced to me by Mr. Elisha Whittlesey,[2] who takes great interest in him. Let him be appointed as soon as he consistently can. A. LINCOLN

May 23, 1861

[1] Parke-Bernet Catalog 841, February 25, 1947, No. 157. Lincoln's memorandum appears, according to the catalog description, on the last page of a three-page petition for an army appointment, signed by John A. Dix, secretary of the Treasury during the last few weeks of Buchanan's administration, and appointed a major general of volunteers by Lincoln on May 16. Lewis has not been identified.

[2] Elisha Whittlesey of Ohio, first comptroller of the Treasury 1849-1857, reappointed by Lincoln to the same office.

To Edwin D. Morgan[1]

His Excellency   Washington, D.C.
Gov. E. D. Morgan.   May 23, 1861

My dear Sir   Will you please state to Gen. Walbridge[2] what are the substantial difficulties about the "fourteen regiments" coming forward? I very much wish to get this matter straight, without wrong to the public service, or to any individual. Yours very truly

A. LINCOLN

P. S. You can talk to Gen. W. confidentially.   A L.

[1] ALS, N. See also Lincoln to Morgan, May 20, *supra.*
[2] Probably Hiram Walbridge, a brigadier general of Ohio militia (1843) who was a New York merchant and ex-congressman (1853-1855).

To Simon Cameron[1]

If the Secretary of War can accept the Regiments named within, I shall be greatly gratified. A. LINCOLN

May 24 [26 ?], 1861

1 Angle, p. 273. Lincoln's endorsement is written on the back of a letter May 21, 1861, signed by the colonels commanding the six regiments of the first brigade of Indiana volunteers. The date may be May 26, as this same endorsement is listed in William D. Morley, Inc. Catalog, October 13, 1944, No. 272.

To Winfield Scott[1]

Lieutenant General Scott   Executive Mansion
My dear Sir   May 24. 1861

What think you of the propriety of yourself, or the more immediate commander—Genl. Mansfield,[2] as I understand—taking the occasion of occupying Alexandria & Arlington Heights, to make a proclamation to the citizens of those places, and vicinity, assuring them that they are not to be despoiled, but can have your protection, if they will accept it, and inviting such as may have left their homes, and business to return?

Mr. Nicolay will show you a Telegram, which will not displease you.[3] Your Obedient Servt.   A. LINCOLN

1 ALS-P, ISLA. Lincoln's suggestion was followed the next day, Charles W. Sandford, major general of New York militia, leading the movement.
2 Joseph K. F. Mansfield, in command of the Department of Washington.
3 The telegram has not been located.

To Ephraim D. and Phoebe Ellsworth[1]

To the Father and Mother of Col.   Washington D.C.
Elmer E. Ellsworth: May 25. 1861

My dear Sir and Madam, In the untimely loss of your noble son, our affliction here, is scarcely less than your own. So much of promised usefulness to one's country, and of bright hopes for one's self and friends, have rarely been so suddenly dashed, as in his fall. In size, in years, and in youthful appearance, a boy only, his power to command men, was surpassingly great. This power, combined with a fine intellect, an indomitable energy, and a taste altogether military, constituted in him, as seemed to me, the best natural talent, in that department, I ever knew. And yet he was singularly modest and deferential in social intercourse. My acquaintance with him began less than two years ago; yet through the latter half of the intervening period, it was as intimate as the disparity of our ages, and my engrossing engagements, would permit. To me, he appeared to have no indulgences or pastimes; and I never heard him utter a profane, or an intemperate word. What was conclusive of his good heart, he never forgot his parents. The honors he labored for so laudably, and, in the sad end, so gallantly gave his life, he meant for them, no less than for himself.

In the hope that it may be no intrusion upon the sacredness of your sorrow, I have ventured to address you this tribute to the memory of my young friend, and your brave and early fallen child.

May God give you that consolation which is beyond all earthly power. Sincerely your friend in a common affliction—

A. LINCOLN

[1] ALS, CSmH. Elmer E. Ellsworth was killed at Alexandria, Virginia, May 24. See Lincoln to Cameron, March 5, and to Ellsworth, April 15, *supra*, and notes. Ephraim D. Ellsworth acknowledged Lincoln's letter, June 19, 1861, with ". . . grateful thanks for your kindness to and interest you have shown in our beloved son. . . ." (DLC-RTL).

To Simon Cameron[1]

Hon. Simon Cameron   Washington D.C.
Sec. of War.   May 26th 1861.

Dear Sir,   I am very much inclined to accept Col. Einsteins Regiment and wish you would have it mustered into service as soon as possible if in any way consistent with our arrangements. Your truly   A. LINCOLN

[1] LS, DLC-Cameron Papers. Colonel Max Einstein's Twenty-seventh Pennsylvania, reorganized at Philadelphia after return from the Baltimore riots, was accepted and mustered in, May 30-31, 1861.

To Washington A. Bartlett[1]

Washington, May 27, 1861.

Col. W. A. Bartlett, New York: The Naval Brigade was to go to Fort Monroe without trouble to the Government, and must so go or not at all.   A. LINCOLN.

[1] Tarbell (Appendix), p. 341. Lincoln had received a communication from Bray & Merwin of New York, May 25, 1861: "We have recd an order from Col. Bartlett Naval Brigade for twenty five hundred pair shoes . . . drawers . . . socks . . . bandana handkerchiefs . . . shall we deliver them upon your authority. . . ." (DLC-RTL). Bartlett replied to Lincoln, May 27, "Merwin & Bray had no authority to telegraph to you about our contract . . . it was not our fault we could not have suspected it. . . . We are ready & will sail as ordered . . . without troubling you. Your letter & teleg[rap]h recd. . . ." (DLC-RTL). Lincoln's letter to Bartlett, presumably dated May 25, is not extant. Bartlett had been a lieutenant in the Navy, and served as the first American alcalde of San Francisco in 1846. In April, 1861, he organized a brigade of seamen, but there is no record of his service in the army in 1861.

To Simon Cameron[1]

Hon. Sec. of War   Executive Mansion
My dear Sir: May 27. 1861
    If there be any vacancy of a cadetship at West-Point, at the special request of Mr. Senator Harris, I wish to appoint Jared L. Rathborn to it, provided he fills the conditions. Yours truly
                          A. LINCOLN

[1] ALS, DNA WR RG 94, U.S. Military Academy, 1861, No. 695, Box 79. At request of Senator Ira Harris, Jared L. Rathbone was appointed from New York.

Lorenzo Thomas to William S. Harney[1]

Washington, D.C., May 27, 1861.

Sir: The President observes with concern that, notwithstanding the pledge of the State authorities to cooperate in preserving peace in Missouri, loyal citizens in great numbers continue to be driven from their homes. It is immaterial whether these outrages continue from inability or indisposition on the part of the State authorities to prevent them. It is enough that they continue to devolve on you the duty of putting a stop to them summarily by the force under your command, to be aided by such troops as you may require from Kansas, Iowa, and Illinois. The professions of loyalty to the Union by the State authorities of Missouri are not to be relied upon. They have already falsified their professions too often, and are too far committed to secession to be entitled to your confidence, and you can only be sure of their desisting from their wicked purposes when it is out of their power to prosecute them. You will therefore be unceasingly watchful of their movements, and not permit the clamors of their partizans and opponents of the wise measures already taken to prevent you from checking every movement against the government, however disguised under the pretended State authority. The authority of the United States is paramount, and whenever it is apparent that a movement, whether by color of State authority or not, is hostile, you will not hesitate to put it down.

    I am, sir, very respectfully your obedient servant,
               L. THOMAS, Adjutant-General.

[1] NH, VI, 288-89. That Lincoln drafted this letter for Adjutant General Thomas is possible, but the original has not been located. It is included in the present work on the basis of Nicolay and Hay's inclusion of it in the *Complete Works,* and in the absence of satisfactory evidence to the contrary.

To Carl Schurz[1]

May 27, 1861

If it will make no confusion, Let all the german Regiments be of those going to Fort-Monroe.

This will only, at most, transform, and not change the proportions going there and coming here.   LINCOLN

May 27. 1861.

[1] ALS, DLC-Schurz Papers. See Lincoln to Schurz, May 16, *supra.*

To Lorenzo Thomas[1]

Gen. Thomas,   Executive Mansion, May 27, 1861.

The three gentlemen who will hand you this note, belong to an Artillery Company at Baltimore who wish to get into the United States Service . . . and . . . if you advise it, I will receive them. I hate to reject any offer from what is called a Southern State. . . .

A. LINCOLN

[1] Tracy, p. 184. Concerning this fragmentary text, there is no available identification of the men involved, but the New York *Herald*, May 28, 1861, reports the Eagle Artillery of Baltimore accepted by the president. There is no official record of the acceptance of the Eagle Artillery, however, until July, 1863.

Endorsement: Order of Simon Cameron to Illinois and Indiana Regiments[1]

May 28, 1861.

Let this order be entered as it now stands, I holding for further consideration the subject-matter of what I have erased.

A. LINCOLN.

[1] OR, III, I, 240. Cameron's order (*ibid.*) is given as follows, with no indication of Lincoln's erasures:

"War Department, Washington, May 28, 1861.

"The six regiments of troops in Indiana and the six regiments in Illinois, all which are now in the service of the United States, and commonly called three-months' men, or any one or more of said regiments, may forthwith or as soon as practicable report their readiness to Major-General McClellan, and by, him, or under his order, be received in and attached to the longer service, commonly called three-years' men; provided that no officer or private is held under obligation to such change, and no one of said regiments shall be received into said longer service in which regiment more than one-fifth their number decline the change; and in cases of regiments received, the individuals declining, being not more than one-fifth of the whole, may be discharged at once, their places to be supplied as fast as possible by voluntary recruits. Any of the aforesaid regiments not being transferred to the longer service, according to the terms of the order, will remain in their present three-month service.

"By special order of the President: SIMON CAMERON,
Secretary of War."

Endorsement: Petition of Citizens
of Pekin, Illinois, for Pardon of James Foley[1]

May 28, 1861

The within Petitioners, are my intimate acquaintances, and are most respectable people. Will Judge Bates—Atty. General—please see whether their prayer *can* be granted?　　　A LINCOLN

May 28. 1861

[1] AES, ORB. James Foley was, according to the petition, a former resident of Pekin, Illinois, who had joined the army and had been convicted of murder. The document bears no other endorsements. Reverend Thomas J. Mooney, chaplain of the Sixty-ninth New York Militia, wrote Lincoln June 14, 1861, ". . . to present my most sincere and grateful thanks together with those of our worthy Colonel, and officers . . . for the clemency and great mercy which you have extended towards James Foley in commuting the sentence of death . . . to that of imprisonment. . . ." (DLC-RTL).

To Gideon Welles[1]

Hon: Secretary of the Navy　　　　　Executive Mansion
My dear Sir　　　　　　　　　　　　　May 28. 1861

A friend of mine, residing at Chicago, Illinois—Mr. C. Beckwith —has a lady-relative—Miss Elizabeth Smith—at St. Marks, in Florida, whom he much desires to have brought away from there; and he has been induced to think that some of our vessels connected with the blockade could effect this without much trouble. If this is practicable I shall be obliged if you will direct it to be done. Yours truly　　　　　　　　　　　　　　　A. LINCOLN

[1] ALS, DNA WR NB RG 45, Executive Letters, No. 153. Welles to Lincoln, August 7, 1861, encloses copies of the reports of naval officers who failed in their efforts to remove Miss Smith from the South (DLC-RTL).

To Winfield Scott[1]

[May 29, 1861]

For Lieut. Genl. Scott—

A few days ago I said to the commissioner of Indian affairs that I would appoint whoever he named for Superintendent of Indian affairs in Washington. The commissioner tells me he has intimated

[1] AE, DLC-RTL. Lincoln's incomplete endorsement appears at bottom of Scott to Caleb B. Smith, May 27, 1861, following Smith's endorsement concurring in Scott's recommendation, May 29. Scott's letter introduces the bearer Bion F. Kendall, a native of Maine resident in Washington Territory, who had ". . . executed a confidential mission for me of great danger & importance; taking him thro' nearly all the seceded states. . . ." and who wished to be superintendent of Indian affairs in Washington Territory. Kendall was appointed to the office, July 16, 1861.

To Edward Bates[1]

My Dear Sir   May 30. 1861

Will you do the favor to confer with Mr. Johnson and be preparing to present the argument for the suspension of the Habeas Corpus   Very respectfully yours   A. LINCOLN

The Honorable   I concur

Atty Genl.   William H. Seward

[1] LS-P, ISLA. The result of Reverdy Johnson's conference with Bates is not indicated in any immediate communication from Bates, but on July 5, 1861, the attorney general returned a twenty-six-page opinion, the gist of which was that if suspension was understood to mean ". . . a repeal of all power to issue the writ . . . none but Congress can do it. But if we are at liberty to understand the phrase to mean, that, in case of a great and dangerous rebellion, like the present, the public safety requires the arrest and confinement of persons implicated in that rebellion, I, as freely, declare the opinion that the President has lawful power to *suspend the privilege* of persons arrested under such circumstances." (DLC-RTL).

To Seventh Regiment of New York[1]

THE PRESIDENT returns his thanks to the "Seventh Regiment" of New York, for their delightful serenade of last night.

May 30, 1861

[1] Washington *Evening Star*, May 30, 1861.

To Lorenzo Thomas[1]

I wish Capt. Von Horn's company to be included in Hecker's Regiment from Chicago, Illinois.   A LINCOLN

May 30, 1861

[1] AES, DNA WR RG 94, Adjutant General, Letters Received, 202-P-1861. Lincoln's endorsement appears on John Von Horn to Lincoln, May 30, 1861, requesting inclusion of his company in Colonel Frederick Hecker's Twenty-fourth Illinois Volunteers.

To Salmon P. Chase[1]

Hon. Sec. of Treasury,   May 31, 1861

If it is determined, as I suppose, that Mr. Muller be appointed, let it be done at once; as by the above it appears to be necessary.

Yours truly,   A. LINCOLN

May 31, 1861.

[1] Tracy, p. 185. See Lincoln to Chase, May 9, *supra*, and note.

To Caleb B. Smith[1]

May 31, 1861

It is perceived within that Mr. Irvins' friends desire him to be Superintendent of Utah. Is there any such office, other than the Superintendent of Indian Affairs, which has already been filled? Hon's. Messrs Stratton & Nixon of N.J. present this paper to me.

May 31. 1861   A. LINCOLN

[1] ALS, DLC-Nicolay Papers. The accompanying document is no longer with Lincoln's note, and attempts to identify Irvin have failed. The persons presenting the request were John T. Nixon and John L. N. Stratton, representatives from New Jersey.

To Caleb B. Smith[1]

Executive Mansion. Washington 31st. May 1861

I hereby appoint Charles E. Mix to be acting Commissioner of Indian Affairs, during the temporary absence of the Commissioner from the Seat of Government.   ABRAHAM LINCOLN

[1] LS, DNA NR RG 75, Office of Indian Affairs, Letters Received, 1861, Miscellaneous, P-422. William P. Dole was commissioner of Indian affairs.

To Caleb B. Smith[1]

May 31, 1861

When I was a member of Congress a dozen years ago, I boarded with the lady who writes the within letter. She is a most worthy and deserving lady; and if what she desires can be consistently done, I shall be much obliged   I say this sincerely and earnestly.

May 31, 1861   A. LINCOLN

[1] ALS, ORB. Mrs. Ann G. Sprigg, widow of Benjamin Sprigg, kept a boarding house in 1848-1849 on First Street, E., between A Street, S. and East Capitol Street. No record has been found of Mrs. Sprigg's request. On the bottom of the page following Lincoln's note is the following:

"Hon Mr Smith:
"We boarded some months, with Mrs. Sprigg, & found her a most estimable lady & would esteem it a personal favor, if her request, could be granted.
                                                      "MRS. A. LINCOLN"

To Edward Bates[1]

Send up the commissions, according to the within request.

June 1, 1861.   A. LINCOLN

[391]

¹ AES, DNA GE RG 6o, Papers of Attorney General, Segregated Lincoln Material. Lincoln's endorsement appears on the back of Bates to Lincoln, June 1, 1861, "May I appoint for the Western District of Missouri . . . for Attorney Jonas J. Clark/for Marshal James O. Sitton? I have just gotten a telegram from our friend *S. T. Glover* requesting these appointments, & urging speed." Sitton is listed in the office named, as of September 30, 1861, but Robert J. Lackey is listed as attorney on the same date.

To Simon Cameron¹

Hon. Sec. of War.
My dear Sir:

Executive Mansion
June 1. 1861

Mrs. Capt. Burton is very desirous that her husband may be made a Colonel. I do not know him personally; but if it can be done without injustice to other officers of the Regular Army, I would like for her to be obliged. Yours truly   A. LINCOLN.

¹ ALS, DLC-Cameron Papers. Probably Captain Burton was Henry S. Burton of the Third Regiment of Artillery whose promotion to major, sent to the Senate December 6, 1861, was back-dated to May 14.

Memorandum:
Appointment of Edwin S. McCook¹

June 1, 1861

Edwin S. McCook, is excellently well recommended within for a Lieutenancy in the Regular Army, and I hope it can, without injustice to others be given him.   A. LINCOLN
June 1, 1861.

¹ AES-P, ISLA. Edwin S. McCook of Pekin, Illinois, attended the U.S. Naval Academy and served as midshipman 1854-1856. He was not appointed to the regular army, but raised a company and became captain in the Thirty-first Illinois Infantry, September 18, 1861.

Memorandum:
Appointment of William P. Jones, Jr.¹

This applicant hails from Connecticut, and is well recommended. Let him be placed on the list.   A. LINCOLN
June 3, 1861

¹ AES, DNA WR RG 94, U.S. Military Academy, 1861, No. 445, Box 78. Lincoln's endorsement is on the back of a letter of application from William P. Jones, Sr., New York City, June 2, 1861, recommending William P. Jones, Jr., of Stamford, Connecticut. There is no record of an appointment.

Memorandum:
Appointment of Charles L. Thomasson[1]

Let this case stand high for a chance.   A. LINCOLN

June 3, 1861

[1] AES, CSmH. Lincoln's endorsement is on the back of Thomasson to Lincoln, Louisville, Kentucky, May 20, 1861, on the bottom of which is a recommendation by Joshua F. Speed, for appointment of Thomasson as paymaster. He was not appointed to the regular army, but became a captain in the Fifth Kentucky Infantry.

To Simon Cameron[1]

June 4, 1861

I am personally acquainted with Dr. Prince, and know him to be of excellent private character, and a Surgeon of the highest reputation.   A. LINCOLN

June 4, 1861

[1] AES, DNA WR RG 107, Secretary of War, Personnel Appointments, Box 5. Lincoln's endorsement is on the back of Benjamin Norris to Nicolay, Pittsfield, Illinois, May 23, 1861, recommending Dr. David Prince of Jacksonville, Illinois. Dr. Prince was appointed surgeon with rank of major, August 3, 1861.

Reply to Don Marcelino Hurtado[1]

June 4, 1861

Mr. HURTADO: I receive with pleasure a Minister Plenipotentiary from the Republic of the Granadian Confederacy. Your country contains one of the principal highways of commerce and intercourse between the Atlantic and the Pacific States of this Union. The people of the two countries cannot, therefore, be strangers to each other; they must be friends, and in some measure allies. It shall be no fault of mine if they ever cease to be such.

The republican system of government, which has been adopted so generally on this continent, has proved its adaptation to what is the first purpose of government every where—the maintenance of national independence. It is my confident hope and belief that this system will be found, after sufficient trials, to be better adapted every where than any other to other great interests of human society—namely, the preservation of peace, order, and national prosperity. I sincerely hope that this may be the happy result of the experiment of the system in your country.

I bid you welcome, sir, to the society of the capital.

[1] Washington *Daily National Intelligencer*, June 5, 1861. Hurtado presented his credentials as commissioner and envoy extraordinary and minister plenipotentiary of Granada, and made a brief speech to which Lincoln replied.

To Simon Cameron[1]

Hon. Sec. of War   Executive Mansion
My dear Sir   June 5. 1861

Herewith I send a draft for an order giving Gen. McClland [McClellan] discretion to receive a particular company. There is no cheat about it. Mr. Sturges, who brings this to you is a man of large means, and of the highest character.

Inclosed also is Gen. Scott's note, substantially assenting to the order   Yours truly   A. LINCOLN

1 ALS, IHi. William Sturges, a Chicago banker, wrote to Lincoln, May 27, 1861, that his father, Solomon Sturges ". . . left this morning to visit Genl McClellan at Cincinnati. . . . He will see you latter part of the week. We are very anxious the Rifle Company he has armed uniformed & equipped & who have been in camp now for some time should have orders to go to Washington. . . ." (DLC-RTL). The Sturges Rifles went to West Virginia where the company served as McClellan's bodyguard, and upon McClellan's being given command of the Army of the Potomac were transferred to Washington. Search for the draft of Lincoln's order has been of no avail.

To Winfield Scott[1]

Private
Lieut. Genl. Scott   Executive Mansion   June 5. 1861

My dear Sir   Doubtless you begin to understand how disagreeable it is to me to do a thing arbitrarily, when it is unsatisfactory to others associated with me.

I very much wish to appoint Col. Meigs Quarter-Master General, and yet Gen. Cameron does not quite consent. I have come to know Col. Meigs quite well for a short acquaintance, and, so far as I am capable of judging I do not know one who combines the qualities of masculine intellect, learning and experience of the right sort, and physical power of labor and endurance so well as he.

I know he has great confidence in you, always sustaining so far as I have observed, your opinions, against any differing ones.

You will lay me under one more obligation, if you can and will use your influence to remove Gen. Cameron's objection. I scarcely need tell you I have nothing personal in this, having never seen or heard of Col. Meigs, until about the end of last March. Your obt. Servt,   A. LINCOLN

1 LS Copy, DLC-RTL. The copy is in John Hay's handwriting, signed by Lincoln. General Scott wrote Lincoln, [June 5], that "Nothing can be more kind than your courtesy to me in a matter so exclusively within your own competency as the appointment of a quarter Master general. . . . It costs me nothing . . . to support your preference. . . ." (DLC-RTL). Cameron to Lincoln, June 10, introducing Colonel Charles Thomas, the oldest officer in the quartermaster gen-

eral's department, to see Lincoln about his promotion, indicated that Lincoln faced a problem of seniority in the department (*ibid.*). Montgomery C. Meigs, however, was nominated to the Senate, July 13, 1861, to be quartermaster general with rank of brigadier general from June 10, 1861. On August 5, Lincoln communicated to the Senate ". . . an error in the date of the appointment of Brigadier-General Montgomery C. Meigs . . . by which his rank is dated after that of other officers, while his appointment was actually of earlier date. I therefore, to correct this error, renominate . . . to rank as such from the 15th day of May, 1861. . . ." (*Executive Journal*, XI, 543-44). One wonders, in view of the circumstances, whether the misdating of Meigs' appointment in the list of promotions sent to the Senate on July 13 was entirely inadvertent.

Testimonial Written for Ward H. Lamon[1]

Executive Mansion   June 5 1861

The bearer of this, W. H. Lamon, is entirely reliable, and trustworthy.   A. LINCOLN.

[1] ADS, CSmH. Lamon secured this testimonial to expedite his organization of a brigade of Unionist Virginians, who, forced to leave their homes, had concentrated in such places as Chambersburg, Pennsylvania, and Hagerstown, Maryland. See also Lincoln to Lamon, June 25, *infra*.

To Lorenzo Thomas[1]

If no good reason exists to the contrary I should like for Col. Hunter and Mr. Peck to be obliged in this matter.

A. LINCOLN
June 7, 1861

[1] ES, DNA WR RG 94, Adjutant General, Letters Received, 233-P-1861. Lincoln's endorsement is written in the left margin of David Hunter to Lorenzo Thomas, June 6, 1861, requesting appointment of "Lieut. W. W. Peck, of the 8th. Infantry . . . in the 3d. U.S. Cavalry." William W. Peck, son of Ebenezer Peck of Chicago, was not transferred to Hunter's regiment, but was promoted to captain in the Eleventh Infantry, as of May 14, 1861. See Lincoln to Lorenzo Thomas, June 19, *infra*.

To Simon Cameron[1]

Hon. Sec. of War.   Executive Mansion
My dear Sir   June 8. 1861

Hon. Emerson Etheridge[2] is now with me; and from the information he gives me I am induced to request that you send one thousand stand of Arms to Gen. Prentiss[3] at Cairo, to be delivered by him to such person or persons as he, Mr. Etheredge shall direct. Give Mr. Etheridge an interview, and he will fully explain to you. Yours truly   A. LINCOLN

¹ ALS, IHi.
² Emerson Etheridge of Dresden, Tennessee, ex-congressman (1853-1857, 1859-1861), became clerk of the House of Representatives (July 4, 1861–December 8, 1863).   ³ Brigadier General Benjamin M. Prentiss.

Endorsement: James Cooper to Lincoln¹

June 8, 1861

I can only say that if the War Department can receive this Regiment, I have no objection. I can not take upon my self personally the charge of providing them.   A. LINCOLN

June 8, 1861

¹ AES, RPB. Lincoln's endorsement is on the envelope of Brigadier General Cooper's letter, Camp Carroll, Maryland, June 7, 1861, asking Lincoln's intervention with the War Department to secure acceptance of the Second Maryland Regiment, raised by Captain J. P. Creager without proper authority from the War Department. Below Lincoln's endorsement Montgomery Blair wrote, "I can not understand why there shd be any trouble. The War Dept has called for volunteers from Md for the war & those proposed do not exceed the number called for as I understand it." Some of the companies of the Second Maryland Regiment were accepted in June and the rest in September, 1861.

Endorsement: James Cooper to Lincoln¹

I am sorry Mr. Cooper did not tell us *where* the Regiment is, named within; but still I think it ought to be received.

June 8, 1861   A. LINCOLN

¹ AES, The Rosenbach Company, Philadelphia and New York. This endorsement, or note, probably accompanied the endorsement *supra*, but became separated from the letter of James Cooper.

Memorandum:
Appointment of Christopher Robinson¹

[c. June 8, 1861]

Mr. Senator Simmons, insists that Hon Christopher Robinson of R.I must have something out of the remaining Diplomatic & Consular appointments, and I think Rhode Island should be remembered on that occasion.

Thinks of Chili

¹ AD, DLC-RTL. Lincoln appointed Robinson envoy *pro tem.*, to Peru on June 8 during the Senate recess, and the appointment was confirmed July 15, 1861.

To William H. Seward[1]

Hon. Sec. of State   Executive Mansion
My dear Sir   June 8. 1861

Mr. Wm. W. Richmond whose papers are inclosed within, is very anxious to be Consul to Paris. You know I expect you to name the man for that Consulate. You see he has a note from H. J. Raymond. Give him an interview. Yours truly   A. LINCOLN

[1] ALS, NAuE. For the confusion of the appointment of William W. Richmond of New Orleans with that of William B. Richmond of Memphis, see Lincoln's memoranda c. April 1, *supra*, and August 25, *infra*, and also Lincoln to Seward, August 7, *infra*.

To William H. Seward[1]

Hon. Sec. of State   Executive Mansion
May [*sic*] dear Sir: June 8. 1861

Some days ago, at my request, Mr. Hunter[2] sent a list of the then unfilled diplomatic appointments.

They were, Japan, China, Costa-Rica, Honduras, Venezuela, Paragua. Comr, Chili & Peru.

Japan, I understand, is not to be changed. China, suppose we hold open for Burlingame, if we have to send a different man[3] to Austria. Chili we have since given to Nelson.[4] This leaves open to be disposed of now, so far as I see, Costa-Rica, Honduras, Venezuela, Paragua, Peru, and Constantinople, the latter made vacant by the transfer of Gen. Webb[5] to Brazil.

[1] AL, NAuE.
[2] William Hunter, chief clerk in the State Department.
[3] Anson Burlingame, who was not acceptable to the Austrian government.
[4] Thomas H. Nelson of Indiana.
[5] James W. Webb. The vacancies were filled as follows: Costa Rica, Charles N. Riotte of Texas; Honduras, Hezekiah G. Wells of Michigan; Venezuela, Henry T. Blow of Missouri; Paraguay, Charles A. Washburne of California; Peru, Christopher Robinson of Rhode Island; Constantinople, Edward J. Morris of Pennsylvania.

To Gideon Welles[1]

June 8, 1861

Herewith is a letter of Col. Fremont which contains some information I suppose your Department ought to have. Yours very truly
A. LINCOLN.

[1] Stan. V. Henkels Catalog 1342, January 4, 1924, No. 48c. Frémont was in London at the time and wrote to Francis P. Blair, Sr., May 24, 1861, about the purchase of war steamers by representatives of the Confederacy (Allan Nevins, *Frémont, Pathmarker of the West*, p. 475).

Endorsement:
William Nelson to William H. Seward[1]

[June 9? 1861]

The suggestions within made are approved. Let directions be given
accordingly.   A. LINCOLN.

[1] OR, I, LII, I, 161. Lieutenant William Nelson, U.S. Navy, in charge of
gunboats on the Ohio, wrote to Seward from New York, June 9, 1861, enclosing
a letter received from Mr. Larz Anderson of Cincinnati in which Anderson de-
precated the unit known as the Kentucky Brigade, organized at Cincinnati.
". . . They are not Kentuckians, but an organization gotten up in order that
its officers might be mustered into the service. . . . To send these men to Louisville will do the Union cause a most serious injury. . . . May I ask you to have
this order reconsidered." Lieutenant Nelson was appointed brigadier general of
volunteers in September, 1861.

To Simon Cameron[1]

Hon. Sec. of War   Executive Mansion
My dear Sir   June 10, 1861

If there is any vacancy of a cadetship, for West-Point, which I
have to fill, please give it to James M. Marshall, son of Hon. T. A.
Marshall, of Illinois. Yours truly   A. LINCOLN

[1] ALS, DNA WR RG 94, U.S. Military Academy, 1861, No. 569, Box 79.
Thomas A. Marshall wrote Lincoln, April 14 and May 16, 1861, asking the appointment for his son, and incidentally a brigadier generalship for himself (DLC-
RTL). James M. Marshall was in the fourth class at West Point as of September
30, 1861.

To Simon Cameron[1]

Hon. Sec. of War   Executive Mansion
My dear Sir   June 10– 1861

Please let Col. Montgomery C. Meigs be appointed Quarter-
Master-General. Yours very truly   A. LINCOLN

[1] ALS, owned by Charles W. Olsen, Chicago, Illinois. Concerning Meigs' appointment, see Lincoln's letter to Winfield Scott, June 5, *supra*.

To Simon Cameron[1]

Hon. Sec. of War   Executive Mansion
My dear Sir   June 10, 1861

I am sure that I some time ago, recommended Mr. William Patten, a Lieut. in the N.Y. 7th. to be a Paymaster in the Army; and

I still wish him to be remembered, according to the date of that recommendation. Yours truly   A. LINCOLN

[1] ALS-P, ISLA. William Patten was appointed additional paymaster, June 1, 1861.

To John A. Dahlgren[1]

Capt. Dahlgren,   Executive Mansion
My dear Sir   June 10. 1861
    You have seen Mr. Blunt's new gun. What think you of it? Would the Government do well to purchase some of them? Should they be of the size of the one exhibited? or of different sizes? Yours truly   A. LINCOLN

[1] ALS, ORB. On the envelope Lincoln wrote "Will Capt. Dahlgren please see Mr. Blunt?" See also Lincoln's endorsement, *infra*. Orison Blunt was a leading New York Republican associated with J. G. Syms in the manufacture of guns. In 1862 Blunt made for the U.S. Government a small lot of Enfield pattern rifles, which may be the gun referred to by Lincoln. See Stephen Van Rensselaer, *American Firearms* (1947), and Claud E. Fuller and Richard D. Stewart, *Firearms of the Confederacy* (1944).

Endorsement: John A. Dahlgren to Lincoln[1]

I saw this gun myself, and witnessed some experiments with it; and I really think it worthy the attention of the Government.
June 10, 1861   A. LINCOLN

[1] AES, owned by Wilson F. Harwood, Washington, D.C. Lincoln's endorsement is on the back of Dahlgren's reply to Lincoln's letter of June 10, *supra*, "I have seen Mr Blunt's Gun and was much pleased with it. I think we should have some of them . . . for the present emergency it would be well to adhere to the dimension now constructed."

Endorsement:
Appointment of James B. M. Potter[1]

Respectfully referred to the Secretary of War for his consideration.   A. LINCOLN
    June 10, 1861.

[1] AES, RPB. Lincoln's endorsement is written on the back of Governor William Sprague to Lincoln, June 8, requesting appointment of "my friend General James B. M. Potter" as paymaster in the Regular Army. See Lincoln to Cameron June 11, *infra*, for further developments.

To George B. McClellan[1]

Maj. Gen. McClellan   Washington, Dec. [*sic*]
My dear Sir   June 10. 1861

My friends, Hon. T. A. Marshall, and Hon. A. W. Mack, the bearers of this, I presume are not wholly unknown to you. They are two of our Illinois State Senators, residing respectively at Coles & Kankakee counties. They came here as the representatives of a Company, including themselves, seeking a contract, or contracts, for furnishing provisions for the Army. Fnding that officers of the proper Departments are with you for supplying the West, they now propose to call on you, and them, for the same object. I can do no more than to give assurance that any contract made with them would be faithfully complied with on their part; and that I hope they may obtain some such, on fair and just terms to the government and themselves. They are my friends whom I would be pleased to see obliged. Yours very truly   A. LINCOLN

[1] ALS, DLC-McClellan Papers. Thomas A. Marshall wrote Lincoln, June 16, 1861, "I fear . . . we will fail in accomplishing any thing in the way of a contract. May I not then ask you . . . to make me a brigadier. . . ." (DLC-RTL). Alonzo W. Mack was a banker at Kankakee, Illinois.

Order for Issue of Bonds for Use
of Delaware Indians[1]

June 10, 1861

Whereas, by the treaty of Saxcoxieville, amended by the United States Senate, and finally ratified by the President of the United States on the 22nd. day of August, 1860 a principal object of both parties was the construction of a certain contemplated Railroad therein named; and, to that end, the Leavenworth, Pawnee, and Western Railroad Company were to pay into the United States Treasury, in gold or silver coin, a sum of money afterwards ascertained to be $286,742.15 as the appraised value of certain lands in Kansas belonging to the Delaware tribe of Indians, which sum of money, after expending a sufficient part of it to enable the Indians to commence agricultural pursuits under favorable circumstances, was to be, by the President, for said Indians, invested in safe, and profitable stocks. And whereas the said Railroad Company is not able to pay said sum of money within time, according to said treaty; and whereas the President is of opinion that it is not for the interest of either party that said object of the treaty shall fail;

but not knowing what would be the desire of said Indians on this point; nor knowing whether any part of said sum would be needed to enable the Indians to commence agricultural pursuits under favorable circumstances, but supposing it probable that no part of it would be so needed, as said Indians now have over fifty thousand dollars lying idle in the United States Treasury, therefore

It is directed by the President that said Railroad Company, may execute their Bonds, with interest-warrants, or coupons attached, according to the forms hereto annexed, the principal of which Bonds shall amount to the aggregate sum of $286,742.15 and deposite the same with Archibald Williams of Kansas, hereby appointed to receive and receipt for the same, to be by him transmitted to the Commissioner of Indian Affairs for the use of said Indians; and also shall, in due and proper form, execute, a mortgage upon one hundred thousand acres of the land contemplated in, and by said treaty, to aid in the construction of said Railroad, the said one hundred thousand acres to be the lands designated in the letter of the Commissioner of Indian Affairs to the Secretary of the Interior, dated May 29th. 1861.

Said mortgage to be conditioned for the full payment of said Bonds, both as to interest and principal, and that on any failure to pay either when due, all right and interest of said Railroad Company in and to said mortgaged land, and also to all such of said land not mortgaged, as shall not at that time, be earned and patented, according to said treaty, shall be forfeited, and said land again become the absolute property of the United States in trust for said Indians; and said mortgaged lands to be in no event patented to said until said Bonds, principal and interest shall be fully paid. And upon said Bonds being so made and deposited, and said mortgage being so executed, and duly recorded in Leavenworth county, Kansas, all matters, so far as not necessarily varied by this arrangement, shall proceed in conformity to said treaty, as if the money had been paid by said Railroad Company, and had been invested by the President in said Railroad Bonds. Provided always that this arrangement shall be of no effect, until Archibald Williams, Judge of the United States Court for the District of Kansas, shall have indorsed a certificate upon this paper, that he has carefully examined the same, and also the Bonds and mortgage offered in compliance with its provis[ions], and has found that Bonds, and mortgage do in fact, comply with, and fulfil said provisions; and also that he has had before him, the chiefs and head men named in said treaty, as John Connor, Sax-cox-ie, Ne-con-he-con, and Rock-a-to-wha, and has fully explained to them the nature and effect of this departure from the terms of said treaty, and that they freely assented to the same.   ABRAHAM LINCOLN.

June 10. 1861.

¹ ADS, DNA FS RG 11, General Records of the U.S. Government, No. 317, "Treaty with the Delawares at Leavenworth City, Kansas, July 2, 1861." The order as reproduced is entirely in Lincoln's handwriting, and his endorsement "Approved, as forms, June. 10. 1861. A. Lincoln" appears on the accompanying forms of bonds and interest warrants. See Lincoln to the Senate, July 19, *infra*.

To Simon Cameron¹

Washington, June 11. 1861.

The Government has already accepted ten Regiments from the State of Indiana. I think at least six more ought to be received from that state. Two to be those of Col. James W. McMillan & Col. William L. Brown, and the other four to be designated by the Governor of the State of Indiana; and to be received into the volunteer service of the U.S. according to the "Plan of organization," in the General Order of the War Department No. 15—when they report to Major General McClellan, in condition to pass muster according to that Order. And, with the approval of the Secretary of War to be indorsed hereon, and a copy left in his Department, I direct that the whole six, or any small number of said Regiments be received.   A. LINCOLN.

¹ ALS, RPB. On the same day Cameron communicated to Governor Oliver P. Morton, Lincoln's call for six additional regiments, two of them commanded by Colonel William L. Brown and Colonel James W. McMillin (OR, III, I, 265). Morton to Lincoln, June 19, 1861, protested Lincoln's appointment of colonels: "Without intending to cast any reflections upon the character or fitness of the men appointed, I beg leave to state that I know of no reason making it necessary to take the appointing power from the Executive of the State. . . ." (DLC-RTL). Cameron to Morton, June 23, assured the governor that he regretted the embarrassment, ". . . nothing could have been further from the intention of the President or of this Department. . . ." (OR, III, I, 291).

To Simon Cameron¹

Hon. Sec. of War.   Executive Mansion
My dear Sir   June 11. 1861

Do please give these Pennsylvania friends of yours a chance for One Regiment. Say to them, as has been said to some others—"Present your Regiment in working form, and it will be received." Yours truly   A. LINCOLN

¹ ALS, DLC-Cameron Papers.

To Simon Cameron[1]

June 11, 1861

I have just inclosed to you the recommendation of Gov. Sprague that Gen. James B. M. Potter, be appointed a Paymaster. Immediately afterwards, the Paymaster General called, protesting, as I wrote you, against all these appointments being made from civil life. He said, however, there will be a large number of these appointments, to be made for the volunteers. Can we not fill the first two from the Regular Army, & then give Gen. Potter a chance? We owe Rhode-Island and Gov. Sprague, a good deal, because they give us such good troops, and no trouble.

June. 11. 1861

A. LINCOLN

[1] AES, RPB. Lincoln's endorsement is written on one side of a scrap of paper, the other side of which bears Lincoln's note of March 27, 1862, *infra*, concerning Potter's transfer to the Regular Army. Potter was appointed additional paymaster of Volunteers, June 1, 1861, and on July 15, 1864, was appointed major and paymaster in the Regular Army.

To William P. Dole[1]

Hon. W. P. Dole   Executive Mansion
Comr. of Ind. Affrs.   June [c.11], 1861

My dear Sir   Some time ago I directed you to designate a suitable person to be Superintendent of Indian Affairs in Washington Territory, saying I would appoint the person you would so designate. You designated Anson Dart; and I now have the following reasons for not appointing him all coming to my knowledge since I gave you the direction mentioned.

1st.   A member of the present Cabinet tells me that during Genl. Taylor's administration Dart distinctly tendered money to him for his influence to get an office from Gen. Taylor.

2nd.   A member of the present H.R. from Wisconsin writes me over his own name that Dart is an immoral and dishonest man; and that if nominated, he will go before the Senate and procure his rejection if possible.

3rd.   One of the Senators from Oregon tells me that Dart's character is very bad in that county; that he is universally understood out there to have left his family at home, and kept a prostitute while there; and that, if nominated, he will, in the Senate, procure his rejection if possible.

4th.   The other Senator from Oregon tells me Dart's character is very odious and bad in that county; and that Dart, last winter, distinctly proposed to him that if he would procure his appoint-

[403]

ment to the Oregon Indian Superintendency, he would give him a thousand dollars the day the appointment should be made, and five hundred a year, as long as he should hold the office.

I presume you knew nothing of these things; and that neither you or I could knowingly be for such a man. Yours truly

A. LINCOLN

1 ALS copy or draft, DLC-RTL. The date of this letter must have been on or after June 11, for Lincoln refers to the letter from Representative John F. Potter, June 11, 1861, maintaining that Anson Dart of Wisconsin, former superintendent of Indian affairs in Oregon (1850-1853) ". . . is in every way unfit for that or any other position. . . . And if his appointment shall be made, I will go before the Senate and there protest. . . ." (DLC-RTL). See Lincoln to Winfield Scott, [May 29], *supra*, and note concerning the appointment of Bion F. Kendall.

To Henry W. Hoffman[1]

Collector at Baltimore   Executive Mansion
My dear Sir: June 11. 1861

Can you not give Mr. Balloch[2] the Inspectorship he desires? I shall be obliged if you will. Yours truly   A. LINCOLN

1 ALS, DLM.   2 "Mr. Balloch" has not been identified.

To Simon Cameron[1]

June 12, 1861

With the concurrence of the Secretary of War, and also of the Governor of Massachusetts, with the evidence of the latter the same is in ready condition to move, I direct that the Regiment within mentioned, be mustered into the service of the United States.

June 12. 1861.   A. LINCOLN

1 AES, IHi. Lincoln's endorsement is written on the back of a letter from Roman Catholic Bishop John B. Fitzpatrick of Boston, June 11, 1861, recommending that the Fourteenth Massachusetts, a regiment composed largely of Irish, be accepted by the government. Cameron's endorsement below Lincoln's is as follows: "I approve this order on the condition that this regiment appear at Harrisburg Penna . . . in *ten* days from tomorrow." The regiment was mustered in July 5, 1861, and later became the First Massachusetts Heavy Artillery.

To Simon Cameron[1]

June 12, 1861

I think Joseph J. Reynolds, of Indiana, ought to be a Brigadier General, and, perhaps, the thing done at once. He is a West-Point man, and is well recommended, particularly by the Governor of Indiana.   A. LINCOLN

June 12, 1861.

1 AES, DLC. Lincoln's endorsement is written on the back of a letter from Governor Oliver P. Morton to Lincoln, June 9, 1861, authorizing the bearer, "Hon. A. S. White . . . to ask the appointment of Gen Joseph J. Reynolds as Brig General. . . . I have already in two despatches asked for his appointment but have received no answer. . . ." Joseph J. Reynolds' appointment, dating from May 17, was submitted to the Senate July 29, and confirmed August 5, 1861.

To Simon Cameron[1]

Hon. Sec. of War—   Executive Mansion
My dear Sir: June 12, 1861

Hon. John Van Dyke, Hon. W. A. Newell, and Hon Courtlandt Parker, all of New-Jersey, now present, ask that Moses F Webb, of their State be made a Pay-Master in the Army. This is a good recommendation; and I think N.J. is entitled to that much. Yours truly   A. LINCOLN.

1 ALS, DNA WR RG 107, Secretary of War, Personnel Appointments, Box 6. The recommendation of New Jersey congressman William A. Newell, Newark attorney Courtland Parker, and Judge John Van Dyke of the New Jersey Supreme Court was followed, Moses F. Webb being appointed additional paymaster, August 5, 1861. Lincoln's letter is accompanied by an undated letter from Senator Edward D. Baker to Cameron, making the same recommendation.

To Simon Cameron[1]

Hon. Secretary of War.   Executive Mansion, June 13, 1861.

My dear Sir: I think it is entirely safe to accept a fifth regiment from Michigan, and with your approbation I should say a regiment presented by Col. T. B. W. Stockton, ready for service within two weeks from now, will be received. Look at Colonel Stockton's testimonials. Yours truly,   A. LINCOLN.

1 OR, III, I, 269. Colonel Thomas B. W. Stockton's Sixteenth Michigan Volunteers were accepted and left Detroit for Washington on September 16, 1861.

To Simon Cameron[1]

Hon. Secretary of War: Executive Mansion, June 13, 1861.

My dear Sir: There is, it seems, a regiment in Massachusetts commanded by Fletcher Webster, and which Hon. Daniel Webster's old friends very much wish to get into the service. If it can be received with the approval of your Department and the consent of the Governor of Massachusetts I shall indeed be much gratified. Give Mr. Ashmun a chance to explain fully. Yours truly,

A. LINCOLN.

1 OR, III, I, 269. Colonel Fletcher Webster's Twelfth Massachusetts Regiment was mustered into federal service June 26, 1861.

To Simon Cameron[1]

Hon. Sec. of War   June 13, 1861

Please say to Col. A. T. McReynolds, that when he will present the Cavalry Regiment according to the within authority they will be received under him as they would have been under Carl Schurz.

June 13, 1861   A. LINCOLN

[1] Copy, ISLA. Lincoln's endorsement is written on the back of Schurz to Major Andrew T. McReynolds, June 5, 1861, requesting McReynolds to take command of the First New York Cavalry. Schurz wrote, "Being ordered by the President to leave for my diplomatic post at Madrid I am obliged to dissolve my connection with the Cavalry-Regiment. . . . I would invite you to see the authorities at Washington . . . inducing them to ratify this transfer of authority."

To Simon Cameron[1]

Hon. Sec. of War: Executive Mansion
Dear Sir   June 13, 1861

You intimated to me, as I remember, some doubt of Col. Riker's Regiment of Anderson Zouaves being a reality. Col. Baker[2] assures me that he personally knows it is a reality; and being so, with the consent of the Governor of New-York, I desire that it be received.

Yours truly   A. LINCOLN

[1] ALS, IHi. Colonel John L. Riker's regiment, designated the Sixty-second New York Infantry was mustered into federal service June 30–July 1, 1861.

[2] Probably Senator Edward D. Baker of Oregon, who was made a brigadier general of Volunteers in July, with appointment dating from May 17.

To Caleb B. Smith[1]

Hon. Sec. of Interior   Executive Mansion
My dear Sir: June 13. 1861

Col. Baker was with me yesterday; and herewith I return you his list for Oregon appointments.[2] Please make out and send me Commissions according to it. You see at the foot of the list on the back of the paper he has added one in his own hand writing. Put it in with the rest. Yours truly   A. LINCOLN

[1] ALS, DNA NR RG 48, Applications, Indian Agencies, etc., Oregon, Box 1267.

[2] Senator Edward D. Baker's accompanying list, under date of April 8, 1861, is as follows: B. J. Pengra, surveyor general; William T. Matlock, receiver at Oregon City; William A. Starkweather, register at Oregon City; John Kelly,

register at Roseburg; George E. Briggs, receiver at Roseburg; William H. Rector, superintendent of Indian affairs; William H. Barnhart, William Logan, and Charles Hutchins, Indian agents. The appointments were made as listed.

To Simon Cameron[1]

Hon. Sec. of War   Executive Mansion
My dear Sir   June 14. 1861
 Let Hon. John A. Dix be a Major General of Volunteers. Let Captain John Pope of the U.S.A. and Hon. Stephen A. Hurlbut of Ills. each be a Brigadier General, of (Illinois) volunteers. I understand Gen. Scott wishes an officer now in the Army by the name of [blank] Rosencrantz,[2] to be a Brigadier General in the new Regular Army; and if so, let it be done. Yours truly A. LINCOLN

[1] ALS, DNA WR RG 94, Adjutant General, Letters Received, 222-P.
[2] "William S. Rosecrans" is written on the bottom of the letter in a different hand. Rosecrans' appointment was made dating back to May 16, 1861.

Memorandum: Appointment of John Pope and Stephen A. Hurlbut[1]

My direction to have Pope & Hurlbut appointed Brigadier Generals seems to have been in point, so far as relates to the within.
June 14. 1861   A. LINCOLN

[1] AES, DLC-Cameron Papers. Lincoln's endorsement is written on the back of a telegram received from Governor Richard Yates of Illinois, June 14, 1861: "It is certainly the design of the secessionists of Missouri to attempt the immediate expulsion of the federal troops from that state   This renders the appointment of the superior officers in this state a necessity."

To Salmon P. Chase[1]

June 15, 1861
To the Secretary of the Treasury of the United States:
 You will please issue a Warrant to Wm. H Carryl and Brother for the sum of Seven Thousand Five Hundred dollars for the purpose of furnishing the President's House, in accordance with the act of Feb. 20. 1861.   ABRAHAM LINCOLN.
Executive Mansion
 June 15. 1861

[1] LS, DNA RG 217, General Accounting Office. The letter accompanied a bill rendered by "Wm. H. Carryl & Bro.," May 29, 1861, in the amount of $7,500, for furnishings for the Executive Mansion, which Lincoln approved and referred to Chase on June 17.

Endorsement: John A. Andrew
to Hiram Walbridge[1]

With the concurrence of the Secretary of War, let the ten Regiments named within be called for and accepted.

June 15, 1861.   A. LINCOLN

[1] AES, DLC-Cameron Papers. Governor Andrew wrote General Walbridge, June 12, 1861, ". . . if you can procure—in addition to the last requisition upon this state for six regiments . . . a further requisition for ten Regiments thoroughly armed, equipped, clothed, and provided with tents, baggage train, rations, and subsistence stores—these advances will be made by this state . . . within forty days from the reception of the order here. . . ." Cameron to Walbridge, June 17, 1861, instructed Walbridge to ". . . advise Governor Andrew that the necessary requisition will immediately be made. . . ." (OR, III, I, 275.)

Endorsement: Charles H. Farrell
to Simon P. Hanscom[1]

If this Regiment is such as represented within, I think it ought to be accepted.   A. LINCOLN

June 15, 1861

[1] AES, The Rosenbach Company, Philadelphia and New York. Charles H. Farrell of the New York *Herald* wrote Simon P. Hanscom of the Washington *National Republican*, June 12, 1861, recommending that "Colonel Joachim Maidof the commandant of the Eleventh Regiment, (Washington Rifles) New York State Troops" and his regiment be accepted for the period of six months. The Eleventh New York was not mustered into federal service until June, 1862.

To Edward Bates[1]

Hon. Attorney General   Executive Mansion
My dear Sir: June 17. 1861.

You remember Allen A. Burton was appointed an Associate Justice of the Supreme Court of Dakota Ty. Since then I have given him a different place; and the judgeship of course becomes vacant. I now will thank you if you will send me a Commission for Joseph L. Williams, of Tenn. to fill the vacancy in said Associate Judgeship in Dakota Territory. Yours very truly   A. LINCOLN

[1] ALS, DNA GE RG 60, Papers of Attorney General, Segregated Lincoln Material. Allen A. Burton of Lancaster, Kentucky, was appointed minister to New Granada, and Joseph L. Williams, ex-congressman (1837-1843) of Knoxville, Tennessee, received the Dakota judgeship.

[408]

To Simon Cameron[1]

Hon. Sec. of War   Executive Mansion
My dear Sir   June 17. 1861

After examining the list presented for Officers of the Addition to the Regular Army, I deem it a little unfortunate, that they are drawn from the different States in such unequal proportions, a single State furnishing nearly one fourth of the whole; still I think we have not time now to break up and reconstruct the card. The few modifications I desire to make are as follows:

1st. Let Col. Robert Anderson be appointed a Brigadier General; and Col. William H. Emory take his place on the card, as Colonel of the 15th Regiment of Infantry.[2]

2nd. I wish Oliver L. Shepherd, now Captain in the 3rd Infantry, and Major by brevet, to be a Lieutenant Colonel, you to find the place for him.[3]

3rd. I wish Abner Doubleday, now a Captain in the 1st Artillery, to be a Major in the similar corps if possible, you to find a place for him.[4]

4th. I wish Adam J. Slemmer now a first Lieutenant in same Regiment last mentioned, to be a Major in a similar corps, if possible, you to find a place for him.[5]

5th. If he desires it, I would also like for Capt. Theodore Talbot, who escorted my messenger to Gov. Pickens last April, to be a Major.[6]

6th. Because of his relationship to the late Senator Douglas, I wish James Madison Cutts, Jr. to be a Captain in some part of this new corps.[7]

7th. At the very urgent solicitation of Hon Mr. Van Wyck, I wish Horatio B. Reed to be a Second Lieutenant in this new corps.[8]

8th. I also wish Francis E. Brownell, who stood by Col. Ellsworth at his death, to be a Second Lieutenant in this corps.[9] Yours truly

A. LINCOLN

[1] Angle, p. 277; ALS-F, ISLA (first page only). The list of Regular Army promotions went to the Senate July 31, 1861, the date of appointment being designated as May 14, 1861.

[2] Lieutenant Colonel William H. Emory was appointed lieutenant colonel of the Third Cavalry, Brevet Major Fitz-John Porter, receiving the colonelcy of the Fifteenth Infantry.

[3] Oliver L. Shepherd was appointed lieutenant colonel of the Eighteenth Infantry.

[4] Abner Doubleday was appointed major of the Seventeenth Infantry.

[5] Adam J. Slemmer was appointed major, May 14.

[6] Theodore Talbot was promoted to major, August 3, 1861.

[7] James M. Cutts, Jr., brother-in-law of Stephen A. Douglas, was appointed captain in the Eleventh Infantry.

[8] Horatio B. Reed was appointed second lieutenant in the Fifth Artillery. Representative Charles H. Van Wyck of New York was his sponsor.

[9] Francis E. Brownell was appointed second lieutenant in the Eleventh Infantry.

To Simon Cameron[1]

June 17, 1861

I will thank the Secretary of War, if he will have us furnished, the "Navy-revolvers and Sabre" as desired within, so that Mrs. L. can send them with her compliments. Mr. Fry is an acquaintance of hers, and a good & brave man.   A. LINCOLN

June 17, 1861.

[1] AES, IHi. Lincoln's endorsement is written on the back of an extract copied from "a letter from John Fry of Boyle County Kentucky." Fry expected ". . . to take command of the Company. . . . It is impossible to procure *here,* such accoutrements as are necessary, and I should like to get a pair of *Navy size revolvers,* and a sabre. . . ."

To Simon Cameron[1]

Hon. Sec of War   Executive Mansion
My dear Sir   June 17, 1861

With your concurrence, and that of the Governor of Indiana, I am in favor of accepting into what we call the three years service, any number not exceeding four additional Regiments, from that State. Probably they should come from the triangular region between the Ohio & Wabash rivers, including my own old boyhood home.

Please see Hon. C. M. Allen, Speaker of the Ia.[2] H.R. and unless you perceive good reason to the contrary, make up an order for him according to the above. Yours truly   A. LINCOLN

[1] ALS, InHi-Mitten Collection. Cameron to Oliver P. Morton, June 19, 1861, notified the governor of the War Department's willingness to accept the additional regiments (OR, III, I, 279).   [2] Lincoln's abbreviation for Indiana.

To Simon Cameron[1]

Hon. Sec. of War   Executive Mansion   June 17. 1861

My dear Sir   With your concurrence, and that of the Governor of Ohio, I am in favor of receiving into what we call the three years service, any number not exceeding six additional Regiments from that State. Unless you perceive good reason to the contrary, please see Hon. John A. Gurley, who bears this, and make an order corresponding with the above. Yours truly   A. LINCOLN

1 ALS, owned by Roy G. Fitzgerald, Dayton, Ohio.
2 Representative John A. Gurley of Cincinnati. Cameron's order has not been located.

To Gideon Welles[1]

Hon. Sec. of Navy   Executive Mansion   June 17. 1861.

My dear Sir: Gen. Rousseau, introduces to me Charles E. Anderson, whom he wishes to have appointed a Paymaster in the Navy. As I have no doubt of his fitness for the place, and as the appointment would be a Kentucky appointment, I think it ought to be made so soon as it consistently can. Yours truly   A. LINCOLN.

1 ALS, CSmH. Lovell H. Rousseau of Louisville, brigadier general of the Kentucky Home Guards, was appointed brigadier general of Volunteers, October 1, 1861, but there is no record of a Navy appointment for Anderson.

To Richard Yates[1]

Gov. R. Yates   Washington,
Springfield, Ills   June 17, 1861

The President has raised no one from a Captain to a General in the Regular Army; and the Officers of the Army are not willing that he should. Capt. Pope's own letter asking to be a Brigadier General of Volunteers is now before me.

1 ADf, DLC-RTL. The draft was apparently of a telegram. John Pope to Lincoln, June 16, 1861, has a postscript dated June 17, as follows: "Gov. Yates has just shown me your despatch stating that you had not appointed any Capt. to General—McDowell was only a brevet major. . . . Meigs . . . was Captain of Engineers. I applied for appointment of General of Volunteers for . . . it seemed certain that I could not help having my juniors in rank from Pennsylvania appointed over my head. . . . Col Stone, Col Franklin & Col Porter are all my juniors. . . ." (DLC-RTL). A telegram signed by Jesse K. Dubois, William Butler, and Ozias M. Hatch, June 16, used peremptory language, "expect & demand" that Pope's promotion be in the Regular Army, and a further telegram from them signed also by Richard Yates, June 17, said we ". . . . insist upon his appointment without regard to army prejudices. . . ." (DLC-RTL). Pope's appointment remained as brigadier general of Volunteers.

To Winfield Scott[1]

June 18, 1861

I wish to oblige Mr. Attorney General Bates in the matter mentioned within, and will do so upon the conditions that Lieut. General Scott shall be of opinion I have the lawful power, and that there will be no military impropriety in it. Will Gen. Scott please say?   A. LINCOLN

June 18. 1861

1 AES, MoSHi. Edward Bates wrote June 17, 1861, asking that James B. Eads of St. Louis be appointed commissary of subsistence upon request of Brigadier General Nathaniel Lyon. There is no reply from Scott or record of the famous engineer's appointment to commissioned service, but he was soon to be called upon to design and build armor-plated gunboats for the army's use on the Mississippi.

To Gideon Welles[1]

Hon. Sec. of Navy   Executive Mansion
My dear Sir   June 18. 1861

This will introduce Mr. H. D. Stover who wishes a short talk with you about gun-boats. Please give him a hearing. Yours truly

A. LINCOLN

1ALS, PHi. Stover was a contractor at Philadelphia.

To Ninian W. Edwards[1]

Hon. N. W. Edwards   Washington D.C.   June 19, 1861

My dear Sir: It pains me to hear you speak of being ruined in your pecuniary affairs. I still hope you are injured only, and not ruined.[2] When you wrote me some time ago in reference to looking up something in the Departments here, I thought I would inquire into the thing and write you, but the extraordinary pressure upon me diverted me from it, and soon it passed out of my mind. The thing you proposed, it seemed to me, I ought to understand myself before it was set on foot by my direction or permission; and I really had no *time* to make myself acquainted with it. Nor have I yet. And yet I am unwilling, of course, that you should be deprived of a chance to make something, if it can be done without injustice to the Government, or to any individual. If you choose to come here and point out to me how this can be done, I shall not only not object, but shall be gratified to be able to oblige you. Your friend as ever   A. LINCOLN

1 ALS, ICHi. There are no letters from Edwards in the Lincoln Papers which seem related to his request for aid in the form of an appointment, but an undated letter of Orville H. Browning to Edwards (probably August, 1861) promises to see the president and demand a place for him: "If you were, as I supposed, rich, and able to help yourself . . . I would not do this. . . ." (DLC-RTL). Edwards was appointed captain and commissary of subsistence, August 8, 1861.
2 The first two sentences have been crossed out on the manuscript.

To Joseph K. F. Mansfield[1]

Gen. Mansfield   Executive Mansion June 19, 1861

My dear Sir: The inclosed papers of Col. Joseph Hooker speak for themselves. He desires to have the command of a Regiment.

Ought he to have it? and can it be done? and how? Please consult Gen. Scott, and say if he and you would like Col. Hooker to have a command. Yours very truly   A. LINCOLN

¹ ALS, DLC-RTL. General Mansfield to Lincoln, June 19, 1861: "I should be highly gratified to see Col Hooker a Col in the Regular Army. . . . Yet in consultation with the Commanding General I find him unwilling to entertain the subject." (DLC-RTL). Joseph Hooker had been brevetted lieutenant colonel September 13, 1847, for bravery at Chapultepec, but resigned from the army in 1853. At the end of the Mexican War, he incurred the enmity of Winfield Scott by giving testimony in favor of General Gideon J. Pillow before the court of inquiry investigating Pillow's disloyalty to Scott. Hooker had to be content with appointment as brigadier general of Volunteers, as of May 17, 1861.

To Lorenzo Thomas¹

Gen. Thomas.   Executive Mansion
My dear Sir,   June 19. 1861

Let William W. Peck² be made a 1st. Lieutenant in Col. Hunter's Regiment of Cavalry, as you and I talked this morning.

Also let William A. Dubois,³ of Ills. be made a 2nd. Lieut. as we spoke this morning. Yours truly   A. LINCOLN

P.S. If Mr. Peck can be made a Captain of Infantry, that is preferred; but if that can not be done, let him be sure to be 1st. Lieutenancy in Col. Hunter's Regiment.   A. LINCOLN

P.S. 2nd. If James Curtis,⁴ of Illinois, can be made a 1st. or 2 Lieut. let it be done. He is a West Point cadet, and resigned some time ago.   A. LINCOLN

¹ ALS-P, ISLA.
² See endorsement, Lincoln to Lorenzo Thomas, June 7, *supra*.
³ William A. Dubois, son of Jesse K. Dubois, was a sergeant in the Seventh Illinois Infantry, mustered out July 25, 1861, and appointed August 1 a second lieutenant in the Regiment of Mounted Riflemen, later designated the Third Cavalry, of the Regular Army.
⁴ James Curtis, West Point graduate in 1851, resigned as first lieutenant January 15, 1857. He was appointed first lieutenant in the Fifteenth Infantry, Regular Army.

To Benjamin F. Butler¹

Executive Mansion   June 20th 1861.

I hereby authorize Major General B. F. Butler, if in his discretion he shall deem it necessary and advisable, to appoint Rev. C. W. Dennison a Chaplain of the Volunteer Hospital at Fortress Monroe, during such period of time and under such regulations as he shall prescribe.   A. LINCOLN

¹ LS, DLC-Butler Papers. Reverend Charles W. Dennison was appointed hospital chaplain, but not until July 31, 1862, is the appointment of record.

To Simon Cameron[1]

Hon. Secretary of War.   Executive Mansion, June 20, 1861.

My dear Sir:—Since you spoke to me yesterday about General J. H. Lane, of Kansas, I have been reflecting upon the subject, and have concluded that we need the services of such a man out there at once; that we better appoint him a brigadier-general of volunteers to-day, and send him off with such authority to raise a force (I think two regiments better than three, but as to this I am not particular) as you think will get him into actual work quickest. Tell him when he starts to put it through. Not to be writing or telegraphing back here, but put it through. Yours truly,

A. LINCOLN.

[1] OR, III, I, 280-81; NH, VI, 294. Both sources give also, Cameron's endorsement: "General Lane has been authorized to raise two additional regiments of volunteers." Senator James H. Lane to Lincoln, June 20, 1861, requested permission to raise the two additional regiments ". . . in the existing necessity. . . ." (OR, III, I, 282).

To Winfield Scott[1]

State Department, June 20, 1861.

The Lieutenant-General
Commanding the Armies of the United States:

You or any officer you may designate will, in your discretion, suspend the writ of *habeas corpus* so far as may relate to Major Chase, lately of the Engineer Corps of the Army of the United States, now alleged to be guilty of treasonable practices against this government.   ABRAHAM LINCOLN.

By the President:
WILLIAM H. SEWARD.

[1] OR, II, II, 193; James D. Richardson, *A Compilation of the Messages and Papers of the Presidents, 1789-1897* (Published by Authority of Congress, 1900), VI, 19. Although the *Official Records* prints this order under date of January 20, 1862, as addressed to "Maj. Gen. George B. McClellan, Commanding Armies of the United States," there seems to be little doubt that the order was issued June 20, 1861, as printed by Richardson. The original is missing from the National Archives, but the register of letters received by the adjutant general, lists it under date of June 20, 1861 (DNA WR RG 94, 875-P), and the original has been cataloged for sale at auction under the date of June 20, 1861 (American Art Association Anderson Galleries, Sale 3995, November 10, 1932, No. 61). Major William Henry Chase resigned from the U.S. Army, October 31, 1856. In 1861 he was commissioned colonel and major general of Florida state troops in the Confederate Army.

To Simon Cameron[1]

June 22, 1861

If agreeable to the Secretary of War, I approve the receiving one of the regiments already accepted from Indiana, organized and equipped as a cavalry regiment.   A. LINCOLN.

[1] OR, III, I, 275. Lincoln's endorsement is written on a letter from Governor Oliver P. Morton, June 17, 1861, introducing Robert Dale Owen, author, reformer, and ex-congressman (1843-1847) ". . . authorized to present for your consideration our cavalry regiment being now raised upon the border. . . ." Cameron communicated Lincoln's acceptance ". . . . conditioned, however, that it shall be one, or take the place of one, of infantry already accepted. . . ." (*Ibid.*, p. 291).

To Heads of Bureaus[1]

June 22, 1861

To the Heads of Bureaus in the War, Navy and other Departments.

You will please, under the direction of my private Secretary, make to me such abstract reports, as will show the number of men now enlisted as soldiers or seamen in the service of the United States, or mustered into the service as State Militia or Volunteers, the state of their equipment and drill, the time of their probable readiness for active service, and the place of rendezvous or present station. Also (if practicable) like information in regard to the organization of military forces in the Free States, under State authority. Also the number and kind of arms and ammunition furnished, and yet on hand, and being manufactured. Also the number and description of War vessels and transports at present owned or chartered by the government, where and on what service at present stationed and the number description and time of probable readiness for service of those being prepared.   A LINCOLN
Washington   June 22, 1861.

[1] Copy, DNA WR RG 156, Office of Chief of Ordnance, WD 760. The copy also has an endorsement signed by Simon Cameron and Gideon Welles, "Please assist Mr Nicolay in obtaining all the information he desires."

To James W. Ripley[1]

June 22, 1861

This introduces to Gen. Ripley, the Hon. Robt. Dale Owen, of Ia,[2] an inteligent, disinterested, and patriotic gentleman, who wishes to talk briefly about arms.   A. LINCOLN
June 22. 1861.

¹ ALS, THaroL. This introduction is misdated (NH, XI, 116) January 22, 1861. Owen was appointed by Governor Oliver P. Morton as agent to purchase arms in Europe for Indiana troops.   ² Indiana.

To William H. Seward¹

Hon. Sec. of State   Executive Mansion
My dear Sir   June 24. 1861

I think we would as well have a Cabinet meeting at 12 to-day. Please have the members notified. Yours truly   A. LINCOLN

¹ ALS, PHi.

To Simon Cameron¹

Hon. Sec. of War   Executive Mansion
My dear Sir: June 25. 1861

Col. Richard D. Goodwin, wishes to tender another Regiment from New-York. With your concurrence, and the consent of the Governor of New-York, I have no objection. Please give him a short interview, and look at the notice of his Regiment which he will show you in the New-York Tribune.² Yours truly   A. LINCOLN

¹ ALS, owned by Henry R. Benjamin, New York City. Colonel Richard D. Goodwin was authorized July 22, 1861, to recruit the regiment known as the President's Life Guard, which became a part of the Fifty-ninth New York Infantry. Goodwin was not retained as colonel and was not commissioned.
² The *Tribune,* June 23, 1861, published a notice of the organization of the President's Life Guard.

To Ward H. Lamon¹

Col W. H. Lamon   Washington, D.C.
My dear Sir—   June 25. 1861

I spoke to the Secretary of War yesterday, and he consents, & so do I, that as fast as you get companies, you may procure a U.S. officer, and have them mustered in. Have this done quietly; because we can not do the labor of adopting it as a general practice. Yours as ever   A. LINCOLN

¹ ALS, CSmH. On June 18, 1861, Lamon reported from Williamsport, Maryland, on his recruitment of Virginians: "The refugees are still coming from the 'sacred soil'—(that formerly flowed with milk & honey)—I wish you would see Mr Cameron and get him to authorise me to have those Virginians mustered . . . without reference to the minimum number. . . . I fear an enormous expense individually in provisioning the men as they come. . . . Lieut Smalley . . . Qt-Master and Commissary—is unwilling to muster in the men until each

particular Co. shall have 85 men. . . ." (DLC-RTL). Lamon was "Colonel" by appointment of Governor Yates of Illinois, February 9, 1861, but had no federal commission in the army.

To Queen Victoria[1]

June 26, 1861

Abraham Lincoln,
President of the United States of America,
To Her Majesty Victoria,
Queen of the United Kingdom
of Great Britain and Ireland,
&c,   &c,   &c.

Great and Good Friend:

I have received the letter in which you have made known to me the affliction you have sustained in the death of your justly lamented parent, the Duchess of Kent. I tender to you my sincere condolence, with that of the whole American people, in this great bereavement, and pray God to have Your Majesty and your whole Royal Family constantly under his gracious protection and care.

Written at Washington, this twenty-sixth day of June, in the year of our Lord one thousand eight hundred and sixty-one. Your Good Friend,   ABRAHAM LINCOLN.

By the President:

WILLIAM H. SEWARD, Secretary of State.

[1] LS, Public Record Office, London, England.

To Joseph G. Totten[1]

Gen. Totten.   Executive Mansion   June 27th 1861.

Dear Sir: I have appointed the following persons as cadets "at large" to the Military Academy at West Point, to fill existing vacancies:

Charles Henry Breckenridge[2]   Ky.
J. Hollins McBlair[3]   N.J.
Cyrus M. Allen Jr[4]   Vincennes,   Ind.
William H. Redwood Junr.[5]   Washington   D. C.

Your obt Servt.

ABRAHAM LINCOLN

[1] LS, DNA WR RG 94, U.S. Military Academy, 1861, No. 67, Box 77.
[2] Cadet, September 1, 1861–June 23, 1865.
[3] John Hollins McBlair, Jr., was commissioned first lieutenant in the new Fifteenth Infantry of the Regular Army and did not attend West Point.
[4] Cadet, September 1, 1861–June 23, 1865.   [5] No record of appointment.

To William H. Seward[1]

Hon. Sec. of State.   Executive Mansion
My dear Sir,   June 29. 1861.

Please send a Commission for Theodore Canissius, of Ills as Consul to Vienna. The place is but $1000, and not much sought; and I must relieve myself of the Dr. Illinoisian, tho, he be. Yours truly
A. LINCOLN.

[1] Copy, DLC-RTL. Gustave Koerner to Lincoln, June 13, 1861, recommended Canisius for appointment and added: "I am not aware that a single one of the many Germans, who have been recognized by your administration, was in your favor at Chicago. Now this does seem strange, and it ought to be remedied. . . ." (DLC-RTL). Canisius received the appointment.

List of Army Promotions[1]

[c. July, 1861]

List of officers I wish to remember, when I make appointments from the officers of the regular Army—

    Maj. Anderson
    Capt. Doubleday
    Capt Foster—
    Maj. Hunter
    Lieut. Slemmer—His pretty wife says, a major, or first captain.

[1] AD, DLC-RTL. This undated memorandum was written prior to July 13, 1861, on which date Lincoln sent to the Senate Robert Anderson's promotion to brigadier general. Abner Doubleday's promotion to major, Sanford Foster's reappointment as captain, David Hunter's promotion to colonel, and Adam J. Slemmer's promotion to major—all were made with the list of Regular Army appointments submitted under date of July 31 and received by the Senate August 2, 1861.

Memorandum: Appointment of James Shields and Michael Corcoran[1]

[c. July, 1861]

Private

Thomas Francis Meagher, as well as Senator Latham & Gen. Denver, desire the appointment of Shields.[2]

Bishop Hughes thinks Corcoran should be appointed; and my own judgment concurs in both cases.[3]

[1] AD, IHi.
[2] James Shields, Lincoln's former political opponent in Illinois, now of California, was appointed brigadier general of Volunteers, August 19, 1861. His supporters as listed were: Thomas F. Meagher, major of the Sixty-ninth New York Regiment, who was also promoted to brigadier; James W. Denver, brevetted major general in the Mexican war, who had served under President

Buchanan as governor of Kansas and commissioner of Indian affairs; and Senator Milton S. Latham of California.

3 Michael Corcoran, colonel of the Sixty-ninth New York Regiment, recommended by Roman Catholic Archbishop John J. Hughes of New York, was appointed brigadier general of Volunteers July 21, 1861.

To Winfield Scott[1]

July 2, 1861

To the Commanding General of the Army of the United States.

You are engaged in repressing an insurrection against the laws of the United States. If, at any point, on or in the vicinity of any military line which is now, or which shall be used, between the City of New York and the City of Washington, you find resistance which renders it necessary to suspend the writ of Habeas Corpus for the Public Safety, you, personally, or through the Officer in command, at the point where resistance occurs, are authorized to suspend that writ.

Given under my hand, and the Seal of the United States, at the City of Washington, this second day of
[L.S.]   July, A.D. 1861, and of the Independence of the United States the 85th.   ABRAHAM LINCOLN

By the President of the United States:

WILLIAM H. SEWARD, Secretary of State.

1 DS, NN.

To James W. Ripley[1]

Gen. Ripley   Executive Mansion
My dear Sir   July 3, 1861

Senator McDougal[1], of California, brings you this. I wish you would oblige him, if possible, about furnishing arms for a certain Regiment[2] in which he feels a peculiar interest. If you can oblige him in this, I shall be personally obliged. Yours truly

A. LINCOLN

1 ALS, IHi. The envelope is addressed by Lincoln: "Gen. Ripley/ From the President,/ asking an interview/ for Senator McDougal."

2 The regiment was probably the First California, raised in Pennsylvania by Edward D. Baker.

To William H. Seward[1]

Hon. Sec. of State   Executive Mansion July 3. 1861

My dear Sir   Gen. Scott had sent me a copy of the despatch, of which you kindly sent one.[2] Thanks to both him and you.

Please assemble the Cabinet at 12 to-day, to look over the Message, and reports.

And now, suppose you step over at once, and let us see Gen. Scott, Gen. Cameron, about assigning a position to Gen. Fremont?[3]

Yours as ever   A LINCOLN

[1] ALS, NAuE.

[2] The dispatch was probably that of July 2, from Major General Robert Patterson at Black River, near Martinsburg, announcing that he had routed 10,000 rebels with the loss of three killed and ten wounded.

[3] *General Orders No. 40*, July 3, created the Western Department including Illinois and all west of the Mississippi, with Frémont in command.

Temperance Declaration[1]

[c. July 4, 1861]

Temperance Declaration of Eleven Presidents
of the United States.

Being satisfied from observation and experience, as well as from medical testimony, that ardent spirits, as a drink, is not only needless, but hurtful and that the entire disuse of it would tend to promote the health, the virtue and happiness of the community: we hereby express our conviction, that should the citizens of the United States, and especially all young men, discountenance entirely the use of it, they would not only promote their own personal benefit, but the good of the country and of the world.

James Madison,	James K. Polk,
John Quincy Adams,	Zachary Taylor,
Andrew Jackson,	Millard Fillmore,
Martin Van Buren,	Franklin Pierce,
John Tyler,	James Buchanan,

Abraham Lincoln.

[1] *Journal of the American Temperance Union: and The New-York Prohibitionist*, August, 1861, XXIV, No. 8. The declaration as printed is accompanied by a letter from Edward C. Delavan, ex-wine merchant and noted temperance worker and lecturer, dated July 4, 1861, which reads in part:

"President Lincoln has recently returned me, signed, the Presidential Temperance Declaration.

"In 1833, I obtained the signatures of Presidents Madison, Jackson, and Adams. . . . As new Presidents have been elected, the parchment . . . has been sent to Washington, and in every case returned signed.

"President Harrison died before I had an opportunity of sending the certificate. . . ."

Fragment of Draft of Message to Congress[1]

[July 4, 1861]

Random 6.

I recommend that you give the legal means for making this contest a short, and a decisive one—that you authorize to be applied to the work, at least three hundred thousand men, and three hundred millions of dollars. That number of men is less than one twelfth[2] of those of proper ages, within those regions where *all* are willing to engage; and the sum is less than an eighteenth[3] of the money-value owned by the men who are ready to devote the whole. A right result will be worth more to the world than ten times the men, and ten times the money. The evidence reaching us from the people leaves no doubt that the material for the work is abundant; and that it needs only the hand of legislation to give it legal sanction; and the hand of the Executive to give it practical shape and efficiency. The departments here have had more trouble to avoid receiving troops faster than they could provide them than from any other cause. In a word, the people will save their government, if the government itself will allow them.

[1] AD, DLC-RTL. The single page of manuscript is a preliminary draft of the twentieth paragraph of the Message of July 4, *infra*.
[2] "Tenth" deleted, "twelfth" inserted.
[3] "Tenth" deleted, "eighteenth" inserted.

Message to Congress in Special Session[1]

July 4, 1861

Fellow-citizens of the Senate and House of Representatives:

Having[2] been convened on an extraordinary occasion, as authorized by the Constitution, your attention is not called to any ordinary subject of legislation.

At the beginning of the present Presidential term, four months

[1] AD, first proof sheets with autograph revisions, second proof sheets, two copies, (1) with revisions by William H. Seward for the most part in the handwriting of Frederick W. Seward, (2) with Lincoln's final revisions, DLC-RTL. Although engrossed official copies of Lincoln's later Messages are in the National Archives, no official copy of the Message of July 4, 1861, has been found. The text reproduced here is that of the second proof containing Lincoln's final revisions, which, with the exception of minor changes in punctuation, are noted in the succeeding footnotes. Variants, emendations, and deletions made by Lincoln in the manuscript and on the first proof are also indicated in the footnotes. Minor inconsistencies in usage occurring in Lincoln's manuscript and autograph changes in the proof sheets have been made to conform with the printed proof, but Lincoln's paragraphing, punctuation and capitalization in the manuscript and autograph corrections have been retained in some cases even though not followed by the printers who set the proofs.
[2] The first paragraph revised to the present text in the manuscript, stood originally as follows: "Having convened you on an extraordinary occasion as contemplated by the Constitution, I do not ask your attention to any ordinary subject of legislation. You will act on your own judgment and pleasure whether you will consider any such."

ago,[3] the functions of the Federal Government were found to be generally[4] suspended within the several States of South Carolina, Georgia, Alabama, Mississippi, Louisiana, and Florida, excepting only those of the Post Office Department.

Within these States, all the Forts, Arsenals, Dock-yards, Custom-houses, and the like, including the movable and stationary property in, and about them, had been seized, and were held in open hostility to this Government, excepting only Forts Pickens, Taylor, and Jefferson, on, and near the Florida coast, and Fort Sumter, in Charleston harbor, South Carolina. The Forts thus seized had been put in improved condition; new ones had been built; and armed forces had been organized, and were organizing, all avowedly with the same hostile purpose.

The Forts remaining in the possession of the Federal government, in, and near, these States, were either[5] besieged or menaced by warlike preparations; and especially Fort Sumter was nearly surrounded by well-protected hostile batteries, with guns equal in quality to the best of its own, and outnumbering the latter as perhaps ten[6] to one. A disproportionate share,[7] of the Federal muskets and rifles,[8] had somehow found their way into these States, and had been seized, to be used against the government. Accumulations of the public revenue, lying within them,[9] had been seized for the same object. The Navy was scattered[10] in distant seas; leaving but a very small part of it within the immediate reach of the government. Officers[11] of the Federal Army and Navy, had resigned in great numbers; and, of those resigning, a large proportion had taken up arms against the government. Simultaneously, and in connection, with all this, the purpose to sever the Federal Union, was openly avowed. In accordance with this purpose, an ordinance

---

[3] "All" standing in the manuscript and first proof, deleted at this point in the second proof by Seward. Deletion adopted by Lincoln.

[4] "Entirely" in the manuscript, changed by Seward in the second proof to "generally." Adopted by Lincoln.

[5] "Either beseiged or" inserted by Seward in the second proof. Adopted by Lincoln.

[6] "Perhaps ten" inserted by Lincoln in the blank space which had stood from manuscript to second proof.

[7] "Both in number and quality," in manuscript and first proof, deleted in second proof.

[8] "Arms and ammunition," in the manuscript and first proof, deleted in second proof, and "muskets and rifles" inserted.

[9] "These States" in the manuscript and first proof, changed by Seward to "them" in second proof. Adopted by Lincoln.

[10] "And" in the manuscript and first proof, deleted at this point in the second proof by Seward. Deletion adopted by Lincoln.

[11] "The officers" in the manuscript and first proof; "The" deleted in the second proof by Seward. Deletion adopted by Lincoln.

had been adopted in each of these States, declaring the States, respectively, to be separated from the National Union. A[12] formula for instituting a combined government of these states had been promulgated; and this illegal organization, in the character of confederate States was already invoking recognition, aid, and intervention, from Foreign Powers.

Finding this condition of things, and believing it to be an imperative duty upon the incoming Executive, to prevent, if possible, the consummation of such attempt to destroy the Federal Union, a choice of means to that end became indispensable. This choice was made; and was declared in the Inaugural address. The policy chosen looked to the exhaustion of all peaceful measures, before a resort to any stronger ones. It sought only to hold the public places and property, not already wrested from the Government, and to collect the revenue; relying for the rest, on time, discussion, and the ballot-box. It promised a continuance of the mails, at government expense, to the very people who were resisting the government; and it gave repeated pledges against any disturbance to any of the people, or any of their rights. Of all that which a president might constitutionally, and justifiably, do in such a case, everything was foreborne, without which, it was believed possible to keep the government on foot.

On the 5th of March, (the present incumbent's first full day in office) a letter of Major Anderson, commanding at Fort Sumter, written on the 28th of February, and received at the War Department on the 4th of March, was, by that Department, placed in his hands. This letter expressed the professional opinion of the writer, that re-inforcements could not be thrown into that Fort within the time for his relief, rendered necessary by the limited supply of provisions, and with a view of holding possession of the same, with a force of less than twenty thousand good, and well-disciplined men. This opinion was concurred in by all the officers of his command; and their *memoranda* on the subject, were made enclosures of Major Anderson's letter. The whole was immediately laid before Lieutenant General Scott, who at once concurred with Major Anderson in opinion. On reflection,[13] however, he took full

[12] This sentence was slightly revised by Lincoln from Seward's suggestion in the second proof. The manuscript and first proof read as follows: "Also the forms of establishing a federal government of these States, with departments, and provisions, similar to our own, had been gone through; and this supposed Federal government, under the name and style of 'The Confederate States of America,' had assumed national independence, and was suing for it's recognition by the powers of the earth."

[13] "At the request of the executive," in the manuscript, replaced by "On reflection," in first proof.

time, consulting with other officers, both of the Army and the Navy; and, at the end of four days, came reluctantly, but decidedly, to the same conclusion as before. He also stated[14] at the same time that no such sufficient force was then at the control of the Government, or could be raised, and brought to the ground, within the time when the provisions in the Fort would be exhausted. In a purely military point of view, this reduced the duty of the administration, in the case, to the mere matter of getting the garrison safely out of the Fort.[15]

It was[16] believed, however, that to so abandon that position, under the circumstances,[17] would be utterly ruinous; that the *necessity* under which it was to be done, would not be fully understood—that, by many, it would be construed as a part of a *voluntary* policy—that, at home, it would discourage the friends of the Union, embolden its adversaries, and go far to insure to the latter, a recognition[18] abroad—that, in fact, it would be our national destruction consummated. This could not be allowed.[19] Starvation was not yet upon the garrison; and ere it would be reached, *Fort Pickens* might be reinforced. This last, would be a clear indication of *policy*, and would better enable the country to accept the evacuation of Fort Sumter, as a military *necessity*. An order was at once directed to be sent for the landing of the troops from the Steamship Brooklyn, into Fort Pickens. This order could not go by land, but must take the longer, and slower route by sea. The first return news from the order was received just one week before the fall of Fort Sumter. The news itself was, that the officer commanding the Sabine, to which vessel the troops had been transferred from the Brooklyn, acting upon some *quasi* armistice of the late administration, (and[20] of the existence of which, the present administration, up to the time the order was despatched, had only too vague and uncertain rumors, to fix attention) had refused to land the troops. To now re-inforce Fort Pickens, before a crisis would be

[14] "Informed the executive," in the manuscript, replaced by "stated," in first proof.

[15] The following sentence deleted from the manuscript at this point: "In fact, General Scott advised that this should be done at once."

[16] "The executive," in the manuscript, changed to "It was" in first proof.

[17] "Under the circumstances" inserted by Seward and adopted by Lincoln in the second proof.

[18] "Of independence," in the manuscript and first proof, deleted at this point by Seward. Deletion adopted by Lincoln.

[19] "The administration hesitated." in the manuscript, changed in first proof to the sentence in the text.

[20] The portion in parentheses appears in the manuscript as a revision of the following: "and of the existence of which the present administration had not been notified."

reached at Fort Sumter was impossible—rendered so by the near exhaustion of provisions in the latter-named Fort. In precaution against such a conjuncture, the government had, a few days before, commenced preparing an expedition, as well adapted as might be, to relieve Fort Sumter, which expedition was intended to be ultimately used, or not, according to circumstances. The strongest anticipated case, for using it, was now presented; and it was resolved to send it forward. As had been intended, in this contingency, it was also resolved to notify the Governor of South Carolina, that he might expect an attempt would be made to provision the Fort; and that, if the attempt should not be resisted, there would be no effort to throw in men, arms, or ammunition, without further notice, or in case of an attack upon the Fort. This notice was accordingly given; whereupon the Fort was attacked, and bombarded to its fall, without even awaiting the arrival of the provisioning expedition.

It is thus seen that the assault upon, and reduction of, Fort Sumter, was, in no sense, a matter of self defence on the part of the assailants. They well knew that the garrison in the Fort could, by no possibility, commit aggression upon them. They knew—they were expressly notified—that the giving of bread to the few brave and hungry[21] men of the garrison, was all which would on that occasion[22] be attempted, unless themselves, by resisting so much, should provoke more. They knew that this Government desired to keep the garrison in the Fort, not to assail[23] them, but merely to maintain visible possession, and thus to preserve the Union from actual, and immediate dissolution—trusting, as herein-before stated, to time, discussion, and the ballot-box, for final adjustment; and they assailed, and reduced the Fort, for precisely the reverse object—to drive out the visible authority of the Federal Union, and thus force it to immediate dissolution.

That this was their object, the Executive well understood; and having said to them in the inaugural address, "You can have no conflict without being yourselves the aggressors," he took pains, not only to keep this declaration good, but also to keep the case so free from the power of ingenious sophistry,[24] as that the world should not be able to misunderstand it. By the affair at Fort Sumter, with its surrounding circumstances, that point was reached. Then, and thereby, the assailants of the Government, began the conflict of

---

21 "But starving" changed in the manuscript to "and hungry."
22 "On that occasion" inserted by Seward and adopted by Lincoln in the second proof.   23 "Aggress upon" changed in the manuscript to "assail."
24 "Mystification" changed in the manuscript to "ingenious sophistry."

arms, without a gun in sight, or in expectancy, to return their fire, save only the few in the Fort, sent to that harbor, years before, for their own protection, and still ready to give that protection, in whatever was lawful. In this act, discarding all else, they have forced upon the country, the distinct issue: "Immediate dissolution, or blood."

And this issue embraces more than the fate of these United States. It presents to the whole family of man, the question, whether a constitutional[25] republic, or a democracy—a government of the people, by the same people—can, or cannot, maintain its territorial integrity, against its own domestic foes. It presents the question, whether discontented individuals, too few in numbers to control administration, according to organic law, in any case, can always, upon the pretences made in this case, or on any other pretences, or arbitrarily, without any pretence, break up their Government, and thus practically put an end to free government upon the earth. It forces us to ask: "Is there, in all republics, this inherent, and fatal weakness?" "Must a government, of necessity, be too *strong* for the liberties of its own people, or too *weak* to maintain its own existence?"

So viewing the issue, no choice was left[26] but to call out the war power[27] of the Government; and so to resist force, employed for its destruction, by force, for its preservation.

The call was made; and the response of the country was most gratifying;[28] surpassing, in unanimity and spirit, the most sanguine expectation. Yet none of the States commonly called Slavestates, except Delaware,[29] gave a Regiment through regular State organization. A few regiments have been organized within some others[30] of those states, by individual enterprise, and received into the government[31] service. Of course the seceded States, so called, (and to which Texas had been joined about the time of the inauguration,) gave no troops to the cause of the Union. The border States, so called, were not uniform in their actions; some of them being almost *for* the Union, while in[32] others—as Virginia, North

25 "Constitutional republic, or a" inserted in second proof.
26 "The administration had no choice left," in the manuscript, changed to the present text in first proof.
27 "Military power" changed in the manuscript to "war-power."
28 "To the administration," in the manuscript, deleted at this point in first proof.
29 "Except patriotic Delaware" inserted by Seward and "except Delaware," adopted by Lincoln in second proof.
30 "Others" inserted in second proof.
31 "United States service" changed in the manuscript to "government service." 32 "In" inserted in second proof.

Carolina, Tennessee, and Arkansas—the[33] Union sentiment was nearly repressed, and silenced. The course taken in Virginia was the most remarkable—perhaps the most important. A convention, elected by the people of that State, to consider this very question of disrupting the Federal Union, was in session at the capital of Virginia when Fort Sumter fell. To this body the people had chosen a large majority of *professed* Union men. Almost immediately after the fall of Sumter, many[34] members of that majority went over to the original disunion minority, and, with them, adopted an ordinance for withdrawing the State from the Union. Whether this change was wrought by their great approval of the assault upon Sumter, or their great resentment at the government's resistance to that assault, is not definitely known. Although[35] they submitted the ordinance, for ratification, to a vote of the people, to be taken on a day then[36] somewhat more than a month distant,[37] the convention, and the Legislature, (which was also in session at the same time and place) with leading men of the State, not members of either, immediately commenced acting, as if the State were[38] already out of the Union. They pushed military preparations vigorously forward all over the state. They seized the United States Armory at Harper's Ferry, and the Navy-yard at Gosport, near Norfolk. They received—perhaps invited—into their state, large bodies of troops, with their warlike appointments, from the so-called seceded[39] States. They formally entered into a treaty of temporary alliance, and co-operation with the so-called "Confederate States," [40] and sent members to their Congress at Montgomery. And, finally, they permitted the insurrectionary government to be transferred to their capital at Richmond.

The people of Virginia have thus allowed this giant insurrection to make its nest within her borders; and this government has no choice left but to deal with it, *where* it finds it. And it has the less regret, as the loyal citizens have, in due form, claimed its protec-

---

[33] "Were apparantly, *quite* against it," in the manuscript and first proof replaced in second proof with the conclusion of the sentence as reproduced here.

[34] "Nearly all the" changed in the manuscript to "many."

[35] "They, however, submitted," in the manuscript, changed in first proof to "Although they submitted."

[36] "Then" in the manuscript, omitted in first proof, and inserted in the second proof.

[37] Period and new sentence beginning here in manuscript, changed in first proof to the present text.

[38] "Was," in the manuscript and first proof, changed in the second proof to "were."

[39] "Confederate" changed in the manuscript to "seceded."

[40] "Confederate States of America," in the manuscript and first proof, changed to "Confederate States" by Seward and adopted by Lincoln in second proof.

tion. Those loyal[41] citizens, this government is bound to recognize, and protect, as being Virginia.

In[42] the border States, so called—in fact, the middle states— there are those who favor a policy which they call "armed neutrality"—that is, an arming of those states to prevent the Union forces passing one way, or the disunion, the other, over their soil. This would be disunion completed.[43] Figuratively speaking, it would be the building of an impassable wall along the line of separation. And yet, not quite an impassable one; for, under the guise of neutrality, it would tie the hands of the Union men, and freely pass supplies from among them, to the insurrectionists, which it could not do as an open enemy. At a stroke, it would take all the trouble off the hands of secession, except only what proceeds from the external blockade. It would do for the disunionists that which, of all things, they most desire—feed them well, and give them disunion without a struggle of their own. It recognizes no fidelity to the Constitution, no obligation to maintain the Union; and while[44] very many who have favored it are, doubtless, loyal citizens, it is, nevertheless, treason in effect.

Recurring to the action of the government, it may be stated that, at first, a call was made for seventy-five thousand militia; and rapidly following this, a proclamation was issued for closing the ports of the insurrectionary districts by proceedings in the nature of Blockade. So far all was believed to be strictly legal. At this point the insurrectionists announced their purpose to enter upon the practice of privateering.[45]

[41] The sentence "Those citizens are Virginia," in the manuscript, changed in first proof to the sentence of the present text. Three additional sentences in Lincoln's autograph appear immediately following this sentence inserted at bottom of page ten of first proof, but were deleted in favor of the full paragraph autograph insertion (see note 42) at the same point. The deleted sentences are as follows: "Suppose two respectable gentlemen, both of whom have sworn to support the constitution of the United States, shall each, at the same time, claim to be Governor of Virginia. Which of the two should this government recognize? Him who disregards, or him who keeps, his oath, in this respect?"

[42] This paragraph, not in the manuscript, occurs in first proof as an autograph page inserted.

[43] "Consummated," in the autograph insertion in first proof, changed in the second proof to "completed."

[44] "While they may not all be traitors who have favored it, the thing is, in fact, treason in disguise," in the autograph insertion in first proof, changed by Seward to the reading adopted by Lincoln in the second proof, Lincoln adding the word "doubtless" to Seward's revision. "Treason" is amended to "very injurious" in the Congressional Globe Appendix, which is followed by Nicolay and Hay, suggesting further revision before release for publication.

[45] Seward deleted, and Lincoln adopted in second proof, the sentence stand-

Other calls were made for volunteers,[46] to serve three years, unless sooner discharged; and also for large additions to the regular Army and Navy. These measures, whether strictly legal or not, were ventured upon, under what appeared to be a popular demand, and a public necessity; trusting, then as now, that Congress would readily ratify them. It is believed that nothing has been done beyond the constitutional competency of Congress.[47]

Soon after the first call for militia, it[48] was considered a duty to authorize the Commanding General, in proper cases, according to his discretion, to suspend the privilege of the writ of habeas corpus; or, in other words, to arrest, and detain, without resort to the ordinary processes and forms of law, such individuals as he might deem dangerous to the public safety. This[49] authority has purposely been exercised but very sparingly. Nevertheless, the legality and propriety of what has been done under it, are questioned; and[50] the attention of the country has been called to the proposi-

---

ing next in the manuscript and first proof, as follows: "On more mature reflection, with observation on current events, it was [the administration] concluded that the measures adopted were inadequate to the occasion, both by reason of the very limited time the militia would be held to serve, and the general insufficiency of numbers in the regular land and naval forces." Lincoln had changed "the administration concluded," appearing in the manuscript, to "it was concluded" in first proof.

46 "Accordingly another call was made for ——— volunteers," in the manuscript and first proof, changed by Seward to the present reading adopted in the second proof.

47 Two short paragraphs as revised in the manuscript and first proof are deleted at this point in the second proof by Seward. Deletion adopted by Lincoln. They are as follows:

"Whether the proceedings in the nature of blockade, be technically a blockade, scarcely needs to be considered; since foreign nations only claim what we concede, that, as between them and us, the strict law of blockade shall apply.

"The attention of Congress is sought in aid of this means for suppressing the insurrection, as the one affording at once, the greatest efficiency, and least danger to life, of any at the control of the government."

48 "I felt it my duty," in the manuscript, revised in first proof to "it was considered a duty."

49 "At my verbal request, as well as by the Generals own inclination, this authority has been exercised," in the manuscript, revised in first proof to "This authority has purposely been exercised."

50 The remainder of this sentence, the next two sentences, and the beginning of the next, were revised in first proof to the present text. In the manuscript they are as follows: "and I have been reminded from a high quarter that one who is sworn to 'take care that the laws be faithfully executed' should not himself be one to violate them. ["So I think" deleted in the manuscript.] Of course I gave some consideration to the questions of power, and propriety, before I acted in this matter. The whole of the laws which I was sworn to take care that they be faithfully executed, were being resisted, and failing to be executed, in nearly one third of the states. Must I have allowed them," etc.

tion that one who is sworn to "take care that the laws be faithfully executed," should not himself violate them. Of course some consideration was given to the questions of power, and propriety, before this matter was acted upon. The whole of the laws which were required to be faithfully executed, were being resisted, and failing of execution, in nearly one-third of the States. Must they be allowed to finally fail of execution, even had it been perfectly clear, that by the use of the means necessary to their execution, some single law, made in such extreme tenderness of the citizen's liberty, that[51] practically, it relieves more of the guilty, than of the innocent, should, to a very limited extent, be violated? To state the question more directly, are all the laws, *but one*, to go unexecuted, and the government itself go to pieces, lest that one be violated?[52] Even[53] in such a case, would not the official oath be broken, if the government should be overthrown, when it was believed that disregarding the single law, would tend to preserve it? But it was not believed that this question was presented. It was not believed that any law was violated. The provision of the Constitution that "The privilege of the writ of habeas corpus, shall not be suspended unless when, in cases of rebellion or invasion, the public safety may require it," is equivalent to a provision—is a provision—that such privilege may be suspended when, in cases of rebellion, or invasion, the public safety *does* require it. It[54] was decided that we have a case of rebellion, and that the public safety does require the qualified suspension of the privilege of the writ[55] which was[56] authorized to be made. Now it is insisted that Congress, and not the Executive, is vested with this power. But the Constitution itself, is silent as to which, or who, is to exercise the power; and as

[51] In the manuscript the remainder of this sentence originally read that "more rogues than honest men find shelter under it, should, to a very limited extent, be violated?" This was first revised to read as follows: "that practically more of the guilty than [of] the innocent, find shelter under it," etc. The second revision on the manuscript stands in the first proof and thereafter, except for the insertion "of" in first proof as indicated in brackets.

[52] "Violated," in the first proof, changed by Seward in the second proof to "broken." Not adopted by Lincoln.

[53] This and the next two sentences inserted in first proof in Lincoln's autograph revised three sentences in the manuscript which read as follows: "Even in such a case I should consider my official oath broken if I should allow the government to be overthrown, when I might think the disregarding the single law would tend to preserve it. But, in this case I was not, in my own judgment, driven to this ground. In my opinion I violated no law."

[54] "I decided," in the manuscript, revised to "It was decided" in first proof.

[55] "Of habeas corpus," in the manuscript and first proof, deleted in second proof.

[56] "Which I authorized," in the manuscript, revised to "which was authorized," in first proof.

the provision was[57] plainly made for a dangerous emergency, it[58] cannot be believed[59] the framers of the instrument intended, that in every case, the danger should run its course, until Congress could be called together; the very assembling of which might be prevented, as was intended in this case, by the rebellion.

No[60] more extended argument is now offered; as an opinion, at some length, will probably be presented by the Attorney General. Whether there shall be any legislation upon the subject, and if any, what, is[61] submitted entirely to the better judgment of Congress.

The forbearance of this government had been so extraordinary, and so long continued, as to lead some foreign nations to shape their action as if they supposed the early destruction of our national Union was probable. While this, on discovery, gave the Executive some concern, he is now happy to say[62] that the sovereignty, and rights of the United States, are now everywhere practically respected by foreign powers; and a general sympathy with the country is manifested throughout the world.

The reports of the Secretaries of the Treasury, War, and the Navy, will give the information in detail deemed necessary, and convenient for your deliberation, and action; while the Executive, and all the Departments, will stand ready to supply omissions, or to communicate new facts, considered important for you to know.

It[63] is now recommended that you give the legal means for making this contest a short, and a decisive one; that you[64] place at the control of the government, for the work, at least four hundred

57 "Plainly was made" in the manuscript, revised to "was plainly made" in first proof.
58 "I can not bring myself to believe that the framers of that instrument," in the manuscript, revised to the present text in first proof.
59 "That" in first proof, deleted in second proof.
60 This sentence is inserted in Lincoln's autograph in first proof, replacing the following, in the manuscript: "I enter upon no more extended argument; as an opinion, at some length, will be presented by the Attorney General."
61 "I submit," in the manuscript, revised to "is submitted" in first proof.
62 The remainder of this sentence is inserted in second proof by Seward and adopted by Lincoln, with minor changes in punctuation, in place of the following in the manuscript and first proof: "he finds no cause of complaint against the present course of any foreign power, upon this subject."
63 "I now ask," in the manuscript, revised to "It is now recommended" in first proof.
64 The remainder of this sentence is revised to its present text in the second proof from the following wording in the manuscript and first proof: "that you authorize to be applied to the work at least —— hundred thousand men, and three hundred millions of dollars." Seward had inserted "if necessary" following "work" and "4" in the blank space. Lincoln adopted only the latter suggestion.

thousand men, and four hundred millions of dollars. That number of men is about one tenth[65] of those of proper ages within the regions where, apparently,[66] *all* are willing to engage; and the sum is less than a twentythird[67] part of the money value owned by the men who seem[68] ready to devote the whole. A debt of six hundred millions of dollars *now*, is a less sum per head, than was the debt of our revolution, when we came out of that struggle; and the money value in the country now, bears even a greater proportion to what it was *then*, than does the population. Surely each man has as strong a motive *now*, to *preserve* our liberties, as each had *then*, to *establish* them.

A right result, at this time, will be worth more to the world, than ten times the men, and ten times the money.[69] The evidence reaching us from the country, leaves no doubt, that the material for the work is abundant; and that it needs only the hand of legislation to give it legal sanction, and the hand of the Executive to give it practical shape and efficiency. One[70] of the greatest perplexities of the government, is to avoid receiving troops faster than it can provide for them. In a word, the people will save their government, if the government itself, will do its part, only indifferently well.

It might seem, at first thought, to be of[71] little difference whether the present movement at the South be called "secession" or "rebellion." The movers, however, well understand the difference. At the beginning, they knew they could never raise their treason to any respectable magnitude, by any name which implies *violation* of law. They knew their people possessed as much of moral sense, as much of devotion to law and order, and as much pride in, and reverence for, the history, and government, of their common country, as any other civilized, and patriotic people. They knew they could make no advancement directly in the teeth of these strong and noble sentiments. Accordingly they commenced by an

[65] "Less than one twelfth," in the manuscript and first proof, changed in second proof to "about one tenth."

[66] "Apparently" inserted in first proof.

[67] "Thirtieth," in the manuscript and first proof, changed in second proof to "twentythird."

[68] "Are," in the manuscript, changed to "seem" in first proof.

[69] "It will cost," in the manuscript and first proof at the end of this sentence, deleted in second proof.

[70] This sentence was inserted in the manuscript in place of the following: "The War Department has great trouble to avoid receiving troops faster than it can provide them." Although Lincoln kept "provide them" in his revision, the printer made it "provide for them," in second proof.

[71] "Of" not in the manuscript, but printed in first proof and kept in second proof.

insidious debauching of the public mind.[72] They invented an[73] ingenious sophism, which, if conceded, was followed by perfectly logical steps, through all the incidents, to the complete destruction of the Union. The sophism itself[74] is, that any state of the Union may, *consistently* with the national Constitution, and therefore *lawfully*, and *peacefully*, withdraw from the Union, without the consent of the Union, or of any other state. The little disguise that the supposed right is to be exercised only for just cause, themselves to be the[75] sole judge of its justice, is too thin to merit any notice.

With rebellion thus sugar-coated, they have been drugging the public mind of their section for more than thirty years; and, until at length, they have brought many good men to a willingness to take up arms against the government the day *after* some assemblage of men have enacted the farcical pretence of taking their State out of the Union, who could have been brought to no such thing the day *before*.

This sophism derives much—perhaps the whole—of its currency, from the assumption, that there is some omnipotent, and sacred supremacy, pertaining to a *State*—to each State of our Federal Union. Our States have neither more, nor less power, than that reserved to them, in the Union, by the Constitution—no one of them ever having been a State *out* of the Union. The original ones passed into the Union even *before* they cast off their British colonial dependence; and the new ones each came into the Union directly from a condition of dependence, excepting Texas. And even Texas, in its temporary independence, was never designated a State. The new ones only took the designation of States, on coming into the Union, while that name was first adopted for the old ones, in, and by, the Declaration of Independence. Therein the "United Colonies" were declared to be "Free and Independent States"; but, even then, the object plainly was not to declare their independence of *one another*, or of the *Union;* but directly the contrary, as their mutual pledge, and their mutual action, before, at the time,[76] and afterwards, abundantly show. The express plighting of faith, by each and all of the original thirteen, in the Articles of Confederation, two years later, that the Union shall

---

[72] "Morals" in the manuscript changed to "mind."

[73] "A single," in the manuscript, changed to "an" in first proof.

[74] "Was, and," standing at this point in the manuscript and first proof, deleted in second proof. Italics in this sentence were added in first proof.

[75] "The" not in the manuscript, but is in first proof.

[76] "Then" in the manuscript, changed to "at the time" in three pages of manuscript revision which replaced page eighteen of the first proof.

be perpetual, is most conclusive. Having never been States, either in substance, or in name, *outside* of the Union, whence this magical omnipotence of "State rights," asserting a claim of power[77] to lawfully destroy the Union itself? Much is said about the "sovereignty" of the States; but the word, even, is not in the national Constitution; nor, as is[78] believed, in any of the State constitutions. What[79] is a "sovereignty," in the political sense of the term? Would it be far wrong to define it "A political community, without a political superior"? Tested by this, no one of our States, except Texas, ever was a sovereignty. And even Texas gave up the character on coming into the Union; by which act, she acknowledged the Constitution of the United States, and the laws and treaties of the United States made in pursuance of the Constitution, to be, for her, the supreme law of the land. The States have their *status* IN the Union, and they have no other *legal status*. If they break from this, they[80] can only do so against law, and by revolution. The[81] Union, and not themselves separately, procured their independence, and their liberty. By conquest, or purchase, the Union gave each of them, whatever of independence, and liberty, it has. The Union is older than any of the States; and, in fact, it created them as States.[82] Originally,[83] some dependent colonies

[77] "Of power" appears in manuscript revision of first proof, but not in the original manuscript.

[78] "I believe" in the original manuscript, changed to "is believed" in the autograph revision of page eighteen in first proof.

[79] Four sentences beginning here are not in the manuscript but appear in the autograph revision of page eighteen of first proof.

[80] "It can only be against law, and by revolution," in the manuscript, changed to "they can only do so, against law, and by revolution" in autograph revision of page eighteen in first proof.

[81] This sentence and the next do not appear in the manuscript, but are in the autograph revision of page eighteen of first proof.

[82] The sentence appearing next in the manuscript pages inserted to replace page eighteen of first proof, is deleted in second proof: "As states, the Union gave birth to them." This sentence was itself a revision of a longer sentence in the original manuscript: "As states, they were *born* into the Union, not one of them, except Texas, ever having had a State Constitution, independent of the Union."

[83] The remainder of this paragraph and the next paragraph are as revised in first proof. The manuscript version is as follows: "Unquestionably they have the powers reserved to them by the constitution; but in those, are not included all conceiveable powers, however mischievous or destructive; but such only, as were known in the world, at the time, as governmental powers; and surely a power to destroy the government itself, was not intended to be among these. And if not intended, it has no existence.

"The right of revolution, is never a legal right. The very term implies the breaking, and not the abiding by, organic law. At most, it is but a moral right, when exercised for a morally justifiable cause. When exercised without such a cause revolution is no right, but simply a wicked exercise of physical power."

made the Union; and, in turn, the Union threw off their old dependence, for them,[84] and made them States, such as they are. Not one of them ever had a State constitution, independent of the Union. Of course, it is not forgotten that all the new States framed their constitutions, before they entered the Union; nevertheless, dependent upon, and preparatory to, coming into the Union.

Unquestionably the States have the powers, and rights, reserved to them in, and by the National Constitution; but among these,[85] surely, are not included all conceivable powers, however mischievous, or destructive; but, at most, such only, as were known in the world, at the time, as governmental powers; and certainly, a power to destroy the government itself, had never been known as a governmental—as a merely administrative power. This relative matter of National power, and State rights, as a principle, is no other than the principle of *generality*, and *locality*. Whatever concerns the whole, should be confided to the whole—to the general government; while, whatever concerns *only* the State, should be left exclusively, to the State. This is all there is of original principle about it. Whether the National Constitution, in defining boundaries between the two, has applied the principle with exact accuracy, is not to be questioned. We are all bound by that defining, without question.

What[86] is now combatted, is the position that secession is *consistent* with the Constitution—is *lawful*, and *peaceful*. It is not contended that there is any express law for it; and nothing should ever be implied as law, which leads to unjust, or absurd consequences. The nation purchased, with money, the countries out of which several of these States were formed. Is it just that they shall go off without leave, and without refunding? The nation paid very large sums, (in the aggregate, I believe, nearly a hundred millions) to relieve Florida of the aboriginal tribes. Is it just that she shall now be off without consent, or without making any return? The nation is now in debt for money applied to the benefit of these so-called seceding States, in common with the rest. Is it just, either that[87] creditors shall go unpaid, or the remaining States pay the

[84] "For them" inserted in second proof.

[85] "Those," in the manuscript pages replacing page eighteen in first proof, changed to "these" in second proof.

[86] "I am combatting the position that secession is consistent with the constitution—is peaceful, and lawful," in the manuscript, revised to the present text in first proof.

[87] "The creditors," in the manuscript and first proof, changed to "creditors" in second proof.

whole? A part of the present national debt was contracted to pay the old debts of Texas. Is it just that she shall leave, and pay no part of this herself?

Again, if one State may secede, so may another; and when all shall have seceded, none is left to pay the debts. Is this quite just to creditors? Did we notify them of this sage view of ours, when we borrowed their money? If we now recognize this doctrine, by allowing the seceders to go in peace, it is difficult to see what we can[88] do, if others choose to go, or to extort terms upon which they will promise to remain.[89]

The seceders insist that our Constitution admits of secession. They have assumed to make a National Constitution of their own, in which,[90] of necessity, they have either *discarded*, or *retained*, the right of secession, as they insist, it exists in ours. If they have discarded it, they thereby admit that, on principle, it ought not to be in ours. If they have retained it, by their own construction of ours they show that[91] to be consistent they must secede from one another, whenever they shall find it the easiest way of settling their debts, or effecting any other selfish, or unjust object. The principle itself is one of disintegration, and upon which no government can possibly endure.

If all the States, save one, should assert the power to *drive* that one out of the Union, it is presumed the whole class of seceder politicians would at once deny the power, and denounce the act as the greatest outrage upon State rights. But suppose that precisely the same act, instead of being called "driving the one out," should be called "the seceding of the others from that one," it would be exactly what the seceders claim to do; unless, indeed,[92] they make the point, that the one, because it is a minority, may rightfully do, what the others, because they are a majority, may not rightfully do. These politicians are subtle, and profound, on the rights

---

[88] "Are to" in the manuscript, changed to "can" in first proof.

[89] "In such case, shall we find any more lenders of money, however much we may need them?" appearing at this point in the manuscript, deleted in first proof.

[90] The remainder of this sentence and the next two are revised in first proof and second proof to the present text. In the manuscript they appear as follows: "they have departed from ours, in this respect, or they have not. If they have departed from ours, they thereby admit that ours ought to be as they have made theirs, cutting off the right of secession. If they have not departed from ours, by their own theoretic and practical construction of ours, which they copy in this respect, they show that they will secede from one another, whenever they shall find it the easiest way of settling their debts, or effecting any other selfish, or unjust object."

[91] "They will," in first proof, replaced in the second proof with "to be consistent they must."   [92] "Indeed" inserted in first proof.

of minorities.[93] They[94] are not partial to that power which made the Constitution, and speaks from the preamble, calling itself "We, the People."

It may well be questioned whether there is, to-day, a majority of the legally qualified voters of any State, except perhaps[95] South Carolina, in favor of disunion. There is much reason to believe that[96] the Union men are the majority in many, if not in every other one, of the so-called seceded States. The contrary has not been demonstrated in any one of them. It is ventured to affirm[97] this, even of Virginia and Tennessee; for the result of an election, held in military camps, where the bayonets are all on one side of the question voted upon, can scarcely be considered as demonstrating[98] popular sentiment. At such an election, all that large class who are, at once, *for* the Union, and *against* coercion, would be coerced to vote against the Union.[99]

It may be affirmed, without extravagance, that the free institutions we enjoy, have developed the powers, and improved the condition, of our whole people, beyond any example in the world. Of this we now have a striking, and an impressive illustration. So large an army as the government has now on foot, was never before known, without a soldier in it, but who had taken his place there, of his own free choice. But more than this: there are many single Regiments whose members, one and another, possess full practical knowledge of all the arts, sciences, professions, and whatever else, whether useful or elegant, is known in the world; and there is scarcely one, from which there could not be selected, a President, a Cabinet, a Congress, and perhaps a Court, abundantly competent to administer the government itself. Nor do I say[100] this is not true, also, in the army of our late friends, now adversaries, in this contest; but if it is, so much better the reason why

93 "Ever elevating them above the rights of majorities," appearing in the manuscript at this point, deleted in first proof.

94 In the manuscript and first proof the beginning of this sentence reads, "The dread of their existence is that power. . . ." etc., changed in second proof to the present text.

95 "Perhaps" inserted by Seward and adopted by Lincoln in second proof.

96 "That" inserted in first proof.

97 "Say," in the manuscript, changed to "affirm" in first proof.

98 "Demonstrative of" as misprinted in first proof, corrected by Lincoln to "demonstrating."

99 "And even others, more decidedly for the Union, in sentiment, would be carried the same way," appearing at this point in the manuscript, deleted in first proof.

100 "Nor do I know that," in the manuscript and first proof, changed by Seward to "I do not say that," and revised by Lincoln in second proof to the present text.

the government, which has conferred such benefits on both them and us, should not be broken up. Whoever, in any section, proposes to abandon such a government, would do well to consider, in deference to what principle it is, that he does it—what better he is likely to get in its stead—whether the substitute will give, or be intended to give, so much of good to the people. There are some foreshadowings on this subject. Our adversaries have adopted some Declarations of Independence; in which, unlike the good old one, penned by Jefferson, they omit the words "all men are created equal." Why? They have adopted a temporary national constitution, in the preamble of which, unlike our good old one, signed by Washington, they omit "We, the People," and substitute "We, the deputies of the sovereign and independent States." Why?[101] Why this deliberate pressing out of view, the rights of men, and the authority of the people?

This is essentially a People's contest. On the side of the Union, it is a struggle for maintaining in the world, that form, and substance of government, whose leading object is, to elevate the condition of men—to lift artificial weights from all shoulders—to clear the paths of laudable pursuit for all—to afford all, an unfettered start, and a fair chance, in the race of life. Yielding to partial, and temporary departures, from necessity, this is the leading object of the government for whose existence we contend.

I am most happy to believe that the plain people understand, and appreciate this. It is worthy of note, that while in this, the government's hour of trial, large numbers of those in the Army and Navy, who have been favored with the offices, have resigned, and proved[102] false to the[103] hand which had pampered them, not one common soldier, or common sailor is[104] is known to have deserted his flag.

Great[105] honor is due to those officers who remain true, despite the example of their treacherous associates; but the greatest honor, and most important fact of all, is the unanimous firmness of the common soldiers, and common sailors. To the last man, so far as known,[106] they have successfully resisted the traitorous efforts of those, whose commands, but an hour before, they obeyed as abso-

---

101 "Why this?" in the manuscript, changed to "Why?" in first proof.

102 "Played," in the manuscript and first proof, changed to "proved" in second proof.

103 "Very," in the manuscript and first proof, deleted in second proof.

104 "Has," in the manuscript and first proof, changed to "is known to have" in second proof.

105 "Greater" in the manuscript and first proof, changed in second proof to "Great." 106 "So far as known" inserted in second proof.

lute law. This is the patriotic instinct of the plain people. They understand, without an argument, that[107] destroying the government, which was made by Washington, means no good to them.

Our popular government has often been called an experiment. Two points in it, our people have already settled—the successful *establishing*, and the successful *administering* of it. One still remains—its[108] successful *maintenance*[109] against a formidable [internal][110] attempt to overthrow it. It is now for them to demonstrate to the world, that those who can fairly carry an election, can also suppress a rebellion[111]—that ballots are the rightful, and peaceful, successors of bullets; and that when ballots have fairly, and constitutionally, decided, there can be no successful appeal, back to bullets; that[112] there can be no successful appeal, except to ballots themselves, at succeeding elections. Such will be a great lesson of peace; teaching men that what they cannot take by an election, neither can they take it by a war—teaching all, the folly of being the beginners of a war.

Lest there be some uneasiness in the minds of candid men, as to what is to be the course of the government, towards the Southern States, *after* the rebellion shall have been suppressed, the Executive deems it proper to say, it will be his purpose then, as ever. to be guided by the Constitution, and the laws; and that he probably will have no different understanding of the powers, and duties of the Federal government, relatively[113] to the rights of the States, and the people, under the Constitution, than that expressed in the inaugural address.[114]

He desires to preserve the government, that it may be administered for all, as it was administered by the men who made it. Loyal citizens everywhere, have the right to claim this of their government; and the government has no right to withhold, or neglect it. It is not perceived that, in giving it, there is any coer-

107 "The," in the manuscript and first proof, deleted in second proof.

108 "The," in the manuscript and first proof, changed to "it's" in second proof.

109 "Of it," at this point in the manuscript and first proof, deleted in second proof.

110 "Internal" inserted at this point as printed in the *Congressional Globe Appendix* which is followed by Nicolay and Hay.

111 "That those who can *not* carry an election, can not destroy the government," appearing at this point in the manuscript, deleted in first proof.

112 The remainder of this sentence inserted in first proof.

113 "Relative," in the manuscript and first proof, changed to "relatively" in second proof.

114 The manuscript ends at this point. The remainder of the Message was composed after first proof had been set.

cion, any conquest, or any subjugation,[115] in any just sense of those terms.

The Constitution provides, and all the States have accepted the provision, that "The United States shall guarantee to every State in this Union a republican form of government." But, if a State may lawfully go out of the Union, having done so, it may also discard the republican form of government; so that to prevent its going out, is an indispensable *means*, to the *end*, of maintaining the guaranty mentioned; and when an end is lawful and obligatory, the indispensable means to it, are also lawful, and obligatory.

It was with the deepest regret that the Executive found the duty of employing the war-power, in defence of the government, forced upon him. He could but perform this duty, or surrender the existence of the government. No[116] compromise, by public servants, could, in this case, be a cure; not that compromises are not often proper, but that no popular government can long survive a marked precedent, that those who carry an election, can only save the government from immediate destruction, by giving up the main point, upon which the people gave the election. The people themselves, and not their servants, can safely reverse their own deliberate decisions. As a private citizen, the Executive[117] could not have consented that these institutions shall perish; much less could he, in betrayal of so vast, and so sacred a trust, as these free people had confided to him. He felt that he had no moral right to shrink; nor even to count the chances of his own life, in what might follow. In full view of his great responsibility, he has, so far, done what he has deemed his duty. You will now, according to your own judgment, perform yours. He sincerely hopes that your views, and your action, may so accord with his, as to assure all faithful citizens, who have been disturbed in their rights, of a certain, and speedy restoration to them, under the Constitution, and the laws.

[115] "Which any honest man should regret," which concludes this sentence in Lincoln's autograph insertion at this point in the first proof, is changed by Seward in the second proof to "or any deprivation of any citizen of any right of life, liberty, or pursuit of happiness, guaranteed to him by the Constitution or the laws of the land." Lincoln did not follow Seward's revision, but changed the conclusion of the sentence to the present text, and added the next paragraph following.

[116] This sentence and the next are revised in the autograph pages of first proof to the present text. As first written they were as follows: "No compromise could, in his judgment, be a cure; but, at best, could only be a little more lingering death to our popular institutions. No popular government can long survive a precedent, that those who have carried an election, *must*, on pain of death to the government itself, surrender the point upon which the people gave the election."

[117] "He," in the autograph pages of revision at the end of the first proof, changed to "the Executive" in second proof.

And having thus chosen our course, without guile, and with pure purpose, let us renew our trust in God,[118] and go forward without fear, and with manly hearts.   ABRAHAM LINCOLN
July 4, 1861.

[118] "In the justness of God" as first written, revised to "in God" in the autograph pages of first proof.

Memorandum:
Appointment of Horatio N. Taft, Jr.[1]

[July 4, 1861]

Horatio N. Taft, the boy-bearer of this, wishes to be a page. By the within, his father seems to be willing; and, as he is a play-mate of my little boys, I am quite willing.   A. LINCOLN

[1] AES, owned by Leo MacDonough, Huntington Park, California. Lincoln wrote the endorsement on the back of a note dated July 4, 1861, from Horatio N. Taft, chief examiner in the patent office. Appointed by President Buchanan, Taft was retained by Lincoln because of his staunch Union sympathies. His note reads: "Should the President feel disposed to favor the request of the bearer my son who seems determined to assert his *Independence*, his kindness would be highly appreciated." Since page boys are not listed in the *U.S. Official Register* as of September 30, 1861, the outcome of the boy's application has not been determined.

Remarks at a Review of New York Regiments[1]

July 4, 1861

Gentlemen: I trust you will not censure me for thus appearing before you, and assuming such a prominent position, for there is a kind of rule that constrains me to do so. I am aware that you are more desirous of having Gen. Scott appear before you than myself, and I therefore take great pleasure in introducing him to you.

Gentlemen, I appear before you in obedience to your call; not, however, to make a speech. I have made a great many poor speeches in my life, and I feel considerably relieved now to know that the dignity of the position in which I have been placed does not permit me to expose myself any longer. ["Go on!" and laughter.] I therefore take shelter, most gladly, in standing back and allowing you to hear speeches from gentlemen who are so very much more able to make them than myself. ["Go on!"] I thank you for the kindness of your call, but I must keep good my word, and not be led into a speech, as I told you I did not appear for that purpose. [Laughter and applause.]

[1] Washington, D.C., *National Republican,* July 8, 1861. Following the review of the New York regiments, the president introduced General Winfield Scott, members of the cabinet, and other officers on the platform, most of whom made short speeches. Lincoln's further remarks were in response to the call of the crowd.

To Simon Cameron[1]

Hon Sec. of War.   Executive Mansion
My dear Sir   July 6. 1861

The friends of Capt. Julius Hayden, of the 2nd. Infantry in the old Regular Army, wish him to be appointed a Paymaster. I do not know him personally; but I do know some of his friends. It is said he stands well in the Army, and has been over brevetted. Please place his name where it will be remembered, and considered, when appointments of this sort are made. Yours truly

A. LINCOLN

[1] ALS, IHi. Julius Hayden, brevetted captain, August 20, 1847, and commissioned to permanent rank June 30, 1850, was appointed major in the Tenth Infantry, March 15, 1862.

To Caleb B. Smith[1]

Hon. Sec. of Interior   Executive Mansion July 6. 1861

My dear Sir: Please ask the Comr. of Indian Affairs, and of the Genl. Land Office to come with you, and see me at once.[2] I want the assistance of all of you in overhauling the list of appointments a little before I send them to the Senate. Yours truly

A. LINCOLN

[1] ALS-P, ISLA.   [2] William P. Dole and James M. Edmunds.

To Simon Cameron[1]

Hon. Sec. of War   Executive Mansion
My dear Sir   July 8. 1861

L. Eugene Yorke, of New-Jersey, ought, if possible, to be appointed a Lieutent [*sic*] in the Army. Mr. Nixon, Member of Congress, very much desires this appointment; & I would like for him to be obliged. Your Obt. Servt.   A. LINCOLN

[1] ALS, owned by Edward C. Stone, Boston, Massachusetts. Louis E. Yorke, recommended by Representative John T. Nixon of New Jersey, was appointed captain in the Thirteenth Infantry, August 5, 1861.

To Simon Cameron[1]

Hon. Sec. of War   Executive Mansion
My dear Sir   July 8. 1861
    Please lose no time, in giving an interview to Adjt. Genl. Wheat
of Western Virginia, and furnishing him, if possible with what
arms, equipage &c. &c. he needs. This is very important, and
should not be neglected or delayed. Yours truly   A. LINCOLN

[1] ALS-P, ISLA. Adjutant General James S. Wheat's inability to get action
from the War Department brought a letter from Virginia Unionist Representative John S. Carlile, who became U.S. Senator July 9, replacing Robert M. T.
Hunter: "House of Representatives, July 8, 1861. . . . Complaint is made out
of the State that we are not defending ourselves. How can we, without arms . . .
or anything of defense in our hands? I have written again and again to the Secretary of War. . . ." (OR, III, I, 323-24).

To Richard D. Goodwin[1]

Richard D. Goodwin   Executive Mansion July 8 1861
    My Dear Sir—If when Congress shall have acted in the prem-
ises it shall so have acted as to authorise me to receive Regiments
of troops into the United States Service and you shall then have
a bona fide Regiment on foot ready and prepared according to the
law that may be to be mustered into the U S Service present this
letter to me without delay and I will accept your Regiment upon
the conditions stated   Yours &c   A LINCOLN

[1] Copy, DNA WR RG 107, Secretary of War, Personnel Appointments,
Box 34. See Lincoln to Cameron, June 25, 1861, *supra*, about Goodwin's regiment.

Memorandum:
Appointment of Charles J. Simons[1]

[c. July 8, 1861]
    Mr. Senator Harris, of N.Y. especially desires the appointment
to West Point, of —— Simons, not of N.Y. but son of a foreign-
Missionary from some one of the Western States, himself now at
Exeter Academy N.H.

[1] AE, DNA WR RG 94, U.S. Military Academy, 1861, No. 793, Box 79. Lincoln's endorsement is written on the envelope of a letter from Clara Harris to
her father, July 8, 1861. Charles J. Simons did not receive an appointment to
West Point, but enlisted at Exeter on June 12, 1862, as sergeant in the Ninth New
Hampshire Volunteers.

To Gideon Welles[1]

[c. July 9, 1861]

James M. Chambers was appointed Navy Agent at Philadelphia, some days ago. Send over the Commission. Yours   LINCOLN

[1] Parke-Bernet Catalog 344, February 8-9, 1939, No. 240; Stan. V. Henkels Catalog 1342, January 4, 1924, No. 39. The text is the same in the two sources except for the last sentence, in which Henkels gives "me" instead of "over." Not James M. Chambers, but James S. Chambers was nominated by Lincoln on July 9, 1861. He was confirmed by the Senate on July 19.

To Simon B. Buckner[1]

July 10, 1861

It is my duty, as I conceive, to suppress an insurrection existing within the United States. I wish to do this with the least possible disturbance, or annoyance to well disposed people anywhere. So far I have not sent an armed force into Kentucky; nor have I any present purpose to do so. I sincerely desire that no necessity for it may be presented; but I mean to say nothing which shall hereafter embarrass me in the performance of what may seem to be my duty.

(Copy of this delivered to Gen. Buckner this 10th. day of July 1861.[)]

[1] ADf, DLC-RTL. Governor Beriah Magoffin of Kentucky wrote Lincoln, June 25, 1861, that he was sending Simon B. Buckner, inspector general of the Kentucky State Guard ". . . to communicate with you in my behalf. . . ." (DLC-RTL). The object of Buckner's mission was to secure Lincoln's approval of Kentucky's "neutrality." Buckner was offered a brigadier generalship, but declined and later accepted a similar commission in the Confederate Army.

To James Mandeville Carlisle[1]

J. Mandeville Carlisle.   July 10, 1861.

I wish much to have your opinion, confidentially, on the effect of these measures, if they be passed. Will the Resolution remove the difficulties which you suggested, as preventing the condemnation of vessels captured for B[r]each of the Blockade? Will it have the effect in cases of vessels already captured hereafter? Taking the Resolution and the Bill together—do they leave the President the option of continuing a Blockade under the laws of Nations? . . .   A. L.

[1] Hertz, II, 840. James M. Carlisle, a Washington attorney, was retained by various Central and South American governments and the British legation as legal adviser. The specific resolution and bill about which Lincoln asked an opinion have not been determined.

Memorandum:
Appointment of David H. Wheeler[1]

[July 10, 1861]

A Mr. Morse[2] has been appointed from Iowa to this place, & the Iowa delegation say he is unfit for the place.

[1] AE, DNA FS RG 59, Appointments, Box 401. Lincoln's endorsement is written on the letter of James Harlan, James W. Grimes, and William Vandever, July 10, 1861, recommending David H. Wheeler for consul at Genoa.

[2] Lincoln had nominated Charles E. Moss (not "Morse") for consul at Genoa, July 9, and withdrew the nomination in favor of that of David H. Wheeler under date of July —, 1861 (*Executive Journal*, July 20, 1861).

To William H. Seward[1]

[c. July 10. 1861]

Let it be done.   LINCOLN.

[1] Anderson Galleries Catalog 1669, October 16-19, 1922, No. 695. According to the catalog description Lincoln's endorsement appears on a letter from Seward about appointing Richard Robertson of California as consul. On July 10, 1861, Richard L. Robertson was nominated consul at Mazatlan. He was confirmed by the Senate on July 26.

To Simon Cameron[1]

Hon. Sec. of War   Executive Mansion
My dear Sir   July 11. 1861

Hon. John Covode presents the name of William D. Slack, for a Lieutenancy. Mr. Covode says he has not had one for his District; and I think he ought to have this, especially as the young man is generally very competent & proper & has considerable military experience. Yours truly   A. LINCOLN

[1] ALS, DLC-Cameron Papers. Lincoln enclosed a letter from H. A. and S. D. Dudley of Brady's Bend, Pennsylvania, to Representative Covode, asking the appointment. There is no record of Slack's appointment.

To Hannibal Hamlin[1]

[July 11? 1861]

Will the Vice-President please please [*sic*] procure Professor Hitchcock to preach, as indicated by Gov. Morgan? Yours as ever
A. LINCOLN

[1] AES, CSmH. Lincoln's endorsement is written on the back of a letter from Edwin D. Morgan to Lincoln, dated July 8, 1861, recommending a sermon which

Morgan had heard preached by Reverend Roswell D. Hitchcock, professor at Union Theological Seminary, New York City. "Professor Hitchcock is going to Washington. . . . can you not get him to preach . . . next Sunday morning—and go yourself & hear him. His sermon will do great good. . . ."

To the House of Representatives[1]

To the House of Representatives.   July 11, 1861

In answer to the Resolution of the House of Representatives of the 9th instant, requesting a copy of correspondence upon the subject of the incorporation of the Dominican Republic with the Spanish Monarchy, I transmit a report from the Secretary of State, to whom the Resolution was referred.   ABRAHAM LINCOLN

Washington, 11th July, 1861.

[1] DS, DNA RG 233, Executive Documents, Thirty-seventh Congress, No. 3. The accompanying message from Secretary Seward reported ". . . that it is not deemed advisable to communicate the correspondence at this juncture." The resolution (*House Journal*, July 9, p. 53) requested the President to inform the House ". . . what protest, if any, our government has made against the insolent and aggressive conduct of the Spanish government."

Memorandum:
Appointment of William H. Acker[1]

July 11, 1861

Presented by Mr. Senator Rice, who personally desires that William H. Acker, Capt. in 1st. Minnesota Regt. now near Alexandria, shall be a first Lieut. of infantry—and Mr Rice must be obliged in this as soon as it can be done.   A. LINCOLN

July 11. 1861.

[1] AES, DLC-Cameron Papers. Lincoln's endorsement is written on the back of a letter from William Crooks of St. Paul, Minnesota, to Senator Henry M. Rice, July 4, 1861, requesting that William H. Acker be appointed to the Regular Army. Senator Rice also endorsed the letter: "Mr. Ackers father is a Republican member of our Legislature . . . no better appointment could be made." Acker was appointed captain in the Sixteenth Infantry, dated back to May 14, 1861.

Memorandum:
Appointment of James H. Armsby[1]

July 11, 1861

To-day—July 11, 1861—Mr. Senator Harris, especially requests that Dr. James H. Armsby, may be given some consulate on the continent, of $1500-or-$2000.

[1] AD, DLC-RTL. Armsby was appointed to the consulship at Naples, at $1500.

To the Senate[1]

To the Senate of the United States. July 11, 1861

I transmit to the Senate for its consideration with a view to ratification, a Convention between the United States and Denmark, in the subject of deserting seamen, signed in this City on the 11th instant. ABRAHAM LINCOLN

Washington, July 11, 1861.

[1] DS, DNA RG 46, Senate, 37B B3. On July 17 the Senate unanimously adopted a resolution of ratification.

To William H. Seward[1]

July 11, 1861

Hon. John P. Veree of Pa. wishes George Hogg, to be appointed Consul to Trinidad; and as the place has fees only, suppose we end our responsibility to him by giving it to him at this time.

[1] Copy, ISLA. The copy in the Association files was made some years ago from the original endorsement on a letter from Representative John Verree, which was at that time in the appointment papers of the State Department in The National Archives. Efforts to locate the original for the present citation have failed. Lincoln's nomination of George Hogg for consul at Trinidad, July 12, was confirmed by the Senate, July 26, 1861.

To Gideon Welles[1]

Hon. Sec. of Navy Executive Mansion
My dear Sir July 11. 1861

Mr. George Opdyke, of New-York, especially requests the appointment of Justin H. Howard, as a Pay-master in the Navy; and if it can be done consistently, let it. Yours truly A. LINCOLN

[1] ALS, IHi. There is no record of the appointment of Justin H. Howard to a commission in the Navy.

To Edward Bates[1]

Hon. Atty. General Executive Mansion
My dear Sir July 12. 1861.

In your nominations sent me is one for "Christopher C. Hewett, of *Illinois*" for Chief Justice of Washington Territory. My memorandum shows that I appointed the *man* to the *place*, but not as of *Illinois*; and as I do not know the man personally, or by reputation, I think there is some mistake about his being of *Illinois*.

Please see if my note, directing his appointment designates as "of Illinois." Yours truly   A. LINCOLN

[1] ALS, DNA GE RG 60, Papers of Attorney General, Segregated Lincoln Material. Richard Bates to Edward Bates, July 13, 1861: "In reply to your inquiry when refering to me the letter of the President of the 12th inst. . . . The commission of Judge Hewitt, was, by his direction, sent to 'Dundee Kane County *Illinois*' and his letter acknowledging its receipt is dated at that place. . . ." (DLC-RTL). Hewitt had migrated from Illinois to Seattle about 1850. His appointment is listed as from Washington Territory in the *U.S. Official Register*.

Memorandum:
Appointment of George S. Ford[1]

[c. July 13, 1861]

Kellogg wants to make a swap in this case.

[1] AE, DNA RG 94, U.S. Military Academy, 1861, No. 295, Box 78. Lincoln's endorsement is written on a letter from John D. Caton, July 13, 1861, recommending appointment of the son of the late Governor Thomas Ford of Illinois to West Point. Representative William Kellogg's own son William, Jr., received the appointment from his father's district, and since George S. Ford received no appointment, the "swap" must have fallen through.

Appointment of John A. Graham[1]

Washington   July 15th. 1861

John A. Graham, is hereby appointed to discharge the duties of Register of the Treasury, during the temporary absence of L. E. Chittenden, from Washington.   ABRAHAM LINCOLN

[1] DS, DLC. John A. Graham was chief clerk in the register's office.

To Simon Cameron[1]

July 15, 1861

The father of the young man—Levi Davis—within recommended for a Lieutenancy, is a very highly valued friend of mine, of long standing; and Col. Paine—to say nothing of others—who recommends him, is a fine officer educated at West Point, and who served in the Florida War. I therefore hope a Lieutenancy can be found for him.   A. LINCOLN

July 15. 1861.

[1] AES-P, ISLA. Lincoln's endorsement is written on the back of a letter from Colonel Eleazar A. Paine of the Ninth Illinois Volunteers, Cairo, Illinois, July 3, 1861, recommending Levi Davis, Jr. for a second lieutenancy. There is no record of a commission for Levi Davis prior to January, 1863, when First Sergeant Levi Davis of the Ninety-seventh Illinois was commissioned second lieutenant.

Memorandum:
Appointment of Joseph G. Knapp[1]

[c. July 15, 1861]

Mr. Senator Doolittle, of Wis. especially wishes Joseph G. Knapp to be a Judge in New-Mexico.

[1] AE, DNA RG 60, Papers of Attorney General, Appointments, New Mexico, Box 659. Lincoln's endorsement is written on the envelope of a letter signed by James R. Doolittle and others, July 15, 1861, requesting Knapp's appointment. Lincoln's nomination of Joseph G. Knapp of Wisconsin as associate justice for New Mexico was confirmed by the Senate, August 5, 1861. See Lincoln to Bates, August 5, *infra*.

Memorandum: Defeat at Vienna, Virginia[1]

[July 15, 1861]

A, day or two before the disaster at Vienna, Gen. Tyler[2] had by orders, with a force gone on the same road three miles beyond that point, and returned past it, seeing neither battery or troops—of which Gen. Schenck had been notified. The morning of the disaster Gen. Schenck received the order under which he acted, which is in words and figures following.

(Here insert it)[3]

As appears by the order, Gen. Schenck was not ordered to go himself, but merely to send a regiment; and he went himself, because the Colonels of both his regiments happened to be absent; but he took Col McCook's regt.;[4] and Col. McCook overtook, and joined him before the disaster occurred; and to whom, (he being a regularly educated military man) the order was at once shown, and Gen S. did nothing afterwards but upon his full concurrence. It is not time, as has been stated, that any notice was given Gen. Schenck of a battery, being at Vienna. It is true that a country-man told Gen. Schenck he had heard there were troops at Vienna. He was asked if he had seen them, and he said not; he was asked if he had seen any one who had seen them; and he said not; but he had seen a man who had *heard* there were troops there. This was heard by Col. McCook as well as Gen. Schenck; and on consultation, they agreed that it was but a vague rumor.

It is a fact, that not one officer, or private, who was present at the disaster, has ever cast a word of blame upon either Gen. Schenck, or Col. McCook; but, on the contrary, they are all anxious to have another trial under the same officers.

[449]

1 ADf, DLC-RTL. On June 17, 1861, the First Ohio Regiment of Brigadier General Robert C. Schenck's brigade, in transit on the Loudon and Hampshire Railroad under orders from the adjutant general's office, were attacked by Confederate artillery near Vienna, left the train and went into the woods. According to Schenck's report, the engineer took off with the locomotive, leaving the cars and the regiment behind. Robert C. Schenck to Lincoln, July 15, 1861, enclosed the order of June 17 and returned Lincoln's memorandum ". . . which is all right." (DLC-RTL). The memorandum appears to have been prepared by Lincoln on the basis of Schenck's personal report to the president, made in an effort to clear himself of charges of neglect.

2 Brigadier General Daniel Tyler.

3 The order which Lincoln intended to insert is printed in the *Official Records*, I, II, 125, as follows:

"Headquarters Department Northeastern Virginia,
"Arlington, June 17, 1861.

"Brigadier-General Schenck, Commanding Ohio Brigade:
"Sir: The general commanding directs that you send one of the regiments of your command, on a train of cars, up the Loudon and Hampshire Railroad to the point where it crosses the wagon-road running from Fort Corcoran (opposite Georgetown) southerly into Virginia.

"The regiment, being established at that point, will by suitable patrols, feel the way along the road towards Falls Church and Vienna, moving, however, with caution, and making it a special duty to guard effectually the railroad bridges and to look to the track. The regiment will go supplied for a tour of duty of twenty-four hours, and will move on the arrival at your camp of a train of cars ordered for that purpose, and will relieve all the troops of Colonel Hunter's brigade now guarding the line.

"I am, sir, very respectfully, your obedient servant,
"JAMES B. FRY,
"Assistant Adjutant General."

4 Alexander M. McCook, colonel of the First Ohio.

To the Senate and House of Representatives[1]

July [16] 1861

To the Senate and House of Representatives:

I transmit to Congress a copy of correspondence between the Secretary of State and Her Britannic Majesty's Envoy Extraordinary and Minister Plenipotentiary accredited to this Government, relative to an Exhibition of the products of Industry of all nations which is to take place at London in the course of next year. As citizens of the United States may justly pride themselves upon their proficiency in industrial arts, it is desirable that they should have proper facilities towards taking part in the Exhibition. With this view, I recommend such legislation by Congress at this session as may be necessary for that purpose.   ABRAHAM LINCOLN

Washington, July, 1861.

1 DS, DNA RG 233, Original Executive Documents, No. 8. This copy in the House records is endorsed by the clerk, "July 16 1861. Read, referred to the Com-

mittee on Manufactures and ordered to be printed." A joint resolution, approved July 27, 1861, appropriated $2,000, and authorized the president to take such measures as he deemed best to facilitate a proper representation of the United States at the exhibition.

To Simon Cameron[1]

July 17, 1861

If it be ascertained at the War Department that the President has legal authority to make an appointment such as is asked within, and Gen. Scott is of opinion it will be available for good, then let it be done.   A. LINCOLN

July 17, 1861

[1] AES, owned by Alfred W. Stern, Chicago, Illinois. Lincoln's endorsement appears on a memorial written by Governor William A. Buckingham of Connecticut and signed by numerous public men, requesting the appointment of James B. Merwin to a commission in the army and assignment to temperance work among the soldiers. Lincoln's endorsement is followed by recommendations signed by Winfield Scott and Benjamin F. Butler. According to Merwin's account (*The Christian Advocate*, February 6, 1919, pp. 166-67), the appointment was made, but no record of an appointment has been found prior to June 13, 1862, when Merwin was appointed hospital chaplain. See further Lincoln to Benjamin F. Larned, July 1, 1862, *infra*.

To Simon Cameron[1]

This case must not be neglected when Brigadier Generals are to be appointed for the Ohio forces.   A L.

July 17, 1861

[1] AES, owned by R. E. Burdick, New York City. Lincoln's endorsement is written on a letter signed by Ohio members of congress recommending Newton Schleich, Democratic leader of the Ohio Senate, who had been appointed brigadier of Ohio State Troops by Governor Dennison. Schleich served from April 1 to September 23, 1862, as colonel of the Sixty-first Ohio Volunteers.

To Simon Cameron[1]

I think Col. Kelly's son ought to be appointed, if possible

July 18, 1861   A. LINCOLN

[1] AES, DLC-Cameron Papers. Lincoln's endorsement is written on the back of a letter from John S. Carlile to Lincoln, dated July 17, 1861, enclosing a letter from Brigadier General Benjamin F. Kelley, West Virginia Infantry, wounded ". . . in the action at Philippi," who wished his son Benjamin, Jr., to have a commission. The son was made assistant quartermaster of Volunteers with rank of captain, March 18, 1864.

To Salmon P. Chase[1]

(*Private.*)

Executive Mansion, July 18, 1861.

My dear Sir: I can scarcely avoid an "unpleasantness," not to say a difficulty, or rupture, respectively with Mr. Senator King and Mr. Speaker Grow, unless I can find a place for each a man. Mr. Grow, knowing I have Mr. King on hand, as well as himself, was here this morning, insisting that the second and fifth auditorships are still open, and that I might give them to Mr. King's man and to his. Is the fact so? Are those places open? If they are, you would both oblige and relieve me by letting them go as indicated. Grow's man is Joseph E. Streeter,[2] really of Illinois (no acquaintance of mine), but, as Grow says, to be charged to Pennsylvania. King's man is ———— Smith,[3] of Minnesota. I neither know him nor remember his Christian name as given by Mr. King. Yours as ever,   A. LINCOLN.

[1] NH, VI, 329-30. Chase wrote to Lincoln, July 6, 1861, "Senator King presented the papers of a Mr. Smith [Simeon Smith?] of Minn. for auditor and recommended another Mr Smith [Delano T. Smith] of Minn. for the like place.
"He withdrew the papers of the first Mr. Smith & the other Mr. Smith was made Chief Clerk in the 3d Auditor's office sometime ago, with an understanding that he wd be recommended for appointment as Auditor when the public interests seem to allow. . . ." (DLC-RTL). On July 19, Chase replied to Lincoln's letter of July 18, "Neither of the places . . . can be fairly considered as open. One is promised with your sanction to the gentleman who now fills the chief clerkship [Ezra B. French?]. . . . For the other you have named several gentlemen. . . ." (DLC-RTL). Ezra B. French was second auditor and John C. Underwood fifth auditor, as of September 30, 1861.

[2] Joseph E. Streeter was nominated associate justice of Nebraska Territory, December 9, 1861, and confirmed January 22, 1862.

[3] Probably Simeon Smith. See memorandum, April 2, *supra*, and note.

Memorandum:
Appointment of Second and Fifth Auditors[1]

July 18, 1861

Mr. Speaker Grow says, the 5th & 2nd. Auditorships are both open to appointments.

To-day wrote Sec. of Treasury asking these places for Mr. Grow's and Mr. King's men.   A L.

July 18, 1861.

[1] ADS, DLC-RTL. See Lincoln to Chase, *supra*.

Memorandum:
Appointments Recommended by James R. Doolittle[1]

Please add this to Mr. Senator Doolittle's list sent in a day or two ago.   A. LINCOLN

July 19, 1861.

1 AES, owned by Charles W. Olsen, Chicago, Illinois. This note appears on a letter from Senator Doolittle, July 19, 1861, recommending appointment of C. Seth Cushman as first lieutenant and Charles L. Noggle as second lieutenant in the new regiments of the Regular Army. Noggle was appointed to the Second Infantry, and Cushman to the Fourteenth Infantry.

To the Senate[1]

To the Senate of the United States: July 19, 1861

I transmit to the Senate, for its advice with a view to a formal execution of the instrument, the draft of a treaty informally agreed upon between the United States and the Delaware tribe of Indians, relative to certain lands of that tribe.

Washington, 19th July, 1861.   ABRAHAM LINCOLN.

1 *Executive Journal*, XI, 473. See order for issue of bonds for use of Delawares, June 10, *supra*, and Lincoln to Orville H. Browning, July 20, *infra*. The treaty was ratified by the Senate, August 6, 1861.

To the Senate and House of Representatives[1]

July 19, 1861

To the Senate and House of Representatives:

As the United States have, in common with Great Britain and France, a deep interest in the preservation and developement of the fisheries adjacent to the Northeastern coast and Islands of this continent, it seems proper that we should concert with the Governments of those countries such measures as may be conducive to those important objects. With this view, I transmit to Congress a copy of a correspondence between the Secretary of State and the British Minister here, in which the latter proposes, on behalf of his Government, the appointment of a Joint Commission to inquire into the matter, in order that such ulterior measures may be adopted as may be advisable for the objects proposed. Such legislation is recommended as may be necessary to enable the Executive to provide for a Commissioner on behalf of the United States.

Washington, 19th. July, 1861.   ABRAHAM LINCOLN

[453]

[1] DS, DNA RG 233, Original Executive Document. Referred to the Senate committee on foreign relations, the message was reported by Senator Sumner on July 23 with a recommendation that further consideration be postponed to the first Monday in December.

To William H. Seward[1]

Hon. Sec. of State   Executive Mansion
My dear Sir   July 19, 1861

I wish to see you a moment this morning on a matter of no great moment. Will you please call? Yours truly   A. LINCOLN

[1] ALS, RPB.

To Lorenzo Thomas[1]

July 19, 1861.

I have agreed, and do agree, that the two Indiana regiments named within shall be accepted if the act of Congress shall admit of it. Let there be no further question about it.   A. LINCOLN

[1] OR, III, I, 339-40; NH, XI, 120. The original letter is missing from the National Archives, but is listed in the register of letters received by the adjutant general (DNA WR RG 94). Robert D. Owen to Cameron, July 20, 1861, enclosed a copy of Lincoln's note with the comment, ". . . I desire to express my regret that there should have been any conflict of opinion on this subject, and to add that I entirely concur . . . that there should be but one uniform term of enlistment, namely, for three years or during the war. I desire further to add that I shall use my influence with the Governor to induce him to propose to these regiments to enlist on the above terms. . . ." (OR, III, I, 339-40).

To Elisha Whittlesey[1]

July 19, 1861

I desire that the Treasury Department will devise a system or plan for disbursing the appropriation mentioned within; and if, according to said plan, disbursing agents are to be appointed I shall be ready to appoint them, on the recommendation of that Department. In case of Indiana, I am satisfied with Jonathan S. Harvey,[2] named within as disbursing agent   A. LINCOLN
July 19. 1861.

[1] AES, CSmH. Lincoln's endorsement is written on a letter from Cameron to Lincoln, dated July 19, 1861, referring a letter from Elisha Whittlesey, comptroller of the treasury, in regard to the mode of refunding monies advanced by the states for equipping Volunteers. Whittlesey recommended and Cameron

agreed that the disbursements should be made by agents appointed by the Treasury instead of by the War Department.

² There is no record of Jonathan S. Harvey's appointment as agent of the Treasury.

To Orville H. Browning[1]

Hon. O. H. Browning   Executive Mansion
My dear Sir: July 20, 1861

To-day I send to the Senate the arrangement made through Mr. Williams[2] with the Delaware Indians, asking their advice as to the making a formal treaty of it, as it already is in substance. On very full reflection I have thought this course the safest and best. I will thank you if you will move an amendment in about these words: "Provided that no part of said lands, shall be patented, until the money price for such part shall have been fully paid; and provided further that time shall be extended, so that the rights of said Railroad Company under the treaty to which this is supplemental, shall not be forfeited until ————————[3]

These provisos for the perfect security of the Indians on the one hand; and for the benefit of the Co. on the other. The blank you will fill of course. Yours as ever   A. LINCOLN

[1] ALS, ORB.
[2] Lincoln's old friend Archibald Williams, whom Lincoln had appointed U.S. district judge for Kansas.
[3] Lincoln's proposed amendment was expanded to include certain other matters and passed the Senate, August 6, 1861.

To Simon Cameron[1]

July 20, 1861.

The Secretary of War has my approbation to sign this letter.

A. LINCOLN.

[1] OR, III, I, 339. The letter which Lincoln approved was from Cameron to Representative Francis Thomas of Maryland, authorizing organization of four regiments of loyal citizens ". . . on both sides of the Potomac River from the Monocacy to the west boundary of Maryland, for the protection of the canal and of the property and persons of loyal citizens. . . ." (*Ibid.*, I, 338-39).

To Simon Cameron[1]

Sec. of War please give this man a hearing.

July 20 1861   A. LINCOLN

[1] Parke-Bernet Catalog 315, November 18-19, 1941, No. 325. According to the catalog description, Lincoln's endorsement appears on the back of ". . . a warrant appointing J. S. Hill a First Sergeant in the Washington Light Infantry."

To John W. Forney[1]

PRIVATE

Hon. J. W. Forney   Executive Mansion
My dear Sir   July 20. 1861

There is a young man here by the name of Sympson (Senator Browning will give you his christian name) to whom the giving of some place, if in your power, would greatly oblige me. His father is one of my best friends whom I have not, so far, been able to recognize in any substantial way. Yours very truly

A. LINCOLN

[1] ALS-P, ISLA. John W. Forney had been elected secretary of the Senate on July 15. Orville H. Browning's *Diary* records on this date, "I . . . wrote a note to the President to try and get him [Forney] to give Sam Sympson a place." Samuel A. Sympson was the son of Lincoln's old friend Alexander Sympson, but it seems that an older brother, Coleman C. Sympson, got the job, since the *U.S. Official Register*, 1863, lists "C. C. Simpson of Illinois" as clerk in the Senate.

To Caleb B. Smith[1]

If the place is vacant, give it to Mr. Coleman, as indicated within.   A. LINCOLN

July 20, 1861.

[1] AES, DNA NR RG 48, Applications, Indian Agencies, Box 1271. Lincoln's endorsement is written on a letter from William P. Dole and Caleb B. Smith, July 19, 1861, recommending Isaac Coleman of Indiana. The *U.S. Official Register*, 1863, lists Isaac Coleman as agent for Choctaws.

Memorandum: John Wilson's Regiment[1]

Let Mr. Wilson bring the Regiment in 40 hours, or if need be, in a few hours more.   A. LINCOLN

July 22, 1861

[1] AES, owned by S. H. McVitty, Salem, Virginia. Lincoln's endorsement is written on the back of a letter from Wilson, Washington, July 22, 1861, offering ". . . the services of my head and hands, for any duty in which you may wish to employ me. . . . On the 6th. I tendered the services of an efficient Regt. from Chicago—they are ready—& could reach here in 40 hours. . . ." Of several persons bearing the name "John Wilson" who may have been Lincoln's correspondent in this instance the best probability seems to be the John Wilson who was land agent of the Illinois Central Railroad in Chicago. A letter from Simon Cameron to Colonel Charles Knobelsdorf of Chicago, July 22, 1861, accepting the North Western Rifle Regiment, later the Forty-fourth Illinois Infantry, suggests that this may be the regiment equipped by Wilson (Chicago *Tribune*, July 24, 1861).

To Simon Cameron[1]

If there be a vacancy, I desire that C. C. Campbell be appointed
a captain of Artillery.   A. LINCOLN
July 23, 1861.

[1] AES, IHi. Lincoln's endorsement is written on a memorial, July 8, 1861,
signed by officers at Camp Defiance, Cairo, Illinois, recommending the appointment of Charles C. Campbell as captain of artillery in the Regular Army. The
document also bears Lyman Trumbull's concurrence dated July 23, 1861. Campbell did not receive the appointment to the Regular Army, but was made major
of the First Illinois Light Artillery, October 23, 1861.

Memoranda of Military Policy
Suggested by the Bull Run Defeat[1]

July 23. 1861.

1 Let the plan for making the Blockade effective be pushed
forward with all possible despatch.

2 Let the volunteer forces at Fort-Monroe & vicinity—under
Genl. Butler—be constantly drilled, disciplined, and instructed
without more for the present.

3. Let Baltimore be held, as now, with a gentle, but firm, and
certain hand.

4 Let the force now under Patterson, or Banks, be strength-
ened, and made secure in it's position.[2]

5. Let the forces in Western Virginia act, till further orders,
according to instructions, or orders from Gen. McClellan.

6. [Let] Gen. Fremont push forward his organization, and op-
perations in the West as rapidly as possible, giving rather special
attention to Missouri.

7 Let the forces late before Manassas, except the three months
men, be reorganized as rapidly as possible, in their camps here
and about Arlington

8. Let the three months forces, who decline to enter the longer
service, be discharged as rapidly as circumstances will permit.

9 Let the new volunteer forces be brought forward as fast as
possible; and especially into the camps on the two sides of the
river here.

July 27, 1861[3]

When the foregoing shall have been substantially attended to—

1. Let Manassas junction, (or some point on one or other of the
railroads near it;); and Strasburg, be seized, and permanently

held, with an open line from Washington to Manassas; and and [*sic*] open line from Harper's Ferry to Strasburg—the military men to find the way of doing these.

2.   This done, a joint movement from Cairo on Memphis; and from Cincinnati on East Tennessee.

1 AD, DLC-RTL.
2 The forces operating near Harpers Ferry were not yet under command of General Nathaniel P. Banks. The order removing General Robert Patterson from command had been issued on July 19, but did not take effect until July 27. Patterson was held responsible for the defeat at Bull Run by reason of his failure to immobilize the Confederate forces under General Joseph E. Johnston.
3 The memoranda under this date continue on the same page with 8 and 9, above.

Remarks to the Sixty-Ninth New York Regiment[1]

July 23, 1861

The President and Secretary Seward visited the fortifications over the river to-day. Arriving at Fort Corcoran they were received by the gallant New York Sixty-ninth with the greatest enthusiasm. The President asked if they intended to re-enlist? The reply was that "they would if the President desired it." He announced emphatically that he did, and wrote them a letter complimenting them upon their brave and heroic conduct, and expressing the hope that the whole regiment would re-enlist.[2] This was received with cheers, and the determination expressed to go in for the war and stand by the government and the old flag forever.

1 New York *Herald*, July 24, 1861.
2 The letter is not of further record.

To Charles S. Olden[1]

Washington, D.C.,
The Governor of New Jersey: July 24, 1861.

Sir: Together with the regiments of three-years' volunteers which the Government already has in service from your State, enough to make eight in all, if tendered in a reasonable time, will be accepted, the new regiments to be taken, as far as convenient, from the three-months' men and officers just discharged, and to be organized, equipped, and sent forward as fast as single regiments are ready, on the same terms as were those already in the service from that State. Your obedient servant,   A. LINCOLN.

[Endorsement.]

This order is entered in the War Department, and the Governor of New Jersey is authorized to furnish the regiments with wagons and horses.   S. CAMERON, Secretary of War.

¹ OR, III, I, 365. Governor Olden replied August 3, 1861, that ". . . New Jersey will respond as promptly as possible. . . ." (DLC-RTL).

To Simon Cameron¹

July 25, 1861

Let the four Artillery companies which have been in actual service at Cairo for some time, be mustered in regularly for the three years service, and so done that they be paid from the begi[nning] of their actual ser[vice.]   A. LINCOL[N]
July 25 [1861]

¹ AES, RPB. Lincoln's endorsement is written on an envelope in which letters from Governor Richard Yates and William Thomas, army auditor for Illinois, had been delivered to the president. Yates' letter has not been found, but a telegram which Secretary Seward sent by Lincoln's direction on July 25, informed Yates that "Your sixteen regiments of infantry and battalion of artillery will be accepted. . . ." (OR, III, I, 349).

To the House of Representatives¹

To the House of Representatives: July 25, 1861

In answer to the resolution of the House of Representatives of the 15th instant, requesting a copy of the correspondence between this government and foreign powers on the subject of the existing insurrection in the United States, I transmit a report from the Secretary of State.   ABRAHAM LINCOLN.
Washington, July 25, 1861.

¹ Thirty-seventh Congress, First Session, *House of Representatives Executive Document No. 12.* Lincoln's communication was accompanied by one from Secretary Seward of the same date which deemed it inexpedient "to communicate the correspondence called for."

To the House of Representatives¹

To the House of Representatives: July 25, 1861

In answer to the resolution of the House of Representatives of the 22d instant, requesting a copy of the correspondence between this government and foreign powers with reference to maritime rights, I transmit a report from the Secretary of State.

Washington, July 25, 1861.   ABRAHAM LINCOLN.

[1] Thirty-seventh Congress, First Session, *House of Representatives Executive Document No. 13.* Secretary Seward's communication of the same date expressed the opinion that ". . . communication of the correspondence called for would not at this time comport with the public interest."

To Winfield Scott[1]

Will Lieut. Genl. Scott please see Professor Lowe, once more about his balloon?   A LINCOLN
July 25, 1861.

[1] ALS, DNM-Lowe Collection. On June 18, 1861, Professor Thaddeus S. C. Lowe of Cincinnati, Ohio, had demonstrated the practicability of using his balloon for purposes of military observation, by taking up a telegraph wire and sending the president the "first telegram ever dispatched from an aerial station." Although Lincoln saw General Scott about the balloon immediately thereafter, the general was not enthusiastic, and Lincoln's note was written more than a month later. Lowe was later employed by General McClellan to make balloon observations of enemy activity.

To William H. Seward[1]

Hon: Sec. of State   July 25, 1861
Dear Sir   The bearer of this wishes to have a son appointed consul to Spezia; and if you have no objection, I have none
July 25. 1861   A. LINCOLN

[1] ALS, DNA FS RG 59, Appointments, Box 370. Lincoln's note is written on a letter from Senator James W. Grimes introducing the father of William T. Rice of Boston, Massachusetts, who wished his son appointed consul. The *U.S. Official Register*, 1861, lists William T. Rice as consul at Spezia.

To Lorenzo Thomas[1]

July 25, 1861
If the Adjutant General can get the Regiment together on the terms proposed, I think it will be a good corps, and ought to be accepted.   A. LINCOLN
July 25, 1861.

[1] AES, owned by L. E. Dicke, Evanston, Illinois. Lincoln's endorsement is written on the back of a letter from Charles B. Stuart of Elmira, New York, written from Washington, July 23, offering to organize a regiment of engineers and mechanics. The regiment was authorized on September 20 as the Fiftieth New York Infantry and was designated Fiftieth New York Engineers on October 22, 1861.

To the War Department[1]

[c.July 25, 1861?]

Col. Wallace, bearer of this, commands one of the Illinois Regiments, just ordered to be received, wishes a copy of the order to take to Illinois. Please let him have it.   A. LINCOLN

[1] ALS, IHi. Lincoln's note is written on the back of a card bearing Ward H. Lamon's note "*To the door keeper at White House.* This will be handed you by *Major Wallace* of Ills. one of Mr Lincolns best friends. Show him at once to Mr. Lincoln's room if you can do so. Ward H. Lamon." William H. L. Wallace's regiment, the Eleventh Illinois, was mustered July 25, 1861.

To Simon Cameron[1]

Hon. Secretary of War   Executive Mansion
Dear Sir   July 26, 1861.

Please let Reuben B. Hatch of Illinois, be appointed an Assistant Quartermaster, and assigned to the Brigade of General Prentiss, in Illinois.

Also let Speed Butler of Illinois be appointed Commissary of Subsistence, and assigned to the Brigade of General Pope, in Illinois
          Your obedient Servant   ABRAHAM LINCOLN.

[1] LS, IHi. Reuben B. Hatch of Meredosia, Illinois, brother of Ozias M. Hatch, was appointed assistant quartermaster of Volunteers with rank of captain, August 3, 1861. Speed Butler, son of Lincoln's old friend William Butler, was appointed commissary of subsistence, August 3, 1861, and on September 1, became major of the Fifth Illinois Cavalry.

To Simon Cameron[1]

July 26, 1861

Lewis E. Johnson, desires to be a Paymaster of Volunteers. He is the son of Hon. Reverdy Johnson who much desires the appointment   A. LINCOLN.
July 26, 1861.

I wish this to be done when the time comes.   A.L.

[1] Newark Galleries Catalog 128, December 5, 1930, No. 156. Lewis (Louis) E. Johnson was nominated additional paymaster July 31 to rank from June 1, 1861.

To the House of Representatives[1]

To the House of Representatives: July 27, 1861

In answer to the resolution of the House of Representatives of the 24th instant, asking the grounds, reasons, and evidence upon which

[461]

the police commissioners of Baltimore were arrested, and are now detained as prisoners at Fort McHenry, I have to state that it is judged to be incompatible with the public interest at this time to furnish the information called for by the resolution.

Washington, July 27, 1861.   ABRAHAM LINCOLN.

[1] Thirty-seventh Congress, First Session, *House of Representatives Executive Document No. 16.* The arrest of the police commissioners of Baltimore for secession activities was ordered by Winfield Scott, June 24, 1861 (OR, I, II, 138-39).

Memorandum:
Appointment of Walter D. McIndoe[1]

[c.July 27, 1861]

Wisconsin Delegation propose that the nomination of Henry Martin, as Sup. Ind. Affs. be withdrawn; and Walter D. McIndoe, of Wis be substituted.

[1] AE, DNA NR RG 48, Applications, Indian Agencies, Utah, Box 1267. Lincoln's memorandum is written on the back of a letter of July 27, 1861, signed by Senator James R. Doolittle, Senator Timothy O. Howe, and Representative John F. Potter, recommending the change in appointment. James D. Doty of Wisconsin is listed in the *U.S. Official Register,* 1861, as superintendent of Indian affairs for Utah.

To the Senate[1]

July 27, 1861

To the Senate: In answer to the resolution of the Senate of the 25th instant, relative to the instructions to the ministers of the United States abroad, in reference to the rebellion now existing in the southern portion of the Union, I transmit a report from the Secretary of State.   ABRAHAM LINCOLN.

Washington, July 27, 1861.

[1] Thirty-seventh Congress, First Session, *Senate Executive Document No. 5.* Secretary Seward's accompanying communication of the same date declared that ". . . it is not deemed expedient to communicate the instructions called for."

To Simon Cameron[1]

The within are good recommendations, & I respectfully submit the case to the Sec. of War.   A. LINCOLN

July 29, 1861.

[1] AES, DLC-Cameron Papers. Lincoln's endorsement is written on the back of the last of several letters recommending that William M. Este, a native of Ohio and citizen of San Francisco, California, be granted a commission. Este was appointed second lieutenant in the Twenty-sixth Ohio Infantry, December 17, 1861.

To Simon Cameron[1]

Hon. Sec. of War.   Executive Mansion
My dear Sir   July 29, 1861
  I understand that by an existing law, there is to be a Paymaster
for every two regiments of volunteers. With this understanding I
wish to appoint Valentine C. Hanna of Indiana one of these Pay-
masters; and that it be done at once, or put on a list so that it will
certainly be done in due course. Yours truly   A. LINCOLN.

[1] ALS, CSmH. Valentine C. Hanna was appointed additional paymaster, August 15, 1861.

To Simon Cameron[1]

Hon. Sec. of War—   Executive Mansion
My dear Sir: July 29. 1861
  At various times certain men have been named as Brigadier Generals of Volunteers, and most of whom have already been acting in
that capacity. As the Volunteer bill is now a law, I will thank you
to send me blank nominations of them to be laid before the Senate.
So far as I can remember, they are Pope and Hurlbut of Ills: Reynolds of Ia.[2] Curtis of Iowa, Cox and Schenck of Ohio, McCall of
Penn. and Kearney, of New-Jersey—and there may be others not
recollected by me, whose names your records will show. Butler,
Banks and Dix also were named as *Major* Generals of Volunteers;
and their nominations should also be sent. Let them, in the nominations, be designated as of *Volunteers* without assigning them to any
particular corps, or States.
  I am not sure whether Lyons was appointed for volunteers or for
regulars. McClellan, Fremont, Anderson & Rosecrantz, were appointed for regulars; and I think their nominations are already
before the Senate. Yours truly   A. LINCOLN

[1] ALS, DLC-Cameron Papers. Cameron's letter to Lincoln, July 29, 1861, cor-
roborated the fact that nominations for McClellan, Frémont, Mansfield, Mc-
Dowell, Anderson, and Rosecrans for the Regular Army had already been sent
to the Senate, and promised to attend to the others (DLC-RTL). The nominations
of Major Generals Nathaniel P. Banks, John A. Dix, and Benjamin F. Butler;
Brigadier Generals Nathaniel Lyon, John Pope, George A. McCall, Samuel R.
Curtis, Philip Kearny, Joseph J. Reynolds, Rufus King, Jacob D. Cox, Stephen A.
Hurlbut, Franz Sigel, Robert C. Schenck, and Benjamin M. Prentiss—all to the
Volunteers—were sent to the Senate July 29, with appointments dating from May
16, 1861, for the first three named, and May 17 for the others.
[2] Abbreviation for Indiana.

To Simon Cameron[1]

July 29, 1861

If it is possible to furnish 5000 stand of Arms to the State Govt. at Wheeling, without endangering other points too much, let it be done.

The bearer of this an intelligent gentleman from there, whom please see a moment   A. LINCOLN
July 29. 1861

[1] AES, DLC-RTL. Lincoln's endorsement is written on a letter from John S. Carlile introducing James W. Paxton and Daniel Lamb of Wheeling, Virginia. Thomas A. Scott, acting secretary of war, informed Carlile, August 6, 1861, that ". . . 2,000 rifled arms were ordered . . . to Western Virginia. . . . One thousand of the arms . . . to be delivered to J. W. Paxton and Daniel Lamb. . . ." (OR, III, I, 389).

To Hannibal Hamlin[1]

Hon: H. Hamlin,   Executive Office,
President of the Senate   July 29th 1861

Sir, I transmit, herewith, to be laid before the Senate, for its constitutional action thereon, Articles of agreement, and convention with accompanying papers.   ABRAHAM LINCOLN

[1] DS, DNA RG 46, Senate 37B C2. The treaty with the Arapahoe and Cheyenne Indians was amended and ratified by the Senate, August 6, 1861.

To the Kentucky Delegation in Congress[1]

Executive Mansion July 29, 1861.

Gentlemen of the Kentucky delegation, who are for the Union— I somewhat wish to authorize my friend Jesse Bayles to raise a Kentucky Regiment; but I do not wish to do it without your consent. If you consent, please write so, at the bottom of this. Yours truly
A. LINCOLN

I repeat, I would like for Col. Bayles to raise a Regiment of Cavalry, whenever the Union men of Kentucky desire, or consent to it.
Aug. 5. 1861.   A. LINCOLN

[1] ALS, The Rosenbach Company, Philadelphia and New York. On the bottom of the letter is the delegation's endorsement, "We consent—" signed by Representatives Robert Mallory, Henry Grider, George W. Dunlap, James S. Jackson, and Charles A. Wickliffe. Lincoln's endorsement of August 5 is written on the verso. Jesse Bayles organized the Fourth Kentucky Cavalry at Louisville and served as colonel until April 14, 1863.

To the Senate[1]

July 30, 1861

To the Senate of the United States: In answer to the resolution of the Senate of the 19th instant, requesting information concerning the *quasi* armistice alluded to in my message of the 4th instant, I transmit a report from the Secretary of the Navy.

July 30, 1861.   ABRAHAM LINCOLN.

[1] Thirty-seventh Congress, First Session, *Senate Executive Document No. 7.* The accompanying communication from Gideon Welles of the same date, reported that ". . . it is believed the communication of the information called for would not, at this time, comport with the public interest." The Senate resolution of July 19 requested the president to communicate ". . . the character of the *quasi* armistice . . . by reason of which the commander of the frigate Sabine refused to transfer the United States troops into Fort Pickens, in obedience to his orders. . . ." (*Senate Journal,* July 19, 1861, p. 62). Captain Henry A. Adams in command of the *Sabine* had refused to follow an order issued by Winfield Scott to Captain Israel Vogdes in command of troops sent to reinforce Fort Pickens, on the grounds that he (Adams) had not received orders from his superiors (i.e., the Navy), and on the further grounds that an agreement was still in existence between the U.S. Government and the state of Florida, not to reinforce Fort Pickens. The purported agreement was negotiated prior to Lincoln's inauguration and the secession of Florida, and was in fact merely a temporary verbal agreement and not a signed armistice. An order from Secretary Welles, sent by Lieutenant John L. Worden of the Navy, finally reached Adams, and Fort Pickens was reinforced on the night of April 12. Worden was arrested on his return trip by land and held by the Confederacy until an exchange of prisoners brought his release seven months later.

To the Senate[1]

July 30, 1861

To the Senate of the United States: In answer to the resolution of the Senate of the 23d instant, requesting information concerning the imprisonment of Lieut. John J. Worden [John L. Worden][2] of the United States navy, I transmit a report from the Secretary of the Navy.   ABRAHAM LINCOLN.

July 30, 1861.

[1] Thirty-seventh Congress, First Session, *Senate Executive Document No. 6.* The accompanying communication from Gideon Welles of July 29, 1861, reported that ". . . communication of the information called for would not, at this time, comport with the public interest." See also Lincoln's message, *supra* and note.
[2] Brackets are in the source.

To John C. Frémont[1]

July 31, 1861

The writer of the within I personally know to be a most reliable man, both for integrity and judgment; and as the matters he speaks of are in Gen. Fremont's field, I submit them to him asking his special attention to the [*sic*] them. A. LINCOLN

July 31, 1861

1 AES, DLC-RTL. Lincoln's endorsement is written on a letter from Colonel John M. Palmer, Headquarters, Fourteenth Regiment of Illinois Volunteers, Sturgeon, Missouri, July 24, 1861, to Senator Lyman Trumbull. Palmer reported many secessionists in the area and recommended organizing and arming the loyal citizens. Lincoln forwarded Palmer's letter to Frémont, and Frémont returned it enclosed with his reply, August 5, that the ". . . plan suggested . . . is about what Genl Frémont has been doing. . . ." (DLC-RTL).

Memorandum:
Appointment of Thomas H. Dudley[1]

July 31, 1861

It is said Mr. Dudley is acting as Vice-Consul at Paris, & would like to remain awhile. Let us remember this whenever we think of appointing a Consul to Paris. A.L.

July 31. 1861

1 AES, DNA FS RG 59, Appointments, Box 276. Lincoln's endorsement is written on a letter from John T. Nixon and others, undated, requesting that Thomas H. Dudley of Camden, New Jersey, be allowed to remain in Paris until his health was restored. Dudley was nominated consul at Liverpool, December 23, 1861, and confirmed by the Senate, February 19, 1862.

To United States Marshals[1]

July 31, 1861

The Marshal of the United States in the vicinity of forts where political prisoners are held, will supply decent lodging and subsistence for such prisoners unless they shall prefer to provide in those respects for themselves, in which cases they will be allowed to do so by the commanding officers in charge.

Approved, and the Secretary of State will transmit the order, to Marshals, the Lieutenant General, and Secretary of the Interior.

31 July 1861. ABRAHAM LINCOLN.

1 Copy, DNA WR RG 94, Adjutant General, Letters Received, P 878.

To Simon Cameron[1]

Executive Mansion, August 1, 1861.

My dear Sir: Herewith I enclose you a resolution of the Senate inquiring whether Hon. James H. Lane, of Kansas, has been appointed a general in the army of the United States; and if yea, whether he has accepted the appointment. Will you please furnish me, as soon as possible, copies of all record entries and correspondence upon the subject which are in your department, together with a brief statement of your personal knowledge of whatever may contribute to a free[2] and fair statement of the case? Yours truly,

Hon. Secretary of War. A. LINCOLN.

[1] Thirty-seventh Congress, First Session, *Senate Executive Document No. 8.* The original letter is missing (DNA WR RG 107). As printed in *Senate Executive Document No. 8,* it is No. 2 of the several documents transmitted by Lincoln on August 5 in response to the Senate resolution of July 31. See Lincoln to the Senate, August 5, *infra.*   [2] NH, VI, 337, reads "full" instead of "free."

To Simon Cameron[1]

Gen. Mansfield wishes Charles H. Hosmer to be a 2nd. Lieut.; and so let it be done. A. LINCOLN

Aug. 1, 1861.

[1] ALS, DLC-Cameron Papers. Charles H. Hosmer of Illinois was nominated to the Senate as second lieutenant in the First Infantry on August 1 and confirmed August 5, 1861.

To Simon Cameron[1]

Let the within named be a Pay-Master of Volunteers if a place for him can be found A. L

Aug. 1, 1861

[1] AES, IHi. Lincoln's endorsement is written on a recommendation, signed by eight Illinois congressmen, for George Phelps of Fulton County, Illinois. Phelps was nominated paymaster on August 2 and confirmed by the Senate on August 5, 1861.

To the Senate[1]

To the Senate of the United States. August 1, 1861

I submit herewith for consideration, with a view to ratification, a Postal Convention between the United States of America and the United Mexican States, concluded by their respective Plenipotentiaries on the 31st. ultimo. ABRAHAM LINCOLN

Washington 1 August 1861

[1] DS, DNA RG 46, Senate 37B B10. The treaty was ratified without amendment on August 6, 1861.

To the Tycoon of Japan[1]

August 1, 1861

Abraham Lincoln, President of the United States of America.

To His Majesty the Tycoon of Japan.

Great and Good Friend: I have received the letter which you have addressed to me on the subject of a desired extension of the time stipulated by Treaty for the opening of certain ports and cities in Japan. The question is surrounded with many difficulties. While it is my earnest desire to consult the convenience of Your Majesty and to accede so far as I can to your reasonable wishes so kindly expressed, the interests of the United States must, nevertheless, have due consideration. Townsend Harris, Minister Resident near Your Majesty, will be fully instructed as to the views of this Government, and will make them known to you at large. I do not permit myself to doubt that these views will meet with Your Majesty's approval, for they proceed not less from a just regard for the interest and prosperity of your Empire than from considerations affecting our own welfare and honor.

Wishing abundant prosperity and length of years to the great State over which you preside, I pray God to have Your Majesty always in His safe and holy keeping.

Written at the City of Washington this first day of August, 1861.

Your Good Friend, ABRAHAM LINCOLN.

By the President:

WILLIAM H. SEWARD, Secretary of State.

[1] Copy, DNA FS RG 59, Communications to Foreign Sovereigns and States, III, 176-77. Secretary Seward's communication to the ministers of foreign affairs of the Tycoon on the same date calls attention to the fact that "The subject, however, has been complicated by the yet unpunished and unatoned homicide of Mr. Heusken, our late Secretary of Legation. You must be aware that the first element of national fraternity is the safety of the persons charged with the conduct of their mutual intercourse and relations." (*Ibid.*). Henry C. J. Heusken of New York had been assassinated January 14, 1861.

To Simon Cameron[1]

August 2, 1861

Maj. Genl Butler is empowered to raise a brigade of not exceeding five thousand men with the proper proportions of artillery and mounted men and the same troops to organise and equip and arm with such serviceable arms as he may deem fit provided the expense shall not exceed the expense paid by the United States for like equipment or Material for like troops—and provided the Secretary of War concurs in this. A. LINCOLN

Aug. 2 1861

1 DS-P, ISLA. This document is in Benjamin F. Butler's handwriting with the exception of "and provided the Secretary of War concurs in this," and the signature. Butler's authorization from the War Department did not come, however, until September 12. See the draft of an order authorizing Butler to raise a Volunteer force, September 10, and Lincoln's telegram to the New England Governors, September 11, *infra*.

To John C. Frémont[1]

To Major Genl. Fremont,   Washington, August 2d 1861.

 Godfrey Aigner, M.D. has been selected by the Sanitary Commission to visit the camps of a portion of your department, to report upon circumstances affecting their health, and to advise the officers in regard to means for sustaining and improving the sanitary condition of their men. As Doctor Aigner will only act consistently with the strictest rules of military discipline, and as it will be his duty to sustain your authority and meet your wishes in all respects, your countenance, aid and support is confidently requested to be extended to him, in facilitating his movements and strengthening his influence. Yours truly   A. LINCOLN

1 LS, owned by Charles W. Olsen, Chicago, Illinois. Dr. Godfrey Aigner of New York was one of six special commissioners assigned by the Sanitary Commission to inspect military camps.

To the House of Representatives[1]

To the House of Representatives: August 2, 1861

 In answer to the resolution of the House of Representatives of yesterday, requesting information regarding the imprisonment of loyal citizens of the United States by the forces now in rebellion against this Government, I transmit a report from the Secretary of State, and the copy of a telegraphic despatch by which it was accompanied.   ABRAHAM LINCOLN.

Washington, 2d. Augt., 1861.

1 DS, DNA RG 233, Original Executive Documents, Thirty-seventh Congress, First Session, No. 17. Seward to Lincoln, August 2, 1861, notified the president that the only information he had on the subject was the telegram which he enclosed, as follows: "(Received August 1, 1861.—From Richmond, Va., July 31.) I am here a prisoner. Ely, Arnold Harris, and McGraw are also here. C. Huson, Jr." According to the New York *Times*, July 29, 1861, Arnold Harris, ex-publisher of the Washington, D. C. *States*, and Henry S. Magraw of Pennsylvania, had gone to Bull Run to recover the body of Colonel James Cameron of the Seventy-ninth New York, brother of Simon Cameron. Representative Alfred Ely of New York who had gone out to watch the battle was captured and held for six months. C. Huson, Jr., was probably the son of Calvin Huson of New York, a commissioner in the State Department.

To the Senate[1]

To the Senate of the United States August 2, 1861

The Resolution of your Honorable body which is herewith returned, has been submitted to the Secretary of Navy, who has made the Report upon it, which I have the honor to inclose herewith.

I have the honor to add that the same rule stated by the Secretary of the Navy, is found in Section 5 of the Army Regulations published in 1861. It certainly is competent for Congress to change this rule by law; but it is respectfully suggested that a rule of so long standing, and of so extensive application, should not be hastily changed; nor by any authority less than the full law-making power. ABRAHAM LINCOLN

August 2. 1861.

[1] ADS, DNA RG 46, Thirty-seventh Congress, First Session, Senate 37B A6, Box 9. The Senate resolution directed that the nominations of a list of second lieutenants in the Marine Corps be returned to the president and that ". . . the Senate are of opinion that rank and position in the Army, Navy, or Marine Corps should not be left to be decided by lot, but that, all other things being equal, preference should be given to age." (*Executive Journal*, July 31, p. 493). Secretary Welles replied that according to Army and Navy regulations ". . . questions respecting the rank of officers arising from the sameness of dates in commissions of the same grade shall be decided . . . . by lottery among such as have not been in the military service of the United States." (*Ibid.*, August 3, p. 527). Senator Hale from the committee on Naval Affairs reported August 5, that Secretary Welles' citation of regulations ". . . has not the slightest reference to the case under consideration. . . ." because the regulation applied only to ". . . officers of different regiments or corps. It is not to be resorted to, then, until the other tests provided are exhausted, but between officers of the same date of the same regiment or corps the order of appointment prevails. It is believed that this order of appointment has never . . . been fixed by lot, and if it shall be allowed in the present instance . . . will be of the most demoralizing character. . . ." (*Ibid.*, p. 548). But Senator Hale's resolution to send a copy of the report to the president was voted down.

To Hamilton R. Gamble[1]

August 3, 1861

To His Excellency H R Gamble Govr of Missouri Jefferson City

In reply to your message directed to the President—I am directed to say that If,[2] by a proclamation, you promise security to citizens in arms who voluntarily return to their allegiance, and become peaceable, and loyal, this government will, cause the promise to be respected. SIMON CAMERON

War Deptmt Secy of War

Washington Aug 3, 1861

[1] ADf, DLC-Cameron Papers. Hamilton R. Gamble had been inaugurated governor of Missouri on July 31. On August 5, he issued a proclamation that

". . . If those citizens, who at the call of the late Governor have taken up arms, choose to return voluntarily to their homes . . . they will find in the present Executive a determination to afford them all the security in his power. . . ." (New York *Tribune*, August 6, 1861). Although Cameron's message, composed in part by Lincoln, appears in the *Tribune* along with the proclamation, Gamble's message directed to the president has not been located.

[2] The draft in the Cameron Papers has the remainder of this sentence in Lincoln's autograph.

To Thomas A. Scott[1]

Executive Mansion,

Hon. Asst. Secretary of War.   Aug. 3, 1861.

Gen'l Scroggs of New York wishes to raise a military corps for service of the government and I shall be satisfied with any arrangement you may make with him at the department on the subject. Yours very truly,   A. LINCOLN.

[1] Tracy, p. 191. Thomas A. Scott of Pennsylvania had been nominated assistant secretary of war, August 3, 1861. Brigadier General Gustavus A. Scroggs of the New York Militia was authorized to recruit a regiment known as the Fourth Regiment, Eagle Brigade. It was not fully recruited and when the troops were transferred to the Seventy-eighth New York Infantry, Scroggs was not transferred or commissioned.

To William H. Seward[1]

I wish the applicant within named to have a $1500 consulate; and, if possible, to be within the German States.   A.L.

Aug. 3. 1861.

[1] AES, DNA FS RG 59, Appointments, Box 332. Lincoln's endorsement is written on the back of a brief of papers recommending Jacob T. Lockhart, secretary of the Republican state committee of Indiana, for an unspecified consulate. Lockhart received no consulate, but is listed in the *U.S. Official Register*, 1861, as Indian agent of the Nevada superintendency.

To Edward Bates[1]

Hon. Attorney General   Executive Mansion

My dear Sir: August 5. 1861

As you are anxious that Fletcher M. Haight shall be Jud[g]e of the Southern District of California, send me the nomination.[2] Also, at the request of the Wisconsin members, I conclude that Joseph G. Knapp shall be an Associate Justice in New-Mexico, in place of ——— Blackwood.[3] Yours truly   A. LINCOLN

[1] ALS-P, ISLA.
[2] Fletcher M. Haight's nomination was sent to the Senate on August 5.
[3] Joseph G. Knapp was appointed in place of William G. Blackwood. See memorandum c. July 15, *supra*.

To Simon Cameron[1]

[c.August 5, 1861]

Mr. John A. Ford, as is seen by the within papers is or was well recommended by his neighbors for post master at Petersburg. The change of sentiment since then has driven him from his home and he now seeks the appointment of second lieutenant in the army. I hope it can be conveniently given him.   A. LINCOLN.

Unless there is some confusion not known to me let Mr. Ford be appointed.   A.L.

[1] Copy, ISLA. The copies of Lincoln's endorsements are undated, but on August 5, Lincoln nominated John A. Ford of Virginia for appointment as first lieutenant in the Thirteenth Infantry, and the Senate confirmed the appointment the same day. In addition to Lincoln's endorsements, Ford's papers carry an endorsement by Winfield Scott as follows: "Mr. Ford served honorably in the Mexican War"; and by Cameron as follows: "General Thomas—Please appoint for it."

To Simon Cameron[1]

Hon. Sec. of War   Executive Mansion
My dear Sir   August 5. 1861

Col. John M. Wallace, commanding a Regiment,[2] now at Harper's Ferry, has become unable to ride a horse; and therefore his friends wish him to be a Paymaster; and I too, think it ought to be done.

Could you not also put in George A. Mitchell, for a Paymastership; as even then, Indiana will not have a large share. Yours truly   A. LINCOLN

[1] ALS, IHi. John M. Wallace and George A. Mitchell were both appointed paymasters on August 5, 1861.
[2] Lincoln wrote and deleted "recently at Cumberland" at this point.

To Simon Cameron[1]

Would it not be as well to appoint James Cooper, Brigadier General, & B. W. Perkins Quarter-Master, as Cooper recommends?
Aug. 5. 1861   A. LINCOLN

[1] AES, RPB. Lincoln's endorsement is written on the envelope enclosing Cooper's letter to Benjamin W. Perkins of August 1, and Cooper's letter to Cameron dated August 6, 1861. Cooper, in command of Maryland troops since May 11, 1861, was nominated to the Senate December 6, 1861, as brigadier general of Volunteers, his commission to date from May 17, 1861, and was confirmed by the Senate February 3, 1862. Benjamin W. Perkins was nominated to the Senate on the same date but was rejected on February 10, 1862.

To Simon Cameron[1]

The within is reliable, & I ask respectful attention to it.

Aug. 5, 1861.   A L.

[1] AES, owned by Richard F. Lufkin, Boston, Massachusetts. Lincoln's endorsement is written on the back of a letter from James C. Conkling, recommending that a regiment raised by William O. Jones in Sangamon, Morgan, Scott, and Menard counties in Illinois, be accepted. William O. Jones resigned as lieutenant colonel of the Forty-sixth Illinois Infantry shortly after it was mustered in December, 1861.

To Simon Cameron[1]

It appears to me that the appointment within recommended, would be proper; but I refer it to the Secretary of War.

Aug. 5, 1861   A. LINCOLN

[1] AES, IHi. Lincoln's endorsement is written on a letter from Montgomery Blair, August 5, 1861, endorsed in concurrence by Edward Bates and others, recommending Captain Amos F. Garrison of Missouri, formerly of the Commissary Department, for appointment as commissary in the Army of the United States. Garrison was appointed captain and commissary of Volunteers on August 7, 1861.

Memorandum:
Appointment of Edward E. Sharp[1]

When the time comes, this appointment ought to be made.

Aug. 5. 1861.   A. L

[1] AES, DNA WR RG 94, U.S. Military Academy, 1861, No. 750, Box 79. Lincoln's endorsement is written on a letter from Representative James S. Rollins of Missouri, August 4, 1861, recommending Edward E. Sharp for appointment at large to West Point. Although Lincoln again endorsed the appointment on January 27, 1862, as "A very strong case," no appointment was made.

To the Senate[1]

August 5, 1861

To the Senate of the United States: In answer to the resolution of your honorable body of date July 31, 1861, requesting the President to inform the Senate whether the Hon. James H. Lane, a member of that body from Kansas, has been appointed a brigadier general in the army of the United States, and if so, whether he has accepted such appointment, I have the honor to transmit herewith certain papers, numbered 1, 2, 3, 4, 5, 6, and 7, which, taken together, explain themselves, and which contain all the information I possess

[473]

upon the questions propounded. It was my intention, as shown by my letter of June 20, 1861, to appoint Hon. James H. Lane, of Kansas, a brigadier general of United States volunteers, in anticipation of the act of Congress, since passed, for raising such volunteers; and I have no further knowledge upon the subject, except as derived from the papers herewith enclosed.   ABRAHAM LINCOLN.

Executive Mansion, August 5, 1861.

[1] Thirty-seventh Congress, First Session, *Senate Executive Document No. 8.* The original cannot be located (DNA WR RG 46). The papers transmitted by Lincoln are printed in *Senate Executive Document No. 8* as follows: 1. copy of the Senate resolution of July 31; 2. Lincoln to Cameron, August 1 (*vide supra*); 3. copy of Lincoln to Cameron, June 20 (*vide supra*); 4. copy of Lorenzo Thomas to Lincoln, July 15, informing the president that the letter of appointment for Lane directed on June 20 had been sent to Lincoln for signature but had not been returned; 5. copy of Lorenzo Thomas to Lane, July 26, reminding Lane that he has not signified his acceptance of the appointment; 6. Lane to Thomas, July 28, notifying that when the Kansas Brigade is organized and he learns their wishes as to a commander he will signify his acceptance or non-acceptance.

To Rufus F. Andrews[1]

Hon. Rufus F. Andrews   Washington,
My dear Sir: August 6, 1861

Mr. James Morss, wishes to be Deputy-Surveyor at New-York. I do not know him personally, except for the last few days; but the testimonials he has presented interest me enough for him, to induce me to ask for him a fair and careful consideration of his case. Yours very truly   A. LINCOLN

[1] ALS, Munson-Williams-Proctor Institute, Utica, New York. James Morss is not listed as appointed in the *U.S. Official Register*, 1861.

To Simon Cameron[1]

August 6, 1861.

. . . . Let these appointments be sent me immediately, unless there be some objection not known to me.

[1] *The Collector*, July-August, 1946, J 1488. The description accompanying this fragmentary text indicates that Lincoln's letter asked appointments for Samuel Simmons of Missouri; Joseph S. York, Bradford R. Wood, Jr., and Charles A. Place of New York; and Merritt H. Insley of Kansas. All were appointed as follows: Simmons, captain and commissary of subsistence of Volunteers, August 29; York, captain Fifteenth U.S. Infantry, August 29; Wood, first lieutenant Forty-fourth New York Infantry, August 30; Place, second lieutenant Fifteenth New York Engineers, August 27; Insley, captain and assistant quartermaster of Volunteers, August 6, 1861.

To William H. Seward[1]

Hon. Sec. of State—   Executive Mansion
My dear Sir   August 6. 1861
    Theodore D. Edwards, on good recommendations was appointed
Attorney for Colorado Territory, and declines it.
    He is a Kentuckian, and declines the office; and asks to be Con-
sul to Demarara.
    I do not find an applicant for it on our list; and I do not object
to his having it. Yours truly   A. LINCOLN.

1 ALS, NAuE. See Lincoln to Seward, September 17, *infra*.

To Edward Bates[1]

Atty. Genl. please preserve these.
    Aug. 7, 1861   A L.

1 AES, InFtwL. Lincoln's endorsement is written on a recommendation of
certain Kentucky congressmen, dated July 31, 1861, for the appointment of Jeremiah T. Boyle as U.S. district judge in Kentucky. Boyle was not appointed to
a judgeship, but became a brigadier general of Volunteers on November 9, 1861.

To Simon Cameron[1]

Hon. Secretary of War   Executive Mansion, Aug. 7. 1861
    My dear Sir: The within paper, as you see, is by Hon. John S.
Phelps, and Hon. Frank P. Blair Jr. both members of the present
Congress from Missouri. The object is to get up an efficient force
of *Missourians* in the South Western part of the State. It ought to
be done; and Mr. Phelps ought to have general Superintendence of
it. I see by a private report to me from the Department, that 18
regiments are already *accepted* from Missouri.[2] Can it not be arranged that *part* of them (not yet organized, as I understand) may
be taken from the locality mentioned, and put under the control of
Mr. Phelps? And let him have discretion to accept them for a
shorter term than three years, or the war; understanding, however
that he will get them for the full term if he can. I hope this can
be done, because Mr. Phelps is too zealous & efficient; and understands his ground too well for us to lose his service. Of course provision for arming, equiping &c. must be made. Mr. Phelps is here,
& wishes to carry home with him, authority for this matter. Yours
truly   A. LINCOLN

1 ALS-F, American Art Association Catalog, February 20-21, 1928, No. 258.
John S. Phelps of Springfield, Missouri, and Francis P. Blair, Jr., wrote Lincoln
on August 6, 1861, recommending that additional troops be raised in Missouri,
enlisted for six months if desirable, to ". . . repel the threatened invasions . . .

[475]

to invade Arkansas, and . . . to keep the Indians west of that state in subjection. . . ." (OR, I, III, 430). Thomas A. Scott to Phelps, August 8, 1861, authorized ". . . five regiments of infantry and one . . . of cavalry for six months, or . . . the duration of the war. . . ." (*Ibid.*, III, I, 392).
² Thomas A. Scott to Lincoln, August 3, 1861 (DLC-RTL).

To Simon Cameron[1]

August 7, 1861

Gov. Koerner, who proposes within to raise additional forces for us, is one of the most reliable of men. If the Department can safely promise to take the troops, it can be done with as much reliance on Gov. Koerner, as on any other man.   A LINCOLN

Aug. 7. 1861

¹ Stan. V. Henkels Catalog, May 19, 1925, No. 142. Lincoln's endorsement is described as written on the back of a letter from Trumbull to Lincoln, dated August 7, 1861, forwarding and endorsing Koerner's offer to raise more German regiments. See Lincoln to Koerner, August 8, *infra.*

To Simon Cameron[1]

Hon. Sec. of War   Executive Mansion
My dear Sir: August 7, 1861

Senator Lane, of Kansas wishes appointments for Kansas volunteers—as follow.

A. C. Wilder, to be Assist. Com. of Subsistence.[2]
Dr. *Rufus Gilpatrick*, to be a Brigade Surgeon—[3]
Henry J. Adams, to be a Paymaster[4]
Dr. *W. W. Updegraff*, to be a Paymaster—[5]

I am satisfied that these appointments be made.   A. LINCOLN

¹ ALS-P, ISLA.   ² A. Carter Wilder was appointed August 7, 1861.
³ No record of the appointment of Rufus Gilpatrick has been found, but several references to his service in connection with an expedition into Indian territory occur in the *Official Records*. He was killed at Webber's Falls, Cherokee Nation, April 25, 1863, while dressing wounds of a Confederate soldier.
⁴ Henry J. Adams was appointed September 5, 1861.
⁵ W. W. Updegraff's appointment is not of record, but he served later as first lieutenant, Third Brigade of Kansas Militia.

Designation of William P. Dole to Present Treaty to the Delaware Indians[1]

Washington, August 7. 1861

I designate William P. Dole, Commissioner of Indian Affa[i]rs, to present the treaty, as amended, mentioned above, to the Indians[2] for their acceptance; and to take such acceptance, if freely given,

with the signatures of said Indians;[3] and to certify his proceedings
herein to the Executive. ABRAHAM LINCOLN

[1] AES, DNA FS RG 11, General Records, No. 317, Treaty with the Delawares
at Leavenworth City, Kansas, July 2, 1861. Lincoln's endorsement is written on
the bottom of the copy of the Senate resolution amending and ratifying the
treaty, August 6, 1861.

[2] "Through their chiefs & Head men" inserted at this point in another hand.

[3] Semicolon changed to comma and "chiefs & Head" inserted in another
hand.

To James S. Jackson[1]

Hon: James S. Jackson   Washington,
My dear Sir   Aug. 7. 1861

If you will, with the concurrence of the Union members of Congress, of Kentucky, raise a Regiment of Cavalry in that State, it
shall be received into the U.S. service—yourself to be Colonel, and,
if you please, Capt. R. Johnson[2] to be Lieut. Colonel. Yours very
truly   A. LINCOLN

[1] ALS, The Rosenbach Company, Philadelphia and New York. Representative
James S. Jackson organized the Third Kentucky Cavalry, which was mustered
into U.S. service on December 31, 1861. He was made brigadier general of Volunteers July 10, 1862, and was killed at the battle of Perryville, October 8, 1862.

[2] Richard W. Johnson was appointed brigadier general of Volunteers October 11,
1861, before the Third Kentucky Cavalry was fully organized.

To John A. McClernand[1]

Hon. John A McClernand   Executive Mansion.
My Dear Sir,   Aug. 7th. 1861.

You having been appointed a Brigadier General of Illinois Volunteers—

Your Brigade will consist of four regiments—if convenient and
desirable—*one* company of cavalry in *each* regiment and *two* artillery companies. Any four regiments which will be agreeable to
you and to one another, will be agreeable to me. One Regt of Hon
John A. Logan, one of Hon P B Fouke, one of Hon J. N. Coler, and
one of Hon B. C. Cook, will be entirely satisfactory to me[2]—or if
any one of these Regiments fail, take any other that is agreeable to
you and to the regiment. In all this, I think it will conduce to harmony for you to confer with Major General Fremont.

A. LINCOLN.

[1] Copy, DLC-RTL. The copy was enclosed by McClernand to Lincoln, January
3, 1862.

[2] Philip B. Fouke was colonel of the Thirtieth Illinois; John A. Logan, colonel
of the Thirty-first Illinois; William N. Coler, colonel of the Twenty-fifth Illinois; Burton C. Cook, not appointed.

Memorandum: Appointment of John Matthews[1]

Let Dr. John Matthews be a Regimental Surgeon for Kentucky volunteers.   A. LINCOLN

     Aug. 7. 1861.

[1] AES, owned by Dale Carnegie, Forest Hills, New York. Lincoln's endorsement has been clipped from the papers on which it was written. Dr. John Matthews was regimental surgeon in the Fifth Kentucky Infantry.

To Winfield Scott[1]

Lieut. Gen'l. Scott.   Executive Mansion, August 7, 1861.

     My dear Sir: If it be true, as is intimated to me that you think Gen'l Wool should go to Fortress Monroe, let him be ordered there at once. Yours very truly,   A. LINCOLN.

[1] Tracy, p. 192. Major General John E. Wool took command at Fort Monroe, August 17, 1861, relieving Benjamin F. Butler. Edwin D. Morgan had written to Lincoln, August 5, 1861, ". . . Against the distinguished and loyal General Officer in command at Fortress Monroe I should be the last to make complaint. . . . But . . . the duty of disciplining undrilled troops could be most safely committed to an experienced army officer. . . . I beg to propose . . . Major General Wool. . . ." (DLC-RTL).

To William H. Seward[1]

Hon. Sec. of State   Executive Mansion
My dear Sir   August 7. 1861

     I have all the while intended for you to appoint the Consul to Paris. Senator Simmons thinks you now wish to appoint William B. Richmond, of Tenn; and if this is so, send me the Commission at once, & I will sign it. Yours truly   A. LINCOLN

[1] ALS, NAuE. See Lincoln's memorandum concerning this appointment, c. April 1, Lincoln to Seward concerning the appointment of William W. Richmond, June 8, *supra*, and Lincoln's memorandum concerning the same, August 25, *infra*. Senator James F. Simmons of Rhode Island undoubtedly recommended William B. Richmond for the appointment, and through confusion of the names was listed as a supporter of William W. Richmond. Recommendations by Senator Andrew Johnson of Tennessee for both men are also involved in the confused cases. Lincoln was under the impression that William W. Richmond was claiming Senator Simmons' sponsorship under false pretenses.

To Gideon Welles[1]

                               [August 7, 1861]

     I have just received this, and now refer it to the Secretary of the Navy.

[1] *Naval Records*, I, XVI, 618. Lincoln's endorsement is on a telegram received from Bellamy Storer, judge of the Superior Court of Cincinnati, August

7, 1861, stating that "Private information to me from Savannah assures me that [Josiah] Tattnall is about to move against the blockading fleet. He has six armed tugs. Have we a squadron large enough to oppose him?" Secretary Welles forwarded the information to Flag Officer William Mervine in command of the squadron at Key West, Florida.

To Simon Cameron[1]

Hon. Sec. of War   Executive Mansion Aug. 8. 1861

My dear Sir   Edward Ellsworth, first couisin to Col. Ellsworth who fell at Alexandria, is a non-commissioned officer in the 4th. Regiment of Michigan volunteers, now stationed at the Relay House, wishes to be a 2nd. Lieut. in the Army. He is present while I write this; and he is an intelligent, and an exceedingly wary appearing young man of 20 years' age. I shall be glad if a place can be found for him   Yours truly   A. LINCOLN

[1] ALS, ORB. Edward A. Ellsworth was appointed second lieutenant in the Eleventh Infantry to date from October 24, 1861, and promoted to first lieutenant as of the same date, according to the War Department's list of promotions dated March 15, 1862, and confirmed by the Senate on April 14, 1862.

To Gustave P. Koerner[1]

Hon. G. Koerner   Washington, D.C. Aug. 8. 1861

My dear Sir Your despatch, saying application of German Brigade is withdrawn is just received. Without occupying our standpoint, you can not conceive how this subject embarrasses us. We have promises out to more than four hundred Regiments, which, if they all come, are more than we want. If they *all* come, we could not take yours, if they do *not* all come we shall want yours; and yet we have no possible means of knowing whether they will all come or not. I hope you will make due allowance for the embarrassment this produces. Yours truly   A. LINCOLN

[1] ALS, MoSHi. Gustave P. Koerner had to abandon his plan for raising a regiment of Germans because the competition for re-enlisting the three-months troops into three-years-or-the-war regiments, already approved, left fewer men available than he had anticipated (*Memoirs of Gustave Koerner*, edited by Thomas J. McCormack, II, 164).

To Lorenzo Thomas[1]

Adjutant Genl. Thomas.   Executive Mansion
My dear Sir   August 9. 1861

By the appointment of —— Marcy, this morning, as Inspector General, a vacancy of Pay-master, as you said, was made. Oblige

Mr. Senator King, by giving that place to Simeon Smith of Minnesota. Yours truly   A. LINCOLN

¹ ALS, IHi. Randolph B. Marcy was appointed inspector general August 9, and commissioned brigadier general of Volunteers September 23, 1861. Simeon Smith received the appointment in lieu of a place in the Treasury. See Lincoln to Chase, July 18, *supra*.

To Simon Cameron[1]

Let Alexander Bielaski be appointed an Aid de camp, with the rank of Captain, to Brigadier General McClernand.   A. LINCOLN
August 10. 1861.

¹ AES, Polish Roman Catholic Union, Chicago, Illinois. Lincoln's endorsement follows a recommendation by Winfield Scott written on the back of John A. McClernand to Scott, August 10, 1861, asking that Alexander Bielaski be appointed ". . . my aid de camp." Bielaski was appointed with rank of captain August 10, and was killed at the battle of Belmont, Missouri, November 7, 1861. McClernand to Lincoln September 11, however, refers to Bielaski's commission having been revoked (see Lincoln to Lorenzo Thomas, September 17, *infra*).

To Simon Cameron[1]

Hon. Sec. of War.   Executive Mansion
My dear Sir   August 10. 1861
    If Ohio is not already overstocked with Paymasterships of Volunteers, let Richard P. L. Baber have one. I personally wish this done.
Yours truly   A. LINCOLN

¹ ALS, DLC-Cameron Papers. Richard P. L. Baber, active Republican of Columbus, Ohio, was appointed additional paymaster, September 12, 1861, having declined appointment as consul at Matanzas, Cuba (Seward to Lincoln, July 25, 1861, DLC-RTL).

To Simon Cameron[1]

Hon. Sec. of War   Executive Mansion
My dear Sir   August 10. 1861
    It is said Capt. McKnabb, or, McNabb, in Utah, has been dismissed from the Army on the charge of being a disunionist; and that he wishes a hearing to enable him to show that the charge is false. Fair play is a jewell. Give him a chance if you can. Yours truly   A. LINCOLN

¹ ALS, DLC-Cameron Papers. Captain John McNab of the Tenth Infantry, in command at Fort Laramie, had been dismissed July 1, 1861, on grounds of disloyalty. There is no record of his reinstatement.

To George B. McClellan[1]

Can Gen. McClellan suggest what is to be done in the within
case?   A. LINCOLN
Augt. 10, 1861

[1] AES, ORB. Lincoln's endorsement is written on William S. Rosecrans' telegram dated at Clarksburg, August 10, detailing the need for officers and drill
masters with "military education," to lead and train the raw troops in Western
Virginia.

Pass for Messrs. Blakey and Veluzat[1]

Messrs. Blakey & Valuzat, should have passes to visit our camps
over the River, if they apply for them.   A. LINCOLN
Aug. 10, 1861

[1] ADS, NHi. The men to whom Lincoln gave the card containing his recommendation for a pass were probably George D. Blakey of Bowling Green, Kentucky, and Joel S. Veluzat, a first lieutenant in the Thirteenth Kentucky Infantry.

To William H. Seward[1]

I do not object to Senator McDougal being obliged by the appointment of the within named.   A. LINCOLN
Aug. 10, 1861

[1] AES, DNA FS RG 59, Appointments, Box 272. Lincoln's endorsement is written on the back of James A. McDougall to Lincoln, August 6, 1861, recommending Israel S. Diehl of California for consul ". . . at Smyrna or to some post in
the East. . . . Mr. Diehl has long and prominently been identified with those
reformatory movements which have done so much to benefit the people of the
Pacific coast. . . ." Diehl was appointed consul at Batavia, Java, August 12,
1861.

To William H. Seward[1]

No. 8

Augustus Haight, of Judge Sloan's District—for a Consulship. Let
it be fairly considered.   A L.
August 10. 1861.

[1] AES, DNA FS RG 59, Appointments, Box 299. Lincoln's endorsement is written on an envelope addressed by Lincoln to "Hon Sec. of State." Wisconsin Representative Andrew S. Sloan's candidate for a consulship is not listed as
appointed to office.

Proclamation of a National Fast Day[1]

August 12, 1861

By the President of the United States of America:

A Proclamation.

Whereas a joint Committee of both Houses of Congress has waited on the President of the United States, and requested him to "recommend a day of public humiliation, prayer and fasting, to be observed by the people of the United States with religious solemnities, and the offering of fervent supplications to Almighty God for the safety and welfare of these States, His blessings on their arms, and a speedy restoration of peace:"—

And whereas it is fit and becoming in all people, at all times, to acknowledge and revere the Supreme Government of God; to bow in humble submission to his chastisements; to confess and deplore their sins and transgressions in the full conviction that the fear of the Lord is the beginning of wisdom; and to pray, with all fervency and contrition, for the pardon of their past offences, and for a blessing upon their present and prospective action:

And whereas, when our own beloved Country, once, by the blessing of God, united, prosperous and happy, is now afflicted with faction and civil war, it is peculiarly fit for us to recognize the hand of God in this terrible visitation, and in sorrowful remembrance of our own faults and crimes as a nation and as individuals, to humble ourselves before Him, and to pray for His mercy,—to pray that we may be spared further punishment, though most justly deserved; that our arms may be blessed and made effectual for the re-establishment of law, order and peace, throughout the wide extent of our country; and that the inestimable boon of civil and religious liberty, earned under His guidance and blessing, by the labors and sufferings of our fathers, may be restored in all its original excellence:—

Therefore, I, Abraham Lincoln, President of the United States, do appoint the last Thursday in September next, as a day of humiliation, prayer and fasting for all the people of the nation. And I do earnestly recommend to all the People, and especially to all ministers and teachers of religion of all denominations, and to all heads of families, to observe and keep that day according to their several creeds and modes of worship, in all humility and with all religious solemnity, to the end that the united prayer of the nation may ascend to the Throne of Grace and bring down plentiful blessings upon our Country.

In testimony whereof, I have hereunto set my hand, and caused the Seal of the United States to be affixed, this 12th.
[L.S.] day of August A.D. 1861, and of the Independence of the United States of America the 86th.

By the President: ABRAHAM LINCOLN.

WILLIAM H. SEWARD, Secretary of State.

[1] DS, DNA FS RG 11, Proclamations.

To Simon Cameron[1]

Hon. Sec. of War   Executive Mansion
My dear Sir   August 13. 1861

Let *now* Brigadier Genl. David Hunter be a Major General of Volunteers to be assigned to a Division of Illinois Volunteers. Also let George H. Stoneman, and William F. Smith, both now in the service, each be a Brigadier General of Volunteers. Also Henry W. Benham, a Brigadier General of Volunteers. I mean Capt. Benham, so often spoken of, and am not sure I have his christian name correct; but you will know.[2] Yours truly   A. LINCOLN

[1] ALS-P, ISLA. The four appointments were made August 13, according to Lincoln's instructions.

[2] Henry W. Benham had been appointed major in the corps of engineers on August 6.

To William H. Seward[1]

Hon. Mr. Babbit presents this, & I ask respectful attention to it.   A. LINCOLN

    Aug. 13. 1861

[1] AES, DNA FS RG 59, Appointments, Box 263. Lincoln's endorsement is written on the back of a letter written by Representative Elijah Babbitt of Pennsylvania, August 13, 1861, recommending Allen A. Craig for a consulship, preferably at Glasgow. Craig is not listed as appointed to any consulship.

To William H. Seward[1]

Why may not this young man have Venice, which is only $750– or Nice, which has Fees only? Senator Pomeroy is very anxious for it.

    Aug. 13. 1861.   A. LINCOLN

[1] AES, DNA FS RG 59, Appointments, Box 242. Lincoln's endorsement is written on the back of the application and list of recommendations of Antonio Buchignani for the consulship at Venice or Nice, August– 1861. No appointment for Buchignani is listed in the *U.S. Official Register*, 1861, but in 1863 he is listed as messenger in the House of Representatives.

To Winfield Scott[1]

August 14, 1861

I have only a slight acquaintance with Mr. Villard, as a gentlemanly newspaper correspondent; and as such I commend him to others.   A LINCOLN

Aug. 14. 1861.

[1] AES, DLC-RTL. Lincoln's endorsement is written on the back of Henry Villard's letter, undated, offering his services ". . . in supplying General Scott with whatever information of usefulness to him I shall be able to collect during my stay in Memphis, Richmond, New Orleans & other points I propose to visit. . . ." There is no indication in Villard's *Memoirs* that anything came of this offer, but his tour was fully reported in the New York *Herald* and is extensively recounted in Villard's *Memoirs* (I, 200 ff.).

To Lorenzo Thomas[1]

August 14, 1861

It is said Capt. Dallas was rejected by the Senate through mistake. If Gen. Thomas can be satisfied, to a reasonable degree of certainty, that this is true, let Capt. Dallas be reappointed at once.

Aug. 14. 1861   A. LINCOLN

[1] AES, owned by R. E. Burdick, New York City. Lincoln's endorsement is written on a letter from Brigadier General William B. Franklin, August 12, requesting that the case of Alexander J. Dallas, whose appointment as captain in the Twelfth Infantry had been rejected by the Senate on August 5, be reconsidered on the basis of information furnished by Franklin. Below Lincoln's endorsement is the following:

"It was stated in the Military Comtee. of Senate, that Capt. Dallas was *dismissed* from the Navy & Marine Corps. This caused his rejection. Had the truth been known, he would have been confirmed by the Senate & endorsed by the Comtee. without doubt. In my opinion a great wrong has been done this gentleman.   "MILTON S. LATHAM

"Aug 15./61   of S. Mil. Comtee.
"I concur in the above
H WILSON"

Dallas had served (1846-1851) as midshipman in the Navy. See Lincoln's further communication to Thomas in this case, August 17, *infra*.

To John C. Frémont[1]

Washington, August 15, 1861.

Been answering your messages ever since day before yesterday. Do you receive the answers? The War Department has notified all the governors you designate to forward all available force. So telegraphed you. Have you received these messages? Answer immediately.   A. LINCOLN

Major General Frémont.

[484]

1 Thirty-seventh Congress, Third Session, *Senate Reports*, No. 8, III, 115. *Senate Report No. 8* dates this telegram August 5, 1861, but this is obviously a misprint, as Lincoln's telegram is printed in sequence following communications of August 14, and Frémont replied on August 15, "Dispatch rec'd. Answer recd from Messrs. Blair & Scott yesterday & today from secty of war." (DLC-RTL). Following the Confederate advances of early August in Southwest Missouri and up the Mississippi River, Frémont was frantically requesting reinforcements for his command.

To John A. Gurley[1]

Washington, D.C., August 15, 1861.

John A. Gurley, Cincinnati, Ohio: The Grosbeck regiment is ordered to join Frémont at once. Has it gone? Answer immediately.

A. LINCOLN.

1 NH, VI, 344. Gurley's telegram to Lincoln from Cincinnati, August 14, asked authority to send "the Groesbeck Regt." to Frémont. In reply to the above telegram, Gurley informed Lincoln, August 15, that the regiment had not gone but "Will go soon." (DLC-RTL). The regiment commanded by Colonel John Groesbeck became the Thirty-ninth Ohio Infantry.

To Oliver P. Morton[1]

War Department,
Washington City   August 15, 1861—9:20 a.m.

Governor Morton, Indiana: Start your four regiments to Saint Louis at the earliest moment possible. Get such harness as may be necessary for your rifled guns. Do not delay a single regiment, but hasten everything forward as soon as any one regiment is ready. Have your three additional regiments organized at once. We shall endeavor to send you the arms this week.   A. LINCOLN.

1 OR, III, I, 413. Morton to Cameron, August 14: "Will start four regiments to Saint Louis day after to-morrow. I have . . . three battalions of rifled cannon . . . but have no harness. . . . Will have three additional regiments ready in six days, but they have no arms. . . ." (*Ibid.*, p. 410).

To James Pollock[1]

Hon. James Pollock   Washington, August 15, 1861

My dear Sir You must make a job of it, and provide a place for the bearer of this, Elias Wampole. Make a job of it with the Collector, and have it done. You *can* do it for me, and you *must*. Yours as ever   A. LINCOLN

1 ALS, PHC. James Pollock, former governor of Pennsylvania (1855-1858), was director of the mint at Philadelphia. The *U.S. Official Register* does not list Elias Wampole in 1861, but in 1863, he appears as consul at Laguayra, Venezuela,

appointed from Pennsylvania. William B. Thomas, collector of customs at Philadelphia, wrote to Lincoln August 22, that Pollock had called with Lincoln's letter recommending Wampole, but that since Wampole was really a citizen of Illinois he should get an office there (DLC-Nicolay Papers). Wampole had formerly resided in Menard County, Illinois, where he doubtless made Lincoln's acquaintance.

To Simon Cameron[1]

Hon. Sec. of War   Executive Mansion
My dear Sir   Aug. 16. 1861
   If there is a letter in your Dept. written by Col. Cass of Mass. 9th. in relation to trial of Michael H. Macnamara, by a Court Marshal [*sic*], please send it to me—by the bearer.

                                          A. LINCOLN

[1] ALS, DLC-Cameron Papers. There is no reply from Cameron in the Lincoln Papers. Colonel Thomas Cass was in command of the Ninth Massachusetts Infantry, from which First Lieutenant Michael H. McNamara, of Company E, was dismissed on September 10, 1861. McNamara enlisted again as a private August 14, 1862, and was mustered out as sergeant June 21, 1864.

To Simon Cameron[1]

I believe the writer of this is our Gen. Thomas, M.C. of Maryland; and if so, let the man he recommends be appointed.
   Aug. 16. 1861   A. LINCOLN

[1] AES, IHi. Lincoln's endorsement appears on a letter from Representative Francis Thomas, Washington, August 16, 1861, requesting appointment as lieutenant of George M. Downey, "who on account of his earnest devoted support of your administration has been forced to leave his home at Piedmont Virginia. . . ." Downey was appointed first lieutenant in the Fourteenth U.S. Infantry on October 26, 1861.

Memorandum:
Appointment of Clarence Darling[1]

                          Executive Mansion   Aug. 16. 1861
To-day William A. Darling, of New-York, and a Presidential Elector last year, calls and asks that his son, Clarence Darling, not 16 till Oct. 1862 — be a Cadet at West. Point. I file this for a memorandum till the time comes.   A. LINCOLN

[1] ADS, DLC-RTL. There is no record of the appointment of Clarence Darling.

Proclamation Forbidding Intercourse with Rebel States[1]

August 16, 1861

By the President of the United States of America.

A Proclamation

Whereas, on the 15th. day of April, 1861, the President of the United States, in view of an insurrection against the Laws Constitution and Government of the United States which had broken out within the States of South Carolina Georgia, Alabama, Florida, Mississippi, Louisiana & Texas, and in pursuance of the provisions of the Act entitled "An Act to provide for calling forth the militia to execute the laws of the Union, suppress insurrections, and repel invasions, and to repeal the act now in force for that purpose," approved Feb. 28th., 1795, did call forth the militia to suppress said insurrection and to cause the Laws of the Union to be duly executed, and the insurgents have failed to disperse by the time directed by the President, and whereas such insurrection has since broken out and yet exists within the States of Virginia, North Carolina, Tennessee and Arkansas; and whereas the insurgents in all the said States claim to act under the authority thereof, and such claim is not disclaimed or repudiated by the persons exercising the functions of government in such State or States, or in the part or parts thereof in which such combinations exist, nor has such insurrection been suppressed by said States; Now, therefore, I, Abraham Lincoln, President of the United States, in pursuance of an Act of Congress approved July 13, 1861, do hereby declare that the inhabitants of the said States of Georgia, South Carolina, Virginia, North Carolina, Tennessee, Alabama, Louisiana, Texas, Arkansas, Mississippi & Florida (except the inhabitants of that part of the State of Virginia lying west of the Allegheny Mountains and of such other parts of that State & the other States hereinbefore named as may maintain a loyal adhesion to the Union and the Constitution, or may be from time to time occupied and controlled by forces of the United States engaged in the dispersion of said insurgents,) are in a state of insurrection against the United States, and that all commercial intercourse between the same and the inhabitants thereof, with the exceptions aforesaid, and the citizens of other States and other parts of the United States is unlawful, and will remain unlawful until such insurrection shall cease or has been suppressed; that all goods and chattels, wares and merchandize, coming from any of said States, with the exceptions aforesaid.

[487]

into other parts of the United States, without the special license and permission of the President through the Secretary of the Treasury, or proceeding to any of said States, with the exceptions aforesaid, by land or water, together with the vessel or vehicle conveying the same, or conveying persons to or from said States with said exceptions, will be forfeited to the United States; and that from and after Fifteen Days from the issuing of this Proclamation, all ships and vessels belonging in whole or in part to any citizen or inhabitant of any of said States with said exceptions found at sea or in any port of the United States, will be forfeited to the United States; and I hereby enjoin upon all District Attorneys, Marshals and Officers of the Revenue and of the Military and Naval Forces of the United States to be vigilant in the execution of said Act, and in the enforcement of the penalties and forfeitures imposed or declared by it; leaving any party who may think himself aggrieved thereby to his application to the Secretary of the Treasury for the remission of any penalty or forfeiture, which the said Secretary is authorized by law to grant if, in his judgment, the special circumstances of any case shall require such remission.

In witness whereof, I have hereunto set my hand and caused the Seal of the United States to be affixed.

[L.S.]   Done at the City of Washington, this 16th day of August, in the year of our Lord 1861, and of the Independence of the United States the Eighty-sixth.

By the President: ABRAHAM LINCOLN.

WILLIAM H. SEWARD, Secretary of State.

[1] D, DNA FS RG 11, Proclamations. Both the signatures of Lincoln and Seward are in the handwriting of Seward.

To Simon Cameron[1]

Hon. Sec. of War   Executive Mansion
My dear Sir   August 17, 1861

These gentlemen—Samuel Gamage, and Charles R. Saunders—are Californians, who were well recommended for offices which have been given to others. I am now willing that they should be appointed Pay-Masters of Volunteers, as Californians. Yours truly

A. LINCOLN

[1] ALS, DLC-Cameron Papers. Samuel Gamage was appointed captain and commissary of subsistence of Volunteers September 7, 1861. Charles R. Saunders was appointed additional paymaster of Volunteers September 5, 1861, but was rejected by the Senate March 6, 1862. See Lincoln's memoranda to Cameron on these appointments, August 29, and September 4, *infra*.

To Simon Cameron[1]

Hon. Secretary of War: Executive Mansion, August 17, 1861.

My dear Sir: Unless there be reason to the contrary, not known to me, make out a commission for Simon [B.] Buckner, of Kentucky, as a brigadier-general of volunteers. It is to be put into the hands of General Anderson, and delivered to General Buckner or not, at the discretion of General Anderson. Of course it is to remain a secret unless and until the commission is delivered. Yours, truly,

A. LINCOLN.

[*Indorsement.*]

Same day made.

[1] OR, I, IV, 255. Simon B. Buckner declined the appointment and accepted a commission as brigadier general in the Confederate Army. Brackets are in the source.

To Simon Cameron[1]

Hon. Sec. of War   Executive Mansion
My dear Sir—   August 17– 1861

Let Henry Wager Halleck, of California, be appointed a Major General in the *Regular Army*. I make this appointment on Gen. Scott's recommendation; and I am sure he said to me verbally that the appointment is to be in the Regular Army, though a memorandum on the subject handed me by one of his aids, says "of volunteers" Perhaps the Adjt. [Genl. should communicate with] Genl. Scott, on the question.[2] Yours truly   A. LINCOLN

[1] ALS, DLC-Cameron Papers. Henry W. Halleck was appointed major general in the Regular Army, August 19, 1861.
[2] Lincoln obviously failed to complete his thought between "Adjt." at the end of one line and "Genl. Scott" at the beginning of the next. The bracketed insertion has been supplied by the editors.

To Simon Cameron[1]

August 17, 1861

If it be according to the law, & the rules, let Thomas M. Key be appointed, as requested within by Gen. McClellan. For a reason, in no wise disrespectful to Gen. McClellan, nor derogatory to Col. Sackett, I can not, as yet, appoint him.   A. LINCOLN.

Aug. 17. 1861.

[1] AES, NN. Lincoln's endorsement is written on the back of George B. McClellan's letter of August 16, 1861, requesting Thomas M. Key be appointed his aide-de-camp with rank of colonel, and that Lieutenant Delos B. Sacket be appointed inspector general with rank of colonel. Key was appointed August 19, and Sacket October 1, 1861.

To Simon Cameron[1]

Let George A. Flagg named within be appointed an Assistant Quar-Master, of Volunteers.   A. LINCOLN
     Aug. 17, 1861.

[1] AES, IHi. Lincoln's endorsement is written on the back of a duplicate copy of a letter of John L. King to Caleb B. Smith, Chicago, March 24, 1861, asking that George A. Flagg of Chicago be appointed to some territorial land office. Flagg was appointed captain and assistant quartermaster of Volunteers on September 10, 1861.

To Isabel II[1]

August 17, 1861

Abraham Lincoln,
President of the United States of America.
To Her Majesty Isabel II,
     By the Grace of God and the Constitution
          of the Spanish Monarchy, Queen of Spain,
                         &c.,   &c.

Great and Good Friend: I have received the letter which Your Majesty was pleased to address to me on the 22nd. day of June, last, announcing the birth of an Infanta, upon whom had been bestowed in sacred baptism the names of Maria del Pilar Berenguela Isabel Francisca de Asis Christina Sebastiana Gabriela Francisca Caracciola Saturnina.

I participate in the satisfaction afforded by this happy event, and offer to Your Majesty my sincere congratulations upon the occasion.

May God have Your Majesty always in His safe and holy keeping! Your Good Friend,   ABRAHAM LINCOLN.
     Washington, August 17, 1861.
     By the President:
          WILLIAM H. SEWARD, Secretary of State.

[1] Copy, DNA FS RG 59, Communications to Foreign Sovereigns and States, III, 178-79.

To William H. Seward[1]

August 17, 1861

Mr. J. Wagner Jermon, was an applicant for Consul to Glasgow, & now wishes Melbourne. If the latter is open, the Sec. of State can fill it according to his pleasure, giving fair consideration to Mr. Jermon's claim.   A LINCOLN

Aug. 17. 1861

1 AES, DNA FS RG 59, Appointments, Box 317. J. Wagner Jermon of Philadelphia received neither appointment.

To William H. Seward[1]

August 17, 1861

I, herein, send the Sec. of State, a new application for the Consulate at Melbo[u]rne. The applicant is a New-Yorker; and as the Secretary will see, is very well recommended.   A. LINCOLN

Aug. 17. 1861.

1 AES, DNA FS RG 59, Appointments, Box 407. Charles C. Yeaton, the applicant, did not receive the appointment.

To Lorenzo Thomas[1]

August 17, 1861

I repeat that if Adjutant Genl. Thomas is reasonably well satisfied that Capt. Dallas was rejected by the Senate through misappre-[hen]sion of facts, he is to be re-appointed. It is the opinion of the Adjutant General, and of Genl. Franklin, as shown by what they have written written [sic] within, that he is a good officer.   Aug. 17. 1861.   A. LINCOLN

1 AES, owned by R. E. Burdick, New York City. See Lincoln's earlier endorsement in this case, August 14, supra. Alexander J. Dallas' reappointment was confirmed by the Senate February 20, 1862.

To George B. McClellan[1]

[c. August 18, 1861]

Gen. McClellan please read and return these.   A L

1 AES, DLC-RTL. Lincoln's endorsement is written on a letter from John S. Carlile to Salmon P. Chase, August 18, 1861, describing conditions in Western Virginia.

To Simon Cameron[1]

Hon. Sec. of War   Executive Mansion
My dear Sir   August 19, 1861

At the request of Brigadier General Anderson, I have concluded to appoint George H. Thomas, of the 2nd. Cavalry, a Brigadier General of Volunteers.[2]

[491]

Also, let the Hon. James Shields, now of California, be appointed a Brigadier General of Volunteers.[3]

Also, Col. Michael Corcoran, now a prisoner at Richmond.[4]

Yours truly   A. LINCOLN

[1] ALS, owned by Frederick M. Dearborn, New York City.

[2] George H. Thomas, under appointment dated August 17, was assigned to duty in Kentucky organizing troops.

[3] James Shields was appointed August 19.

[4] Colonel Michael Corcoran of the Sixty-ninth New York Regiment had been captured at the Battle of Bull Run, and remained a prisoner until August 15, 1862. His appointment as brigadier general dated back to July 21, 1861, was not sent to the Senate until December 23, 1862, but along with numerous others on the list of that date was returned to the president because of an error of reference to the act under which the appointments were made. Confirmation of the appointment by the Senate was finally made March 11, 1863.

To Simon Cameron[1]

August 19, 1861

In view of the abundant evidence of the efficiency and valuable service of Capt. Leib, as an Assistant Quarter Master, and especially that borne by Generals Rosecrans, Kelly & Oakes, within, I think he should be re-appointed to his place, unless it is known that some change of magnitude, was made, and proved against him before the Senate.   A. LINCOLN

Aug. 19. 1861.

[1] AES, IHi. Charles Leib of Illinois had been appointed first lieutenant in the Eleventh Infantry of the Regular Army, May 14, 1861, but was rejected by the Senate August 5. In spite of recommendations from his superiors (Brigadier General William S. Rosecrans, Brigadier General Benjamin F. Kelley, and Major James Oakes) upon which he was reappointed, he was again rejected by the Senate both as first lieutenant and as captain and assistant quartermaster, to which rank he had been advanced as of May 21, 1861.

To Simon Cameron[1]

Hon. Sec. of War: Executive Mansion   Aug. 19. 1861.

I understand Mr. Edwards left here a Commissary of subsistence; *but not assigned to any particular Brigade.*[2] If this be so, let Josiah M. Lucas, formerly of Illinois, now of D.C. be Commissary of Subsistence, and assigned to Genl. McClernand's Brigade.[3] Yours truly   A. LINCOLN

[1] ALS, IHi.

[2] Ninian W. Edwards was appointed captain and commissary of subsistence of Volunteers, August 8, 1861.

[3] Cameron endorsed this appointment on the bottom of this letter, August 22, and the appointment was made as of that date.

To Simon Cameron[1]

I think the personal favor within asked by Mr. Stratton ought to be granted, if possible.   A. LINCOLN

Aug. 19. 1861.

[1] AES, DNA WR RG 107, Secretary of War, Personnel Appointments, Box 12. Lincoln's endorsement is written on the back of Representative John L. N. Stratton's letter of May 4, 1861, recommending Samuel H. Howell of New Jersey for a clerkship. Howell is listed in the *U.S. Official Register*, 1863, as paymaster's clerk in the War Department.

To William H. Seward[1]

August 19, 1861

I think the case of Major Jewell is one of merit; and that we ought to find something for him, even if we can not find a consulship. Will the Sec. of State please consider this?   A. LINCOLN

Aug. 19. 1861.

[1] AES, DNA FS RG 59, Appointments, Box 318. Lincoln's endorsement is written on the back of a letter from J. Grey Jewell of Mississippi, "(late)—Major comd'g 2nd. Batn. D.C. Volunteers," asking for a consulship. The *U.S. Official Record*, 1863, lists him as a clerk in the sixth auditor's office.

To Lorenzo Thomas[1]

If appointments of Pay-Masters are not already too numerous, let Mr. Senator Harlan be obliged by the appointment within requested.   A. LINCOLN

Aug. 19. 1861.

[1] AES, RPB. Lincoln's endorsement is written on a letter from Senator James Harlan, July 4, 1861, recommending appointment of Alvin Walker of New York as paymaster. Walker was appointed September 10, 1861.

To Lorenzo Thomas[1]

August 19, 1861

Mr. Nicholas Vedder, is within recommended for a Volunteer Paymastership by our Illinois Democratic members of Congress, now heartily aiding us in the war, and is a good man withal, which I think are sufficient reasons for me to direct that he be appointed.

Aug. 19, 1861.   A. LINCOLN

[1] AES, owned by R. E. Burdick, New York City. Lincoln's endorsement is written on the back of an undated letter from Illinois members of congress, recommending the appointment of Nicholas Vedder of Greene County, Illinois. Vedder, who had been appointed secretary of the Senate committee on Territories under the chairmanship of Stephen A. Douglas in 1856, was appointed additional paymaster of Volunteers, September 5, 1861.

To Gideon Welles[1]

Respectfully submitted to the Navy Department, with request for a respectful consideration.   A. LINCOLN.

Aug. 19, 1861.

[1] American Art Association Catalog, May 6, 1915, No. 316. According to the catalog description, Lincoln's endorsement is written on the back of a letter from Edward C. Carrington, recommending Captain S. E. Arnold for a commission in the Marine Corps. There is no record of the appointment.

To Simon Cameron[1]

Hon. Sec. of War   Executive Mansion
Sir.   Aug. 20. 1861

Gen. McClellan requests that John F. Reynolds, and William F. Barry be appointed Brigadier Generals of volunteers; and so let it be done. Yours truly   A. LINCOLN

[1] Copy, ISLA. The letter bears Cameron's endorsement "Let it be done." Both appointments were made on this date. John F. Reynolds, West Point 1841, was lieutenant colonel of the Fourteenth Infantry. William F. Barry, West Point 1838, was major in the Fifth Artillery.

To Simon Cameron[1]

Unless there be some reason, not known to me, let the appointments, as above suggested by Gen. Thomas, be made.

August 20. 1861.   A. LINCOLN

[1] AES, DLC-Cameron Papers. Lincoln's endorsement is written on a letter from Representative Francis Thomas of Maryland, August 20, 1861, recommending the appointment of William P. Maulsby, colonel; Lewis P. Fiery, major; and Charles E. Rail, lieutenant colonel, of the First Maryland Regiment, Potomac Home Brigade. No record has been found of federal appointment in these cases.

To William H. Seward[1]

Hon. Sec. of State   Executive Mansion
My dear Sir.   August 20. 1861

Mr. Zebina Eastman, of Chicago, Ills. is one of the earliest, and most efficient of our free-soil laborers. If a position, with even moderate pay, could be found for him in England, he is just the man to reach the sympathies of the English people, to the extent that he can come in contact with them. He is more than a common man, in his sphere; and I shall be very glad if you can find out, or fix out for him, some such place as I have indicated. Yours truly

A. LINCOLN

[1] ALS, NAuE. Zebina Eastman, Chicago newspaper editor and abolitionist, is listed in the *U.S. Official Register*, 1861, as consul at Bristol.

To Francis P. Blair, Jr.[1]

August 21, 1861

I repeat, I will commission the officers of Missouri Volunteers.
Colonel Blair.   A. LINCOLN.

[1] Thirty-seventh Congress, Third Session, *Senate Reports*, No. 108, III, 115.
Colonel Francis P. Blair, Jr., telegraphed Montgomery Blair, August 21, 1861, "It
is necessary for the president to commission our officers as . . . the law of this
state . . . make[s] it impossible to act under it . . . at present no officer in the
Missouri service has a commission. . . ." (DLC-RTL).

To Simon Cameron[1]

I shall be gratified if Mr. Hertford can retain the place he now
holds in the War Department.   A. LINCOLN
Aug. 21, 1861

[1] AES, DLC-Cameron Papers. Lincoln's endorsement is written on the back
of a letter from Joseph Hertford, August 19, 1861. A temporary clerk in the War
Department, friend of Leonard Swett and Ward H. Lamon and an ex-Chicagoan,
Hertford apparently did not keep his War Department position, but in 1862 secured a place in the Bureau of Internal Revenue.

To Edward Bates[1]

August 22, 1861

Will the Attorney General please make out pardons in the Missouri cases he and I spoke of, and place them in my hands?

[1] American Art Association Anderson Galleries Catalog 3781, October 30, 1929,
No. 90. Bates to Lincoln, August 24, 1861, "It was my fault not to enquire at
what time you wd need the Mo. pardon, & the draft of your letter to Gov. Gamble.
I leave them now—12.15 p.m. having changed your draft in no respect, except
in the addition of a short sentence, which, it seemed to me, might tend to conciliate good feeling in Mo." (DLC-RTL). Lincoln's letter to Governor Hamilton
R. Gamble is presumably not extant and the pardons have not been located.

To Simon Cameron[1]

Hon. Secretary of War.   Executive Mansion, August 22, 1861.
    Sir: Victor B. Bell, now of Colorado, is one of my most valued
friends; and one of the best, if not the very best clerk I ever knew.
I would like for him to be an Asst. Quarter Master or Commissary
of Subsistence of Volunteers.
    Can you not fix it for me? Yours truly,   A. LINCOLN.
August 22, 1861.

[495]

¹ Tracy, p. 193. Victor B. Bell, who had served as representative from Wabash County in the Illinois House of Representatives (1853-1854), is not of record for either appointment.

To Simon Cameron¹

Let the Appointment within requested, be made.   A. LINCOLN.
Aug. 22, 1861.

¹ AES, owned by R. S. Ruwitch, Chicago, Illinois. Lincoln's endorsement is written on a letter from General George B. McClellan, August 22, 1861, asking appointment of Richard B. Irwin of the District of Columbia as captain and aide-de-camp. Irwin's appointment, made the same day, was confirmed by the Senate on February 3, 1862.

To Simon Cameron¹

Hon. Sec. of War   Executive Mansion
Sir   August 22. 1861
   My impression is that few Assistant Quarter-Masters, or Commissaries of Subsistence, for volunteers, have, as yet, been appointed from Ohio. If I am right in this, let Willard Slocum, of Ohio be appointed to one, or the other of those offices. Yours truly
                                                    A. LINCOLN

¹ ALS, DLC-Cameron Papers. Willard Slocum of Ohio had resigned his place as captain in the Twenty-third Ohio on July 18, and was appointed first lieutenant and adjutant of the One Hundred Twentieth Ohio Infantry, August 25, 1862. There is no record of his appointment as per Lincoln's recommendation in this letter.

Concerning Mr. Rutherford¹

Is there anything in the "Marble line" which could be given Mr. Rutherford?   A. L.
Aug. 22, 1861.

¹ ADS, CSmH. Rutherford has not been identified.

Endorsement¹

I think that the young man within recommended, ought to be appointed, if possible. There is some peculiar reason for it.
Aug. 22, 1861.   A. LINCOLN

¹ Tracy, p. 194. Efforts to locate the document and to identify the case have failed.

To Beriah Magoffin[1]

To His Excellency   Washington, D.C.
B. Magoffin   August 24. 1861
Governor of the State of Kentucky.

Sir: Your letter of the 19th. Inst. in which you *"urge the removal from the limits of Kentucky of the military force now organized, and in camp within said State"* is received.

I may not possess full and precisely accurate knowledge upon this subject; but I believe it is true that there is a military force in camp within Kentucky, acting by authority of the United States, which force is not very large, and is not now being augmented.

I also believe that some arms have been furnished to this force by the United States.

I also believe this force consists exclusively of Kentuckians, having their camp in the immediate vicinity of their own homes, and not assailing, or menacing, any of the good people of Kentucky.

In all I have done in the premises, I have acted upon the urgent solicitation of many Kentuckians, and in accordance with what I believed, and still believe, to be the wish of a majority of all the Union-loving people of Kentucky.

While I have conversed on this subject with many eminent men of Kentucky, including a large majority of her Members of Congress, I do not remember that any one of them, or any other person, except your Excellency and the bearers of your Excellency's letter, has urged me to remove the military force from Kentucky, or to disband it. One other very worthy citizen of Kentucky did solicit me to have the augmenting of the force suspended for a time.

Taking all the means within my reach to form a judgment, I do not believe it is the popular wish of Kentucky that this force shall be removed beyond her limits; and, with this impression, I must respectfully decline to so remove it.

I most cordially sympathize with your Excellency, in the wish to preserve the peace of my own native State, Kentucky; but it is with regret I search, and can not find, in your not very short letter, any declaration, or intimation, that you entertain any desire for the preservation of the Federal Union. Your Obedient Servant,

A. LINCOLN

[1] ALS, IHi; ALS copy, DLC-RTL. Governor Magoffin's letter of August 19, protested recruitment and establishment of camps in Kentucky ". . . without the advice or consent of the Authorities of the State. . . ." (DLC-RTL). Although the state legislature remained loyal, Magoffin persisted in his declared "neutrality" and acted in sympathy with the Confederacy until August, 1862, when he resigned.

To Caleb B. Smith[1]

August 24, 1861

I do not know Mr. Jones. Mr. Shackelford who writes the within I know to be a good man. I have no objection to Mr. Jones having an Indian Agency, if there be one not disposed of or committed.

Aug. 24, 1861   A. LINCOLN

[1] AES, DNA NR RG 48, Applications, Indian Agencies, Miscellaneous 1857-1864, Box 1268. Lincoln's endorsement is written on a letter from James M. Shackelford of Richmond, Kentucky, August 14, 1861, asking appointment of Dr. William W. Jones of Madison County, Kentucky, to an Indian agency. No appointment is listed in the *U.S. Official Register*.

To Lorenzo Thomas[1]

Let the appointment be made, as within requested.

Aug. 24, 1861.   A. LINCOLN

[1] AES, RPB. Lincoln's endorsement is written on a letter from George B. McClellan, August 23, 1861, requesting appointment of Thomas T. Gantt of St. Louis ". . . an Aid de Camp to myself with the rank of Colonel." The appointment was made on August 26, 1861.

Memorandum:
Appointment of William W. Richmond[1]

August 25, 1861

Will Mr. Richmond distinctly declare that he did not write a letter to Mrs. L. giving Senator *Simmons'* name, as one of his backers for a Consulate?   A.L.

Aug. 25, 1861

[1] AES, IHi. Lincoln's endorsement is written on the back of William W. Richmond to Lincoln, Washington, August 25, 1861, complaining of Lincoln's refusal to see him ". . . upon the supposition that I was unworthy of that common courtesy: that you supposed I had unauthorisedly drawn money from the Treasury and that I had substituted myself for some one else!" Richmond explained that he had acted in good faith, supposing himself legitimately appointed, but that he was not William B. Richmond. He also denied having listed Senator Simmons among his supporters. Unfortunately his letter addressed to Mrs. Lincoln August 8, 1861 (DLC-RTL), did list Senator Simmons among the references, and Lincoln's dubiety, when he was confronted by the senator's denial, is readily understood. In Richmond's letter to Mrs. Lincoln, Senator Simmons' name occurs among several others inserted after the letter was written, as names of persons whom Richmond had been told were supporting his application. Richmond explained to Lincoln in a letter of September 21, 1861, that the copy of the unfortunate letter retained by himself did not contain any of the names listed. As a result of the confusion, neither William B. Richmond nor William W. Richmond received the consulship at Paris, and William B. Richmond was further disappointed in failing of confirmation for the consulship at Tunis when Lincoln withdrew his nomination, March 24, 1862. See also Lincoln to Seward, August 7, *supra*.

To Simon Cameron[1]

Unless there be some reason to the contrary unknown to me, let Gen. Richardson be gratified in the appointment of his Staff.

Aug. 26. 1861.   A. LINCOLN

[1] AES, IHi. Lincoln's endorsement appears on a letter from Brigadier General Israel B. Richardson, Camp near Arlington, Fort Albany, August 24, 1861, asking that his request made "five weeks since" for appointments to his staff be expedited as follows: John Mason Norvell, adjutant of the Second Michigan Infantry, to be assistant adjutant general with rank of captain; Edward S. Earle, adjutant of the Third Michigan Infantry, to be brigade commissary with rank of captain; Christopher W. Leffingwell of Michigan, to be brigade quartermaster with rank of major. Norvell was appointed on August 30, Earle on September 9, and Leffingwell on September 10, but Leffingwell failed to be confirmed by the Senate.

To Salmon P. Chase[1]

To the Secretary of the Treasury,   August 26, 1861

Sir, You are hereby authorised and directed to make such advances to any agent appointed under the Act of Congress approved 31 July 1861, as may be required by the Secretary of War, as necessary to the faithful and prompt discharge of the duties of such agent.   ABRAHAM LINCOLN

Executive Mansion
        August 26, 1861.

[1] LS, DNA FI RG 56, General Records, Treasury Department, Series AB, 1861, II, 5.

To John C. Frémont[1]

Washington, August 26, 1861.

Intelligent gentlemen at Louisville say the presence of Rousseau's regiment is needed there. Pardon us for countermanding your order to him to join your department.   A. LINCOLN.

General Frémont.

[1] Thirty-seventh Congress, Third Session, *Senate Reports*, No. 108, III, 117. Bland Ballard, James Speed, Joshua F. Speed, and others telegraphed Lincoln August 24, ". . . In our opinions passing events show that . . . [Rousseau's regiment] are required here & they should be detained here if possible." (DLC-RTL).

To Montgomery C. Meigs[1]

Gnl. Meigs.   [August 27, 1861]

Mr. Wilmore & Mr Dewey[2] of Kentucky have six hundred mules, of a size larger than the Army standard, which they say you decline buying for the reason that the smaller ones, purchased by you had been got at a price, eight dollars less than the man demanded for them. In consideration of the service that larger animals will be used for in the coming winter campaign, we think the price should not prevent the purchase & therefore recommend it.

SIMON CAMERON

A. LINCOLN

[1] LS, DLC-Chase Papers. The letter, or draft, is in Cameron's handwriting and is signed by both Cameron and Lincoln. The date is that assigned to the document in the Chase Papers.   [2] Unidentified.

To Winfield Scott[1]

August 27, 1861

Will Lieutenant-General Scott see the bearer[2] and write briefly on the within letter of the Governor of New Jersey what can be done in the premises.   A. LINCOLN.

[1] OR, III, I, 450. Lincoln's endorsement is written on a letter from Governor Charles S. Olden, August 24, 1861, ". . . I can raise, uniform, arm, and equip the regiments from this state. . . . but I cannot find men . . . competent to lead the regiments. . . . I feel that the General Government owes it to this State to furnish at least colonels. . . ." (*Ibid.*, 451-52). Assistant Adjutant General Edward D. Townsend endorsed, August 28, "The General-in-chief assents to the detail of Captain [Samuel H.] Starr . . . and Lieut. J[oseph] L. K. Smith . . . to command regiments of volunteers from New Jersey. . . ." (*Ibid.*).

[2] Barker Gummere.

To Simon Cameron[1]

August 28, 1861

The writer of the within desired me to sign my name to it. I know not whether it is right or wrong. Yesterday I think I sent you a letter of his, endorsed in such way as I thought proper.[2]

Aug. 28. 1861.   A. LINCOLN

[1] AES, DLC-Cameron Papers. Lincoln's endorsement is written on a letter prepared by L. A. Bargie as follows: "L. A. Bargie, who proposes to go to Colorado Territory, to assist in the organisation of a Regiment there, wishes to obtain some military books, and some side-arms. I request that you will direct them to be given to him."   [2] The endorsement has not been located.

To Simon Cameron[1]

August 28, 1861

Mr. Bell was very well recommended for one of the high offices in the Customs for San Francisco; but among the many applicants so recommended, did not succeed   A. LINCOLN

Aug. 28, 1861

1 AES, owned by Milton H. Shutes, Oakland, California. Lincoln's endorsement is written on the envelope of a letter from Samuel Bell to Senator James A. McDougall of California, August 14, 1861, requesting appointment as paymaster. There is no record of his appointment.

To Simon Cameron[1]

I am quite willing that Senator Harris shall be gratified in the request made within.   A. LINCOLN

Aug. 28. 1861.

1 AES, IHi. Lincoln's endorsement is written on a note from Senator Ira Harris requesting that James B. Swain of New York City be appointed quartermaster with rank of major. Swain was appointed second lieutenant in the First Cavalry Regular Army, November 1, 1861.

To Simon Cameron[1]

August 28, 1861

I personally know Mr. Tanner to be an active, intelligent business-like man, & I understand him to be of unimpeachable character.   A. LINCOLN

Aug. 28, 1861

1 AES, owned by Herman Blum, Blumhaven Library, Philadelphia. Lincoln's endorsement is written on a letter from Philip Dorsheimer, a prominent Republican of Buffalo, New York, August 22, 1861, recommending Henry Tanner of Buffalo for local commissary. There is no record of Tanner's appointment.

To Simon Cameron[1]

These are good recommendations, as the Sec. of War will see. I ask respectful consideration for them.   A. LINCOLN

Aug. 29, 1861

1 AES-P, ISLA. Lincoln's endorsement is written on the back of a letter from Bland Ballard, Louisville, Kentucky, August 20, 1861, asking that his brother-in-law William P. McDowell, a cousin of Brigadier General Irvin McDowell, be given a commission. Although the middle initial is not clearly "P" in Ballard's letter, it seems possible that William P. McDowell, appointed first lieutenant and adjutant in the Fifteenth Kentucky Infantry December 14, 1861, was the same man.

To Simon Cameron[1]

I am quite as willing that Mr. Gamage or Saunders shall be an Assistant Quarter Master, or Commissary, as to be a Paymaster.

Aug. 29. 1861   A. LINCOLN

¹ AES, DLC-Cameron Papers. Lincoln's endorsement is written on a letter from General James W. Denver, August 26, 1861, stating that although he had no objection to Samuel Gamage's and Charles R. Saunders' appointment to places ". . . on the staff of the Cal. expedition . . . it is due to fair dealing to state that today Gen. Cameron, Sec. of War, told me . . . he had appointed Staff officers enough for the whole army and that he could make no new appointments until those already appointed were assigned to duty." See also Lincoln to Cameron August 17, *supra*, and September 4, *infra*, in regard to these appointments.

To Simon Cameron¹

August 29, 1861

The writer of this was an M.C. from N.J. when I was from Ills, and has since been Governor of New-Jersey. If his brother can now consistently be made a Pay-Master, I shall be glad of it—if not, let his name be placed so he can have a chance at no very distant day.   A. LINCOLN

Aug. 29, 1861

¹ AES, owned by R. E. Burdick, New York City. Lincoln's endorsement is written on the back of a letter from William A. Newell of Allentown, New Jersey, August 28, 1861, requesting appointment of his brother John W. Newell as paymaster. The appointment was made September 5, 1861.

To Salmon P. Chase¹

Sec. of Treasury please see J. S. Beard, bearer of this.

Aug. 29, 1861   A. LINCOLN

¹ ALS, IBloHi. Joseph S. Beard was a resident of Bloomington, Illinois, who had lost his job in the Post Office Department as route agent in Illinois. No Treasury Department appointment is of record, but the *U.S. Official Register* lists "Joseph L. Beard" as route agent in Illinois, which suggests that Beard was reappointed to his old job, the *Register* being in error as to the middle initial.

To Winfield Scott¹

Sent to me by the Attorney General, and now respectfully submitted to Lieut. General Scott.   A. LINCOLN

Aug. 29, 1861.

¹ AES, DLC-RTL. Lincoln's endorsement is written on the back of a letter from Nicholas P. Trist of Philadelphia to Edward Bates, August 26, 1861, calling attention to the atrocities committed by Union marauders, and suggesting that steps should be taken to punish crimes of rape, murder, etc. General Scott's reply of August 30, written below Lincoln's endorsement, called attention to the fact that the same strict order which he had issued during the Mexican War to curb marauding had been sent to Senator Lyman Trumbull for insertion in a judiciary bill to punish marauders.

To Winfield Scott[1]

August 29, 1861

Will Gen. Scott please give his opinion whether anything, and if anything, what should be done in Major Cross' case.

Aug. 29, 1861.   A. LINCOLN

I am unwilling to act in this case in opposition to Gen. Scott's views.   A. LINCOLN

Sep. 6, 1861

[1] AES, RPB. Lincoln's endorsements are written on a letter from Major Osborn Cross, San Francisco, California, July 29, 1861, asking that the president remit the remainder of his suspension from duty. Major Cross, a disbursing officer, had been court-martialed for a deficiency in his accounts which ". . . *was paid up by me nearly one year* before I was brought before a Court Martial, even at that time a greater portion was shown to accrue from errors. . . . I have been a disbursing officer over thirty three years, and . . . not *a dollar* has been lost. . . ." General Scott's reply of September 5, written between Lincoln's endorsements, declined to recommend further clemency. Major Cross was returned to duty when his suspension expired and was promoted to lieutenant colonel, February 26, 1863.

To Lorenzo Thomas[1]

If the places are not already full, let Dr. Anthony Dignowitz, be examined for an appointment as a surgeon.   A. LINCOLN

Aug. 29, 1861

[1] ALS, The Rosenbach Company, Philadelphia and New York. Dr. Anthony M. Dignowitz wrote Lincoln from Baltimore, June 15, 1861, that he would like to serve his adopted country (DLC-Nicolay Papers), and General Don C. Buell wrote October 22, 1861, recommending him for an appointment, as a Texas citizen whose Union sympathies had forced him to leave the state (DLC-RTL), but no record has been found of his appointment.

To Lorenzo Thomas[1]

Let the appointment be made, as within requested by Genl. McClellan.   A. LINCOLN

Aug. 30, 1861

[1] Parke-Bernet Catalog 972, May 17, 1948, No. 299. According to the catalog description, Lincoln's endorsement is written on the last page of a letter from McClellan, August 30, 1861. The register of letters received by the adjutant general (DNA WR RG 94) indicates that this missing item concerned the appointment of Major Lawrence P. Graham, as brigadier general, and the appointment of seven other officers recommended by McClellan. Graham was appointed August 31, 1861.

[503]

To Simon Cameron[1]

August 31, 1861

Respectfully submitted to the War Department, with the remark that if arms were in the hands of a Union Regiment in N.C. they probably would not remain in their hands long.

Aug. 31. 1861.   A. LINCOLN

[1] AES, DLC-Cameron Papers. Lincoln's endorsement is written on the back of a letter from Charles H. Foster, Salisbury, North Carolina, August 9, 1861, to Ward H. Lamon, tendering the services of a regiment of loyal North Carolinians if it can be accepted and equipped. Foster, an unconditional Union candidate, was elected to congress in the First Congressional District of North Carolina, in November, 1861, under a provisional state government which later collapsed. Congress denied him his seat on the ground that he had received only 400 votes in a district of 9,000 voters.

To Acting Secretary of State[1]

Hon. Sec. of State   Executive Mansion
Dear Sir   Aug. 31. 1861

Mr. Eastman says the person appointed Consul to Cardiff declines. If so, please let it stand till Mr. W. H. Seward, arrives. I believe he sympathizes with me in the wish to make Mr. Eastman's position somewhat elegible. Yours truly   A. LINCOLN

[1] ALS, NAuE. James C. Slaght of Brooklyn, New York, declined appointment as consul to Cardiff, England, on being offered a captaincy in the quartermaster's department, to which he was appointed September 2, 1861. Zebina Eastman was appointed consul to Bristol rather than Cardiff.

To George B. McClellan[1]

[September, 1861]

May I not now appoint Stevens a Brig. Genl? I wish to do it.

Maj. Genl. McClellan.   A LINCOLN

[1] ALS, DLC-McClellan Papers. Isaac I. Stevens who had taken command of the Seventy-ninth New York Infantry to replace Colonel James Cameron, killed at Bull Run, was a West Point graduate (1835) who had resigned as brevet major in 1853 to become governor of Washington Territory. Humiliated by the rapid advancement of his juniors over him, he was on the point of resigning (Frederick A. Aiken to Seward, September 25, 1861, DLC-RTL), but was appointed brigadier general of Volunteers, September 28, 1861.

To Simon Cameron[1]

Hon. Sec. of War.   Executive Mansion
My dear Sir: Sep. 2. 1861

Let Brigadier Generals of volunteers be appointed as follow:
    Daniel E. Sickles, of New-York.
    O. O. Howard, and Charles D. Jameson, of Maine—

[504]

A. Mc. D. McCook, of Ohio—
Ebenezer Dumont, Robert H. Milroy, and Lewis Wallace, of Indiana.
William A. Richardson, and Eleazer A. Paine, of Illinois.
Yours truly   A. LINCOLN

1 ALS, IHi. Colonel Daniel E. Sickles of the Seventieth New York, Colonel Oliver O. Howard of the Third Maine, Colonel Charles D. Jameson of the Second Maine, Captain Alexander McDowell McCook of the Third Infantry Regular Army, Colonel Ebenezer Dumont of the Seventh Indiana, Colonel Robert H. Milroy of the Ninth Indiana, Colonel Lewis Wallace of the Eleventh Indiana, and Colonel Eleazer A. Paine of the Ninth Illinois were all appointed brigadiers on September 3, 1861. William A. Richardson's appointment of the same date seems not to have been accepted as there is no record of his service as brigadier.

To Simon Cameron[1]

[c. September 2, 1861]

I think it is well that P. is away from the N.H. people. He will do less harm anywhere else; and, by *when* he has gone, his neighbors will understand him better.   A. L.

1 AES, DLC-Cameron Papers. Lincoln's endorsement is written on a letter by Henry McFarland, editor of the Concord, New Hampshire, *The Statesman* to M. B. Goodwin, September 2, 1861, which Cameron had referred to the president. McFarland noted that ". . . Ex President Pierce is at Louisville, Ky. There is a very general suspicion here that his mission there is not one friendly to the government. . . . If the government has any way to observe his motions I hope it will do so. . . ."

To Simon Cameron[1]

Let the appointments be made as recommended by Genl. McClellan   A LINCOLN
Sep. 2. 1861.

1 AES, RPB. Lincoln's endorsement is written on the back of McClellan's letter to Cameron, August 29, 1861, recommending that Major Lawrence P. Graham of the Second Dragoons and Colonel John Sedgwick of the Fourth Cavalry be appointed brigadiers. Both appointments were made, dated as of August 31, 1861.

To Simon Cameron[1]

Let the appointment be made as within requested.
Sept. 2. 1861   A. LINCOLN

1 AES, owned by Richard F. Lufkin, Boston, Massachusetts. Lincoln's endorsement has been removed from attendant papers. Beneath the endorsement, Brigadier General James W. Ripley endorsed on September 14:
"Respectfully returned. As directed I have to report in this case. That Lt.

[505]

Harris has not been in service three months, and is not eligible to this appointment, under the 36th. Paragraph of army regulations, until he shall have served with his corps at least three years. So urgent is the demand for the services of Ordnance Officers on their appropriate duties that none can be spared for detached service, without great injury to the operations of the Department which have been already much crippled by the withdrawal of officers for such service. It will be a lasting disadvantage to any young officer of the ordnance Corps to detach him from his appropriate duties, before he has had an opportunity to attain a practical knowledge of them and may injure him professionally for life. These are serious objections—both as regards the public interest and those of the officer himself—which were probably not known or considered, when this paper was endorsed."

Lieutenant William H. Harris, son of Senator Ira Harris of New York, graduated from West Point in June, 1861, and on August 3, was commissioned second lieutenant in the Ordnance Department.

To John C. Frémont[1]

Private and confidential.

Major General Fremont: Washington D.C. Sept. 2, 1861.

My dear Sir: Two points in your proclamation of August 30th give me some anxiety. First,[2] should you shoot a man, according to the proclamation, the Confederates would very certainly shoot our best man in their hands in retaliation; and so, man for man, indefinitely. It is therefore my order that you allow no man to be shot, under the proclamation, without first having my approbation or consent.

Secondly,[3] I think there is great danger that the closing paragraph, in relation to the confiscation of property, and the liberating slaves of traiterous owners, will alarm our Southern Union friends, and turn them against us—perhaps ruin our rather fair prospect for Kentucky. Allow me therefore to ask, that you will as of your own motion, modify that paragraph so as to conform to the *first* and *fourth* sections of the act of Congress, entitled, "An act to confiscate property used for insurrectionary purposes," approved August, 6th, 1861, and a copy of which act I herewith send you. This letter is written in a spirit of caution and not of censure.

I send it by a special messenger, in order that it may certainly and speedily reach you. Yours very truly A. LINCOLN

[Endorsement]

Copy of letter sent to Gen. Fremont, by special messenger leaving Washington Sep. 3. 1861.

[1] Copy, DLC-RTL. The copy is in Nicolay's handwriting but the endorsement is in Lincoln's handwriting. Among the adverse reactions to Frémont's proclamation was a telegram from James Speed, Louisville, September 3, 1861, which expressed the positive opinion that ". . . that foolish proclamation of Fremont.

. . . will crush out every vistage of a union party in the state. . . ." (DLC-RTL).

2 Frémont's reply of September 8, in regard to this point was as follows: "I do not think the enemy can either misconstrue it, or urge any thing against it, or undertake . . . unusual retaliation. . . . The article does not at all refer to ordinary prisoners of war. . . . I have to ask that you will permit me to carry out upon the spot the provisions of the proclamation in this respect. . . ." (DLC-RTL). The language of Frémont's proclamation, however, was: "All persons who shall be taken with arms in their hands within these lines shall be tried by court-martial, and if found guilty will be shot." (OR, I, III, 466-67).

3 Frémont's reply of September 8, in regard to this point was, "If . . . your better judgement still decides that I am wrong in the article respecting the liberation of slaves, I have to ask that you will openly direct me to make the correction. . . . I acted with full deliberation and . . . the conviction that it was . . . right and necessary. I still think so." (DLC-RTL).

To Simon Cameron[1]

Gen. Cooper has all the while been under the special care of Gen. Cameron; and I am quite willing it should continue so.

Sep. 3. 1861. A. LINCOLN

1 AES, IHi. Lincoln's endorsement is written on a letter from Brigadier General James Cooper to Cameron, August 30, 1861, suggesting that David P. DeWitt and John Sommers be appointed majors, and that ". . . an able and experienced officer as Chief of my Staff . . . [be appointed] as early as practicable." DeWitt was appointed major September 21, and Sommers was appointed colonel October 8, 1861, in the Maryland Volunteers.

Appointment of Gustavus V. Fox[1]

Executive Mansion 4 September, 1861

During the temporary absence of the Hon: Gideon Welles, Secretary of the Navy, from the seat of Government, I hereby appoint Mr. Gustavus V. Fox, Assistant Secretary of the Navy, Acting Secretary of the Navy. ABRAHAM LINCOLN.

1 *Confidential Correspondence of Gustavus Vasa Fox* . . . , edited by Robert M. Thompson and Richard Wainright (New York, 1918), I, 371.

To Simon Cameron[1]

September 4, 1861

If there is any vacant place, of Regimental Quarter-Master, or Commisary, which can fairly be charged to California, do let Mr. Samuel Gamage have it. A. LINCOLN

Sept. 4. 1861.

1 AES, owned by Edgar Jessup, Piedmont, California. Lincoln's endorsement is written on the back of a copy of Lincoln to Cameron, August 17, 1861 (*supra*). See also the note dated August 29, *supra*.

To Simon Cameron[1]

September 4, 1861

I sincerely wish Mr. Hawley be made a Brigade Commissary of Subsistance. In his worthiness, & the interest felt for him by good people, his case is something more than a common one, & I hope he be appointed.   A. LINCOLN

Sep. 4. 1861.

[1] AES, CCamStJ. Lincoln's endorsement is written on a letter from Samuel Bowles, Springfield, Massachusetts, August 23, 1861, recommending William A. Hawley for an appointment. William A. Hawley "of Illinois" was appointed quartermaster with rank of captain, October 31, 1861, but it is not certain that he was the same man recommended by Bowles.

To Simon Cameron[1]

September 4, 1861.

I think provision should at once be made for organizing a force in Eastern Maryland, as recommended by Governor Hicks and General Dix. Let it be done at once, if possible.   A. LINCOLN

[1] OR, III, I, 480. Lincoln's endorsement is written on a letter from Governor Thomas H. Hicks to Cameron, September 3, 1861, introducing Colonel Arthur G. Willis and asking that he be furnished with tents and subsistence for the First Regiment of Maryland Eastern Shore Infantry and that the Second Regiment should be organized forthwith.

To Simon Cameron[1]

September 4, 1861

Mr. Linton had ample recommendations for another office; he served three months with the N.J. troops, as I understand; and I suppose he is very worthy of the place he now seeks. I ask a careful consideration of his case.   A. LINCOLN

Sep. 4. 1861.

[1] AES, IHi. Lincoln's endorsement is written on the back of a letter from John L. Linton of Beverly, New Jersey, September 3, 1861, asking appointment to the quartermaster department. Although he had served as quartermaster in the Fourth New Jersey Militia, April 27—July 31, 1861, no further appointment is of record.

To Heads of Departments and Bureaus[1]

I shall be very glad if any of the Heads of Departments, or Bureaus, can give this lady some suitable employment.

Sept. 4. 1861.   A. LINCOLN

¹ AES, owned by Charles W. Olsen, Chicago, Illinois. According to a clipping
from an unidentified printed source pasted below this note, Lincoln's recommendation referred to "Miss Anne Mary Griffin, for many years a clerk in Washington," but the *U.S. Official Register* does not list her.

To William H. Seward¹

September 4, 1861

If there is a Consulate at St. Helena, which is open, I have no objection to its' going to Mr. *William Moran,* especially as he brings
a letter from Hon Thadeus Stevens who has not troubled us much.

Sept. 4. 1861   A. LINCOLN

¹ AES, DNA FS RG 59, Appointments, Box 348. Lincoln's endorsement is
written on a letter from Representative Thaddeus Stevens, dated August 29, 1861,
recommending William Moran of Pennsylvania. Although the New York *Tribune,* September 24, 1861, lists William Moran as consul to St. Helena, appointed
September 6, the *U.S. Official Register* does not list him either in 1861 or 1863.

To William H. Seward¹

September 4, 1861

It is said the Governorship of Washington Territory is vacant &
within it is asked that it shall not be filled without a hearing. Sec.
of State, please remember this.   A. LINCOLN

Sept. 4. 1861

¹ AES, DNA FS RG 59, Appointments, Box 281. Lincoln's endorsement is written on a letter from Charles Evans, Philadelphia, to William D. Kelley, September 2, 1861, asking that in his interview with the president, Kelley remember
Elwood Evans for the governorship of Washington. William Pickering of Illinois
was appointed governor (see Lincoln to Pickering, October 7, *infra*), but Elwood
Evans was later nominated secretary of Washington Territory, January 7, 1863.

To Simon Cameron¹

I approve the carrying this through carefully, cautiously, and
expeditiously. Avoid conflicts and interference.

Sep 5. 1861.   A. LINCOLN.

¹ Copy, DLC-Cameron Papers. The copy of Lincoln's endorsement is on a copy
of a letter to Cameron from "Herman Boker & Co./ 50 Cliff Street New York,"
September 4, 1861, offering 100,000 rifled percussion muskets and 18,000 sabres,
purchased in Europe, subject to inspection and approval.

To Simon Cameron¹

September 5, 1861

President Lincoln's opinion
(Given to Sec'y Cameron, Sec'y of War)

Regarding the stoppage of the emoluments of Col. Gates under
the provisions of the 20th. Section of the Act of Congress 3rd. Aug

1861 "I have examined the 20th. Section of the Act of Congress entitled an Act for the better organization of the Army, approved 3rd. Aug. 1861 and am of opinion that officers, whose cases fall within it, should be paid according to the old law up to the passage of the new (3 Aug. 1861) (signed) A. LINCOLN
Sept 5th. 1861.

A true copy from the original, which was sent to the Hon. Sec'y of War, Mr Cameron. 5 Sept. 1861. (signed) WM. GATES
Col. U.S.A.

This opinion was not regarded by Mr. Cameron or any other person—(not an order) they said.

[Endorsement: To Edward Bates][2]

Will the Attorney General please say whether the within is, or is not a sound legal opinion? A. LINCOLN
Aug. 18, 1864

[1] Copy and AES, DLC-RTL. The original opinion written by Lincoln has not been located. The endorsement of August 18, 1864, is in Lincoln's autograph on the back of the copy. Gates wrote to Lincoln, September 28, 1861, ". . . I received your confirmation of your first opinion . . . and presented it with the first opinion to the Pay Master General and demanded a restoration of the money stopped out of my pay for the month of August last—which he declined . . . without an order from the War Depart. . . ." (DCL-RTL). The twentieth section of the law referred to stipulated that officers when absent from duty more than six months should not receive allowances for servants, forage, etc.

[2] Bates was leaving Washington when Lincoln's communication arrived, and J. Hubley Ashton, assistant attorney general, answered August 26, 1864, "The view expressed by your Excellency . . . is a perfectly sound one. . . ." (*Ibid.*). Whether Gates was ever able to collect has not been determined.

To Winfield Scott[1]

[c. September 5, 1861]
Will Gen. Scott please look at the within and inform me whether the guns were ordered to Cairo yesterday? A. LINCOLN

[1] AES, DLC-RTL. Lincoln's endorsement is written on the back of a translation of a telegram from General Frémont to "Mr. A. J. deZeyk," September 5, 1861. Albert J. Dezeyk, a Hungarian by birth, was a clerk in the Post Office Department, and the explanation for Frémont's sending it in Hungarian seems to be the desire for secrecy. The translation is in part as follows: "Please to communicate with the President . . . The War Vessels of the enemy are all steel plated mounting heavy guns, better armed faster and larger than ours. Their Officers are all of the U.S. Navy, whilst our Officers can not hold their ground after the first fire; there can be no other result than our capture; there is a very urgent want in Cairo of heavy canons. . . . The enemy is beggining to occupy the coast of Kentucky Hyckman Paducah &c. I think, the time, has come to have command extended to those parts (probably means Kentucky). . . ." Scott's reply has not been located.

To William H. Seward[1]

Sec. of State, please see, and converse with Gen. Kimmel, who is a State Senator of Frederick, Maryland.　　　A. LINCOLN

Sep. 5. 1861

[1] ALS, NbO. Anthony Z. Kimmel was commanding general of the Fourth Division of Maryland Militia.

To Simon Cameron[1]

September 6, 1861

Hon. Jno. Crowell of Ohio presents this. Please hear him fully & do the best for him you can.

[1] American Art Association Anderson Galleries Catalog 4221, January 14-15, 1936, No. 350. According to the catalog description this communication is written on a letter from Major George S. Mygatt of the Forty-first Ohio Volunteers. John Crowell, editor and ex-congressman of Cleveland, was a major general of Ohio Militia.

To Simon Cameron[1]

Will War Department please consider the within request of Gov. Pierpont?　　　A. LINCOLN

Sep. 6. 1861

[1] AES, DLC-Cameron Papers. Lincoln's endorsement is written on a letter from Governor Francis H. Peirpoint, Wheeling, Virginia, September 3, 1861, on the necessity for calling out eight or ten Volunteer regiments in West Virginia, Ohio, and Western Pennsylvania to occupy West Virginia and crush out secession. The letter is signed "F. H. Peirpoint," and this spelling is followed throughout the present work rather than "Pierpoint" or "Pierpont," on the assumption that the governor is entitled to spell his name as he chooses, other considerations notwithstanding.

To Lorenzo Thomas[1]

Let Col. Gorman be appointed as recommended by Genl. Scott.

Sep. 6, 1861.　　　A LINCOLN

[1] AES, RPB. Lincoln's endorsement is written on a letter from Lieutenant Colonel Stephen Miller of the First Minnesota Regiment, August 17, 1861, recommending that Colonel Willis A. Gorman of the same regiment be made a brigadier general. Winfield Scott endorsed "I cordially unite in recommending. . . ." Gorman was appointed brigadier general, September 7, 1861.

To Zachariah Chandler[1]

Hon. Z. Chandler   Washington, D.C.
My dear Sir: Sep. 7. 1861
  Dr. William Brodie, of Detroit, is very amply recommended to
be a Surgeon in the Army (volunteers); but understanding that
yourself and Senator Bingham have some objection, I forbear to
act until I can hear from you & him. Please confer with him, and
write me. Looking at the papers here, he ought to be appointed;
and it embarrasses me some to refuse. Yours truly

                                                       A. LINCOLN

  [1] ALS, DLC-Chandler Papers. Dr. William Brodie was appointed brigade surgeon of Volunteers as of August 3, 1861. The appointment was sent to the Senate
December 24, 1861, and rejected January 15, 1862.

Memorandum[1]

The writer of this is a worthy young man, and his father a most
intelligent & valuable citizen.   A. LINCOLN
  Sep. 7. 1861.

  [1] ADS, MeHi. Clipped from the letter to which it refers, this communication
is without further reference.

Memorandum: Interview with Philip L. Fox[1]

                                Executive, Mansion Sep. 7. 1861.
This day Philip L. Fox, of Philadelphia, is introduced to me by
Friend Newton,[2] and says that within this week, in this City,
Gilead Smith, who Mr. Fox says is to sail from New-York next
wednesday, as a government agent to purchase arms in Europe,
called on him (Fox) and, in presence of two others, F. N. Buck,
and Martin Thomas, both of Philda., spoke of arms which Mr. Fox
knew of for sale, and asked Fox what would be the price, and
being told $15–17–& 19– proposed to join in purchasing them and
putting them on the government at $22. to $27. and dividing the
profits. Mr. Buck introduced Smith to Mr. Fox. Mr. Fox says he
replied that he was not a seller, and desired having no more to do
with the matter than to let the government know where the arms
were to be purchased. Mr. Buck and Mr. Thomas call and say
they heard a conversation with Smith & Fox—that Fox was trying
to sell a lot of arms upon the sale of which he, Fox, was to have a
commission of 50 cents per gun—that Smith and not, as they
understood, represent himself to an agent of the government; but
did propose to Fox to join him in getting the guns on to the gov-

ernment at a price which leave a profit for them to divide, & they understood Fox to agree to it. Neither Smith nor Fox professing to be a government agent—nothing appeared wrong in their conversation. Both are men of good character & Smith is brother-in-law to John Edgar Thompson.

1 AD, DLC-RTL. No further record of this deal has been found.

2 Probably Isaac Newton, whom Lincoln nominated commissioner of agriculture May 16, 1862.

To Lorenzo Thomas[1]

Adjt. Genl. please tell me how this case stands.

Sep. 7. 1861.   A. LINCOLN

1 AES, DLC-RTL. Lincoln's endorsement is written on a letter from Joab Wilkinson, Niantic, Illinois, to Nicolay, August 26, 1861, inquiring about his appointment as captain. Lorenzo Thomas endorsed in reply to Lincoln's request that the commission had been sent to the president and as soon as signed would be forwarded. Wilkinson's appointment had been confirmed by the Senate on August 5 and announced in AGO General Orders No. 65, August 23, 1861. Joab Wilkinson was a brother of Senator Morton S. Wilkinson of Minnesota.

To David Hunter[1]

Major Genl. David Hunter   Washington D.C. Sep. 9. 1861

My dear Sir: Gen. Fremont needs assistance which it is difficult to give him. He is losing the confidence of men near him, whose support any man in his position must have to be successful. His cardinal mistake is that he isolates himself, & allows nobody to see him; and by which he does not know what is going on in the very matter he is dealing with. He needs to have, by his side, a man of large experience. Will you not, for me, take that place? Your rank is one grade too high to be ordered to it; but will you not serve the country, and oblige me, by taking it voluntarily?

1 ADf, DLC-RTL. Francis P. Blair, Jr., to Montgomery Blair, September 1, 1861, " . . . Affairs are becoming quite alarming. . . . Men coming here to give information are not allowed to approach Fremont, and go away in disgust . . . . he throws himself behind the reports of his officers who are trying to prevaricate and shield themselves . . . . he still clings to them & refuses to see for himself. . . . My decided opinion is that he should be relieved of his command and a man of ability put in his place." (Ibid.). Winfield Scott to Lincoln, September 5, 1861, "If . . . Hunter could be brought in close relations with . . . Fremont some rash measures might be staved off & good ones accepted by insinuation, but H.'s rank is too high, by one degree to put him on duty as 'the chief of staff'. . . . (ibid.). The letter to Hunter was carried by Montgomery C. Meigs and Montgomery Blair who went to St. Louis to inspect conditions. Hunter was placed in command at Rolla, Missouri, and on October 24, Frémont was ordered to ". . . call Major-General Hunter, of the U. S. Volunteers, to relieve him temporarily in that command, when he (Major-General Frémont) will report to General Headquarters, by letter, for further orders." (OR, I, III, 553).

To William H. Seward[1]

September 9, 1861

If Gov. Bebb has declined, or resigned the Consulship at Tangiers, I have no objection to its' being given to Judge DeLong.

Sep. 9. 1861   A. LINCOLN

If Gov. Bebb has resigned the Consulship at Tangiers, let Judge James DeLong, of Ohio, be appointed to the place.

Sep. 16. 1861   A. LINCOLN

[1] AES, DNA FS RG 59, Appointments, Box 270. Both endorsements are written on the back of a letter of August 1, 1861, from William Bebb, ex-governor of Ohio (1846-1848) who was appointed an examiner in the Patent Office upon refusing the consulship. Bebb recommended James DeLong of Ohio, who was appointed consul at Tangier but was rejected by the Senate July 12, 1862. He was later appointed and confirmed as consul at Aux-Cayes.

To Simon Cameron[1]

September 10, 1861

Mr. Blair, senr. does not make many recommendations; but as is seen, makes this very warmly. I have no doubt Mr. Moses is a most competent & worthy man, & if there be a vacant place not committed to any other good man, I should be pleased for him to be appointed.   A. LINCOLN

Sep. 10. 1861.

[1] AES, DLC-Cameron Papers. Lincoln's endorsement is written on a copy of a letter from Francis P. Blair, Sr., to Cameron, May 9, 1861, recommending appointment of Isaac Moses of New York as paymaster. Moses was appointed assistant adjutant general with rank of captain, September 25, 1861.

To Simon Cameron[1]

Let Charles F. Van Duser, son of the gentleman named within, be appointed a 1st. Lieutenant, if there is any vacancy.

Sept. 10, 1861.   A. LINCOLN

[1] AES, owned by Gordon A. Block, Philadelphia, Pennsylvania. Lincoln's endorsement is written on a letter from John J. Cisco introducing Selah Van Duzer. Charles F. Van Duzer was appointed second lieutenant in the Twelfth Infantry, September 25, 1861.

To Simon Cameron[1]

Let Gov. Morton be obliged by the appointment of Mr. Western, as Qr. Master, or Commissary, if it can consistently be done.

Sep. 10. 1861   A. LINCOLN

1 AES, IHi. Lincoln's endorsement appears on a letter of Governor Oliver P. Morton, August 29, 1861, recommending John Weston of Elkhart, Indiana, for appointment as a brigade quartermaster. No record has been found of Weston's appointment.

Draft of Order Authorizing Benjamin F. Butler to Raise a Volunteer Force[1]

War Department. Washington. Sept 10th. 1861

Major General B. F. Butler, is hereby authorized to raise, organize, arm, uniform and equip a Volunteer force for the War, in the New England States, not exceeding Six (6) Regiments, of the Maximum Standard, of such arms, and in such proportions and in such manner, as he may Judge expedient, and for this purpose, his orders and requisitions on the Quartermasters, Ordnance, and other Staff Departments of the Army, are to be obeyed and answered, provided, the cost of such recruitment, armament and equippment, does not exceed in the aggregate, that of like troops, now, or hereafter raised for the service of the United States. But this order is to be of no effect, unless the Governor of each State from which troops are to be enlisted, shall indorse his approval upon it, or on a copy thereof.

1 ADf-P, ISLA. Only the last sentence is in Lincoln's autograph. The final copy of this order, signed by Cameron and bearing Lincoln's endorsement—"Approved, Sep. 12, 1861/A. Lincoln" (AES-P, ISLA) —does not have the additional sentence inserted by Lincoln, but before Lincoln approved it on September 12, he sent his telegram to the New England Governors, September 11, *infra*.

To Mrs. John C. Frémont[1]

Now, at once.   A. LINCOLN

Sept. 10 [1861]

1 Allan Nevins, *Frémont, Pathmarker of the West* (1939), p. 516. According to Nevins' description, Lincoln sent a card containing this brief communication granting an interview to Mrs. Frémont who brought a letter and verbal communications from her husband. For an account of the interview see the source indicated.

To Justus McKinstry[1]

Washington, September 10, 1861

J. McKinstry, Brigadier General and Quartermaster, St. Louis:

Permit me to introduce James L. Lamb, Esq., of Springfield, Illinois.

I have known Mr. Lamb for a great many years. His reputation for integrity and ability to carry out his engagements are both unquestioned, and I shall be pleased, if consistent with the public good, that you will make purchases of him of any army supplies needed in your Department. Your obedient servant,

A. LINCOLN.

[1] *Vindication of Brig. Gen. J. McKinstry. . . .* (1862), p. 17. Concerning McKinstry's dismissal, see Lincoln's approval of *General Order No. 43*, January 28, 1863, *infra*.

Memorandum: Appointment of John S. Godfrey[1]

[c. September 10, 1861]

Gen: Hooker wishes ——— Godfrey, now Q M. 2nd. N.H. to be appointed a Brigade Q.M. for his Brigade. He is now acting as such. Senator Hale, Hon. Mr. Rollins, & Col. Marston,[2] all back this application.

[1] AD, DLC-RTL. First Lieutenant John S. Godfrey's promotion to captain and assistant quartermaster of Volunteers, dating from September 10, 1861, was sent to the Senate in a list of similar promotions under date of December 21. General Hooker's request may have been made at any time between these dates, but evidence for more specific dating of Lincoln's memorandum has not been found.

[2] Senator John P. Hale and Representative Edward H. Rollins of New Hampshire and Colonel Gilman Marston of the Tenth New Hampshire Infantry.

Order Approving Sentence of William H. Allen[1]

Washington, September 10, 1861.

The proceedings, findings, and sentence of the Court in the case of *Colonel William H. Allen,* 1st Regiment New York Volunteers, are confirmed and approved.   A. LINCOLN.

[1] AGO, *General Orders No. 76*, September 10, 1861. Colonel Allen had been found guilty of disobedience of orders, maliciously causing private property to be destroyed, conduct unbecoming an officer and a gentleman, and breach of arrest, and had been sentenced to be cashiered.

To Simon Cameron[1]

I join in the above recommendation, if the appointment can be made consistently.   A. LINCOLN

Sept. 11, 1861.

[1] AES, owned by E. F. Slater, New York City. Lincoln's endorsement follows the recommendation of George B. McClellan on the back of a letter from William P. Brinton of Jefferson County, Virginia, to Cameron, September 9, 1861, applying for appointment as first lieutenant of Cavalry. This document seems to have become "lost," and no appointment for Brinton is of record. An endorsement on

the back reads "Rec'd A.G.O. for entry Oct 4, 1866." William P. Brinton served, however, in the Fifty-ninth Pennsylvania and became lieutenant colonel of the Eighteenth Pennsylvania Cavalry, March 1, 1863 to September 19, 1864, when he was wounded and captured at Opeguan, Virginia.

To Simon Cameron[1]

Executive Mansion Sep. 11. 1861
This day Gen. Mansfield personally appears, and urges that Horatio G. Wright, of Topographical Engineers, be a Brigadier General of Volunteers, as a Connecticut appointment. Gen. Totten concurs, as Gen. Mansfield says.

[1] ALS, IHi. Horatio G. Wright was appointed brigadier general of Volunteers September 14, 1861.

To Simon Cameron[1]

War Department, please oblige Gen. McClernand, if possible.
Sep. 11, 1861.   A. LINCOLN

[1] AES, owned by Charles Putnam, Jr., Peoria, Illinois. Lincoln's endorsement is written on the back of a telegram from John A. McClernand requesting that First Lieutenant James H. Wilson of the Topographical Engineers be assigned to his staff at Cairo, Illinois. Wilson was assigned instead to the expedition which captured Port Royal, South Carolina, November 7, 1861. See also Lincoln to Lorenzo Thomas, September 17, *infra*.

To Simon Cameron[1]

September 11, 1861
I have before said, and now repeat, that by the within, and other sources of information, I have no doubt of the fitness and worthiness of Mr. Markland to be a Paymaster, and I desire his appointment if it can consist[ent]ly be made.   A. LINCOLN.
Sep. 11, 1861

[1] Stan. V. Henkels Catalog 1262, July 1, 1920, No. 272. According to the catalog description, Lincoln's endorsement is written on the back of a letter from Allen A. Burton, minister to Colombia, September 9, 1861, asking appointment of A. H. Markland as paymaster. No appointment of Markland as paymaster is of record, but the *U.S. Official Register* lists him in 1863 as special agent of the Post Office Department in Tennessee.

To John C. Frémont[1]

Washington, D.C.
Major General John C. Fremont.   Sep. 11. 1861.
Sir: Yours of the 8th. in answer to mine of 2nd. Inst. is just received. Assuming that you, upon the ground, could better judge

of the necessities of your position than I could at this distance, on seeing your proclamation of August 30th. I perceived no general objection to it. The particular clause, however, in relation to the confiscation of property and the liberation of slaves, appeared to me to be objectionable, in it's non-conformity to the Act of Congress passed the 6th. of last August upon the same subjects; and hence I wrote you expressing my wish that that clause should be modified accordingly. Your answer, just received, expresses the preference on your part, that I should make an open order for the modification, which I very cheerfully do. It is therefore ordered that the said clause of said proclamation be so modified, held, and construed, as to conform to, and not to transcend, the provisions on the same subject contained in the act of Congress entitled "An Act to confiscate property used for insurrectionary purposes" Approved, August 6. 1861; and that said act be published at length with this order. Your Obt. Servt   A. LINCOLN.

1 ADfS, DLC-RTL; LS copy, owned by Crosby Noyes Boyd, Washington, D.C. The copy which was given to the press bears Lincoln's endorsement across the top of the first page as follows: "The following letter from the President to Gen. Fremont was transmitted to the latter by mail, on the 12th. Inst." Across the bottom of the second page of the copy Lincoln wrote in parentheses, "The Act referred to commences on page 80, of pamphlet acts of congress of late session." The act of August 6, 1861, section 4, reads as follows: "Provided that any person held to service or labor, by laws of any State, to another, the owner of such claim to labor loses his claim if person held to labor is employed in hostile service against the government." (See Lincoln to Joseph Holt, September 12, *infra*.) On September 16, Frémont telegraphed Lincoln, "I have seen in the papers your published telegram to me. The original has never reached me. Shall I act on that?" (DLC-RTL). Lincoln's reply, if any, to Frémont's query has not been found, but Lorenzo Thomas to Cameron, October 21, 1861, specifies that ". . . one week after the receipt of the President's order modifying General Frémont's proclamation . . . General Frémont . . . required . . . 200 copies of the original proclamation . . . printed and sent immediately to Ironton [Missouri] . . . for distribution through the country. . . ." (OR, I, IV, 543). See also Lincoln to Mrs. Frémont, September 12, *infra*.

To New England Governors[1]

Sept. 11, 1861.

Gen. Butler proposes raising in New-England, six regiments, to be recruited & commanded by himself & to go on special service. I shall be glad if you as Gov. of [blank] will answer by telegraph that you consent.   A. LINCOLN.

SIMON CAMERON,   Prest.
Sec. of War.

1 ADf, RPB. The body of the draft of this telegram is in Lincoln's hand excepting "will" following the blank, left for insertion of the state name. The date, Lin-

coln's name and Cameron's are added in Cameron's handwriting. Benjamin But-
ler's proposed expedition to New Orleans had been under consideration since early
August (see Lincoln to Cameron, August 2 and the draft of an order authorizing
Butler's Volunteer force, September 10, *supra*).

Replies from various New England governors on September 11 giving their
approval are in the *Official Records* (III, I, 498, 499, 509). The text of Lincoln's
letter to the New England governors, September 10, 1861, as printed in *Private
and Official Correspondence of Gen. Benjamin F. Butler* (1917), I, 239, seems to
be incorrect as to date and very unlike Lincoln in its wording. Since there seems
to be no sufficient reason for supposing that Lincoln sent a communication on both
September 10 and 11, the editors have omitted the text of the communication
dated September 10, as printed in the Butler correspondence.

To Simon Cameron[1]

Hon. Sec. of War   Executive Mansion
My dear Sir   Sep. 12. 1861

Mr. Senator Latham asks authority for Don Andreas Pico to
raise a Cavalry Regiment of native Mexican citizens of California.
Hear Senator Latham upon the subject, and if it impresses you favorably you have my approbation. Gen. Stoneman is with Senator Latham, and vouches for the Don, and approves the plan generally   Yours truly   A. LINCOLN

[1] ALS, DLC-Cameron Papers. In spite of General George Stoneman's and
Senator Milton S. Latham's recommendations, there is no record of Don Andreas
Pico's appointment.

To Mrs. John C. Frémont[1]

Mrs. Genl. Fremont   Washington, D.C. Sep. 12. 1861

My dear Madam—Your two notes of to-day are before me. I
answered the letter you bore me from Gen. Fremont, on yesterday; and not hearing from you during the day, I sent the answer
to him by mail.

It is not exactly correct, as you say you were told by the elder
Mr. Blair, to say that I sent Post-Master-General Blair to St. Louis
to examine into that Department, and report. Post-Master-General
Blair did go, with my approbation, to see and converse with Gen.
Fremont as a friend.

I do not feel authorized to furnish you with copies of letters in
my possession without the consent of the writers.

No impression has been made on my mind against the honor or
integrity of Gen. Fremont; and I now enter my protest against
being understood as acting in any hostility towards him. Your Obt.
Servt   A. LINCOLN

1 ADfS, DLC-RTL. See Lincoln to David Hunter, September 9, and Lincoln to Frémont, September 11, *supra*. One of Mrs. Frémont's letters requested Lincoln's answer of September 11, *supra*, already sent by mail, the other specified that she had learned from Francis P. Blair, Sr., of Francis P. Blair, Jr.'s letter to Montgomery Blair September 1, and requested a copy of it ". . . and any other communications . . . which . . . have made the investigation necessary. . . ."

To Joseph Holt[1]

Hon. Joseph Holt   Executive Mansion Sep. 12. 1861

Dear Sir   Yours of this day, in relation to the late proclamation of Gen. Fremont, is received. Yesterday I addressed a letter to him by mail, on the same subject, and which is intended to be made public when he receives it. I herewith send you a copy of that letter, which, perhaps, shows my position as distinctly as any new one I could write. I will thank you to not make it public, until Gen. Fremont shall have had time to receive the original. Your Obt. Servt.   A. LINCOLN

1 ADfS, DLC-RTL. Holt to Lincoln, September 12, 1861, ". . . The proclamation . . . of Genl. Fremont . . . transcends & . . . violates the law. . . ." (*Ibid.*). The copy of the letter which Lincoln enclosed to Holt was released on September 14 (New York *Herald*), but Frémont still had not received the copy sent by mail. See Lincoln to Frémont, September 11, *supra*.

To James W. Ripley[1]

September 12, 1861

Mr. Weston says there is a vacancy of a Military Storekeeper in the Regular Army; and to which he wishes to be appointed. I know nothing of it; but if the head of the Department or Bureau, having the matter in charge, will be satisfied that his appointment is proper, I have no objection   A. LINCOLN

Sep. 12. 1861.

1 ALS, OClWHi. Charles Weston was appointed military storekeeper at the Watertown, Connecticut, Arsenal, but was removed by General James W. Ripley, chief of ordnance, in September, 1862, on charges of neglect of duty and disobedience of orders preferred by Captain Thomas J. Rodman in command. See also Lincoln to George M. Weston, September 28, *infra*.

To Simon Cameron[1]

Sept. 13. 1861

Charles Case, formerly M.C. from the district of Indiana now represented by Hon. Mr. Mitchell, has been, and is working so well for us in the matter of volunteering in Indiana, that Mr. Mitchell is very anxious for him to be offered a Pay-Mastership. I say offered, for Mr. Case has not himself asked for it. . . .

[1] American Art Association Anderson Galleries Catalog 3955, March 4, 1932, No. 121. This incomplete text is all that is available. Representative William Mitchell was a lawyer of Kendallville, Indiana. Charles Case, a lawyer of Fort Wayne, was not nominated to the Senate as an additional paymaster until March 28, 1864, and was confirmed April 20, 1864, after three years of service in the Indiana Volunteers as a commissioned officer ranking progressively from first lieutenant to colonel.

To Simon Cameron[1]

If the appointment within requested can be made according to law, and the rules of the Dept. I shall be pleased for it to be done

Sept. 13, 1861   A. LINCOLN

[1] Copy, DNA WR RG 107, Secretary of War, Personnel Appointments, Box 12. The copy of Lincoln's endorsement is on the back of a copy of a War Department memorandum concerning the application of Sergeant Charles Hancock, "about thirty years of age" to become a second lieutenant in the Marine Corps. Hancock had all the necessary qualifications and recommendations, but according to law, ". . . all applicants must be between the respective ages of 20 & not over 25 years of age." There is no record of his appointment.

To William H. Seward[1]

Sep. 13. 1861.

To-day, Hon. W. P. Thomasson[2] calls to say William Forrester, of Louisville, Ky, who was raised by Mrs. J. F. Speed, ought to be Sec. of Leg. to Chili.

Is it Chili, that Judge Barton[3] goes to? and is there a Sec. of Leg. to Barton's mission? If so, I am willing, I am willing [sic] that William Forrester, above named, shall have it.   A LINCOLN

[1] ALS, NAuE. There is no record of William Forrester's appointment.
[2] William P. Thomasson, formerly congressman from Kentucky (1843-1847).
[3] The name appears to be "Barton," but Lincoln may have referred to Allen A. Burton of Kentucky, appointed minister to New Granada (Colombia).

To Richard Yates[1]

[September 13, 1861]

The bearer of this Victor B. Bell is an Illinoisan, and one of the cleverest and best business men in the State. He wishes to get a

position not lower than Captain in some volunteer Regiment; and I shall be greatly obliged if you can assist him in it.

Please take some special interest in it. You never served a better man, or one who will more amply appreciate and justify what you may do for him. Yours Truly   A. LINCOLN

[1] Copy, IHi-Yates Papers. The copy is contained in Bell to Yates, September 14, 1861, in which Bell says, "I hold a letter of introduction to you from Pres Lincoln, dated on yesterday of which [the] following is a copy. . . ." There is no record of Bell's appointment by Governor Yates. See also Lincoln to Cameron, August 22, *supra*, concerning Bell.

To Edward Bates[1]

September 14, 1861

If the Attorney General knows no objection, I know none, to Mr. Horatio R. Maryman's being a Justice of the Peace for this District.   A. LINCOLN

Sep. 14. 1861.

[1] AES, CSmH. Lincoln's endorsement is written on a letter from Benjamin B. French, commissioner of public buildings, to Edward C. Carrington, August 29, 1861, recommending Horatio R. Maryman. Record of Maryman's appointment has not been found.

To John W. Davis[1]

[September 15?] 1861

The President has read this letter; and he deeply commisserates the condition of any one so distressed as the writer seems to be. He does not know Mr. Davis—only knows him to be one of the arrested Police Commissioners of Baltimore because he says so in this letter. Assuming him to be one of those Commissioners, the President understands Mr. Davis could at the time of his arrest, could at any time since, and can now, be released by taking a full oath of allegiance to the Government of the United States; and that Mr. Davis has not been kept in ignorance of this condition of release. If Mr. Davis is still so hostile to the Government, and so determined to aid its' enemies in destroying it, he makes his own choice.

[1] AES copy, DLC-RTL. The copy of this endorsement was retained by Lincoln when he returned Davis' letter of September 11, on which the original endorsement was written. Davis acknowledged its receipt in a second letter written at Fort Lafayette, New York, September 20, 1861, ". . . if after an imprisonment of nearly three months, I were to procure my release by taking an oath in refer-

ence to my future conduct, my compliance . . . might . . . be construed into an admission . . . that something in my past . . . justified the . . . obligation. . . ." (*Ibid.*).

Statement Concerning Arrests in Maryland[1]

[c. September 15, 1861]

The public safety renders it necessary that the grounds of these arrests should at present be withheld, but at the proper time they will be made public. Of one thing the people of Maryland may rest assured: that no arrest has been made, or will be made, not based on substantial and unmistakable complicity with those in armed rebellion against the Government of the United States. In no case has an arrest been made on mere suspicion, or through personal or partisan animosities, but in all cases the Government is in possession of tangible and unmistakable evidence, which will, when made public, be satisfactory to every loyal citizen.

[1] Baltimore *American*, September 21, 1861. According to the *American*, Lincoln's statement was made "in reply to an inquiry as to the cause of the arrest of Mayor Brown." Secessionist members of the Maryland legislature and certain other public officials, including Mayor George W. Brown of Baltimore, were arrested September 13-16. Many were released on oath or parole from time to time, the last being released November 27, 1862. (See OR, II, I, 563-748.)

To Unidentified Persons[1]

[c. September 15, 1861?]

Gentlemen:—Yours of to-day, with the enclosure from Mr. Ridgely, has been received and referred to General Scott, as I know nothing whatever of the particular case.

May I beg you to consider the difficulties of my position and solicit your kind assistance in it? Our security in the seizing of arms for our destruction will amount to nothing at all, if we are never to make mistakes in searching a place where there are none. I shall continue to do the very best I can to discriminate between *true* and *false* men. In the mean time, let me, once more, beg your assistance in allaying irritations which are unavoidable. Yours, very truly,   A. LINCOLN.

[1] Hertz, II, 856. Hertz printed this letter without date or other reference. No trace of the original manuscript has been found, but the contents of the letter suggest that it may have been written at the time of the Baltimore arrests. The fact that Lincoln answers on the same date the incoming letter was written, suggests that his correspondents were not farther away than Baltimore. "Mr. Ridgely" may have been James L. Ridgely, whom Lincoln appointed collector of internal revenue at Baltimore in December, 1862.

To Robert Anderson[1]

Genl. R. Anderson   [September 16, 1861]
Louisville, Ky.   from Washington

From what you telegraph to-day, I think you better take active command in Kentucky at once. War Department will telegraph you about arms to-morrow.   A. LINCOLN

[1] ALS, owned by Weldon Petz, Detroit, Michigan; copy, DLC-RTL. The original communication is written on a U.S. Military Telegraph blank. Although the original is undated, the copy bears the date September 16, and with the copy there is the copy of Anderson's telegram received on the same date: "We have received positive information that the Tennesseans are invading Kentucky through the Cumberland Gap. We can get plenty of men if we can obtain arms for them. This is of vital importance.   ROBT ANDERSON."

To Simon Cameron[1]

If the facts are as within stated, of which I know not, I have no objection to the appointment as proposed.   A. LINCOLN
Sep. 16. 1861

[1] AES, DLC-RTL. Lincoln's endorsement is written on a letter from General Joseph K. F. Mansfield to Cameron, September 12, 1861, recommending Lieutenant Colonel Samuel W. Owen of the ". . . 1st. Kentucky Cavalry (so called). . . ." for promotion to colonel of that regiment. Below Lincoln's endorsement is the following: "Respectfully returned to the President who is informed that Le Prince Felix de Salm Salm has been appointed the Colonel of this Regiment. SIMON CAMERON, Secy of War." No further record of Prince Salm Salm's connection with the First Kentucky Cavalry has been found, but other sources indicate his service on General Louis Blenker's staff and as colonel of the Eighth New York Infantry (October 31, 1862—April 23, 1863) and of the Sixty-eighth New York Infantry (June 8, 1864—November 30, 1865).

To Simon Cameron[1]

Respectfully submitted to the War Department, asking a fair consideration of this case.
September 16, 1861

[1] *The Flying Quill*, February—March, 1950, No. 57. According to the catalog description, Lincoln's endorsement is on a recommendation of George Stoneman for a brigadier generalship. Stoneman's appointment as brigadier ranking from August 13, 1861, was confirmed by the Senate on March 7, 1862.

To Simon Cameron[1]

                                         September 16, 1861.

Secretary of War please send to General Scott a copy of your dispatch from General Fremont, showing the localities and number of his forces.   A. LINCOLN.

[1] OR, I, III, 493. Lincoln's endorsement is on Frémont's dispatch of September 15 listing a total of 55,693 men (*ibid.*).

To Simon Cameron[1]

I am willing to make Gen. Cadwallader, a Brigadier, or a Major
General, any moment when Gen. Cameron says so.

Sep 16. 1861   A. LINCOLN

[1] AES, DLC-Cameron Papers. Lincoln's endorsement is written on the back of
a page containing copies of letters recommending appointment of George Cadwalader of Philadelphia as brigadier general. An endorsement by George B. Mc-
Clellan of the same date reads in part, "I cannot recommend the appointment. . . . If he be appointed . . . I would respectfully request that he may not
be assigned to duty . . . under my command. . . ." Cadwalader was not nominated to the Senate as major general until March 28, 1862, and was confirmed
April 25.

To Simon Cameron[1]

The Sec. or Asst. Sec. of War can exercise discretion in this case.

Sep. 16. 1861.   A LINCOLN

[1] AES, DLC-Cameron Papers. Lincoln's endorsement is written on the back of
a letter from civil engineer Albert B. Cooley, Philadelphia, August 23, 1861, requesting permission to communicate with his men employed in deepening the
channel of the James River below Richmond, Virginia, under contract with that
city at the outbreak of the war. A previous endorsement by Thomas A. Scott, September 13, recommended Cooley's sending ". . . *open* letters to his men through
Genl Wool Commanding at Fortress Monroe—letters to be forwarded . . . as opportunity . . . may offer."

To Winfield Scott[1]

                                              Executive Mansion,
                                              Washington, D.C.,
Lieutenant-General Scott: September 16, 1861.

My dear Sir: Since conversing with you I have concluded to
request you to frame an order for recruiting North Carolinians at
Fort Hatteras. I suggest it be so framed as for us to accept a smaller force—even a company—if we cannot get a regiment or more.
What is necessary to now say about officers, you will judge. Governor Seward says he has a nephew (Clarence A. Seward, I believe) who would be willing to go and play colonel and assist in
raising the force. Still, it is to be considered whether the North
Carolinians will not prefer officers of their own. I should expect
they would. Yours very truly,   A. LINCOLN.

[1] OR, I, IV, 613. AGO *General Orders No. 79*, September 17, 1861, authorized
the acceptance of services of loyal North Carolinians, not to exceed one regiment,
at Hatteras Inlet. Clarence A. Seward was lieutenant colonel of the Nineteenth
New York Infantry May 22—September 28, 1861, but no other reference to his
military service has been found.

To Caleb B. Smith[1]

Hon. Sec. of Interior   Executive Mansion
My dear Sir   Sep. 16. 1861.

Please please [*sic*] see the bearer, Dr. Lincoln, and hear him as to a Mr. Chesney. Yours truly   A. LINCOLN

[1] ALS, owned by George Gould Lincoln, Washington, D.C. Dr. Nathan S. Lincoln of Washington sought the release of his friend James Chesney, a native of South Carolina who had been dismissed from his post as clerk in the Pension Office on August 30, 1861, and imprisoned because of an intercepted letter to his son in the Confederate Army. Chesney was released through the influence of his friends (Jeanie Gould Lincoln, "Out With Mosby's Men," *Peterson's Magazine*, December, 1888, pp. 532-33).

To Gideon Welles[1]

Hon. Sec. of Navy   Executive Mansion
My dear Sir   Sept. 16. 1861

Judge Peters[2] says that Robert Mitchell, of Darlington District, South Carolina, wishes to enter the Naval [Academy], and that the M.C. of the District would have nominated him had it not been for secession. I do not know the young man; but if he be shown to be loyal, and qualified & suitable in other respects, I think you might appoint him. Yours truly   A. LINCOLN

[1] ALS-P, ISLA. There is no record of Robert Mitchell's appointment.
[2] John H. Peters.

To Simon Cameron[1]

I personally know Mr. Parsons, & have no doubt he would make a good Paymaster, Qtr. Master, or Commissary.   A. LINCOLN
Sep. 17. 1861.

[1] AES, DNA WR RG 107, Secretary of War, Personnel Appointments, Box 4. Lincoln's endorsement is written on the back of letters from Henry D. Bacon and Hiram Barney, September 6, 1861, recommending Lewis B. Parsons for an appointment. Parsons was appointed captain and quartermaster of Volunteers, October 31, 1861.

To Winfield Scott[1]

September 17, 1861

Will Lieut. Gen. Scott please consider, and inform me what can be, and ought to be done as a recognition of the gallantry of the officers who fought with Gen. Lyon at Wilson's creek?
Sep. 17. 1861.   A LINCOLN

¹ ALS, RPB. No reply from Scott has been located, but a joint resolution of congress, approved December 24, and printed in AGO *General Orders No. 111,* December 30, 1861, gave recognition to the late Brigadier General Nathaniel Lyon and authorized each regiment engaged in the battle of Springfield, Missouri ". . . to bear upon its colors the word 'Springfield' embroidered in letters of gold. . . ." (OR, I, III, 93).

To William H. Seward¹

Respectfully submitted to the State Department, with the inquiry "Has Edwards yet gone to Demarara?   A LINCOLN
Sep. 17. 1861.

¹ AES, DNA FS RG 59, Appointments, Box 358. Lincoln's endorsement is written on the back of a testimonial of John L. Pfau, September 16, 1861, as to the disloyalty of Reverend Charles A. Page of Newport, Kentucky. Below Lincoln's endorsement is Seward's reply, "No. He has not gone—and I advise that his commission be revoked. WHS." The only apparent connection between the cases of Page and Theodore D. Edwards, appointed consul at Demerara, British Guiana, is that both were Kentuckians accused of disloyalty. The *U.S. Official Register* lists Edwards as consul, as of September 30, 1861, but in 1863 the consulship at Demerara is vacant. See Lincoln to Seward, August 6, *supra.*

To Lorenzo Thomas¹

September 17, 1861

Gen. McClernand, has shown great energy, and industry. He sat in Congress to the end of the session; and since then has effected certainly as much as any other Brig: Genl. in organizing forces. He is now in full command at Cairo, & without an aid. Please let him have the one he asks for within.   A. LINCOLN
Sep. 17. 1861.

¹ AES, owned by R. E. Burdick, New York City. Lincoln's endorsement is written on the back of McClernand's letter of September 11, 1861, explaining more fully than his telegram of the same date (see Lincoln to Cameron, September 11, *supra*) his need as commanding officer at Cairo, Illinois, for a staff officer and asking again for the assignment of First Lieutenant James H. Wilson: ". . . all this work I have done without a staff— without an adjutant, and even without an aid, for the commission of Capt. Bielaski has been revoked." A lengthy endorsement by Lieutenant Colonel Hartman Bache, Bureau of Topographical Engineers, September 18, explained that Lieutenant Wilson had been assigned to recruiting a company of enlisted men and that other generals (Dix, Anderson, and Samuel R. Curtis) were ahead of McClernand with requests for a staff officer from the Bureau.

To Simon Cameron¹

Hon. Sec. of War   Executive Mansion Sept. 18. 1861
My dear Sir: To guard against misunderstanding I think fit to say that the joint expedition of the Army and Navy agreed upon

some time since, and in which Gen. T. W. Sherman was and is to bear a conspicuous part, is in no wise to be abandoned, but must be ready to move by the first of, or very early in, October. Let all preparations go forward accordingly. Yours truly   A. LINCOLN

[1] ALS, owned by Edward C. Stone, Boston, Massachusetts. Brigadier General Thomas W. Sherman commanded the Army units of the expedition which left Hampton Roads, Virginia, October 29, and occupied Port Royal, South Carolina, November 7, 1861. See the same letter to Welles, *infra*.

To William H. Seward[1]

Hon. Sec. of State   Executive Mansion
My dear Sir   Sep. 18. 1861
    Mr. Williams wants a Consulship. If you can find one he is willing to take, I have no objection. Yours truly   A. LINCOLN

[1] ALS, DNA FS RG 59, Appointments, Box 404. William R. Williams is not listed as consul either in 1861 or 1863 in the *U.S. Official Register*.

To Gideon Welles[1]

Hon. Sec. of Navy.   Executive Mansion Sept. 18, 1861
    My dear Sir To guard against misunderstanding I think fit to say that the joint expedition of the Army and Navy, agreed upon some time since, and in which Gen. T. W. Sherman was, and is to bear a conspicuous part, is in nowise to be abandoned, but must be ready to move by the first of, or very early in October. Let all preparations go forward accordingly. Yours truly
                                                           A. LINCOLN

[1] ALS, DNA WR NB RG 45, Executive Letters, No. 129. See the same letter to Cameron and note, *supra*.

To William S. Wood[1]

If the items of this bill are correct, in all respects, let it be paid out of fund for furnishing Presidential Mansion.
    Sep. 18. 1861.   A. LINCOLN

[1] AES, DNA RG 217, General Accounting Office. Lincoln's endorsement is on the back of a bill rendered by John Alexander to the commissioner of Public Buildings in the amount of $335.50 for materials and labor in erecting a large tent on the "Presidents Grounds . . . June 27, July 3, 6, 10, 13, 17, 20, 1861." Commissioner Wood endorsed "I certify the above to be correct. W. S. Wood."

To Simon Cameron[1]

Sec. of War, please see the bearer—Mrs. Warren.

Sep. 19. 1861   A. LINCOLN

[1] ALS, RPB. Mrs. Warren has not been identified.

To Simon Cameron[1]

September 19, 1861

Let Staff officers be appointed for Gen. Paine, as within requested.
Gen: Camron perceives that our friend Leonard Swett is one of
them.   A. LINCOLN

Sep. 19. 1861.

[1] AES, IHi. Lincoln's endorsement appears on a letter of Brigadier General Eleazar A. Paine to Lorenzo Thomas, Paducah, Kentucky, September 12, 1861, asking the following appointments to his staff:
"Leonard Swett, Asst. Adjt. Genl. Richard E. Davis Brigade Commissary Algernon S. Baxter Brigade Qr. Master Ephraim Gilmore Aid, Captain Phelps Paine aid, 1st Lieut."
Swett was appointed on November 16, but the appointment was cancelled. Davis and Baxter were appointed on November 23. No record of the appointment of Gilmore has been found. Phelps Paine was appointed lieutenant and assistant adjutant general of Volunteers as of October 23, 1861.

To Winfield Scott[1]

September 19, 1861

These papers have been handed me by James Baker, the father. If
the boy be under eighteen is he entitled to a discharge? And if so,
how is the fact as to age, to be ascertained?   A. LINCOLN

Sep. 19. 1861.

[1] AES, DLC-RTL. Lincoln's endorsement is written on the back of a deposition by James Baker, September 17, 1861, requesting a discharge for his only son Almon Baker, a minor, who had enlisted without his father's consent, and was at the time a member of Company G, Second Michigan Infantry. Scott's endorsement written immediately below Lincoln's cites an act of congress, September 28, 1850, under which the boy should be discharged ". . . upon evidence being produced satisfactory to the Secretary that the recruit was a minor. . . ."

To Simon Cameron[1]

Hon. Sec. of War   Executive Mansion
My dear Sir: Sep. 20. 1861

There are pressing demands for arms both at St. Louis and at
Louisville; while I do not know that any can be spared for either
place. If, however, with your better knowledge of the facts, you

can spare any for St. Louis, to the extent of four or five thousand let them be shipped to the order of Gov. Gamble. Yours truly

A. LINCOLN

[1] ALS, DLC-Cameron Papers. Governor Gamble telegraphed Edward Bates, September 17, "For God's sake get me arms for infantry & cavalry"; and Joshua F. Speed telegraphed twice on September 17: ". . . Men plenty but no arms. . . ."; ". . . Our men cannot go into camp without arms, as they can at the North; as we have enemies at home. . . ." (DLC-RTL).

To Simon Cameron[1]

And I sent, this morning, an order for Todd's appointment, on the back of Gen. McClellan's letter recommending three others.

Sep. 20. 1861.   A. LINCOLN

[1] AES, DLC-Cameron Papers. Lincoln's endorsement is written on the back of a note from Cameron, "Genl. Thomas has called to say he recommends the apptment of Mr. Todd as a Brigade General." Lincoln's endorsement on McClellan's letter has not been located, but John B. S. Todd was appointed brigadier general of Volunteers September 19, 1861.

To Simon Cameron[1]

If there be a vacancy, let Charles Weston be appointed a Military Store-Keeper, as indicated within by Gen. Ripley.

Sep. 20. 1861   A. LINCOLN

[1] AES, IHi. Lincoln's endorsement appears on a letter from Brigadier General James W. Ripley, September 19, 1861, recommending Charles Weston of Maine for appointment as military storekeeper in the Ordnance Department. See Lincoln to Ripley, September 12, 1861, *supra*.

Memorandum:
Appointment of Henry D. Wallen, Jr.[1]

[c. September 21, 1861]
West-Point.

I wish this case to be specially attended to.   A. LINCOLN

[1] AES, DNA WR RG 94, U.S. Military Academy, 1861, No. 908, Box 80. Lincoln's endorsement is written on a letter from Cameron to Mrs. Laura L. Wallen, New York City, September 21, 1861, promising an appointment for her son ". . . in January or February next. . . ." See Lincoln to Joseph G. Totten, January 18, 1862, *infra*.

To William H. Seward[1]

[c. September 21, 1861]

Mr. Miller, the old gentleman concerning whom Maj. Ramsay writes the within letter, is employed, and for a long time has been, at the Arsenal. He is now implicated for disloyalty by some evidence before the Congressional Investigating Committee now in session in this City, and is in danger of discharge. I have seen him, and believe him to be loyal. Please see him, and talk with him; and if he makes the same impression upon you, administer the Oath of Allegiance to him, & give him a request to the War Department that he be allowed to retain his place.   A. LINCOLN.

Hon. Sec. of State.

[1] Hertz, II, 881 (n.d.). George D. Ramsay wrote to Representative John F. Potter, December 11, 1861, in reply to a query concerning what disposition had been made of employees listed by the committee on loyalty of government employees, "Mr. [Isaac S.] Miller was reinstated on the 21st September, at the request of the honorable Secretary of State, and with the approbation and . . . direction of the . . . Secretary of War." (Thirty-seventh Congress, Second Session, *House of Representatives Report No. 16*, p. 8).

To Orville H. Browning[1]

Private & confidential.

Hon. O. H. Browning   Executive Mansion
My dear Sir   Washington Sept 22d 1861.

Yours of the 17th is just received; and coming from you, I confess it astonishes me. That you should object to my adhering to a law, which you had assisted in making, and presenting to me, less than a month before, is odd enough. But this is a very small part. Genl. Fremont's proclamation, as to confiscation of property, and the liberation of slaves, is *purely political,* and not within the range of *military* law, or necessity. If a commanding General finds a necessity to seize the farm of a private owner, for a pasture, an encampment, or a fortification, he has the right to do so, and to so hold it, as long as the necessity lasts; and this is within military law, because within military necessity. But to say the farm shall no longer belong to the owner, or his heirs forever; and this as well when the farm is not needed for military purposes as when it is, is purely political, without the savor of military law about it. And the same is true of slaves. If the General needs them, he can seize them, and use them; but when the need is past, it is not for him to fix their permanent future condition. That must be settled according to laws made by law-makers, and not by military proclamations. The proclamation in the point in question, is simply "dictatorship." It assumes that the general may do *anything* he pleases—confiscate the lands and free the slaves of *loyal* people, as well as of disloyal ones. And going the whole figure I have no doubt would be more popular with some thoughtless people, than that which has been done! But I cannot assume this reckless position; nor allow others to assume it on my responsibility. You speak of it as being the only means of *saving* the government. On the contrary it is itself the surrender of the government. Can it be pretended that it is any longer the government of the U.S.—any government of Constitution and laws,—wherein a General, or a President, may make permanent rules of property by proclamation?

I do not say Congress might not with propriety pass a law, on the point, just such as General Fremont proclaimed. I do not say I might not, as a member of Congress, vote for it. What I object to, is, that I as President, shall expressly or impliedly seize and exercise the permanent legislative functions of the government.

So much as to principle. Now as to policy. No doubt the thing was popular in some quarters, and would have been more so if it had been a general declaration of emancipation. The Kentucky Legislature would not budge till that proclamation was modified; and Gen. Anderson telegraphed me that on the news of Gen. Fremont having actually issued deeds of manumission, a whole company of our Volunteers threw down their arms and disbanded. I was so assured, as to think it probable, that the very arms we had furnished Kentucky would be turned against us. I think to lose Kentucky is nearly the same as to lose the whole game. Kentucky gone, we can not hold Missouri, nor, as I think, Maryland. These all against us, and the job on our hands is too large for us. We would as well consent to separation at once, including the surrender of this capitol. On the contrary, if you will give up your restlessness for new positions, and back me manfully on the grounds upon which you and other kind friends gave me the election, and have approved in my public documents, we shall go through triumphantly.

You must not understand I took my course on the proclamation *because* of Kentucky. I took the same ground in a private letter to General Fremont before I heard from Kentucky.

You think I am inconsistent because I did not also forbid Gen. Fremont to shoot men under the proclamation. I understand that part to be within military law; but I also think, and so privately wrote Gen. Fremont, that it is impolitic in this, that our adversaries have the power, and will certainly exercise it, to shoot as many of our men as we shoot of theirs. I did not say this in the public letter, because it is a subject I prefer not to discuss in the hearing of our enemies.

There has been no thought of removing Gen. Fremont on any ground connected with his proclamation; and if there has been any wish for his removal on any ground, our mutual friend Sam. Glover can probably tell you what it was. I hope no real necessity for it exists on any ground.

Suppose you write to Hurlbut and get him to resign.[2] Your friend as ever   A. LINCOLN

[1] LS, IHi; ADfS and LS copy, DLC-RTL. The letter which is in the Illinois State Historical Library is the one received by Browning. It bears further minor emendations in Lincoln's handwriting and provides the final text as reproduced here. Browning to Lincoln, September 17, 1861, is in the Lincoln Papers, but scarcely requires summary in view of Lincoln's explicit references.

[2] Browning's reply of September 30 is sixteen pages in length and contains an insert in regard to Lincoln's cryptic suggestion concerning Stephen A. Hurlbut as follows: "I could not tell, for the life of me, whether you were serious, or whether you was *poking* a little irony at me. If I thought you were in earnest I would certainly do it, as I could with great propriety, having in my possession his written pledge to resign if he drank a drop of liquor after going into the service. He has violated his pledge, and behaved badly, and ought to resign." (DLC-RTL). Hurlbut did not resign, of course, but served with distinction throughout the war. One of the charges preferred against General Frémont, however, was that he had permitted Hurlbut to ". . . remain in command of the forces . . . in Northern Missouri from the tenth-day of August . . . to about the tenth-day of September . . . , knowing him . . . to be a common drunkard and unfit all of said time to command. . . ." (Charges preferred by Francis P. Blair, Jr., against John C. Frémont, October 2, enclosed in Blair to Lincoln, October 3, 1861 (DLC-RTL).

To John C. Frémont[1]

Washington, September 22, 1861.

Governor Morton telegraphs as follows: Colonel Lane [Love],[2] just arrived by special train, represents Owensboro, 40 miles above Evansville, in possession of secessionists. Green river is navigable. Owensboro, must be seized. We want a gunboat sent up from Paducah for that purpose. Send up the gunboat if, in your discretion, you think it right. Perhaps you had better order those in charge of the Ohio river to guard it vigilantly at all points.

Major General Frémont.   A. LINCOLN.

[1] Thirty-seventh Congress, Third Session, *Senate Reports*, No. 108, Report of the Joint Committee on the Conduct of the War, Part III, pp. 148-49; also in *Official Records*, I, IV, 265. Frémont telegraphed Lincoln the same day, "I have immediately ordered Captain [Andrew H.] Foote with gunboat to . . . Owensborough, and will take measures to guard the Ohio." (OR, I, IV, 265).

[2] Both sources are in error in naming "Colonel Lane." Morton's telegram (DLC-RTL) reads "Love" instead of "Lane," and undoubtedly refers to Lieutenant Colonel S. Palace Love of the Eleventh Kentucky Infantry, which was organized from Green River counties in Kentucky and was encamped at Owensboro.

To Oliver P. Morton[1]

To Gov O P Morton   Sept 22d 1861.
        By Telegraph from Washington   1861
Have just ordered Gen Fremont to send up gun Boat if he can
spare it   A LINCOLN

1 Copy, In. The copy received by Morton is written on a Western Union Telegraph Company blank.

To Montgomery C. Meigs[1]

September 23, 1861
The within recommendations of James H. McKay are excellent
and most ample and proper and he should be appointed if there
be any vacancy   A. LINCOLN
        Sept 23. 1861

1 AES, owned by Mary L. Callwell, San Francisco, California. Lincoln's endorsement is written on an envelope. The papers referred to are no longer with
the endorsement. James H. McKay of Illinois was nominated to the Senate as
captain and assistant quartermaster of Volunteers, April 7, and confirmed April
14, 1862.

Endorsement:
Release of Imprisoned Secessionists[1]

[c. September 24, 1861]
Were sent to Fort Lafayette by the military authorities of Kentucky and it would be improper for me to intervene without further knowledge of the facts than I now possess.   A. LINCOLN.

1 OR, II, II, 808. Lincoln's endorsement is on a communication from George D.
Prentice, September 24, 1861, asking release of ex-Governor Charles S. Morehead, Reuben T. Durrett, and M. W. Barr, arrested in Louisville, Kentucky. See
also Lincoln to Seward, October 4, infra.

Memorandum About Guns[1]

Executive Mansion, Washington, Sep. 24. 1861.
    If twenty guns, and a carriage and appointments to each, shall
be made equal, or superior to the Ellsworth gun & carriage, exhibited some time since to Capt. Kingsbury,[2] and more recently to
me, the quality to be judged of by Capt. Kingsbury; and shall be
delivered to the Government of the U.S. at this city, within sixty
days from this date, I will advise that they be paid for at the price
of three hundred and fifty dollars for each gun, with its' carriage

and appointments—and in addition will advise that reasonable charges for transportation from Worcester, in Massachusetts to this city, be paid. Will also advise that forty cents per pound be paid for all good amunition, suitable for said guns which shall be furnished with said guns, provided the amount does not exceed two hundred rounds to each gun.   A. LINCOLN

¹ ADS, DLC-RTL. Eli Thayer, ex-representative from Massachusetts (1857-1861), wrote Lincoln on September 21, 1861, suggesting in the interest of increased efficiency of Union troops, "The formation of Light Artillery Brigades. . . . The cannon to be drawn by the soldiers. . . . The cannon best adapted to this service is the one called the 'Ellsworth Gun,' from his [Elmer E. Ellsworth] having first ordered such for the use of his Zouave regiment." (DLC-RTL).
² On November 30, 1861, Captain Charles P. Kingsbury of the Ordnance Department certified the receipt and performance of the cannon presented by Thayer (DLC-RTL).

To Lorenzo Thomas¹

Adjt. General, please answer this, or have it answered.
Sep. 24, 1861   A. LINCOLN

¹ AES, DLC-RTL. Lincoln's endorsement is written on a telegram from Colonel John B. Turchin, Camp Dennison, Ohio, September 23, explaining that his regiment, the Nineteenth Illinois, had ". . . one hundred & fifty (150) men disabled by rail road accident about one hundred (100) men sick. . . . Our uniforms shirts & shoes worn out. The men not paid for two (2) months. Our equipments are sent . . . to Washington. The Regt is ordered to Louisville. . . . which way shall we go. . . ." Below Lincoln's endorsement is an endorsement by Absalom Baird, A.G.O., that a telegram had been sent to Turchin "to obey the orders of his General."

To Simon Cameron¹

The within recommendations of Mr. Millard are ample; and I shall be gratified if a place can be found for him.
Sep. 25. 1861   A. LINCOLN

Please see Mr. Millard   A.L.

¹ AES, IHi. Lincoln's endorsements are written on an envelope which Lincoln addressed "Hon. Sec. of War." The papers referred to are no longer with the envelope, and "Mr. Millard" has not been identified.

To Simon Cameron¹

Sec. of War, please see Mr. Denny, of Mass.
Sep. 25. 1861.   A. LINCOLN

¹ ALS-P, ISLA. Lincoln's note is written on a small card. Denny may have been Christopher C. Denny, clothing manufacturer of Leicester, Massachusetts.

To Simon Cameron[1]

Hon. Sec. of War   Executive Mansion
My dear Sir: Sep. 25. 1861
  I am called upon for aid to Colorado Territory. Please see the
Messenger of Gov. Gilpin, and his despatches, and with the assist-
ance of Genl. Scott, provide as well for that territory, as a con-
sideration of the whole public service will admit. Yours truly
                                                   A. LINCOLN

  [1] ALS, IHi. The accompanying envelope is endorsed by Lincoln "Please see
the bearer, Messenger from Gov. Gilpin/ A.L." Governor William Gilpin had
sent a letter to Cameron by messenger Benjamin R. Pegram, dated August 26,
1861, asking ". . . essential supplies . . . 10,000 muskets, rifles, and equipments. . . ." (OR, I, III, 496).

To Winfield Scott[1]

Lieut. Genl. Scott   Executive Mansion
My dear Sir   Sep. 25. 1861
  The bearer of this—Mr. Pancoast—represents that he resides in
Hampshire County, Va. on the Maryland border, in an isolated
neighborhood of Union people, who are suffering for *salt*. He
wants permission to take a limited supply for that neighborhood
from Hagerstown through our lines. He says the nature of the
country does not admit of the article being carried from where
he will take it to any secession region.
  I know not whether his request is admissable; but thinking you
will better understand the matter than I, I send him to you. Very
truly   A. LINCOLN

  [1] ALS-P, ISLA. Samuel A. Pancoast was given approval for his project and
also secured the approval of Virginia authorities, but upon charges of specula-
tion was arrested and imprisoned at Richmond in November, 1861 (OR, II, II,
1530-45).

To William H. Seward[1]

                                          September 25, 1861
Mr. Clark thinks the Consulship at *Tahiti* is vacant; and if the
Secretary of State knows no objection, I know none, to Mr. Clark's
having the appointment.   A. LINCOLN
  Sep. 25. 1861

  [1] AES, NAuE. Lincoln's endorsement appears on a letter from A. H. Clark,
Washington, September 25, 1861:
  "In March last I was recommended for the Consulship of Acapulco.

"Of the number of those who recommended me are gentlemen now holding important federal positions in California and elsewhere. I am fully endorsed in the State Department by Senators Harlan, McDougall and Latham.

"My application for Acapulco was unsuccessful, and I respectfully ask the Consulship for Tahiti, made vacant by the death of Mr [Visesimus] Turner who was appointed from California."

No record of Clark's appointment has been found.

To Caleb B. Smith[1]

September 25, 1861

Has Dr. Stephenson, Congressional Librarian, resigned? Is there any vacancy of Assistant Congressional Librarian? . . . .

[1] Metropolitan Art Association Catalog, April 1, 1914, No. 563. This incomplete text is all that is available. John G. Stephenson had not resigned, apparently, for he was still librarian in 1863. There may have been a vacancy as assistant librarian, however, for assistant librarian L. L. Tilden was replaced by George A. Morris of Ohio in the *U.S. Official Register* for 1863.

Appointment of William L. Hodge[1]

Executive Mansion September 26, 1861.

I hereby appoint William L. Hodge Acting Secretary of the Treasury during the absence of the Secretary commencing on Friday, the 27th inst.   ABRAHAM LINCOLN

[1] DS, owned by Foreman M. Lebold, Chicago, Illinois. Both Secretary Chase and Assistant Secretary George Harrington being absent from Washington, Lincoln appointed Hodge, who had been assistant secretary during the Fillmore administration, but who had no federal office in 1861.

To Oliver P. Morton[1]

To O P Morton   Sept 26   1861
By Telegraph from Washington 1861

We are supplying all the demands for arms as fast as we can we expect to order a lot to you tomorrow   I think there is no concentration of Railroads at Muldroughs Hill   a week ago we heard that the enemy was encamped on Muldroughs hill   now our friends are encamped upon it & the enemies pickets are in sight   that is an improvement   A. LINCOLN

[1] Copy, In. The copy received by Governor Morton is written on a Western Union blank, without punctuation. Morton's telegram to Thomas A. Scott, September 25, 1861, advised that ". . . The recruiting business in Indiana will stop if guns are not furnished. . . . My state has done well. Has stripped herself of arms for the Government and the war is now upon her borders. . . . I wish this shown to the President." (DLC-RTL). Morton to Lincoln, September 26, reported

the enemy's pickets ". . . in sight of Muldraugh's Hill about forty (40) miles from Louisville, from that point they can communicate by rail with every seceded state but Texas & Arkansas. . . ." (*Ibid.*).

To Samuel T. Glover[1]

Sent from Washington [September 27, 1861?]

To Samuel T. Glover, Esq St. Louis, Mo.

What news from up river?—Lexington, Booneville, or Jefferson City? Please answer.   A. LINCOLN

[1] ALS, owned by Henry R. Benjamin, New York City. The date of this telegram is derived from Glover's telegram in reply, received at 12:45 A.M., September 28, 1861. The time of dispatch recorded on Lincoln's telegram by the operator is "5.15 PM." Glover's reply is as follows: "We have dispatch that [James H.] Lane has captured at Osceola large supply train of Raines [James S. Rains, Missouri State Guard, Confederate] & [Sterling] Price & one hundred thousand dollars in money No other news" (DLC-RTL).

Following the action at Boonville, Missouri, on September 13, Lexington, Missouri, was besieged until September 20, when it surrendered to Confederate forces.

To Montgomery C. Meigs[1]

Q. M. Genl.

Please do the proper thing as to the within.

Sep. 27. 1861   A. LINCOLN

[1] AES, DLC-RTL. Lincoln's endorsement is written on a telegram from William Thomas, secretary of the Illinois department of army auditors, Springfield, Illinois, September 25, 1861, "We hear nothing from Washington. Mulligan's brigade is on our hands and no money to purchase a ration. We have sent over fifty thousand (50,000) men . . . without a Quarter Master. . . ." (DLC-RTL). Colonel James A. Mulligan of the Twenty-third Illinois Infantry was offered, but declined, appointment as brigadier general. Meigs' endorsement in reply to Lincoln's is as follows: "Capt. [Asher R.] Eddy a regular quarter master is ordered to Springfield to assist the Governor."

To William H. Seward[1]

September 27, 1861

I am entirely willing that Mr. Slade shall be appointed to any consulship not already disposed of, except the *single* one which the Sec. of State understands without my now mentioning.

Sep. 27. 1861   A. LINCOLN

[1] AES, NAuE. Lincoln's endorsement is on a letter from Edward Bates to Lincoln, September 23, 1861, asking a consulship for William Slade of Cleveland, Ohio. Slade was nominated to the Senate for the consulship at Nice, March 21, and confirmed March 31, 1862.

To James G. Bennett[1]

Private & confidential.

Mr. James Gorden Bennett   Washington, D.C.

My dear Sir   Sept. 28. 1861

Last evening Mr. Wickoff solicited me for a pass, or permission to a gentleman whose name I forget, to accompany one of our vessels down the Potomac to-day, as a reporter of the Herald, saying the Sec. of the Navy had refused, while he had given the privilege to reporters of other papers. It was too late at night for me to see the Secretary, and I had to decline giving the permission, because he the Sec, might have a sufficient reason unknown to me. I write this to assure you that the administration will not discriminate against the Herald, especially while it sustains us so generously, and the cause of the country so ably as it has been doing. Your Obt. Servt.   A. LINCOLN

[1] ALS-F, Grand Rapids, Michigan, *Press*, February 12, 1927. This letter is misdated September 22, 1861, in Hertz, II, 842. Bennett replied October 22, 1861, regretting that "Mr. Wikoff gave you any trouble. . . . Before that application by Mr. W, but unknown to him the Secretary of the Navy had very kindly facilitated [?] another of my correspondents all that was required. . . ." (DLC-RTL). Henry Wikoff, author, adventurer, and sometime British agent was correspondent for the New York *Herald.*

To Simon Cameron[1]

September 28, 1861

To-day, Sep. 28, 1861, Hon. Messrs. Dunn, Mitchell and Porter, and John D. Defrees, Mr. Donnohue, Fletcher, and Jones, all of Indiana, call and ask that Thomas A. Morris of that state be a Major General of Volunteers, and they say such is the wish of the entire Indiana Delegation in Congress.

[1] AES, IHi. William M. Dunn, William Mitchell, and Albert G. Porter were U.S. representatives, and John D. Defrees was superintendent of public printing. The other men named were probably D. C. Donnohue of Greencastle, Calvin Fletcher of Indianapolis, and Aquilla Jones of Greencastle. Thomas A. Morris received no federal appointment as major general, but his biographical sketch in *Appletons' Cyclopaedia* says he was offered and declined the appointment

To Simon Cameron[1]

September 28, 1861

I think the case is sufficiently made for Gen'l Wade to be appointed.

[1] American Art Association Anderson Galleries Catalog 3913, May 6, 1931, No. 45. According to the catalog description, Lincoln's endorsement is written on the back of a letter from Melancthon S. Wade of Cincinnati, who was appointed brigadier general of Volunteers, October 1, 1861.

To William H. Seward[1]

The writer of the letter of which this is a copy, is one of the best
men I know.   A. LINCOLN

Sep. 28. 1861

[1] AES, DNA FS RG 59, Appointments, Box 241. Lincoln's endorsement is on
the back of a copy of a letter from Lincoln's old friend James N. Brown, written
from Springfield, Illinois, September 21, 1861, recommending Thomas Brown,
editor of the *Ohio Farmer* at Cleveland, for a consulship. Thomas Brown is not
listed as consul either in 1861 or 1863.

To William H. Seward[1]

Hon. Sec. of State   Executive Mansion
My dear Sir   Sep. 28. 1861

I do not believe the duty is appropriately yours, but I will thank
you if you will have this Indian treaty & amendments put in
shape for publication, and also a draft of a proclamation in regard
to it prepared. The accompanying notes of the Comr. of Indian
Affairs, and of Mr. Usher, Atty for the indians, show, I think, that
all is satisfactory now   Yours truly   A. LINCOLN

[1] ALS, DNA FS RG 11, General Records of the U.S. Government, No. 317,
Treaty with the Delawares at Leavenworth City, Kansas, July 2, 1861. The treaty
proclamation was signed by Lincoln October 4, 1861.

To George M. Weston[1]

Geo. M. Weston, Esq   Executive Mansion
My dear Sir: Sep. 28. 1861

Some time ago I told your brother if he would Get Gen. Ripley
to say he desired his (your brother's) appointment as Military
Store keeper, I would be inclined to appoint him. He brought me
a note from Gen. Ripley saying he was competent, but in which he
did *not* say he wished his appointment, and seemed to think he had
got what I suggested. I, however, wrote the Sec. of War, favorable
to his appointment. This morning your brother came to me again,
having found in the newspapers that somebody else [had been ap-
pointed] to the office, and insisted that there is still another place.
I went to Gen. Ripley, who told me plainly, he did *not* ask for his
appointment, and could not be induced to ask for it. I have got the
Sec. of War to promise to try to fix a place for him. Yours truly
                                                           A. LINCOLN

[1] ALS, owned by Mrs. William F. Whiting, Holyoke, Massachusetts. See Lin-
coln to James W. Ripley, September 12, *supra*, in regard to appointment for
Charles Weston. George M. Weston was a lawyer and newspaperman of Augusta,
Maine.

To Oliver P. Morton[1]

To Gov O P Morton   Sept 29   1861
           By Telegraph from Washington   1861

I have just shown your message to Gen Scott   He says he will be glad if the Report of Zollicoffers having left Cumberland Gap shall be confirmed   I intend writing you today   Arms going to you and Anderson as fast as we can send them

                                   A LINCOLN

[1] Copy, In. The copy received by Governor Morton is written on a Western Union blank, without punctuation. Governor Morton's message concerning Confederate Brigadier General Felix K. Zollicoffer's movements has not been located.

To Oliver P. Morton[1]

Washington, D.C. Sep. 29, 1861

His Excellency Gov. O. P. Morton: Your letter by the hand of Mr. Prunk[2] was received yesterday. I write this letter because I wish you to believe of us (as we certainly believe of you) that we are doing the very best we can. You do not receive arms from us as fast as you need them; but it is because we have not near enough to meet all the pressing demands; and we are obliged to share around what we have, sending the larger share to the points which appear to need them most. We have great hope that our own supply will be ample before long, so that you and all others can have as many as you need. I see an article in an Indianapolis newspaper denouncing me for not answering your letter sent by a special messenger two or three weeks ago. I did make what I thought the best answer I could to that letter. As I remember, it asked for ten heavy guns to be distributed, with some troops, at Lawrenceburgh, Madison, New-Albany and Evansville; and I ordered the guns, and directed you to send the troops if you had them.

As to Kentucky, you do not estimate that state as more important than I do; but I am compelled to watch all points. While I write this I am, if not in *range*, at least in *hearing* of cannon-shot, from an army of enemies more than a hundred thousand strong. I do not expect them to capture this city; but I *know* they would, if I were to send the men and arms from here, to defend Louisville, of which there is not a single hostile armed soldier within forty miles, nor any force known to be moving upon it from any distance.

It is true, the Army in our front may make a half circle around Southward, and move on Louisville; but when they do, we will make a half circle around Northward, and meet them; and in the mean time we will get up what forces we can from other sources to also meet them.

I hope Zollicoffer has left Cumberland Gap (though I fear he has not) because, if he has, I rather infer he did it because of his dred of Camp Dick Robinson, re-inforced from Cincinnati, moving on him, than because of his intention to move on Louis-ville.[3] But if he does go round and re-inforce Buckner, let Dick Robinson come round and re-inforce Sherman, and the thing is substantially as it was when Zollicoffer left Cumberland Gap. I state this as an illustration; for in fact, I think if the Gap is left open to us Dick Robinson should take it and hold it; while Indiana, and the vicinity of Louisville in Kentucky, can re-inforce Sherman faster than Zollicoffer can Buckner.

You requested that Lt. Col. Wood,[4] of the Army, should be appointed a Brigadier General   I will only say that very formidable objection has been made to this from Indiana. Yours very truly   A. LINCOLN

[1] ADfS, DLC-RTL; LS, CSmH. Governor Morton telegraphed Lincoln September 26, 1861, in reply to Lincoln's telegram of the same date (*supra*), "It is true there is no concentration of rail roads at Mull Droughs Hill but the road running thence south connections with rail roads running to nearly every confederate state. From the spirit of your despatch & from other information I am satisfied my despatches in regard to Kentucky are not highly honored. . . ." (DLC-RTL).

[2] Morton's letter introduced Dr. Daniel H. Prunk of Indianapolis ". . . bearer of despatches from me. . . ." a surgeon in the Nineteenth and Twentieth Indiana Volunteers.

[3] Richard M. Robinson furnished the land near Bryantsville, Kentucky, on which the camp was established.

[4] Thomas J. Wood was appointed brigadier general of Volunteers October 11, 1861.

To Benjamin B. French[1]

September 30, 1861

I do not recollect having any acquaintance with Esqr. Ferguson; but if the Comr. of Pub. Buildings inclines to appoint him to any place, I have no objection   A. LINCOLN

Sep. 30. 1861.

[1] AES, CSmH. Lincoln's endorsement is written on a letter from Reverend E. P. Phelps, Baltimore Conference, Methodist Episcopal Church, September 28, 1861, recommending B. W. Ferguson, ". . . a justice of the Peace in Washington . . . . and a decided Union man . . . ." for an appointment ". . . under the commissioner of Public Buildings. . . ." Benjamin B. French of New Hampshire had recently been appointed commissioner, but no record has been found of B. W. Ferguson's appointment.

To George B. McClellan[1]

Will Gen McClellan please see Pay-Master Whitney a moment?
Sep. 30. 1861   A LINCOLN

[1] ALS-P, ISLA. Henry C. Whitney had been appointed paymaster August 6, 1861.

To Winfield Scott[1]

September 30, 1861

The Sanitary Commission is doing a work of great humanity, and of direct practical value to the nation, in this time of its trial. It is entitled to the gratitude and confidence of the people, and I trust it will be generously supported. There is no agency through which voluntary offerings of patriotism can be more effectively made.   A. LINCOLN.

Winfield Scott.
Washington, September 30, 1861.

[1] New York *Tribune*, October 7, 1861. Frederick L. Olmstead of the Sanitary Commission wrote Lincoln, September 30, 1861, "The Quarter Master General has informed the Sanitary Commission that some scarcity of blankets is for the present to be apprehended. The commission proposes to supply hospitals as far as possible from private stores, by which means a considerable quantity will be set free for the men in active service. Without announcing the deficiency the Secretary of the Commission is about to issue a circular soliciting donations and respectfully requests a line from the President recommending the purpose of the Commission to the confidence of the public." (DLC-RTL).

To Edward Bates[1]

[October, 1861]

William McKay, wishes to be a Judge in Colorado. He was recommended for Judge of Kansas, & his papers are in the Atty Genls. Dept.

[1] AD, DNA RG 60, Papers of Attorney General, Appointments, Kansas, Box 405. William McKay is not of record as appointed to office either in Kansas or Colorado.

To Simon Cameron[1]

Honorable Sec. of War: Executive Mansion, October 1st, 1861.

My dear Sir: The Postmaster-General and myself have special reasons for wishing to oblige Mr. Benj. F. Watson, of Lawrence,

Mass. He has been appointed an Assistant Paymaster or Paymaster of Volunteers, but he wishes the same post in the regular Army. If there is any vacancy, not committed to any other person, let Mr. Watson have it. If there be no such vacancy, oblige him, as far as you can, by sending him to service at the place which suits him best. Yours truly, A. LINCOLN

[1] Tracy, pp. 194-95. Benjamin F. Watson, appointed additional paymaster of Volunteers, September 5, 1861, had been postmaster at Lawrence, Massachusetts, under Pierce and Buchanan, but had been removed because it was understood by the Post Office Department that he had accepted a commission in the Sixth Massachusetts Infantry, a three-months regiment. Upon being mustered out August 2, Watson learned of his removal and telegraphed Lincoln. According to Watson's account, Lincoln's reply of August 8 (presumably not extant), enclosing a memorandum from the postmaster general, explained as follows: "If I signed a paper, in making a change in the office, it was among others, without my being conscious of this particular one. . . . I shall talk fully with the Postmaster-General on the subject when I next see him." (Benjamin F. Watson, "Abraham Lincoln as Seen by a Life-Long Democrat, After Going through Baltimore," *Abraham Lincoln Tributes* . . . . introduction by The Rev. William Hayes Ward, D.D., New York, 1895, p. 139.)

Memorandum for a Plan of Campaign[1]

[c. October 1, 1861]

On, or about the 5th. of October, (the exact day to be determined hereafter) I wish a movement made to seize and hold a point on the Railroad connecting Virginia and Tennesse, near the Mountain pass called Cumberland Gap.

That point is now guarded against us by Zolicoffer, with 6000 or 8000, rebels at Barboursville, Kentucky, say twentyfive miles from the Gap towards Lexington.

We have a force of 5000 or 6000, under General Thomas,[2] at Camp Dick Robinson, about twentyfive miles from Lexington, and seventyfive from Zollicoffer's camp on the road between the two, which is not a Railroad, anywhere between Lexington and the point to be seized—and along the whole length of which the Union sentiment among the people largely predominates.

We have military possession of the Railroads from Cincinnati to Lexington, and from Louisville to Lexington, and some Home Guards under General Crittenden[3] are on the latter line.

We have possession of the Railroad from Louisville to Nashville, Tenn, so far as Muldrough's Hill, about forty miles, and the rebels have possession of that road all South of there. At the Hill we have a force of 8000 under Gen. Sherman;[4] and about an equal force of rebels is a very short distance South, under under [sic] Gen. Buckner.

We have a large force at Paducah, and a smaller at Fort-Holt, both on the Kentucky side, with some at Bird's Point, Cairo, Mound City, Evansville, & New-Albany, all on the other side; and all which, with the Gun-Boats on the River, are, perhaps, sufficient to guard the Ohio from Louisville to it's mouth.

About supplies of troops, my general idea is that all from Wisconsin, Minesota, Iowa, Illinois, Missouri, and Kansas, not now elsewhere, be left to *Fremont*.

All from Indiana and Michigan, not now elsewhere, be sent to Anderson at Louisville.

All from Ohio, needed in Western Virginia be sent there; and any remainder, be sent to Mitchell[5] at Cincinnati, for Anderson.

All East of the Mountains be appropriated to McClellan, and to the coast.

As to movements, my idea is that the one for the coast,[6] and that on Cumberland Gap be simultaneous; and that, in the mean time, preparation, vigilant watching, and the defensive only be acted upon—(this however, not to apply to Fremonts operations in Northern and middle Missouri)—that before these movements, Thomas and Sherman shall respectively watch, but not attack Zollicoffer, and Buckner.

That when the coast and Gap movements shall be ready, Sherman is merely to stand fast; while all at Cincincinnati [sic], and all at Louisville with all on the lines, concentrate rapidly at Lexington, and thence to Thomas' camp joining him, and the whole thence upon the Gap.

It is for the Military men to decide whether they can find a pass through the mountains at or near the Gap, which can not be defended by the enemy, with a greatly inferior force, and what is to be done in regard to this.

The Coast and Gap movements made, Generals McClellan and Fremont, in their respective Departments, will avail themselves of any advantages the diversions may present.

[1] AD, The Rosenbach Company, Philadelphia and New York. The exact date of this document cannot be established from its contents, and it may have been composed a few days earlier. Orders for the movement on Cumberland Gap may be found in OR, I, IV, 294-306.   [2] George H. Thomas.
[3] Thomas L. Crittenden.   [4] William T. Sherman.
[5] Ormsby M. Mitchel.
[6] The "coast movement" referred to was certainly the November 7 expedition which took Port Royal, South Carolina, with General Thomas W. Sherman commanding the Army forces.

To Padischah Abd ul Aziz Khan[1]

October 2, 1861

Abraham Lincoln,
President of the United States of America.

To His Imperial Majesty Abd ul Aziz Khan,
Padischah of the Empire of the Ottoman Family.

Great and Good Friend: I have received the letter which Your Majesty has been pleased to address to me, communicating intelligence of the demise of Your Majesty's honored brother, His late Imperial Majesty Abd ul Mejid Khan, and of your own accession to the throne of your ancestors. Assuring you of my deep sympathy at the death of your august brother, who was the constant friend of the United States, I beg leave to offer to Your Majesty my sincere and hearty congratulations upon your accession to his throne, with my best wishes that your reign may be happy and glorious to yourself and prosperous to your realm. Permit me also to assure Your Majesty of my constant and earnest desire to maintain the amity and good correspondence which have always subsisted and still prevail between the two nations, and that nothing shall be omitted on my part to cultivate and promote the friendly sentiments always entertained and cherished by this Government in its relations with His late Majesty. And so I recommend Your Majesty to the protection of the Almighty.

Written at Washington, the second day of October, Anno Domini 1861. Your Good Friend,   ABRAHAM LINCOLN.

By the President:

WILLIAM H. SEWARD, Secretary of State.

[1] Copy, DNA FS RG 59, Communications to Foreign Sovereigns and States, III, 179-80.

Inscription on Photograph Given to Mrs. Lucy G. Speed[1]

For Mrs. Lucy G. Speed, from whose pious hand I accepted the present of an Oxford Bible twenty years ago.   A. LINCOLN
Washington, D.C. October 3, 1861

[1] The photograph is now owned by Mrs. Elise C. Railey, Louisville, Kentucky. Mrs. Speed was the mother of Joshua F. Speed, whom Lincoln visited in August and September, 1841.

To Isabel II[1]

October 3, 1861

Abraham Lincoln,
President of the United States of America.

To Her Majesty Doña Isabel II,
By the Grace of God and the Constitution
of the Spanish Monarchy, Queen of Spain,
&c., &c., &c.

Great and Good Friend: I have received the letter which Your Majesty was pleased to address to me on the 12th. of August, last, conveying the melancholy tidings of the decease of Her Royal Highness the Infanta Doña Maria de Regla, Your Majesty's niece.

I participate in the grief occasioned by this sad event and offer to Your Majesty and to your royal household my sincere condolence.

May God have Your Majesty always in His safe and holy keeping! Your Good Friend, ABRAHAM LINCOLN.

Washington, October 3, 1861.

[1] Copy, DNA FS RG 59, Communications to Foreign Sovereigns and States, III, 180-81.

To William H. Seward[1]

I think these papers better remain in the State Department.

Oct. 3. 1861. A.L.

[1] AES, DNA FS RG 59, Appointments, Box 279. Lincoln's endorsement is written on an envelope containing papers of Theodore D. Edwards (*vide supra*, September 17, 1861).

To William H. Seward[1]

October 3, 1861

James Mitchell, the writer of one of the within letters, I know, and like. He was, for years, colonization agent, for Indiana; and I suppose, by what he says, being a democrat, he was removed by our friends. He is a *Methodist* of good standing, and Governor Wright especially wishes him to be cared for. His first care, as you see by his letter, is for his brother-in-law, *G. F. Savitz*. I will be really obliged, if the Secretary of State can find something for this brother-in-law. Will he please try? A. LINCOLN

Oct. 3. 1861.

[1] AES, NAuE. Lincoln's endorsement has been removed from the accompanying letter. No record of an appointment for G. F. Savitz has been found.

To Caleb B. Smith[1]

Executive Office   October 3d. 1861
Let the reservation be established as recommended by the Secretary of the Interior.   A. Lincoln.

[1] Copy, DNA NR RG 75, Office of Indian Affairs, Executive Order File. The copy of Lincoln's order is written on the bottom of the page containing a copy of Smith's letter of October 3, 1861, recommending that the Uintah Valley in Utah be set apart as an Indian reservation.

To Edward Bates[1]

Hon. Attorney General   Executive Mansion
My dear Sir: Oct. 4. 1861
Let Joseph E. Streeter, of Illinois, be appointed to the vacant Judgeship in Nebraska Territory.   A. Lincoln

[1] ALS, DNA GE RG 60, Papers of Attorney General, Segregated Lincoln Material. Joseph E. Streeter of Joliet, Illinois, brother-in-law of Speaker of the House Galusha Grow, was appointed associate justice of Nebraska, and died in office in February, 1863.

To Simon Cameron[1]

The writer of this is a very dear friend of mine, whom I would much wish to oblige.   A. Lincoln
Oct. 4. 1861.

[1] AES, IHi. Lincoln's endorsement is written on a letter from Nathan M. Knapp, Winchester, Illinois, September 18, 1861, requesting "some sort of appointment of my son, Jno. Sullivan Knapp, who is a private in . . . 14th Ill. Vols. . . . Can he not be put to some service that will get him out of the ranks. . . ." John S. Knapp was appointed second lieutenant in the Seventeenth U.S. Infantry on October 24, 1861.

General Order Concerning Flag Officers[1]

General Order.
Executive of the United States.
4th. October, 1861.
Flag Officers of the United States Navy, authorized to wear a square flag at the mizzen-mast head, will take rank with Major Generals of the United States Army.   Abraham Lincoln

[1] DS, DNA WR NB RG 45, Executive Letters, No. 12.

To William H. Seward[1]

Hon. Secretary of State.   Executive Mansion, October 4, 1861.

My dear Sir: Please see Mr. Walker, well vouched as a Union man and son-in-law of Governor Morehead, and pleading for his release. I understand the Kentucky arrests were not made by special direction from here, and I am willing if you are that any of the parties may be released when James Guthrie and James Speed think they should be. Yours, truly,   A. LINCOLN.

[1] OR, II, II, 809. Ex-governor Charles S. Morehead was paroled January 6, 1862, on request of Samuel J. Walker, on condition that he neither enter Kentucky or any other state in insurrection nor act or correspond against the authority of the U.S. (*Ibid.*, p. 825).

To Whom It May Concern[1]

Whom it may concern   Washington, D.C. Oct. 4, 1861

This will introduce Mr. A. C. Badger formerly of Louisville, Kentucky. He is a reliable, and most worthy gentleman; and as such I commend him to all with whom he may meet.

A. LINCOLN

[1] ALS, CtY. Alpheus C. Badger was in the banking business at Chicago, Illinois.

To Samuel R. Curtis[1]

Brig: Genl. S. R. Curtis   Washington, D.C.
My dear Sir: Oct. 7. 1861.

Without prejudice, and looking to nothing but justice, and the public interest, I am greatly perplexed about Gen: Fremont: In your position, you can not but have a correct judgment in the case; and I beseech you to answer Gen. Cameron, when he hands you this, "Ought Gen: Fremont to be relieved from, or retained in his present command?" It shall be entirely confidential; but you can perceive how indispensable it is to justice & the public service, that I should have, an intelligent unprejudiced, and judicious opinion from some professional Military man on the spot, to assist me in the case. Yours very truly   A. LINCOLN

[1] ALS, IHi. This letter was delivered to General Curtis by Simon Cameron on October 12. Cameron carried also a letter from Lincoln to Frémont which is presumably not extant but is mentioned by Cameron in his letters to Lincoln of October 12 and 14 (DLC-RTL). Curtis replied under date of October 12, "The question you propose . . . seems easily answered. It is only a question of manner and time. . . ." (*Ibid.*). Cameron's letter of October 14 related an interview in which Frémont ". . . . made an earnest appeal to me. . . . In reply to this appeal, I told him that I would withhold the order [for his removal] until my return

to Washington. . . ." (*Ibid.*). The copy of Winfield Scott's order removing Frémont which is in the Lincoln Papers bears the date October 7, but appears in the *Official Records* (I, III, 553) under date of October 24, 1861. While Cameron was in St. Louis, Montgomery Blair was in the North sounding out leading persons on Frémont's removal. His letters of October 5 and 7 related that William C. Bryant, Horace Greeley, Governor John A. Andrew and others, received the proposed removal very well (*ibid.*).

To William Dennison[1]

His Excellency: Washington, D.C.
Gov. Dennison   Oct. 7. 1861

My dear Sir: Mr. Gurley tells me there are Six Regiments now in service from Ohio, who have not been commissioned either by *you* or *me*. I shall be glad if you will commission the officers, as I understand they are very uncomfortably situated, not knowing where they belong, or whether they belong anywhere; and as I do not wish to commission them over your head. Yours very truly

                                A. LINCOLN

P.S. If you perceive no valid objection, let the commissions date, from the time they ought to have had them   A.L.

[1] ALS, IHi. This letter was delivered by John A. Gurley on October 16, and Governor Dennison replied on the same date that the regiments ". . . organized under the authority of Genl Fremont, now in this State and in Missouri. . . ." would be promptly commissioned (DLC-RTL).

To William Pickering[1]

Genl. Pickering: Executive Mansion   Oct. 7. 1861

You wish to be Governor of Washington. Last spring when I appointed Dr. Jayne,[2] I was greatly pressed to appoint a man presented by the Methodist people through Bishop Simpson & others, and I then said, if I should appoint another Governor of a Territory from Illinois, it should be their man. I do not *know* that their man will accept that to Washington; but it must be offered to him; and if he declines it, you may have, it. Your Obt. Servt.

                                A. LINCOLN

[1] ALS, owned by Misses Catherine and Martha Pickering, and Mrs. Mary Streever, Jamaica, New York. William H. Wallace, Lincoln's first appointee as governor of Washington Territory, resigned upon becoming delegate to congress. Bishop Matthew Simpson's candidate was John Evans of Chicago, who declined the appointment on October 28, in view of ". . . the remoteness of that Territory rendering a residence there incompatible with occasional attention to my interests in Illinois. . . ." (DLC-RTL.) William Pickering's appointment was confirmed by the Senate December 19, 1861.

[2] William Jayne, governor of Dakota Territory, nominated to the Senate March 23, confirmed March 27, 1861.

To William H. Seward[1]

I shall be very glad to see the Secretaries at the time mentioned.
Oct. 7. 1861.   A. LINCOLN

[1] AES, NAuE. Lincoln's endorsement appears on a letter from Seward, October 7, 1861: "General Cameron and I will come at 2 o'clock this afternoon to confer with you, if you are willing."

To William H. Seward and Caleb B. Smith[1]

October 7, 1861

The within papers show that the Agricultural societies of most of the North-Western States wish John W. Hoyt, of Wisconsin to have a particular place in connection with the World's fair. I wish the Sec. of State, and Sec. of Interior, to fully consider the claim they present, and to give due weight to it.   A. LINCOLN
Oct. 7. 1861.

[1] AES, DNA FS RG 59, Appointments, Box 313. John W. Hoyt was not appointed one of the U.S. commissioners to the London exhibition, but was appointed a commissioner from the state of Wisconsin (*Appletons' Cyclopaedia*).

To Simon Cameron[1]

October 10, 1861

Sec. of War, please see Col, Barret, and see if you can not agree with him about taking his Cavalry Regt. to Kansas & the Indian frontier.   A. LINCOLN
Oct. 10, 1861.

[1] ALS-P, ISLA. Lincoln's note was probably written for Colonel James A. Barret of Springfield, Illinois, in command of the Tenth Illinois Cavalry, mustered in November 25, 1861.

To George D. Ramsay and John A. Dahlgren[1]

Will Major Ramsey, or Capt. Dahlgren, please find work for Michael Donavan?   A. LINCOLN
Oct. 10, 1861

[1] AES, DLC-RTL. Lincoln's endorsement is written on a letter from Mrs. Mary Buckley, October 1861, asking employment for her brother Michael Donovan, who had formerly been employed at the Washington Arsenal, of which Major George D. Ramsay was at this time in command.

To Lorenzo Thomas[1]

[c. October 10, 1861]

Col. C. F. Ruff—for Brig. Genl. in regular Army. Dr. McClintock is strongly in favor of him.

[1] AE, RPB. Lincoln's endorsement is written on the back of a copy of Governor Andrew G. Curtin's letter, October 10, 1861, recommending Charles F. Ruff of Pennsylvania, for appointment as brigadier general. Dr. McClintock was probably John McClintock, Methodist minister of Pennsylvania, at the time pastor of the American Chapel in Paris, France. There is no record of Ruff's appointment.

To Pacha Mohammed Said[1]

October 11, 1861

Abraham Lincoln,
President of the United States of America

To His Highness Mohammed Said Pacha,

Viceroy of Egypt and its Dependencies &c., &c. &c., Great and Good Friend: I have received from Mr. Thayer, Consul General of the United States at Alexandria, a full account of the liberal, enlightened and energetic proceedings which, on his complaint, you have adopted in bringing to speedy and condign punishment the parties, subjects of Your Highness in Upper Egypt, who were concerned in an act of cruel persecution against Faris, an agent of certain Christian missionaries in Upper Egypt. I pray Your Highness to be assured that those proceedings, at once so prompt and so just, will be regarded as a new and unmistakable proof equally of Your Highness' friendship for the United States, and of the firmness, integrity and wisdom with which the Government of Your Highness is conducted. Wishing you great prosperity and success, I am, Your Friend,   ABRAHAM LINCOLN

Washington, October 11, 1861.

By the President:

WILLIAM H. SEWARD, Secretary of State.

[1] Copy, DNA FS RG 59, Communications to Foreign Sovereigns and States, III, 181. Faris-El-Hakim, a Syrian physician employed by American missionaries in selling and distributing Bibles, had been mobbed and imprisoned. Upon charges brought by William S. Thayer, thirteen men had been assessed fines totaling $5,000 as damages for Faris, and to avoid delay the Viceroy had advanced the sum for prompt payment.

To Whom It May Concern[1]

Whom it May Concern: Executive Mansion, Oct. 11, 1861.

The bearer of this, Hugh Roden, says he is a drummer in the seventh regiment New Jersey volunteers, and wishes to be transferred to the second regiment New Jersey volunteers, to be with his brother, who is in the latter regiment. If it will not injuriously affect the service, I shall be glad for him to be obliged.

A. LINCOLN.

1 Troy, New York, *Daily Times*, August 13, 1881 (from the Newark *Advertiser*). There is no record of the transfer requested by Hugh Roden. He was mustered out of Company K, Seventh New Jersey Infantry, October 7, 1864, and his brother George Roden was mustered out of the Second New Jersey Infantry, June 21, 1864.

Memorandum:
Appointment of Charles Ernenwine[1]

Oct. 12. 1861

Charles Ernenwine, of Philadelphia, is a Bavarian Officer,—in this country from 1849—was Lieut. Col. to the Penn. 21st. now out of service. He wishes a respectable place in the service.

1 AD, DLC-RTL. There is no record of further federal service on the part of Ernenwine who served as lieutenant colonel in the Twenty-first Pennsylvania, a three-months regiment, April 15–August 8, 1861.

Memorandum: Appointment of John Spicer[1]

October 12, 1861

Today, Oct. 12. 1861. B. C. Cook, of Ills, calls and says *John Spicer*, his brother-in-law, has done the duties from the beginning, of Q.M. & Com. in Gen. Popes Brigade—and wishes to be regularly appointed to one or the other place. That J. W. Shaffer,[2] appointed Q.M. & Speed Butler, appointed Com; each went to Pope & finding Spicer there yielded to him, Shaffer getting into Hunter's staff, & Butler becoming Aid to Pope. Thus it stood till Spicer was hurt at fall of bridge & Mr. C does not know how it is since.

1 AD, DLC-RTL. First Lieutenant John Spicer of the Twentieth Illinois Infantry was dismissed August 20 and appointed commissary of subsistence of Volunteers September 10, 1861. He was dismissed from service August 16, 1862.

2 John W. Shaffer, appointed captain and quartermaster of Volunteers August 3, 1861, served throughout the war, being brevetted brigadier general of Volunteers March 13, 1865, for service as chief of staff of the Army of the James in the campaign before Richmond in 1864.

To William H. Seward[1]

October 12, 1861

I did not know that Foster had a consulship; and if he had, I am astonished that he declines it. Let the Sec of State take the whole case & do as he pleases with it.   A. LINCOLN

Oct. 12. 1861

1 AES, RPB. Lincoln's endorsement is written on the back of a telegram from Thomas Foster of Minnesota, declining appointment as consul to Tahiti. Foster's appointment was announced in the New York *Tribune*, October 7, 1861, but is not otherwise of record. The *U.S. Official Register* lists Alexander Salmon, consul at Tahiti as of September 30, 1861.

To Winfield Scott[1]

Lieut. Gen. Winfield Scott: Washington, October 14, 1861.

The military line of the United States for the suppression of the insurrection may be extended so far as Bangor in Maine. You and any officer acting under your authority are hereby authorized to suspend the writ of habeas corpus in any place between that place and the city of Washington. ABRAHAM LINCOLN.

By the President:

  WILLIAM H. SEWARD, Secretary of State.

[1] OR, II, II, 109.

To Caleb B. Smith[1]

Washington, October 14, 1861.

Dear Sir: How is this? I supposed I was appointing for Register of Wills a *citizen of this District*. Now the commission comes to me "Moses Kelly, of *New Hampshire*." I do not like this. Yours truly,

  A. LINCOLN.

[1] NH, VII, 8. Smith replied October 15, 1861, "Moses Kelly came to this District in 1841 from New Hampshire and has resided here continuously ever since. He . . . married here & has raised a family here. He has been a constant voter here for twenty years and is an owner of real estate here. . . ." (DLC-RTL). Kelly had been chief clerk in the Department of Interior, to which office Smith appointed his son Walton J. Smith (New York *Tribune*, October 17, 1861). See also Lincoln to Caleb B. Smith October 16, *infra*.

To Edward Bates[1]

Hon. Atty. General Executive Mansion
My dear Sir Oct. 15. 1861

I have just looked over your opinion in Capt. Stansbury's case, & for which I thank you.

Please return to me the Capt's letter, with Gen. Scott's endorsement on it. Yours truly A. LINCOLN

[1] ALS, DNA GE RG 60, Papers of Attorney General, Segregated Lincoln Material. Captain Howard Stansbury of the Topographical Engineers was retired from duty September 28, 1861.

To Edward Bates[1]

Will the Attorney General please have this case attended to as soon as reasonably convenient? A. LINCOLN
Oct 15. 1861

[1] AES, DNA RG 204, U.S. Pardon Attorney, A 354. Lincoln's endorsement is written on a letter from Charles P. Sengstack, former warden of the District Penitentiary, October 10, 1861, recommending a pardon for Isaac Lambert. Bates replied October 19, "The case of *Isaac Lambert* . . . has been examined by me several times. My *feelings* were enlisted on the side of mercy. . . . I cannot yet affirmatively recommend his pardon. . . . I shall be really glad to learn that you . . . find in the case, a proper occasion for the exercise of your merciful power. . . ." (DLC-RTL). See further, Lincoln to Bates, June 11, 1862.

To Simon Cameron[1]

October [c. 15] 1861

I would like for Hon. D. S. Dickinson to be obliged in this case

Oct. 1861.   A. LINCOLN

[1] AES, DLC-Cameron Papers. Lincoln's endorsement is written on a letter from Daniel S. Dickinson, Binghamton, New York, October 15, 1861, recommending ". . . my friend and neighbour Harris G. Ro[d]gers. . . ." for appointment as paymaster. Rodgers was appointed additional paymaster of Volunteers October 22, 1862.

To Simon Cameron[1]

Very respectfully submitted to the Secretary of War, as being an ample recommendation.   A. LINCOLN

Oct 15. 1861

[1] AES, Herbert Wells Fay Collection. Lincoln's endorsement is written on a letter signed by John A. Logan and others, August 1, 1861, recommending L. B. Colby of New York for an army appointment. No appointment is of record.

To Montgomery C. Meigs[1]

Q.M. Genl. Meigs   Executive Mansion
My dear Sir   Oct. 15. 1861

This introduces Mr. Thomas H. Clay, son of the late Hon. Henry Clay. He calls on business; and I shall be pleased for you to oblige him as far as possible, consistently with the public interest. Yours truly   A. LINCOLN

[1] ALS, IHi. Thomas H. Clay's business errand has not been determined. Lincoln appointed him minister to Nicaragua, October 21, 1862.

To Edward Bates[1]

Hon. Attorney General   Executive Mansion
My dear Sir: Oct. 16. 1861

Please send a commission for Bland Ballard, as District Judge for the District of Kentucky. Yours truly   A. LINCOLN

¹ ALS, DNA GE RG 60, Papers of Attorney General, Segregated Lincoln Material. Bland Ballard was appointed to replace Thomas B. Munroe who ". . . has joined the rebels." (New York *Times*, October 19, 1861).

Memorandum:
Appointment of Frank E. Foster¹

Oct. 16. 1861

To-day, Gov. Chase brings to my notice the name of "Frank E. Foster" of Follett Foster & Co, Columbus O. I wish to get something for him.

¹ AD, DLC-RTL. No appointment for Foster has been found.

To Caleb B. Smith¹

What do you think of this?   A.L.
Oct. 16, 1861.

¹ AES-P, ISLA. Lincoln's endorsement is written on a letter from Amos Reed, clerk of the House committee investigating charges of disloyalty, October 16, 1861, stating that testimony had been taken before the committee "seriously impeaching the loyalty of Mr. [Moses] Kelley," late chief clerk of the Department of Interior. Smith replied October 19, 1861, "On the 9th inst. I received a letter from Hon John F. Potter Chairman of the Com. furnishing me a list of all the persons employed in this Department against whom evidence of disloyalty had been adduced before the Com. Mr. Kelly's name does not appear in the list. . . ." (DLC-RTL). The Potter Investigating Committee adjourned October 9, reporting evidence of treason on the part of 472 federal employees (New York *Tribune*, October 10, 1861). Moses Kelly's appointment as register of wills was allowed to stand (see Lincoln to Smith, October 14, *supra*).

To George D. Ramsay¹

Majr. Ramsay   Executive Mansion
My dear Sir   Oct. 17, 1861
The lady—bearer of this—says she has two sons who want to work. Set them at it, if possible. Wanting to work is so rare a merit, that it should be encouraged   Yours truly

A. LINCOLN

¹ ALS, ORB. The bearer cannot be identified, but see Lincoln to Ramsay, October 10, *supra*. Mrs. Mary Buckley, a widow with six children, may have appealed to Lincoln a second time for aid.

To Simon Cameron¹

This matter should be attended to at once   A.L.
Oct. 18. 1861.

1 AES, DNA WR RG 107, Secretary of War, Letters Received, M 539. Lincoln's endorsement is written on an official copy of a letter from Governor John A. Andrew to General Benjamin F. Butler, October 5, 1861, protesting Butler's personal recruitment efforts in Massachusetts and making particular reference to reports that Butler was offering bounties for enlistments in his expedition (see Lincoln to New England Governors, September 11, *supra*). Governor Andrew went to Washington to protest in person the unfair competition of two recruiting authorities operating within the state of Massachusetts. The record of the controversy, which continued into 1862, may be found in the *Official Records* (III, I, 810-66).

Memorandum:
Appointment of Hiram Shaw and William V. Wolfe[1]

For the sake of Kentucky and the memory of Henry Clay I would like these appointments to be made as soon as practicable.

Oct. 18. 1861.   A.L.

1 AES, DLC-RTL. Lincoln's endorsement is written on a letter from Thomas H. Clay, October 17, 1861, requesting appointment of Hiram Shaw of Lexington, and William V. Wolfe of Louisville, Kentucky, as paymasters. There is no record of either man's appointment as paymaster, but William V. Wolfe served as first lieutenant in the Fifteenth Kentucky Infantry.

To Thomas W. Sherman[1]

General Thomas W. Sherman,   Washington,
Annapolis, Md.:   October 18, 1861.

Your dispatch of yesterday received and shown to General McClellan. I have promised him to not break his army here without his consent.

I do not think I shall go to Annapolis.   A. LINCOLN.

1 OR, I, VI, 181. George B. McClellan to Thomas A. Scott, October 17, 1861, ". . . I will not consent to one other man being detached from this army for that [Port Royal] expedition. . . . No outside expedition can effect the result. . . ." (*ibid.*, p. 179). Sherman to Lincoln, October 17, 1861, "Necessity compels me to address the President direct & ask that the 79th N York Highlanders . . . be ordered here [Annapolis]. . . . We commence embarking tomorrow morning. . . ." (DLC-RTL).

To Salmon P. Chase[1]

Sir: Washington   October 19. 1861

I request that you will give to the Collector of Customs at New-York the necessary instructions to secure the free admission of the goods, specified in the accompanying Invoice and Bill of Lading, imported per Steamer "Glasgow" for the use of the Presidential mansion   [A. LINCOLN]

Hon: S. P. Chase, Secretary of the Treasury

[1] LS, DNA FI RG 56, General Records, Treasury Department, Series AB, 1861, Letters from Executive Officers, II, 6. The signature has been clipped from the letter. An endorsement on the back of the letter specifies, "Attended to Oct 19/61."

Memorandum: Appointment of F. M. Murray[1]

Whenever a Paymaster-Quarter-Master, or Commissary, can be appointed for Paducah, Ky Mr. Murray ought to be the man.

Oct. 19, 1861. A. LINCOLN

[1] AES, DLC-RTL. Lincoln's endorsement is written on a letter from L. T. Trimble, Paducah, Kentucky, October 6, 1861, introducing F. M. Murray. Murray had written Lincoln from Paris, Kentucky, September 5, 1861, "For the sin of having given my best support to your claims . . . I have been . . . an exile from my home and family. My residence is in . . . Paducah . . . where . . . I was engaged in the practice of law. . . ." (DLC-RTL). There is no record of an appointment for Murray.

To Frank Fuller[1]

Frank Fuller. Washington D.C
     Gov. Utah— Oct 20 1861
Sir.

The completion of the Telegraph to Great Salt Lake City is auspicious of the Stability & Union of the Republic.

The Government reciprocates your Congratulations

ABRAHAM LINCOLN

[1] Copy, owned by Miss Eileen Thorne, Jackson Heights, New York. The operator's copy of the telegram is written on a blank of the Pacific Telegraph Company. Lincoln replied to a telegram of the same date from Fuller, secretary of state and acting governor of Utah, celebrating the opening of telegraph wires to Salt Lake City. The text of Fuller's telegram appears in the New York *Herald*, October 21, 1861, as follows:

"To the President of the United States:— Great Salt Lake City.
"Utah, whose citizens strenuously resist all imputations of disloyalty, congratulates the President upon the completion of an enterprise which spans the continent, unites two oceans and connects remote extremities of the body politic with the great government heart. May the whole system speedily thrill with quickened pulsations of that heart, the parricidal hand of political treason be punished, and the entire sisterhood of States join hands in glad reunion around the national fireside. "FRANK FULLER,
"Acting Governor of Utah."

To Simon Cameron[1]

Respectfully submitted to Sec. of War—about a Regt. & not an officer A.L.
Oct. 21, 1861

1 AES, ORB. Lincoln's endorsement is written on a letter from Joshua F. Speed, October 18, 1861, requesting that a regiment of cavalry under "Col. Bowles" (probably William M. Bolles, colonel of the Second West Virginia Cavalry), stationed at Parkersburg, West Virginia, be sent to Kentucky and assigned to Jeremiah T. Boyle's brigade.

To Simon Cameron[1]

Sec. of War, please see Mr. T. H. Clay, son of the late Hon. Henry Clay.　　　　　　　　　　　　　　　　　　　　　　A. LINCOLN

Oct. 21, 1861

1 ALS-P, ISLA. See Lincoln's memorandum, October 18, *supra*.

To Joseph Hooker[1]

[October 21, 1861]

If agreeable to Genl. Hooker, let the time be 4 o'clock, P.M. Tuesday, October 22, 1861.　　　　　　　　　　　　A. LINCOLN

1 AES, owned by Alfred W. Stern, Chicago, Illinois. Lincoln's endorsement is written on a letter from Brigadier General Hooker, October 21, 1861, inviting the president to appoint the day and be present at the first raising of the flag on newly completed Fort Lincoln.

To John J. Hughes[1]

Archbishop Hughes　　　　　　　Washington, DC. Oct. 21. 1861.

Rt. Rev. Sir: I am sure you will pardon me if, in my ignorance, I do not address [you] with technical correctness. I find no law authorizing the appointment of Chaplains for our *hospitals;* and yet the services of chaplains are more needed, perhaps, in the hospitals, than with the healthy soldiers in the field. With this view, I have given a sort of quasi appointment, (a copy of which I inclose) to each of three protestant ministers, who have accepted, and entered upon the duties.

If you perceive no objection, I will thank you to give me the name or names of one or more suitable persons of the Catholic Church, to whom I may with propriety, tender the same service.

Many thanks for your kind, and judicious letters to Gov. Seward, and which he regularly allows me both the pleasure and the profit of perusing.

With the highest respect Your Obt. Servt.　　　　A. LINCOLN

1 ADfS, DLC-RTL. In the Lincoln Papers there are several letters from Archbishop Hughes but none of them is concerned with the appointment of hospital

chaplains. See Lincoln's form letter appointing hospital chaplains submitted with the Annual Message to Congress, December 3, *infra*. Archbishop Francis P. Kenrick of Baltimore assigned Reverend Francis X. Boyle and Reverend F. M. Magrath to the performance of the duties of chaplain, October 24, 1861 (*ibid.*).

To Officer in Command at Poolesville, Maryland[1]

Executive Mansion, October 21, 1861– 10 p.m.

Officer in Command at Poolesville:

Send a mounted messenger to the battle-ground and bring me information from General Stone. I want the particulars as to result of engagement and the relative position of the forces for the night, their numbers, and such other information as will give me a correct understanding of affairs.   A. LINCOLN.

[1] OR, I, LI, I, 498. Captain Francis G. Young of the Seventy-first Pennsylvania Volunteers telegraphed Lincoln of the death of his old friend, General Edward D. Baker, at 5 P.M., October 21 (DLC-RTL). General Charles P. Stone replied to Lincoln's telegram at 10:35 P.M., that it was "impossible to give full particulars of what is yet inexplicable to me. . . . We have still possession of Harrisons Island and some fifteen hundred men on the Va side opposite Edwards Ferry. . . . Our killed & wounded may reach 200. Number of prisoners unknown." (*Ibid.*). A second telegram from Captain Young, October 21, gave particulars of the battle of Ball's Bluff (*ibid.*).

To Montgomery C. Meigs[1]

Submitted to Q.M. General. Washburne, who sends this, is an M.C, and one of an investigating Committee now at St. Louis.

Oct. 22. 1861.   A LINCOLN

[1] AES, IHi. Lincoln's endorsement appears on a telegram from Elihu B. Washburne, St. Louis via Springfield, October 21, 1861:

"Yours recd. [Major Robert] Allen prostrated by some kind of sickness. Committee still think the public interest imperatively demands some able and incorruptible regular Army quarter master to be sent here immdy. This is sent like former despatch from Springfield as we dont dare trust St Louis telegraph."

Concerning conditions at St. Louis, see Lincoln's communications to Curtis and Hunter, October 24, 1861, *infra*. Lincoln's communication to which Washburne replied has not been found. Meigs endorsed below Lincoln's endorsement on October 23: "I have consulted Secy of War Order Maj [Robert E.] Clary to proceed with all despatch to St Louis relieve Maj Allen until Maj Allen recovers from his present illness sufficiently to return to duty. When Maj Allen recovers Maj Clary will proceed to the writer or report by letter to Gen Rosecrans & take charge of the QM Depot in that Dept. locating himself where he can best supervise & control it."

To Caleb B. Smith[1]

Executive Mansion,

Hon. Sec. of Interior   Washington, Oct. 23, 1861

My dear Sir: If you can think to mention the next time I see you, I will tell you more fully what Mr. Lewis says of the cases noted by him on the inclosed cards. Very truly yours,

A. LINCOLN

1 Tracy, pp. 195-96. "Mr. Lewis" has not been identified.

To Caleb B. Smith[1]

Sir   Washington Oct [23?] 1861

The proposed contract for Coal and privileges at the Isthmus of Chiriqui, with suggestions & my conditional approval thereon—has been returned from the Navy Department because of the pressing business therein which does not allow the Secretary time to examine the subject

It is therefore referred to you with authority to act, and you are hereby authorized to carry the contract into effect, should the result of your examination be satisfactory and establish that it will prove of sufficient value to the government. The War, Navy, Post Office & Interior Departments may all derive benefits from this proposed contract. The latter under the law of 3d March 1819 requires heavy appropriations for the transport & support of captured Africans. It is possible that a modification of that law may make it a measure of great economy to direct there negroes to some of the unocupied lands of Central America, and the present contract, may if well considered and arranged, be the introduction to this, and an equally desirable measure to secure the removal of negroes from this country. I therefore recommend that all these points be considered and that the contract be so drawn as to secure such advantages as may in your judgement seem desirable for the United States to hold.

To Hon Caleb Smith
    Secretary of the Interior

1 Copy or draft, DLC-RTL. The bracketed date is that assigned to the document in the Lincoln Papers. Not in Lincoln's handwriting, the copy or draft may be what Lincoln sent or intended to send to Smith, but Lincoln's endorsement to Smith, October 24, *infra*, seems to indicate conclusively that the project was turned over to the Interior Department at this time. The Chiriqui Improvement Company headed by Ambrose W. Thompson of Philadelphia had in 1855 obtained control of several hundred thousand acres in Panama. On August 8 Thompson proposed to the Navy Department to deliver coal at the Chiriqui Lagoon for

one-half the price the government then paid (Thompson to Welles, August 8, 1861, DLC-RTL). Ninian W. Edwards, whom Lincoln had asked to examine the project, gave his approval (Edwards to Lincoln, August 9, 1861, *ibid.*). For further developments, see Lincoln to Smith, October 24, *infra.*

To Samuel R. Curtis[1]

Executive Mansion,
Brig: Genl. S. R. Curtis   Washington, Oct. 24, 1861.

Dear Sir On receipt of this, with the accompanying inclosures, you will take safe, certain, and suitable measures to have the inclosure addressed to Major General Fremont, delivered to him, with all reasonable despatch—subject to these conditions only, that if, when Gen. Fremont shall be reached by the messenger (yourself, or any one sent by you) he shall then have, in personal command, fought and won a battle, or shall then be actually in a battle, or shall then be in the immediate presence of the enemy, in expectation of a battle, it is not to be delivered, but held for further orders. After, and not till after, the delivery to Gen. Fremont, let the inclosure addressed to Gen. Hunter be delivered to him. Your Obt. Servt.   A. LINCOLN

[1] ALS, IHi. The enclosures referred to were undoubtedly *General Orders No. 18* and Lincoln's letter to General David Hunter, *infra*. It seems obvious, however, that after writing this letter to Curtis, Lincoln decided to withhold the letter to Hunter until a later date, thus allowing time for General Hunter to assume command before receiving Lincoln's suggestions (see Lincoln to Curtis, October 28, *infra*). *General Orders No. 18* (OR, I, III, 553) is as follows:

"Headquarters of the Army,
"Washington, October 24, 1861.

"Major-General Frémont, of the U.S. Army, the present commander of the Western Department of the same, will, on the receipt of this order, call Major-General Hunter, of the U.S. Volunteers, to relieve him temporarily in that command, when he (Major-General Frémont) will report to General Headquarters, by letter, for further orders.   "WINFIELD SCOTT.

"By command: E. D. TOWNSEND,
"Assistant Adjutant-General."

Lincoln's precaution in withholding the letter to Hunter was justified, for General Frémont attempted to prevent the delivery of *General Orders No. 18*. Leonard Swett, by whom Lincoln dispatched the letter to Curtis, related the circumstances at length in a letter dated November 9, 1861, which reads in part as follows:

"Tuesday morning [October 29], I went immediately to Genl. Curtis . . . but I could not see him until evening . . . . we found numerous obstacles to the delivery of the order. It had unfortunately been announced in the New York papers, that the order was coming. Several St Louis men, who knew me came out on the same train. . . . It was therefore thought by Genl' Curtis & myself that my connection with it might be suspected and some other person should take it through the lines. . . . Gen'l Curtis knew nothing of the character of these orders except what I, a stranger to him, told him. In the event of trouble, which he feared, it might be necessary for him . . . to *know* what it contained. . . . I opened one of the orders, took several copies, after which, the Genl enclosed it in a new envellop and directed it as before.

"The trouble of delivery was to get some reliable man, who had legitimate business inside Gen'l Frémont's lines. Capt [Ezekiel] Boyden, of Champaign Co. Ills . . . was selected as one, and Capt McKinney [Thomas J. McKenny?] . . . as the other. . . . McKinney took the originals and delivered them first.

"He arrived at Fremonts camp, at five oclock am. [November 1] having rode on horseback the two nights and day previous, having gone by Rolla. After waiting about five hours, and learning that there was no immediate prospect of battle, he applied at head quarters for admission The aid . . . told him he must make known his errand He declined, stating he must see the Gen'l & could confer with no one else I omitted to say he was dressed for the trip like a country farmer. . . . Finally he was admitted. When the Gen'l read the order he said excitedly "Sir, how did you get through my lines," when informed the Gen'l dismissed him. In a few moments . . . the aid came to him and told him not tell [*sic*] in camp the character of the order In a few moments more he came back again asking if Hunter knew of this To this . . . he responded as directed that a messenger had gone by Sedalia to give him a duplicate The messenger then tried to find where Hunter was. The soldiers did not know and the Genl's friends could not or would not tell. He tried to get a pass out of camp That was refused About eleven oclock at night, he overheard the password With that and an old pass of Gen'l Curtis he started & got out The next day [November 2] about twelve oclock he found Hunter. . . .

"The following facts I learn from Capt J W Shaffer of Freeport As soon as the order arrived, Fremont ordered all his men to arms He sent back for Hunter'[s] division to march all night which they did, to join in the battle in the morning. When morning came, Fremont issued his Farewell address and left without giving any information about the Gov property There went with him, his body guard, 50 Indians and a paymaster with between 200000 & 300,000$ The paymaster was arrested here last night and has some of the money. Hunter on taking command send [*sic*] cavalry scouts in all directions for from 30 to 40 miles but of course there was no enemy. . . .

"Let me tell a few more things which I have tried to investigate candidly & believe to be true. Gen'l Fremont has talked about his signature to unlawful orders being above law & to be obeyed The german people have talked about making him Dictator Some of his officers in quite high standing have talked so too."

Frémont's order relinquishing his command to General Hunter was issued under date of November 2 (*General Orders No. 28, OR*, I, III, 559).

Date Due

DEC 2 3 '81 OCT 2 3 1989			
MAR 2 1 2001			
ℊℬ	PRINTED	IN U. S. A.	